Iron Lazar

Frontispiece. L. M. Kaganovich as People's Commissar for Rail Transport in 1935

Iron Lazar

A Political Biography of Lazar Kaganovich

E. A. Rees

ANTHEM PRESS
LONDON · NEW YORK · DELHI

Anthem Press
An imprint of Wimbledon Publishing Company
www.anthempress.com

This edition first published in UK and USA 2013
by ANTHEM PRESS
75–76 Blackfriars Road, London SE1 8HA, UK
or PO Box 9779, London SW19 7ZG, UK
and
244 Madison Ave. #116, New York, NY 10016, USA

First published in hardback by Anthem Press in 2012

Copyright © E. A. Rees 2013

The author asserts the moral right to be identified as the author of this work.

All rights reserved. Without limiting the rights under copyright reserved above,
no part of this publication may be reproduced, stored or introduced into
a retrieval system, or transmitted, in any form or by any means
(electronic, mechanical, photocopying, recording or otherwise),
without the prior written permission of both the copyright
owner and the above publisher of this book.

British Library Cataloguing-in-Publication Data
A catalogue record for this book is available from the British Library.

Library of Congress Cataloging-in-Publication Data
The Library of Congress has cataloged the hardcover edition as follows:
Rees, E. A.
"Iron Lazar" : a political biography of Lazar Kaganovich / E.A. Rees.
pages ; cm
Includes bibliographical references and index.
ISBN 978-0-85728-349-8 (hardback : alkaline paper)
1. Kaganovich, L. M. (Lazar' Moiseevich), 1893–1991.
2. Cabinet officers–Soviet Union–Biography. 3. Politicians–Soviet Union–Biography.
4. Communist leadership–Soviet Union. 5. Soviet Union–Politics
and government–1936–1953. I. Title.
DK268.K27R44 2012
947.084092–dc23
[B]
2011045061

ISBN-13: 978 1 78308 057 1 (Pbk)
ISBN-10: 1 78308 057 4 (Pbk)

This title is also available as an ebook.

TABLE OF CONTENTS

List of Figures   vii
Introduction   ix

Chapter 1	The Making of a Bolshevik, 1893–1917	1
Chapter 2	Red Terror and Civil War, 1918–1921	19
Chapter 3	Building the Monolithic Party, 1922–1927	41
Chapter 4	Ukrainian Party Boss, 1925–1928	61
Chapter 5	The Triumph of the Stalin Faction, 1928–1929	81
Chapter 6	Revolution from Above, 1928–1935	101
Chapter 7	Stalin's Deputy, 1930–1935	123
Chapter 8	Moscow Party Boss, 1930–1935	145
Chapter 9	Boss of Rail Transport, 1935–1937	165
Chapter 10	Political and Social Revolution through Terror, 1936–1938	183
Chapter 11	The Man	203
Chapter 12	The Despot's Creature, 1939–1953	229
Chapter 13	De-Stalinization and Nemesis, 1953–1991	249
Conclusion		271

Notes   281
Bibliography   333
Name Index   347
Subject Index   355

LIST OF FIGURES

Frontispiece	L. M. Kaganovich as People's Commissar for Rail Transport in 1935	ii
Figure 1	L. M. Kaganovich with his wife Maria in Saratov in 1917	11
Figure 2	L. M. Kaganovich in Tashkent in 1920	34
Figure 3	Some of the Politburo leaders in 1929: G. K. Ordzhonikidze, K. E. Voroshilov, V. V. Kuibyshev, I. V. Stalin, M. I. Kalinin, L. M. Kaganovich and S. M. Kirov	124
Figure 4	L. M. Kaganovich and I. V. Stalin photographed in the Kremlin grounds on 1 May 1934	132
Figure 5	N. S. Khrushchev and L. M. Kaganovich with the builders of the Moscow Metro in 1935	157
Figure 6	I. V. Stalin, A. A. Zhdanov, L. M. Kaganovich, A. I. Mikoyan and K. E. Voroshilov stand beside the body of G. K. Ordzhonikidze, February 1937	189
Figure 7	Stalin and Kaganovich. Sculpture by Rakitina and Eletskaya, probably 1933 or 1934	213
Figure 8	L. M. Kaganovich with his wife Maria and their daughter Maia in 1934	216
Figure 9	L. M. Kaganovich before his expulsion from the Presidium in 1957	260

INTRODUCTION

As a leading figure in the shaping of the Stalinist state, Lazar Kaganovich has, not without cause, had a bad press. He has been treated as the *bête noir* of the Stalin era, as a kind of ogre; vilified by Trotsky, depicted as a Stalinist sycophant by Khrushchev, denounced by delegates to the XXI Party Congress as one of the architects of the Great Terror. In the post-Soviet Russia, he was characterised as the ambitious, self-hating Jew who showed little loyalty to his fellow compatriots. He was heavily implicated in many of the worst of Stalin's crimes and evokes little sympathy. At the same time, the works dealing with his life and career are often oversimplified, producing a caricature with little subtlety or nuance. This work attempts to draw a fuller picture of Kaganovich as a political actor, to understand his contribution to the creation of the Stalinist system. But the study is above all about the nature of the inner dynamics of the ruling group, and of its transformation over time. Stalin cannot be understood without understanding the role of his deputies, while the role of his deputies cannot be understood without understanding Stalin.

The Stalinist leadership had no figures of standing comparable to Trotsky or Bukharin under Lenin. Its intellectual formation was much narrower, less cosmopolitan, and more provincial. Many had only limited formal education and were essentially self-educated. Kaganovich has no claim to be considered an intellectual or theoretician. He is of interest as a political executive, administrator, organizer, and troubleshooter. The Stalinist system manifested some polycratic features, whereby institutions in certain periods exercised significant degrees of autonomy. The heads of these institutions exerted considerable influence in their own spheres and on government policy. But Kaganovich's career illustrates in a much starker manner than that of any other of Stalin's deputies, the transformation of the Stalinist leadership over time, the impact of the political and moral choices that were made by these individuals and the repercussions this carried for the regime and for themselves as individuals.

This study seeks to interpret the factors that influenced the general development of the Stalinist system. It focuses on the functions assumed by individuals, their ideological world view and their psychological make-up.

In contrast to the work of Erik van Ree that stresses the extent to which Stalin's thought derived from Marxist and Leninist precedents, the author has elsewhere argued the importance of a more cynical *realpolitik* – revolutionary Machiavellianism – as a central factor in shaping the ideology and policies of the Bolshevik leadership.[1] Machiavelli argued that it was not possible to rule innocently, to rule without dirtying one's hands, but this form of political realism still leaves unanswered the question of how far the resort to coercive, illegal or amoral measures might be judged to be prudent or commensurate. The embrace of dubious means and inhumane methods carried dangers for the state itself and for the agents of the state.

This work explores the Soviet regime's development over time, examines the degree to which the Stalinist regime differed from the Leninist regime and the extent to which the former laid the foundation for the latter. The Stalinist system was shaped by ideology, cultural factors, situational factors, in terms of domestic and external constraints, but it was also shaped by personal and psychological factors – the mindset of leaders and the impact of that on the psychology of the organizations they led.[2] The work examines the function of subordinate leaders under conditions of dictatorial and despotic rule, the way in which they functioned and the way they subsequently explained and rationalized their role. The centrality of Stalin's contribution in shaping the history of the period requires some effort to address the question of his psychology and its bearing on state policy (see Chapter 11).

The writing of political biographies of the leaders of the Stalin era raises other questions: Were Stalin's colleagues mere ciphers or did they help shape policy as independent actors? What were the dynamics of leadership politics within the oligarchic order of the 1920s and within the system of personal dictatorship which developed in the early 1930s? How much was the regime's development shaped by circumstances and how much shaped by Bolshevism – in terms of its ideology, methods and mindset? Here, we explore how individual Bolsheviks fashioned their own images, identities and personas.[3] At the same time, we examine the demands which Bolshevism as a movement made on its adherents, the pressure of the collective discipline of the ruling group, the strong factional and clientele nature of Soviet politics and the pressures of bureaucratic politics, whereby individuals identified with the offices which they held. But Bolshevism aspired to reshape social identities, not only by education and persuasion, through its power to define its friends and enemies, but also by recourse to administrative and coercive methods.[4]

The study of Soviet history since the 1980s has been bedevilled by the debate between the totalitarian school and the revisionist school. This biography eschews both approaches. The totalitarian school highlighted important aspects of the political regime of Soviet communism, the role of ideology, the reliance on coercive and terroristic means to enforce its dictates. It was best represented by Carl J. Friedrich and Zbigniew K. Brzezinski, with their six-point syndrome, but represented by figures such as Leonard Schapiro, Adam Ulam, Richard Pipes and Robert Conquest. This approach was no doubt constrained by the understanding of the time, and may have oversimplified aspects of the regime. Attempts by revisionists to dismiss this as a product of right-wing ideas, as being driven by anticommunism, is simplistic and reveals a deep misunderstanding of the origins and roots of the concept in the 1930s.

The revisionist school emerged in the 1980s, heralded by Sheila Fitzpatrick, its principal representatives being J. Arch Getty, Roberta Manning, Robert Thurston and William Chase. This school now dominates the American academic scene. The revisionist school, in its attempts to write a social and cultural history of the Stalin era, has fallen into another trap: the elevation of the social and the cultural as though they can be discussed in isolation from the political. Revisionism displays a degree of political naivety, and a tendency to normalize and relativize the Stalinist system. The focus on the social and cultural aspects of the regime has been allied to attempts to depict the system of political leadership as driven by pressures from below. The identification of polycratic aspects of the Soviet party-state, including institutional and regional lobbies, should not be confused with pluralistic decision making. Polycratic structures can coexist with dictatorship and despotic forms of rule.

The polarization of debate between the totalitarian and revisionist camps reflects an ideological stasis that impedes scholarship. The division is clearly conceived of as carrying political implications – the totalitarian camp is anti-Soviet, anti-Communist, whereas the Revisionist school claims a degree of objectivity but is seen by its critics as apologists for the Stalin regime. The replacement of a 'top down' totalitarian model by a 'bottom up' social-cultural revisionist approach to explain the Soviet regime hardly amounts to an advance in theoretical sophistication. One one-sided approach is replaced by another one-sided approach.

An alternative, non-revisionist, non-totalitarian approach is represented by luminaries such as E. H. Carr, Stephen Cohen, R. V. Daniels, R. W. Davies, Isaac Deutscher, Moshe Lewin and Alec Nove. This approach recognizes the central importance of politics, but seeks to place political developments in their domestic and international context. This approach sees the Soviet regime as a modernising government, constrained by objective limits as determined by economic and social realities, but within these constraints, the political leadership faced real choices, and the choices made had a determining effect in shaping its future course.

The approach, based on close archival research, remains strongly exemplified by the work of historians such as Oleg Khlevniuk. This work sets itself in this tradition. It focuses primarily on the political nature of the regime. It does not eschew the possibility of useful comparisons between the Soviet regime and other authoritarian regimes of the era. It does not shy away from examining the nature of the system of dictatorial rule instituted in the USSR under Stalin, nor does it avoid examining the Great Terror as a stage in the establishment of a system of tyrannical rule in the USSR. It is based on the assumption that the Soviet regime's development was shaped not only by domestic and international circumstances, but was also influenced by the nature of the political leadership under Stalin. In this, an important role has to be played by the study of the ideology, language and psychology of the Soviet leadership.

The totalitarian school depicts Stalin as a ruler who dominated the life of the Soviet Union from soon after Lenin's death, and who ruthlessly used his power to transform the state and society in accordance with the dictates of Marxism-Leninism. Carl A. Linden characterized the system of Soviet power after 1917 as a form of 'ideocratic despotism'.[5] In sharp contrast, 'revisionist' historiography has posed the question of whether Stalin was a 'weak' ruler, pushed by institutional pressures, popular opinion and the struggle among his deputies.[6]

Between these two positions, a third approach focuses on the interplay between a centralized party-state driven by its own ideology and the wider society shaped by problems of governance, development, the preservation of domestic and external security. This approach highlights the choices, political and ethical, confronting the regime. The Soviet regime was profoundly changed by the way it assumed the functions of a regime of modernization.[7] Bertrand Russell had already cogently noted in 1920 that the Bolshevik regime had abandoned communism for modernization, but argued that this would be a project shaped by ideology and by the negation of the Enlightenment's attitude of rigour, scepticism and toleration of contending ideas about science and society.[8] Stalinism might be seen as a species of 'developmental dictatorship' which offers the basis for comparative study with other regimes.[9]

The Soviet regime was guided by Marxist ideology, and this coloured its conception of development. Three variant developmental strategies were attempted – War Communism, the New Economic Policy (NEP) and the Command Administrative Economy. Each of these systems had its own coherence. The concept of 'developmental dictatorship' addresses the crucial problems associated with modernization and the overcoming of backwardness. The political, economic, social and cultural realms were interconnected. Domestic developments were shaped by the external environment. Investment choices made in one area profoundly affected policies in other areas. Policy failures had a profound impact on the way in which the political system responded. Whilst the Soviet system underwent a profound transformation under the pressures of carrying through its developmental agenda, the leadership faced real choices. The choices made were determined by the perceptions, motives and ideas of its political leaders.

Most scholars accept that Stalin acquired dictatorial power, but there remains disagreement as to the chronology of this transition. There also remains considerable confusion in the literature as how to characterize Stalin – as oligarch, autocrat, dictator, despot or tyrant. The terminology employed reflects more than semantic nuances; it points to a fundamental difference in interpreting the internal dynamics of the ruling group. Stalin has been described as a 'neo-patrimonial' leader within a collective leadership.[10] Oleg Khlevniuk argues that Stalin became a dictator after 1936.[11] Professor Stephen Wheatcroft has characterized the ruling group as 'team Stalin', but argues that in the final years the system became one of tyrannical rule.[12] The ruling group might alternatively be characterized as a cabal, camarilla, circle, clan, clique, coterie or faction. T. H. Rigby compared Stalin's relations with his immediate subordinates to that of a gangland boss and his men.[13] Andrea Graziosi argues that the terms used within the Stalin group to designate the leader – *vozhd'* (leader), *khozyain* (boss), *roditel'* (guardian or father) – were also associated with mafia or criminal argot.[14] Rigby and Graziosi point to the importance of the 'criminalization' of the leading group's actions and mentality.

Four periods of Stalin's rule can be demarcated: (1) from 1924 to 1928, as the leading figure with an oligarchic system, in which no faction was dominant; (2) 1929 up to 1933, as leader of the triumphant Stalinist faction, with Stalin clearly more than *primus inter pares*; (3) from 1933 to 1936 as personal dictatorship; and (4) from 1936 to 1953, as despotic ruler. The period of the war 1941–45 marks a phase of its own but does not contradict this basic chronology. The transition from each phase to the next followed a certain inherent logic. Stalin, of course, was neither omnipotent nor omniscient, and continued throughout his period of rule to rely on his deputies. The contributions of Stalin's subordinates can only be understood in relation to the changing nature of this system of leadership.[15] But the study of the Stalin era can also help us refine our categories and concepts, to define more precisely what constitutes dictatorship, where it is appropriate and where it is an inappropriate category.

As a political biography, this work is above all an examination of politics from above, and about the importance of agency, the role of the political leadership and the contribution of one individual within that leadership, and thus about intention, motivation and calculation. The study eschews the traditional totalitarian and the revisionist and post-revisionist conceptions of

Soviet politics, and seeks to offer an alternative conception of the way in which the Soviet system evolved. In this, it seeks to draw on alternative theoretical conceptions of the nature of politics and society, and of their interactions.

It starts from the premise that politics was the principal and determining factor in shaping the Soviet regime. It emphasises Lenin's restricted conception of politics.[16] The Soviet system systematically dismantled the limited 'public sphere' and embryonic civil society that had emerged in the late tsarist period.[17] An emergent legal culture was subsumed by a regime of state lawlessness.[18] The Bolshevization of language transformed the concepts and categories in which political and social issues could be discussed.[19] Real public opinion gave way to popular opinion or popular moods that the government sought to gauge and direct.[20] Underlying the relations of state and society lay a profound crisis of legitimation, which the regime sought to manage through a strategy of self-legitimation.[21] The regime that emerged thus was endowed with strong cultic aspects that manifested, in large part, the features of a 'political religion'.[22] Class, ethnic, and gender identities and even individual identities were ascribed, mediated and manipulated by the state.[23] The elaboration of the party-state as the supreme political and ethical arbiter involved an attack on individual conscience and on the integrity of the self.[24]

The best biography of Kaganovich is in Italian by Loris Marcucci, *Il Commissario di Ferro di Stalin*, but this is based only on secondary sources.[25] The brief biography by Roy Medvedev in *All Stalin's Men* remains useful,[26] as is the more extended treatment in *Zhelezni yastreb*.[27] There is also the short study of Kaganovich by the Ukrainian historian Yuri Shapoval.[28] The biography by Stuart Kahan, *The Wolf in the Kremlin*,[29] supposedly by the American nephew of Kaganovich, adds little to existing knowledge and its reliability as a source is questionable.[30] Kaganovich himself asserted that his American relatives denied that Stuart Kahan was related to them.[31]

The basic details of Kaganovich's career are given in various older Soviet reference works.[32] In 1996 Kaganovich's memoirs, *Pamyatnye zapiski rabochego, kommunista-bol'shevika, profsoyuznogo, partiinogo i sovetskogo rabotnika*, were published.[33] These memoirs, written between 1961 and 1985, are useful on his childhood, early revolutionary career and the role he played in 1917, during the Civil War, and the early years in the party Secretariat after 1922. However, for most of the Stalin era, the memoirs are of limited use and have to be handled with great circumspection.[34] There are also Kaganovich's conversations with the Russian journalist Feliks Chuev, *Tak govoril Kaganovich: Ispoved' stalinskogo apostola* (*Thus Spake Kaganovich: Confessions of a Stalinist Apostle*),[35] and with the historian G. A. Kumanev.[36] These works are characterized by significant silences and omissions that illustrate Kaganovich's own 'state of denial'.

The publication of a wealth of archival documents and a great number of books and articles based on archival sources over the last fifteen years has made possible a much fuller account of the internal workings of the Stalinist regime and the internal debates on matters of policy. Of particular significance has been the publication of the correspondence between Stalin and Kaganovich from 1931 to 1936, when Kaganovich was at the height of his influence.[37]

In this study we trace the evolution of the leadership of the Soviet regime. The changes at the apex of the political system were intimately connected to wider developments within the party-state apparatus and in its relationship with the wider society. The career of Kaganovich as a case study illustrates these developments. In this, it raises questions about the nature of authoritarian rule and of the rationality of the whole system.

Chapter 1

THE MAKING OF A BOLSHEVIK, 1893–1917

The Russian Empire in which Lazar Kaganovich grew up was convulsed by upheavals which threatened the very survival of the state. Under Nicholas II, the autocracy sought to transform itself into a modernizing state. The industrialization drive, directed by finance minister Sergei Witte in the 1890s, had a profound impact on the whole country. The defeat of the imperial navy and army by Japan in the Far East in 1904–5 administered a major shock to the state. Peasant resentments and working-class protests ignited the abortive 1905 revolution. The dynasty's claims to legitimacy were seriously compromised. The tsar's gestures toward constitutional reform by means of the October Manifesto were followed by a new repression under Piotr Stolypin combined with an attempt to reform agriculture. From 1909 onward, the rearmament drive stimulated economic recovery. The tsarist regime was beset by the dilemma of promoting industrial development while dealing with the backwardness of agriculture, and preserving Russia's standing as a major power while addressing the demands for domestic reform.

The autocracy was heavily dependent on the support of privileged society and of the backing provided by the state administration, the police and the armed forces. The advocates of constitutional reform drew on a narrow base of middle-class support. Peasant radicalism posed a direct threat to the existence of landed interests. The working class, although numerically small, was characterized by its radical temper. The non-Russian nationalities provided the base for secessionist movements. The political opposition in Russia was strongly revolutionary in outlook – Socialist Revolutionary, Social Democratic, Trudoviki, Bundist and Anarchist. Russian Marxists, perplexed by the failure of a Russian bourgeois revolution, embraced a militant, revolutionary variant of Marxism that rejected reformism. From 1905 to 1917 the society was polarized between the advocates of autocratic order and of revolutionary transformation.

Lazar Kaganovich's early life was shaped by the stresses and tensions through which the society passed in these years. It was influenced by the political choices that were available, as expressed by the various political parties. But individuals are not simply the product of circumstances, they are active agents who interpret their circumstances, who make choices in their lives and fashion their own identities. The early life of Kaganovich illustrates what he shared in common with the generation of young radicals that grew up in this period and what was distinctive about his own experience. It sheds light on the way in which he became a Bolshevik and highlights the nature of Bolshevism as a political movement in this period and its appeal to revolutionary, young workers.

Family and Childhood

Lazar Moiseevich Kaganovich was born and brought up in the village of Kabany, Kiev province, 30 kilometres from Chernobyl. This was part of the region of Polese that constituted part of the Jewish pale of settlement. The surrounding countryside, well wooded with rivers and lakes, was rich in wildlife.[1] According to Kaganovich's recollections, Kabany had about 300 households, of which five to ten were rich 'kulaks' and 30 were well-to-do peasants. He recalled how the poor peasants and landless labourers (*batraks*) were exploited by the kulaks and middle peasants.[2] The population was predominantly Ukrainian, with some Byelorussians and Jews. Ukrainian was the language of the village. The Jewish families lived together in what was termed the 'colony', which comprised about 20 families, most of whom were poor artisans. The Kaganovich family was the only Jewish family to live outside the colony, but they had relatives and friends in the colony.

Kaganovich's father, Moisei, was born in Kabany in 1863, and lived there all his life. He had a brother who emigrated to America. Moisei received no education and began work at 13 years of age as an agricultural labourer, then worked in timber felling, and then in a wood-resin tar factory. His wife, Genia Dubinskaya, was born and grew up in a small town near Chernobyl in a family of coppersmiths. Genia gave birth to thirteen children, of whom six survived – five sons (Izrail, Aron, Mikhail, Yuli and Lazar) and one daughter (Rachel). Lazar was born on 23 November 1893.[3] The youngest and the favourite, he was the 'Benjamin of the family'.

The family was poor and their circumstances became more difficult when Moisei was badly burnt in an accident with a boiler at work. His health remained poor thereafter, and he died of bronchial asthma in 1923. Moisei leased a plot of land to grow potatoes, vegetables and buckwheat. He tried to go on seasonal work at a local brickyard, with Yuli and Lazar to help him. But Genia became the main breadwinner, through dressmaking, dying wool and baking. The children also earned money picking sugarbeet on the nearby Khorvat estate. The family received help from Genia's brother, Mikhail. Things eased when the two eldest sons began work, Izrail in timber felling, and Aron as a joiner. The family was able to move from their earth-and-turf hovel (*stepka*) to a larger one-room, wooden-planked cottage (*khat*). They slept on benches.[4] But they now had a stove and oil lamps, with more space to entertain friends and neighbours, and the house often overflowed with people.[5]

Lazar Kaganovich's brother Mikhail began work in 1903 as a metal worker in Chernobyl and then Kiev. In 1905 he joined the Russian Social Democratic Party and, in Kaganovich's words, became 'a fearless revolutionary'. The Russo–Japanese War stirred popular ferment, while the land question continued to agitate the peasants. At the village of Lubyanka, three kilometres from Kabany, there was a peasant uprising.[6] The grenadiers, who were sent to suppress it, were quartered in Kabany. The poor peasants of Kabany, Kaganovich recalled, sympathized with their neighbours in Lubyanka.

The population of Kabany was mixed, and Kaganovich recalled that the children of the poor and middle peasants – Russian, Ukrainian, Jews, Poles and Byelorussians – socialised freely. Zionist ideas had little influence among the poor Jewish workers, and among Russian and Ukrainian workers there was little anti-Semitism. However, the Jewish population of Kabany was well aware of the pogroms in Odessa, Kishinev and elsewhere.[7]

Although his parents were practically illiterate, they brought up their children with intelligence and tact. It was a close family. They lived modestly and were self-reliant. Mosei had a quiet temperament, never scolded the children, but was serious and supportive. Genia was an important influence. Kaganovich describes her as proud, religious and with a love of life.[8] After the marriage of her daughter Rachel, Yuli and Lazar had to help at home. The children were brought up with a love of labour and a sense of social justice.

The family name 'Kaganovich' (pronounced ka·gan·o·vich, with the stress on the 'o') was the same in root as Kagan, Kahan and Cohen, indicating a family descended from a rabbi. The memoirs make no mention of the family attending the synagogue, nor of their observation of Jewish customs and rituals. We might infer that they were still quite conventional in these matters.[9] In his personal file written in the early twenties, Lazar recorded that he knew Russian, Ukrainian and had a weak command of Yiddish.[10]

Kaganovich attended a Jewish school (*kheder*) attached to the synagogue in the Jewish colony. Thereafter, the Jewish families enlisted the services of a teacher from Chernobyl, but this school was closed down by the school inspector.[11] He was then sent with his brother Yuli to a school in Martynovich, where they were taught the Bible and the Talmud, Russian and general subjects. The two brothers travelled from Kabany to Martynovich, taking their food with them and staying in lodgings. The school gave him the basis for self-education and a passion for self-improvement. Yuli, Lazar recalled, was his favourite brother;

he had a kindly disposition. But he himself, he admits, was temperamentally closer to his brother Mikhail, and had a 'stormy character'.[12]

He finished school at the age of thirteen, and was then apprenticed to a blacksmith in the nearby town of Khochava.[13] In the local library he immersed himself in reading the literary classics, Dickens and Victor Hugo.[14] As well as the Russian classics, he read the brochures and newspapers which Mikhail brought from Kiev. Kaganovich recounts that as an adolescent he was quite widely read in history.[15]

In his memoirs Kaganovich refers to how in his youth he was attracted by the Book of Amos in the Hebrew Bible – with its condemnation of the rich and powerful.[16] It also depicts a jealous and vengeful God, Yahweh, 'the God of Armies', who directs his wrath at the children of Israel for their transgressions. We can only speculate as to how far he was drawn by the same apocalyptic and messianic side of Bolshevism.

Maxim Gorky was a favourite author. His stories from this period deal with the life of the lower classes and celebrate the strong figures who, by an assertion of will, were able to master their fate, and carry a strong Nietzschean theme. He also admired the German Social Democrat Wilhelm Liebknecht's tale *The Spider and the Fly*.[17] The gist of this story is that the downtrodden and the oppressed, though weak and divided, can assert themselves through organization and leadership. His first introduction to philosophy was Spinoza's *Ethics*, and for a time, he recalled, he was drawn to 'idealistic pessimism' before embracing a materialist understanding of history.[18] When he had money, he visited the bookshops. The purchase of a lamp to allow him to read at night was an important event.

The World of Work

His career as an apprentice blacksmith was short-lived. He moved to Kiev and there worked with his brother Mikhail in a scrap metal yard. They stayed in a dosshouse in Nizhnyi Val. As a result of illness brought on by this work, he had to return home to recuperate for three months. Through tutoring the children of his uncle Aron in Russian, he was able to raise enough money to return to Kiev.

There, he took a series of heavy manual jobs, working twelve hours a day for meagre wages.[19] He worked mainly in the bustling district of Podol, with its shops, workshops, large enterprises, wharves and ship repair yards. Many of the owners and a large proportion of the workers were Jews. In prolonged periods of unemployment, he spent his time on Kreshatik Boulevard and Bibikovsky Boulevard. In observing the lives of the various social classes, he recalls, he came to despise the unfeeling rich and scorn the petty bourgeoisie. At 14 years of age in 1907, he began working as a shoemaker in factories and workshops. When he was just 16 years old, he organized his first worker self-education group.[20] His attitude toward the working class, however, was not uncritical; he sharply distinguished between the backward and progressive elements in the proletariat. The possibility of further study at school or university was an impossible dream, but it may be that there was a stage in his teens when he aspired to such a course.[21]

Kiev was a large, prosperous city, a centre of administration, education and culture. It possessed a large middle class and politically was fairly quiescent but developed into a stronghold of Ukrainian nationalism. Among the revolutionary parties, the Bolsheviks competed with Zionists, Bundists, Socialist Revolutionaries, Mensheviks and Anarchists to recruit Jewish youth. The political repression following the defeat of the 1905 revolution slowly ebbed. Gradually, political opposition began to revive, with the Kiev Social Democrats issuing leaflets on 1 May 1910. The revolutionaries directed their attention at the city's large contingent of railway workers. The district of Podol had a particular reputation because of its many politically educated, young workers.

Kiev, with its cosmopolitan make up – Ukrainians, Russians, Poles, Germans, and Jews – was a place where racial animosities could easily be stirred. In 1911 the infamous Beilis case took place, in which a Jewish worker from the city was accused of the ritual murder of a Christian child. Anti-Semitic feelings were whipped up by the Black Hundred organizations, 'The Union of the Archangel Mikhail' and 'The Twin-Headed Eagle', with the connivance of leading public figures, including the minister of justice. Radical parties mobilized in protest and on 4 October many factories, especially in Podol, went on a demonstrative strike. The assassination of Piotr Stolypin, the prime minister, in the Kiev Opera House on 1 September 1911, caused a huge stir, with attempts by 'The Twin-Headed Eagle' to whip up a pogrom. The Bolsheviks took measures to protect themselves and to rebuff this threat.

Kaganovich only joined the Bolshevik party after these momentous events. In his retirement he claimed that he was introduced to the Bolsheviks by his brother Mikhail and had joined the party in August 1911.[22] He declared: 'I entered the Great university of the revolution, the university of the great party – the university of Lenin!'[23] This is not quite true. In his autobiographical sketch, which he was required to write for the party in the early 1920s, he revealed that his initial contact with revolutionaries was with Grabovsky, a Menshevik with whom he worked. He established links with the Bolsheviks only after January 1912, and he appears to have become a member later that year.[24] Notwithstanding his claim to see his brother Mikhail as a role model, Lazar Kaganovich joined the Bolshevik party seven years after him.

The Bolshevik party, headed by V. I. Lenin, represented the most revolutionary wing of Russian Social Democracy. For self-educated workers, Marxism offered a powerful tool for analysing the world, and engendered a great self-confidence. Admission into the party was closely regulated, and membership was coveted by young radicals. The two brothers defined themselves as Bolsheviks, not Mensheviks or Socialist Revolutionaries, and they had rejected the main Jewish socialist organization, the Bund.[25] Three other brothers – Aron, Izrail and Yuli – joined the Bolshevik party after the Revolution, but, Kaganovich claims, their attitude was revolutionary before then.[26]

The choice of the Bolshevik party was significant in another sense. The Menshevik party was stronger than the Bolsheviks in Ukraine and the south generally, even in key industrial centres such as Ekaterinoslav. The Mensheviks recruited strongly from the national minorities, such as Jews and Georgians, whereas the Bolsheviks recruited predominantly from the Great Russians, although a significant number of their leading figures were Jews. The Bolsheviks were successful in recruiting young workers who had newly arrived in industry. By 1907 the Bolshevik party had about 46,000 members.[27] For a core who became members, this was to be a lifetime's commitment. Lenin's conception of the vanguard party, guided by a doctrinaire reading of Marxism, as outlined in 'What is to Be Done?' of 1903, led several fellow Marxists to characterize him as a 'Jacobin'. Bolshevism, as critics such as Nikolai Berdayev and Semon Frank were quick to point out, manifested a form of quasi-religious messianism, moral and legal nihilism, and subscribed to a form of party idolatry.[28]

Kaganovich recalls that he began studying Lenin's works, and his article 'Stolypin and Revolution', written following Stolypin's assassination, made a big impression. While liberal journalists deplored this outrage, Lenin characterized Stolypin as the head of the 'counter-revolutionary government', the 'arch-hangman', and an organizer of Black Hundred gangs and anti-Semitic pogroms. The 'semi-Asiatic, feudal Russian monarchy', Lenin declared, could defend itself only 'by the most infamous, most disgusting, vile and cruel means.'[29]

In 1911 a Kiev city party conference elected a committee.[30] Yu. L. Pyatakov, the son of a wealthy Kiev sugar magnate, who had been expelled from St. Petersburg as a student agitator, was its leader. Another prominent member was Evgeniya Bosh. In June 1912 the arrest of Pyatakov and other committee members precipitated the collapse of the city's party organization. In 1917 Pyatakov and Bosh returned to take charge of the Kiev party organization, but by this time Kaganovich had moved elsewhere.

An underground group of Social Democrats met in a garret on Nizhnyi Val. The meetings were often attended by the sisters Maria and Liza Markovna

Privorotskaya. Together with Roza Vorob'evaya (Grinshpon), they distributed *Igla* (Needle), the paper of the hosiery workers union, and other agitational literature among Kiev's women workers.³¹ In 1912 Kaganovich and Maria Privorotskaya were married.³² Born in 1894 of Jewish parents, she started work as a young girl in hosiery enterprises. She was active in the workers' revolutionary movement, joining the Bolshevik party in 1909, when just fifteen years of age. Whether they married in a synagogue or registry office is unclear.

In 1912 a number of the trade unions in Kiev were legalized, but the more militant Bolshevik-controlled leather workers union, of which Kaganovich was a member, was only legalized at the beginning of 1913. The Social Democrats participated in the election campaign to the IV Duma. They fought with strike-breakers hired by employers who sought to play on ethnic divisions to divide the workers. In Kiev, the Bolsheviks, Mensheviks and Bundists used clubs – the Society for the Dissemination of Education to the People, and the Scientific-Technical Club – as front organizations, a cover for agitation work and illegal meetings. Kaganovich as a member of the Podol district party committee (*raikom*) worked as an agitator, organized self-education groups, and campaigned for the legalization of the leatherworkers union. Lacking the necessary residence permit, he was obliged to change accommodations to avoid arrest. In the factories, labour organization was severely weakened by the Stolypin reaction, with employers calling in the police to deal with troublemakers.

In 1913 Kaganovich and his wife lived in a flat at 31 Yaroslavsky Street. Their home became a meeting place for other Bolsheviks. They organized circles to study political economy and the Communist Manifesto, and produced revolutionary posters and leaflets which they distributed in the workers' quarters of Kiev. L. A. Sheinin, one of the group, later recalled Kaganovich's skill in conspiratorial activities.³³

In early 1914, against the background of mounting labour unrest, a group of Kiev Bolsheviks were sent into exile. A demonstration was organized at the railway station, with Kaganovich brandishing a banner. He was arrested and released after questioning, but his flat was put under police surveillance, and he had to move elsewhere. The decision by the authorities to prohibit the celebration of the centenary of the birth of the Ukrainian poet and revolutionary democrat Taras Shevchenko in March 1914 was also used by the Kiev party committee to denounce the tsarist empire as a 'prison of the nationalities'.

Kaganovich's memoirs significantly ignore any reference to Kiev Marxists who later fell afoul of Stalin. He makes no reference to Leon Trotsky, who lived in Kiev for a brief period after 1905 and acted as the correspondent of the journal *Kievskaya Mysl'* on the Balkan Wars (1912–14).³⁴ He is silent about Pyatakov and Bosh, who supported Trotsky in the 1920s, although he must have known both of them. Similarly, he makes no mention of Yan Gamarnik, a student at Kiev University, and V. P. Zatonsky, a member of the Marxist Borot'bist group, both of whom became prominent under the Soviet regime.

The Great War

In August 1914 Russia went to war with Germany and Austro-Hungary despite former interior minister P. N. Durnovo's warning that a prolonged war carried the serious danger of revolution. Initially, the war cut off the rising tide of labour unrest and produced a rallying of patriotic feelings. The Bolsheviks in Kiev ineffectually attempted to campaign against the war. Efforts to organize the city's party organization were aided by the arrival of Stanislav Kosior. Although just 25 years of age, he was regarded as an experienced Bolshevik. In an interview in 1991, Kaganovich spoke of Kosior as a friend and father figure (*roditel'*) who had examined him in political economy and Marxism, and had co-opted him onto the Kiev city party committee in 1915.[35]

In the first half of 1915 Degtiarev, Veinberg and other leaders of the Kiev party committee were arrested, while Kosior fled the city. Kaganovich records that he himself was arrested and sent back to Kabany, but he soon returned to Kiev. He and his wife left Kiev in October. In 1916, under the pseudonym Stomakhin, he worked in a shoe factory in Ekaterinoslav (Dnepropretrovsk) and became chairman of an illegal trade union. The Old Bolshevik Serafim Gopner, in her memoirs, recalled that, on her return from emigration in the summer of 1916, in the town 'there worked the still very young but already tempered and energetic L. M. Kaganovich (Boris)' – a member of the district and all-city committee. He was linked with other party activists, notably the leaders of the party organization of the Briansk works.[36]

Kaganovich was fired for organizing a strike at the shoe factory where he worked. The workers came out on strike for six weeks, demanding his reinstatement. The workers' demand was met, but, as a result of what Kaganovich called 'accusations by a provocateur', he had to flee to Melitopol' where he worked under the name of Gol'denberg and became chairman of an underground union of bootmakers and an organizer of Bolshevik groups.[37]

In the second half of 1916 Kaganovich and his wife moved to Yuzovka, the industrial centre of the Donbass, dominated by the New Russia Metallurgical Company, founded by the Welsh ironmaster John Hughes. He worked there under the name Boris Kosherovich (Yiddish-kosher), a sign that he had both pride in his Jewish background and a sign that he was not without a sense of humour, but also an indication that he was clearly recognizable as a Jew. He worked in a shoe factory and was the leader of the Bolshevik organization. At Yuzovka he organized an illegal union of bootmakers, which successfully carried out a number of strikes.

The February Revolution

The crisis of the Romanov dynasty culminated in the abdication of Nicholas II on 2 March 1917, with power passing to the Provisional Government. The abdication was triggered by a wave of popular protest which was exacerbated by the economic crisis caused by the war. The implosion of the regime reflected a loss of authority and its desertion by even those institutions and social groups that had acted as its bulwark. The limited constitutional reforms attempted in 1905 came unstuck. The tsarist regime's attempt to chart a course of development – Sergei Witte's programme of industrial development and Piotr Stolypin's programme of agrarian reform – had failed to create a basis for the regime to stabilize itself.

The Romanov dynasty was engulfed by a rising tide of popular protest, On 25 February 1917 mass meetings were organized in the works and mines in the Donbass, and Kaganovich spoke at a meeting at the New Putilov works. On 1 March 1917 in Yuzovka, the Bolsheviks held two meetings, one of which was attended by the Menshevik-Internationalists. The well-known Yuzovka Bolshevik F. Zaitsev recalled that Kaganovich spoke at this meeting, defending the Bolshevik line of turning the imperialist war into a civil war.[38]

The first time Kaganovich spoke at a mass meeting was on 3 March when he addressed a meeting of several thousand miners and metal workers in Yuzovka. He discovered that he had a talent for oratory. At one such meeting, he first met Nikita Khrushchev, not then a Bolshevik but a representative of the workers of the Ruchenkov mines.[39] In Yuzovka the Menshevik Defencists and the Bolsheviks battled for control of the newly constituted local soviet. The Bolshevik gained a majority on its executive committee and Boris Koshevorich (Kaganovich) was elected as deputy chairman.[40] On 10 March he became a member of the Yuzovka unified committee of the Russian Social Democratic Labour Party (the RSDLP), which included Bolsheviks and Menshevik-Internationalists.[41]

In April 1917 he returned to Kiev and there was conscripted into the army. In his memoirs, he simply implies that the party sent him into the army to work as an agitator. At Kiev, he asserts, he fell afoul of various Mensheviks and Socialist Revolutionaries, who, via the soldiers' section of the Kiev Soviet, arranged for him to be transferred from Kiev to Saratov, which had a garrison of 50,000 soldiers.[42]

From May 1917 Kaganovich served in the 7th company of the 42nd Infantry Regiment in Saratov. He was elected a member of the executive committee of the soviet of workers and soldiers deputies and a member of the Saratov committee of the party. In the middle of May, a general meeting of party members of the military organization was held. At this, Kaganovich asserts, he clashed with the Old Bolshevik V. P. Milyutin regarding Lenin's April Theses. The meeting established the Military Organization of the Saratov RSDLP, which worked under the city and province party committee. Kaganovich was elected as its chairman.[43]

By 10 June, the Saratov Bolshevik party organization had a membership of 2,500 and its military organization had 400 members.[44] Kerensky's June offensive produced a major shift in the mood of the soldiers. The elections for the soviet prompted intense struggle in the barracks. Kaganovich claims that he was arrested on a pretext by Socialist Revolutionary officers and held for two days.[45] The Bolsheviks used the soldiers' self-help organizations (*zemliachestva*) to propagandize among the great non-party mass of soldiers and to extend their influence into the countryside.

Kaganovich attended the All-Russian Conference of Bolshevik military party organizations in Petrograd, as a representative of the Georgian army.[46] The conference, held in the Kshesinsky palace, opened on 16 June. His first visit to the capital – Piter – made a big impression on him.[47] He participated in the 'White Nights Meetings' in the Vyborg-side working class district. He and V. Antonov-Ovseenko addressed a mass meeting at the Aivazov factory, where Maria Spiridonova, the prominent Socialist Revolutionary (SR), and various Mensheviks were speaking. The two became close friends.[48]

Addressing the All-Russian Conference of Bolshevik Military Organizations on June 20, Lenin opposed the radicals in the military organization and in the Petrograd party organization who favoured an immediate insurrection. The conference was deeply divided on the issue. Kaganovich and N. V. Krylenko argued in favour of the Leninist line in opposition to the radicals led by A. Vasiliev and Shemaev. Kaganovich argued that most of the people were following the SRs and Mensheviks. The Bolsheviks had to win over popular support before embarking on the insurrectionary course, or otherwise a premature attempt to take power might pitch the proletariat into a disastrous civil war.[49]

On Nikolai Podvoisky's suggestion, Kaganovich issued greetings to Lenin on behalf of Old Bolsheviks of the Military Organization. He heard I. V. Stalin's report which argued against the idea of forming national units in the army. He was involved in drafting the conference resolution, and for the first time met Stalin, who, he recalled, showed great tact in handling questions.[50] He also met Vyacheslav Molotov, who headed the Central Committee's Information Department.[51]

The conference elected an All-Russian Bureau of Military Party Organizations attached to the Central Committee of the RSDLP (Bolsheviks). The bureau was chaired by N. I. Podvoisky. The relatively unknown Kaganovich was one of the eleven members.[52] The radicals in the bureau – V. I. Nevsky, N. I. Podvoisky, K. A. Mekhonoshin, N. K. Belyakov, A. Ya. Semashko – played the leading part in promoting the mood that led to the insurrectionary attempt during the famous July Days.[53]

The members of the bureau were intended to remain in Petrograd after the conference to direct the work of the Military Organization. Podvoisky and Yakov Sverdlov tried to persuade Kaganovich to stay and work in Petrograd, but he insisted on returning to Saratov.[54] He travelled via Moscow, where the Moscow party committee sent him to the Skobelev monument to address a meeting – organized by the Socialist Revolutionaries – which was also addressed by Nikolai Bukharin.[55]

He returned to Saratov. In the second half of June, Valerian Kuibyshev arrived in the town, and lectured on 'Revolution and counter-revolution'. Kaganovich and Kuibyshev were to form a close friendship. After the July days, an anti-Bolshevik campaign was launched. Kaganovich was accused of going to Petrograd without authorization; he was arrested and listed with other Bolshevik activists to be dispatched to the front. At Gomel' station, the Polese committee of the Bolshevik party intervened to block his further transportation. He and other arrested soldiers were released.[56]

The Polese committee of the Bolshevik party operated in what is present-day Belarus. Polese encompassed the territory of the Jewish pale, with Gomel' as its principal centre, and also included Kaganovich's home region. He was

Figure 1. L. M. Kaganovich with his wife Maria in Saratov in 1917

elected a member of the Gomel' soviet of workers and soldiers deputies. He was also elected chairman of the Polese Bolshevik party bureau, which also included T. M. Privorotsky (responsible secretary – and Kaganovich's brother-in-law), Mendel Khataevich (deputy chairman) and five other members. Kaganovich assumed general leadership and was in charge of mass political work among the workers, soldiers and peasants, and he also headed the special military commission. His wife Maria worked in the Polese soviet's section for work among women.[57]

From September 1917 Kaganovich worked in Gomel'. Following the abortive counter-revolutionary coup, headed by the Supreme Military Commander General Lavr Kornilov, at the end of August the Bolsheviks rallied strong support among railway workers and soldiers, many of whom joined the Red Guards. Kaganovich also sat on the board of the Gomel' union of leatherworkers, who in September–October struck in support of a strike by fellow workers in Moscow. The Bolsheviks and the Bund fought intensely to gain influence amongst Jewish workers. As a Bolshevik who could speak Yiddish, Kaganovich was a major asset. As a result of a debate, Kaganovich claimed, the leading Bundist, Mark Liber, was sent packing from Gomel'.[58]

Kaganovich, as a member of the All-Russian Bureau of Military Organizations of the Bolsheviks, was elected chairman of a delegation to go to Petrograd in order to lobby for the publishing of the tsarist government's secret treaties, to end the war and to conclude peace. However, because of the difficult situation in Gomel', he was unable to go.

The October Revolution in Gomel' and Mogiliev

On 16 October, the province conference of the Soviets, held in Minsk, witnessed a clash between the Bolsheviks and their critics. Kaganovich spoke as representative of the Gomel' soviet, denouncing the bankruptcy of the 'social conciliators', arguing that the masses were increasingly supporting the Bolsheviks. After the conference, he discussed the military situation with A. F. Myasnikov, leader of Minsk province party committee. Myasnikov noted that the Central Committee had referred to him as 'very energetic and fervent', and proposed that he be nominated as a candidate for election to the Constituent Assembly.[59]

The Polese committee's Military Commission, led by Kaganovich, began organizing and arming the Red Guards for insurrection. The Polese committee, through the Gomel' soviet, led the campaign among the soldiers. It secured the release of soldiers who had been imprisoned in June 1917, some of whom had been accused of killing their commanding officer who had ordered them to fire on their fellow soldiers.[60]

In October, there were fears that front-line units would be deployed to suppress the revolutionary movement in Petrograd and Moscow. The Polese committee, with the help of railway workers, succeeded in impeding the movement of these units. Kaganovich and others were involved in propagandizing the Cossack and other regiments to turn them against the government and against their own officers.[61] On 28 October the Provisional Government was overthrown and the new Soviet government, comprising an alliance of the Bolsheviks and the Left Socialist Revolutionaries, under Lenin was proclaimed in Petrograd. By this time the Polese committee's military revolutionary committee had control of Gomel'.[62]

The Supreme Military High Command's headquarters (Stavka), based in Mogiliev, became the major centre of opposition to the new Bolshevik government. The Stavka proposed to transfer itself to Kiev to link up with the Ukrainian nationalist forces of Petlyura and to escape the advancing army of Bolshevik soldiers and sailors led by Krylenko. Socialist Revolutionary leaders, including Viktor Chernov, had gathered in Mogiliev and were considering forming a government there.[63] The Mogiliev soviet was dominated by Socialist Revolutionaries and Menshevik Defencists, and refused to recognize the new Soviet government's appointee, Krylenko, as Supreme Commander. On 31 October, Kaganovich, in disguise, and using the name Zheleznoi (Iron) visited Mogiliev. The Mogiliev railway workers, on Kaganovich's suggestion, adopted the tactics of the Gomel' railway workers to frustrate the movement of the Stavka to Kiev. A pro-Bolshevik battalion of the Grigorievsky cavalry assisted in withholding transport facilities to the Stavka.[64] By the middle of November, Krylenko had gained control of Mogiliev.

Kaganovich visited the Stavka of the Supreme High Command of Krylenko.[65] Krylenko proposed that Kaganovich join him in Petrograd to work on plans for the creation of a new Soviet army. Kaganovich also had contact with Myasnikov, who was Krylenko's deputy, and with whom he had worked in Minsk and Gomel'.

In the middle of December Kaganovich presided over the third congress of soviets of Mogiliev province. On his initiative, the Mensheviks were expelled from the unified Social Democratic organization and a purely Bolshevik organization was formed. The Soviet established an Extraordinary Commission (Cheka) to combat counter-revolution, headed by Privorotsky, who went on to become a leading Chekist.[66]

Kaganovich's activities in Minsk and the western region need to be set in context. This was no backwater, but a major stronghold of Bolshevik support. The results of the elections to the Constituent Assembly at the end of 1917 showed that the Bolshevik party commanded large support in Petrograd and Moscow, the two capitals, in the major industrial regions and in the army. Their support in the countryside was very weak. The Bolsheviks gained large support in the Western–Byelorussian region with its large Jewish population, especially in Minsk, Vitebsk and Smolensk.[67]

The unfolding of the revolutionary crisis in Russia from February to October 1917 was influenced by the war and the crisis in the army. For the Provisional Government and for the Bolsheviks, control over the armed forces was a decisive factor. The Bolshevik seizure of power in October was facilitated by their control over the Red Guards in the capital and the support they had within the army via the Military Organization. The surge of popular support for the Bolsheviks in the autumn of 1917 gave them 24 per cent of the vote in the elections to the Constituent Assembly. The Bolshevik opposition to war commanded wide approval, especially in the army. Their commitment to the granting of land to the peasants defused potential peasant opposition.

The Bolsheviks were not the plaything of historical forces. They were able to harness, channel and guide the popular movement at crucial stages. Lenin's decisions on doctrine and tactics had profound implications. He adopted a position of intransigent opposition to the Provisional Government and was contemptuous of the Socialist Revolutionary and Menshevik parties. It was his decision to reject the idea of a broad-based socialist government in October, and his decision to disperse the Constituent Assembly in January 1918. The October Revolution was predicated on the Bolsheviks' belief that it would act as a trigger for a socialist revolution on a European and global scale. But the Bolshevik–Left SR government lacked popular legitimacy. The domestic economic crisis was exacerbated, and the threat of a German advance increased as the army disintegrated. The October seizure of power was the inevitable prelude to civil war.

Creating the Red Army

Kaganovich was elected as a deputy to the Constituent Assembly on the Bolshevik list. The assembly met in Petrograd on 5 January 1918. He arrived the following day, after the assembly had been dispersed, and attended the meeting of the Congress of Deputies where Lenin defended his decision to dissolve the assembly. In his memoirs, he records his strong approval of this decision, arguing that the Bolshevik party, in a revolutionary situation, could not be constrained by legal niceties.[69]

On 8 January 1918 Kaganovich, as a delegate, attended the III All-Russian Congress of Workers and Soldiers deputies. There he heard Sverdlov and Lenin defending their decision to disperse the assembly, Stalin's speech on the nationalities policy and Zatonsky's speech on the establishment of a Ukrainian Soviet government. In his memoirs, he claims that at the congress he berated Yuli Martov, leader of the Mensheviks, over his refusal to endorse the October seizure of power. At this congress, he was elected a member of its Central Executive Committee of the Congress of Deputies and for the next forty years was to remain a member of this body and its successors, theoretically the supreme organ of the Soviet Republic.

At the congress, Lenin issued a directive for the creation of a new Soviet army. The All-Russian Bureau of Military Party Organizations, attached to the Central Committee, was assigned the task of drafting the decree. The new People's Commissariat of Military-Naval Affairs (NKVMDel) was established.[70] Nikolai Podvoisky, who was charged with drawing up the decree, recruited Kaganovich onto the drafting committee.[71] A meeting with Lenin made a big impression on him. When introduced, Kaganovich recounted, Lenin recalled his speech to the Conference of Bolshevik Army Organizations in June 1917. On 16 January the Soviet government (the Council of People's Commissars or Sovnarkom) issued the decree, incorporating some of Lenin's amendments, on establishing the Red Army.[72]

The All-Russian Collegium for Organizing the Workers' and Peasants' Red Army, headed by Podvoisky, attached to NKVMDel was given the task of forming the army. After discussion with Sverdlov, Kaganovich was relieved as head of the Polese party organization and was assigned to work in the collegium. He referred to Podvoisky as 'my unfailing friend and boss'. The collegium's small staff was housed in the Marinsky palace. Kaganovich worked 12 to 14 hours a day as a commissar in the Agitation-Propaganda Department. The department also issued a newspaper, *Workers and Peasants Red Army and Fleet*. He lived in the Astoria hotel, where conditions were good but the food supply was very bad. His wife Maria worked in the administration of Central Executive Committee of the Congress of Deputies.[73]

The threat of a German invasion prompted an upsurge in army recruitment. On 1 March the German army seized Kiev, and military units were formed in Ukraine to repel them.[74] On 3 March the Treaty of Brest-Litovsk was signed.[75] The treaty was bitterly opposed by the Left Communists, and precipitated the departure of the Left Socialist Revolutionaries from the government. Kaganovich supported the treaty, and later expressed disapproval of Trotsky's handling of these talks. He scathingly rejected the policy of revolutionary war advocated by the Left Communists and Left Socialist Revolutionaries.[76]

In the spring of 1918 the seat of the Soviet government was transferred from Petrograd to Moscow. The All-Russian Collegium was housed on Sretensky Boulevard. In April 1918, on the recommendation of Podvoisky and Mekhonoshin, Kaganovich was appointed to the Organization-Agitation Department of the All-Russian Collegium for Organizing the Red Army, on a salary of 500 rubles a month. He was housed at the hotel Alpine Rose on Kuznetsky Most.[77]

On 25–26 March a conference of the provincial military sections of the Moscow military region was convened. Its chairman was Mikhail Frunze, whom Kaganovich had known in Minsk in 1917. The main report was given by Podvoisky, who proposed to speedily create an army of 1.5 million men.[78] By June the Red Army, the Red Guards and the food supply and partisan units numbered about half a million men. The authority of the officers was reestablished, and the elected soldiers' committees were disbanded. Conscription was introduced to boost the army's ranks.[79]

Kaganovich, in his memoirs written long after in his retirement, disparaged Trotsky's role in creating the Red Army, giving most of the credit to Lenin, Sverdlov and Stalin, while emphasizing the practical role of the All-Russian Collegium under Podvoisky.[80] By June 1918 the All-Russian Collegium had been dissolved and its officials dispersed. Kaganovich was employed for a month as a worker at the Mercury factory in Moscow,[81] before accepting Podvoisky's invitation to join the Higher Military Inspectorate. But before he took up this new post, his career took a new turn.

Kaganovich's account of his early life stands at variance with other hostile accounts. In 1933 a writer in the Menshevik journal claimed that Kaganovich had become a worker during the war in order to avoid military service, and that prior to this he had been an 'intellectual without specific profession'. Moreover, it was asserted that for a period he worked in a department store in Kiev, but left after accusations of theft.[82] After his political fall in 1957, some Old Bolsheviks cast aspersions on his early revolutionary career, accusing him of supporting the Provisional Government in March 1917, of siding with the Mensheviks and of enthusiastically volunteering to join the army.[83] These accounts are suspect and are contradicted by other sources.[84] Allegations that he had been an active Zionist in his early years are also unfounded.[85]

While the accusations directed at Kaganovich need to be read with caution, his own account of his early life is not entirely straightforward. No satisfactory explanation is offered for his delay in joining the Bolshevik party. This suggests that in his early teens he may have contemplated a career other than the revolutionary course which he adopted in 1912. The circumstances behind his departure to Melitopol in 1916 are unclear. The memoirs offer no real explanation as to how he avoided being conscripted into the army from 1914 to 1917 or of the circumstances under which he was finally enlisted.

Although Kaganovich had strong intellectual interests, he belonged more to the category of the revolutionary worker autodidact. Photographs of him from these early years show a handsome, dapperly dressed young man in coat, collar and tie, with a fresh face and well-groomed, dark, wavy hair and, in some pictures, a moustache. His eyes (which were blue) gaze confidently into the camera. He appears as the conscious worker aspiring to dignity, but he might easily be taken for a student or young intellectual.[86]

Attempts to trace Kaganovich's adherence to the revolutionary cause to some psychological roots yield little. He was a well-adjusted individual. In his memoirs he wrote nostalgically of his childhood, describing his upbringing in a stable and warm family, and recalled with affection his native region. The deprivations of a straitened childhood and thwarted ambition for advancement via education fuelled a sense of grievance against the injustice of the *ancien regime*. Undoubtedly, the disabilities imposed on Jews was a factor in his radicalization. His political outlook was forged during the aftermath of the 1905 Revolution, by the Stolypin reaction and the Great War. His adherence to Bolshevism was to be absolute, colouring all aspects of his existence, and lasted the whole of his life. It was a choice that was to bring great power and status, but which was also to make extraordinary demands.

Conclusion

Kaganovich was a remarkably self-possessed man. His formal education was limited, but he was intelligent, quick-witted and had boundless energy. He was an accomplished orator, a good organizer and a natural leader who possessed a real charismatic quality. He came from the milieu of the small-town Ukrainian Jewish artisans who were being proletarianized. He belonged to that substantial group of deracinated, radicalized Jewish workers and intellectuals, who made up a significant component of the revolutionary movement. He was what Gramsci termed an organic intellectual of the working class who were proud of their self-identity as class-conscious workers and part of the revolutionary vanguard. He won a reputation as a leading activist in Kiev and the Donbass. After being conscripted into the army, his role in the Bolshevik Military Organization dramatically propelled his career. During the October Revolution he worked in the big Jewish centres of Minsk, Gomel' and Mogiliev.

He was a committed trade unionist and worked in legal and semilegal unions from 1911 onward. In his memoirs, he emphasized that his allegiance to the trade unions was instrumental in turning him into a Bolshevik.[87] He was an ardent, idealistic revolutionary. He subscribed to Lenin's doctrinaire, uncompromising conception of socialism and his views on party organization. He embraced a cosequentialist view of ethics, that the ends justified the means. He did not lack courage, and was self-controlled and focused. Like other Bolsheviks, there was something ascetic, puritanical, self-righteous in his makeup. As with many revolutionaries, his marriage was one of revolutionary comrades. His clandestine political and trade union activities tempered a personality already characterized by its toughness and resilience. The October Revolution opened up new vistas for him, and at the age of 24, his career was about to take off dramatically.

Lenin's conception of socialism was coloured by utopian aspirations, untempered by engagement in practical affairs of state and economic management. The Bolsheviks' attempt to realize the unrealizeable carried with it the danger of the perversion of the idealistic project with profound consequences for themselves and the regime they had created. Dostoevsky, writing of modern revolutionary socialism, prophesied that the attempt to realize its aims would produce "such darkness, such chaos, something so coarse, so blind, so inhuman that the entire edifice would crumble away to the accompaniment of the maledictions of mankind, even before it would finally have been constructed".[88] In that, Dostoevsky proved a better prophet and a more perceptive thinker than Lenin.

Chapter 2
RED TERROR AND CIVIL WAR, 1918–1921

In October 1917 the Bolsheviks, in coalition with the Left SRs, established their government, the Council of People's Commissars (Sovnarkom). The new regime offered unprecedented opportunities for advancement to a wide cohort of party members and sympathizers. The consolidation of the Soviet state became the overriding priority of the regime. The winter of 1917–18 witnessed a collapse of industrial production and acute problems of food supply in the urban centres. The dispersal of the Constituent Assembly in January 1918 was perceived, even by some Bolsheviks, as an illegal usurpation of power. The advancing German armies threatened to overthrow the Soviet regime. By the summer of 1918 the first phase of the Civil War had begun, with the White Armies of Kolchak, Denikin, Yudenich and Wrangel in league with the interventionist forces from Britain, France, America and Japan. The failure of the European revolution left the Russian revolutionary government beleaguered and isolated. In this period Kaganovich underwent a baptism of fire into the realities of revolutionary politics and into the practicalities of *realpolitik* in major battle fronts such as Nizhnyi Novgorod, Voronezh and Turkestan.

Nizhnyi Novgorod

In 1918 Kaganovich was sent by the Central Committee to Nizhnyi Novgorod initially as a party agitator.[1] On 26 May the province party committee heard a report on behalf of the Central Committee from N. A. Semashko, who had close links with the city, and on his recommendation the committee co-opted Kaganovich and one other as members.[2] Kaganovich served as the Bolshevik political chief of Nizhnyi Novgorod from June 1918 until September 1919. This period in his career is glossed over in his memoirs.[3] According to him, the appointment was authorized by Sverdlov with Lenin's approval.[4]

Nizhnyi Novgorod (Nizhnyi or Nizhegorod) was a major industrial centre with a strong revolutionary tradition. In October 1917 the Bolsheviks, in alliance with the Left SRs, took control of the Nizhnyi soviet, with I. P. Romanov elected as chairman of the province soviet executive committee (*gubispolkom*).[5] The party's position was buttressed by the Cheka and the Revolutionary Tribunal (established in March 1918) and the Military Commissariat.[6] The alliance between the Bolsheviks and the Left SRs broke down in March 1918 over the question of the signing of the Treaty of Brest-Litovsk. The city held a commanding position on the Volga, and constituted a major Bolshevik outpost during the Civil War.

Popular opinion in Nizhnyi was highly critical of Bolshevik method and policies. In March 1918 the local authorities accused the Mensheviks and Right SRs of stirring up the workers of the great Sormovo engineering works.[7] On 23 April there was an attempted uprising in Nizhnyi, allegedly fomented by an unlikely alliance of Anarchists and Kadets, exploiting the discontent within the army. Trotsky reported on the great reluctance of workers in Nizhnyi to join the Red Army.[8] Bolshevik grain requisitioning provoked strong opposition in the countryside. In the province alone in 1918 there were some 40 peasant risings against the Bolshevik authorities that were attributed to SR, Menshevik and White Guard agitation.[9] The risings peaked in the summer of 1918 and were brutally suppressed.[10]

On 11 June Sovnarkom established the committees of poor peasants (*kombedy*). In Nizhnyi and elsewhere the *kombedy* were employed for grain requisitioning, directing their actions against the kulaks, 'speculators', and even against the middle peasants. They worked in league with the Cheka and revolutionary tribunals. On 20 June the Nizhnyi province Cheka ordered the surrender of all civilian-held firearms.[11] The province party committee placed a special armed detachment of 100 communists at the disposal of the Cheka to conduct mass searches and to combat counter-revolution.[12]

On 10 June a conference of 200 worker delegates (representing, according to different estimates, 40,000 or 100,000 workers) convened in Sormovo as a focus of worker opposition to Bolshevik rule. The meeting was disrupted by the Red Guards, who rampaged through the workers' district, shooting wildly, killing two and wounding several dozen. The next day the conference called for a general strike against the Bolshevik authorities. The Mensheviks lodged a protest with the All-Russian Central Executive Committee of Soviets. A Menshevik report at this time spoke of the workers of Nizhnyi as having completely deserted the Bolsheviks.[13]

On 18 June Sormovo went on strike and shops, cafes and businesses closed in sympathy. The same day, the crowd released from the local prison 105 local capitalists, arrested by the Cheka for non-payment of a levy imposed on them by the Nizhnyi soviet.[14] The strike lasted several days. The Sormovo Cheka arrested the strike leaders, and the Nizhnyi province soviet confiscated all enterprises which had closed.[15] In accordance with the Sovnarkom decree of

26 June nationalizing all large industrial enterprises, the state took over the giant Sormovo, Kulebansky and Vyksynsky works in Nizhnyi.

The introduction of what became known as 'War Communism' in the summer of 1918 was intended as a leap into the new communist order. It was ideologically driven and only in part dictated by the needs of managing a civil war economy. Large, medium and small-scale industries were nationalized. Grain was gathered by forcible requisitioning. In the countryside, the Bolsheviks sought to mobilize the poor peasants via the poor-peasants committee against not only the kulaks, but also against the middle peasants.[16] The Nizhnyi party committee enthusiastically embraced these policies.

In June the IV Nizhnyi Province Party Conference elected a new party committee with Kaganovich as chairman.[17] He replaced M. S. Sergushev, a worker and long-standing Bolshevik, who remained as a committee member.

At the end of June the II Province Congress of Soviets witnessed heated exchanges between the Bolsheviks and the Left SRs. Kaganovich vigorously defended the Treaty of Brest-Litovsk: 'Our task is not to die with honour, but to preserve the Soviet republic, whatever the odds... Thus, it is laughable to shout about war when we have absolutely nothing.'[18] V. G. Zaks, for the Left SRs, continued to advocate revolutionary war against Germany. He denounced the 'food supply dictatorship', warning that the *kombedy* would provoke more peasant risings, and lead to a diminution of the acreage sown. The Bolsheviks' agrarian policy, based on the poor peasants (*bedniaks*), was doomed to fail.[19] The Bolshevik-dominated congress ignored these warnings and approved the policy on peace and a resolution on the committee of poor peasants

On 27 June the Nizhnyi province Bolshevik party committee condemned the threat by the Left SRs to withdraw from the province soviet executive committee, declaring that it did not fear to rule alone, and would 'resolutely stand at its post'.[20] The V All-Russian Congress of Soviets, which met on 5 July, finalized the split between the Bolsheviks and the Left SRs. The assassination of the German ambassador, Count Mirbach, was followed by the attempted putsch of the Left SRs in Moscow on 6 July. Three days later, the Nizhnyi province soviet executive committee closed down the newspaper of the Left SRs and on 11 July, expelled the Left SRs from its ranks.[21]

In response, the SRs staged political risings in Yaroslavl, Murom and Rybinsk. Yaroslavl was not relieved until 21 July, with the sending in of Cheka detachments from Petrograd and elsewhere. The Cheka detachment from Nizhnyi, led by N. A. Bulganin, played an important part in the repression which ensued. Fifty-seven of the insurgents were shot, and a special commission sent to the town sentenced another 350 to death.[22]

The Red Terror in Nizhnyi Novgorod

By summer, the position of the Bolshevik government was precarious – deserted by Left SRs, threatened by peasant rebellion and working class discontent. The commencement of the allied intervention also deepened the mood of despair. The Czechoslovak Legion, which supported the Socialist Revolutionary Komuch government, seized Simbirsk, Samara and Izhev and took Kazan on 6 July. Against this background, the decision to execute all the members of the royal family was taken. In July–August, Lenin instructed local Bolshevik leaders to institute a policy of terror, to execute and take as hostage rich peasants who withheld grain and to ruthlessly suppress peasant rebellions.[23]

On 7 August Trotsky, as People's Commissar for War, was appointed commander of the Revolutionary Military Council (Revvoensoviet) of the Eastern Front. He later described Nizhnyi as Moscow's bastion against the Czechoslovak Legion and as the main supply base for the Fifth Army.[24] Two days later, Lenin, after discussing the situation with Ya. Kh. Peters, acting chairman of the Cheka, sent an urgent letter to G. F. Fedorov, chairman of the Nizhnyi province soviet executive committee.[25] He instructed him to immediately establish a 'troika of the dictatorship' to suppress the threat of a White Guard rising. There then followed a series of blood-curdling injunctions: 'to institute immediately a mass terror', 'to shoot and deport hundreds of prostitutes who get the soldiers drunk, former officers, *etc.*'; those found in possession of weapons to be shot; Mensheviks and other unreliables to be deported en masse. Lenin also assigned F. F. Raskol'nikov and K. Kh. Danishevsky, members of the Revvoensoviet of the Eastern Front, to Nizhnyi to assist in suppressing the threatened counter-revolution.[26]

On 10 August the Nizhnyi province party committee established a Military Revolutionary Committee (MRC) with full power. It comprised five members, including the heads of the local soviets, Cheka and Military committees, with Kaganovich as head of the province party committee.[27] The following day, Lenin issued instructions to the MRC for the defence of the city. The MRC drew up plans for the city's defence, including proposals for the creation of a concentration camp to hold arrested army officers.[28]

On 16 August Ya. Z. Vorob'ev, head of the province Cheka, reported to the first Nizhnyi province conference of the Cheka and the Military Commissars on the arrest of members of the local bourgeoisie, army officers, kulaks, former police and Okhrana officers.[29] Three days later, Lenin instructed Raskol'nikov, of the Revvoensoviet of the Eastern Front, to send forces to Kazan and to Nizhnyi to establish revolutionary order.[30] On 22 August the MRC discussed plans for the evacuation of the city.[31] The following day, the MRC ordered the mobilization of all party workers between 18 and 28 years of age.[32]

Efforts were made to rally working class support behind the regime.³³ Some smaller factories, under Bolshevik control, passed resolutions of support, but the party's influence in the major factories was weak. At the Vyksynsky works, with 8,000 employees, there was virtually no party organization by August, while at Sormovo, with 15,000 workers, party membership had slumped from 1,200 in March to 107 by September.³⁴

G. Ya. Sokolnikov, a Central Committee emissary, addressed a poorly attended meeting at the Sormovo works on 30 August and upbraided them for their inactivity, chiding them that, in 1905, they had been in the front rank of the fighters for the freedom of the working class. Kaganovich, in his speech, berated the workers for failing to support the Bolshevik authorities:

> And what have you Sormovichi done to secure grain? Have you organized a single food supply detachment? Have you – 15,000 strong mass – sent one detachment to the front to struggle with the Czechoslovaks to win Volga grain? No! You have done nothing!³⁵

A party activist from Nizhnyi reported to the Secretariat in Moscow that the situation in the city left an 'oppressive image', and that the mobilization of activists for the front had precipitated a collapse of membership numbers.³⁶

On 30 August Lenin was wounded in an assassination attempt in Moscow. The All-Russian Central Executive Committee immediately called for reprisals. *Pravda* even implied that the bourgeoisie as a class should be exterminated. The suggestion was repeated by Georgi Zinoviev in Petrograd.³⁷ On 4 September a telegram signed by G. I. Petrovsky instructed local soviets to carry out a Red Terror in earnest.³⁸ Six days later Sovnarkom published its decree 'On Red Terror', drafted by Felix Dzerzhinsky, head of the Cheka, and Sverdlov,³⁹ which gave the actions retrospective legal cover.

On the day of the attempted assassination, the MRC of Nizhnyi resolved 'to answer the terror of the bourgeoisie with the Red Terror' by shooting bourgeois hostages and by instituting 'mass terror against the bourgeoisie and its minions.'⁴⁰ Already on 31 August the Nizhnyi Cheka reported that they had shot 41 people 'from the bourgeois camp' and seized up to 700 people as hostages.⁴¹ The shooting of unarmed hostages in flagrant violation of the rules of war set an ominous precedent of class justice. The conduct of the terror in Nizhnyi is shrouded in mystery and local newspapers of the period are hard to find.

On 3 September mass meetings were held in the province and supportive resolutions were passed.⁴² At this time the MRC co-opted V. I. Mezhlauk as a member, and decided to place Sormovo and other works under military discipline. The Military Revolutionary Committee appointed a commandant responsible for all defence matters, the registering of arms and the imposition of a curfew. On16 September it ordered the confiscation of the property of the bourgeoisie who had fled the town, while those who remained were to be arrested and held in a specially built 'concentration camp'.[43]

Kazan was recaptured on 10 September and the threat to Nizhnyi was lifted. The town was decked out in red flags in celebration.[44] Those associated with Trotsky in the campaign to free Kazan – I. I. Vatsetis, Ivan Smirnov, A. P. Rozengolts, F. F. Raskol'nikov, N. Muralov and K. K. Yurenev – now dominated military affairs.[45] On 19 September the Nizhnyi province party committee, on a report from Kaganovich, disbanded the MRC and transferred its functions to the province party committee.[46] The height of the Red Terror in Nizhnyi city and province had passed, but the repression did not end.

The V Province Party Conference in Nizhnyi Novgorod

The V Nizhnyi Province Party Conference opened on 25 October. Kaganovich delivered the main report, outlining the regime's beleaguered position and the 'desertion' of the proletariat by the urban and rural petty bourgeoisie. This isolation was itself turned into a virtue:

> The dictatorship is rendered in its most pure, most naked form, the dictatorship of the proletariat, without any petty bourgeois dilution. And once the dictatorship belongs to the proletariat, once this class has only one party, it means that the dictatorship belongs to the party, the party of communists.[47]

Here was a clear statement of the substitution of the party for the class, made all the more acute by the desertion of the regime by the workers in the major enterprises. Bolshevik power came to rest on the four pillars – the party, the Cheka, the Red Army and the state bureaucracy.

Kaganovich called on the party to turn itself into an 'iron-mailed fist' of the proletarian dictatorship, extending its control into the soviets, the trade unions, and the poor peasant committees. The merging of the province party and province soviet newspapers into one – *Nizhegorodskaya kommuna* – was a fusion of party and soviet functions to which he was to return to again. The strictures of the 'party dictatorship', Kaganovich declared, should be applied to its own members, so as to eradicate internal dissension and to establish 'unanimity'. The party, he argued, should not immerse itself in the details of administration. He outlined a vision of party-state relations which was to have an enduring impact. With startling frankness he stressed the party's role was to lead, but not overtly. The party should secretly instruct the Cheka or the

Military Tribunal to carry out arrests and executions, but should not directly involve itself in these matters, adding, 'nobody must know about this; you will not see in the press accusations from the province committee of the party'.[48] Here we have one of the most explicit statements of the 'Machiavellianism' that underpinned Bolshevik power.

In his speech, he referred cryptically to the events in Nizhnyi of August–September. Following the attempt on Lenin's life, when the slogan 'Long live the Red Terror' had been proclaimed, the Nizhny province party committee 'did not lag behind' and although he refused to divulge the numbers of those arrested and shot, he declared 'The counter-revolutionary bourgeoisie and kulakdom was absolutely smashed not only here but in the whole province.'[49] The conference elected a new province party committee, with Kaganovich as chairman.[50]

The Situation after the Red Terror

The 'Red Terror' left the province stunned. Attempts were made to justify these decisions by turning the handful of Bolsheviks killed by peasant insurgents into martyrs. In December 1918 the local party newspaper carried a poem, dedicated to Kaganovich, by the socialist poet Sergei Malashkin. Entitled 'Silver Knell of Autumn' (*Serebryannyi zvon listopada*), it evokes a melancholic mood and alludes to the Red Terror. This is a time, the poet says, not for regret or reproach, but a time when comrades should come together, to drink and be of good heart.[51] Evidently, these terrible actions weighed on the conscience of some Bolsheviks, although the notion of dulling one's conscience with drink has an ominous ring.

After the terror, Nizhnyi remained under the control of the Cheka and the Revolutionary Tribunal. The newspaper *Nizhegorodskaya kommuna* carried daily reports of searches carried out, with lists of individuals arrested. On 22 December the province party committee issued an order, signed by Kaganovich and Sergushev, for enlisting up to 10 per cent of all party members into the armed forces. Orders were issued for party members to assist in collecting arms.[52]

On 25 October the Nizhnyi Party Conference sent greetings to Karl Liebknecht as the leader of the imminent German revolution.[53] In November the local press hailed the expected Austrian and German revolutions.[54] This heady optimism was dispelled in January 1919 with the news of the murder of Liebknecht and Rosa Luxemburg. Kaganovich's admiration for Luxemburg as a revolutionary leader suggests that he probably knew little of her criticisms of the authoritarian aspects of Leninism.

In December Lenin dispatched Stalin and Dzerzhinsky to investigate the reasons for the fall of Perm and to take measures to stabilize the military situation. At the end of the month Trotsky visited Nizhnyi and delivered a speech at the Sovetsky Theatre on the situation on the Eastern Front, and also addressed a meeting of 10,000 at the Sormovo works.[55] The same day, in *Pravda*, he strongly defended the controversial policy of employing former tsarist officers in the Red Army.[56] His imposition of ruthless military discipline, including the shooting of commanders and political commissars, provoked an outcry in the party.[57]

Kaganovich as Head of the Nizhnyi Novgorod Soviet Executive Committee

On 16 January 1919 the Nizhnyi province soviet executive committee elected a new presidium, chaired by Kaganovich.[58] In the face of public indignation, the head of the province Cheka, Vorob'ev, and his assistants, including Bulganin, were forced to resign. Bulganin, himself a native of Nizhnyi, played a prominent role both in suppressing the Left SRs rising in Yaroslavl, and in organizing the Red Terror in Nizhnyi. His Cheka colleagues attracted particular odium and were known as 'Bulganin's goons'.[59] On 29 January the province soviet executive committee, on the insistence of the centre, abolished the Cheka at district (*uezd*) level, with the exception of four districts. Kaganovich reported that they would seek to overturn this ruling.[60]

From January to September 1919 Kaganovich served as chairman of the province soviet executive committee. He gave up his post as chairman of the province party committee, which was occupied by Sergushev, although he delivered the report in this capacity at the VI Province Party Conference in February.[61] Kaganovich remained the dominant political figure in Nizhnyi. One of the reasons for this demarcation of party and soviet functions was the outcry caused by the excesses of the Cheka.

'To the Party Congress'

Kaganovich began to elaborate his ideas on party and soviet administration which he had presented to the province party conference in October. On 11 December in a report to the province party committee, he complained of the weakness of the local party leadership and proposed that the Central Committee create its own bureau to monitor party work in the localities. Other speakers complained that the Central Committee weakened local party organizations by taking the best workers for itself.[62]

In January *Nizhegorodskaya kommuna* published Kaganovich's article entitled 'To the party congress', addressed to the forthcoming VIII Party Congress. This was Kaganovich's first major venture into print, and it was an extraordinary debut. It dealt with three issues: party organization at national and local level, the organization of the Red Army and the future of the Cheka. Provincial party committees, he maintained, often contravened official policies out of ignorance and lack of clear directives. The solution was to introduce the 'strictest centralism'. The Central Committee should set up a political committee and an organizational committee to manage its affairs and expand the role of its Secretariat in overseeing local party bodies. The party should not hesitate to employ bourgeois specialists and tsarist army officers and turn them into 'servants' of the proletarian dictatorship. The party should not 'play at soldiers', but create a powerful army, based on proletarian consciousness, possessing real military expertise.[63] Party cells in the Red Army should have no say on operational matters, but should exercise close political supervision over the former tsarist officers. The strictest discipline should be enforced: the military department should not flinch from shooting party members who breached discipline.

Kaganovich's article was published a few days after Trotsky's visit to Nizhnyi. It endorsed Trotsky's controversial policy of shooting military commanders and commissars for breaches of discipline. It also endorsed the policy of employing former tsarist officers. This policy was strongly opposed by Stalin and K. E. Voroshilov, commanders of the Southern Front, and also by Zinoviev and Yuri Larin. In March 1919 Lenin, at a meeting of Sovnarkom, raised the question of dispensing with the services of these officers. Trotsky pointed out that the Red Army employed 30,000 former tsarist officers and that the very suggestion was 'infantile'.[64]

On 1 March *Pravda* gave an account of Kaganovich's article in *Nizhegorodskaya kommuna*, and on 4 March it published the thesis of the Nizhnyi Party Conference on party organization. It proposed transforming the party onto a hierarchically ordered and disciplined body, with full documentation and assignment of all party members (especially those with long pre-revolutionary party membership – *stazh*). The criteria for party admission had to be tightened up in order to stem the influx of petty bourgeois elements and careerists. The party had to transform itself into a real force in organizing soviet construction. In an obvious rejoinder to the criticisms levelled at the Nizhnyi Cheka, the thesis praised the Extraordinary Commissions as the 'fighting organs of the proletarian dictatorship'. It rejected calls for the liquidation of the district Cheka as inexpedient. Concerning military organization, the thesis also warned that they should 'not go too far' in granting powers to officers, and took issue with the Central Committee's instructions to reduce the power of the party cells in the army.[65]

Kaganovich's proposals coincided with the thinking of the centre. In January the Central Committee decided to set up two subcommittees and to call them the Political Bureau (*Politburo*) and the Organizational Bureau (*Orgburo*). The publication of Kaganovich's proposal in *Pravda* on 5 February prompted Klavdiya Sverdlova, of the party Secretariat, to protest to Sergushev, chairman of the Nizhnyi province party committee, insisting that there was a strong centre, but lamely admitting that the centre's resolutions often simply 'hang in the air'.[66]

On 4 March, at the VI Province Party Conference, Kaganovich defended his thesis on party centralization. The conference unanimously approved his organizational thesis for presentation at the coming party congress. A new province party committee of seven members was elected.[67] The congress also elected Kaganovich, Sergushev and four others as delegates to the VIII Russian Party Congress.[68]

The VIII Party Congress in March was dominated by the question of party organization, particularly within the army. Yakov Sverdlov, who had advocated increased central control over provincial party organization, died before the congress opened.[69] Both Zinoviev and Lenin tried to reassure the delegates that the Central Committee and the Secretariat would henceforth approach their work in a more planned and organized fashion.[70]

The exasperation of local party organization with the lack of guidance and support provided by the centre was expressed by the Democratic Centralists, headed by T. V. Sapronov, V. Maksimov and V. V. Osinsky. While demanding the strengthening of the central party bodies and the proletarianization of their composition, they also demanded greater accountability to the membership through party conferences that should be held every three months. They also stressed the importance of restoring soviet democracy and preserving party and soviet bodies as distinct and separate entities.[71]

At the congress, Kaganovich elaborated on his ideas on party organization, arguing that it was necessary to appoint at each level a presidium or collegium of about three 'responsible party workers' devoted exclusively to managing party work. In this he anticipated the future party structure based on committees at each administrative tier (what later was designated as *obkom*, *gubkom*, *gorkom*, *raikom*). At the level of the Central Committee, there should be a bureau or 'organizational commission' of leading party workers, who would be released from all other work. This again anticipated the future Orgburo. Party work had to be placed on a new footing, rejecting 'artisanship'. In this he envisaged a unified administrative party structure: 'Every party organization must have its own secretariat.'[72]

In contrast to the Democratic Centralists, who saw the party's authority as being derived from the elected soviets, Kaganovich reversed the order: 'the party is the source of the strength and power of soviet work'; the soviets were strong in the regions where the party was strong. Local party organizations lacked material resources, and consequently, he argued, they should siphon off funds from the agitation department of the provincial soviets, adding, lest there be any confusion, 'This must be done using state resources.'[73] The provincial party committees should closely oversee the district and village committees. He criticized Zinoviev's thesis on national sections in the party, arguing that such sections be subordinated to the local party committees and demanded that their role and rights be more clearly defined. He urged measures to strengthen the rural party organization and to use the journal *Ezhenedelnik 'Pravdy'* as a guide for local party workers.

The congress passed a resolution on strengthening democracy in the soviets and a second resolution on increased centralization and 'military discipline' in the party.[74] But the main outcome of the congress was the creation of the Politburo and Orgburo alongside the party Secretariat. The Politburo members were Lenin, Lev Kamenev, Trotsky, Stalin, N. N. Krestinsky, and the candidate members were Zinoviev, N. I. Bukharin and M. I. Kalinin. Stalin was appointed to the Politburo and Orgburo, providing a direct link between the two.[75] Lenin now endorsed the policy of employing military specialists, which the congress confirmed.[76] Most of Kaganovich's demands had been met. At the congress, Lenin criticized a document issued by the Nizhnyi province party committee, which declared as its aim to levy an extraordinary tax on the middle peasants. Sergushev, for the province party committee, insisted that this was a typographical error, an explanation that Lenin accepted.[77]

The Bolsheviks' policy of establishing the *kombedy*, one of the issues behind the rift with the Left SRs in July 1918, alienated the middle peasants and proved to be a colossal blunder driven by ideological intransigence. The congress called for a more attentive attitude to the middle peasants. Trotsky claimed credit for this change of policy, which was dictated by the situation on the Volga, where the Red Army faced the problem of conscripting recruits and procuring grain while combating the threat of counter-revolution.[78] On 28 March Kaganovich, in his report to the province soviet, highlighted the central message of the VIII Party Congress, the vital necessity of winning over the middle peasants.[79]

The Situation in Nizhnyi Novgorod in 1919

Through the winter and spring, the food supply crisis and a typhus epidemic dominated the lives of the population in Nizhnyi. The worsening economic and political situation brought a tightening of repression. On 29 March the Nizhnyi province soviet executive committee resolved, on the basis of a Central Committee decree, to retain Cheka officials in their posts and to reappoint Vorob'ev as chairman of the province Cheka.[80] On 4 April *Pravda* reported on one grain requisitioning operation in the province which had left fifty peasants dead.[81]

In the spring, major strikes at Sormovo, Tula, Petrograd and Moscow underlined the regime's loss of support. Workers' resolutions in Sormovo and elsewhere demanded a cessation of the Civil War, fair elections, the abolition of privileges for Communists and the convocation of the Constituent Assembly. The authorities closed the plant, arrested activists and withheld food rations from the strikers.[82] On 9 April Kaganovich reported to the province party committee on measures taken to end strikes at the Briansk Arsenal and the Novaya Etna works, which he blamed on Menshevik and SR agitators.[83]

The Bolshevik party organization in Nizhnyi grew from 6,128 in March 1918 to 11,130 by March 1919. This increase, however, masked a veritable haemorrhage of proletarian members from the giant enterprises. The party Secretariat continued to monitor the situation at these works.[84] Vlas Chubar' was sent to Nizhnyi, co-opted onto the province party committee, and given a special mandate to oversee the Sormovo works.[85]

Bolshevik policy fuelled peasant hostilities and prompted a huge growth in the Green movement.[86] In August, it was reported that an army of the 'Greens' was active in the province.[87] New alarms were sounded with the threat of Kolchak on the Eastern Front. On 12 April Trotsky visited Nizhnyi and addressed a meeting of Red Sailors of the Volga flotilla.[88] Four days later, Kaganovich reported to the Nizhnyi province soviet executive committee on organizing the Eastern Front and imposing strict labour discipline in industry. The party's policy of conciliating the middle peasants was to be fully applied. A major drive was launched to apprehend military deserters, a problem which assumed a huge scale in 1919. He also proposed to re-establish the Cheka in the districts where they had been disbanded in January.[89]

Semashko, a Central Committee plenipotentiary sent to Nizhnyi, instructed the province soviet executive committee on its obligations in organizing support for the front. On 20 April he reported to the Central Committee that he had received a fair reception at Sormovo, where he had addressed them on the need to repulse Kolchak and institute a full mobilization.[90]

On 3 May Kaganovich again addressed the province soviet executive committee on the defence of Kazan and on securing supplies for the Red Army. A week later, Semashko, Kaganovich and Sergushev reported to the province party plenum on strengthening the rear and organizing support for the front. They again highlighted the importance of good relations with the middle peasants. In June the province soviet had to send representatives to neighbouring provinces to secure food supplies. The crisis was exacerbated by the fuel shortage that led to the closure of a number of metal works.[91]

On 3 July Krupskaya visited Nizhnyi.[92] The same day, Kaganovich reported to the province soviet executive committee on the situation in the province: strikes, arson, worker discontent and critical shortage of food and fuel. He again highlighted the Cheka's central role in fighting counter-revolution and preserving order. He also reported on his visit to Moscow to discuss with the People's Commissariat for Procurement measures to secure food supplies for the province.[93] He had discussions with Lenin, he later recalled, and grain was made available.[94] The following day he addressed the trade union conference in Nizhnyi on the food supply situation. The conference passed a resolution supporting Soviet power.[95]

At the VII Province Party Conference in July, Kaganovich demanded that the party be militarized and that all party secretaries be held personally accountable for all decisions taken in their name.[96] Sergushev was confirmed as chairman of the province party committee. Kaganovich at the end of the month was confirmed as chairman of the presidium of the province soviet executive committee.[97]

Voronezh

In the summer of 1919 Denikin's forces advanced from the south and threatened Moscow. The Central Committee assigned large numbers of soldiers to the Southern Front, where Trotsky had command.[98] The situation of the Eastern Front had stabilised and in August the Nizhegorod authorities assigned thousands of Red Army men and volunteers to the campaign. The leading local officials in Nizhnyi – the chairman of the province party committee (Sergushev), the chairman of the province soviet executive committee (Kaganovich), the head of *gubcheka* (Vorob'ev), the province party committee secretary (Mordovtsev) and others – volunteered.[99] The province party committee, however, refused Kaganovich permission. He travelled to Moscow and gained the consent of both Elena Stasova and Lenin to be assigned to Voronezh as a Central Committee plenipotentiary and as chairman of the province Military Revolutionary Committee.[100]

On 3 September Kaganovich arrived in Voronezh by freight train. He was enlisted into a special detachment for the defence of the city and took charge of the party's political department (*politotdel*). The battle for the city raged for four days, until the Bolsheviks triumphed on 13 September. On his departure from the city on 19 September, Kadrashov, chairman of the province party committee, gave him a document which acknowledged that 'during the battle for Voronezh, he, with rifle in hand, had fought in the leading positions.'[101] He returned to Moscow on 25 September and reported to the Secretariat. On his advice, Kadrashov was replaced.

On 1 October Denikin's forces captured Voronezh. According to Kaganovich, he was summoned by Stasova to go and see Lenin, who told him that Stalin was being assigned to the Southern Front and that the recapture of the town was a top priority. With Trotsky's transfer to defend Petrograd against Yudenich's forces, Stalin assumed command of the front. On 24 October Voronezh was liberated, and within hours a celebratory meeting was convened on III International Square. In his address, Kaganovich, on behalf of the revolutionary committee and the province party committee, praised the role of Budennyi's cavalry in the victory.[102]

Kaganovich, as chairman of the province Military Revolutionary Committee, worked closely with the Red Army. On 28 October he issued Order No. 1, on restoring normality, which included instructions on respecting the rights of believers to hold divine services and to chime the bells. The hospitals were reopened to deal with an outbreak of typhus. At the funeral of the combatants who fell in the operation to force a crossing of the Don, Budennyi and Kaganovich delivered orations and the service was attended by priests.[103] Budennyi and Kaganovich remained close friends thereafter. Kaganovich subsequently became chairman of the province soviet executive committee and led party and soviet construction work in Voronezh province.

On 5 December the VII All-Russian Congress of Soviets opened in the Bolshoi Theatre in Moscow. Kaganovich was elected to the presidium as Kaganovich-Voronezhsky, to distinguish him from P. K. Kaganovich, a food supply commissar in Simbirsk province.[104] In the debate, Kaganovich dismissed Kalinin's charge that he favoured local control over industrial enterprises, declaring that he had been accused of being an arch-centralizer.[105] At the congress, he claimed, Lenin questioned him and V. M. Molotov, his successor as chairman of the Nizhnyi soviet executive committee, regarding the situation in the town.[106]

In 1920 Kaganovich (using the pseudonym Voronezhsky) published *Kak stroitsia sovetskaya vlast'* ('How soviet power is built'), based on his reports to the Voronezh Province Congress of Soviets in January and to the All-Russian Central Executive Committee of Soviets in February. The main theme was the need for the centre, through the provincial and district soviets, to establish direct connections with the people.[107]

The brutalizing effect of the Civil War on this generation of Bolshevik leaders and activists was lasting. Lenin, in October 1920, addressing the Komsomol congress, advanced a crude consequentialist conception of morality, declaring 'our morality is entirely subordinated to the interests of the class struggle of the proletariat.'[108] The dictatorship of the proletariat was not a law-governed state, but was guided by revolutionary expediency. In his polemical attack on Karl Kautsky, Trotsky in *Terrorism and Communism* in 1920 justified Bolshevik terror tactics. The Bolshevik resort to terror was not simply reactive, but also proactive. This opened an ideological and ethical chasm between Communism and Social Democracy. Like other Bolsheviks, Kaganovich imbibed the party ethic which subordinated individual conscience to the party's dictates and to the higher laws of 'necessity'.

The Turkestan Front, 1920–1922

With victory in the Civil War in sight, the Soviet government directed its attention to securing control of its periphery, especially in Moslem Central Asia (Turkestan). In 1916, following a major revolt, the region was placed under martial law and large-scale settlement of Russian peasants in the region was initiated.[109] In October 1917 the Tashkent Soviet of Workers' and Soldiers' Deputies, made up mainly of Russian railway workers, seized power in Turkestan. Russian revolutionaries thereafter proceeded to create a Bolshevik party organization. A rival government based in Kokand was crushed by the Red Guards in February 1918. An attempted rebellion in Tashkent in January 1919 was brutally suppressed.

Soviet control of Turkestan was confined to the city of Tashkent. By the end of 1919 there were over 20,000 armed insurgents fighting the Bolsheviks. The Bolsheviks branded the rebels as brigands (Basmachi), but they called themselves Beklar Hareketi (the Freeman's Movement), led by former officials, landlords and imams. In February 1919, the Tashkent Soviet organized the First Extraordinary Congress for the Liquidation of the Basmachi. In July 1919 Moscow dispatched Mikhail Frunze and the Fifth Army to conquer Turkestan.

On 8 October 1919 the Bolshevik leadership sent the newly formed Turkkomission (Turkestan Commission of the Russian Communist Party) to Tashkent to study the situation. Its membership included a number of senior party and military leaders.[110] As a result, in July 1920 Moscow disbanded the Russian-dominated Tashkent Soviet and replaced it with a Provisional Central Committee composed of Russian and Moslem Bolshevik supporters. The Central Committee created its Turkestan bureau (Turkburo), headed by Sokolnikov, with the aim of strengthening party work in the region. A Central Committee resolution of 29 June assigned the task of administering the region jointly to the Turkburo and Turkkomission.

In July the Central Committee assigned Kaganovich to Turkestan.[111] He read up on the region in the library of the People's Commissariat of Nationalities. He reported to Lenin on the situation in Voronezh and discussed with him his new responsibilities in Turkestan.[112] His journey from Moscow to Tashkent took 23 days, and he found the city ravaged by cold and famine.[113] Hundreds of experienced party workers were assigned to Turkestan. These

Figure 2. L. M. Kaganovich in Tashkent in 1920

included two figures who had worked with him in Nizhnyi and Voronezh, namely Sergushev and Bulganin.

A Central Committee order appointed Kaganovich as a member of the Turkburo, the Turkkomission and of Sovnarkom Turkestan.[114] He also became a member of the Military Revolutionary Committee and chairman of the reformed Tashkent town soviet. A proposal to make him deputy chairman of Sovnarkom Turkestan met strong opposition and on Sokolnikov's advice, he was instead made head of the People's Commissariat of Workers' and Peasants' Inspection (NKRKI or Rabkrin); paralleling the role that Stalin had of oversight of the central Soviet government as head of the NKRKI of the Russian Federation.[115] In the autumn of 1920, following a Turkkomission decree on grain requisitioning to deal with the acute food supply crisis, Kaganovich acted as the plenipotentiary of the People's Commissariat of Procurement of RSFSR in Tashkent.[116]

Kaganovich led the V Congress of the Communist Party of Turkestan from 12 to 18 September. His report stressed the need to combat colonialist attitudes toward the native Moslem population and to purge and educate the party. He supported G. I. Safarov's stance on the national question, which aimed to win over the Muslim population. Citing Lenin's views, he stressed the importance of policy in Turkestan for Soviet international policy in the East, with Turkestan setting a model and becoming a 'centre for revolution in the East'.[117] Safarov, the main Bolshevik authority on Tukestan, in his book *Colonial Revolution in Turkestan*, bemoaned the insensitivity of many communists to the aspirations of the native population and argued that Soviet power in Turkestan rested on a thin layer of Russian railway workers.[118]

At the IX Congress of Soviets of Turkestan, Kaganovich, on behalf of the Turkburo and Turkkomission, reported on economic reconstruction and state building.[119] The congress approved a new constitution for the republic (drafted by Frunze, Kuibyshev and Kaganovich), based on the RSFSR's constitution, which gave the state a clearer class character, and disenfranchised the propertied classes. It approved the transfer of land to the landless labourers and the dispossession of landowners including those termed as Russian kulak colonizers.[120]

Kaganovich accepted the Turkestan assignment, although he feared that Maria, his wife, who suffered from tuberculosis, would find the climate uncongenial. She had held leading posts on the city party committees in Nizhnyi and in Voronezh. In 1919, when Kaganovich was assigned to Voronezh, she and their daughter Maia, ended up in Kursk, together with Sergushev and Vorob'ev, where the latter was killed. With Stasova's help, Kaganovich's wife and daughter were sent to Moscow and then returned to Nizhnyi. In Turkestan, Maria Kaganovich worked as deputy commissar of the People's Commissariat of Social Welfare, and was a member of the Tashkent province party committee.

The military operation against the Basmachi began in earnest in October 1920. In a letter to Lenin, Stalin advocated adopting the tactics aimed at isolating the insurgents employed by G. K. (Sergo) Ordzhonikidze in the Caucasus.[121] A major role in this struggle was played by the Chekists, Peters, Privorotsky and Bulganin. The Young Turk Enver Pasha, assisted by the Turkish authorities and British intelligence, was active in fomenting Basmachi rebellion in Turkestan as a means of destabilizing the Soviet regime.

In 1920 Kaganovich published a book on the establishment of Soviet power in Turkestan, *Pamyatnaya knizhka sovetskogo stroitelya* (Memoir Book of Soviet Construction). It was dedicated 'to the First and Great World Soviet Builder, the Leader (*Vozhd'*) of the October Revolution, Vladimir Ilich Lenin'. This was one of the first manuals devoted to the practical organization and work methods of the soviets. It stressed the high standards of selflessness required of officials and the need to combat the remnants of colonial and feudal attitudes to gain popular consent.[122]

The X Party Congress and the Trade Union Controversy

At the end of 1920 the debate on the role of the trade unions in the socialist state erupted. Trotsky argued for the merging of the trade unions into the state apparatus and for the militarization of labour. The Workers' Opposition, headed by A. G. Shlyapnikov and Alexandra Kollontai, with a strong base in the powerful metalworkers union, argued for industry to be placed under trade union control. Lenin advocated a compromise, preserving the independence of the trade unions to protect the interests of their members, but retaining control of industry firmly in the hands of the state.

The debate in Tashkent was intense, with the Workers' Opposition, led by Pravdin, enjoying strong support amongst the railway workers.[123] Kaganovich, in an article in *Izvestiya TurkTsIK* on 30 January 1921, defended Lenin's views.[124] He deputized as chairman of the Turkburo during Sokolnikov's absence caused by illness, and summoned a joint session of the Turkburo and the Central Committee of the Communist Party of Turkestan in which the Leninists had the majority. The meeting decided to take the issue to the rank and file, beginning with the party cells in the railway district. As a result, the city party conference supported Lenin's position on the trade unions.[125] The All-Turkestan territorial party conference, on 11–14 February, debated the role of the trade unions. Kaganovich gave the main report on the trade unions in defence of Lenin's position, E. A. Preobrazhensky gave a subreport presenting Trotsky's views, and Pravdin outlined the views of the Workers' Opposition. After intense debate, the Leninists won a large majority.[126]

The X Party Congress, overshadowed by the Kronstadt revolt and its bloody suppression, marked a momentous turning point in the history of the Bolshevik party, which greatly strengthened the advocates of centralization and discipline. The congress approved Lenin's resolution on 'Party Unity', which outlawed factions and condemned the Workers' Opposition as an 'anarcho-syndicalist deviation' incompatible with membership of the party. The Control Commission was established to enforce party discipline. Kaganovich voted for both resolutions.[127]

Stalin delivered his report on the nationalities question, in which he outlined an alliance between the Russian workers and the peasants of other nationalities as providing the basis of political stability of the new regime. Safarov, in a subreport on behalf of the Turkestan delegation, argued that Soviet power was in danger of perpetuating the old tsarist system of Russian colonial dominance.[128] Safarov, after Lenin's death, became a supporter of Zinoviev. Subsequent Stalinist histories refer to serious disagreements between Stalin and Safarov over the nationalities question and struggles between Kaganovich and Safarov for control of the Tashkent party, but these appear to be later constructions.[129]

In 1921 the Central Committee assigned Kaganovich to head the Organization Department of the Central Council of the Trade Unions (VTsSPS) in the struggle with the Workers' Opposition. He also worked in the Moscow Union of Leather Workers, in the Zamoskvorech'e district party committee, headed by the 'never to be forgotten' Roza Zemlyachka, an Old Bolshevik, who, in 1920, with Bela Kun, oversaw the massacre of White Officers in the Crimea and went on to become a hard-line Stalinist. He became a member of the party cell in the large Krasnyi Postavshchik factory. Many of the women workers supported Kollontai, but the enterprise, Kaganovich recalled, was turned into a Leninist stronghold. He remained a member of this cell until 1961.[130]

The IV Congress of Trade Unions met in May 1921 with Kaganovich as one of the delegates. At the congress, demands for the trade unions to be freed of party control were condemned by the Leninists. Mikhail Tomsky, the leading Bolshevik trade unionist, who had been elected to the Politburo in April, refused to endorse the Leninist line, and as punishment, was assigned by Lenin to work in Turkestan.[131]

The NEP in Turkestan

In 1921 the Bolshevik government effected a major change in policy. This was dictated by the Kronstadt rising, the strike wave in Petrograd and the growing peasant revolt. War Communism was abandoned and the New Economic Policy (NEP) was introduced. The restoration of the market, partial privatization of industry, and the replacement of forcible grain requisitioning with a tax in kind was seen as a retreat to capitalism and widely perceived in the party as a capitulation. Lenin justified the NEP as a strategic retreat before the socialist offensive could be renewed.

The introduction of the NEP was extremely controversial and generated strong resistance within the party. In Turkestan it was associated with moves to try to revive the economy and through concessions and land reform, to win over the native population and to encourage the Basmachi to surrender.[132] But in July Lenin instructed the leadership in Tashkent to provide grain to deal with the unfolding famine in Russia.[133] In May Tomsky replaced Sokolnikov as head of the Turkkomission and Turkburo. He soon clashed with Safarov over the way the NEP was being introduced in Turkestan and over the question over nationalities policy.[134] Lenin dispatched Adolph Ioffe to sort out the row with instructions that Soviet rule in Central Asia should not be construed as imperialist.[135] In January 1922 Stalin reported to Lenin that the party congress in Turkestan had taken a position of principle not to accord a privileged position to the Russians. Lenin expressed his satisfaction.[136]

Kaganovich, for a second time, was commanded to Turkestan as a member of the Turkburo. In January–February 1922 he addressed a number of meetings and conferences on NEP's role in unifying workers and peasants. On 7 March he reported to the VI Party Congress of Turkestan on the role of the trade unions under the NEP. In March–April Kaganovich, as one of the Turkestan delegates, attended the XI Party Congress in Moscow. The congress set up a commission, which included Stalin, Dzerzhinsky, S. M. Kirov, Kaganovich, and E. M. Yaroslavsky to look into the activities of the 'Twenty-Two', the leaders of the Workers' Opposition. The congress resolution censured Shlyapnikov, Kollontai and S. P. Medvedev for flouting party directives.[137]

Thereafter, Soviet power was gradually consolidated in Turkestan. In April the Central Committee created a commission, headed by Ordzhonikidze, to lead the fight against the Basmachi.[138] In May the Turkburo was reorganized into the Central Asia Bureau, chaired by Yan Rudzutak. On 4 August Enver Pasha was killed in a clash with Soviet forces. The struggle with the *Basmachi* in the Ferghana valley and Eastern Bukhara continued until 1925.

Conclusion

Kaganovich played a much more important role in party affairs during the Civil War than has previously been recognized. He was assigned by the centre to impose order in Nizhnyi Novgorod and oversaw the Red Terror in August–September 1918. These terrible actions, which included authorizing the shooting of hostages, were a formative stage in his career. These were rationalized as part of the life-and-death struggle of the revolution. In his memoirs and later interviews, he elided his role in these events. In Nizhny, Voronezh and Tashkent, he was a member of the Military Revolutionary Committee and a strong supporter of the Cheka. Kaganovich's firefighting activities in these hot spots confirmed his reputation as a resolute and dependable party worker. His rapid promotion attests both to his abilities and to his skill in cultivating powerful patrons.

Already in 1918 Kaganovich emerged as one of the most articulate advocates of the party's militarization and a supporter of a fusing of the party and soviet state apparatus, and of substituting the party for the déclassé proletariat. He advanced these ideas, not as a local party maverick, but a man closely connected with the central party authorities, as a boss of one of the main front line centres. These organizational principles, already entrenched under Lenin, provided the basis for the future Stalinist state. Tens of thousands of party, Cheka and Red Army officers, their mentality shaped by the Civil War, rose to political prominence in the following decade. While Kaganovich was one of the first Bolsheviks to broach the question of using the soviets as a transmission belt between state and society, he was always dismissive of the libertarian currents in Bolshevism, exemplified by the Workers' Opposition and the Democratic Centralists.[139]

Contrary to Roy Medvedev's assertion that Lenin knew little of him, Kaganovich stressed the several occasions on which they had met.[140] In 1918–19, He was associated with Trotsky, but in 1920-21 in the trade union debate, he emerged as a staunch Leninist. In 1991 he recalled that, in this period, he knew Trotsky well, but had clashed with him on several occasions; Trotsky, he argued, was a talented man, a great orator, but as a politician and strategist, he was much inferior to Stalin.[141] Only after 1921 did he begin to forge his close association with Stalin. But his links with Trotsky in 1919–20 were always a potential embarrassment, of which Kaganovich and Stalin must both have been very conscious.

Chapter 3

BUILDING THE MONOLITHIC PARTY, 1922–1927

Kaganovich emerged from the Civil War as one of the new elite of proletarian, revolutionary administrators who were to have a decisive influence in shaping the political development of the state in the coming era. The ending of the Civil War left the new Bolshevik regime in a state of disorientation. A series of crises – the Kronstadt rebellion, the strike movement, and the peasants' revolts – had compelled a démarche, the abandonment of War Communism and the introduction of the New Economic Policy (NEP). This was widely resented by party activists as a capitulation to capitalism. The Bolshevik regime lacked legitimacy and its social base was seriously eroded. The failure of the European revolution, forced the Soviet regime to come to terms with the realities of capitalist encirclement. The party strove to consolidate its power by outlawing other parties and by imposing as ban on factions within the Bolshevik party itself. The one-party state rested on the administrative might and coercive capacity of the party, the state apparatus, the Cheka and the Red Army.

The new regime sought to legitimize itself as the embodiment of the 'dictatorship of the proletariat'. But this was a party that in a sense substituted itself for a declassed proletariat. It bolstered its self-legitimation through its claim to embody a wider good, and through profession of a consequentialist morality. The ideals of communism were left in suspension as the regime orientated itself to a new task, assuming the role of a developmental dictatorship. From 1922 the regime sought to recuperate and renew its strength. Through the NEP it strove to rebuild the economy and to find a new accommodation with society. It attempted to build support among the non–Russian peoples. A central tenet of the new approach was the priority accorded to the party as the central institution around which the whole structure of power was built and which ensured control over the society. Notwithstanding the major retreat forced upon it, the regime remained convinced of its right to rule and of the viability of its ideology as a guide to action.

The Party Secretariat

Kaganovich's career in 1922 entered a new phase. Having distinguished himself in Nizhny Novgorod, Voronezh and Tashkent and having proved himself a loyal Leninist in the trade union controversy, he was now brought into the very centre of government. As part of the strengthening of the Bolshevik one-party state, the XI Party Congress in March–April 1922 invested great powers in the party Secretariat. This was also part of the Leninist group's manoeuvres to maintain control over the party in opposition to Trotsky and his supporters.[1] Stalin was elected as general secretary with Molotov and Kuibyshev elected as secretaries. Molotov was already a prominent party figure, and already a candidate member of the Politburo.[2] Kuibyshev, a leader of the Left Communists in 1918, had worked his way back into official favour in Turkestan and by his role in fighting the Workers' Opposition in his former base of Samara in 1921.

Kuibyshev informed Kaganovich that, with Lenin's approval, it had been decided that he should work in the Secretariat. A meeting was arranged with Stalin. He was offered the post as head of the Secretariat's Organization and Instruction Department (Orgotdel). Although he expressed uncertainty as to whether he could cope with these new responsibilities, Stalin reported that Kuibyshev, who had worked with Kaganovich in Turkestan, had recommended him and vouched for his courage, solidity and self-confidence.[3]

The Orgotdel's function was to maintain day-to-day contact with the lower party bodies, to issue and transmit orders and directives, answer queries and to assess the performance of subordinate bodies in fulfilling party policy. It was also responsible for issuing press communiqués. In May 1921 the Orgotdel was provided with a staff of instructors and inspectors whose task was to check on the implementation of party policy. Alongside the Orgotdel was the Records and Assignment Department (Uchraspred), headed by S. I. Syrtsov, which oversaw cadre appointments.[4]

Stalin proposed that Kaganovich should present a lecture to the communists of the Orgotdel on the history of the Leninist party. This, he later recalled, was a test which Stalin had set for him. He wrote the lecture after consulting Molotov and Kuibyshev and after discussions with Old Bolsheviks such as M. F. Vladimirsky, S. I. Mitskevich, Roza Zemlyachka and Nikolai Podvoisky. It was in effect a restatement of the principles of party organization outlined in Lenin's 'What is to Be Done?' with its stress on the primacy of the party, its restrictive view of party democracy, its elevation of the role of the intellectuals, its selective conception of party membership and its doctrinal rigidity.[5]

Kaganovich, as head of Orgotdel, worked under Molotov. In the Orgotdel, He had two deputies, Okhlopkov and Lepa, who had worked with him in

Lenin, in his final articles, offered guidance on the future development of the Soviet regime. In the 'Tax in Kind' and 'On Co-operation' he argued for the continuation of the NEP as a means of promoting economic recovery while conciliating the peasants. He urged care in ensuring harmony between the Russians and the non-Russian nationalities. In 'How we should reorganize Rabkrin' and 'Better Fewer, But Better', he highlighted the inefficiency of the state and economic administration and advanced proposals to create a self-regulating mechanisms to ensure that the proletarian dictatorship did not lapse into a system of arbitrary rule.

The XII Party Congress

By 1923 the transformation of the Bolshevik party into a monolithic organization was well advanced, and it was a trend promoted not simply by Stalin, but by other party figures, notably Zinoviev and Trotsky.[14] In the final months of Lenin's life the process was accelerated.

At the XII Party Congress in April 1923, Trotsky reported on the 'scissors' crisis, the growing disparity between the price of industrial and agricultural goods. It also heard Stalin's report on the nationalities question and adopted a landmark resolution that granted major concessions to non-Russian people as regards language and culture and the policy of indigenization (*korenizatsiya*). The congress also discussed Lenin's plan for the reorganization of the system of party and state control and his controversial scheme to unify the party's Central Control Commission (CCC) and the Peoples' Commissariat of Workers' and Peasants' Inspection (NKRKI, or Rabkrin). Kaganovich, as a member of the Mandate Commission, had to answer the queries of delegates concerning Lenin's final articles.[15]

One of the main reports was presented by Leonid Krasin, the People's Commissar for Foreign Trade. He was the leading figure on the right of the party, a strong spokesman for the managers and engineers, and a strong defender of the NEP. He was one of the Bolshevik leaders with actual experience in running a modern company, having been in charge of the Siemens company's activities in Russia. In an article in *Pravda*, he denounced Lenin's plans for the reorganization of the control agencies CCC-Rabkrin, arguing that it reflected a simplistic military model for administration which bore no relation to the way Western administrative systems were organized. He warned that such an administrative system carried grave dangers as regards decision making.

He was accused of promoting a managerialist, technocratic view of socialism, which through the extension of the NEP, would lead, it was alleged, to a capitalist restoration. He was condemned for lacking faith in the capacities of the party and its proletarian cadres to build socialism. Kaganovich, in his memoirs, described Krasin's speech as that of a 'pretender for the post of prime minister'.[16] As it transpired, the chairmanship of Sovnarkom, vacated by Lenin's death in 1924, passed to Alexei Rykov.

The congress approved the plans to join the Central Control Commission-People's Commissariat of Workers' and Peasants' Inspection (CCC-Rabkrin). Initially conceived by Lenin as a self-correcting mechanism for regulating the operation of the party-state apparatus, it quickly became a formidable instrument of control over the party-state apparatus.[17] Kuibyshev, who was relieved from his post as party secretary, was appointed head of CCC-Rabkrin. In his memoirs, Kaganovich recounted the assistance he, as head of Orgotdel, had rendered to Kuibyshev ('my friend') in organizing the control agency and in selecting suitable cadres for this work.[18] The Secretariat and the new CCC-Rabkrin emerged as the real powerhouse of the Stalin group.

Krasin's vision of administration, based on Western models, differed fundamentally from the centralizing, militarized, control-dominated, hierarchical trends in Soviet administrative practice. Lenin favoured the military model, and this was the option strongly favoured by Stalin. Following Krasin's defeat in 1923, the Soviet party-state was relentlessly restructured on the military model, in which process Kaganovich played a conspicuous part.

The congress elected Kaganovich as a candidate member of the Central Committee. The congress also passed a resolution, based on Stalin's report, on strengthening the Uchraspred in the centre and the localities. In July 1923, the Central Committee enlarged the number of posts in the state and economic apparatus which were in Uchraspred's gift.[19]

Trotsky and the Left Opposition, 1923–1924

With Lenin incapacitated, the triumvirate of Zinoviev, Kamenev and Stalin moved to isolate Trotsky in the struggle for the succession. Stalin's grip over the central party apparatus prompted concern, reflected in Zinoviev's famous convocation of a secret meeting of party leaders at Kislovodsk in September 1923 to discuss the situation. At this time, the famous 'scissors crisis', reflecting the disparity between agricultural and industrial prices, prompted a crisis in urban–rural trade. Wage arrears fuelled mounting labour discontent, and provoked a rash of strikes. The Orgotdel monitored the developing crisis, and Kaganovich reported directly to Stalin.[20] The Central Committee set up three commissions to look into the divergence of industrial and agricultural prices, to examine delays in wage payment and to examine internal party matters.

On 15 October 1923 the 'Platform of the 46' was issued by Trotsky's supporters.[21] It denounced the leadership's economic policy and the undermining of internal party democracy. On the Secretariat's instructions, the Orgotdel ordered local party secretaries to prohibit distribution of this fractional document.[22] One of its signatories was Kaganovich, but this was not L. M. Kaganovich, as has been supposed, but P. K. Kaganovich, an official of the People's Commissariat of Trade and a Trotskyist.[23] Might the omission of the signatory's initials have been a piece of mischief making, an attempt to cast aspersions on one of Stalin's allies?

A joint plenum of the Central Committee and CCC in October condemned the views of Trotsky and his supporters. Zinoviev and Kamenev demanded Trotsky's removal from the Politburo, but Stalin advocated a more cautious line. The Orgotdel maintained daily operative contact with local party bodies, and closely followed the course of the debates. The situation in Moscow, Kaganovich relates, was especially tense, where Trotsky had organized his own centre, headed by Serebryakov. Kaganovich reported to Stalin on the ineffectual efforts of the Moscow party committee, headed by I. A. Zelensky, to fight the Trotskyites. Stalin summoned Zelensky and ordered him to take resolute measures. He sent Kaganovich to assist the Moscow party committee in this work, advising him, 'You don't need to be diplomatic here, take matters into your hands.'[24] Kaganovich waged a relentless struggle against the Trotskyites, demanding reports from party secretaries on the situation in their districts (*raions*). He addressed meetings of the Moscow party propagandists and attended meetings of the party cells, including a meeting of communist students at the Plekhanov Institute, which was a Trotskyist hotbed. At the district party conference in Zamoskvorech'e district, the opposition censured party secretary Roza Zemlyachka and denounced Kaganovich as 'the CC's commissar in the Zamoskvorech'e district'.[25]

Kaganovich also addressed a meeting of Old Bolsheviks of the Moscow party organization on the threat which Trotsky and his supporters posed to Leninism. A number of the Old Bolsheviks who spoke rebuked the Moscow party committee for not having summoned their help earlier and for failing to develop a more energetic response. M. F. Vladimirsky, I. I. Skvortsov-Stepanov, Litvin-Sedoi, M. F. Shkiryatov and A. A. Solts pledged their support for the leadership.[26] Kaganovich later recounted that Stalin's self-critical speech at an open session of the Krasnaya Presnya district party committee won over many activists, but that Trotsky's article 'To the party meetings', published in *Pravda*, had rekindled the struggle.

For ten days an intense struggle was fought against the Trotskyists. The Central Committee's position was approved at a meeting of Moscow party activists on 11 December, and the plenum of Moscow party committee three days later. The Secretariat and Orgburo heard reports from the district party committees on the discussions, and submitted proposals to the Politburo.[27]

The internal party debate on party democracy, the last such open discussion, was then abruptly terminated. In his memoirs, Kaganovich repeats the official view that Trotsky drew his support in Moscow from student and military cells and not from the workers' cells.[28] In fact, Trotsky had drawn strong support from the workers' cells and this was the reason why the debate was halted.[29]

In January 1924, at the XIII Party Conference, Stalin, as general secretary, provided a blunt defence of party monolithism, arguing that party democracy was entirely dependent on internal and external conditions and might at some point, as during the Civil War, have to be suspended and the party militarized. The Bolsheviks were 'Lenin's disciples' and the ban on factions secretly adopted at the X Party Congress, had now been enshrined in the conference resolution. The party had to be transformed into a 'party of steel'. He dismissed the opposition's charges of bureaucratic degeneration by which the apparatus now dominated the party.[30]

Lenin died on 21 January. The following day, Kaganovich attended a commemorative meeting of his party cell at the Krasnyi Postavshchik leatherworks. Much later, he recalled Stalin's love for Lenin and his great grief at his death.[31] Stalin's pronouncements venerate Lenin as a revolutionary, prophet, leader and father figure and offer an important clue to his mindset with its absolutist, totalistic conceptions of the world. The embalming of the leader's body, placed on display in the Mausoleum, reflected a quasi-religious conception of socialism and a cultic interpretation of politics that was to become an intrinsic part of Bolshevik culture.

The XIII Party Congress

At the XIII Party Congress in May 1924, Molotov and Kaganovich were elected to the congress commission on party construction and were the main authors of the resolution on this issue.[32] In the report of the Revision Commission, Kursky revealed that from April 1923 to April 1924, the Secretariat and Orgburo had examined some 7,726 questions. The enormous burden placed on the Secretariat meant that important matters were often left to meetings of the heads of sectors, chaired by I. I. Korotkov or Kaganovich.[33] Kaganovich had day-to-day contact with the officials of the Central Committee apparatus and the Secretariat and Orgburo.[34]

At the congress, Stalin weathered the revelations of Lenin's 'Testament', which had called for his removal from the post of party general secretary. Stalin at this stage even offered to resign. Immediately after the congress, the Central Committee elected Bukharin as a full member of the Politburo, and elected Mikhail Frunze, F. E. Dzerzhinsky and G. Ya. Sokolnikov as candidate members. The Central Committee was enlarged from 40 to 53 members.

Kaganovich, who had chaired the congress mandate commission, was elected a full member of the Central Committee and a member of both the Secretariat and the Orgburo.[35]

Following the congress, the Orgotdel and Uchraspred were merged to form the Organization and Assignment Department (*Orgraspred*) aimed at putting the work of cadres' appointments on a firmer footing. Kaganovich became the head of Orgraspred.[36] S. I. Syrtsov was appointed head of the Secretariat's Agitation and Propaganda Department.[37] Orgraspred was closely involved in developing the *nomenklatura* system. In 1924, at a meeting of the Orgburo, Dzerzhinsky protested that, as chairman of Vesenkha and a candidate member of the Politburo, he could not appoint cadres without the approval of Kaganovich and the Orgraspred.[38] By contrast, in May 1924 Molotov instructed Kaganovich to respond to the request from G. V. Chicherin, People's Commissar for Foreign Affairs (NKInDel) for help to find qualified personnel.[39]

The Orgotdel and Orgraspred had a wide brief. In 1922 Kaganovich was involved in setting rules for party work in those enterprises privatized under the NEP.[40] In 1923–25, he was involved in setting the borders and organizing the administration of the new autonomous republics in Central Asia and the Caucasus.[41] In 1924 he was involved in organizing party cells in the army and the navy.[42] At the XV Party Congress in December 1927, Kursky credited Kaganovich with Orgraspred's successful work in cadre assignments.[43]

At the Central Committee plenum, in August 1924, the triumvirate of Stalin, Kamenev and Zinoviev established a 'ruling collective', headed by a septemvirate of Bukharin, Zinoviev, Kamenev, Rykov, Stalin, Tomsky and Kuibyshev, plus candidate members Dzerzhinsky, Kalinin, Molotov, N. A. Uglanov and Frunze. The aim was to exclude Trotsky from decision making by bypassing the Politburo. These individuals were bound by strict discipline. Kaganovich became one of the members of the 'ruling collective'.[44]

Stalin projected himself as Lenin's rightful heir. His speech, 'Trotskyism and Leninism', delivered to a party faction of the All-Union Central Council of the Trade Unions (VTsSPS) on 19 November 1924 initiated the ideological assault on Trotsky, branding him as an advocate of state terror. The joint Central Committee-CCC plenum, on 17–20 January 1925, accused Trotsky of attempting to replace Leninism with Trotskyism. 'Socialism in One Country' was now propounded as the true Leninist conception of international development of the revolution, in opposition to the Trotsky's 'Permanent Revolution'. Stalin presented himself as the staunch defender of NEP, the advocate of cooperation with the peasantry and moderate industrialization, whilst attacking critics of official policy as adventuristic and a deviation from the course advocated by Lenin in his final articles.

The Lenin Enrolment

On the day of Lenin's funeral, Zinoviev proposed the rapid expansion of party membership from 700,000 to 1 million, to be made up mainly of workers from the bench.[45] The XIII Party Congress, in May1924, authorized the Lenin enrolment. The Orgburo was charged with organizing the selection and education of these new recruits, and Kaganovich was appointed chairman of the commission to oversee this work.[46] On 8 December he presented a report on this question to the Orgburo. Local party committees were to select the best workers for party membership and were to involve them in party work and place them in positions in the state, trade union and other organizations.[47]

The XIV Party Conference, in April 1925, welcomed the admission of 200,000 workers into the party's ranks. Kaganovich reported to the Central Committee plenum on work among the new recruits, after which the special commission set up for this work was disbanded.[48] The enrolment was presented as a step to strengthen the party's links with the proletariat, but oppositionists saw it as a means to dilute the party's ranks with politically unsophisticated and malleable members. In its battle with the opposition following Lenin's death, the recruits of the Lenin enrolment provided dependable ballast for the leadership in its struggle with the opposition.

Stalin used the recruitment drive to fundamentally rewrite the history of the Bolshevik party, promoting the idea of the monolithic party derived from Lenin's 'What is to Be Done?'[49] His *Foundations of Leninism*, based on lectures delivered at Sverdlov University in April 1924 and dedicated to the recruits of the Lenin enrolment, codified this version of party organization and ideology. Control over ideology was central to gaining control of the party.

Kaganovich also contributed to the process. His pamphlet, *Kak postroena RKP (Bol'shevikov): Ob ustave partii* (How the RKP (Bolsheviks) is built: concerning the party statutes), for use in instructing the new members, was published in 1924. In substance, this was the lecture which Kaganovich delivered to the Orgotdel in 1922. He made no claim to originality, but stressed how he had consulted closely with Stalin and others over its contents. The pamphlet closely followed Stalin's speech to the XIII Party Conference and quoted the general secretary to the effect that the Bolsheviks did not 'fetishize the question of democracy'.[50] It identified four cardinal principles of Bolshevik party organization – activism, discipline, centralism and the factory cells – as the basic units of the party. Moreover, the party, through its cells, led the mass organizations. Kaganovich stressed Lenin's insistence on 'iron discipline', strict adherence to party rules, tight control of admission into the party, regular purges of the membership, the enforcement of the 'ban on factions and strict subordination of all lower bodies to higher bodies. His conception of 'democratic centralism' was highly centralist.

Kaganovich's pamphlet was republished in at least twelve different editions in the next two years.[51] It was reissued as *Kak postroena VKP(b)* in 1927 and 1929, with the subtitle 'What workers entering the VKP(b) must know'. The four cardinal principles of party organization were no longer outlined in so stark a fashion, but the stress on centralism remained. Echoing Stalin's views, the priority was to create a party of iron discipline and monolithic unity. The failure of the Paris Commune, he asserted, stemmed from the absence of a 'conscious organized leadership', of a 'strong class party'.[52]

Kaganovich adopted Stalin's conception of the Bolshevik party as following a straight line of development from Lenin's model of the vanguard party outlined in 'What is to Be Done?' He had little faith in the self-creativity of the masses, and contemptuously dismissed the more libertarian currents in Bolshevism as naïve and sentimental.[53] What counted was organization, with the unfettered power of the party-state embodying the 'dictatorship of the proletariat'. Like Stalin, he held an essentially statist conception of socialism, in which the party and state apparatus were fused.

The Lenin enrolment marked a fundamental step in recreating the Bolshevik party. The party leadership, disillusioned with the capacity of the working class to act as a dependable base of support, substituted the party itself for the proletariat. The party-state was hailed as embodying the 'proletarian dictatorship' unconstrained by law, while the party's right to rule was expounded as a cardinal principle of communist ethics. The highest duty of a party member was obedience, with the obligation to inform the party authorities of fractional and dissident activity. Bolsheviks, as politically conscious, disciplined, party members, were required to subordinate individual personal consideration to the interests of the party.

Strengthening the Soviets

The Soviet regime after 1921 was isolated from the people, in particular from the peasantry and non-Russian peoples. The regime's weakness in the countryside was underlined by the peasant boycott of soviet elections.[54] The revolt of the Georgian peasants in August 1924, which was suppressed with exemplary force, dramatized the crisis, and forced the government to make further concessions to the peasantry.[55] This policy lay at the heart of the party's strategy of alliance (*smychka*) with the peasantry, the policy of 'face to the countryside' and the policy of concession on prices and taxes. All this was justified with reference to Lenin's later writings.

Kaganovich had established a reputation as an authority in the organization of soviets in Voronezh and Turkestan, and in 1923 he published a work on soviet self-government.[56] On 20 October 1924 he was made chairman of a new Orgburo commission, charged with strengthening the soviets. The commission was to remain active for the next four years. He set up four subcommissions; (1) the organization of the soviets, (2) the economic functions of the soviets, (3) the rural soviets and (4) the soviets in the republics.[57] On 25 October the Central Committee plenum discussed the matter. On the eve of the meeting, Stalin and Kaganovich addressed a gathering of secretaries of rural party cells. Kaganovich highlighted the need to improve the work of the rural soviets, linking 'the centralism of state power with the broadest local self-government'.[58]

In January 1925 a conference on the revitalization of the soviets was held, chaired by Kalinin.[59] Kaganovich, who presented the main report, advanced measures to further strengthen the soviets and to conciliate the peasants by granting the soviets their own budgets, strengthening 'revolutionary legality' and combating bureaucracy, corruption and irregularities.[60] In April a second conference was held, at which he again stressed the need to strengthen the soviets and to secure the legal rights of electors to vote. The term kulak was too loosely interpreted, and voters were often disqualified merely because they had criticized the president of a rural district executive committee or village soviet.[61]

On 27 April 1925 Kaganovich, addressing the XIV Party Conference, claimed that the party's policy of 'face to the countryside', through economic concessions and steps to revitalize the soviets, was transforming peasant attitudes. It was essential that soviet delegates did not feel that 'decisions have been predetermined in the narrow collegium of the party committee'. The rural party had to retain its leadership of the soviets, but allow the soviets their own area of discretion.[62] On 28 April he delivered the opening address to the newly formed Institute of Soviet Construction attached to the Communist Academy on the revitalization of the soviets.[63] He became head of this Institute and used it to promote his ideas.

With the rise of the Leningrad Opposition in 1925, the leadership's policy of concessions to the kulaks and middle peasants came under strong fire. At the Central Committee plenum in July 1926 Trotsky condemned the pro-kulak policy and the bias against industry. The plenum discussed the 1925–26 soviet elections, based on a report by Molotov and Kaganovich, and condemned the extension of the franchise in 1924 to the kulaks and other petty bourgeois elements. Trotsky dismissed the motion presented by Kaganovich as being insufficiently critical of past policy.[64] Although Kaganovich continued to defend the policy of revitalizing the soviets from a class perspective, a major shift in policy was now affected.[65] After 1926 the kulaks were again barred from voting in soviet elections.

The importance of strengthening the soviets was stressed by the XIV Party Conference and the XIV Party Congress. In October 1927 Stalin underlined this strategy in opposition to Zinoviev and Kamenev's policy of 'dekulakization' and restoring the *kombedy* as part of a new class war in the countryside. The revitalization of the soviets was central to the strategy of winning over the middle peasants. This policy in the countryside was complemented by the policy of industrializing the country.[66]

The Leningrad Opposition, 1925

Official economic policy aimed at stabilizing the currency, giving priority to agriculture and granting concessions to the peasantry. Under NEP, the People's Commissariat of Finance (NKFin), headed by Sokolnikov, reached the height of its influence. Kaganovich's links with Sokolnikov stretched back to Nizhnyi Novgorod and Turkestan. At the XI Party Congress, Kaganovich was elected to the commission charged with reviewing Sokolnikov's thesis on the state budget.[67] In 1924 the new currency reform, with the introduction of the gold-backed chervonets ruble, was implemented. According to Kaganovich, Sokolnikov proposed to Stalin that he, Kaganovich, be made his deputy in NKFin.[68]

Following Trotsky's defeat, new rifts appeared within the ruling triumvirate. Alarmed by Stalin's concentration of party power in his own hands, Zinoviev and Kamenev chose economic policy as the key issue on which to challenge him. They demanded a reversal of the concessions made to the peasantry, which, they alleged, were strengthening the kulaks, and they urged measures to protect working-class living standards and to promote the growth of heavy industry. Zinoviev and Kamenev drew their support from a broad constituency, including Sokolnikov and Krupskaya and, briefly, even Dzerzhinsky. Stalin was compelled to lean on the 'rightist' elements in the Politburo, notably Bukharin, Tomsky and Rykov.

On 5 March 1925 the Politburo, in a move against the Leningrad Opposition, dispatched a commission including Yaroslavsky, Kaganovich and Uglanov to Leningrad to investigate the Komsomol organization which was suspected of disloyalty. The Leningrad party organization distanced itself from the pronouncements of the local Komsomol officials. In Moscow, the commission questioned the Komsomol's Central Committee and it was severely purged.[69]

Kaganovich strongly supported the diumvirate of Stalin and Bukharin. Although appointed as general secretary of the Ukrainian Communist Party in April 1925 (see Chapter 4), he continued to play an active part in the internal party struggles at all-union level. In 1925 the Moscow and Ukrainian party organizations were in the forefront of the struggle against the Leningrad Opposition.[70]

The moves against Zinoviev's supporters in Ukraine produced a counter-attack from his power base in Leningrad. I. Vardin, in *Leningradskaya Pravda* in December 1925, directed his fire mainly at Bukharin, but also censured Kuibyshev, Uglanov and Kaganovich, and ended with a call to 'eradicate the current phenomenon of a Right deviation armed with Left SR phrases'.[71] This was clearly a reference to the Left SRs support for soviet democracy and for the middle peasants in 1918.

At the IX All-Ukrainian Party Congress, held in Kharkov from 6–12 December 1925, Kaganovich strongly defended official policy. The Soviet regime, he argued, was subject to a twofold encirclement – that of the peasant economy with its 22 million households, and that of international capitalism. Two dangers had to be avoided, the overestimation and underestimation of the kulaks. In a sweeping attack on Trotsky, he strongly defended the concept of party monolithism. Marx, he argued, had envisaged the proletarian dictatorship as a 'ruthless dictatorship'.[72] The role of the CCC and the GPU was to realize this end. He rejected accusations of dictatorship within the party, arguing that Lenin had always defended party unity against the demands of the Mensheviks and other opportunists for 'freedom of speech', which was invariably a mask for factionalism and for disseminating revisionist ideas.

At the XIV Party Congress in December 1925 Kamenev denounced Stalin's methods of operation, the rise of the theory of the 'leader', and the growing concentration of power in the Secretariat. Zinoviev and Sokolnikov echoed these concerns. Molotov, however, insisted that the Orgburo and Secretariat remained subordinate to the Politburo.[73]

Kaganovich scathingly attacked the oppositionists, accusing Zinoviev of pessimism, and failing to advance any practical programme. On the peasant question, he noted that the kulaks were particularly strong in Ukraine, and that differentiation was growing more rapidly there than elsewhere, but he rejected the Joint Opposition's charge that this was a consequence of official policy (see Chapter 4).[74] Zinoviev's call for horses for the horseless households was pure sloganizing, as 40 per cent of households (10 million) were without horses, while his attack on 'speculators' threatened to alienate those middle peasants who were engaged in trade. Zinoviev's article, 'The Philosophy of the Epoch', of September 1925, ostensibly an attack on the émigré N. V. Ustrialov's advocacy of a capitalist restoration in Russia under the NEP, Kaganovich asserted, was in fact directed primarily at discrediting Bukharin.[75]

Krupskaya asserted that official policy meant that poor peasants were paying higher taxes than in the previous year. Kaganovich responded that the Ukrainian party organization had set up a special commission to examine the matter. They had freed 22 per cent of poor peasant households (1.2 million) from taxes and organized some 400,000 households (mainly poor peasants) into cooperatives. However, he did not deny Krupskaya's claim that the Ukrainian leadership had provided the greatest relief to the well-to-do peasants.[76] They had expended great efforts to involve millions of middle peasants in the soviets. They had fought the tendency to use 'methods of War Communism', of pressure and illegal measures, at local level. He accused Zinoviev, Kamenev and Sokolnikov of 'empty demagogy', criticizing official policy without advancing any practical alternatives. He defended Bukharin, who had retracted his slogan calling on the peasants to enrich themselves.

The Joint Opposition

Kaganovich reported on the results of the XIV Party Congress to the party activists of Kharkov.[77] The proletariat, which by 1921 had become déclassé, had been strengthened. The party, Kaganovich asserted, was strong enough not to need to expel Trotsky from its ranks, although Zinoviev and Kamenev had wanted him expelled from the Politburo and the Central Committee. Zinoviev wished to neutralize the middle peasants, rather than winning them over as Lenin had argued in 'On Co-operation'. The party, he declared, had the capacity to undertake 'dekulakization', and thus to contain the kulak danger. He endorsed Stalin's views on building 'Socialism in One Country'. The Russian Revolution could avoid the danger of Thermidor, by strengthening the party's links with the working class as a check on the peasantry and other petty bourgeois elements.

The British General Strike in May–June 1926 was a crucial factor in the formation of the Joint Opposition. The issue was debated in the Politburo and produced an open clash at the session of 3 June. The defeat of the General Strike embarrassed the Politburo leadership by discrediting its policy of seeking alliances with Labourite and Social Democratic parties and trade unions in Europe.

Tomsky as head of the All-Union Central Council of the Trade Unions (VTsSPS) had set up the Red International of Labour Unions (widely known as Profintern) based in Moscow as a rival to the social democratic International Federation of Trade Unions (IFTU), based in Amsterdam. However, as part of a more conciliatory foreign policy, Tomsky, on behalf of VTsSPS, in 1923 extended feelers to the IFTU on the subject of trade union unity. When it became obvious that the IFTU would not consider a merger with the Profintern, VTsSPS began negotiations to affiliate with the Amsterdam International. The IFTU was seen by the left of the Communist Party of the

Soviet Union as a revisionist social democratic body. VTsSPS's attempt to join the IFTU was viewed as a capitulation, and the abandonment of any hope for revolutionary advance in the capitalist West.[78]

Kaganovich strongly supported Tomsky's line on the IFTU. In 1926, in the new membership books issued to the trade unions affiliated to VTsSPS, the old section concerning adherence to the Profintern was deleted. In a speech in Kharkov, Kaganovich spoke in favour of Soviet trade unions entering the IFTU. The left wing of the party denounced this as evidence of a capitulation to social democracy. Kaganovich riposted, claiming that the stenographer in Kharkov had misinterpreted his words. Oppositionists from Kharkov, however, asserted that Kaganovich had himself carefully corrected the stenographic report.[79] This was one of his rare political slips. Thereafter, the oppositionists referred to him as the 'Amsterdamer'. At the Central Committee plenum in October 1927, Trotsky again raked up the charge against Kaganovich.[80]

At the Central Committee plenum in July 1926, Kamenev, Zinoviev and Trotsky spoke out against Stalin, and castigated agricultural and industrial policy. Kaganovich strongly defended the official line. Industrial wages, he acknowledged, remained low and for miners and metal workers, they were still below pre-war levels. He accused the opposition of trying to incite the less politically conscious workers against the Central Committee. On 12 July, on the prompting of VTsSPS and Tomsky, the Politburo had decided to raise the wages of industrial workers. This, he asserted, was before Pyatakov, one of Trotsky's closest allies, had posed the question at the Central Committee-CCC plenum that month.

Kaganovich denounced the Joint Opposition for their lack of constructive suggestions, and chided them as faint hearts who did not believe in the possibility of building socialism in Russia without world revolution. The Joint Opposition, he maintained, contained disparate elements, from Sokolnikov, who advocated the 'agrarianization' of the country, to Trotsky, who wanted an industrial 'leap forward' to Preobrazhensky, who wished to turn the countryside into a colony of industrialization. The party, he argued, needed a cautious, realistic policy in its dealings with the kulaks and the peasantry. He noted that in 1924 Kamenev and Zinoviev had chided him as a 'semi-Trotskyist' because he had opposed their proposal to expel Trotsky from the Politburo, while in 1926 they concluded an alliance with him.

Kaganovich reported to the party activists on the results of the joint Central Committee-CCC plenum in July 1926.[81] He defended Tomsky from the attacks of the Joint Opposition regarding trade union policy and links with the IFTU. He accused Trotsky of advocating an ultraleftist, sectarian course on foreign policy and praised Stalin's sober analysis of the temporary stabilization of capitalism, arguing that the defence of the USSR was the revolutionary's paramount consideration. The plenum ousted Zinoviev from the Politburo and replaced him with Yan Rudzutak, and elected five loyalists as candidate members: Anastas Mikoyan, Andrei Andreev, Sergo Ordzhonikidze, Sergei Kirov and Kaganovich.[82]

At the Ukrainian Central Committee plenum, on 3–4 August 1926, Kaganovich again denounced the opposition's 'pettiness' and 'intellectual poverty'. He struck a note of pathos, accusing the Joint Opposition, through their denial of the possibility of building 'Socialism in One Country', of destroying hope:

> And in fact, what the devil, how can the workers and peasants dream, suffer and build if they do not have the confidence that they are building. For what then should they build, for what then should they dream, for what then should they suffer?[83]

In October 1926 the Central Committee plenum expelled Trotsky and Kamenev from the Politburo. At this time Trotsky perspicaciously foresaw that Stalin, in consolidating his 'one man rule', could not tolerate figures of the stature of Bukharin, Tomsky or Rykov in the Politburo, preferring, lesser, more pliant figures, such as Uglanov, Kaganovich and G. I. Petrovsky.[84] At the XV Party Conference, in October–November 1926, Kaganovich led the attack on the Joint Opposition, condemning their antipeasant stance: 'Theirs is the road of plundering the peasantry, a pernicious road, no matter how much Trotsky and Zinoviev may protest against this – such indeed are their slogans'. He mocked Trotsky's insistence on the 'right of free speech', a right which Trotsky himself, at the XI Party Congress, had denied to the Workers' Opposition, to Medvedev and Shlyapnikov, who at least were 'Old Bolsheviks'. Trotsky himself, he asserted, had now embarked on the 'Kronstadt road'.[85]

Through his outspoken attacks on the Joint Opposition, and through his ruthless actions in suppressing the oppositionists in Ukraine (see Chapter 4), Kaganovich established a reputation as one of Stalin's most forthright supporters. Trotsky, at the Central Committee plenum in February 1927, lambasted Kaganovich's ad hominem attacks and demagogic methods in blackening the opposition.[86]

At the joint Central Committee–Central Control Commission plenum in August 1927, Ordzhonikidze proposed that both Zinoviev and Kamenev be expelled from the Central Committee. Trotsky, in a wide-ranging speech, renewed his attack on 'Socialism in One Country'. The speech was repeatedly interrupted by shouts and interjections, with Kaganovich prominent in barracking Trotsky, raking up past differences between him and Lenin.[87]

The barracking of oppositionists and the breaking up of meetings had been well developed by Kaganovich in Ukraine.

The 'Platform of the Opposition', issued in September 1927, identified three tendencies within the party: the Right (Rykov, Tomsky), the Joint Opposition on the left (Trotsky, Zinoviev and Kamenev) and the Centrism of the official apparatus (Stalin, Molotov, Uglanov, Kaganovich, Mikoyan and Kirov). The 'centrist-official group', it argued, 'least of all expresses the attitudes of any broad mass, but it is trying – not without success – to substitute itself for the party'. It represented the caste of 'administrators' in the party – state, economic organizations and the trade unions who numbered tens of thousands. 'Among these there is no small number of "worker" bureaucrats – former workers, that is, who have lost all connections with the mass of workers.'[88] The triumph of the party machine under the general secretary's control was reflected in the derisory number of votes that the Joint Opposition candidates won in elections in these years. The left experienced this defeat as a bitter and crushing blow, with some, such as Adolf Ioffe and Evgeniya Bosh, choosing suicide.

Conclusion

In the period up to 1927, during the struggle with the Joint Opposition, Stalin worked in close harmony with Bukharin, Rykov and Tomsky. He astutely sought to project himself as Lenin's true heir. He used the party apparatus to build up his power, but also exploited the remnants of the party's democratic traditions. Kaganovich used tactics against the Trotskyists in Moscow similar to those he had used in Tashkent against the Workers Opposition, and which Kuibyshev had used in Samara, namely, the mobilization of the party rank and file. The same tactics were to be employed against the Zinovievites in Leningrad, and against the Joint Opposition. The Lenin enrolment was used to change the party's composition and to re-educate it membership.

Kaganovich's appointment to the Secretariat in 1922 brought him into Stalin's inner circle. Stalin, Molotov, Kuibyshev and Kaganovich represented the core of the emergent Stalin group. Kaganovich was the young, inexperienced newcomer who had to prove himself. The reorganized Central Control Commission – Rabkrin – became another key element in this power structure. The alliance drew in individuals connected to Stalin from his Caucasian days – Ordzhonikidze, Abel Yenukidze, Kirov and Mikoyan. The alliance also included members of the Tsaritsyn group, most notably Voroshilov and Budennyi. The command structure of the central party-state apparatus was streamlined, with hierarchical control established over subordinate structures, and rigorous control established over cadre appointments. Stalin, and Kaganovich as his pupil, legitimized this as a realization of Lenin's conception of party organization as outlined in 'What is to Be Done?' The struggle for the succession revolved around institutional manoeuvres, definitions of Leninism and the crucial issue of the future of the NEP.

For Kaganovich, the best period of work with Stalin was from 1922 to 1925. Stalin heeded Lenin's rebuke and adopted a more collegial style of leadership. Stalin would often invite Kaganovich, Molotov and Bukharin to his *dacha* for long convivial gatherings.[89] At this time, the party leadership still behaved with considerable informality, as he later recalled:

> This was a period when we worked to begin with at Vozdvizhena and then we moved to Staraya ploshchad (Old Square), working until twelve, half past twelve or one o'clock. Then, we would go by foot to the Kremlin via Ilinka. We went, me, Molotov, Kuibyshev and whoever else. We went along the street, I remember, in winter, he [Stalin] in fur hat, with ear-flaps flapping... We laughed and joked, he would say something, we would speak, throwing out jokes at one another...so to speak, just joking. Those watching from the side, would ask: who were this company? The security almost didn't exist. It was very small. Maybe one or two people went that was all.... That was the kind of period it was. It was a happy period of life. And Stalin was in a good mood. Sometimes we would sit for ages around a table chatting.[90]

From 1923 to 1928 Stalin, who was renowned for his domineering, egotistical manner, affected a more open, benign character. Chastened by Lenin's words about him in the 'Testament' and sensing his weakness, he depicted himself as modest and even self-deprecating. He projected himself as Lenin's disciple, determined to defend him against all those like Trotsky who could be depicted as one intent on self-aggrandisement.

The political struggle for succession after Lenin's death was a struggle of groups and factions. The main contenders for power – Stalin, Trotsky, Zinoviev and Kamenev – had their own constituencies of supporters, reflecting the central importance of informal clientele networks in Russian politics. This lent to the succession struggle a particular intensity and bitterness. Stalin built up his group on the basis of Civil War contacts and his men in the party Secretariat. This was seen as the general secretary's coterie, people bound to him by shared ideas and a common interest in seeking to control the party. Stalin's personality invested this group with a particular outlook: it was shaped less by ideology or ideas than by loyalty to him; it defined itself as a group in opposition to other groups and other leadership contenders. It met and socialized together, thus circumventing the institutional power vested in the Politburo. The office of party general secretary became de facto the post of party leader invested with immense real and symbolic power. Stalin's cliquish and conspiratorial methods of rule reflected an enduring feature of his modus operandi. His opportunism, his ruthless manoeuvring and single-minded pursuit of power took his rivals by surprise and poisoned party relations. His deputies, such as Molotov and Kaganovich, viewed this lack of scruples as evidence of the general secretary's supreme tactical astuteness, proof of his formidable political skill.

Chapter 4

UKRAINIAN PARTY BOSS, 1925–1928

In 1925 Stalin appointed Kaganovich as general secretary of the Ukrainian Communist Party. This was his first major assignment and a sign of the high regard in which he was held. The appointment was part of the shuffling of personnel in the struggle for succession following Lenin's death. The Ukrainian leadership was deeply divided over key issues concerning the best way to consolidate Soviet power, the nature of the Soviet federal system and the degree of autonomy to be retained by the republic within the USSR. Nationalities policy and the measures taken to placate Ukrainian national feeling, embodied in the strategy of 'Ukrainization', generated intense disagreement. Economic policy provided another issues of conflict. The struggle to control Ukraine was bound up with the wider struggle to gain control of the party at the all-union level. With his assignment to Ukraine, Kaganovich was required to steer a course between the contending factions in the republic while satisfying Stalin's desire to consolidate his control.

The New Economic Policy was primarily an economic strategy aimed at fostering economic recovery by using the market, taxation and pricing policy. But NEP was also a political strategy. Within the limitation of the one-party state, an attempt was made to nurture a degree of popular compliance, if not consent, for the Soviet regime. Within this framework a broader strategy for the development of the Soviet regime began to be evolved. This was based on winning the support of the non-Russian peoples. From 1925 there was a relaxation of the party's policy of religious persecution. It encompassed attempts to foster greater political support through the revitalization of the local soviets. NEP was thus a broad developmental strategy. Kaganovich's role as party boss of Ukraine illustrates the way in which this strategy evolved and the internal contradictions within this policy that led to its undoing.

Ukrainian General Secretary

Stalin's relations with the Ukrainian leadership were strained over differences concerning the handling of Trotsky, following the publication of the latter's article 'Lessons of October'. The Politburo, in January 1925, sacked Trotsky from the chairmanship of Military Revolutionary Council (Revvoensoviet) and replaced him with Frunze. Stalin and a majority of the Politburo majority proposed that Trotsky be retained in the Politburo, while Zinoviev and Kamenev, favoured his expulsion from its ranks. Stalin communicated these developments to the general secretary of the Ukrainian Communist Party, Emmanuel Kviring. The Ukrainian Central Committee supported the demands of Zinoviev and Kamenev for Trotsky's expulsion from the Politburo.[1] At the joint plenum of the all-union Central Committee and Central Control Commission the same month, Kamenev proposed that Stalin be appointed as chairman of the Revvoensoviet, with the aim of removing him from the post of general secretary. Kviring, at a meeting in Stalin's Kremlin apartment, advanced the same proposal, which Stalin indignantly rejected.[2]

To appease Stalin's wrath, the Ukrainian Central Committee sent a note to the all-union Central Committee on 23 February. It recanted its error in supporting Kamenev and Zinoviev, whom it now reprimanded for undermining party unity.[3] This failed to satisfy Stalin. Under pressure, the Ukrainian Politburo, on 20 March, acceded to Kviring's 'request' to be relieved of his post as general secretary. Moreover, it 'categorically insisted' that the all-union Central Committee should appoint V. M. Molotov as general secretary of the Ukrainian Communist Party.[4]

On 26 March the all-union Politburo agreed to send Kaganovich to Ukraine.[5] Evidently, Stalin could not afford to lose Molotov, although Kaganovich asserts that Molotov turned down the post.[6] In terms of seniority, Molotov far outranked Kaganovich. Kaganovich, just 31 years of age, who only eight years earlier had left Ukraine as a shoemaker, now returned as its party leader. His appointment was strongly resented by senior Ukrainian leaders, such as G. I. Petrovsky and V. Ya. Chubar'.[7] Although Kaganovich had been born in Ukraine and spoke Ukrainian fluently enough for public speeches, as a Jew, he was also a target of anti-Semitism, both within the party and the wider society. He took with him a team of aides with the purpose of taking control of the Ukrainian party.

Despite its reservations, the Ukrainian Politburo on 3 April confirmed Kaganovich's appointment. This was confirmed two days later by the Ukrainian Central Committee plenum, on the proposal of G. I. Petrovsky.[8] Kaganovich was relieved as secretary of the all-union Central Committee and A. Bubnov was appointed in his place.[9] Kviring was transferred to the post of deputy chairman of Vesenkha USSR. Before his departure for Kharkov, Kaganovich discussed with Stalin the situation in the republic. Stalin derisively remarked that, in a Politburo of seven, there were fourteen opinions.[10] He was sent to Ukraine to strengthen support behind the official line, since Petrovsky and others were suspected of vacillating towards Zinoviev and Kamenev.[11] He was also to block demands for greater Ukrainian autonomy.

The Ukrainian Government

The Ukrainian Communist Party was a relatively weak organization that had been in effect installed in power by the Red Army. In 1919 it had just 16,363 members.[12] In 1920 it absorbed the small left-wing nationalist party the Borot'bist, a number of whose former members, such as A. Ya. Shumsky, G. F. Grin'ko and V. P. Zatonsky, were to occupy senior positions in the party.[13] Ukraine had a population of 21 million, 89 per cent of whom were peasants, the great majority of whom were Ukrainian speakers, although the large cities were predominantly Russian-speaking. The XII Party Congress in 1922, in a resolution drafted by Stalin, approved a more conciliatory nationalities policy based on concessions on cultural and language matters and the strategy of of *korenizatsiya*, the recruitment of officials from the titular nationality of the republics. This policy was to be pursued while preserving the Communist Party's monopoly of power and preserving the integrity of the Union. Although incorporated into the USSR in 1922, Ukraine still retained some autonomy. Members of the Ukrainian Politburo, such as Chubar', Petrovsky, and I. Klimenko, strongly defended the Republic's interests in the all-union Central Committee.

Kaganovich's first speech to the Ukrainian Central Committee in April 1925, created a good impression. *Izvestiya* reported that his address to the IX All-Ukrainian Congress of Soviets on 3 May was enthusiastically received. The USSR, he declared, was to serve as a model for the proletariat of the West and the oppressed nationalities of the East to show them how the problem of government (*vlast*) was to be solved. The Leninist system offered every worker and peasant the chance to participate in government. He called for renewed efforts to raise the cultural level of the population and to fight illiteracy and noted 'a colossal growth of Ukrainian culture'.[14]

Following the IX All-Ukrainian Party Congress in December 1925, the Central Committee elected a Politburo comprising Kaganovich, Petrovsky (chairman of the Central Executive Committee of Ukraine), Chubar' (chairman of Sovnarkom Ukraine), M. L. Rukhimovich (chairman of Vesenkha Ukraine), A. Radchenko (chairman of the Ukrainian trade unions), Klimenko (party secretary), Zatonsky (head of the Political Administration of the Military District), N. A. Skrypnik (People's Commissar of Justice and chief procurator) and K. O. Kirkizh (secretary of Kharkov *gubkom*).[15] Skrypnik, an Old Bolshevik, was responsible for drafting the main resolutions on Ukrainization adopted by the Ukrainian Central Committee during Kaganovich's tenure. In 1926 the Ukrainian Institute of Marxism-Leninism appointed him to the chair on the nationality question.[16]

Kaganovich encountered considerable difficulties in managing the fractious conflicts between different local elites in Ukraine, which reflected factional interests, regional interests and different ideological positions. The 'Ekaterinoslavites' (Dnepropetrovsk), headed by Petrovsky and A. Medvedev, clashed with the 'Donbassites', led by A. Mikheenko and V. Moiseenko. There were also the party clans of Kharkov and Kiev to contend with.[17] The dominance of the industrial centres was challenged by the agricultural provinces of the Right Bank.

The isolation of the communist authorities from the society in Ukraine, as in the USSR, remained a problem. As general secretary, Kaganovich received detailed weekly reports from the Central Committee's Information-Statistical Department.[18] The Ukrainian GPU, in one of its regular reports to him on 3 September 1925, documented widespread dissatisfaction amongst workers fuelled by high unemployment, with widespread anti-Semitism, with workers and peasants denouncing the 'dominance of the red nobility of Yids'.[19]

Kaganovich and the Economic Development of Ukraine

As general secretary, Kaganovich supported economic concessions to the peasantry as part of the policy of 'face to the countryside!' The drive to revitalize the soviets aimed also to strengthen the regime's links with the peasants. In a speech in May 1925 to the IX Congress of Soviets of Ukraine, he stressed that the recovery of agriculture was to be the basis for the restoration of industry, with cheap manufactured goods supplying the peasant market.[20] The middle peasants, he insisted, had to be won over. Kamenev, chairman of Sovnarkom's Council of Labour and Defence (STO), who attended the congress as the representative of the Moscow leadership, outlined further measures to relax controls over private agriculture as a means of stimulating production.[21] But the needs of industry were not to be neglected, with the congress adopting a special resolution on industrial development, including a project for building a giant hydroelectric station on the Dnieper River.[22]

Concessions to the peasantry, however, did not mean an abandonment of class policies. The committees of poor peasants, which had been set up during the Civil War, were retained in Ukraine, although they had been disbanded in the Russian Federation. In 1925 Kaganovich and Petrovsky, in consultation with Stalin, agreed to retain the committees despite strong opposition from Klimenko, secretary of the Ukrainian Central Committee, who argued for their abolition.[23]

At the Ukrainian Central Committee plenum in July 1925, Kaganovich defended the policy of cutting the prices of industrial goods and reducing the tax on the peasantry.[24] The Ukrainian tax assessments for 1925 gave maximum relief to the well-to-do peasants.[25] The Ukrainian Central Executive Committee opposed this line and favoured a firm class policy in taxation. Petrovsky, its chairman, in a barely disguised attack on Kaganovich's policies, belaboured 'bourgeois' tendencies in party policy, particularly the indulgent attitude toward the middle and well-to-do peasants.[26]

The tax cuts on private peasant agriculture reduced the Ukrainian government's revenue and limited its ability to fund new investment for industry. The Ukrainian Politburo on 28 August 1925, while stressing its commitment to the Union, overrode Kaganovich's objections and resolved to include tax revenues from union industries and trade organizations which were located in Ukraine in the Ukrainian budget.[27] In the end, this decision was overturned by Moscow.[28]

Ukrainization in Practice

Kaganovich was a strong advocate of promoting the use of Ukrainian language and culture and advancing Ukrainian cadres in all institutions. In this he had the backing of the leadership in Moscow. However, he was beset by criticism from the Ukrainians, from those who thought the policy went too far and those who thought it did not go far enough. The Ukrainian Politburo on 3 April approved proposals for the Ukrainization of the Komsomol, the trade unions and soviets. It agreed also to publish the journals *Kommunist* and *Krasnaya Armiya* in Ukrainian.[29] On 10 April Kaganovich was appointed chairman of the Ukrainian Politburo's Commission on Ukrainization. A week later the Ukrainian Politburo approved his proposals for the full use of the Ukrainian language in the party.[30] The Ukrainian Central Committee also set 1 January 1926 as the deadline for the full use of Ukrainian in the state administration. Addressing a conference of the Kiev Military District, he argued that the use of Ukrainian in the army was vital if it was to avoid the appearance of an alien occupying force.[31]

On 6 April, at the Ukrainian Central Committee plenum, dissent over the policy of Ukrainization surfaced. A. Shumsky, a former Borot'bist and People's Commissar of Education in Ukraine and the most vocal advocate of Ukrainization in the government, admonished the slow progress in implementing the policy and the failure of the party to fully apply it. He reproved the literary journals *Ukraina* and *Chervonyi shliakh* for having published works which 'have nothing in common with communism'. Trade union leaders F. Ugarov, A. Radchenko and K. Gulyi berated Shumsky's report and charged him with bourgeois nationalism. Kaganovich defended Shumsky, and his call to Ukrainize the party was approved.[32]

Ukrainization was now rigorously enforced.[33] The number of schools in the republic using Ukrainian increased from 6,150 in 1922 to 15,148 in 1927. By 1927, 2 million children were being taught in Ukrainian.[34] The Ukrainian language press's circulation rose from 90,000 in 1924 to 612,000 in 1926.[35] The proportion of Ukrainians in the Ukrainian Communist Party rose from 30 per cent in 1923 to 52 per cent in 1927.[36] This effort was slowed down in 1926–27 in the new drive to increase the recruitment of workers into the party.[37] The issuing of the protocols of the Ukrainian Politburo in Ukrainian for the first time in January 1927 signalled a commitment to Ukrainization at the highest level.[38]

For ardent Ukrainizers, this was all too modest and a sop to cover the progressive erosion of Ukrainian sovereignty. Ukrainization was strongly opposed by the Russian-speaking party and trade union leaders in the urban and industrial districts, and by many officials of state administrative and economic institutions in Ukraine. The left wing of the party opposed the policy, arguing that it would alienate the party's core support among the Russian speaking working class. Kaganovich was caught in the middle between the most radical exponents of Ukrainization and its most vehement critics.

At the end of October 1925, Shumsky, as a member of the Comintern's Executive Committee, was received by Stalin together with leaders of the Communist Party of Western Ukraine, which operated underground in Poland. He complained that Ukrainization was being implemented too slowly, and was being obstructed by party and trade union officials. He asked to be transferred from Ukraine, and gave as his reason his differences with Kaganovich. He proposed that Kaganovich be replaced as general secretary by either Chubar', Petrovsky or Skrypnik. Stalin is said to have responded emolliently, 'You (*ty*) Aleksandr Yakovlevich are right, but it is too early.'[39]

At the IX All-Ukrainian Party Congress in December Kaganovich strongly defended Ukrainization, stressing the need to train state officials who were fluent in the language. This did not appease his critics. P. Solodub complained of the overcentralization of power in the party and accused Kaganovich of pursuing a policy which was both too pro-Ukrainian and too pro-kulak. I. Dashkovsky condemned the internal regime in the Ukrainian party, whereby anyone who dissented from the line of Kaganovich and Stalin was branded a deviationist. Lobanov, who claimed to speak in the name of the working class, scolded the leadership for failing to address the causes of worker dissatisfaction.[40] Kaganovich dismissed the criticisms of his personal style of leadership and affirmed his commitment to Ukrainization.

Mikhail Kalinin, who attended the congress as the representative of the all-union Politburo, defended Kaganovich's position as Ukrainian general secretary: 'Kaganovich now, is also a Ukrainian and a patriot no less than any of us'. The real threat to the republic, he claimed, came not from Soviet centralization but from Ukrainian autonomism.[41]

The Struggle against the Zinoviev-Kamenev Opposition

In the developing split between Stalin, Zinoviev and Kamenev, the Ukrainian leadership backed Kaganovich's line and supported Stalin. The IX Congress of the Ukrainian Communist Party in December 1925 sharply rebuked the 'New Opposition' and demanded action to uphold party unity and discipline. Members of the Ukrainian Politburo were sent to Kiev, the Donbass and Dnepropetrovsk to neutralize the opposition. The re-election of party organizations in Ukraine in September–October 1925 was used to further weaken the dissidents.[42]

At the XIV All-Union Party Congress the same month, the Ukrainian delegates – Kaganovich, Petrovsky, P. P. Postyshev, A. Medvedev, N. A. Skrypnik and D. Z. Lebed' – were prominent in attacking Kamenev and Zinoviev.[43] Chubar' proposed the removal of Kamenev's report on economic construction and this was adopted. In response, Krupskaya and Kamenev accused Kaganovich of pursuing a 'pro-kulak' policy in Ukraine. Zinoviev seized on the speech of Petrovsky in July 1925 to indict the Ukrainian party's policy on agriculture and to drive a wedge between Petrovsky and Kaganovich. Kaganovich accused Zinoviev of misrepresenting his views and of 'tearing a single quotation' out of context.[44]

In January 1926 Petrovsky was elected a candidate member of the all-union Politburo. This appears to have been the price which Stalin paid to secure his loyalty and to compensate him for the slight of having Kaganovich appointed over his head as the Ukrainian general secretary in 1925. Just five months later, Kaganovich was elevated to this rank.

On 19 March 1926 the Ukrainian Politburo heard Zatonsky's preliminary report on the results of Ukrainization. This provoked another acrimonious clash between Shumsky and other Ukrainian leaders. Kaganovich declared, 'We cannot compulsorily Ukrainize the Russian workers', a proposition which the Politburo adopted unanimously.[45] A letter signed by Kaganovich and Chubar' was sent to all Central Committee members accusing Shumsky of waging a personal campaign against Kaganovich.

These heated exchanges prompted Stalin himself to intervene. On 26 April he sent a letter to Kaganovich and the Ukrainian Central Committee in which he outlined official policy.[46] He accepted that Shumsky had identified as an important trend the widespread movement in favour of Ukrainian language and culture. It was essential to correct those party and soviet officials who were 'still imbued with a spirit of irony and scepticism towards Ukrainian culture and Ukrainian social life'. At the same time, Stalin accused Shumsky of serious errors. Firstly, he insisted the proletariat could not be 'Ukrainized from above'. Secondly, Shumsky ignored the dark side of the process of Ukrainization, whereby the non-communist intelligentsia set the interests of Ukraine in opposition to those of Moscow. He denounced an article by the poet Mykola Khvylovy entitled 'Away from Moscow', which called for 'the immediate de-Russification of the proletariat' and for Ukrainian literature to be developed free of Russian dictates.

In this dispute Stalin effected a certain distance. In a passage which was omitted from his Collected Works, he chided Kaganovich: '[I]t is possible that Kaganovich has certain defects, of over-administration. It is possible, that organizational assault in reality, in practice influences comrade Kaganovich.'[47] In the unpublished postscript, Stalin also asserted that ex-Borot'bists such as Shumsky should be drawn into leading party posts.

Shumsky's demand for Kaganovich's recall from Ukraine was widely known. In May 1926, at a session of the Ukrainian Politburo, I. Yakir, commander of the Ukrainian Military District and a close personal friend of Kaganovich, rebuked Shumsky: 'Shumsky irresponsibly said to Stalin that the organization was administered by mechanical methods, and that Kaganovich was an organizer but not a politician.'[48] Shumsky recounted his exchange with Stalin: 'I declared that I would remain working in Ukraine, even under Kaganovich, although I doubted that any good would come of this, since the circumstances for work had been made very difficult.'[49]

On 12 May the Ukrainian Politburo discussed Zatonsky's report on Ukrainization. The debate exposed a serious rift between the majority of the Ukrainian leadership and the ex-Borot'bists. Kaganovich, in a major speech, defended Ukrainization from a class position that was clearly directed at Shumsky. In Ukraine, he declared, two cultures competed for dominance: a Soviet-proletarian, socialist culture, influenced by the Communist Party, and an anti-Soviet culture, which reflected the aspirations of the kulaks, the Nepmen and the non-communist intelligentsia. He again insisted that nobody could forcefully Ukrainize Russian workers. The party had to struggle resolutely with 'the ideological distortion of opposing Ukrainian culture to Russian culture, of opposing Ukraine to Moscow', as expounded by Khvylovy and his supporters.

There followed a stormy debate in which Postyshev, M. Demchenko and K. Sukhomlin berated Shumsky, Khvylovy, Solodub and Doroshkevich. Grin'ko, chairman of the Ukrainian Gosplan and himself an ex-*Borot'bist*, strongly defended Shumsky, condemned the Ukrainophobe pronouncements of certain Moscow leaders and the prevailing tendency towards Russification in Ukraine. He described Kaganovich's appointment in Ukraine as temporary and insisted that Shumsky be brought into the Ukrainian Politburo and that other Ukrainians be promoted as province party committee secretaries. Chubar' scorned Grin'ko's ideas on cadre reassignment. F. Korniushin, secretary of the Ukrainian party Central Committee, accused Shumsky and Grin'ko of attempting to seize power in the Politburo.

Shumsky rejected this accusation and declared that most Russians in the party bore a 'suspicious, unfriendly, not to say harsh attitude towards the Ukrainian communist'. His Borot'bist past was raked up against him. In his speech he also recounted his exchange with Stalin. In reply, Kaganovich emphatically denied that he was guilty of an overadministrative approach and claimed that he had always striven 'to work in a friendly, Bolshevik manner'. He also condemned Shumsky for 'group work' against the Central Committee, virtually a charge of factionalism. At the end of the session, Chubar' called for unity, stressing that the general secretary should remain in his post, and rebuked Shumsky for having broached with Stalin the issue of Kaganovich's leadership.[50] In reality, Kaganovich's relations with Chubar' and Petrovsky were already severely strained.

At the Ukrainian Central Committee plenum on 2–6 June, a report by Zatonsky on Ukrainization provoked yet another stormy exchange. Members of the Central Committee A. A. Ivanov, A. Berezin, and the two Donbass secretaries A. Mikheenko and V. Moiseenko, demanded that no monopoly should be given to the Ukrainian language and culture. Gulyi charged the former Borot'bists with factionalism under a national cover. Chubar', Skrypnik and Petrovsky again accused Shumsky of sheltering nationalist 'deviationists' amongst the writers. Shumsky countered that the Ukrainian Communist Party was still predominantly a Russian body and insisted that Ukrainian cultural policy should be decided in Kharkov, not in Moscow.[51] One of Shumsky's supporters, Solodub, warned that the piecemeal erosion of sovereignty threatened 'Ukrainian statehood'. Grin'ko again repeated his view that Kaganovich was a temporary figure in Ukraine, although the time was not yet expedient for his removal.

Despite illness, Kaganovich resolved to speak. He denied the charge that Ukrainization was simply a ploy and criticized Shumsky's pronouncement to the Politburo session on 12 May. He underlined the international significance of Ukrainization as a model of Soviet national development for people in the West. While conceding that Great Russian chauvinism was still a greater danger than Ukrainian chauvinism, he condemned Khvylovy for attempting to set the path of Ukrainian cultural development in opposition to Russia's at a time when a 'united front' with the Russian proletariat was vital. He was supported by Petrovsky and Zatonsky. In his concluding words, Zatonsky declared, 'We think that a time will come when we will dispense with comrade Kaganovich, but this will be when we have principled divergences, and at present we have none. At present, he follows the party line. This is how he leads.'[52]

On 6 June a closed session of the plenum was held. Beforehand, the Politburo agreed on a compromise resolution to safeguard its unity. At the closed session, Kaganovich, in an agitated state, stressed his desire to work in a comradely manner, a statement which Shumsky welcomed. The resolution of the closed session condemned the claims made concerning Kaganovich's lack of 'organic contact with Ukraine', a position from which Shumsky and Grin'ko had dissociated themselves. It also expressed its 'full political and comradely confidence' in Kaganovich and the existing Politburo.[53] The plenum unanimously endorsed Kaganovich's tempo in carrying out Ukrainization.

In July Kaganovich was elected candidate member of the all-union Politburo, and thereafter was allowed a freer hand to deal with Shumsky. The Ukrainian Politburo appointed Zatonsky as chairman of its commission on Ukrainization.[54] An attack was launched on the 'super-Ukrainizers' and 'national deviationists'.[55] In November Shumsky was relieved as chief editor of the journal *Chervonyi shliakh*, and was replaced as commissar for education.[56] However, this was balanced by the dismissal of a substantial number of officials in Kiev and Dnepropetrovsk who opposed Ukrainization.[57]

The War Scare of 1927

In July 1927 Stalin, in an article in *Pravda*, 'Note on Contemporary Themes', highlighted the growing threat of war.[58] This aimed to unsettle the Joint Opposition and to provide a pretext for strengthening party control. The Ukrainian leadership responded on cue with alarming warnings on Polish threats to Soviet security. V. A. Balitsky, head of the Ukrainian GPU, submitted a report to Kaganovich on the revival of the 'Ukrainian counter-revolution'. Pilsudski's coup in Poland in 1926, the report argued, had had an important impact on opinion in Ukraine, and that the kulaks, together with elements of the intelligentsia, constituted the main social base of anti-Soviet opposition.[59]

In July–August Kaganovich undertook a month-long tour of the Ukrainian border provinces, addressing sessions of the province bureaus on the situation.[60] On 1 September Balitsky submitted a report on the situation in the border provinces to Kaganovich. In the event of war, he asserted, the poor and middle peasants would fight for the Soviet government and that only a minority of kulaks looked forward to a war and the prospect of the overthrow of Soviet power. On 13 September he addressed the Ukrainian Politburo's Commission for Investigating the Frontier, outlining the importance of land reorganization and population transfers from the border zone to strengthen security. In these weeks, he also had meetings with peasants and soldiers, aimed at assessing their mood.[61]

Ukrainization under Attack

In 1926–27 the question of the nationalities policy became embroiled in the struggle between the party leadership and the Joint Opposition, with the latter attempting to make common cause with the dissidents in Ukraine. They argued that Ukrainization served to strengthen the Ukrainian nationalist bourgeoisie, that it was strongly opposed by the Russian-speaking workers who provided the core support for the Bolshevik regime and that it encouraged autonomist sentiments that weakened the union.

In the winter of 1926 Yuri Larin, in an article in *Bol'shevik*, argued that the policy of encouraging local languages and cultures had unleashed a form of 'zoological Russophobia'. He singled out for censure Khvylovy's article 'Away from Moscow' and an article by Skrypnik in *Ukrainskii Bol'shevik*. He condemned the 'compulsory' Ukrainization of the trade unions, with proceedings being conducted in the Ukrainian language, which many Ukrainian workers did not understand.[62] In 1927 V. Vaganyan, a signatory of the Oppositionist 'Declaration of the 83', published a book, *O natsional'noi kulture*, which dismissed Ukrainization as a costly and 'reactionary experiment' which slowed down the cultural development of the masses.[63] At the Central Control Commission presidium in June 1927, Zinoviev accused the Ukrainian Communist Party of violating the CPSU's nationalities policy by discriminating against the Russian-speaking workers.

At the joint plenum of the Ukrainian Central Committee and Central Control Commission, in February–March 1927, Kaganovich reproved Larin for promoting a Russian chauvinist deviation and charged Shumsky with espousing Ukrainian nationalist ideology. The aim of Ukrainization, he argued, was not to raise the level of national consciousness, but rather to defuse the language and cultural issue and to secure the more effective integration of Ukraine into the USSR, in part through the development of its productive forces. He supported Skrypnik's line in implementing Ukrainization. He denied Shumsky's claim that the atmosphere inside the party was hostile to the Ukrainians, noting that nine Ukrainians had been promoted as province party secretaries. He stressed that they were ready to work with the ex-Borot'bists.[64]

The joint plenum of the Ukrainian Central Committee and Central Control Commission in June condemned Shumsky's views. It also censured the leadership of the Communist Party of Western Ukraine (KPZU), and particularly its leader Karlo Maksimovich, for its support for Shumsky. *Bol'shevik* at the end of 1927 published a stinging attack on Vaganyan and Larin.[65]

The X Congress of the Ukrainian Communist Party was held in Kharkov, 20–29 November, and was attended by Rykov. In his report, Kaganovich insisted that the line of Ukrainian Communist Party was that of the CPSU.[66] Ukraine was at the forefront of the drive to develop Soviet nationality policy. Western imperialism, in league with the Ukrainian White Guards, was intent on turning Ukraine into a colony of the West. The October Revolution, Kaganovich claimed, had liberated the Ukrainians and other non-Russian peoples. The Bolsheviks were reviving the Ukrainian nation, formerly considered a 'non-historic nation'. He boasted of the achievements of Ukrainization, declaring, 'We placed in charge of the cultural front one of the best, most senior Bolshevik-Leninists, Nikolai Alekseyevich Skrypnik.' He dismissed Larin, Vaganyan and Zinoviev as representatives of a Russian nationalist deviation in the CPSU. While it was necessary to Ukrainize the party and state apparatus, he insisted, there would be no compulsory Ukrainization of the proletariat.

The Comintern discussed the Ukrainian issue on several occasions.[67] The Ukrainian Central Committee discounted the Comintern's Executive Committee charge that they were promoting a nationalist deviation and in turn warned of a Russian nationalist deviation in the CPSU, while also criticizing any attempt to separate Ukraine from the USSR. The V Congress of the Comintern underlined the importance of Soviet policy in Ukraine for the countries of Central and Eastern Europe, where the revolutionary movement, it argued, was developing.

Kaganovich rebutted the charges of 'Russian chauvinists' who claimed that Ukrainization was being imposed 'from above', but he also castigated the nationalist deviationists inside the Ukrainian Communist Party. He repulsed the assertions that Ukraine had lost its statehood. The relations between Ukraine and the RSFSR, he argued, should serve as a model for relations between the USSR and future socialist republics such as the future Polish Soviet Socialist Republic.[68]

Economic Policy in Ukraine, 1926–1927

Kaganovich in 1925 was accused by Zinoviev and Kamenev of pursuing a Rightist pro-peasant policy. In 1926 he became a strong supporter of industrial growth. The XIV Party Congress committed the party to a policy of industrialization. Kaganovich reported on the results of the congress to the Kharkov party activists. Socialism was being built in the USSR via the NEP and the 'alliance' of workers and peasants. It was necessary to strengthen the country's defences. Industry was now the vanguard of the economy.

The contradictions between state industry and peasant agriculture had to be resolved by economic, not administrative, means. He continued to defend Lenin's stance that agriculture could be socialized through the development of cooperatives.[69]

On 10 March 1926 the Ukrainian Politburo discussed the near insolvency of two Ukrainian trusts, Yugostal and the Southern Machine-Building trust (Yuzhmashtrest). The session was attended by Dzerzhinsky, head of Vesenkha USSR, who proposed that Yuzhmashtrest be declared bankrupt and that other branches of Ukrainian industry should cover its debts. Members of the Ukrainian Politburo responded indignantly. Kaganovich introduced a proposal requesting more finance and credit for the Ukrainian trusts from the all-union Central Committee.[70] At the Ukrainian Central Committee plenum in April 1926, he insisted that state investment be channelled into the metal and coal industries, the two most neglected sectors.[71] On 10 May the Ukrainian Politburo again raised the question of rapidly resolving the financial problems of Yugostal with the all-union party Central Committee.[72]

In July Kaganovich argued that the Soviet state had demonstrated its ability to control private capital, reflected in the growing role of the cooperatives in trade.[73] Ukraine's heavy industry had suffered badly during the Civil War. Huge investment was already being made in Yugostal. He declared that the Communist Party's first priority was 'the growth of our socialist industry and the forcing of the industrialization of the country' and that Ukraine had to occupy one of the foremost places in the all-union plan for building new works. In agriculture, the kulaks were to be kept in check through the development of cooperatives, the expansion of the collective farms (*kolkhozy*) and state farms (*sovkhozy*) and by curtailing the provision of credit.

Kuibyshev, who took over as chairman of Vesenkha USSR following Dzerzhinsky's death in August 1926, pursued a more assertive policy of industrialization and in this was supported by the Ukrainian industrial lobby. Kaganovich and Kuibyshev were friends from their days in Turkestan. Ukraine had powerful advocates as vice chairmen in Vesenkha USSR, notably Pyatakov, Kviring and M. L. Rukhimovich. Kviring was transferred from Vesenkha USSR to Gosplan USSR in December 1926. Grin'ko was transferred from Ukraine to Gosplan USSR in November 1926 after clashing with Kaganovich in Ukraine.

A commission, headed by Trotsky, worked out detailed proposals for the building of the hydroelectric station on the Dnieper River (Dneprostroi), which the Ukrainian leadership had approved in May 1925. At the Central Committee plenum in April 1926, Stalin expressed reservations regarding the wisdom of committing so much investment to one project.[74] Kaganovich strongly supported the scheme.[75] In October the Ukrainian Politburo sent

Kaganovich and Chubar' to Moscow to lobby for the project.[76] Kaganovich reported to the Ukrainian party leadership in February–March 1927 that they had succeeded in obtaining approval for the dam.[77] Stalin now supported Dneprostroi, but on the understanding that Ukraine itself should finance a large part of the project.

In October the XV all-union Party Conference, on a report from Chubar', listed the Dnieper hydroelectric station as a 'shock task' for the USSR as a whole.[78] Chubar' reported to the Ukrainian Politburo on the need for Ukraine to find additional resources for the project, above those allocated by Moscow. On 26 November the Ukrainian Politburo established a special commission of the Ukrainian Central Executive Committee to assist Dneprostroi, chaired by him.[79] The funding of the project was hotly debated. On 2 February 1927, at a meeting of the Ukrainian Politburo, Shumsky vehemently denied the charges of Kaganovich and Petrovsky that he had opposed Dneprostroi, asserting only that he had demanded guarantees that it would be financed out of the all-union, rather than the Ukrainian, budget.[80]

These controversies concerning the funding of individual projects were part of a wider debate on financing the industrialization program. Kaganovich, like the rest of the Stalinist group, continued to defend the official policy of holding down the price of grain, while simultaneously forcing down the price of manufactured goods. This severely limited the state's scope for accumulating funds for industrial investment.

Addressing the Ukrainian Communist Party conference on 17 October 1926, Kaganovich endorsed the 'regime of economy' campaign as a means of funding the industrialization drive. He warned also of the growing power of the kulaks, and the need to use the committees of poor peasants as a check on their power.[81] Various speakers accused him of destroying internal party democracy and of pursuing a pro-peasant policy. The conference resolution condemned the Joint Opposition for its lack of faith in 'Socialism in One Country', for seeking to separate the party from the working class and for advocating policies which would rupture relations between the working class and the peasantry.

At the all-union Central Committee plenum on 8 February 1927 Kaganovich accused the Joint Opposition of demagoguery on economic policy. The government's industrial policy was constrained by the difficulty of imposing a heavier tax burden on the peasantry. Industry had to find additional internal resources to fund new investment through the rationalization drive and the 'regime of economy' campaign which was provoking strong opposition from workers in the main industrial areas. He stressed the importance of the Dneprostroi project. Moreover, new investment was urgently required for the renewal of the metallurgical works of Yugostal, Kramatorsk and

Yuzhmashtrest. At the same time, he acknowledged that the situation was equally critical at other works, such as Sormovo in Nizhnyi Novgorod, where his brother Mikhail was chairman of the soviet economic council.[82]

In May the Ukrainian Politburo noted with approval the positive outcome of Kuibyshev's visit to Ukraine, with his tour of the reconstruction work at Yuzhmashtrest, the Nikolaev works and the Kharkov, Kiev and Odessa agricultural implements works. The Ukrainian leadership and Vesenkha USSR had evidently found common ground regarding the future development of heavy industry in Ukraine.[83] Kaganovich, at the X Ukrainian Communist Party Congress in November, argued that Ukraine's share of USSR industrial production and investment was modestly increasing and welcomed the all-union Central Committee's decision to proceed with the electrification of the country. Industrialization would strengthen the socialist element in the economy, but this was to be achieved through self-financing, rationalization, cost cutting and measures to boost labour productivity.[84]

At the XV Party Congress in December 1927, Kaganovich highlighted the impact of the war scare of the autumn on Ukraine. He emphasized his commitment to the policy of accelerated industrialization, especially for metallurgy and machine- building, where Ukraine would have precedence. But he rejected any suggestions that he was speaking as a provincial lobbyist (*oblastnik*).[85] However, the prominence assigned to the industrialization of Ukraine gave him ammunition against the nationalist wing of the Ukrainian party, which argued that Ukraine was losing its sovereignty and being turned into a colony. From 1925 onward, the Ukrainian and Urals party organizations were locked in a bitter struggle over priority in investment for the reconstruction of the metallurgical industry.[86]

The Struggle against the Joint Opposition

At the Ukrainian Central Committee plenum, in June 1926, Kaganovich rounded on the Joint Opposition for exploiting the difficult international situation and of trying to use anti-Soviet moods for their own advantage. On 14 July the Ukrainian party secretariat instructed local party organizations to expel the oppositionists from the party.[87] In September the Ukrainian Politburo and presidium of the Central Control Commission, in a joint resolution written by Kaganovich, condemned 'the criminal, corrupting activities of the Trotskyist opposition'.[88] In November, on the orders of the Ukrainian Politburo, nine opposition leaders were arrested.

The Joint Opposition had high hopes of winning support in Ukraine. Khristian Rakovsky visited Ukraine to lead the Trotskyist agitation on the tenth anniversary of the October Revolution.[89] Kaganovich, in his memoirs, recounted the stormy reception which had been organized for him.⁹⁰ He was rebuffed in Kharkov, Dnepropetrovsk and Zaporozhe and had not dared to go to the Donbass. At Dnepropetrovsk a detachment of Red Army men blowing police whistles disrupted the meeting and dragged Rakovsky from the tribune. Rakovsky denounced these tactics as 'social fascism'.⁹¹ Kaganovich was not abashed to claim the result as a great victory for the official line, citing the derisory number of votes won by speakers from the Joint Opposition at party meetings. At the XV all-union Party Congress, 11 members of the Ukrainian delegation denounced the opposition. After the congress, the arrests and exile of oppositionists from Ukraine continued.

Kaganovich sought to consolidate his position through personnel transfers. In October 1926 P. P. Postyshev replaced Kirkizh as secretary of the Kharkov city party organization.⁹² Kirkizh, who was supported by Chubar', was appointed head of the Ukrainian Central Control Commission. He quickly fell out with Kaganovich, who accused him of supporting Rykov and Tomsky against Stalin. In January 1927 he was ousted as chairman of Central Control Commission and was replaced by V. P. Zatonsky.⁹³ However, in 1927 Zatonsky's relations with Kaganovich became soured.⁹⁴

At the Ukrainian Central Committee plenum in February–March, Kirkizh identified two opposing groups in the Ukrainian Politburo: the first included Kaganovich, Petrovsky and Zatonsky, and the second, Chubar', Klimenko and Radchenko.⁹⁵ At the All-Ukrainian Congress of Trade Unions in 1927, Kaganovich sought to discredit its chairman Radchenko, stressing the need for party control over the unions in realizing the programme of industrialization.⁹⁶ This provided a harbinger of the attack on Tomsky and VTsSPS in 1928. Kaganovich also worked to strengthen his position by building up his network of clients among provincial party leaders. He appointed V. Chernyavsky in Odessa, F. Kornyushin in Kiev, and advanced V. Stroganov, P. Terekhov and Khrushchev in the Donbass. In the autumn of 1927 a number of first secretaries of the province committees were replaced, on the pretext of advancing Ukrainians.⁹⁷

In March 1928 Shumsky's supporters gained control of the Communist Party of Western Ukraine (KPZU).⁹⁸ In a report to the Kharkov party activists, Kaganovich insisted that, while fighting against Shumskyism, the party had also to set its face against Great Russian chauvinism. He censured officials who displayed a dismissive attitude to the Ukrainian language, insisting on the need to carry through the 'great process of Ukrainization', but it had to be based on proletarian elements. The joint plenum of the Ukrainian Central Committee and Central Control Commission had 'given a rebuff to the slanders' of the KPZU that there was no Ukrainization in Soviet Ukraine, and that the Ukrainian Communist Party promoted a Great Russian policy.

The Grain Crisis of 1927–1928

In the autumn of 1927 the regime faced mounting difficulties with grain procurement, exacerbated by the inadequate supply of manufactured goods to the countryside. The all-union Politburo, on 24 December, dispatched plenipotentiaries to the most important grain-producing region to secure supplies.[99] Kaganovich oversaw the application of emergency measures in Ukraine. In March 1928, at a session of the all-union Politburo, Kaganovich, Chubar' and Petrovsky opposed a proposal to import 130,000 tons of grain to deal with the supply crisis, promising Stalin that they would find sufficient grain in Ukraine.

The Ukrainian Central Committee–Central Control Commission plenum, which met 12–16 March, heard a GPU report on the grain procurement campaign. Some delegates expressed alarm at its detrimental impact on the mood of the middle and poor peasants and even among the workers. Degtiarev noted that the campaign was sapping the morale of soldiers in the army. Kaganovich warned against 'panic'. The campaign for grain collection from January to March was greatly intensified.[100] The plenum voted to increase pressure on the kulaks.[101]

In his report to the plenum, Kaganovich declared that the grain crisis stemmed from a central contradiction between the planned socialist economy and peasant agriculture geared to the market. The inadequate supply of manufactured goods being sent to the countryside threatened to destabilize the industrial-financial plan and the gold-backed ruble, the *chervonets*. The grain procurement campaign encountered strong resistance in Mariupol, Melitopol and Zaporozhe. Pressure had to be applied to secure the grain, but he warned against excesses, disorders and 'sadistic tendencies'. The domestic crisis was directly linked to the threat of war. Robespierre's fall during the French Revolution, he recalled, had stemmed from such a crisis. But he dismissed the Trotskyist opposition charge of Thermidor as idiocy. The Soviet state was demonstrating its power over the kulaks.[102]

Addressing Kharkov party activists at the end of March, Kaganovich sharply shifted his ground on agrarian policy.[103] The Ukrainian party organization had drafted 10,000 people into the countryside in the preceding two months. As a result, they had achieved a 'sharp leap forward' in grain collections, which disproved the opposition's 'slanderous lies' that the Central Committee was pursuing a 'pro-kulak' policy. He conceded that the interests of the middle peasants had been infringed, with cases of 'stupid bungling and abuse of power'. The *kombedy* were weak and needed to be revived with 'tens, hundreds of thousands of real, actual poor peasants'. The sowing campaign, he noted, was 'directed in the channel of the collectivization of agriculture', orientated on wining the support of the poor and middle peasants. Kaganovich declared that in 'strengthening the political and economic might of the dictatorship of the proletariat' they did not need to wear kid gloves.[104]

A key role in the developing power struggle inside the party was played by the Shakhty affair, which developed in the spring of 1928. This was to have a lasting impact on the regime's relations with the bourgeois specialists (see Chapter 5).

Kaganovich's Removal as General Secretary

By 1928 Kaganovich's relations with other members of the Ukrainian leadership were severely strained. According to Khrushchev, he was opposed by Chubar' and Petrovsky. Petrovsky courted the Dnepropetrovsk lobby, which previously had backed Kviring. Kaganovich relied on the party leaders of the Donbass and particularly the Yuzovka party organization, which had a special status as the proletarian bedrock of the party, which incited some jealousy in Kharkov.[105] Kaganovich thus came to rely on those Ukrainian leaders who were least sympathetic to Ukrainization. At the XV all-union Party Congress in December 1927, Chubar' and Petrovsky pressed Stalin to recall Kaganovich. Stalin accused them of anti-Semitism.[106] Molotov was required to 'pacify' the dispute between the Ukrainian leaders.[107]

The last months of Kaganovich's leadership of the Ukrainian party were marked by great acrimony. His handling of the grain procurement crisis was sharply criticized by a number of provincial party committee secretaries. The dispute between Skrypnik and Shumsky over Ukrainization again flared up. The Ukrainian party was not, Skrypnik asserted, 'controlled by Kaganovich's group'. Ukraine was not a colony exploited by Moscow. Such views amounted to a 'petty bourgeois ideologically fascist line'.[108]

This prompted a strong rejoinder. In April Shumsky, Maksimovich and Grin'ko and other Ukrainians, whom Kaganovich had ousted and who were working in Moscow, sent a sharply worded protest to the all-union Politburo concerning Skrypnik's allegations, and also deplored Kaganovich's role. On 12 April the Ukrainian Politburo, at a closed session in Moscow, criticized the declaration. It was alleged that inside the all-union Politburo, Bukharin sympathized with the views of Shumsky, Maksimovich and Grin'ko.[109]

In June the Ukrainian leadership met with Stalin to discuss grain procurement. Several days later, at the Ukrainian Central Committee plenum, Chubar' reported that at the very end of the meeting, 'Stalin turned to me and, in the absence of Molotov, said "we are thinking of recalling Kaganovich from you"'.[110] Chubar' responded, saying that when Kaganovich had arrived in Ukraine, he had greeted him as a colleague and had supported him.[111] The implication was that this trust had been forfeited.

The Ukrainian Central Committee plenum in June 1928 paid tribute to Kaganovich's contribution as general secretary and requested that the all-union Central Committee retain him in his post. However, A. Odintsov, in dissent, accused Kaganovich of having scattered the old Ukrainian cadres and of employing inadmissible methods in party leadership. Postyshev, Kaganovich's protégé, interjected to deny Odintsov's charge that the Ukrainian Politburo and Central Committee were 'pawns, playthings in Kaganovich's hands' and demanded that such rumour mongers be expelled from the Central Committee.[112] The all-union Politburo on 7 July reappointed Kaganovich as secretary of the all-union Central Committee. Three days later, the Ukrainian Politburo, at a session in Moscow, acceded to his request to be released from his duties as Ukrainian general secretary.

In Bukharin's view, Stalin 'bought' the Ukrainians by withdrawing Kaganovich from Ukraine.[113] Chubar' scathingly indicted his personalized and dictatorial style of leadership: 'Mutual confidence, mutual control by us was breached, such that we could not believe one another... Questions were resolved behind the backs of the Politburo, on the side.'[114] The historian Stephen Cohen, with some hyperbole, writes of Kaganovich's 'three year tyranny in Kharkov'.[115] These authoritarian methods reflected the Stalin group's endeavours to impose control over the republic's factionalized political groupings. But they undoubtedly also reflected Kaganovich's personal style.

Kaganovich was succeeded as the new Ukrainian general secretary by Stansilav Kosior. He had served as party secretary of the Siberian region and in January 1926 was transferred to the Central Committee's Secretariat. In 1927 he became a candidate member of the Politburo. Kaganovich undoubtedly played a key role in the promotion of his old mentor.[116] Chubar' remained as chairman of the Ukrainian Sovnarkom. Under Kosior, Skrypnik retained great influence on questions pertaining to industrial investment policy and Ukrainization.[117]

Conclusion

Kaganovich's brief tenure as Ukrainian general secretary covered an important moment in the history of the Ukrainian Soviet Socialist Republic. Ukrainization was promoted in order to broaden the regime's base of popular support. It was a policy which ran in parallel with the economic relaxation introduced by NEP. In this, Kaganovich had to steer a course between the advocates and the critics of Ukrainization. This conciliatory policy was to flounder on the fundamental conflict between the supporters of the Ukrainian language and the supporters of the Russian language, the latter of which included the party's proletarian support base in industrial Donbass. Kaganovich helped secure the

Ukrainian party's support for Stalin, but his authoritarian style provoked the ire of many republican leaders.

In this period, Kaganovich and Molotov were Stalin's closest and most dependable aides. Stalin had not yet consolidated his control of the Politburo. A disciplined Stalinist faction had not yet formed. Thus, as general secretary in Ukraine, Kaganovich was allowed some leeway and displayed some degree of independence. Moreover, Stalin, in 1926, over the row between Kaganovich and Shumsky, felt free to leave his aide in the lurch. Stalin adopted a more conciliatory policy towards Shumsky, but in the end, allowed Kaganovich to terminate his political career. In the struggle with the Joint Opposition, Kaganovich undoubtedly acted as Stalin's agent. But in 1928, to discomfit the 'Rightists' in the Politburo and to appease the Ukrainians, the general secretary decided it was prudent to remove him from the republic. In a position where he was not fully in control, Stalin was required to show tact and diplomacy in his handling of people.

As Ukrainian general secretary, Kaganovich, having staunchly defended the NEP in 1924–25, became an enthusiastic advocate of industrialization. Kaganovich and the Ukrainian lobby, in alliance with Kuibyshev and Vesenkha, may well have been instrumental in shifting Stalin toward embracing a policy of industrialization. To fund this programme, the policy of concessions to the peasantry, which he had been instrumental in promoting, was abandoned. In 1927–28 he became an outspoken advocate of forcible grain requisitioning, measures he had earlier condemned, and a defender of moves to curb the power of the kulaks. This policy shift, by antagonizing the peasantry, ran directly counter to those policies aimed at winning their support through the revitalization of the soviets and Ukrainization. At the same time, the priority of financing industrialization gave birth to the 'regime of economy' campaign, which antagonized workers and led to the drive to reorientate the trade unions to assist in the work.

Chapter 5

THE TRIUMPH OF THE STALIN FACTION, 1928–1929

Stalin, in his struggle with the Joint Opposition in 1926–27, relied on the support of the 'Rightists' – Bukharin, Rykov and Tomsky. This alliance came under mounting stress; the grain crisis of 1927 posed the question of the viability of the NEP as a policy that could deliver rapid industrial growth; the defeat of the British General Strike and the suppression of the Chinese Communist Party represented two major setbacks in foreign policy in 1926. The Politburo leadership was taken unawares by these developments. It was vigorously attacked by the Joint Opposition for its lack of foresight. Stalin responded with the 'left turn' on domestic and foreign policy, returning to the class warfare rhetoric of the early Soviet period. This abrupt policy change surprised his allies and caused deep division within the Politburo. Trotsky's prediction that the defeat of the Joint Opposition would precipitate a new split between Stalin and Bukharin proved prescient. On this basis, the Stalin group was constituted. The struggle between the Stalinist group and the Rightists was a battle not only to control key institutions, but also to control the economy and to construct a new developmental strategy that went beyond the confines of NEP.

Kaganovich's role in this period casts light on the formation of the Stalin group, its policies and tactics. Its strategy accorded priority to the expansion of heavy industry, which involved turning the terms of trade against the peasantry and procuring grain at low prices, by compulsion where necessary. Leading advocates of industry were V. V. Kuibyshev, head of Vesenkha, and G. M. Krzhizhanovsky, head of Gosplan. Kaganovich, as Ukrainian party secretary, was a strong supporter. The regional industrial lobbies of Ukraine and the Urals clamoured for priority to be given to industrial investment. This precipitated a clash in the Politburo and was strongly opposed by the leading economic commissariats of the NEP era – the commissariats of finance, trade and agriculture.

The abandonment of the NEP ran counter to Lenin's final precepts on the future management of the economy. It posed serious dangers in terms of exacerbating relations with the peasantry and the working class. The view of economic historians is that the NEP could have provided a basis for future industrial growth within the confines of the market economy, and based on trade between industry and agriculture.[1] But the new policy reflected the growing confidence of the regime in its ability to force the pace of industrial growth. It stemmed also from the real problem of the growing gap between the Soviet economy and that of the most advanced capitalist states, and the related lag in Soviet military capabilities. The absence of foreign investment and credits, however, carried serious implications with regard to the domestic funding of the industrialization drive.

The XV Party Congress

The XV Party Congress in December 1927 saw the comprehensive defeat of the Joint Opposition, with Trotsky denouncing the Bonapartist and Caesarist tendencies in the Soviet leadership. The congress met while the grain collection campaign was in progress. The general secretary's report highlighted the new priority accorded to the industrialization of the country. He complained of the slow growth of agriculture and argued that the only solution was 'a transformation to the collective cultivation of the soil on the basis of a new and higher technique'. He noted the 'elements of a goods famine' and the inadequate supply of manufactured goods going to the countryside as the inevitable debit side of the policy of industrialization, which would continue for 'the next few years'.[2]

Kaganovich, who spoke after Stalin, supported giving priority to the development of heavy industry, citing the achievements of Ukrainian industry. He brushed aside current difficulties in grain procurement as 'inevitable in so huge a work of construction as ours'.[3] He launched a powerful assault on the Joint Opposition. Following the severing of Anglo-Soviet relations, the party, following Lenin's precepts, had successfully exploited inter-imperialist rivalries 'to turn our weakness into our strength', to avert the danger of war. It was necessary, he argued, to strengthen communist influence within the Red Army. He savaged Trotsky's imprudent words on the opposition's ambivalence as regards its willingness to defend the Soviet regime in the face of capitalist threats – the so-called 'Clemeanceau' thesis. He insisted that based on his one-month tour of the Ukrainian border region, the population in the event of war would rally to the Soviet government. It was necessary to continue with the Leninist nationalities policy. The steady economic revival in the preceding two years had raised living standards for the mass of the people.[4]

The Joint Opposition, Kaganovich argued, had tried unsuccessfully to exploit popular discontent over wages, but the admission into the party of

70,000 of the best, most advanced proletarians gave the lie to the charge of bureaucratic degeneration, declaring, 'The proletariat stays with its party.' He sought historical justification for the monolithic unity imposed on the party: the defeat of the Paris Commune had stemmed from the absence of a strong, centralized, disciplined party, an error that the Bolsheviks were not to repeat.[5] The speech contained a sinister warning. Whereas the Mensheviks had taken fifteen years to transform themselves into 'an active counter-revolutionary force', in the conditions of revolution, dissident groups within the party had undergone the same transformation in two to three years. He continued, 'We are not coy young ladies, we are obliged to pose the question politically thus, as it is posed by history, as Lenin taught us.'[6] The opposition demonstration at the Yaroslavl station on the tenth anniversary of the October Revolution, he declared, was an 'antiparty', 'counter-revolutionary' action. The Central Committee and Central Control Commission had to take resolute measures to ensure there was no repetition. Trotskyist views were incompatible with party membership and those who clung to this position should be expelled from its ranks.

The Grain Crisis

The grain procurement crisis was produced in part by the government's commitment to forced industrial development, which resulted in a lowering of the official price paid for grain and a reduction in the supply of manufactured goods to the countryside. In January 1928 Stalin went to Siberia, and his closest associates – Anastas Mikoyan, Andrei Zhdanov, Nikolai Shvernik and Andreev – took charge of other regional operations.[7] Kaganovich, as general secretary of the Ukrainian Communist Party, was a forthright exponent of forcible grain seizure. He now defended a policy of exploiting the peasants, a policy which, when advocated by Zinoviev and Trotsky, he had denounced only in November 1926. These measures, on which hinged the future of the NEP, caused a deepening crisis between Stalin and his erstwhile supporters, Bukharin, Rykov and Tomsky.

The party Central Committee plenum, in early July, brought to the surface the simmering dispute regarding agrarian policy. V. V. Osinsky warned of the breakdown of the link with the peasantry. A. I. Stetsky declared that 'they are saying in the countryside, that 1919 and 1920 have returned'. G. Ya Sokolnikov spoke in favour of raising agricultural prices. Even Andreev attributed peasant hostility not to incidental 'excesses', but to the fact that they had seized the basic reserves of the middle peasants.[8]

Kaganovich identified as the main problem in agriculture the control exercised by the kulaks over grain marketing. He conceded that errors had been committed, but warned against any judgemental attitude towards a policy that had been carried out by the whole party. They were pursuing a centrist course: they should not elevate extraordinary measures into a permanent system, as some comrades wanted. The Soviet state, he argued, would continue to rely on 'administrative-political influence in the economy', and where necessary, they would invoke the criminal code. While the well-to-do peasants had wavered, the middle peasants as a whole had not allied with the kulaks against the Soviet government. Class struggle was intensifying, he alleged, with the kulaks leading all the risings in those districts afflicted by grain shortages. He predicted that 'In future grain collection campaigns, we will clash with the cruel opposition of the kulaks.' The party had to mobilize the activists and speed up the pace of procurements.[9]

Rykov castigated Kaganovich's disingenuousness and according to Sokolnikov, 'made mincemeat of him'.[10] He accused him of using sophistry to justify emergency measures as a policy applicable at all times and in all circumstances and of invoking the methods of War Communism.[11] Kaganovich's uncompromising stand drew much of the fire which might otherwise have been directed at Stalin. In a conciliatory gesture, the Central Committee unanimously agreed to repeal the extraordinary measures applied in the first half of 1928 and to normalize methods of grain purchasing.[12]

This concession reflected the strength of the 'Rightists' within the Politburo: Bukharin was the party's leading theoretician, Rykov was the head of government as chairman of Sovnarkom and STO, and Tomsky was head of the All-Union Central Council of the Trade Unions (VTsSPS). They drew support from other local leaders, most notably Uglanov, the head of the Moscow party organization. They enjoyed considerable support in the commissariats of finance, trade and agriculture. In the summer of 1928 Bukharin thought that he commanded a majority in the Politburo. He confided to Kamenev that Stalin was 'an unprincipled intriguer who subordinates everything to his appetite for power', with the warning 'He will strangle us', and that Stalin was a Genghis Khan.[13]

In June 1928 Stalin recalled Kaganovich from the post of general secretary of the Ukrainian Communist Party. This was intended to appease the Ukrainian leadership, particularly G. I. Petrovsky, and to defuse any attempt by Bukharin to cultivate their support. The move wrong-footed the 'Rightists' in the Politburo, creating an impression that Stalin was amenable to compromise and that the undertakings on avoiding administrative measures in future grain procurement campaigns would be adhered to. This turned out to be nothing more than a tactical ploy.

N. A. Uglanov and the Moscow party committee followed the 'Rightist' line. Kaganovich was entrusted with the task of breaking their power in the capital.

He and other officials of the Central Committee worked to organize a revolt from below, following a well-tried strategy, establishing close cooperation with the districts of Moscow. In October, 50 secretaries of cells from the Rogozhsko-Simonovsky district sent a letter to the Central Committee denouncing the factional activity of district party secretary, N. Pen'kov, who was one of Uglanov's men. This set an example for activists in other districts.[14]

Bukharin believed that Stalin intended to oust Uglanov and appoint Kaganovich in his place.[15] In October, at the plenum of the Moscow Party Committee, Stalin denounced the 'Rightist danger' in the Moscow party leadership. But Stalin evidently decided that to put Kaganovich into this sensitive post would be too provocative a step, and instead appointed Molotov.[16] This, however, was a temporary appointment, and a few months later Molotov was replaced by K.Ya. Bauman.

Kaganovich's recall also served to strengthen the central party apparatus. Stalin delegated the running of the party Secretariat and Orgburo entirely to Molotov and Kaganovich, and very rarely attended the formal meetings of either of these two bodies. Stalin ordered that Kaganovich should chair the meetings of the Secretariat. He was to concentrate on cadre assignments, overseeing policy in the countryside, and dealing with the political situation in Moscow.[17] In August, Tomsky protested to Molotov regarding an official communiqué that Kaganovich had been elected as chairman of the Orgburo. No such post existed, he insisted, although individuals acted as chairmen at both Politburo and Orgburo meetings. Molotov undertook to correct the error.[18] The Secretariat and Orgburo had been depleted by the loss of leading officials. A. A. Andreev was transferred to the North Caucasus, D. E. Sulimov to the Urals, N. M. Shvernik to Urals, I. M. Varekis to the Central Black Earth region, Boris Sheboldaev to the Lower Volga, Mendel Khataevich to the Central Volga and Bauman to Moscow.[19]

In the Secretariat, Kaganovich directed the work of the party instructors. He, more than anyone, was the person responsible for developing the role of the instructors as a vital part of the party's machinery of administration. The chief task of the instructors, as defined by the Central Committee resolution of 14 January 1929, was to check the work of party organizations in enforcing the policies of industrialization and collectivization, mobilizing the party rank and file, and monitoring cadres policy. In February, Kaganovich published a short article, 'Concerning the Work of the Instructors', in which he rejected Menshevikists' and Trotskyists' 'slanders' that the party apparatus had become the enemy of party democracy. The party apparatus, he insisted, was the instrument which ensured that policy was implemented. The 'responsible instructor' had a vital function; they should concentrate on major issues, and needed to be fully 'politicized'.[20]

The Shakhty Affair

In June 1927 the execution by the OGPU (the Unified State Political Administration, the secret police) of twenty 'monarchist whiteguards' who were accused of terrorist, sabotage and espionage activities in league with foreign intelligence agencies was used by Stalin to fan the fears of war.[21] The war scare of 1927 and the attack on the kulaks in connection with the grain crisis marked a return to the class warfare rhetoric of the early Soviet period.

This campaign also played on widespread popular hostility towards the bourgeois specialists in industry. This acquired a new dimension in the spring of 1928 when 53 engineers in the coal mining industry in the North Caucasus town of Shakhty were accused of wrecking and working in league with the former owners of the mines. Their trial lasted from May until the end of July. The affair was initiated by E. G. Evdokimov, head of the OGPU in Shakhty in the North Caucasus region, who appealed, over the head of V. R. Menzhinsky, his boss in the OGPU, directly to Stalin. Menzhinsky, V. V. Kuibyshev and G. K. Ordzhonikidze viewed the charge of widespread wrecking with scepticism. Stalin sanctioned the campaign against the bourgeois specialists, brushing aside calls by Bukharin and Rykov for restraint.

Kaganovich played no significant part in initiating the affair, but he played a crucial role in developing and justifying the attack on the bourgeois specialists. The Ukrainian Central Committee in March 1928 discussed the issue of economic counter-revolution.[22] On 24 April V. A. Balitsky, the head of the Ukrainian GPU, and I. Blat, head of the GPU's Economic Administration, presented reports to Kaganovich on counter-revolution in Donbass. These reports elaborated an extensive conspiracy linked to Polish, French and German intelligence agencies, former mine owners and various opposition centres in Moscow and Kharkov. The conspirators had allegedly penetrated the main mine administration, Donugol', and had seized 'all the main commanding heights'. Engineers, it reported, retained a deep aversion to the communist regime; many showed a contemptuous attitude towards workers, and some engaged in sabotage. Eighty-four officials had been arrested.[23] Kaganovich reported to the Ukrainian Komsomol congress on the lessons of the Shakhty affair. In April and June the Central Committee of the Ukraine discussed the matter and the all-union Central Committee approved a resolution on the training of new specialists.[24]

In the wake of the trial, Stalin, Molotov and Kaganovich vocally advocated the advancement of young proletarians onto technical and training courses and their promotion to positions of responsibility as part of a programme to create a new Soviet intelligentsia.[25] Kaganovich headed a special Central Committee commission which oversaw the training and promotion of new technical and administrative cadres. This work was developed as a major field of party activity in the next five years.

In the autumn of 1928, at the request of Kaganovich's commission, the OGPU conducted a social and political survey of 9,000 engineers and other specialists in the state's economic apparatus. After a year of 'hard' investigation, he reported the preliminary results to the Central Committee in November 1929. The OGPU, he asserted, had uncovered an organized war against Soviet power. Five hundred specialists had been arrested on wrecking charges. Former 'big' capitalists and landowners accounted for 29 per cent of that number, and the rest were drawn from the non-gentry intelligentsia. Of the 106 arrested on the railways, 62 per cent came from the ranks of the old honorary nobility, trading class and clergy. This was adduced as proof that the campaign was coordinated by the 'commanding elite of the old capitalist order'.[26] In his report, he listed 23 leading industrial specialists who were under arrest. These included S. A. Khrennikov and V. I. Zhdanov, the former heads of the metal trust Gomzy and later high specialists in Glavmetall; D. N. Shvetsov, the former head of the Leningrad shipbuilding trust and then head of Gipromez; Taube and Gartman, chief engineers of Gosplan's industrial section; A. Svistyn, technical director of Yugostal and other prominent members of the trust's management board. These specialists, led by Khrennikov, figured as key defendants in the Industrial Party trial a year later. Among the arrested railway specialist was K. N. von Mekk, who was executed in 1930. Kaganovich rebuked Bukharin, who he accused of advocating a technocratic order run by engineers and managers.[27] Wreckers and spies, he alleged, had infiltrated the planning and administrative organs and industrial enterprises, creating constant crises in various branches of the economy. But he offered an olive branch: Most of those arrested were 'big shots' (*tyzy*), former owners and managers of industry, like von-Mekk. The majority of the old specialists were working honourably, and the party would give them its support.[28]

In his report, Kaganovich called for strict discipline in the higher technical schools and for the purging of the ranks of rectors, deans and academic staff of hostile elements. Party and Komsomol members should be given preferential access to these schools. The training of cadres had to be speeded up as a matter of urgency: 'It is necessary that the proletariat master knowledge and science, then we will feel ourselves to be firm and confident in the field of trade, finance, and agriculture.'[29] He berated the People's Commissariat of Enlightenment (*Narkompros*) for its penchant for producing 'artists and ballet dancers'. The resolution stressed the urgency of promoting young graduates and former workers to 'positions of command'.[30]

The promotion of a new generation of proletarian cadres was part of the 'revolution from above', a part of the cultural revolution aimed at effecting a major change in consciousness and behaviour.³¹ Stalin used the campaign to force the split with the 'Rightists', but also to pressure vacillators such as Kalinin.³² The trial was instrumental in constructing the internal enemy – the spy, the wrecker, the terrorist in league with the foreign enemy. This was presented as an assertion of a principled, resolute Bolshevik conception of vigilance and class justice. It played on a broad popular anxiety shaped by the Civil War and the foreign intervention.

The Trade Unions

The industrialization drive was hampered by the lack of investment. The government responded with its 'regime of economy' campaign aimed at reducing the costs of maintaining the state administration. The rationalization drive in industry was aimed at improving efficiency, cutting costs so as to allow prices to be lowered and to allow an increase in profit accumulation which could be reinvested in industry.

The campaign antagonized workers and provoked a strong trade union backlash. The All-Union Central Council of the Trade Unions (VTsSPS) headed by Tomsky was a bastion of the Right. By early November 1928 Stalin's campaign to discredit his leadership prompted union officials to complain of 'an atmosphere making it completely impossible to work'.³³ The Central Committee plenum that month admonished those in its ranks who favoured a slackening of the tempo of industrialization. The youth organizations' newspaper, *Komsomolskaya Pravda*, spearheaded the attack on the unions. Kaganovich was assigned a crucial role in the campaign against the trade unions, having already played a leading role in the campaign to restructure the Ukrainian trade unions in 1927.

At the VIII Trade Union Congress in December, Stalin's supporters, led by Kuibyshev (Vesenkha) and Ordzhonikidze (Central Control Commission-Rabkrin) extolled all-out heavy industrialization, and highlighted the role of the trade unions in raising productivity. By contrast, Tomsky and his associates opposed an industrial drive that would victimize the working class and transform the trade unions into 'houses of detention'.³⁴ Tomsky found himself in a minority in the party caucus which controlled the congress agenda. On 24 December, having heard a report by A. I. Dogadov, the caucus endorsed the Central Committee's policy on industrialization by a large majority. It reproved the Soviet trade union movement for adopting a 'purely workers' point of view and called for an 'intensified struggle against the danger of the Right and against any compromise with it'.³⁵

Molotov sought Tomsky's consent to appoint Kaganovich to the presidium of VTsSPS. Tomsky objected to the assignment of a 'political commissar' to control the unions. Kaganovich would become the focus of all those who opposed the official line of the Council, especially those from the Ukrainian delegation, creating a civil war within it at a time when unity of leadership was vital.[36] On Politburo instructions, the caucus voted to co-opt five Stalin appointees, including Kaganovich and I. A. Akulov, onto the presidium. Kaganovich's appointment was carried only by a majority of 28 to 24.[37] Defeated, Tomsky again tendered his resignation, which was rejected, but he thereafter refused to return to his post.[38] The first step taken by Kaganovich was to pressure the Moscow City Trade Union Council and VTsSPS's presidium to expel Tomsky's supporters.[39]

On 9 February 1929 a joint session of the Politburo and the presidium of Central Control Commission censured Bukharin, and accused Tomsky of establishing a 'feudal principality in the trade unions'.[40] On 23 April the Central Committee censured Bukharin, Rykov and Tomsky for setting the trade unions in opposition to the party and relieved Tomsky of his post in VTsSPS. N. M. Shvernik became the effective head of VTsSPS, bringing the union under the control of the Stalinist group.

Kaganovich continued to exercise oversight of the unions. In September 1929 the VTsSPS plenum launched the campaign 'face to production', directed at tightening labour discipline, which caused a sharp deterioration in working and living conditions. Addressing a meeting of Moscow activists in November, Kaganovich acknowledged that the 'extremely pressurized tempos of our construction' had created serious difficulties for the working class. The government had sought to alleviate the situation by improving housing conditions, wages and food supplies. The trade unions, he complained, had supported only a 'tortoise tempo' of industrialization, which Tomsky had justified as defending the unions from party control.[41] The Bolsheviks, he argued, had always adhered to the Leninist line concerning the party's close alliance with the trade unions as schools of communism. Many trade unionists, while denouncing the 'Rightists', still clung to old habits and practices. It was necessary to raise the cultural level of trade union cadres, and to advance 'new fresh strata of proletarians' into trade union work.

In January 1930 Kaganovich summoned all communists to involve themselves in production meetings, in shock brigades and in socialist emulation. While a small group of shock-workers was waging a heroic struggle, one section of the workers, he complained, mocked those they labelled 'shock-worker-idiots' (*chudaki-udarniki*). They had to raise the backward elements among the working class in order to fulfil the industrial-financial plan. It was necessary to ensure that this revolution occurred not only in the brains of the 'elite' of the trade union movement, but among lower links of the trade union movement and among the broad working mass. Able workers, he urged, should be promoted to leading posts: 'There are thousands of such workers, tens of thousands. It is necessary only to receive them, to find them and to promote them to work.'[42]

At the XVI Party Congress in June–July, Kaganovich branded Tomsky's opposition to rapid industrialization as opportunism. In 1928 the party, he asserted, had been compelled to intervene and change the leadership of the trade unions. This, he bluntly conceded, might be a violation of 'proletarian democracy', but the party did not fetishize democracy, but saw it as 'a means for defending the working class, for the best fulfilment of its socialist task.'[43] This marked an important step in rationalizing the power of the party-state apparatus, in the infantilization of society, and the progressive dismantling of the 'public sphere' and of civil society.

It was essential, Kaganovich argued, to increase the number of communists in key points in the factories, shops and brigades. Notwithstanding the efforts to involve communists in production through the Leninist enrolment, only 15–20 per cent of communist workers were involved in socialist emulation and shock-work. He was strongly critical of egalitarian production communes, but viewed the production meetings in the factories more favourably and supported the idea of making the heads of production meetings assistants to the director of the enterprise.[44] The congress resolved to extend the practice.[45]

The party's Central Control Commission purged the trade unions. In 1930 the Central Committee oversaw the re-election campaign of the factory committees. As a result, a new stratum of workers, mostly shock-workers, was advanced into the factory committees. Kaganovich continued to closely monitor the work of the trade unions.[46] The Stalinist leadership sought to mobilize working-class support through its new radical rhetoric directed against class enemies, through the mass recruitment of industrial workers into the Communist Party, through the mobilization of workers behind the production campaigns in industry and through the campaign of the 'Twenty-five Thousanders' behind the collectivization drive in the countryside.

The Komsomol

In the struggle for the 'general line', the Stalinists directed their appeal in particular towards youth. In his report to the Komsomol congress in May 1928, Stalin outlined a more interventionist role for the state in socialist construction. In this, he stressed the need to control the state both from above and from below through a policy of mass mobilization. The Komsomol's leadership was changed, with A. V. Kosarev elected as its head, and it became a strong supporter of the official line. The Central Committee, on 11 February 1929, approved guidelines for developing the policies of the Komsomol.[47]

At the end of October 1929 Kaganovich, addressing the First Moscow Province Conference of the Komsomol, appealed to young activists to rally round the party.[48] The strains of the industrialization drive, he acknowledged, caused dissatisfaction amongst some workers and cadres. The party, he asserted, had chosen a middle path between two hypothetical extremes, Trotskyists 'superindustrialization' and 'Rightist' capitulation to peasant pressure. This was a favourite rhetorical device. In reality, it is difficult to imagine how a 'superindustrialist' programme would have differed from that actually pursued in 1929. The party's policy was presented as a reaction to the actions of the kulaks. Those who buried their grain in the ground and refused to sell it to the proletarian state, Kaganovich argued, were waging class warfare against the state's policy to reconstruct agriculture on socialist lines.

Kaganovich appealed to the Komsomol to assist the party in enforcing the Leninist line. The Right deviation needed to be taught the basics of Leninism: 'Lenin taught not only by persuasion and entreaties, but Lenin took up the ideological Bolshevik cudgel and belaboured and taught Bolshevism.' In a period of intensified class conflict, the Komsomol had to proletarianize its ranks and expel careerist and kulak elements. The Shakhty affair had exposed the unreliability of the old specialists. The Komsomol had to assist in preparing its worker members for study in the higher technical educational institutions. In the years of revolution, the party had not hesitated to promote 24-year-olds as commanders, as leaders of provinces. Here he alluded to his own election as party secretary of Nizhnyi Novgorod in 1918. He promised that those who applied themselves to real affairs would be fully supported. The party required 'hundreds of thousands of literate, cultured cadres'. But Komsomol members were reluctant to be sent to the countryside where the class struggle was most intense. The Komsomol needed to rekindle the idealism of the Bolshevik 'undergrounders', develop self-criticism and to overcome the defeatists and 'whimperers' in their ranks. He offered a glimpse of the radiant future that awaited them: 'In ten to fifteen years' time, the country will be unrecognizable.'[49]

The Soviets

Kaganovich, as head of the Institute of Soviet Construction attached to the Communist Academy, continued to oversee the campaign to revitalize the soviets as a way of broadening the regime's base of support. After 1926, this policy was increasingly informed by the regime's new class policy in the countryside. Largely in response to the attacks from the Joint Opposition, the participation of kulaks in soviet elections, which had been permitted in 1924 and 1925, was halted in 1926. This marked a major retreat from the policies of the NEP and provided a clear indication of the limits of Bolshevik 'managed democracy'. In 1926 Kaganovich published *The Party and the Soviets*, in which he rejected Zinoviev's assertion that the proletarian dictatorship had become a party dictatorship, insisting that the soviets provided the regime with its base of mass support.[50]

In 1928 the Smolensk scandal, which revealed collusion between local party-soviet officials and kulaks, was used to highlight the dangers of regime degeneration stemming from the class policies of NEP.[51] The 1928–29 election campaign was launched in earnest at a conference in Moscow in October 1928, with reports by Kaganovich and Abel Yenukidze. The soviets, Kaganovich declared, were not merely mass organizations but organs of government. The party, while leading the soviets and putting forward its candidates, should not 'crush the will of the electors'. It should mobilize the landless labourers, poor peasants and a majority of the middle peasants in order to isolate the kulaks. Alluding to the Smolensk scandal, he warned of the growing power of the kulaks.[52]

Kaganovich also reported on the coming soviet elections to the Institute of Soviet Construction and to the All-Union Meeting for Soviet Elections. Soviet elections in the USSR, like elections in capitalist states, he asserted, 'must lead and always lead to the strengthening of class supremacy and the instrument of that class supremacy – the state administration'. Electoral procedures had to be improved, with the aim of reducing abstentionism (or 'absenteeism' as Kaganovich significantly termed it) in the elections.[53] He noted the weakness of the soviets in the national republics, as highlighted by the commission, headed by A. S. Kiselev which visited Semipalatinsk and Kazakhstan. The soviets had to implement the party's class policy. It was necessary to promote a new generation of cadres from among the proletariat, the poor peasants and landless labourers, and to mobilize the masses and unite them around the party.

He offered an insight into the Stalin groups' conception of the Soviet state: 'With us, the interests of the masses and the interests of the state are one and the same.' The Soviet state, as a proletarian state, aimed to strengthen its power, to industrialize the country and to involve the masses in its work. He echoed Stalin's claim that class struggle intensified in the transition to socialism. Social differentiation was growing in the countryside, and the rural proletariat was being pitched into conflict with 'the kulak, speculators, the mir-eater', who savagely opposed government policies.

For the peasantry, Kaganovich asserted, there could be no return to capitalism, which would disadvantage the middle peasants. The middle peasants, aggrieved by high taxes and the low prices paid for grain, were swayed in their allegiance against Soviet power by the kulaks. But the government's room for concessions was limited because of its commitment to industrial investment. Industrialization would facilitate the transformation of agriculture. A firm proletarian policy, as Lenin had advocated, would check vacillation. Forced industrialization, he acknowledged, was causing privations and deep dissatisfaction among workers, many of whom displayed 'petty bourgeois' attitudes, adding, 'It is impossible to flatter workers and say that all workers are free from such influences.'[54] Hostile class elements and remnants of the Mensheviks and SRs 'from their subterranean holes' would try to use the elections to discredit the party. The class struggle, Kaganovich asserted, was intensifying, reflected in conflicts of the landless labourers and poor peasants against the kulaks, and in various anti-Soviets acts of murder and torture. His role in reviving the soviets provided the background for his work in promoting the Urals-Siberian method of grain procurement in 1928–29.

The Urals-Siberian Method of Grain Procurement

In July 1928 the Central Committee plenum suspended the use of emergency measures which had been used in the early months of the year to secure grain supplies. A new approach to grain requisitioning was needed.[55] Kaganovich, in *Bol'shevik* in October 1928, proposed to make the village soviets responsible for allocating the tax burden between households, with the aim of transferring most of the burden onto the kulak and rich peasant households.[56] On 29 November 1928 the Politburo instructed local party organizations to speed up grain collection, through a mass political campaign in the countryside.[57]

As the grain crisis persisted, bread rationing was introduced in December.[58] Following the ruin of the autumn sowing in the southern regions, the procurement targets for the eastern regions (Siberia, the Urals, Kazakhstan, Bashkirya and the Volga) were significantly raised.[59] The Politburo discussed the issue with the regional party secretaries I. D. Kabakov (Urals) and A. P. Smirnov (Siberia) and turned down their petitions for targets to be lowered.[60] At a joint meeting of the Politburo and the presidium of the Central Control Commission, Bukharin, responding to Stalin's suggestion that the state needed to extract a 'tribute' from the peasantry, accused the leadership of 'the military-feudal exploitation of the peasantry'.[61]

On 4 March the Politburo dispatched Kaganovich to the Urals. On 13 March he participated in the meeting of the Urals province party committee bureau, which endorsed the use of 'social methods' as the main method of grain collection.[62] He also visited northern Kazakhstan and western Siberia to stimulate grain collection. According to Rykov, Kaganovich proposed by telegram that measures for a social boycott of those withholding grain should be sent to Politburo members for their approval, without convening a formal meeting of the Politburo. Rykov, however, insisted on placing the matter on the Politburo's agenda, because it contradicted existing policy which barred the resort to extraordinary measures.[63]

On 20 March the Politburo, ignoring the views of the Rightists, approved Kaganovich's proposal to extend this method of grain procurement to Kazakhstan, the Urals and Siberia. Compulsory quotas were to be levied on each village. Those who refused to cooperate were to be subject to boycott, which involved their expulsion from the cooperatives, suspension of the supply of industrial goods, refusal to mill their grain, exclusion of their children from the schools, the levying of fines and even deportation.[64]

Kaganovich consulted with the Siberian provincial leaders concerning this new policy. Already, on 21 March, the Siberian Territorial Party Committee bureau directed the district committees to 'transmit the firm tasks for procurement to individual villages in a voluntary manner (on the initiative of the poor peasants and *aktiv*)'.[65] This was the first announcement of the introduction of this tactic in Siberia. On 27 March the Siberian bureau adopted Kaganovich's proposal to supplement the use of social pressure with force, where necessary.[66]

Kaganovich then toured the two main grain growing areas of Rubtsovsk and Barnaul districts.[67] Addressing the IX Urals Province Party Conference, in April 1929, he stressed the danger of war, as noted by the VI Comintern congress. He highlighted the alleged growth of terrorist acts perpetrated by kulaks against the Soviet regime, and accused the 'Rights' of undermining the party's class position. He denied that extraordinary measures had been applied that year, arguing that only social influence had been used. He also rejected the claim that the middle peasants were hostile to Soviet policies.[68]

At the united Central Committee–Central Control Commission plenum of April 1929, Stalin dubbed the measures employed in grain collection as the 'Urals-Siberian method' (USM). The implication was that this was a local initiative which the centre had adopted. Historians have taken conflicting positions on the origins of the USM, as to whether is emanated from the centre or from the regions.[69] In fact, the initiative came from the centre and its author was Kaganovich. At the plenum, the 'Rightists' denounced the USM as heralding the end of the NEP. Tomsky accused Kaganovich of promoting 'extraordinary measures' in the disguise of 'social initiative'.[70] Bukharin attacked the Stalinist theory of the intensification of class struggle in the process of socialist construction and warned that the USM would create a vicious circle of declining grain supplies, which would elicit yet more extraordinary measures. He proposed creating a manoeuvrable grain reserve through imports.[71]

Kaganovich strongly defended the USM as a strategy of grain procurement. Notwithstanding the measures taken to raise grain prices and to improve the supply of consumer goods to the countryside, the kulaks still withheld their grain, thus openly challenging the Soviet government. The USM, he claimed, would allow the party to win the support of the majority of peasants for grain collection. He rejected Bukharin's formulation that 'the united front of the village is against us'.[72] Only by intensifying the struggle against the kulaks, he insisted, could the Soviet government win the support of the poor and middle peasants. The kulaks, he claimed, dominated the village assembly and manipulated the poor peasants by getting them drunk. The Soviet government, he insisted, had not abandoned recourse to legal measures.[73]

S. I. Syrtsov, from Siberia, denied that the NEP was being abolished and justified the USM as a step to the planned regulation of agriculture through collectivization.[74] Mikoyan rejected Bukharin's proposal to import grain, while Molotov defended the USM.[75] Stalin repudiated the 'Rightists' attempts to equate the USM with extraordinary measures, while justifying the extraction of a 'tribute' from the peasantry to support the industrialization drive. He rejected Bukharin's charge that they were engaged in the 'military-feudal exploitation of the peasantry'. He justified the USM, 'based on the principle of self-imposed obligations' of peasant communities, but added that there was no political measure undertaken by the party that was not accompanied by some excesses.[76]

The plenum's resolution denounced Bukharin and his group for opposing the party's agricultural policies and threatened them with expulsion from the Politburo. Thereafter, the USM was developed as a 'mass political campaign'. On 27 June the Politburo abolished any time limit on its application and imposed stiffer legal penalties against kulaks that resisted grain collection.[77] In the winter of 1929–30 the USM as a strategy effectively collapsed. Addressing the All-Union Meeting on Soviet Construction in January 1930, Kaganovich complained that 'the gigantic wave of collectivization' was growing despite the inaction of the rural village soviets and their failure to heed orders from Central Executive Committee (TsIK) of the Congress of Soviets. As a result, the task of carrying through the collectivization drive fell largely on the shoulders of the party-state apparatus. The Red Army was also required to provide trained workers for the *kolkhozy*.[78]

Kaganovich as Theoretician

The Stalin group worked systematically to weaken Bukharin's strong support among party intellectuals. Kaganovich, as head of the Institute of Soviet

Construction, led the campaign in the Communist Academy and in the Institute of Red Professors. In an address to the Institute of Soviet State and Law on 4 November 1929, he made a belated attack on Bukharin's article 'Notes of an Economist', published in September 1928, and sought to project himself as a party theoretician. The Soviet state, he bluntly asserted, was not a 'law-governed state'; rather 'our laws are determined by revolutionary expediency at each given moment. The state is a superstructure above the economic basis; but this does not exclude the active reverse influence of the state on the economic basis, but presupposes it.' Through the use of 'extra-economic measures', 'the whole force of the laws of the proletarian state' was being employed to drive out the law of value and to strengthen planning. The concept 'rule of law' was a bourgeois juridical concept at variance with a true Marxist-Leninist conception of the state.[79]

Kaganovich accused Bukharin of committing an egregious error and conceding an important point to social democracy 'by admitting, first, the very possibility of an organized capitalism, and by admitting, second, that the imperialist state acquires a directly commanding role in the economy'. According to Kaganovich, the opposite was true; the capitalist state was losing what remained of its independence. Bukharin and the 'Rightists' were in reality direct descendants of the former Left Communists of 1918. Bukharin, in 'Notes of an Economist', claimed to stand as the spokesman for the 'leftist' defence of the Leninist 'state commune' and had denied that 'the law-governed nature of the intensification of the class struggle in the reconstruction period'.[80] Bukharin, he declared, feared centralization, feared the Hobbesian 'Leviathan'. By implication, the Stalinist group embraced Leviathan, paradoxically strengthening the proletarian dictatorship supposedly in order to create the commune.

Kaganovich argued that Lenin, already in 1916, had dissented from Bukharin regarding the withering away of the state, arguing that it was a long process that proceeded in the conditions of intensified class struggle and not in the circumstances of an idyll of 'class peace.'[81] The party remained resolutely committed to the struggle against bureaucracy and to involving the masses in its work. This was a time, he argued, when the party had to mobilize the full might of the proletarian state to defeat its class enemies. It was state power which made the building of socialism possible.

At the Central Committee plenum in November 1929 Kaganovich rejected the arguments of the Rightists and Trotskyists that party democracy was dead, with a bureaucratized structure dominated by the secretarial apparatus ruling over a passive membership. The Trotskyist position on freedom of debate, he insisted, led logically to the toleration of a deviation – the establishment of a second Central Committee – a position the Bolsheviks had never accepted.

In the preceding year, he claimed, class struggle had sharply intensified. But whereas the Trotskyists and Rightist had predicted a crash, it had, instead, been a year of triumph. He advocated 'the maximum possible tempo of industrialization'. They had confounded the sceptics and the entire bourgeois world, who had viewed the Five-Year Plan as a 'fantasy'. The USSR was becoming a 'metal country', and possessed unrivalled resources for future development.[82]

Kaganovich's views, like those of the Stalin group in general, reflected the narrowest, class-reductionist, conception of politics and the state, where the party itself defined who the proletariat was and what the interests of the proletariat were. The implication of this for state authoritarianism, for the public sphere, for public opinion, for democracy, for elementary rules of accountability of the state, were profound and far-reaching,

The Stalin Group

In the struggle with the 'Rightists' the general secretary constructed around himself a group of supporters at the heart of which were Molotov, Kaganovich and Kuibyshev. Even Voroshilov in the summer of 1927 expressed grave misgivings concerning Stalin's handling of policy issues.[83] The war scare of 1927 served to discomfit the oppositionists, while justifying tighter discipline. According to Kaganovich, it was Stalin who personally inserted into the XV Party Congress resolution, the clause on the military importance of industrialization.[84] This was a clear move to accommodate the concerns of the military. The crisis in the countryside demoralized the peasant conscripts in the Red Army at a time when the war scare heightened alarm regarding the country's security. In October 1928 a commission led by Ordzhonikidze, Kaganovich and Bubnov was set up to strengthen political training and education in the army.[85] In 1928 Ordzhonikidze, as head of the Central Control Commission, tried to act as a mediator between the Stalin group and the left, and drew censure for being too accommodating. However, Stalin's 'left turn' provided the basis for wining over some of these dissidents. By the autumn of 1928 Ordzhonikidze, Voroshilov, Mikoyan and, with greater reserve, Andreev and Kalinin had embraced the new line.

The Stalin group's organizing centre was the party's Orgburo and Secretariat. Politburo commissions were employed to control the debate, enforcing collective responsibility for decisions as a means of isolating dissent. Stalin also relied on the Central Control Commission-Rabkrin – the agency of party and state control – headed by Ordzhonikidze in the drive against the Rightists, and as a key policy-making centre for industry and agriculture.[86] It was in this period that Kaganovich forged a close relationship with

Ordzhonikidze, whom he described as 'my best friend'.[87] In 1929–30 they stood out as the two coming men in the Stalinist group.

Bukharin was ousted from the Politburo in November 1929. This marked the defeat of the Right Opposition. Tomsky lost his Politburo seat in July 1930, and Rykov was expelled in December 1930. The Stalin group gained unchallenged control of the party-state apparatus Stalin had constructed this alliance of individuals from the second rank of the leadership. His low regard for those around him is supported by his reported statement to Bukharin, 'You and I are the Himalayas, the rest are nonentities'.[88] Anna Larina records that her husband, Bukharin, considered that Stalin preferred to surround himself with faceless, submissive figures.[89]

Conclusion

In 1928 Stalin effected a sharp turn to the left in domestic and foreign policy. In this he acted under the pressure of events and the barbs from the Joint Opposition. But he was able to turn the situation to his advantage, constructing a strategy based on three elements (1) the war scare linked to the threat from the internal enemies of the Soviet regime; (2) the grain crisis and the anti-kulak campaign and (3) the attack on the bourgeois specialists. This was the basis for a new radical offensive aimed at the mobilization of the activists directed at transforming the economy and fundamentally changing the mentality of the peasantry and of the working class. This strategy pushed his relations with his colleagues Bukharin, Rykov and Tomsky to breaking point. Around these campaigns, Stalin developed a series of policies that broke decisively with the NEP and were used as a part of a general attack on the 'Rightists'. Through this strategy Stalin built a coalition of individuals and institutional leaders held together by ideological conviction and shared interests.

While the general secretary was the architect of the strategy of the emergent group, other members contributed in shaping policy and developing initiatives. Kaganovich and Molotov were Stalin's chief lieutenants. Isaac Deutscher perceptively identified the two as 'left Stalinists'.[90] In 1927, having been a defender of the NEP, Kaganovich became a strong advocate of industrialization, an ardent proponent of collectivization and of the struggle against the kulaks. The policies that he had promoted in Ukraine in 1926–27 were transposed to the all-union level in 1928. Having played a key role in militarizing the party's command structures, he was instrumental in extending these principles to the trade unions and the Komsomol. While dismissive of the claims of democracy in these organizations, he was an enthusiastic advocate of promoting workers and young engineers into positions of authority. These developments were rationalized in terms of the intensifying class struggle and the need to mobilize the regime's organizational and human resources to carry through the 'revolution from above'. The strategy of 'cultural revolution' was thus a necessary concomitant of the new developmental strategy of the Stalin group.

Kaganovich emerged as the most articulate spokesman of the Stalin group as regards its conception of the Soviet state, in terms of justifying its total claims and elaborating its systematic moves to destroy the remnants of the public sphere and of civil society as part of a statist conception of socialism. The defeat of the Right marked the final stage in the dismantling of internal party democracy. Kaganovich was a leading practitioner of organizing the revolt of the activists, which had been employed against Trotsky, the Leningrad Opposition and the Joint Opposition and was again employed against the Right in the trade unions and in the Moscow party organization. The Stalin group also used this tactic to legitimize itself by posing not as a faction based on the apparatus, but as the spokesmen of the rank and file. But the destruction of the public sphere created an amorphous society in which 'public opinion' was replaced by an unstructured popular opinion and public moods. On this foundation, Kaganovich was to play a key role in promoting the cultic aspects of Communist power and above all, the cult of the leader.

Chapter 6

REVOLUTION FROM ABOVE, 1928–1935

With the defeat of the Right Opposition, Stalin, Molotov and Kaganovich, constituting a form of triumvirate, assumed full control of the party-state machine. In January 1930 the policy of all-out collectivization and dekulakization was launched. The 'revolution from above' placed the party Secretariat, under Kaganovich and Molotov, at the centre of the drive to mobilize the party, to assign cadres and to enforce policy. Industrial policy was shaped by Gosplan, Vesenkha and officials of CCC-Rabkrin, which, under the leadership of Ordzhonikidze, took over Vesenkha in November 1930.[1] The economic commissariats responsible for the management of the NEP, especially the People's Commissariat of Agriculture and the People's Commissariat of Finance, were downgraded.[2] The cause of industrialization was advanced by the strong regional lobbies of Ukraine and the Urals.[3] Stalin, at the XVI Party Congress dismissed the Trotskyists as 'the most extreme minimalists and the most wretched capitulators' on industrial tempos and continued to indulge in the wildest fantasies regarding economic growth.[4] These ideological and institutional pressures led to an extraordinary radicalization of policies in which the whole of the ruling group was caught up, which carried serious implications for the economy and for the future of the regime itself.

The collectivization of agriculture was a long-term goal of the Bolsheviks. In 1917 it was abandoned, as the peasant revolution in the countryside destroyed the large landed estates. The system of small peasant holdings that thereafter dominated was inefficient and technically backward. It gave the peasants control over agricultural production, and the marketing of agricultural produce became highly dependent on the maintenance of favourable terms of trade for the peasantry. This imposed limits, via state taxation policy and pricing policy, on the accumulation of resources for industrial investment. Collectivization was seen as a solution to the problem of backwardness through the reorganizing of agriculture into large state and collective farms as a basis for mechanization and modernization. It was intended to block the growth of a putative capitalist class amongst the kulaks.

The capitalist path of development that Stolypin had attempted after 1906 was closed off. In the 1920s peasant agriculture displayed a potential for development as witnessed the recovery of output under NEP after 1921. The path of socialist development was viewed by Lenin in 1923 as being achieved via voluntary cooperatives. The coercive use of requisitioning as employed during the Civil War era was to be avoided. However, with the new priority accorded to industrial growth from 1927 onward, the obstacles imposed on future development by peasant agriculture became a matter of concern. Bukharin and the Rightists argued that NEP should be retained and that industrialization could be pursued within these constraints. The position of the Stalin group conceived of a new developmental strategy with a reassertion of the party's ideological goal of socialist development. This involved the prioritization of investment in heavy industry. In agriculture, the party-state was reorientated to ensure its capacity to extract grain from the countryside in the face of peasant opposition, through the decision to collectivize agriculture and 'dekulakization'.

Collectivization and Dekulakization

The Stalin's groups' commitment to collectivization reflected a number of shared assumptions. A belief that priority for industrial development meant that agriculture would have to be squeezed to release the necessary resources. They believed that collectivization, the socialization of agriculture, would provide the basis for a rapid modernization of this sector. Their rigid and simplistic class conception of peasant society was supported by L. Kritsman and the Institute of Agrarian Marxists. The view was rejected by A. V. Chayanov as reflecting a fundamental misunderstanding of the more organic, fluid nature of peasant society. A key part in shaping agricultural policy was played by CCC-Rabkrin. Its leading authority on agriculture, Ya. A. Yakovlev, who had worked with Stalin and Kaganovich in the central party apparatus in 1923–25, in December 1929 was appointed head of the newly established all-union commissariat of agriculture – NKZem USSR. Other agencies were especially set up to carry out the operation, such as Kolkhoztsentr and Traktortsentr.

The Central Committee plenum, in November 1929, was a critical step in the adoption of the policy of collectivization. On the first day, Kuibyshev assured delegates that the 'middle peasant has moved in a huge avalanche' into the *kolkhozy*. He rebutted Bukharin's accusation that the party was intent on the 'feudal exploitation of the peasantry'.[5] The plenum's resolution called for 'the most decisive measures' against kulak resistance and sabotage.[6]

On 21 November 1929 Kaganovich reported to Moscow party activists on the results of the Central Committee plenum.[7] The first year of the Five-Year Plan had been a year of intensified class struggle, but a year of economic advance. They had secured 92 per cent of the plan for grain procurement (11.2 million tons compared to just 4.3 million tons at the same time in 1928). He anticipated a growth in the number of *kolkhozy* from 33,200 in 1928 to 103,000 in 1930, with membership growing from 1.1 million in 1928 to 15 million in 1930. Kaganovich read aloud a letter from a female party member from the countryside, which spoke of intense kulak opposition to collectivization. The class struggle in the countryside was now 'like at the front'. The most incredible rumours were spreading; that the anti-Christ was in the land and that the world would soon end. The letter concluded with a desperate appeal for help.

Kaganovich emphasized the steps that were being taken to modernize the countryside and to win over the peasantry. He gloried in the fact that the commodity- exchange link between industry and agriculture had replaced the trade link, and this had been attained through 'administrative pressure'. The producer cooperative – which Bukharin advocated – he argued, would have been turned into 'kulak cooperative nests'. The proletarian dictatorship was using its power to transform agriculture, and Bukharin's charge that they were engaging in the 'military-feudal exploitation of the peasantry' reflected a failure to address the real choices facing the party.[8] The USM, however, proved to be a great illusion and Kaganovich, its author, now committed himself enthusiastically to coercive measures.

Most of the principal party leaders – Stalin, Molotov, Kaganovich, Kuibyshev, Mikoyan, Kosior and Rudzutak – and many regional party secretaries, strongly supported the new line in public. Andreev in North Caucasus had been less enthusiastic on the antikulak line of the central leadership, and had argued for the inclusion of kulaks into the new collective farms. He was severely censured for this by Kaganovich.[9] Targets for collectivization were raised as regional secretaries sought to outdo one another.

In December 1929 the Politburo took the decision to collectivize agriculture and to reorganize the 25 million peasant households. Stalin, in his speech of 27 December, announced the policy objective of liquidating the kulaks as a class. On 5 January 1930 the Politburo endorsed the policy of wholesale collectivization. A Politburo's secret directive of 16 February 1930 detailed the way dekulakization was to be conducted.

With the launching of forced collectivization and dekulakization, the party's policy to split the poor and middle peasants from the kulaks, fell apart. On 13 January the Politburo, on a report from Kaganovich, scrapped the Central Committee's departments for work amongst the poor peasants, and its women's department, the Zhenotdel. Both were blamed for failing to mobilize the poor and middle peasants behind the collectivization drive.[10] The village soviets and the rural party organizations were similarly criticized for their laxity.[11] Kaganovich now admitted that all the work of guiding the development of the *kolkhozes* was being done 'directly and exclusively' by men of the party *apparat*.[12] The abolition of the Zhenotdel, he conceded, had been strongly opposed by female comrades.[13] At the XVI Party Congress, he reproached the Zhenotdel for concentrating on social questions and neglecting political education. As a result, peasant women, manipulated by the kulaks, had played the leading role in resisting collectivization. The abolition of the Zhenotdel had 'created a liquidations mood towards work amongst women' but this needed to be resisted.[14]

To enforce collectivization and dekulakization the authorities were compelled to rely on the local party organizations, the courts, the militia, the OGPU, and, in some areas, army detachments. Peasant resistance was broken by recourse to force, deportations, dispossession, forced expulsions and summary executions. The party's Secretariat organized the mobilization of party activists, Komsomol members and rank-and-file workers from the factories to assist in the campaign.[15] The Secretariat's Orgraspred, headed by Nikolai Yezhov, who was also deputy head of NKZem USSR, organized the selection and assignment of cadres.[16]

In February 1930 party leaders were sent to the regions to oversee the spring sowing drive; Kalinin (Central Black Earth region), Ordzhonikidze (Ukraine), Kaganovich (Lower Volga) and Yakovlev (Central Volga).[17] The same month, Kaganovich addressed a rally of worker volunteers being sent to the countryside, the 'Twenty-five Thousanders'. In a two hour rallying speech, he exhorted them:

> Your role is the role of the proletarian leader. There will be difficulties, there will be kulak resistance and sometimes even collective farm resistance, but history is moving in our favour... Either we destroy the kulaks as a class, or the kulaks will grow as a class of capitalists and liquidate the dictatorship of the proletariat.[18]

'Dizzy with Success'

The policy of dekulakization created a humanitarian catastrophe with tens of thousands of families being deported in the middle of winter to inhospitable regions where there was little or no provision for them. In January S. A. Bergavinov, party secretary of the Northern Territory, wrote to Kaganovich to report that the OGPU was inquiring as to whether the region could take 100,000 kulak families, and that the Northern OGPU had agreed to take 50,000–70,000 families.[19]

Collectivization provoked a wave of peasant risings and protests, the intensity of which clearly took the leadership by surprise.[20]

On 2 March 1930 *Pravda* published Stalin's article 'Dizzy with Success' which signalled a retreat on collectivization and heralded a large exodus of peasants from the collective farms. This was bitterly resented by these same officials who had been propelled into battle with the peasantry. In that article and in 'Reply to Collective Farm Comrades', Stalin unloaded the blame for the situation onto local officials.[21] He charged these officials with various personal failings: being light-headed or suffering a temporary mental aberration, 'communist vainglory', 'extreme vanity and conceit', 'fear of acknowledging one's errors,' and behaving like 'blockheads'. This might stand as a thumbnail psychological self-portrait. In listing these failings he was no doubt making clear that he was aware of what was being said of him, and by projecting these failings onto others, he sought to absolve himself of the charge. His strategy of self-justification was to sharply differentiate between the 'correct' policy of the 'general line' and errors in implementation. He was innocent and blameless and bore no responsibility for the policies of which he was the principal author. He was to repeat this line at the XVI Party Congress. How the 'correct' policy had failed to anticipate the problems in its implementation was an issue never addressed.

The Politburo again dispatched Molotov, Ordzhonikidze, Kaganovich and top agricultural officials to the provinces. The peasant risings, far from ending, appear to have intensified in this period. In the Central Black Earth region, Kaganovich, according to a report sent in from Kozlov district to NKZem, ordered district party committees to expel dissentients from the *kolkhozy*, assigning them remote, less fertile land, denying them loans.[22]

In early April Kaganovich was sent to West Siberia temporarily to replace Robert Eikhe, who had been taken ill. At a meeting of the regional party committee bureau, local officials from the districts condemned the lack of support from the central leadership and the centre's attempts to make them scapegoats for its own failings. The bureau, in a top-secret resolution, denounced this attitude as Leftist, stressing the need for self-criticism.

At special conferences in Siberia in early April, Kaganovich harangued local party and soviet leaders for failing to control their subordinates. He promised to expedite the review of peasant complaints of abuses directed against the middle peasants and of wrongful dekulakization. He lambasted the demoralized mood of the local party. He also petitioned Stalin for additional grain supplies for those areas suffering harvest failure in southwest Siberia. He and Eikhe summoned local party organizations to ensure a good sowing campaign. The regional party committee bureau on 21 April, attended by Kaganovich and Eikhe, heard reports from the Procuracy and court officials: 328 officials had been arrested and sentenced for periods of imprisonment and eleven had been sentenced to be shot (in five cases, the sentences had been carried out). Kaganovich, evidently taken aback, demanded to know when the officials had been shot. In response to a case of drunken officials who had murdered a peasant and raped his wife, he coldly inquired, 'Does this mean that they were shot for being drunk?'[23]

Stalin, in his 'Reply to the Collective Farm Comrades' on 3 April, chided the Moscow party for its 'feverish pursuit of inflated collectivization figures'.[24] Soon after, Bauman, who was accused of leftist excesses in carrying out the collectivization policy, was replaced by Kaganovich as first secretary of Moscow province and city committees. He was judged to have the requisite political acumen to affect a retreat on the collectivization front without betraying the confidence of the party activists.

Stalin's report to the XVI Party Congress in June 1930 highlighted the growing crisis in the capitalist world and contrasted this with the growth of the Soviet economy. The threat posed by capitalist encirclement was used to justify the high priority accorded to heavy industry. He provided a stark option: 'Either we vanquish and crush them, the exploiters, or they will vanquish and crush the workers and peasants of the USSR'.[25] He rejected the charge that NEP had been abolished – a position he maintained until 1937! The errors in collectivization he blamed on the 'traditions of Trotskyism in practice', which the party centre had courageously corrected. The offensive against the kulaks had not produced the crisis that the Rightists had direly forecast.

Kaganovich's report to the congress spoke of the fierce class struggle in the countryside, and the 'savage resistance of kulakdom' to collectivization. In the face of 'huge difficulties', the rural communists had performed 'heroic work'. In 1928–30 at least a quarter of a million people had been assigned for work in the countryside. The Red Army had supplied large numbers of cadres for the campaign: in 1927, 31,000; in 1928, 67,000; and in 1929, 180,000. He lauded the 'Twenty-five Thousanders' as a 'whole movement among the workers', with 60,000 volunteering to serve. In the grain *sovkhozy*, there were 70,000 qualified workers, compared to 15,000 in 1928. He censured the failure of the village soviets to assist in this operation. The party's rural organization remained woefully weak. The first grain collection drive had been 'the cleansing flame' to expel kulak elements from the party and to recruit landless peasants.[26] The party needed resolute self-criticism to correct deviations, but he added, '[T]hose who commit leftist excesses, the great majority, with the exception of a small number of semi-Trotskyists, are people who honourably wish to carry out the party line'.[27] The Central Committee would remove district party secretaries who resisted the correction of errors.

In the autumn of 1930 the party renewed its offensive on collectivization. In 1931 intense pressure was applied to force the peasants into the collective farms, with a new wave of mass deportations of kulaks to Kazakhstan and elsewhere. The organization of the deportation and resettlement of those dekulakized was entrusted to two party commissions, one headed by Molotov and another headed by Andreev.[28]

The Famine, 1932–1933

The high procurement targets set for agriculture from 1929 onward depleted the stocks held by the peasant. Nevertheless, the government insisted on persisting with this policy. In the spring of 1932 an attempt was made to deal with the serious food problem. This was referred to as the 'neo-NEP'. A collective farm market was legalized, the artel was proclaimed as the model for collective farms, and the peasants' private plots were legalized. Subsequently, Stalin was to claim credit for allowing the peasant households to have a cow and some livestock. The supply of consumer goods to the countryside was increased. These belated concessions proved too late and inadequate to avert the looming catastrophe.

On 8 May a Politburo commission headed by Kaganovich was established to check the production and supply of mass consumer goods.[29] On 20 May the government issued a resolution on organizing collective farm trade and the trade of individual peasants and on reducing the tax on traded goods. Much of the correspondence between Stalin and Kaganovich in this period was devoted to this subject.[30]

On 20 June the Politburo ordered Molotov and Kaganovich to instruct the party leadership of Central Volga and Lower Volga regions to meet their obligations as regards grain targets.[31] At the end of June, on Stalin's proposal, a meeting of provincial and territorial party secretaries and soviet chairmen was convened. A party resolution on the persistence of kulak resistance demanded measures to 'smash the opposition'.[32]

Ukraine was the major supplier of grain and was crucial for realizing the state's procurement targets. Stalin dispatched Molotov and Kaganovich to the III All-Ukrainian Party Conference, which convened on 6–9 July. In a letter to Kaganovich, Stalin railed at the leadership of Stanislav Kosior and Vlas Chubar' in Ukraine for their opportunism and irresponsibility and asserted that they should be dismissed.[33] Kosior had been elected a full member of the Politburo in 1930 and Chubar' a candidate member of the Politburo in 1926.

At the conference, Ukrainian party and government leaders voiced their concern at the centre's policies. Kosior noted that some areas were already 'seriously short of food' and that many in the Ukrainian Central Committee and at local level considered the delivery plans to be excessive.[34] Skrypnik declared that instead of trying to find the guilty, they should be trying to identify the causes of policy failure. Chubar' blamed the failures on *kolkhoz* gigantism, unrealistic procurement targets and on the exodus of young people from the countryside. He called on Molotov and Kaganovich to see for themselves what the situation was.[35]

Molotov and Kaganovich did not speak until the end and it was clear that the centre's emissaries would have the final say. In his address to the conference on 8 July Kaganovich severely rebuked the party's work in mechanically setting grain collection targets for the districts regardless of local circumstances.[36] But he also rebuked the many district workers at the conference who had censured the work of the Central Committee plenipotentiaries who had been sent to enforce policy. He criticized the party's inactivity and the expectation of activists that grain would flow in 'spontaneously'. Notwithstanding their liquidation as a class, the kulaks, sought from within to undermine the *kolkhozy*. It was necessary to increase the income of *kolkhozniki* and to develop supplementary economic activities in the *kolkhoz* – the rearing of livestock, vegetable growing, artisan production, etc. Communists who feared that this would turn the *kolkhozniki* into kulaks were guilty of the 'crudest mistake.'

Molotov and Kaganovich attributed the failures in grain procurement to political error and weakness. There could be no let-up in collectivization or in the pressure on the *kolkhozy* to supply more grain. Stalin had ordered a delivery of 7.7 million tons of grain from Ukraine. After intense discussions, the Ukrainians got the figure reduced to 6.6 million tons, but this was still far beyond a realistic target.

On 11 August Stalin, in a letter to Kaganovich, complained of the dire situation in Ukraine; Kosior vacillated between the demands of the Central Committee and those of the district party committees; Chubar' was no leader, and S. F. Redens, as head of OGPU, was failing to fight counter-revolution. The Ukrainian party with its 500,000 members, he claimed, was infested with 'conscious and unconscious Petlyuraites' and Polish agents. He proposed that Kaganovich replace Kosior as general secretary of the Ukrainian party. V. A. Balitsky should take over as head of the Ukrainian OGPU and Redens should be demoted to deputy. Chubar' should be replaced as head of Sovnarkom Ukraine by G. G. Grinko. It was necessary to turn Ukraine into a Soviet stronghold and a model republic, 'We must not spare any money on this'. If this was not done, Stalin melodramatically warned, 'we may lose Ukraine'.[37]

Kaganovich proposed that it might be possible instead to 'straighten out' Kosior with a severe tongue lashing, but added, 'It is harder for me to judge than you,'[38] which hinted at his close relationship with Kosior. The note had its effect. Stalin changed his mind and the two Ukrainian leaders retained their posts. Stalin used Kaganovich as a conduit to convey his displeasure with certain officials, but at the same time, Kaganovich could also exert a restraining influence against overimpetuous actions.

In response to the deepening crisis, Stalin himself drafted the law of 7 August, which instituted draconian with punishments for those found guilty of stealing collective farm property and the theft of goods from transport, punishments of execution or imprisonment in a camp for up to ten years. In a telegram to Kaganovich on 4 August, Stalin instructed him, 'Publish it as soon as possible'. Stalin also insisted that the OGPU should shoot on the spot those stealing grain from railway wagons and stores.[39] The law met with opposition in the Politburo. Kaganovich's draft letter omits the names of the Politburo members who criticized the decree.[40] There is a strong probability that those who expressed opposition were Kosior and Chubar', the two Politburo members most directly affected. Some days after the adoption of the decree, Stalin sent Kaganovich a letter on the need to clarify, to the party and punitive organs, the point of these measures.[41] In the following six months under this law, 103,000 people were sentenced by the courts, and 4,800 were shot.[42]

On 17 August Stalin and Molotov instructed Kaganovich to involve the army in the harvest campaign in Ukraine.[43] Economic incentives were also employed to bring grain onto the market. In Moscow, on 8 October, Kaganovich declared that by providing goods for the villages they had 'offended the city.' He charged those who advocated limited grain imports of wishing to strengthen the country's dependence upon the capitalist world.[44]

The Politburo was well aware of the developing crisis in grain supply. In the autumn of 1932, on Stalin's instructions, a Central Committee commission, headed by Kaganovich, was sent to North Caucasus to deal with grain procurement difficulties. A similar commission, headed by Molotov, was sent to Ukraine. These two commissions had a profound impact in shaping policy against the background of the developing famine crisis.[45]

North Caucasus had the reputation of the Soviet Vendée, as a centre of White counter-revolution during the Civil War and an area in which kulak households were dominant. Kaganovich's commission to North Caucasus included M. A. Chernov (the State Committee for Grain Procurement, or KomZag), T. A. Yurkin (NKSovkhoz); A. I. Mikoyan (NKSnab), Ya. B. Gamarnik (Political Department of Red Army), M. F. Shkiryatov (CCC), G. G. Yagoda (OGPU), and A. V. Kosarev (Komsomol).[46]

On 1 November Kaganovich and Mikoyan sent a telegram to Stalin on the situation in North Caucasus, criticizing local party activists who, they asserted, were infected with a pro-'kulak' mood. The villages that failed to meet procurement targets were placed on a blacklist and deprived of manufactured goods.[47] In discussions with the regional party committee leadership, Kaganovich noted that the OGPU had presented revealing evidence on the degeneration of rural communists.[48] Special plenipotentiaries were assigned for each district and special commissions were sent to Kharkov and Saratov, where the resistance was most intense.[49] The Kaganovich delegation ordered a purge of local communists.[50] On 4 November the Central Committee-CCC appointed a special committee, headed by M. F. Shkiryatov, to purge the party organizations of the North Caucasus, parts of Ukraine and Lower Volga[51] This preceded the general party purge begun in April 1933. On 14 November Stalin, Molotov and Kaganovich sent a telegram to the localities forbidding *kolkhoz* trade in grain until they had fulfilled their target for grain procurement.[52]

Addressing a meeting of party secretaries on his arrival in Kuban, Kaganovich cited historical precedent of the deportation of the Cossacks in 1921: 'You don't like to work here, then we deport you. Somebody may object and say that this is illegal. Well, this is not true, it is perfectly legal. You are against Soviet power, you do not want to sow, therefore, in the name of state interests, Soviet power has the right to fight against this behaviour.... We shall reach our aims, comrade secretaries, if not with you, then over your heads.'[53]

Kaganovich toured the districts accompanied by GPU officers, arresting workers, some charged as former 'Whites'. On 20 November he telegrammed Stalin about measures to secure grain targets in the North Caucasus region. Two days later, Stalin sent a telegram to Kaganovich and Boris Sheboldaev, the regional party secretary, authorizing the deportation of 2,000 kulak and well-to-do peasant households from the North Caucasus. The next day Kaganovich addressed a meeting of North Caucasus party bureau, which adopted a tough resolution to combat sabotage of grain collection, to strengthen the *kolkhoz* and to overcome kulak resistance, and censured the district authorities for their weakness and lack of resolve.[54]

About 25 November the North Caucasus regional party bureau and the Rostov city committee and activists held a meeting with Kaganovich in attendance. Sheboldaev's speech underlined the class struggle in the countryside and reproached the party organizations, which did not understand the struggle with the kulaks from within the *kolkhozy*.[55] The meeting resolved to smash all the saboteurs and counter-revolutionaries responsible for the failure of grain collection and the autumn sowing.[56]

Sixteen Cossack villages in the Kuban, including Poltavskaya, Medvedovskaya, Urupskaya and Bagaevskaya, were bombarded and their inhabitants deported by the OGPU to the far north. Military agricultural colonies, such as Krasnoarmeisk, were established in the region.[57] On 27 November the joint plenum of the Politburo and the presidium CCC, authorized a further tightening of repressive measures, with Stalin accusing local communist officials of idealizing the *kolkhozy*, which in reality had been infiltrated by kulaks and other anti-Soviet elements. The wreckers and saboteurs needed to be exposed and rooted out.[58]

Administrative controls were further tightened. On 1 October 1932 a new commissariat for grain and livestock *sovkhozy*, NKSovkhoz under T. A. Yurkin, was set up, thus reducing NKZem's influence. On 12 December the Politburo established the Central Committee's agricultural department (Selkhozotdel), headed by Kaganovich. This effectively placed him in charge of agricultural policy in this crucial period. The Politburo charged Kaganovich, Yakovlev and Yurkin to find candidates to head the Political Administrations in NKZem and NKSovkhoz.[59] On 22 December Kaganovich reported to Stalin on the Ukrainian Politburo's decisions to strengthen grain procurement, with the situation in Kharkov province being especially unsatisfactory. Party leaders, he reported, were being dispatched to various provinces to ensure that policy was properly implemented.[60]

The Central Committee–Central Control Commission Plenum January 1933

Stalin's report, 'Work in the Countryside', delivered to the joint plenum of the CC and CCC on 11 January 1933, highlighted the achievements of the First Five-Year Plan in overcoming the country's age-old backwardness, and in creating, in the shortest possible time, the industrial base for guaranteeing the country's security. In this, he invoked the authority of Lenin. With famine gripping the country, he insisted that the living conditions of both workers and peasants were actually improving. The difficulties faced by the regime were caused by its opponents. He defended the law of August 1932 as a law that made socialist property sacred and inviolable. As he so often did, he distinguished between the correctness of policy, 'the general line' and the shortcomings in its implementation. Policy failures stemmed from the lack of will, commitment and resolve of officials. He highlighted the inconvenience caused to the state by difficulties in grain procurement. Anti-Soviet elements had wormed their way into the collective farms, turning them in to 'nests of counter-revolutionary activity'.[61]

Kaganovich, in a lengthy report to the plenum, castigated the kulaks, offering them as the scapegoats for the catastrophic failure of official policy. The party was in the throes of a new 'Bolshevik offensive'. Agricultural collectivization provided the conditions for the countryside to flourish. While thousands of *kolkhozy* gave excellent results, he admitted that there were a 'huge number' which, because of bad leadership, remained quite unsatisfactory.[62] He stressed Stalin's work in directing policy.[63] The class struggle in the countryside remained acute. Only by breaking kulak resistance had it been possible to consolidate the *kolkhozy*, he claimed, thus confounding the direst warnings of Rykov, Tomsky and Bukharin, who had wished to see a slackening of the class struggle. He insisted that representatives of 'kulakdom' remained in the villages, and echoed Stalin's warnings of anti-Soviet elements who led 'counter-revolutionary agitation', 'terrorized honourable *kolkhozniki*' and were wrecking the *kolkhozy* from within. Many rural cadres, he argued, were infected with the views of N. D. Kondratiev and A. V. Chayanov. The Rightists had now replaced the 'Trotsktyist' bogeymen of 1930.

Kaganovich, ignoring the lack of realism in procurement targets, rebuked those 'tender hearted' local officials and party members – 'traitors to the interests of the toilers' – who failed to enforce policy on grain collection. In the autumn of 1932 many *sovkhozy* had flouted directives from Yurkin, their own commissar, on grain collection and the autumn sowing plans. The rapid growth of the *kolkhozy* and Machine Tractor Stations (MTS) meant that many of their chairmen were recent appointees. The party had sent 50,000 people, from other branches of the economy and from the educational institutions, to agriculture. NKZem and NKSovkhoz needed to promote people from within the *kolkhozy* and *sovkhozy*. Those directors subject to 'bourgeois degeneration tendencies' had to be removed. The *kolkhozniki* had to be reeducated in labour discipline and respect for socialist property by enforcing the 7 August law. Socialist emulation and shock-work was 'extremely weak' and had to be developed. Kaganovich added that, 'To win over the majority in the *kolkhoz* is possible only in struggle with anti-*kolkhoz* elements'.

The most important initiative, announced by both Stalin and Kaganovich was the creation of political departments (*politotdely*) in the *kolkhozy*, *sovkhozy* and MTS, which would be accountable to the Political Administration, which in turn would be linked closely to the party Secretariat. The *politotdely* were to combat wrecking and sabotage. Kaganovich admitted that many district party committees (*raikoms*) bitterly opposed their creation. Stalin roundly admonished the weakness of the *raikoms* in agriculture, which had necessitated this reorganization.[64]

On January 11 the plenum approved measures to strengthen the Central Committee's agricultural department (Selkhozotdel), and confirmed Kaganovich's appointment as its head. On a report by Kaganovich, the *politotdely* were set up in the MTS, *sovkhozy* and *kolkhozy*. A special resolution of the Central Committee sought to define responsibilities and to avoid conflict between the MTS, the *politotdely* and the district party committees (*raikoms*).[65] Large numbers of political workers from the party, the Red Army and OGPU were assigned to work in the *politotdely*. From the outset, a bitter struggle developed between these bodies for precedence in the localities.[66]

The developing famine crisis was met with public silence by the authorities, which was reflected also in a private reticence on the issue. R. W. Davies and

S. G. Wheatcroft write, '[E]ven in the most secret documents the key Soviet leaders, Stalin, Molotov and Kaganovich, had little to say about the reasons for their decisions, or even about the famine itself'.[67] The very word famine was avoided. Kaganovich and Molotov were certainly privy to all the key decisions.

At the end of January 1933 Kaganovich, in North Caucasus, wrote in his diary of kulak opposition taking the form of 'vicious terror', citing a case of a regional party committee representative being immolated. He wrote of cases of death from starvation, but also of feigned starvation and alleged cases of heads of families withholding food from their own children.[68] This illustrates the Stalin group's self-delusion and its strategies of self-rationalization. In February 1933 Stalin instructed Kaganovich and Molotov to block the visit of American press correspondents to Kuban on the grounds that they were spies.[69]

With the famine entering its most terrible phase, Stalin, in early February 1933, addressed the first All-Union Congress of Collective Farm Shock-workers. He stuck a folksy note, stressing the advantages of collectivized agriculture. But he warned against those who loafed in the collective farms, invoking Biblical authority, 'He who does not work, neither shall he eat'.[70] Addressing the same congress, Kaganovich justified the collectivization of agriculture as necessary to achieve industrial growth. Without industrialization, they would have faced war and intervention from West and East. He offered an extravagant defence of the 7 August law as 'this great law' by which the state had secured grain supplies. Such laws, he rhapsodized, 'live for tens and hundreds of years'. There were now 200,000 *kolkhozy* and 5,000 large-scale *sovkhozy*. He stressed the need to ensure the success of the spring sowing campaign. The speech was peppered with homely peasant proverbs as well as references to Stalin as the 'first shock-worker-*kolkhoznik*'.[71]

As summer approached, the crisis eased and repression was relaxed. On 7 May 1933 the Politburo forbade the OGPU in the republics, territories and regions (except the Far Eastern Territory) to impose death sentences.[72] The following day, the Politburo prohibited the mass exiling of peasants.[73] The 1933 harvest was relatively good. In the autumn of that year Kaganovich continued to monitor grain procurements.[74]

Social and Political Costs

The conception of agricultural collectivization was visionary but woefully out of touch with reality. The revolution from above was to be one of the most tragic illustrations of the ill-thought-out attempts by Marxists to socialize agriculture.

In economic terms, the achievements of collectivization were dubious. It gave the regime control over the means to extract agricultural produce from the countryside and allowed it to pursue its goals of industrial development. But the industrialization drive was carried out in bursts, with huge disproportions. The expected transfer of resources from the rural into the urban sector was not achieved in the short term. Instead, resources had to be pumped into the countryside. It produced a catastrophic fall in livestock herds and in the availability of draught power. It massively disrupted food supplies and trade networks. The policy revealed a woeful misunderstanding of the nature of agriculture and the belief that it might be reorganized overnight and that it could quickly catch up in efficiency with the more advanced countries.

The effects of collectivization were far-reaching. It exposed the hollowness of the party's class strategy in the countryside. It undermined the attempts to revive the soviets as a link between state and society; it undid the party's nationalities policy. The policy carried through as a military expedition and as a war on the kulaks. Predictably, it encountered intense peasant opposition.

The crisis of 1932 prompted an upsurge of dissident activity inside the party (see Chapter 7). The central authorities further strengthened their control over the republican and regional party bodies. Pavel Postyshev, a Kaganovich protégé, was assigned to take over the Kharkov party organization. In 1933 Postyshev was made party secretary, member of the Politburo and Orgburo of the Ukrainian party organization. In 1934 he also became a candidate member of the Politburo CPSU.[75]

The collectivization crisis of 1929–30 brought a new assault on the Ukrainian nationalist intelligentsia, while the famine crisis of 1932–33 saw the republic's limited autonomy further curtailed and the concessions associated with cultural and language policy restricted. On 6 February 1933 the joint plenum of the Central Committee and Central Control Commission of Ukraine welcomed the decision of the all-union Central Committee, of January 24, which severely censured the Ukrainian party organization. The plenum declared that the resolution was in direct relation to the III Party Conference and the advice of Molotov and Kaganovich.[76]

In May 1933 an attack on Skypnik was launched by P. P. Lyubchenko, deputy chairman of Sovnarkom Ukraine, in a note to Stalin and Kaganovich.[77] In July it was reported to Kaganovich that Skrypnik had planned to denounce official nationalities policy in Ukraine at the Central Committee-CCC plenum the previous January but had been dissuaded by his wife, who had threatened suicide if he went ahead.[78] In November Kosior sent his report on counter-revolution in Ukrainian nationalism for the Ukrainian Central Committee plenum to Kaganovich for his approval.[79] At the plenum, M. M. Popov branded Skrypnik as the leader of the Ukrainian nationalist deviation.[80] As a result, Skrypnik, whom Kaganovich had lauded in 1928 as the architect of the regime's policy of Ukrainization, committed suicide.[81]

The famine of 1932–33 caused between 5 million and 8 million deaths.[82] Its worst impact was felt in Ukraine, North Caucasus, Lower Volga and Kazakhstan. Whether official policy was directed at destroying the power of the peasantry or was part of a programme to destroy the basis of Ukrainian nationalism are questions still hotly contested.[83] Even at the end of his life, Kaganovich could still not admit the enormity of the tragedy.[84]

Collectivization and dekulakization undoubtedly contributed to the scale of the disaster. The loss of draught power, through the loss of oxen and horses, was a major contributory factor. The forced export of grain from 1928 to 1932 and the government's failure to build up an adequate emergency grain reserve proved disastrous. The Japanese invasion of Manchuria in September 1931 and the fear of war in the Far East undoubtedly influenced grain procurement policy. The leadership viewed the famine less as a humanitarian catastrophe, rather as part of the process whereby the peasantry were disciplined into the workings of the new collective farm system.

The unrealistic procurement targets set by the centre created intense stains with local leaders. In October 1933 I. P. Rumyantsev, first secretary of the Western province party committee, reported that he had received a roasting from Kaganovich and Molotov on account of the province's failure to meet its planned target for flax production.[85]

Stalin's Second Revolution

Kaganovich played a central part in promoting the Stalin cult and bolstering the *vozhd*'s self-image as a second Lenin. Addressing a meeting of the Moscow party activists on 22 May 1933, he asserted that just as Lenin in 1917 had not flinched from propelling the proletariat into a struggle with its enemies, so Stalin in 1928–29 had not feared to launch the proletariat into a struggle with the remnants of capitalism. The 'revolution from above' was now seen as outshining the October Revolution itself:

> It is a small thing to win power, it is a small thing to drive out the capitalists; what is necessary is to destroy the root from which capitalism grows, what is necessary is to change, to reconstruct, the economy of the country.[86]

At the XVII Party Congress, in January–February 1934, Kaganovich described the 'revolution from above' as 'the greatest revolution which human history has known, a revolution which smashed the old economic structure and created a new, *kolkhoz* system on the base of the socialist industrialization of our country.'[87]

They had resolved 'the most difficult task of the proletarian revolution', a clear expression of relief that the regime had surmounted the famine crisis.

He struck a note of patriotic pride, echoing Stalin's speech to the industrial managers in February 1931 contrasting the backwardness and weakness of the country in the past with its transformation into 'one of the most industrialized countries in the world' and a 'a first-class, mighty military force and one of the decisive factors for peace in the whole world.'[88] The struggle with the kulaks, Kaganovich asserted, had been 'one of the most serious, if not *the* most serious, battle with capitalism', as Lenin had foreseen in 1921. The foundations for a socialist economy had been firmly laid. The invocation of Lenin's authority here is significant, given that in 1930 Krupskaya had publicly declared that collectivization had been carried out in a un-Leninist manner (see Chapter 8).

The party strove to strengthen its organization in the Soviet countryside. The percentage of peasants in the party rose from 20.4 per cent in 1930, to 28.5 per cent in 1934. The joint Central Committee–Central Control Commission plenum in January 1933 ordered a new purge of the party apparatus, led by Kaganovich. This fell disproportionately on the rural party organizations. At the XVII Party Congress, Kaganovich rebuffed calls for the abolition of the *politotdely*.[89] The new Commission of Party Control was established to strengthen control over the districts.[90] In 1934 conflict between the *politotdely*, and the *raikom* and the MTS directors intensified.

At the Central Committee plenum in November 1934, Kaganovich delivered a major report on the *politotdely* in the countryside. The *politotdely*, he announced, were to be merged into the district party committees, with some of their heads being found places as party secretaries of the district party committees. He stressed the responsibilities of the district party bodies: 'It is necessary to love party work.'[91] He chaired the commission that produced the resolution that now abolished the *politotdely* in the MTS and the *kolkhozy*, on the grounds that they had completely justified themselves and could now be dispensed with. This marked a retreat by Kaganovich and Stalin, the principal architects of the scheme. The *politotdely* in the *sovkhozy* were retained throughout the thirties.

Following a good harvest in 1934, Stalin instructed Kaganovich and Zhdanov not to allow any relaxation in grain procurement, demanding 'maximum pressure'.[92] He was determined to build up grain reserves in order to facilitate the abolition of bread rationing. Kaganovich visited Ukraine, West Siberia and the Moscow and Chelyabinsk provinces to enforce this campaign. The Chelyabinsk authorities were strongly censured and disciplined for their inaction. In Ukraine, he took a more indulgent line. On 13 September Stalin, in a letter to Politburo colleagues, sharply criticized 'people such as comrade Kaganovich' who bowed before the pressure of local party secretaries from Ukraine and elsewhere for reduced procurement targets. He insisted on a turn to a hard policy.[93]

As the food situation eased, the Central Committee plenum in November 1934, under Stalin's directives, abolished bread rationing which had been in force since the end of 1928. Kaganovich reported that the rationing system had embraced 50 million people, as well as supplies for 24 million people in areas of industrial crops.[94] It was necessary to dispense with this costly administrative apparatus, to develop the trading system and to adjust prices and wages accordingly. The harvest in 1935 was good and in September Kaganovich wrote exultantly to Ordzhonikidze of the procurement operation as an 'absolutely fantastic, stunning victory, a victory of Stalinism.'[95]

Managing the Industrialization Drive

Kaganovich played a less prominent role in overseeing industrial policy than in agriculture. His work in industry became more pronounced only from 1932 onward. One area where his role was significant was in overseeing the trade unions. Just as collectivization aimed to transform the mentality of the peasantry, so the industrialization drive was associated with the transformation of the consciousness of industrial workers, aimed specifically at breaking trade unionist attitudes.

At the XVI Party Congress in June 1930, Stalin boasted that the party was setting targets of investment that made the Trotskyists, with their 'superindustrialist' targets of the mid-1920s, seem 'the most extreme minimalists and the most wretched capitulators.'[96] In the same speech, he blamed the errors in collectivization on Trotskyist excesses perpetrated by local officials! At the Moscow regional party conference, Kaganovich praised the 'Bolshevik tempos' set for industry and noted 'the exceptional role' of Ordzhonikidze's Rabkrin in raising targets. Boldly asserting that 'History gave us no other way but tense plans', he warned the delegates that 'we must live through the next one to one-and-a-half years – they are the most difficult years'. The rewards for this sacrifice would be immense: A prediction by the *New York Times* that the USSR might be the world's second great power in 1940 was an underestimation: 'We are convinced that 1940 will see only one great world power – the USSR.'[97] He praised socialist emulation as a system of incentives which would replace the whip of capitalist competition.[98]

In January 1931 the Central Committee and the All-Union Central Council of the Trade Unions (VTsSPS) adopted a resolution to divide the existing 22 trade unions into 44, organized along branch lines. This was part of the 'face to production' campaign, with the unions being required to concentrate on shock-work and socialist emulation. VTsSPS's powers were to be drastically reduced, with questions related to production being assigned to the unions. At the end of 1931 Kaganovich summoned the trade union leaders and sternly upbraided them.⁹⁹ As part of the new incentive system, wage differentials between different industries and between grades grew sharply.¹⁰⁰

Addressing the IX Congress of Trade Unions in April 1932, Kaganovich criticized the 'huge defects' in their work. Little was being done to re-educate the new millions of workers flooding into industry, many of whom were influenced by 'petty bourgeois survivals and attitudes.' 'We still have many backward workers. We must not flatter the workers. This is not our Bolshevik habit.'¹⁰¹ The trade unions would remain as 'schools of communism'. In a speech to the Moscow city party committee, he highlighted the need to mobilize the support of non-party Bolshevik workers, those who have a 'Bolshevik spirit' but lack a party card, through organizing open meetings of the cells.¹⁰²

At the XVII Party Congress in 1934, Tomsky appeared as a penitent, and was rebuked by Kaganovich and Shvernik for his work as head of VTsSPS in 1928–29 in setting the unions against the party.¹⁰³ Kaganovich reported that the proportion of workers involved in socialist emulation had risen from 29 per cent in January 1931 to 71 per cent by November 1933. There were 5 million shock-workers in industry and transport. Trade union membership had grown by 6 million between 1928 and 1933. The old 'trade unionists' attitudes had been overcome. However, VTsSPS, he complained, was still holding onto powers that should be transferred to the production unions.¹⁰⁴ In the following months a Politburo commission, headed by Kaganovich, restructured the trade union movement, subdividing 47 into 154 unions organized by trade, which weakened the unions still further, turning them into surrogate agencies of industrial management.¹⁰⁵

In 1932 the overheated economy forced the Politburo to sharply reduce capital investment in heavy industry. On 23 July 1932 the Politburo established a commission, headed by Kuibyshev, to deal with mounting difficulties on the industrial front and to secure drastic cuts in capital investment, including 450 million rubles from NKTyazhprom's (the Commissariat of Heavy Industry) plan for the third quarter. Ordzhonikidze, who was easily swayed to threaten resignation, protested vehemently. In a personal letter, Kaganovich attempted to reconcile him to the cut, stressing that the decision had the support of Stalin ('our chief friend'). He added, 'Please don't get upset about it, and especially don't get angry.'¹⁰⁶ Molotov's dispute with Ordzhonikidze on this issue was seemingly patched up by Bukharin's intermediation.¹⁰⁷

In the first quarter of 1933 the Donbass' coal industry experienced acute problems. On Stalin's instructions, a brigade of Central Committee officials, officials of NKTyazhprom and trade unionists, headed by Kaganovich, was dispatched to investigate. Their conclusions were discussed with provincial party committees. In April, he addressed a meeting of Donbass shock-workers on the problem of leadership in the mines, notably the large number of young foremen who lacked experience and authority.[108] The Secretariat approved the commission's work. A Central Committee and Sovnarkom resolution of 8 April, drafted by Kaganovich, Ordzhonikidze and Shvernik, scrapped the functional system in the coal industry and ordered a large-scale transfer of engineering and technical personnel to underground work.[109]

In May, Stalin, Molotov and Kaganovich instructed the mine administrations and the Donetsk province party committee to 'go all out for self-criticism and the checking of fulfilment in all mines and pits without exception' and 'to punish unconditionally all those who smell remotely of sabotage'.[110] On Stalin's instruction, Kaganovich drafted two further resolutions on wages for workers and technical personnel and on strengthening party work and trade union work. At the XVII Party Congress, S. A. Sarkis, the party secretary of the Donbass region, noted Kaganovich's 'huge role' in mobilizing the workers and overcoming strong opposition to the 8 April resolution on transferring skilled men to underground work. The purge of the party ranks carried out by the Shvernik commission had had a beneficial effect. The daily output of coal from the Donbass rose from 117,000 tons in April 1933 to 148,000 tons in January 1934.[111]

In September 1933 Ordzhonikidze and Kaganovich clashed with Stalin over the repression of industrial managers. Stalin, in a letter to Molotov, strongly protested against the Politburo's decision to rebuke V. V. Vyshinsky, the State Procurator, for his remarks regarding wreckers in NKZem and Vesenkha, following attempts by the Procuracy to initiate a case against the Kommunar works for producing incomplete combine harvesters.[112] Mendel Khataevich, secretary of Dnepropetrovsk province party committee, defended the works. In a note to Molotov, Stalin expressed his displeasure: 'I wrote to Kaganovich that to my surprise, he, on this matter, placed himself in the camp of the reactionary elements in the party.'[113] In a note to Kaganovich, Stalin was more restrained:

> It is very bad and dangerous that you (and Molotov) were not able to curb Sergo's bureaucratic impulse with regard to incomplete combines and defended him against Vyshinsky. If you will educate cadres thus then you will not have one honourable party member left in the party. This is disorder.[114]

This was the last recorded instance where the Politburo took a decision that ran counter to the will of the general secretary. The decision was quickly reversed. This provides a concrete measure of the consolidation of

Stalin's dictatorial power, a power that was never again to be challenged by the Politburo.

Conclusion

The regime's developmental strategy embodied in Stalin's 'revolution from above' appealed to powerful strains in Bolshevik ideology and practices. The radicalization of policy making after 1929 led to the headlong push for collectivization, and for the fantastic, exaggerated plans for industrial development that largely destroyed the coherence of the plan. Collectivization was turned into a military operation as part of a socialist offensive, a political crusade aimed at mobilizing the activists and a reversion to the Civil War methods of grain requisitioning. The Stalin faction was united in its commitment to this policy. Collectivization and dekulakization was intended to avert the growth of kulak power and with it the spectre of a capitalist restoration. The policy was also rationalized as the government's response to the intensification of class struggle in the countryside. The 'revolution from above' was conceived as a heroic act of reconstructing the economy and society, of which the suppression of the class enemy was an integral part and justified by historical necessity.

Stalin's own fantastic projections for industry and agriculture contributed to the crisis. But the nature of the state owned, planned economy contained inherent contradictions that generated new problems. The strategy produced a great hypertrophy of the party-state apparatus, increasingly alienated from society, in which the 'the public sphere' was drastically contracted. Bukharin's warning that these measures would lead to the brutalization of the party and the state apparatus proved prescient. Collectivization and dekulakization had as its inevitable concomitant the growth of the Gulag system and the strengthening of the Soviet police state. The 'revolution from above' generated great tensions between the central party leadership and the party in the republics, provinces and districts, the leaders of which were blamed by Stain for policy failures. It was against the background of these successive crises that the general secretary's power was transformed into a system of personal dictatorship.

Kaganovich shared Stalin's vision of the transformation of the country and embraced these brutal policies with commitment and resolve. He contributed to elaborating the regime's own heroic narrative and constructing its idealized self-image. He pioneered the failed strategy of the USM and he was directly involved in enforcing collectivization and dekulakization. The retreat in the spring of 1932 proved inadequate to avert the catastrophic famine that followed. In December 1932 Kaganovich, as head of Selkhozotdel, became the party's leading official in charge of agriculture and architect of the new tighter regime of control reflected in the new *politotdely*. In the winter of 1932–33 he oversaw the purging of the party and the deportation of peasants from North Caucasus. In his pronouncements he echoed and reinforced Stalin's main policy lines and was the most vocal Politburo member in defending the August 1932 law on state property. He acted as Stalin's agent, but in the summer of 1932 and in August 1933 there were rumours of differences between them on agrarian policy,[115] with Stalin on other occasions expressing dissatisfaction with the line taken by his deputy.

The party Secretariat assumed a role of coordination, of reconciling the interests of conflicting institutions, of initiating new policy lines, of preparing new cadres and of organizing steps to remove from positions of power those out of step with the new thinking. But the 'revolution from above' was not well coordinated or well organized. It allowed different institutions to pursue their own agendas. Vesenkha and Gosplan allowed the targets for heavy industry to become hugely inflated. The pressures from regional lobbies of Ukraine and the Urals for new investment in the metallurgical industry contributed to the same trend. The coherence of the plan was undermined. In agriculture the lack of clear directives for collectivization and the encouragement of competition between regional party chiefs to outdo one another in terms of completion of collectivization led to all kinds of excesses. From 1932 onward the leadership was compelled to impose greater order in this state of affairs. But the measures taken were insufficient to avert the famine. Gross errors in the developmental strategy contributed to the growth of political dictatorship. The mechanisms of the planned, state-owned economy took time to settle down. But even when this initial period of resettling down had been realized, serious inefficiencies and disparities in the economy became evident

Chapter 7
STALIN'S DEPUTY, 1930–1935

From 1930 to 1935 Kaganovich was at the height of his power as Stalin's deputy and a full member of the Politburo. As party deputy he balanced Molotov as chairman of Sovnarkom. The stresses associated with the 'revolution from above' brought profound changes in the organization of the work of the party and in its ideology. Kaganovich played a pivotal role in strengthening the party apparatus, which assumed a key role in setting and enforcing policy. The central party apparatus and Sovnarkom became the main directing centres of the developmental dictatorship of the command administrative economy. They set priorities, coordinated subordinate institutions and resolved conflicts. The party assumed the key role in mobilizing support behind this programme and in training cadres to staff the state and economic institutions. The regime became increasingly detached from society. The breakneck pace of industrialization precipitated a deepening crisis in agriculture that resulted in the famine of 1932–33.

The nature of the Soviet political leadership underwent a marked change as the defeat of the Rightists saw the consolidation of the power of the Stalin group. The former Trotskyist V. N. Maksimovsky clearly believed that Stalin already had dictatorial power by 1929. He stressed the historic role of personal dictatorship as a means of resolving difficult issues, but drew a sharp distinction between dictatorship and tyranny and warned of the dangers of dictatorship turning into tyranny.[1] The members of the ruling group were either oblivious to these dangers or chose to ignore them. From 1929 to 1932 Stalin stood at the head of the triumphant group. He was already more than *primus inter pares* among the members of the Politburo. The flourishing of his cult underlined his position of supremacy. After 1932 Stalin's leadership assumed ever more clearly the form of a personal dictatorship.

The Ruling Group

Stalin's 50th birthday, on 21 December 1929, was hailed with unprecedented public celebrations.[2] The celebration can be seen as a testimony to Stalin's narcissistic inflated self-image, and the willingness of his deputies to bolster this self-idealized image. The Central Committee resolution, drafted by Kaganovich, described Stalin as the 'best pupil, heir and successor of Lenin' and proclaimed him the new 'leader' (*vozhd*').[3] A jubilee issue of *Pravda* was devoted to the event, with laudatory articles by the Politburo members. Kaganovich's article 'Stalin and the Party', a concerted attack on the Rightists, asserted 'Treachery in politics always begins with the revision of theory'.[4] By the same logic, he who defined correct theory defined what treachery was. Stalin was elevated as a symbol of unity of the party leadership.[5] Volkogonov asserts that Kaganovich and Molotov wanted the celebration to be more elaborate.[6] Much to the annoyance of Ordzhonikidze and Mikoyan, Kaganovich began to give eulogies in praise of Stalin. According to Mikoyan, Stalin rebuked him on one occasion for his excessive flattery in public speeches.[7] In the early 1930s, for Kaganovich, Stalin was still an 'older' brother or 'best friend' for his closest followers.[8]

With the defeat of the Right, the Stalin faction acquired complete ascendancy in the Politburo. Following the XVI Party Congress in July 1930 the Politburo comprised 10 members: Stalin, Voroshilov, Kaganovich, Kalinin, Kirov, Kosior, Kuibyshev, Molotov, Rykov and Rudzutak. Ordzhonikidze also attended Politburo sessions ex-officio as head of CCC-Rabkrin. According to Voroshilov, Stalin's inner circle included, besides himself, Molotov, Kaganovich, Mikoyan, Kuibyshev and Ordzhonikidze.[9] The composition of this group varied according to different observers.[10]

Figure 3. Some of the Politburo leaders in 1929: G. K. Ordzhonikidze, K. E. Voroshilov, V. V. Kuibyshev, I. V. Stalin, M. I. Kalinin, L. M. Kaganovich and S. M. Kirov

As Stalin's deputy, Kaganovich was the constant recipient of the *vozhd*'s proposals, instructions and thoughts, in what remained a 'master' and 'servant' relationship.[11] In an ingratiating letter from August 1931, he wrote, 'I actually didn't want to tire you, especially in the first days of your holiday, but it must be so – more often than normal, for it's hard for us to rule without you.'[12] At this time, Stalin confided to Kaganovich his concern regarding divisions in the Politburo. The sharp disputes between Ordzhonikidze (Vesenkha) and Molotov (Sovnarkom) and Kuibyshev (Gosplan) revolved around investment and output targets. Stalin spoke of Ordzhonikidze's stubbornness and inflated pride as a cause of friction, with his frequent appeals to the Politburo against the decisions of Sovnarkom and his attempts to revise decisions taken by the Politburo itself. The problem of Kuibyshev's alcoholism also raised concern.

In September 1931 Stalin expressed frustration with the way the Politburo conducted its affairs and warned that these disputes could split the 'ruling group'.[13] He warned Kaganovich that such developments threatened to turn the Politburo into a mere rubber stamp for resolutions from the economic commissariats.[14] He reprimanded Ordzhonikidze, declaring that the Politburo was being turned into a plaything of competing sectional interests.[15]

Within the Politburo there were alliances based on bonds of friendship and shared institutional interests. Molotov and Kuibyshev were close. Ordzhonikidze, Kirov, Kaganovich and Mikoyan were close friends.[16] Kaganovich was also a close friend of Kosior, party secretary of Ukraine. In the 1920s he had been on close relations with Kuibyshev, but this had evidently cooled. Kaganovich was close to Voroshilov, but his closest friend was Ordzhonikidze. Kaganovich's elder brother, Mikhail Kaganovich, was also a close friend of Ordzhonikidze.[17] From 1928 to 1936 he worked as one of Ordzhonikidze's deputies, firstly in CCC-Rabkrin, then, from 1931, in Vesenkha and NKTyazhprom.[18] Like his brother Lazar, he had a reputation as a tough, hard-driving administrator. It was he who was reported as stating that 'the earth should tremble when the director walks around the plant'.[19]

The view of the Politburo as being divided between hardliners and moderates, and between advocates of rapid industrialization versus moderates from 1932–33 onward, a view which originated with Boris Nicolaevskii, needs to be qualified.[20] The archival documents emphasize policy differences based on institutional interests and personal alliances. The heads of key institutions tended to be protective of their own personnel, especially against the encroachments of the police and control agencies.

Stalin employed Kaganovich to effect major personnel changes in the party and government. In September 1931 he instructed his deputy to remove M. L. Rukhimovich and his 'gang' from the head of the transport commissariat NKPS (the People's Commissariat of Ways of Communication). Stalin and Kaganovich brusquely rejected counter-proposals from Molotov and Ordzhonikidze.[21] In a letter to Kaganovich, Stalin also rejected the candidacies of I. V. Kosior (brother of Stanislav Kosior) and Eikhe as deputies for NKPS.[22] He stressed the need for people who were competent and politically loyal.

Kaganovich promoted a number of able, young administrators within the central party apparatus. He advanced Pavel Postyshev, a member of the Ukrainian Politburo from 1926 to 1930, to be secretary of the central Orgburo in 1930.[23] A year later, Stalin blocked a proposal to transfer him from the Secretariat to Sovnarkom.[24] Nikolai Yezhov, who, during collectivization served as deputy narkom (deputy commisar) of NKZem USSR, was appointed head of the Central Committee's cadres section.[25] The Politburo on 27 January 1931, on Kaganovich's recommendation, granted Yezhov the right to attend Politburo meetings.[26] On his recommendation, Georgi Malenkov was appointed deputy head of the Cadres Department.[27]

The Reorganization of the Central Party Apparatus

In 1928 and 1929 the Politburo met on a weekly basis, almost invariably on a Thursday. As its workload grew enormously, Molotov introduced, alongside the formal meetings of the Politburo, weekly working sessions of the Politburo. Whereas the formal sessions discussed policy issues and were attended by members of the Central Committee, the working sessions were devoted to discussing routine issues of legislation and were restricted to Politburo members.

In 1931 Kaganovich drastically reduced the number of Politburo working sessions and in 1933 ended the practice. As a result, a huge number of issues were resolved outside the formal Politburo session through the device of polling members (*oprosom*).[28] The Politburo's decline is confirmed by the surviving stenographic reports of its discussions in the 1920s and 1930s. This restricted policy debate and fostered a system of decision making that was cruder, more limited and more intellectually impoverished.[29]

On 26 January 1930 the Orgburo divided up responsibility among the four secretaries. Stalin was responsible for preparing Politburo sessions and overseeing the work of the Secretariat; Molotov was to lead the departments of culture and propaganda, Kaganovich, the organizational-instruction department and the department of distribution of cadres and Smirnov, the department of agitation.[30]

The Central Committee approved proposals submitted by Kaganovich on reorganizing its own apparatus into seven sectors:[31] Organization-instruction, Assignment, Culture and Propaganda, Agitation and Mass Work,

Secret Department, Administrative Affairs and the Lenin Institute.³² This reconstruction was intended to streamline the apparatus and to allow it to concentrate on four principal functions: checking policy implementation, selecting cadres, mass work, and servicing the needs of the party in the localities. The party Secretariat under Kaganovich was turned into Stalin's effective instrument of rule.³³

The Secret Department of the Central Committee was charged with organizing the work of the Politburo and communicating its commandments to lower institutions. In May 1929 Kaganovich laid down the instructions concerning its organization and function. These included secret communications, 'conspiracy' or *konspiratsiya*, a revealing legacy of the underground years.³⁴ Its work may also have embraced the sensitive issue of eavesdropping on the conversations of party-state officials. In November 1933 the Secretariat ruled that the Secret Department was subordinated directly to Stalin and in his absence, to Kaganovich.³⁵

At the XVI Party Congress in 1930, Kaganovich spoke in favour of organizing the party on 'functional principles' (*functional*), as promoted by CCC-Rabkrin (under Ordzhonikidze).³⁶ This was supposed to produce a specialized, streamlined administrative apparatus and to cut costs. He soon became an arch critic of functionalism as a system that fragmented administrative tasks and weakened leadership.³⁷

Stalin had long regarded the government, under the chairmanship of Rykov, as hostile to him. While Stalin was still on vacation in October 1930, the Politburo members exchanged views on who should take over as chairman of Sovnarkom. Molotov opposed appointing Stalin as head of government.³⁸ Ordzhonikidze proposed Molotov for the post.³⁹ Kaganovich stressed Stalin's great leadership qualities and argued that it was the wish of the party rank and file that he should occupy the post.⁴⁰ Voroshilov informed Stalin that he, Mikoyan, Molotov, Kaganovich and, with some reservations, Kuibyshev favoured his appointment as chairman of Sovnarkom.⁴¹ However, Stalin insisted that Molotov take the post.

Molotov's appointment as chairman of Sovnarkom marked him out as the undoubted number two figure within the Soviet leadership. Kaganovich became the second party secretary after Stalin and was his principal aide. From 1931 to 1938 Kaganovich chaired the meetings of the Orgburo. Up to 1935 he was closely involved in preparing matters in the Secretariat which were then referred to the Orgburo and the Politburo for resolution.⁴²

Politburo sessions were generally chaired by Molotov.⁴³ Stalin preferred to be unencumbered with this chore, intervening himself in discussions or often listening to the debate and summarizing the sense of discussions. The Politburo protocols were signed by Stalin and in his absence, by Kaganovich as the second secretary and Stalin's major-domo in charge of party work.

Each year Stalin was absent from Moscow for several months in the summer from 1931 to 1936. In the meantime, Kaganovich assumed charge. Their correspondence reflects Stalin's constant and close involvement in almost all aspects of decision making. He always had the last say, but initiatives and suggestions often emanated from Kaganovich. The later sat on a plethora of Politburo committees and commissions, received local party leaders, heard their reports and often undertook tours of inspection. Stalin was kept constantly informed on policy matters by courier, by telephone and by visits from leading officials. Often, the notes from Moscow were signed by Kaganovich and Molotov as the two senior figures. These notes commonly ended with the request 'Please let us have your opinion'. Kaganovich never tired of stressing how he and his colleagues agreed with *vozhd'*'s analysis and prescriptions.[44]

Party Recruitment and Mobilization

Kaganovich in 1924–25 oversaw the Lenin enrolment and the campaign to educate the new generation of party members. He also oversaw the huge drive to proletarianize the party's ranks from 1929 to 1933. In January 1930 he reported to a party meeting attached to the Central Committee on the 'mobilization of the activism of the masses'. The 'cultural revolution' reflected the growing size of the industrial proletariat, which by 1930 numbered 3 million, as well as its cultural development. He urged a tightening of censorship over the arts, theatre, cinema and literature and the full use of 'all the levers of the proletarian state' to extend 'communist education'. Agitation had to become 'a mighty tool of mobilizing the masses for the fulfilment of the concrete tasks' of production.[45]

In his speech to the XVI Party Congress in June 1930, Kaganovich reported that 'workers from production' made up 48 per cent of the party membership.[46] He noted the huge expansion of the mass media as part of the 'cultural revolution', but chided the trade unions for spending little on the literacy campaign, using their cultural budget to fund sports, cinema, spectacles and concerts. He noted efforts to involve workers in administration, to replace those hostile elements being purged, and the success in the promotion of native cadres (*korenizatsiya*) in the republics.

From 1927 to 1933 the membership of the CPSU grew from 786,000 to 2.2 million. In this period the proportion of members designated as workers by origin grew from 55 per cent to 65 per cent.[47] The party was at its most proletarian in terms of its social composition in these years. After 1933 membership fell sharply as the party purge was carried out, with preference being given to recruiting members from the new Soviet elite. Membership numbers only returned to the levels of 1933 in 1941 as part of the wartime recruitment drive.

Kaganovich supervised a huge expansion in the programme of party education. From 1930 to 1933 the number of party schools and circles grew from 52,000 to 210,000, with the numbers attending rising from 1 million to 4.5 million. By 1934 there were 130,000 propagandists, the majority of whom were now workers, five times more than in 1928.[48] A central task was to strengthen the primary party organizations and to involve all members in shock-work and socialist competition. To bolster party support in the countryside a major drive was initiated to build up the rural party cells.[49] The number of rural party members grew from 404,000 to 709,000 between 1930 and 1934. Nevertheless, 50 per cent of the *kolkhozy* still lacked a single party member.[50]

Kaganovich exercised a special oversight over the Komsomol. Youth was assigned a privileged place in the Stalinist programme. He lauded the Komsomol as a more dependable ally of the party than the trade unions in the struggle with the Right deviation.[51] At the XVI Party Congress, he praised the Komsomol's role in promoting shock-work and socialist emulation. With a membership of 2.5 million and with a quarter of all industrial workers under 22 years of age, it had a crucial role to play. The Komsomol, with some exceptions in the national republics, had supported the party during collectivization.[52] Addressing the Komsomol congress in January 1931 he praised its work in promoting higher tempos in industry in Magnitogorsk and elsewhere. Youth was the future. 'We need engineer-organizers and not people with diplomas.'[53] He issued a bold prophecy that by the start of the Second Five-Year Plan, the Soviet economy would catch and overtake that of the United States. 'Socialism will be victorious.... You will be the masters of the whole world!'[54]

In November 1933 Kaganovich addressed the Komsomol Central Committee plenum on its fifteenth anniversary, declaring. 'Stalin is the best friend and leader of the Komsomol.'[55] The country's defence, he asserted, was an issue close to the heart of the Komsomol, which provided 40 per cent of army conscripts. The fascist movements, he noted, modelled their youth organizations on the Komsomol. As secretary of Moscow party organization he promoted the Komsomol's work in building the Metro.

Kaganovich was also a patron of the Pioneer organization. In 1930 he urged Pioneers to encourage their parents to participate in socialist emulation campaigns. In conversation with a young Pioneer leader in 1933, he questioned how far they had succeeded in overcoming the 'vestiges of the past' in terms of egotism, vanity and selfishness.[56]

After the tumultuous growth of party membership over the preceding four years, on 10 December 1932, with the crisis in agriculture accelerating, the Politburo authorized a new purge of the party ranks, as part of the drive to tighten discipline. The commission was chaired by Kaganovich.[57] He took charge of the campaign, bypassing Rudzutak, head of CCC, with local commissions reporting directly to him.[58] The drafting in of so many Stalinist hardliners ensured that an uncompromising approach would be taken with wavering and disaffected members.

In May 1933 Kaganovich reported that about half of the party membership (including candidates) of 3.2 million had been screened. The party had to be organized like an army, purged of 'unhealthy elements' and its ideological level raised. Echoing Stalin's words he declared that the party was no longer dealing with open enemies, but rather with 'double dealers', who attacked official policy 'on the sly'. Some party members, he indignantly noted, still considered it quite 'lawful' to discuss the realism of government plans.[59] The party, he asserted, could not require from ordinary workers a sophisticated knowledge of ideology, but sufficient so they did not follow it as a religious faith.[60] In September 1933 Kaganovich reported to his friend Ordzhonikidze that the purge was proceeding well.[61] Rudzutak reported to the XVII Party Congress that 182,500 members, 16.8 per cent of the membership, had been expelled from the party.[62]

Cadre Policy

From the Shakhty trial onward, Stalin, Molotov and Kaganovich were the chief advocates of dismissing bourgeois specialists and advancing a new generation of proletarian cadres in their place. From 1929 to 1935 Kaganovich had charge of cadre policy, and delivered the major reports on the subject to the party congresses. The 'revolution from above' found its most concrete expression in cadre policy.

At the XVI Party Congress Kaganovich reported a huge success in the 'communization' and 'workerization' of the higher technical institutes (*vtyzy*). Gosplan had compiled a five-year plan for training cadres. The number of engineers and technicians in the whole economy was to quadruple from 309,000 to 1,220,000 by the end of the First Five-Year Plan. The proportion of specialists in industry would increase from 2 per cent to 5 per cent of the entire labour force, placing the USSR on a par with Germany. It was necessary to train more cadres for trade, cooperatives and finance. New industrial academies were being opened that offered courses for higher cadres.

Stalin played the key role in initiating the Shakhty trial in 1928 and in authorizing the trial of the Industrial Party and the Menshevik Buro in 1930. The decision not to proceed with the trial of the Labouring Peasants Party was a problem, taken for fear that it might backfire against the background of the debacle in agriculture. Experts in finance and agriculture were purged to eradicate the so-called *Kondratevshchina* and *Chayanovshchina*.

In February and June 1931 Stalin, in two speeches to business executives, called for the older and younger technical specialists to work in harmony, thus signalling an easing of the repression of bourgeois specialists initiated by the Shakhty affair. The Soviet regime lacked sufficient capable, young specialists and had to rely in large measure on the older, more experienced generation. However, Stalin still stressed the long term objective to create a new Soviet intelligentsia drawn from the working class and peasantry.[63]

Kaganovich reported to the XVII Party Congress a huge expansion in the number of higher institutions of education – *vuzy*, *vtyzy* and *tekhnikums* – from 129 in 1928 to 600 in 1933, with the number of students increasing from 348,000 to 1.163 million.[64] A majority of the students were Komsomol and party members.[65] In heavy industry, the number of specialists with completed higher education had risen from 13,700 in 1928 to 50,700 in 1933. The number of agronomists with completed higher education grew from 18,000 in 1928 to 126,000 in 1933. Between 1928 and 1924 some 45,000 specialists had been drafted into agriculture from industry.

The First Five-Year Plan coincided with an unprecedented drive to train cadres for industry and agriculture. This was part of the drive to weaken the influence of the older generation of 'bourgeois specialists' and to advance a new generation of cadres drawn from the working class. Kaganovich effectively oversaw this campaign. Tens of thousands of engineers, technicians and agronomists were trained in this period. These were beneficiaries of the Stalinist regime, but their full advance into positions of power was only to come in 1937–38.[66]

The Consolidation of Stalin's Dictatorship

The defeat of the Rightists removed the last substantial group who opposed Stalin. Internal party debate was suppressed, as the party was turned into an administrative instrument of the developmental dictatorship. But in the wake of the crisis of collectivization and industrialization, dissent continued periodically to surface. In 1930 S. I. Syrtsov and V. V. Lominadze criticized the recklessness of agricultural and industrial policy and Stalin's domination of policy. The matter was referred to a Politburo commission, headed by Ordzhonikidze,[67] and it was discussed at the joint plenum of the Central Committee-CCC in November 1930, with the main report presented by Kaganovich.

In 1932 the deepening crisis in agriculture prompted an upsurge in oppositional activity. The M. N. Ryutin platform condemned the leadership's policy failures. The group of A. P. Smirnov, V. V. Eismont and G. G. Tolmachev

Figure 4. L. M. Kaganovich and I. V. Stalin photographed in the Kremlin grounds on 1 May 1934

group seems to have been largely the fabrication of the secret police. According to Boris Nicolaevskii, Stalin in both cases pressed for the death penalty, but was blocked by the Politburo, with only Kaganovich strongly supporting him.[68] The Politburo stenographic reports on these two cases provide no support for these assertions.[69] It is possible that Kaganovich did take a hard line on the former oppositionists, as he habitually did.

The rise of Stalin's dictatorship was linked to the crisis in agriculture. The law on the theft of state property of August 1932, which Stalin drafted for endorsement by the Politburo, was challenged by at least one Politburo member (possibly Kosior or Chubar'). This apparently was the last case when Politburo members defied his will. At this time, Kaganovich, in a letter of obeisance addressed to 'Dear Comrade Stalin', declared 'I completely and fully agree with your assessment of the state of affairs in the Ukraine'. He now presented himself as his acolyte: 'You have not only the official political right but also the moral right of a comrade to make whatever use you please of what you have made of me as a politician, that is, as your pupil.'[70] During the famine Kaganovich was the most vociferous defender of Stalin's policies.

Kaganovich managed the work of the Politburo and under his stewardship in 1932 and 1933, especially after January 1933, its power and status sharply declined. In 1932 there were 43 meetings, but Stalin attended only 30, being absent for a long spell during the summer months.[71] In 1933 the Politburo met on 24 occasions; in 1934, on 18 occasions; in 1935, just 15 times; in 1936, 9 times and in 1937, just 6 times. After 1934 the Secretariat ceased to meet in formal sessions, but the Orgburo continued to hold such sessions through the 1930s.[72] With the demise of the Politburo, power was increasingly invested in Stalin's own private office.[73]

The meetings in Stalin's Kremlin office dating back to the 1920s became in effect the general secretary's conclave.[74] The regularity of these meeting and the high standing of the officials who attended them indicate an enormous streamlining of the decision-making process. It allowed Stalin to control the political agenda, to dispense with factional intrigues and gave him direct oversight over the work of the party-state apparatus, with leading officials being required to report and to give account of their activities.[75] The Politburo's formal meetings correspondingly declined in power.[76]

The crisis in agriculture in 1932 prompted an upsurge of oppositional activity inside the party. The suicide of Stalin's wife, Nadezhda Alliluyeva, was also in part related to this crisis. Kaganovich delivered one of the funeral orations at Novodevichy. Her death, he later noted, badly affected Stalin.[77] But his testimony, which always aims to humanize Stalin, needs to be read with some scepticism. Stalin seemingly experienced emotions only at a superficial level, was little troubled by the suffering of others and felt no qualms of conscience for inflicting such suffering. Stalin reportedly offered his resignation to the Politburo. This was the prelude to a dramatic increase of his power.

Kaganovich's role as Stalin's deputy in the party apparatus now assumed central importance. In September 1933 Stalin wrote to Molotov, protesting against his plan to take a long vacation, since Kuibyshev might again start to drink and Kaganovich was already overburdened with central and local (Moscow) responsibilities.[78]

The famine crisis brought a drastic tightening of central controls. At the joint Central Committee–Central Control Commission plenum in January 1933, Stalin again, as in April 1930 in the article 'Dizzy with Success', absolved himself of responsibility for the crisis and severely rebuked the republican, provincial and territorial party committees for providing weak leadership.[79] The famine prompted the leadership to rally together as the best way of preserving the regime. Kaganovich, Kirov, Ordzhonikidze and Voroshilov sought to relaunch Stalin's cult as an expression of unity and of their obeisance to the *vozhd'* as the undisputed leader.[80]

The Moscow province and city party conference from 16 to 24 January 1934 was a curious affair which saw a flourishing cult arise around Kaganovich (see Chapter 8). Kaganovich's report anticipated the main decisions of the XVII Party Congress. He highlighted the threat posed by German fascism and Japanese militarism, anticipating the main line in Stalin's report. Kaganovich hailed the 'leader of genius of the party and the working class, the great Stalin', who alone ensured the great victories, domestic and international, achieved by the party.[81]

The XVII Party Congress, the 'congress of victors', marked the rout of the opposition and the apotheosis of the general secretary as the *vozhd'*, the unquestioned leader. As in his address to the CC-CCC in January 1933, Stalin blamed local party leaders for past failures (by implication, the famine). The decision to abolish the Central Control Commission-Rabkrin (see The Reorganization of Party and State Control below) directed responsibility for the failures in agriculture onto the failure of the control organizations to correctly implement policy. The 'general line' was correct; it was implementation that was at fault. The speech was also striking for the stress placed on social hierarchy, its renewed attack on egalitarianism and wage levelling and the training and advancement of the great number of new cadres and technicians.

Many rumours surround the congress, stories of dissent spoken of in the congress corridors, speculations concerning the election of the Central Committee. Mikoyan and Antonov-Ovseenko assert that in the election of the Central Committee, as many as 300 out of 1,225 voting delegates scrubbed Stalin's name from the list and that Kirov won the largest number of votes.

The results were reported by V. P. Zatonsky, head of the audit commission, to Kaganovich, who, after consulting with Stalin, ordered that the ballot papers be destroyed.[82] The opening of the party archives has failed to shed further light on this affair. Not surprisingly, Kaganovich in retirement dismissed these charges as lies.[83]

The unease at the XVII Party Congress reflected deep disquiet, caused primarily by the famine, for which Stalin was held responsible. The effusive praise of Kaganovich at the Moscow party conference early in January (see Chapter 10) may have manifested the same discontent. Although closely allied with Stalin, Kaganovich had the virtue of not being Stalin. In 1934 Kaganovich was at the apex of his career. The reports of the party congress leave little doubt of his popularity among the delegates. Following the congress, Kaganovich was one of the ten members of the Politburo. Stalin, Kaganovich, Kirov and Andrei Zhdanov were elected party secretaries. The first three were also members of the Orgburo.

For a person of Stalin's paranoid sensibilities, the very suspicion of disloyalty was enough. Stalin did not act precipitately – he bided his time. He may well have concluded that to secure his position he had to bring his lieutenants to heel.

Party Organization in 1934

Kaganovich's report to the XVII Party Congress on the 'Organizational Question' complemented the reports of Molotov and Kuibyshev on the Second Five-Year Plan.[84] He demanded measures to strengthen control in the commissariats. He now castigated functionalism as 'a bourgeois method of management' and advocated strengthening one-man management (*edinonachalie*) so as to ensure concrete operative leadership in industry. NKTyazhprom had taken steps to reform its organization, but the commissariats of light industry and agriculture (a kind of 'Bedlam') still suffered from its affects. In an obvious swipe at Molotov and Sovnarkom-STO, who had oversight of the economic commissariats, he warned that the Politburo itself was ready to take the necessary corrective measures.

The Central Committee's growing role in economic matters threatened to eclipse Sovnarkom and STO. Kaganovich declared, 'Our Politburo of the CC is the organ of operative direction of all branches of socialist construction.'[85] He noted how Stalin and the Central Committee had paid close attention to agriculture. In this he contrasted the efficiency of the Central Committee apparatus's handling of business with Molotov's Sovnarkom and STO.[86] At the same time, Ordzhonikidze secured the Politburo's support for a lowering of the targets presented by Molotov and Kuibyshev for heavy industry in the Second Five-Year Plan.

Kaganovich outlined sweeping changes in the structure of the party Secretariat, with the establishment of specialist economic departments to oversee branches of the economy and a department of Leading Party Organs (ORPO) which was to concern itself with cadre assignments and to ensure stricter control over the provincial and regional party committees. These changes were intended to strengthen the role of the party Secretariat in economic management in opposition to Sovnarkom. On 10 March the Politburo assigned responsibility for the Central Committee's departments as follows: Transport Sector, Kaganovich (with Zhdanov as deputy head); Industrial Sector, Yezhov; Agricultural Sector, Zhdanov; Culture-Propaganda Sector, A. I. Stetsky; Leading Party Organs, D. A. Bulatov; Special Sector, A. N. Poskrebyshev and Administrative Affairs of the Central Committee, Ya. E. Brezanovsky.[87] Already on 17 January 1934 the Secretariat ordered that Central Committee apparatus staff could only be appointed and dismissed with the approval of Kaganovich or Stalin.[88]

On 4 June the Politburo divided responsibilities between the three party secretaries: Stalin had charge of Culture-Propaganda, the Special Sector and the work of the Politburo; Kaganovich oversaw the Orgburo, the Industrial Sector, the Transport Sector, the Komsomol and the Commission of Party Control; Zhdanov was assigned the Secretariat, the Agricultural Sector, the Planning-Finance-Trade Sector, Political Administration, the Sector for Leading Party Organs and Administrative Affairs.[89]

The Reorganization of Party and State Control

A major change in party-state organization was the abolition of the once powerful Central Control Commission-Rabkrin. The party and state control bodies were now held responsible for the failure to properly implement official policy. They were in effect made scapegoats for the failure of policy in the countryside that had produced the famine. The decision was first announced by Kaganovich in his speech to the Moscow party conference in January. At this stage, leading officials of CCC-Rabkrin, such as N. K. Antipov, Yaroslavsky, Yakov Peters and Abel Yenukidze, endorsed the reorganization.[90] Other leaders, such as Rudzutak, head of CCC-Rabkrin, were completely taken aback by the decision.[91]

Kaganovich elaborated on the reform in his speech to the congress. CCC-Rabkrin and Sovnarkom's Commission of Implementation would be abolished and replaced by a Commission of Party Control, attached to the Central Committee and by a Commission of Soviet Control, attached to Sovnarkom. The decision was simply announced; it was not open for debate. The membership of these two bodies would be elected by the party congress. Control was to be of a systematic daily character. The implementation of official policy was to be their primary concern. Rudzutak was clearly out of favour and following the party congress, was elected as candidate, not a full member, of the Politburo.

The new Commission of Soviet Control (CSC) was headed by Kuibyshev, whilst the new Commission of Party Control (CPC) was headed by Kaganovich, with Yezhov as his deputy.[92] Addressing the Commission of Party Control's plenum on 28 June 1934, Kaganovich argued that control should become an 'inseparable' part of administration.[93] CPC and CSC were to be 'independent of local organizations', operating through their own plenipotentiaries in the localities. This, he envisaged, might lead to conflicts between the territorial party committees and the plenipotentiaries, but this was no bad thing, and these could be submitted to the party's Central Committee for resolution.[94]

Kaganovich from 1929 onward played a major role in promoting the role of the party instructors in ensuring control over policy implementation in the localities. In September 1934 he declared, '10 thousand to 15 thousand instructors comprise the basic skeleton of the party apparatus.'[95] There was to be no let-up in the struggle with the kulaks and other enemies, and no retreat into 'liberal' methods. He also played a central role in establishing the *politotdely* in the MTS, *kolkhozy* and the *sovkhozy* in January 1933 (see Chapter 6). These measures to militarize the administration of agriculture were extremely controversial and led to a partial dismantling of this system in 1934.

Ideology and Cultural Policy

The triumph of the Stalin group was also reflected in its control over matters of ideology. In 1929 Kaganovich was elected to the Communist Academy and became director of the Institute of Soviet Construction, previously headed by E. B. Pashukanis. In December 1929 Stalin, in his address to the Conference of Marxist Agronomists, called for a resolute attack on theoretical deviations.[96] In June 1930 Kaganovich censured the president of the Communist Academy and eminent Marxist historian Mikhail Pokrovsky.[97] In January 1931 he called for a thorough examination of Pokrovsky's Institute of History.[98] Pokrovsky died in 1932. The repudiation of Pokrovsky went with a rediscovery of narrative history, a new emphasis on the individual in history and a more positive assessment of the progressive aspects of Russia's history.

Stalin's letter to the editors of *Proletarskaya revolyutsiya* in October 1931 marked a major step in tightening control over intellectual life. While purporting to deal with errors in the writing of party history, this was turned into a general directive on non-party ideas in all spheres of thought. Addressing the Institute of Red Professors, Kaganovich highlighted the significance of this letter for the training of communist cadres and for eradicating 'Trotskyist contraband' from party history. All disagreements about current policy had a theoretical basis and stemmed from a perversion of Marxist-Leninist theory.'[99]

The same utilitarian approach was applied to education. The Politburo in August 1931 approved the proposals of Kaganovich's commission on the reform of primary and middle schools. The curriculum was focused more on science and mathematics, with the aim of training pupils for entry into the technical institutes, and preparing them for the world of work. The authority of the school director was reasserted and the influence of public representatives in the schools was curbed.[100]

As party secretary, Kaganovich had oversight of cultural and science policy. In 1930 he authorized the publication of sensitive articles in the press, oversaw the work of Glavlit in the field of censorship, authorized the publication of works on party history and edited the protocols of party meetings.[101] The development of cultural policy reflected the new priorities of Stalin's developmental dictatorship, with the doctrine of 'socialist realism' being proclaimed in 1932. In place of open debate, uniformity in cultural policy was established, with a clear utilitarian role assigned to culture.

In 1932 Kaganovich headed the party commission that dissolved the once powerful Russian Association of Proletarian Writers (RAPP). In 1934 he oversaw the first Congress of Soviet Writers, presided over by Gorky, with the main report presented by A. A. Zhdanov, where the doctrine of 'socialist realism' was formally adopted. Kaganovich kept Stalin (who was on vacation) informed of developments, supervised the drafting of the congress resolution, which was sent to Stalin for his approval, and checked the list of writers to be elected to the presidium.[102] 'Socialist realism' represented the quintessence of Stalin's cultural philosophy, the imposition of a theoretical straightjacket on artists and the elevation of intellectually and aesthetically impoverished ideas as the foundation of progressive, socialist culture.

Stalin's personal preferences exerted a dominating influence, but his deputies were delegated specific responsibilities. Kaganovich acted as a kind of overlord on the cultural front in the early 1930s, with a general oversight over literature, cinema and theatre.[103] He was also a patron of the Union of Architects.[104] Zhdanov became responsible for literature, Voroshilov for the pictorial arts and sculpture, and Platon Kerzhentsev and Molotov, for music. This heralded the triumph of the narrowest kind of 'Marxist-Leninist' philistinism, with political criteria triumphing over aesthetic considerations. Kaganovich was party to the persecution of modernist artists who were out of step with socialist realism as a doctrine.[105] In 1932 Stalin and Kaganovich prohibited the staging of Nikolai Erdman's play *The Suicide*.

Kaganovich and Gorky were on very friendly terms and in these years, kept up a lively correspondence, with Gorky soliciting paper for publication ventures, promoting the needs of young sculptors, advancing plans for a museum of icons and seeking official support to invite the French writer Romain Rolland to visit the USSR.[106] As head of NKPS, Kaganovich in 1935 promoted plans for a collective work by Soviet writers, celebrating the achievements of rail transport, inspired by Gorky's project 'The History of Factories and Works'.[107] Only A. Platonov's short story *Bessmertnie* (The Immortals) appeared.[108] The moral of the story – in which Kaganovich is featured – the tireless efforts of executives to keep the system going, echoes the theme of respect for and trust in the cadres which Stalin promoted.

From 1931 to 1937 Kaganovich closely monitored the work of Soviet cinema. He heard reports on script and film scenarios, on plans for the production for the coming year. This was a field in which Stalin showed a particular interest. In 1931 and 1933 the Orburo reprimanded Soyuzkino for its failure to produce high quality films. Boris Shumyatsky's appointment as head of Soyuzkino brought an improvement in the management of the film industry, which increasingly found favour with the political leadership.[109] From May 1934 onward Stalin, Kaganovich, Shumyatsky and other members of the Politburo and their wives and children would watch films and newsreels. Stalin and Kaganovich held frequent discussions with film directors on individual films. Both were admirers of *Chapaev*, the Soviet classic on the Civil War.[110] But Stalin also authorized the purchase from the west of Chaplin's *Modern Times*.

In 1934 the film *Jolly Fellows* (*Vesely Rebyati*), which featured the leading jazz musician of his day, L. O. Utesov, provoked a strong critical reaction. Bubnov and Antipov of the Orgburo's Cinema Commission denounced it as counter-revolutionary and a manifestation of cultural hooliganism. Kaganovich defended the film. On Stalin and Kaganovich's order, the Orgburo's Cinema Commission was disbanded. Kaganovich issued a statement on the importance of cinema as a form of mass entertainment, the import of which was that ideological rigidity should not constrain the objective of gaining a mass popular audience for Soviet film.[111] This was part of efforts to humanize the Stalinist system. Related to this was his promotion, aided by Utesov, of song and dance ensembles and jazz orchestras among railway workers, in the face of those who had derided jazz as being Western and decadent.[112]

In 1935 Kaganovich strongly criticized the film *Birobidzhan*, about the Jewish autonomous region, and Jewish theatre for its nationalistic spirit. Stalin, at this time, took a more positive view.[113] In 1937 Kaganovich criticised Sergei Eisenstein's film *Bezhin Meadow* as anti-Soviet and argued that he should no longer be assigned work as a director.[114] Stalin played the benign patrician and soon after assigned Eisenstein responsibility for directing the film *Alexander Nevsky*. From January 1937 onward Kaganovich's role in Soviet cinema declined dramatically and was replaced in this sphere by Molotov.

Domestic and External Security

While the Politburo and Stalin's deputies retained influence, Stalin's ability to use repression was held in check. The Politburo decided on matters of sentencing, especially the application of the death sentence in political cases. Kaganovich, as Stalin's deputy, received draft variants of important cases from the chairman of the Military Collegium of the Supreme Court USSR, V. V. Ul'rikh and in consultation with the *vozhd'*, the final decisions were taken.[115]

From 1927 onward Stalin's paranoia became increasingly manifest, as reflected in the Shakhty affair. He was the Politburo figure who was most preoccupied with the search for enemies. In July 1932 he instructed Kaganovich to apprehend OGPU agents in Manchuria whom he suspected of being enemy agents. In August 1932 he warned of foreign specialists working in the country all of whom might be intelligence agents.[116] In 1932–33 the resort to repression in agriculture and on the railways increased dramatically, but in industry this trend was checked. The Metro-Vickers trial in March 1933 did not lead to a second Shakhty affair, partly on account of the restraining influence of Ordzhonikidze's NKTyazhprom on the Procuracy and the OGPU.

Stalin's outlook is also illustrated by the affair of A. S. Nakhaev, a senior officer of Osoaviakhim, the civil defence organization. In August 1934, addressing a detachment of recruits at as camp near Moscow, he called for a popular rising to overthrow the Soviet regime. He was promptly arrested. Kaganovich informed Stalin of the event in restrained terms, communicating Voroshilov's opinion that Nakhaev was a 'psychopath' (he probably meant psychotic). Stalin demanded that Nakhaev be 'eliminated', and, on his insistence, the NKVD (the People's Commissariat of Internal Affairs – the secret police) then fabricated a conspiracy involving foreign intelligence.[117] In December the Politburo referred the case to the military tribunal of the Supreme Court of the USSR.[118] Nakhaev was almost certainly executed.

On 1 December 1934 Sergei Kirov, party secretary of Leningrad, was assassinated. Stalin and other Politburo members travelled to Leningrad to lead the investigation. Kaganovich was left in charge in Moscow. On 10 December a draconian new law (articles 466-79) drafted by Stalin removed the right of appeal and speeded up the procedure for executing those convicted in cases involving 'terror'. The law was widely employed in 1936–38. Twelve days after the assassination, Kaganovich, in a speech to the Moscow party, blamed the Zinovievite antiparty group, and demanded that this counter-revolutionary 'scum' be extirpated completely.[119]

The debate concerning the assassination and the question of Stalin's possible complicity in it gained currency, especially following Khrushchev's speech of 1956 which hinted at Stalin's involvement. Ordzhonikidze thought that the NKVD had been negligent in protecting Kirov.[120] In retirement, both Molotov and Kaganovich rejected the charge that Stalin was implicated in Kirov's murder. According to Kaganovich, 'Stalin loved Kirov...he simply loved him!' and was deeply affected by his death.[121] In November 1990 Kaganovich welcomed the ruling of the Procuracy of the USSR that there was no evidence of Stalin's involvement in plotting Kirov's murder.[122]

Whether Stalin arranged the assassination of Kirov is unclear. He was certainly capable of such an act and the manoeuvres at the XVII Party Congress suggest that he had a motive. However, the evidence suggests that he was not implicated, but rather used the assassination for his own purposes.[123] The downgrading of Kaganovich as Stalin's deputy in 1935, following the rallying of support for him at the Moscow party conference in January 1934, is more clear-cut and illustrates Stalin's extreme sensitivity to anything he saw as a challenge to his authority.

Stalin turned his sights on the OGPU. Its head, Yagoda, in 1928–29 had flirted with the Rightists. In July 1934 OGPU was subsumed into the newly created People's Commissariat of Internal Affairs (NKVD) with Yagoda as its head. A Politburo commission comprising Yagoda, Kaganovich and Kuibyshev, set up to reorganize the security apparatus, failed to find common ground, thus sparking an intense debate on the role of the security apparatus.[124] Kaganovich may have aspired to head the NKVD.[125] Stalin had not yet found a suitable candidate to head the organization and lacked sufficient backing to effect the changes he wanted.

The historian J. Arch Getty rightly notes that in their private correspondence, the leadership used the same language as they did in public in reference to wreckers, spies, counter-revolutionaries, Trotskyists, Rightists, and so forth.[126] The Soviet leaders were trapped by their own categories and concepts. The Stalin–Kaganovich correspondence shows that the leadership was able to address routine technical problems – investment targets, wage policy, taxation, currency matters and the practicalities of abolishing rationing – with some objectivity. However, discussions on security matters tended to evoke set responses. Stalin used the 'enemy syndrome' as a trigger whereby a shift from a non-ideological to an ideological discourse was affected. This was the area in which Stalin's discretion and power was greatest.

The development strategy of the Soviet regime was conditioned by defence and foreign policy considerations and by what the leadership defined as a system of 'capitalist encirclement'. Kaganovich played a secondary role in these areas, but was a participant in the deliberations. In the field of defence policy, Stalin resolved issues mainly in consultation with Voroshilov, minister of war (appointed Marshall in 1935) and the chief military commanders, although in 1930 Stalin clashed sharply with Marshall Mikhail Tukhachevsky on military strategy.[127] In the field of foreign policy, Stalin had the decisive voice, but drew on the advice of colleagues, especially Molotov and Maxim Litvinov, People's Commissar of Foreign Affairs.

On 5 June 1932, on Stalin's proposal, Kaganovich became his deputy in the joint Politburo–Sovnarkom Defence Committee.[128] This was a measure of Stalin's confidence in him. In April 1935 he joined the commission as a member in his own right.[129] Kaganovich was involved in various key foreign policy initiatives: the USSR's decision in December 1933 to join the League of Nations, negotiations with Japan over the sale of the Chinese Easter Railway and fishing agreements, relations with Nazi Germany and reactions to anti-Soviet speeches by Nazi leaders, as well as recognition of the USSR by the United States.[130] In May 1934, on Stalin's proposal, the Politburo charged Kaganovich, Stalin and Kuibyshev with determining the agenda of the congress of Comintern.[131]

In 1931 and 1932 Kaganovich was critical of Litvinov's stance for being too pro-Western.[132] After 1934 he appears to have supported the policy of collective security and popular fronts directed at the rising danger of fascism, but remained critical of Litvinov for being too pro-British.[133] E. A. Gnedin, a senior official of NKInDel, noted in his memoirs how at Politburo sessions Litvinov was treated as an adviser. Gnedin added, 'It is worth noting that Kaganovich responded with sarcasm – even to Molotov's remarks.'[134]

In 1935 Hitler occupied the Rhineland while Mussolini invaded Abyssinia (Ethiopia). The USSR drew closer to France, Great Britain and the United States. In May the Franco–Soviet and Czechoslovak–Soviet Pacts were signed and in July–August the VII Congress of the Communist International, reversing previous revolutionary policies, strongly supported the formation of Popular Fronts against fascism in the Western democratic countries.[135]

Kaganovich does not appear to have supported Molotov's idea of a *rapprochement* with Nazi Germany, and probably supported Stalin's line of seeing whether collective security could work. His correspondence with Ordzhonikidze shows that he was privy to major developments. In September 1936 Stalin entrusted him with the delicate task of arranging the sale of 20 fast-bombers, rifles and ammunition to the Mexican government, with the aim that they be immediately be resold to the Republican government in Spain.[136]

Conclusion

The 'revolution from above' and the creation of the command administrative economy transformed the Soviet regime into a species of developmental dictatorship. It was a system that aspired to a form of 'totalitarian' control over society, based on mass mobilization and an orchestrated consensus. Kaganovich was at the centre of these processes. In 1932–33 he was responsible for the dramatic decline in the formal meetings of the Politburo, which coincided with the consolidation of Stalin's dictatorship. Soon, the deputies were to discover that they were no longer able to control him. The Kirov assassination was used to further strengthen Stalin's power. In 1935 Kaganovich was transferred to economic work and lost his role as Stalin's deputy in the party, but continued in a diminished capacity to oversee aspects of the Politburo's work on the *vozhd"*s behalf.

This system of decision making had profound implications for the way in which policy was made and was intimately linked to major policy failures and miscalculations in agriculture and industry. Kaganovich was one of the principal architects of transforming the central party apparatus and the institution of the party instructors into an instrument of managing and directing the programme of modernization. As Stalin's deputy, he oversaw the work of the Politburo, Secretariat and Orgburo from 1930 to 1935. He played a crucial role in dismantling CCC-Rabkrin, a step towards a more centralized, more rigid system of party and state control He promoted the militarization of party administration, based on the *politodely* in agriculture and transport. He oversaw the drive to enlarge and proletarianize the party ranks and directed the new purge of 1933.

Stalin's dictatorship may have suppressed dissent, but it did not ensure loyalty to the leader. The debacle of collectivization and the famine, and his practice of unloading responsibility onto others, generated intense animosity. This was reflected in the party organizations at district, province and republican level (especially in Ukraine). The abolition of the Central Control Commission-Rabkrin was also a cause of dissatisfaction. The resort to repression against industrial cadres was also an issue of contention. Stalin viewed some of his deputies with distrust and had reason to regard the Central Committee with suspicion. The ruling group's modernization strategy involved the destruction of economic and human capital, while its administrative methods promoted bureaucracy and its strategy of social mobilization restricted the public sphere and civil society.

Chapter 8

MOSCOW PARTY BOSS, 1930–1935

In 1930 Kaganovich became a full member of the Politburo and for the next five years acted as Stalin's deputy in the party. At the same time, he was appointed as first secretary of the Moscow party committee. In this period he acquired a real power base and won a degree of party and public visibility that marked him as a major political figure in the USSR.[1] Moscow, the 'red capital', the headquarters of the party and of the world revolution, was of great symbolic importance. Kaganovich's role as party boss of Moscow, which embraced the city and the province, demonstrated the extent to which Stalin's deputies were allowed a degree of latitude in developing policy as well as the limits to that delegated power. The modernization of the capital was a central part of the regime's developmental programme in which ideological goals were to a significant degree subsumed under more pragmatic considerations. Moscow province was economically one of the most important regions of the USSR, having a population of more than 10 million people, including major towns such as Tula, Kalinin, Kolomna, Serpukhov, Podol'sk, Orekhovo-Zuevo, Ryazan' and Kaluga.

The Political Leadership of Moscow

Following the ousting of Uglanov as the secretary of the Moscow party organization in 1928, the post was temporarily filled by Molotov and then by K. Ya. Bauman. Stalin's article 'Dizzy with Success' in March 1930, signalled a major retreat with regard to collectivization. The Moscow city and province party committees, at a plenum in late March, refused to recant their errors and another plenum had to be convened in early April. Bauman was accused of leftist excesses in collectivization and on 18 April the Politburo relieved him of his post. Stalin appointed Kaganovich in his place, an appointment confirmed by his 'election' to this post by the Moscow party committee plenum.[2] At the XVI Party Congress in June, the Moscow province authorities were severely criticized for excesses during collectivization.[3]

While Kaganovich was in Siberia, Stalin, by telegram, sounded him out on being made first secretary of the Moscow Committee. On his return to Moscow, he had discussions with Stalin on the tasks he was to undertake as the capital's party boss. Stalin's plan to appoint Kaganovich as first secretary of Moscow in 1928, which had then been judged inexpedient, was finally realized.[4] It underlined Stalin's determination to impose his will on the capital. Kaganovich continued to hold down his post as party secretary, testifying both to his enormous capacity for work, and to the very high degree of trust that Stalin placed in him in this period.

In the following months, a number of top officials at district level were replaced and tens and hundreds of new workers and poor peasants were promoted to party and soviet posts. Kaganovich held meetings with party activists of all the districts in the province. Members of the Politburo and secretaries of the Moscow party committee attended district party conferences and met with the activists in the enterprises. The Moscow party committee dispatched propagandists into the countryside in May–June to strengthen the remaining *kolkhozy* after the exodus.[5]

With Kaganovich heavily involved in the work of central party apparatus, much of the work of administering Moscow fell on the shoulders of his deputies, Nikita Khrushchev, K. V. Ryndin, Nikolai Bulganin and Georgi Malenkov.[6] Khrushchev, whose links with Kaganovich had been well established in Ukraine, moved to Moscow in 1928 to study at the Industrial Academy.[7] Notwithstanding his lack of educational qualification, with Kaganovich's patronage he was rapidly promoted. In January 1932 he replaced Ryndin as second secretary of the Moscow city party committee. Kaganovich informed Stalin that Khrushchev had sided with the Troskyists in 1923–24. Nevertheless, Stalin approved his appointment.[8] Like his patron, he lacked education but was possessed of natural talents, a formidable capacity for work and was an unswerving Stalinist.[9]

Nikolai Bulganin served with Kaganovich in Nizhnyi Novgorod and Turkestan during the Civil War, thereafter became an industrial manager and was chairman of the Moscow Soviet from 1931 to 1937.[10] Malenkov, who had worked with Kaganovich in Turkestan and in the Central Committee apparatus, headed the organization section of the Moscow party committee. Yakov Peters, a Stalinist hardliner whose links with Kaganovich stretched back to Turkestan, headed the Moscow party Control Commission.[11] Alexander Bulushev was Kaganovich's assistant from 1931 to 1935 and in 1932–33 he also headed Moscow city party committee's secret department.[12] S. F. Redens, chairman of the Ukrainian GPU in 1934, became head of OGPU for Moscow province and was to spearhead the mass repression there in 1936–38.[13]

According to Timothy J. Colton, Kaganovich packed the Moscow establishment with a personal coterie. Twenty-one ranking Moscow functionaries between 1930 and 1937 (eleven who made it to province party committee or city party secretary) had previously served with Kaganovich in Nizhnyi Novgorod, Voronezh, Turkestan, Ukraine and in the Central Committee's Secretariat. One example was N. Ye. Donenko, Moscow province party committee secretary for transport in 1932–35, who had been Kaganovich's assistant for party cadres in the Secretariat in 1923–24 and head of personnel of the Ukrainian party in 1928–29.[14]

From 1930 to 1933 Peters and the party Control Commission waged a resolute struggle to eradicate dissent and to turn the Moscow party organization into a solid Stalinist bastion. At the Moscow party conference in January 1934, several speakers recalled how the Moscow party organization under Kaganovich had liquidated the *Uglanovshchina* and the 'leftist' deviation of Bauman and had struggled against bureaucracy and 'groupism', mutual guarantees, nepotism, incorrect education of the activists, and family circles.[15] Under his leadership, the Moscow committee took a much closer and direct interest in the work of all district party committees. The Moscow party organization under Uglanov had been racked by internal divisions. The conflict between Sokol'niki and Krasnaya Presnya district had been especially acute.[16] The Krasnaya Presnya and the Orekhovo-zuevsky district party committees had been turned into rightist 'fiefdoms'.[17]

The Reconstruction of the Economy of Moscow and Its Province

Kaganovich reported directly to Stalin on questions relating to Moscow. However, in the Stalin–Kaganovich correspondence from 1931 to 1936 there is only one written report from Kaganovich to Stalin, dated September 1931, on improving the organization of the city's economy.[18] This is highly revealing as to Stalin's trust in his deputy, his willingness to delegate powers to him and to the survival of polycratic aspects in the Soviet system of government.

Agriculture and food supply

Kaganovich's chief task on being appointed party secretary of Moscow was to correct the failings of agricultural policy under Bauman. In adjusting policy, it was necessary to prevent local officials and activists from being completely demoralized by a change of direction. In the summer of 1930 Nadezhda Krupskaya, in a speech to the party conference of the Bauman district in Moscow, charged that collectivization had been carried out in a un-Leninist manner, without proper consultation with the party. The Central Committee bore full responsibility for the ensuing errors, which it could not unload onto the local officials. The attack was clearly directed at Stalin and his article 'Dizzy with Success'. Kaganovich immediately took the floor and upbraided her. Members of the Central Committee, he declared, had no right to criticize the Central Committee's (i.e. the Politburo's) line. Moreover, 'Krupskaya should not think that just because she was Lenin's wife, she has a monopoly on Leninism'.[19] The intemperate nature of the response reflects Kaganovich's style, but suggests also that he had been rattled.

In the autumn of 1930 the collectivization drive in Moscow province was resumed with greater force and severity than under Bauman. In December 1930 the Moscow party committee resolved to turn Moscow province 'from a consuming into a producing region', to ensure adequate food supplies for the capital.[20] On 19 February 1931 Kaganovich, in addressing the Moscow province party committee plenum, identified districts in which the kulaks were supposedly strong and active. In the previous autumn, he revealed, the OGPU had uncovered and liquidated 206 counter-revolutionary 'kulak' groups (with 2,858 participants). There had been attacks on *kolkhoz* property and acts of terror (*terakty*). Members of the Union of the Russian People and members of a church-monarchist group, he alleged, had been involved in stirring up the peasants, while anti-Soviet groups were active in industry. He declared, 'We Bolsheviks, of course, do not idealize the working class as a whole', emphasizing the need for concrete Bolshevik leadership.[21]

In April 1932 food shortages sparked off a series of protests in the textile region of Ivanovo province, neighbouring Moscow province. A major strike, unprecedented since the early 1920s, broke out in Vichuga. On 12 April Kaganovich visited the town. An OGPU detachment firing into the air dispersed the crowds, hundreds were arrested, and the strike movement was quelled. The Central Committee instructed the Ivanovo province party committee to purge its ranks of suspect members. The government took steps to improve food supply to the region.[22] On this visit, he became infuriated when egalitarian-minded local officials refused to take advantage of the privilege of using their own 'special stores' and insisted that their wives and children queue up with everyone else.[23]

On 14 May, in the wake of the strikes, Kaganovich addressed the Moscow city party plenum, outlining the need for change, and stressing the need for responsibilities within the factory to be clearly defined. To strengthen party control, he proposed reducing the total number of cells in the factories and using mainly 'professional' cadres, rather than volunteers.[24] In response to this crisis, Stalin authorized a significant easing of policy. On 20 May 1932 *kolkhoz* sales at market prices were authorized and the right of the peasants to their own plots and livestock was now belatedly recognized.

Kaganovich firmly supported Stalin's hard line on thefts of state property as embodied in the law of 7 August, 1934. On 11 August he delivered a speech to Moscow militiamen on the need to ruthlessly combat thefts of state property and acts of hooliganism as part of a campaign against class enemies and directed at protecting 'revolutionary order'.[25] Addressing the Moscow province and city party conference that month, he took a more moderate line, outlining the role of the party in improving agriculture and in strengthening the *kolkhozy*.[26] It was necessary, he declared, to stimulate rural artisan industries through incentives and tax cuts. The collective farms spent too much on buildings and administration, and not enough on wages. He rejected as nonsensical the views of those who believed that if the peasants had their own plots, this would undermine the collective farms. The Central Committee had decreed against the forcible socialization of livestock. The party should strive simultaneously to strengthen the *kolkhozy* and the individual plots.

In the new socialized sector of agriculture, he revealed, 40 per cent of chairmen of collective farms and brigadiers were between 18 and 21 years of age. He urged more efforts to promote nonparty people and to improve communications between the administration and the collective farm workers. The Central Committee's plans for grain collection should not be mechanically allocated to districts, but should take account of local conditions. The reform of agriculture, he argued, was not a 'neo-NEP as some 'opportunists' suggested. In order to develop markets and to stimulate the flow of goods to the bazaars, a 30-kilometre zone around Moscow was to be freed of state procurement and contracts, except for grain. It was necessary to increase the production of goods of mass consumption for the peasant market.[27]

In his speech to a joint session of the Moscow city and province party committees on 8 October 1932, he again highlighted the need to stimulate trade and to increase the production of goods of mass consumption in order to bring more grain onto the market. The policy of directing consumer goods to the countryside, Kaganovich admitted, had 'offended' the towns. The artisan industry of Moscow province had produced goods worth 400 million rubles per annum before the war. This was now down to 30–40 per cent of the pre-war level. This trend had to be reversed through increased incentives. He blamed the past neglect of this sector on a favourite bugbear, namely, 'leftist' excesses and the underestimation of *kolkhoz* trade.[28]

During the famine crisis of 1932–33 the Moscow region was given privileged treatment, no doubt in part influenced by the disturbances in Ivanovo in early 1932. On 4 July 1933 Kaganovich reported to the Moscow city and province party committees on the success of the spring sowing campaign and on the prospects of turning the province into a producer region. He stressed the important role of the *politotdely* and the Machine Tractor Stations (MTS). The area of collectivized agriculture in Moscow province had increased from 50 to 65 per cent, with the establishment of 2,250 new *kolkhozy*. The sown acreage had increased and mechanization had improved. Rural officials, he argued, should regard individual peasants as 'tomorrow's *kolkhozniki*'; they should avoid exaggerated targets. There should be no repetition of 'Dizzy with Success'.[29]

In September 1933 Kaganovich reported to Stalin a disastrous fall in grain yields in Moscow province caused by torrential rainfall. With the backing of M. A. Chernov, head of the Committee for Grain Procurement, he pleaded for a cut in the province's grain procurement target, which Stalin approved.[30]

As an example of Kaganovich's high-handedness, Roy Medvedev cites his visit, in the autumn of 1933, to Efremov district, Moscow province, to oversee the progress of grain collection and potato harvesting. Officials who resisted the unrealistic targets were abused, dismissed and threatened with imprisonment. Nearly half of the local population of Efremov boarded up their huts and left the district, which had to import grain and potatoes for the next three years.[31]

Despite all this, in 1933, for its achievements in agriculture, Moscow province received the Order of Lenin, while Kaganovich received the same award. In January 1934 Khrushchev claimed that the task set by Kaganovich to transform Moscow province from a consumer to a producer of vegetables and potatoes had been realized.[32] The improvement in the economic situation provided the platform for abolishing bread rationing. In 1934 Malenkov reported to Kaganovich on discontent among the workers of Ivanovo concerning the proposed raising of bread prices. The situation, he claimed, was being exploited by 'counter-revolutionaries' and posed a serious danger which required immediate action.[33]

Industry

While the Moscow party committee, under Uglanov, had concentrated on textiles and light-industrial development in Moscow province, under Kaganovich, the development of machine building, machine tools, chemicals and energy was highlighted.[34] Moscow, like Berlin, had become a major centre for producing electrical equipment.[35] He took a personal interest in the modernization of major works such as Serp i Molot, AMO, Dynamo, Elektrozavod, Vladimir Ilich, Gosnak, Tormoznoi, 24-i works, Krasnyi Bogatyr' and Kauchyk.[36] The Moscow Stalin Motor Works (ZIS), the USSR's largest car producer, was to receive an investment of 474 million rubles during the Second Five-Year Plan.[37] Moscow also became an important centre for the defence industries.[38] Kaganovich assumed responsibility for the rapid conversion of Moscow factories to tank and aircraft production.³⁹ He also promoted the production of aircraft motors at the Frunze works.⁴⁰

The development of the Moscow coal basin was intended to reduce the region's heavy reliance on Donbass coal and to reduce the burden on the railways. In 1934 its output target was raised from 5.5 million tons to 6 million tons.⁴¹ Kaganovich also took the initiative in developing the New Tula (Novotula) metallurgical combine, a works of major defence significance.⁴² He also intervened to improve the quality of production at the Kaganovich Ball Bearing Works.⁴³ Under his direction, the major chemical combines at Bobrikovsky (Stalinogorsk), Voskresensky and Ugresahsky were built.

Light industry was not neglected. Kaganovich attempted to resolve holdups in the textile industry and to promote improvements in the quality of production and to reduce waste.⁴⁴ He reported on low-quality production to the Moscow province conference in September 1933. Despite these interventions, a check of the textile industry in April 1934 revealed that the situation remained largely unchanged.⁴⁵

Moscow constituted the hub of the country's rail network. Under Kaganovich, efforts were undertaken to improve the organization of its operations. He was also closely involved in overseeing the construction of the Moscow-Donbass trunk line, which was the main coal supply line for the capital's industrial and domestic needs.⁴⁶ He promoted the reconstruction of the railway wagon-building works at Kalinin.⁴⁷ He intervened repeatedly in 1932 and 1933 to overcome production problems at the Kolomensky locomotive works. Under his leadership, the electrification of the Moscow suburban rail network began.⁴⁸

The Second Five-Year Plan, as approved by the XVII Party Congress in 1934, assigned a special place to Moscow province as one of the premier economic regions of the country. During the plan period, Moscow province was to receive 10.7 billion (Soviet milliard) rubles of capital investment, 10.9 per cent of a total capital investment of 98.8 billion rubles. Moscow province and the Urals province were the two major recipients of capital investment after the Ukrainian SSR that received 16.8 per cent of total investment. For heavy industry, Moscow was assigned 3.5 billion rubles (9 per cent). This was a compromise figure between Gosplan USSR, which had proposed a figure of 2.6 billion rubles, and Moscow province planning commission had demanded 4 billion rubles.⁴⁹ Moscow province also received the lion's share of investment for light industry, trade, communications, housing and education.⁵⁰

During the Second Five-Year Plan, Moscow province was to further develop its specialization in precise machine building, motor construction, transport machine building, machine tools, instruments and electrotechnology. The capital's scientific-technical expertise was to be placed at the service of the rest of the country.[51] Moscow province, at the end of First Five-Year Plan, was responsible for 40 per cent of the country's light industrial production. This was expected to decline to 28.2 per cent by 1937, notwithstanding an increase of 117 per cent in textile production during the period. Eighty-five per cent of investment was allocated for modernizing and expanding existing enterprises.

The Reconstruction of Moscow

Moscow's reconstruction under Kamenev and Uglanov had proceeded gradually, restricted by economic constraints. From 1929 onward, in response to the competition launched by the Moscow party committee, a series of fantastic schemes for the reconstruction of Moscow was submitted by Russian and international architects: Nikolai Ladovsky's 'dynamic city', German Krasin's 'workers' colonies', the modernist visions of Le Corbusier and Ernst May. Moisei Ginsburg and Leonid Sabsovich advanced proposals for the dissolution of large urban population concentrations, while Kostantin Mel'nikov proposed the creation of a 'green city'.[52]

In 1930 the debate took a new turn. The antiurbanists came under severe attack and were accused of 'Chayanovism.' The Group of Proletarian Architects (VOPRA) denounced the Organization of Modernist Architects (OSA) for its 'utopianism' and 'Westernism'. Three weeks after Kaganovich had taken over as Moscow party secretary, the Central Committee, on 16 May 1930, issued its resolution denouncing Sabsovich and Larin, criticizing 'semi-fantastic' and 'utopian' theories about gaining socialism 'in a single leap' by such means as communal cooking and child rearing or 'the fundamental replanning of existing cities and the construction of new ones at the exclusive expense of the state'. Urban planning had to take account of the state's limited resources when industrialization was the main priority. Moscow's reconstruction was now to be modelled on the experience of other major European capitals.[53] In this, the project of modernization was to a significant degree de-ideologized.

From 1928 to 1933 Moscow city's population grew from 2.3 million to 3.6 million. The Politburo created a commission, including Stalin himself, chaired by Kaganovich to look into the reconstruction of Moscow and other cities. The Central Committee instructed the Moscow soviet to build houses for half a million people in three years.[54] On 28 December 1930 the Moscow party committee adopted its first statement on Moscow's ills: the absence of well-planned urban services, the poor integration of industrial services with industrial construction and inattention to the rising expectations of the capital's population. Kaganovich, in his report to the Central Committee plenum in June 1931 on the reconstruction of the capital, highlighted two major schemes – the construction of the Moscow–Volga canal and the building of the Moscow Metro.[55] Stalin, in his report, endorsed this policy.

Kaganovich reported to the Moscow Soviet in 1931 on the city's transformation. Since 1917 some half a million workers, residents of barracks, dosshouses and cellars had been rehoused in central Moscow in the apartments of the bourgeoisie.[56] The growing population placed great pressure on all public services. He criticized urban development in the capitalist West, and the continuing survival of poverty and poor housing. He had visited Vienna to see how the Austrian Social Democrats had developed their capital and criticized the barrack housing provided by the Social Democratic administration of the city. He emphasized the need to relate the city's development to practical needs; he chided simplistic theoretical formulations which equated different styles of development with particular epochs: petty bourgeois – linear (London); capitalistic – chessboard (New York); feudal – radial (Paris, Moscow).

He insisted that housing development should be based on apartments of two to four rooms in five-storey blocks, with the provision of the necessary services and facilities to hand. He rejected the idea of communal living as something which could be bureaucratically imposed from above. He repudiated any attempt to define narrowly what a 'socialist' city was. Russia's cities, he explained, had become 'socialist' when the Bolshevik government assumed power in 1917. He dismissed as 'nonsense' any suggestion for the 'reduction or self-abolition' of large urban centres. On the contrary, Moscow and other cities had to be brought up 'to the level of the technically advanced cities of Europe'.[57] Urban planning was a matter 'of strictly practical significance, not of abstract theoretical significance'. The planners should remodel historic Moscow, 'build even and correctly interlinked roads, unkink curved and crooked streets and alleys' and demolish its 'tumbledown hovels'.[58]

On 15 June 1931 the Central Committee approved a resolution, based on Kaganovich's report, on developing the urban economy of Moscow and other Soviet cities.[59] The plenum rejected two opposed tendencies – capitalist-style urban gigantomania and schemes for the deurbanization and deindustrialization of the capital. Others, it was alleged, wanted to preserve old Moscow – the Moscow of merchants and priests – and wanted to build a new capital on a new site.[60] The Central Committee instructed the Moscow organizations to prepare a 'scientifically grounded plan' for it as a 'socialist city' and approved its resolution, 'Practical Measures to Improve and Develop the Moscow City Economy'. In July 1932 Kaganovich chaired a meeting of 150 specialists and officials and gave general guidance in line with Stalin's directions 'to proceed first and foremost from the historically established forms of the present city, rebuilding it in accord with the dictates of our epoch'.[61] Priority was given to developing the electric trolley bus system, urban heating through district plants, street lighting, public conveniences, sewage system, roads, bridges, parks and dining facilities and factory canteens.

Addressing the Moscow Soviet in 1931 Kaganovich boasted that in the past five years, 30 million square metres of new housing space had been built in the USSR, an achievement which no bourgeois state in Europe could match. A contemporary British expert on housing noted that in fact, the USSR's performance on this score was far from impressive. The rate of building in Moscow, which was far in excess of that for the USSR as a whole, was well under half the rate of building per capita in the United Kingdom, while the space allowed per family was equivalent to the worst cases of overcrowding in Britain.[62]

During Kaganovich's tenure as party secretary, Moscow's urban landscape was transformed with the building of the vast Moskva hotel, the skyscraper office block of Sovnarkom and Gosplan on Prospekt Marx and the enlargement of the NKVD's Lubyanka headquarters. Street names were relentlessly sovietized. He took a close interest in architecture, became the Politburo's main authority in this field and acted as a patron to architects.[63] In August 1932 he discussed with delegates from the Union of Soviet Architects plans for the reconstruction of Moscow and other cities.[64]

In January 1934, on Kaganovich's initiative, an Academy of Architecture was set up with the task of drafting a plan for the reconstruction of Moscow.[65] He headed the Architectural Planning Commission of the Moscow party committee and Moscow Soviet (Arkhplan). The commission was made up of architects, academics, party and soviet officials and aimed to set the highest standards in architectural and planning work.[66] Arkhplan studied the experience of other countries, especially the reconstruction of Paris by Hausmann. In place of Mosproekt, they had, on Kaganovich's proposal, created special architectural and planning units (*masterskie*) headed by architects. In his speech to the Moscow Soviet plenum in July 1934 Kaganovich spoke of the importance of avoiding 'excesses', a view that Stalin supported.[67]

Moscow was to serve as a model for other Soviet cities. In 1935 Kaganovich instructed Arkhplan that it should strive to relocate factories outside Moscow in order to reduce overcrowding and pollution and to reduce pressure for more housing. In practice, it proved difficult to get industrial trusts to comply and to halt the unplanned building of small factories and workshops within the city.[68]

The first plan was submitted to the Central Committee and Sovnarkom early in 1935. On 10 July 1935 the Central Committee approved the resolution 'Concerning the Master Plan for the Reconstruction of the City of Moscow', co-signed by Stalin and Molotov. The plan envisaged a population of approximately 5 million. The city's territory was expected to more than double, with most of the development being in the southwest, beyond the Lenin Hills. This, according to Khrushchev, was inspired by Kaganovich.[69] In an off-the-record chat with officials, he presented the plan as a 'plan of war'.[70]

The destruction of old Moscow

The reconstruction of Moscow also brought with it very real costs. Under Kaganovich, the destruction of historical monuments in the capital assumed a new scale. Roy Medvedev rightly notes that Stalin had the final say on all major reconstruction plans for Moscow and all proposals to raze historic buildings.[71] Under pressure from the Moscow and all-union authorities, the Academy of Sciences was forced to withdraw protected status from almost all the country's historic monuments which had religious associations.

Stalin insisted on Kropotkinskaya embankment, the site on which stood the cathedral church of Christ the Saviour, for the new Palace of Soviets. The Politburo approved the location.[72] The decision was signed by Stalin, Molotov, Kaganovich, Kalinin and Bulganin.[73] The cathedral was blown up on 5 December 1931, thus removing a central component from the architectural ensemble of central Moscow.[74] The Palace of Soviets, topped with a giant statue of Lenin, a monstrous essay in kitsch, was never built because of the lack of solid foundations. The site was eventually given over to an open-air swimming pool until the cathedral was rebuilt in the 1990s. Kaganovich later argued that he had urged that the Palace of Soviets be built on the Lenin Hills and warned that the demolition of the cathedral would be held against him and would 'call forth a flood of anti-Semitism'.[75]

The famous Sukharev Tower was also destroyed. Kaganovich much later argued that he had initially opposed the decision. Its demolition, he claimed, was necessary to ease traffic flows and was agreed upon after all other options had been explored.[76] In August 1933 architects Igor Grabar', V. I. Zholtovsky and others begged Stalin for it to be spared. Kaganovich asked them to elaborate alternative strategies, but also convoked a meeting of communist architects to call them to arms in the 'raving class struggle' surrounding the issue. Times were such, he protested, that 'we cannot deal with a single decrepit little church without a protest being delivered to us' and the protests were turning Muscovites against the regime.[77]

Before the Revolution, Moscow had 460 Orthodox churches. On 1 January 1930 this was down to 224 and on 1 January 1933, down to about 100.[78] In the Kremlin, the church of the Saviour in the Wood, the most ancient in all Moscow, was demolished in the spring of 1933. Rykov believed that this was because it darkened the windows of the flat that Kaganovich took over in 1932. The Passion Monastery was also destroyed. In July 1934 the Moscow party bureau ordered the destruction of the walls of Kitaigorod (Chinatown), described by the Kaganovich commission as 'a relic of savage and medieval times'. Claims that he advocated the demolition of the Kremlin and St. Basil's are based on unreliable hearsay accounts that reflect the strong animus against him.[79]

When the Iversky Gates and Chapel on Red Square were destroyed, many architects objected, but Kaganovich simply responded, 'My aesthetic conception demands columns of demonstrators from the six districts of Moscow pouring into Red Square simultaneously.'[80] He blamed Khrushchev for destroying much of the capital's architectural patrimony, asserting that he, Kaganovich, had walked the streets of Moscow at night deciding what should be preserved.[81] In fact, however, most of the destruction was done under his reign of revolutionary iconoclasm. Undoubtedly the destruction of ancient and religious monuments provoked widespread and lasting resentment.

Building the Metro

As early as 1900 the Moscow Duma had discussed the question of building a metro system. The issue was revived in 1930 and attracted considerable controversy. Some argued that the money should be spent on expanding other modes of transport in the capital. Gosplan also expressed reservations on account of the high cost involved. Kaganovich claimed that the scheme had been opposed by Rightists and some Leftists.[82] The Politburo discussed the question and unanimously approved the plan. Stalin paid particular attention to the Metro, and Kaganovich, as secretary of Moscow, was an energetic promoter of the project.

In 1931 work began on an experimental sector of the system. In March 1933, at the height of the famine, the Central Committee and Sovnarkom, on a proposal of the Moscow authorities, approved a scheme for 10 interconnecting lines with a length of 80 kilometres.[83] The Second Five-Year Plan draft of January 1934 set a target of investment in Metrostroi of 1.2 billion rubles, with the construction of 36 kilometres of two track lines by 1937.

P. P. Rotert was made director of the project and Y. T. Abakumov, his deputy. Both were mining engineers brought in from the Donbass, together with a large number of miner volunteers.[84] Abakumov was closely associated with Khrushchev. Khrushchev, on Stalin's orders, took charge of the Metro construction project. A disagreement arose regarding the methods of construction, between the German open-trench method

Figure 5. N. S. Khrushchev and L. M. Kaganovich with the builders of the Moscow Metro in 1935

advocated by Rotert, and the English closed-tunnel method, favoured by Khrushchev and Kaganovich. The Politburo opted for the closed-tunnel method.[85] Kaganovich, Khrushchev and Bulganin were closely involved in this work. Kaganovich regularly reported on progress to Stalin and the Politburo. Kaganovich also visited Berlin incognito in order to study the Metro there.[86]

On 29 December 1933 Kaganovich addressed the Moscow Soviet and announced that the party and government had set the seventeenth anniversary of the October Revolution (7 November 1934) as the target date for completing the first phase of the Metro.[87] Moscow factories were required to assign their best engineers and workers to the Metro.

The poet A. I. Bezymensky wrote:

> The Metro you are building
> Fired by Stalin's strength
> Lazar Kaganovich will launch
> On November Seventh.

The date 24 March 1934 was set as the day of an all-Moscow voluntary day of work (*subbotnik*) under the slogan 'All Moscow builds the Metro', with Kaganovich hard at work with a shovel. However, after the shafts had been inspected in April by Molotov, Khrushchev and Bulganin, the timetable was altered. On a report from Kaganovich, the Moscow Soviet set the completion date at 16 July 1934.[88]

Khrushchev, whom Kaganovich placed in charge of Metro construction, later recounted:

> At the time, I still held Lazar Moiseyevich in high esteem. There was no question about his devotion to the Party and to the cause. In the course of chopping firewood, he sent a lot of chips flying, as they say, but he never flagged in strength or energy. He was as stubborn as he was devoted.[89]

A former reporter for the newspaper *Vechernaya Moskva*, A. V. Khrabovitsky, recalled: 'I always saw Khrushchev together with Kaganovich. Kaganovich was the active, powerful one, whereas all I ever heard Khrushchev saying was 'Yes, Lazar Moiseyevich', 'Right, Lazar Moiseyevich.'"[90] According to Abakumov, Kaganovich chose the location of the subway lines and plotted the tunnellers every move: 'He watched over how we put through the shafts, drifts...vaults and walls and constantly visited us and gave us practical instructions on how to work.'[91]

The idea of a collective literary works was then in vogue, with the work on the Belomor canal, edited by Gorky, S. G. Firin and I. L. Averbakh providing the model. Gorky also urged Kaganovich to promote a work on the building of the Metro, and in 1935 *Rasskazy stroitelei metro* was published.

The Moscow–Volga canal

Water supply was one of the main concerns of Moscow city leaders, as growing consumption by industry and domestic users created frequent water shortages and cuts.[92] A Politburo commission considered the matter.[93] On 15 June 1931 the Central Committee plenum, on a report by Kaganovich, proposed to double Moscow's water supply by 1935 by linking the Moskva River with the upper reaches of the Volga.[94]

The scheme was opposed by the Commissariat of Water Transport, while Gosplan was unenthusiastic.[95] Nevertheless, in March 1932 STO, chaired by Molotov, included the canal in the category of national 'shock-work'.[96] The Moscow–Volga canal, longer than the Panama Canal, was the biggest river canal scheme in the world, and was one of the prestige projects of the Second Five-Year Plan.[97] Its cost was originally estimated at 700 million rubles. Kaganovich rejected accusations that it was an unnecessary luxury, stressing the need to guarantee the city's future water supply needs.[98]

On 1 June 1932 Sovnarkom adopted the Dmitrov plan for the canal, 127 kilometres long, the least expensive, and set the completion date as November 1934.[99] Academician S. Ya. Zhuk played an important part in developing the project.[100] It was nominally financed by the Moscow Soviet, but this was a project of national significance with Gosplan and NKTyazhprom closely involved. Construction work began in September 1932. On 5 December the Politburo finally approved the Kaganovich commission's proposal for the course of the canal. It was to be completed by the end of 1935, with STO required to provide 400 million rubles in 1934.[101] Two accounts claim that the scheme was initiated by Stalin.[102] Any project of this scale required Stalin's approval. Kaganovich's role, however, was central.

The Moscow–Volga canal was one of the major project undertaken employing forced labour. In his memoirs, Kaganovich claims that the Moscow party committee was initially reluctant to use such labour.[103] At the end of 1932 the construction was entrusted to OGPU.[104] The Moskanalstroi trust was set up to organize the work. It was headed by L. I. Kogan, who had previously headed the Baltic–White Sea canal (Belomor) project. In 1933, with the completion of the canal, a large number of managers, technicians and forced labourers were transferred to the new project.[105] The Moscow–Volga canal project was better managed than the Belomor canal, with a lower death rate amongst the forced labourers.

The work was undertaken jointly by the Moscow party committee and NKVD, which provided the labour. Some 196,000 prisoners from the Dmitrov camp, headed by S. G. Firin, were employed on this project.[106] Already in April 1934, Khrushchev reported to Kaganovich that at a meeting of the Politburo, Kuibyshev, head of Gosplan, had proposed to delay its completion for financial reasons. Khrushchev and Bulganin had objected. Stalin also strongly opposed any delay on the grounds that he thought it inexpedient to retain a large number of convict labourers in Moscow province over an extended period.[107]

The Moscow Party Conference of January 1934

As head of the Moscow party organization, Kaganovich enjoyed great publicity, but the image he cultivated was that of the unassuming, businesslike executive. Photographs and reports of him in the Moscow press were restrained and he was always depicted as one of the collective leadership of the city party organization. Even critics of the Stalinist regime noted that the cult surrounding him was relatively modest.[108]

The joint IV Moscow province and third city party conference met from 16 to 24 January 1934, ahead of the XVII Party Congress and in a curious way, upstaging the congress.[109] In his report, Kaganovich argued that the USSR would turn itself, during the second *piatiletka*, into the most technically advanced state in Europe.'[110] In the *kolkhozy*, the challenge of the class enemy had been thwarted. He stressed Stalin's close involvement in all aspects of the city's urban economy and plans for the reconstruction of the capital.[111]

Kaganovich anticipated an intensification of the class struggle in the country during the Second Five-Year Plan. The party was like an army going into battle, where the commander had to be resolute, able to choose the right tactics and able to inspire his troops.[112] Moscow had provided many of the activists for the *politotdely* of MTS, railways and construction organizations.[113] There was scarcely a district, party cell, enterprise or mine, it seemed, where his influence had not been directly felt.

Peters reported that the Moscow party Control Commission had disciplined 2,000 members for 'Right' opportunist charges during the grain collection campaign in 1932. Consequently, in 1933–34 only 10.4 per cent of members of the Moscow province party were purged; this was lower than for any other province except Leningrad.[114] In 1933 Shlyapnikov and Medvedev, the leaders of the Workers Opposition of 1921, were finally expelled from the Moscow party.[115] Sokolnikov recanted his past association with the Zinoviev-Kamenev opposition of 1925. He was loudly barracked by the delegates.[116] Kaganovich scathingly denounced his old mentor, charging him with capitulating before the pressure of the kulaks and the world bourgeoisie.[117]

One delegate noted Moscow had become the premier educational centre for the country and that the student body of Moscow, which in the past had sided with the Trotskyists and the Right had become strongly loyalist.[118] The Moscow party committee and Kaganovich were praised for their efforts to improve the schools, stabilizing the curriculum and improving the supply of books.[119] In 1934 the Academy of Sciences was moved from Leningrad to Moscow.

The conference witnessed a remarkable outpouring of praise of Kaganovich. He was addressed in various terms, as a 'talented leader and organizer', an 'intellectual giant', an outstanding orator and theoretician, the 'best comrade-in-arms of comrade Stalin', 'Stalin's best assistant', 'our beloved helmsman', the exponent of the 'Leninist-Stalinist' style of leadership, a model of 'sagacious leadership', 'our best leader, best Stalinist', 'our beloved leader of the Moscow Bolsheviks.'[120] He had ideologically united the Moscow party organization around the Leninist Central Committee and comrade Stalin, establishing the monolithic and steel-like unity of the Moscow organization under the banner of Lenin-Stalin.[121]

Bulganin and Yenukidze praised Kaganovich's 'searching criticism' of projects and his mastery of architectural and technical matters.[122] Kaganovich modestly disclaimed any right to be an expert on the urban economy.[123] The two leading OGPU officials responsible for the Moscow–Volga canal, L. I. Kogan and M. D. Berman, paid effusive praise to Kaganovich's drive and enthusiasm in overseeing the project and his role in solving practical problems.[124] A. A. Sol'ts noted that Kaganovich had called for more attention to be paid to the re-education of convicts, so that ordinary criminals should receive more favourable treatment than political offenders.[125]

Khrushchev paid tribute to Kaganovich's role in resolving basic questions of Metro construction.[126] Matusov, of Metrostroi, praised the work of Kaganovich, Khrushchev and Bulganin in overseeing the construction work. Kaganovich involved himself in resolving technical problems in meetings with specialists and workers and undertook nighttime inspection tours of the underground shafts when his work in the Central Committee and the Moscow party committee was over.[127] I. A. Likhachev, the director of the giant Stalin Motor Works and one of the leading industrial managers in the USSR, praised Kaganovich's part in the building of the works, ensuring its completion on time.[128] Artyunyants, head of the construction of the Stalinogorsk chemical combine, praised Kaganovich's intervention in rescuing the project, which, after an investment of 40 million rubles, was nearly abandoned because of inadequate water supply.[129]

R. P. Eideman, head of Osoaviakhim, reported that Kaganovich had ordered that by the end of the year, 500,000 workers in Moscow should be trained in shooting, and 100,000 trained as Voroshilov riflemen (marksmen). In Moscow, flying, gliding and parachute jumping became mass sports, promoted for their defence role and their part in developing patriotic sentiments.[130] An elderly female delegate recounted how she had placed the portraits of Stalin and Kaganovich near the icon in her home.[131] Several speakers highlighted Kaganovich's efforts to improve workers' living conditions, to get rid of barracks and to improve supplies. Other delegates echoed Kaganovich's warnings regarding the need to ideologically combat German Nazism and its racist theories.[132] The Byelorussian party congress sent their greetings to Kaganovich, and reported that to commemorate his work in Gomel' and Mogiliev in 1917, a subscription had been organized to build a squadron of fighter planes which would bear his name.[133]

While this chorus of praise is stylized and exaggerated, it is difficult to avoid the conclusion that Kaganovich was admired as a forceful and effective administrator. It was a signal from the capital's leaders that with Stalin seriously compromised by the famine, the strengthening of other second-rank leaders might be welcomed. For Kaganovich, such adulation might well have been unwelcome, since such a manifestation would not have passed the paranoid Stalin unnoticed.

Demoted to Economic Administration

The reception that Kaganovich received at the Moscow party conference appears to have irritated Stalin. In the following year he took steps to clip his deputies wings. The first step in 1934, was the appointment of Khrushchev in place of Kaganovich as first secretary of Moscow city party organisation. In February 1935 Kaganovich was appointed head of the People's Commissariat of Transport (NKPS). He now also lost the post of first secretary of the Moscow province party committee to Khrushchev. As a form of compensation, the Politburo ruled, however, that Kaganovich should retain an oversight role over Moscow.[134] At this time he also lost his post as chairman of the Commission of Party Control to his deputy Ezhov. Within the Secretariat his influence was eroded by the rise of Zhdanov, who had succeeded Kirov as Leningrad party boss.

Already in 1935 we see the emergence of a younger cohort of Stalinist leaders. Khrushchev was now elected a candidate member of the Politburo. William Taubman in his biography of Khrushchev refers to him as 'Stalin's pet'.[135] Stalin preferred Khrushchev as Moscow party boss, someone less experienced, more compliant and lacking political weight. Khrushchev's Trotskyist past made him vulnerable and thus easily pressured. This was a snub to Kaganovich. The promotion of his deputy over his head, a man more intellectually limited and administratively less capable than himself, must have been galling. With Khrushchev in charge of Moscow and Zhdanov in charge of Leningrad, Stalin must have calculated that he had strengthened his grip on the two capitals.

These moves were calculated steps to downgrade Kaganovich and to divert him from party work into economic administration. As head of NKPS he was charged with the major task of sorting out the railways. He retained some influence over Moscow, and reaped the credit for what he had achieved there.

On 14 May 1935 to a great fanfare of celebration the Moscow Metro was opened, a 12 kilometre line linking Sokol'niki, Okhotnyi ryad and Gorky Park.[136] Kaganovich delivered the main speech, 'The Victory of the Metropoliten – The Victory of Socialism.' The speech was issued in a finely produced, extensively illustrated, commemorative booklet.[137] He struck a strongly patriotic theme, acknowledged the contribution of foreign specialists, but stressed that the Metro had been built with Soviet equipment and by Soviet workers and specialists. It had cost 700 million rubles. The Moscow Metro was more comfortable than any capitalist system; it raised people's spirits, so that Moscow workers felt 'as though they are in a palace shining with...the light of advancing all-victorious socialism'. He rhapsodized on how art and architecture had been brought together to create this marvel, which gave the lie to the bourgeois calumnies that communists were uncultured barbarians intent on transforming society into a barracks and destroying individuality. They were striving to build a new order: 'We struggle for a new culture, for new labour, for a real radiant beautiful life for all humanity.' In recognition of its role, the Moscow organization of the Komsomol was awarded the Order of Lenin. Kaganovich paid fulsome tribute to Stalin, 'the continuer of genius of Marx, Engels and Lenin'.[138] Newsreels of Stalin's address on the opening of the Moscow Metro were viewed in the Kremlin cinema.[139]

Kaganovich had proposed that the Metro be named in Stalin's honour. However, Stalin, in a letter to the Moscow party committee, insisted that it be named after Kaganovich in recognition of his contribution to the project. On 13 May 1935 the Central Executive Committee of the USSR declared, 'In accordance with the wishes of the builders of the Metropoliten and the Moscow party and Soviet organizations, to assign to the Moscow Metropoliten the name comrade KAGANOVICH, L. M.'[140] This was Kaganovich's great moment. However, Stalin's speech on the opening of the Metro signally failed to mention Kaganovich's contribution, a clear sign of disfavour.[141] The naming of the Metro in his honour might be seen as some compensation for his loss of the post of Moscow party secretary The Moscow Metro retained his name until 1955, when it was renamed in honour of Lenin.

In 1935 and 1936 the Politburo regularly discussed the Moscow–Volga canal's progress with its completion date having been repeatedly delayed.[142] In June 1936 Stalin, Ordzhonikidze, Kaganovich and Yagoda visited the project.[143] In June 1937 the Politburo approved a resolution on the completion of the project, which was named the Moscow Canal.[144] The canal turned Moscow into a major inland port connected to the Black, Caspian, Baltic and White seas. The river station of Rechnoi Vokzal provided the capital with new transport links and recreational facilities.

In November 1935 the double-headed eagles were taken down off the Kremlin towers and replaced by the red stars. The matter was decided between Kaganovich and Stalin, who approved the design of the stars. Their decision was then confirmed by the Politburo and published as a joint Central Committee–Sovnarkom USSR resolution.[145]

Conclusion

Kaganovich's period as head of the Moscow party organization must, by the terms of the Stalinist system, be judged a resounding success. The party organization was turned into a solid bastion of the Stalinist regime. The crisis in agriculture in 1930 was overcome so that Moscow province in 1933 was hailed as the great success story of Soviet agriculture. Moscow was also transformed into one of the country's premier industrial regions. By the end of the 1930s Moscow city and province accounted for about one-fifth of all industrial workers and about a quarter of all industrial production of the USSR. The two giant projects, the Metro and the Moscow–Volga canal, showcased Soviet socialism in action. These examples of the positive achievements of the Soviet regime sustained a new mood of optimism after the trauma of collectivization and dekulakization and offered the hope for a more stable course of future development.

Whilst Kaganovich was one of the arch-opponents of the visionaries of urban planning, he displayed a much greater sense of realism regarding the priorities of urban development in a situation of restricted resources than either the hyper-urbanists or the de-urbanists. But reconstruction also had its negative side, most visibly in the destruction of the capital's ancient monument. The absurd Palace of Soviets was never built. The investment poured into housing, transport and the retail sector barely kept pace with the demands of population growth. In many ways, the reconstruction of the capital reflected the breakneck development of the rest of the country, with its own lags and imbalances. Kaganovich's energetic role in initiating and implementing these changes was central, but without Stalin's support, none of these changes would have been possible.

Kaganovich's leadership of Moscow reveals that within limits, Stalin delegated considerable powers to his deputies. He clearly revelled in the work of reconstructing the capital and had found an outlet for his great energies. He had a talent for promoting able people, and many of those involved in the administration of Moscow went on to make careers at the highest level of state. He cultivated a close working relationship with managers, engineers, architects and planners. The flourishing cult around him suggests that he had a real popular following among the capital's administrative elite. However, Stalin saw his deputy's arrogation of power and his popularity as Moscow party boss as a threat. Twelve months after his canonization by the Moscow party conference in January 1934, Kaganovich was transferred to other duties. This episode well illustrates Stalin's distrustfulness, his jealousy of those who became too popular and his lack of magnanimity.

Chapter 9

BOSS OF RAIL TRANSPORT, 1935–1937

In February 1935 Kaganovich was appointed head of the People's Commissariat of Ways of Communications (NKPS) – the ministry that had charge of the rail transport system.[1] His role in the central party apparatus, the Orgburo and Secretariat was reduced, and he lost the leadership of the Moscow party organization. He was diverted from party work, where he had made his reputation, into economic management, where he had little experience. They railways were the Achilles heel of the Soviet system, and in 1930–33 they had experienced an acute crisis. The railways were the main mode of transport in the USSR, carrying some 80 per cent of all freight. They were also vital for the defence of the country. After the Japanese invasion of Manchuria in 1931 and the rise of Hitler to power in 1933, the Soviet leadership feared the prospect of war in the East and in the West. The railways were a major consumer of the products of heavy industry, and relations between NKPS and Vesenkha/NKTyazhprom were plagued by conflict. Kaganovich's career in this period casts important light on the internal debates of the Stalinist leadership with regard to economic policy.

The Soviet economy in 1934–36 experienced a stable period of development, what Naum Jazny referred to as 'the three good years'. It marked an interlude between the famine and the Great Terror. Notwithstanding the consolidation of Stalin's dictatorial power as party leader, the Soviet political regime retained some of the characteristics of a polycratic system. The NKVD remained a powerful agency, which headed by Genrich Yagoda was not entirely under Stalin's control. The military, under Marshall Mikhail Tukhachevsky, remained a force in its own right. Powerful commissariats, notably NKTyazhprom and NKPS, retained considerable power. Despite the huge investment made in the economy, economic performance was characterized by high levels of waste, inefficiency, imbalances and poor coordination between sectors.

Background, 1933–1934

From 1929 onward, the rail transport system, subject to massive underinvestment, unsuccessfully strove to cope with the huge growth of freight. Successive heads of NKPS had come to grief – Yan Rudzutak, M. L. Rukhimovich and A. A. Andreev. Kaganovich, in his capacity as party secretary, had been involved in overseeing the transport system. On 20 March 1933 the Politburo set up a commission, headed by Kaganovich, for the creation of *politotdely* on the railways.[2] On 10 July a Political Administration of NKPS was set up to oversee the *politotdely* on the 22 lines that made up the rail network.[3] Many of the heads of the *politotdely* were former officials of the Cheka, the Red Army and the Central Committee apparatus.[4] The railways became the most militarized sector of the economy.

On 18 August 1933 a special Politburo commission on railway transport was established, made up of Molotov (chair), Stalin, Kaganovich (deputy chair), Voroshilov, Andreev (head of NKPS), Ordzhonikidze and Blagonravov.[5] The work of the railways regularly found its place in Kaganovich's letters to Stalin. Kaganovich assumed a leading role in the work of the commission, with almost half of his time being devoted at one stage to the work of the railways.

At the XVII Party Congress in 1934 NKPS and its narkom, Andreev, were pilloried by Stalin, Voroshilov, Rudzutak, Kaganovich, Molotov, Kuibyshev and a host of other figures.[6] On 14 February the Politburo confirmed the composition of the powerful Central Committee–Sovnarkom Transport Commission. Kaganovich, who also headed the Central Committee's Transport Section since 1932, was made chairman.[7] The commission members were Stalin, Molotov, Andreev, Ordzhonikidze, Voroshilov and Blagonravov, with S. Gaister as secretary.[8] The composition of the Commission underlined its high status, and was almost the Politburo in another guise.[9]

The Commission imposed very tight control over NKPS. In March 1934 two joint Sovnarkom–Central Committee resolutions dealt with the problems of freight traffic, especially on the main coal carrying Donetsk line.[10] The commission employed Central Committee–Sovnarkom brigades to carry out investigations on individual lines.[11] It heard reports from line directors and heads of *politotdely* on line performances. It received information on the accident rate, reports on specific accidents with dispositions from the Central Committee Transport Section,[12] and reports on the monthly plans and performance of the individual lines.

Kaganovich also headed the Commission of Party Control (CPC), established by the XVII Party Congress, which also closely supervised NKPS. N. N. Zimin, who was transferred from NKPS's Political Administration, headed CPC's railway transport group.[13] In July, Zimin took over as chairman of the Sovnarkom–Central Committee's Transport Section.[14]

In 1933 and 1934, under Andreev, severe measures of repression were applied to train drivers, signalmen, and track workers as a result of the spiralling accident rate. Many cases were brought before the courts, and a great number of death sentences were passed. As a result, skilled personnel fled from the railways into less hazardous occupations.

Intense pressure was applied to NKPS to improve its efficiency. This encountered strong internal resistance. At the All-Union Dispatcher Conference in December strong opposition was voiced against attempts to force up the targets for efficiency.[15] It pronounced that the existing commercial speeds of freight trains of 14 kilometres per hour were a maximum. Kaganovich, in 1937, branded it a 'conference of wreckers', influenced by S. K. Kudrevatov, head of the Scientific Technical Research Institute of Operations and others.[16]

On 17 November the Central Executive Committee and Sovnarkom approved the Second Five-Year Plan, which set investment in the railways at 18.7 milliard rubles in order to overcome past neglect and to 'put the Soviet railways on a par with the best lines of the most advanced capitalist countries'.[17] On 25 December the Politburo raised the loading target for freight wagons to 80,000 (two-axle equivalents) for 1935, compared to a target of 45,000 in the Second Five-Year Plan.[18]

In 1934 the railways achieved the most dramatic improvement in performance since 1930; nevertheless, at the end of the year, 15 million tons of freight remained unshipped.[19] The Central Committee–Sovnarkom Commission on Transport in December 1934 approved an investment on the railways in 1935 of 4,041 million rubles, compared to a planned investment in 1934 of 3,569 million rubles.[20] It blasted a hole in the Second Five-Year Plan, which Gosplan and Sovnarkom had laboured over for so long and which had been approved only one month before. It set a target for freight for 1935 of 358 million tons, an increase of 13 per cent compared to 1934.[21] These, Kuibyshev, chairman of Gosplan, insisted, were minimum targets, the realization of which required strict 'Bolshevik methods of work'.[22]

Kaganovich as Narkom of NKPS

Stalin, who had relied heavily on Kaganovich during the crises years of 1932–33, decided to bring his deputy to heel. The crisis on the railways provided him with his opportunity. On 28 February 1935 Kaganovich, on Stalin's authorization, was appointed head of NKPS in place of Andreev.[23] He lost the post of party secretary of Moscow province to Khrushchev, and he surrendered the chairmanship of the Commission of Party Control (CPC) to his deputy, Nikolai Yezhov.[24] On 3 March he was appointed a member of STO.[25] It is difficult not to see this as a demotion. The Moscow evening paper which reported his assignment to NKPS carried an unusually grim-faced photograph of Kaganovich.[26]

This also provided an opportunity for a major shake-up in the staffing of the central party bodies. On 10 March Andreev was given charge of the Orgburo, the Central Committee's sectors for Industry and Transport and the Department of Administrative Affairs. He had been humiliated by Kaganovich's constant attacks on NKPS. Persistent rumours refer to the deep animosity between the two.[27] Yezhov was appointed as Andreev's deputy and took over as head of the Department of Leading Party Organs.[28] In 1935 he carried out the verification of party documents, which in practice became a party purge. Kaganovich lost a key post to his subordinate, Yezhov, who began to cultivate close links with Stalin and began promoting the CPC as a rival to the NKVD.[29] Andrei Zhdanov, Leningrad party secretary, was also appointed to the central party Secretariat.[30]

NKPS now had a powerful advocate in the Politburo, gaining its most powerful leader since the days of Dzerzhinsky and Trotsky. Stalin had evidently decided to clip Kaganovich's wings and to sideline him into economic work. On his transfer to NKPS, meetings of the engineers, technicians and architects of Metrostroi sent their best wishes for his success in his new post, with fulsome praise of his achievements as head of the Metro project.[31] *Pravda* and *Izvestiya* hailed the appointment of the 'iron narkom'. Meetings of railway workers sent greetings to the 'iron commander', and welcomed the party's close interest in their work.[32]

Kaganovich had no previous experience of railway administration. But he took over at NKPS at a propitious time when new investment was already committed. British diplomatic reports in 1935, repeating current gossip in Moscow, saw this as a double-edged appointment:

> It has been suggested that M. Stalin would not be altogether displeased if M. Kaganovich were to fail; there have been rumours to the effect that M. Kaganovich's increasing prominence has aroused some jealousy in the highest quarters.[33]

The oppositionist press – the Trotskyist *Bulletin' Oppositsii* and the Menshevik *Sotsialisticheskii vestnik* – speculated on Kaganovich as a possible heir to Stalin. In Kaganovich's personal file, a copy of an article on him from the *Christian Science Monitor* of 1 May 1935 entitled 'Is He Driving for Supreme Power in Russia?' is preserved, with a Russian language translation.[34] Nevertheless, in the November celebrations of 1935, as in the previous year, his portrait was second only to those of Stalin in prominence.[35] If Kaganovich felt his transfer to NKPS was a slight, at still only 41 years of age he must have felt that he could afford to bide his time. What is significant is that even an ultraloyalist like Kaganovich could fall under the *vozhd*'s suspicion.

As head of NKPS, Kaganovich had a direct line of communication to Stalin. But NKPS was under intense pressure from Sovnarkom (Molotov), Gosplan (Mezhlauk) and NKFin (Grin'ko) to improve performance and to check the growth of investment. NKPS's relations with NKTyazhprom, which had been very strained, improved dramatically, based on the close bond between Kaganovich and Ordzhonikidze. Molotov protested that Kaganovich and Ordzhonikidze preferred to take issues of contention to the Politburo for resolution.

Kaganovich's appointment invested NKPS with new political significance. He was assisted by four deputy narkoms – G. I. Blagonravov, A. M. Postnikov, Ya. A. Lifshits and Zimin.[36] External supervision of NKPS via the Commission of Party Control (CPC) and the Commission of Soviet Control (CSC), which had been such an irritant to Andreev, diminished. In NKPS, Kaganovich tightened up the commissariat's system of internal control. Zimin took over as head of NKPS's Political Administration.[37] NKPS's links with the NKVD were reinforced. V. A. Kishkin, who had headed the NKVD's Transport Department, was appointed head of NKPS's Sector of Control.[38] A. M. Shanin, a friend of Yagoda's, was appointed head of the NKVD's Transport Department.[39]

Addressing a meeting of leading trade unionists in April, Kaganovich emphasized the role of the union in improving transport. He again condemned the excessive use of the courts but urged greater discipline.[40] In April, the Central Committee–Sovnarkom Commission on Transport was reorganized. Kaganovich remained a member, but Molotov replaced him as chairman.[41]

The Development of Rail Policy, 1935

As head of NKPS, Kaganovich was allowed some latitude in shaping policy, but he was under intense pressure to raise efficiency.[42] He brought his flamboyant and energetic style of leadership to NKPS, identifying himself with the commissariat, appearing at public gatherings dressed in railway uniform. On the Soviet rail network, a cult developed around him. The Soviet historian G. A. Kumanev recalls how in the 1930s, large portraits of Kaganovich alongside smaller portraits of Stalin were displayed even in remote railway stations.[43]

Kaganovich's managerial style was interventionist, maintaining close links with line directors via conferences, telegrams and the telephone. He quickly built up a detailed knowledge of the operations of each line network and of their personnel. His chief technical adviser was Professor V. N. Obraztsov. His two key priorities were to improve the operational efficiency of the railways and to reduce accidents.[44]

On 19 March 1935 Kaganovich issued a new order on the struggle with accidents. This revealed that in 1934, there had been 62,000 accidents and wrecks. Hundreds of people had been killed and thousands injured. The direct material loss amounted to 60 million rubles. This was a 'shameful' and 'disgraceful' state of affairs.[45] Henceforth, he insisted, line directors would be held personally accountable for the accident rate on their lines.[46]

From 1 to 5 April a meeting of NKPS employees was convened in Moscow, attended by Stalin, Kaganovich, Molotov, Ordzhonikidze, Voroshilov, Mikoyan, Andreev, Chubar' and Yezhov. It discussed the fight against accidents.[47] It also addressed the question of speeding up the turnaround time for freight wagons and capital construction work for 1935. A number of technical commissions were set up to work out practical proposals in each of these areas.[48]

In April and May the Central Committee–Sovnarkom Commission on Transport approved a whole series of resolutions on the operative work of the railways, construction work, financial planning and technical supplies.[49] In May it appears the Commission was wound up, ending the system of direct party and government oversight over the railways.

Kaganovich's arrival at NKPS brought a sustained attempt to improve efficiency. In this, he was pitched into a major confrontation with leading administrators and specialists, who argued that large scale investment was required if the railways were to accomplish the new tasks laid on them. Already in February a Politburo commission, headed by Kaganovich, fixed a daily loading target of 60,230 wagons for NKPS in March, compared to 55,700 wagons for 1935.[50] Whilst NKPS's Operational Administration and its Scientific Technical Research Institute of Operations insisted that a daily loading of 55,000–58,000 wagons was a maximum limit, B. Isaev, deputy chairman of NKPS's Scientific Technical Council, suggested that a daily loading of 66,000 wagons was quite feasible.[51]

In two speeches to railway officials and *politotdel* workers in April Kaganovich backed the radical specialists. He raised the loading target for the third and fourth quarter to 67,000 wagons, a target which was then approved by the Politburo.[52] He rounded on the advocates of the 'limit', arguing that the Soviet railways still lagged behind those of the United States and Germany in terms of efficiency. He strongly criticized the excessive and counterproductive use of the courts in dealing with infractions of rules and regulations.[53] According to Kaganovich, this target met strong opposition and only on 1 May, when a loading of 75,934 wagons was attained, was this resistance overcome.[54]

On 14 April Kaganovich signed an NKPS order which condemned the Scientific Technical Research Institute for Operations and the section of the Eastern line of the NKPS's Operational Administration for breaching party and government policy. The leadership and many of the leading specialists were dismissed and denounced.⁵⁵ A further NKPS order on 15 April censured NKPS's Operational Administration and its Scientific Technical Research Institute and called for an end to 'blatant and criminal breaches of state discipline'.⁵⁶

An article in *Pravda* on 11 May by 'Transportnik' (probably Stalin himself) denounced NKPS's Scientific Technical Research Institute of Operations as one of the bastions of the antistate theory of the 'limit'. NKPS's Central Operational Administration's journal, *Eksploitatsiya zheleznykh dorog* and other journals were under their control. The specialists were accused of 'pseudoscientific balderdash'.⁵⁷ At the end of June two new scientific research institutes were created, the Scientific Research Institute of Railway Transport, headed by Obraztsov, and the Scientific Research Institute of Track and Construction, headed by A. A. Lazarevsky.⁵⁸ These institutions were charged with instilling 'revolutionary spirit' into scientific work on transport.⁵⁹

Many railway officials considered NKPS's orders on speeding up the turnaround time for freight wagons and reducing the accident rate to be mutually incompatible. Gosplan's journal, *Planovoe khozyaistvo*, condemned the 'ferocious opposition' of 'reactionary elements' to these two measures which, it claimed, were not incompatible but mutually dependent. NKPS had to 'rout' the 'conservative and bureaucratic elements' that sought to 'sabotage' the improvement of the railways.⁶⁰ New timetables were introduced on 1 June, but met opposition from the Operational Administration, which claimed that passenger transport had been sacrificed to the needs of freight transport.⁶¹

Kaganovich, in NKPS, relaxed Andreev's regime of repression. This seemingly enjoyed Stalin's support. Addressing Red Army graduates on 4 May Stalin acknowledged the improvement in the transport system. Having overcome the dearth of technology, it was now necessary to 'master the technology'; he issued his famous slogan that 'cadres decide everything', but argued that it was also necessary to show a respectful attitude to workers.⁶²

The year 1935 marked a breathing space, a period in which repression was relaxed and in which Stalin cultivated a more benign image as the person dispensing awards for good workers, as the man who had made the concession on the private plot and the cow in 1932, not the man who had presided over the famine. Attempts to humanize the *vozhd'* were reflected in his appearances with representatives of collective farm workers and members of national minorities. Stalin at this time claimed an improvement in the material conditions of the working class: 'Life has improved, comrades. Life has become more joyous'.⁶³

But below the surface a more ominous trend was evident. This was given its clearest expression by Yezhov's report to the Central Committee early in June 1935. The report dealt with the case of Yenukidze, but was developed into an expose of so-called 'terrorist' Trotskyist and other groups active in the central governmental apparatus, the military and in the Kremlin itself. These groups, Yezhov claimed, set as their aim the assassination of Stalin and other leading figures. They were directly connected to the conspirators behind the murder of Kirov. Lev Kamenev and his brother-in-law, N. A. Rosenfeld, were identified as leading figures in this conspiracy.[64] Twelve months later, this became the central narrative of the Great Terror.

In a lengthy report to a meeting of railway employees in July Kaganovich proposed that by 1 October, freight trains should attain the technical speed of 27 kilometres per hour and a commercial speed of 19.4 kilometres per hour, with an average daily run for locomotives of 253 kilometres. The utilization of locomotives was to be improved by 'forcing the boilers' and increasing their hours of operation. These targets, he insisted, could be attained without increasing the accident rate: all that was needed was a change of attitude amongst railway specialists, to 'reconstruct people's brains'.[65] NKPS, he argued, still lacked sufficient trained technicians and engineers. In 1935, NKPS was to receive a further 5,000 engineers from its own *vtuzy*. Kaganovich highlighted the damaging effect which repression in the past had had on NKPS's cadres, creating a state of 'psychological trauma' among some workers. He promised a more solicitous approach to cadres, but warned that those who opposed NKPS's policies would be dealt with ruthlessly: 'This is not an era of rotten liberalism on railway transport, but an era of the most resolute Leninist-Stalinist Bolshevism.'[66]

On 30 July, in recognition of NKPS's achievements, a grand reception was held in the Kremlin for 400 railway workers. It was attended by Stalin, Kaganovich, Ordzhonikidze, Voroshilov and other prominent figures. Kaganovich delivered another extravagant encomium to the *vozhd'* as the 'first engine driver of the Soviet Union', the 'great locomotive driver of history'. He attributed NKPS's success to the attention which the Central Committee and Stalin personally had devoted to it.[67]

In a short address, Stalin demanded that the daily loading target for the railways be raised to 75,000–80,000 wagons.[68] Not to be outdone, Kaganovich pledged that NKPS would attain a daily loading of 80,000 wagons as soon as possible. Additional provision had to be made for repair and maintenance. In July he issued an order for the construction of 200 new wagon repair points at a cost of 70 million rubles, to be completed by the end of the year.[69] He later credited Stalin with this initiative.[70]

On 7 August NKPS issued two orders based on joint Sovnarkom–Central Committee resolutions. The first (No.183/Ts) concerned increasing the speed of locomotives and became a bitter bone of contention between Kaganovich and his critics in NKPS.[71] The second order approved large pay increases for railway workers, the largest increases being awarded to locomotive drivers, with substantial bonuses being offered for those drivers who exceeded the norms for the distances travelled and for time saved.[72]

The Mobilization of the Railway Workers

Under pressure from Sovnarkom and Gosplan to ensure more effective use of investment, NKTyazhProm and NKPS began promoting methods to raise labour efficiency. The initiative originated with Ordzhonikidze of NKTyazhprom and Kaganovich at NKPS, who appear to have worked in concert in promoting the drive. The Donetsk region, headed by its party secretary S. A. Sarkis, was to be the proving ground. Stalin only sanctioned these initiatives when they were already well developed in the autumn of 1935.[73]

In the summer of 1935 the Donetsk province committee began discussions of how to mobilize the internal resources of the Donetsk line. On 1 July locomotive driver P. F. Krivonos increased the average operational speed of his train from 24 to nearly 32 kilometres per hour.[74] On 30–31 August, A. Stakhanov set his record in the coal industry. By September there were 700 locomotive drivers of the Donetsk line involved in the campaign. NKPS began promoting the Krivonos movement as a national campaign, just as NKTyazhprom promoted Stakhanovism in industry.

The Stakhanovite/Krivonosovite movements grew out of the socialist emulation and shock-work campaigns of the First Five-Year Plan. But they were now stimulated by substantial wage incentives and bonuses. On 6 September highly publicized rallies of shock-workers were held throughout the country to mobilize support behind the autumn/winter preparations. Kaganovich's speech to 35,000 Moscow railway workers in Gorky Park attributed the railway's success to the application of Stalin's six conditions for economic success, which he had advanced in June 1931, and to the fact that Bolsheviks and non-party people were rallying around the party.[75]

The First All-Union Congress of the Stakhanovites of Industry and Transport opened on 14 November 1935 in the Kremlin's Great Hall.[76] Kaganovich announced a major breakthrough in boosting railway freight traffic. The Krivonosites had demonstrated that speeds of 40–50 kilometres an hour could be attained by E-type locomotives, confounding the 'limiters' of NKPS's Locomotive Administration, who had regarded speeds of 22–23 kilometres per hour as a norm. The Krivonosite movement provided the surest guarantee that Stalin's target of a daily loading of 80,000 wagons would be attained. If Stalin set NKPS a new target, Kaganovich boasted, the railways would rise to the challenge.[77]

Stalin now hailed the Stakhanovite movement, which, he claimed, had emerged 'spontaneously' from below, in the teeth of managerial opposition.

He offered the slogan: 'New people, new times, new technology'. In NKPS, the views of conservative professors – 'dictators of opinion' – had now been disproved. It had been necessary to give them a 'slap in the teeth' and to dismiss them from NKPS. The Stakhanovite movement, he asserted, 'smashes the old technical norms' and would 'allow free scope to the new forces of the working class'.[78]

On 29 November the Politburo decided to deal with opposition to the Krivonosite movement on the railways by organizing an open trial, with two culprits singled out for exceptional treatment and sentenced to ten years imprisonment.[79]

The Central Committee plenum of 21–25 December 1935 was devoted primarily to the reports from leading economic commissars – Ordzhonikidze, Mikoyan, S. S. Lobov, I. E. Lyubimov and Kaganovich – on the Stakhanovite movement in each sector of the economy. Stalin was absent for most of the plenum. The reports by Ordzhonikidze and Kaganovich were received with acclaim. Kaganovich's report was the high point of the plenum, culminating in 'stormy, long, unceasing applause, turning into an ovation. All stand'. One delegate spoke of Kaganovich's 'brilliant report' and his success in galvanizing the railways to overcome the 'limiters'.[80]

In December 1935 the authority of Ordzhonikidze and Kaganovich was at its height. They were the two figures within the leadership most committed to resolving economic problems through management methods and without recourse to coercion and repression, at least within their own sectors. Neither had any compunction about using coercion against the peasantry. They enjoyed strong support in the Central Committee. Kaganovich's triumph at this plenum demonstrated that his demotion in February 1935 had done nothing to lessen his authority. On the contrary, his success at NKPS has further elevated his reputation. The Ordzhonikidze–Kaganovich line of promoting economic efficiency via the Stakhanovite movement stood in direct opposition to the line of increased repression advocated by Yezhov. At this stage, Stalin had not openly committed himself to one line or another.

The Performance of the Railways in 1935

At the Central Committee plenum on 25 December Kaganovich announced that in 1935, NKPS had carried 390 million tons of freight, 108.2 per cent of the plan target, and an increase of 23 per cent over 1934.[81] In 1935, 3,752 million rubles was invested in the railway, a concrete expression of the government's new commitment to improving rail transport.

Plaudits were showered on Kaganovich. In a celebratory article, *Pravda* hailed this as 'the greatest triumph of the year'. Kaganovich, Stalin's inspired choice as narkom, was the 'most outstanding and talented Bolshevik organizer'.[82] Within two years of the transport crisis being at its height, the official view voiced by Molotov and Mezhlauk was that it had been solved.[83] On 14 January the Central Executive Committee approved NKPS's success in overfulfilling the freight plan targets for 1935.[84]

Holland Hunter attributed the dramatic turnaround in the railways' performance in 1935 to the combined effect of the dramatic increase in investment and the improvement in operational efficiency brought about by Kaganovich's shake-up of NKPS.[85] But his policies, as his critics had warned, pushed up the accident rate. On the entire Soviet rail network in 1934 there were 62,000 category one accidents and wrecks, rising to 69,614 in 1935.[86] The costs of these accidents can only be guessed.

Stalin's attitude to the Stakhanovite movement and his view of the overall economic situation has to be largely inferred. He appears to have viewed the movement as a mechanism by which a huge surge in productivity in all branches of the economy could be realized. The vast investment that had been made since 1928 had not, in his opinion, delivered the growth rates that were expected because of conservatism and obstructionism within the economic institutions. This was allied to a propensity for fantastic projections of future growth.[87]

In a report to the Central Committee on 13 December Kaganovich urged drastic improvement in construction work on the railways using Stakhanovite methods.[88] In a second report, nine days later, he hailed the Krivonosovite movement on the railways as a 'gigantic historical movement', which was part of the socialist transformation of the system on the principle of 'New Country, New People'. The past backwardness of the railways he blamed on the 'limiters' who were held in awe by party officials. He singled out for criticism the Scientific Research Institute of Operations –headed by professor S. K. Kudrevatov, a line director under Denikin – for its 'platform of naked sabotage'.[89]

Kaganovich reported that there were 69,000 Krivonosites on the railways and that through incentives, the movement should be enlarged. Moreover, all workers should receive a basic technical minimum education. The administration had to be purged of class enemies and accident causers. However, he expressed general satisfaction with personnel and in a veiled rebuke to the NKVD and the Commission of Party Control, warned against extreme measures:

> Here what is required is not a campaign purge, but organic, long term, consistent struggle, day in day out, hour by hour, for the purging of our cadres of class-alien elements. Concerning the leading, commanding

cadres, the basic mass of the higher command staff, of railway transport is working quite well. The mood is upbeat and confident. Indeed, the success of 1935 was achieved, in the main, by the very same cadres who worked there earlier.[90]

He lauded Stalin's role in facilitating this triumph –'the greatest man in the world'. However, in 1935 Kaganovich kept in post all the line directors that he had inherited. Some technical specialist, charged as 'limiters', were arrested, but most had been retained, with some being reassigned or demoted. The crisis of the winter season, which so many had anticipated, had not materialized.

A Central Committee resolution outlined a radical agenda to develop the Stakhanovite-Krivonosite movement, to reconstruct the whole science of rail transport on a new basis purged of conservative influences, to develop a large scale programme for the training of railway workers in the technical minimum standards (500,000 workers in 1936) and the promotion of the most successful students into responsible positions.[91] This represented a return to the policies of mass mobilization and the promotion of workers and young graduates of 1929–31, in which Stalin, Molotov, Ordzhonikidze and Kaganovich had played such a crucial role.[92]

The Advance of the Railways, 1936

As a result of its successes in 1935, the stocks of the railways were high. Kaganovich was one of eleven narkoms awarded the Red Banner of Labour on 17 January 1936.[93] In the early months of 1936, railway workers and officials were showered with state awards.[94] The Central Executive Committee approved the renaming of the major lines in honour of past and present Bolshevik leaders; the Perm line became the Kaganovich line.[95]

In 1936 NKPS was increasingly pressed by the People's Commissariat of Defence and by the military establishment, who were perturbed by German and Japanese war preparations.[96] In his report to the Central Executive Committee in January, Tukhachevsky noted with envy the ability of the German railways to transport hundreds of thousands of people around the country during mass festivals.[97] In his speech to railway workers on 30 July Kaganovich stressed the interdependence of Soviet industry, the army and the railways.[98] In September, major military manoeuvres were conducted in Byelorussia on the western front as a demonstration of Soviet military preparedness.

In December 1935 Kaganovich outlined to the Central Committee plenum the plan for the railways for the coming year.[99] Molotov presented the plan to the Central Executive Committee in January 1936. NKPS was to achieve a freight turnover of 457 million tons, an increase of 17 per cent over 1935. A daily loading target of 78,500 wagons was set. Capital investment was set at 5,059 million rubles. NKPS was required to cut construction costs by 11 per cent, introduce further economies and generally improve operational efficiency.[100]

In February 1936 *Pravda* hailed 1935–36 as the 'First Bolshevik Winter on Transport'. Stalin's target, set in July 1935, of a daily loading of 80,000 wagons had been attained.[101] On 3 April *Pravda* published a letter to Stalin, which had supposedly been approved by over half a million railway employees, and which proposed a staggering daily loading target of 100,000 wagons.[102] 1936 was pronounced as 'The Stakhanovite Year'.[103] On 15 April a conference of railway workers in the Kremlin's Great Hall, addressed by Kaganovich, endorsed the new target of 100,000 wagons.[104] However, no date was set for its realization. In the following weeks, the NKPS Soviet approved a series of orders to raise the technical efficiency of the railways by improving the utilization of locomotives and speeding up the movement of trains.[105] These orders provoked intense opposition.[106]

In the winter of 1935–36, serious difficulties were experienced on the eastern lines, which were of critical importance on account of tense relations with Japan.[107] In January–February 1936 Kaganovich, with Politburo authorization, undertook an inspection tour of the far eastern lines.[108] In a series of telegrams to Stalin in January 1936, he spoke of groups of counter-revolutionaries, saboteurs and former kulaks on the Omsk and Tomsk lines. He charged that at the Krasnoyarsk depot, wreckers were in league with Japanese and Polish intelligence and that Trotskyists were sabotaging the Stakhanovite movement. He called on the NKVD to eliminate the spies and class enemies.[109] A special unit of the Supreme Court's Military Collegium followed in Kaganovich's wake. Two were sentenced to death by the court at Krasnoyarsk, while three were sentenced to death and ten to periods of imprisonment at Tomsk.[110]

At the NKPS Soviet in April, Kaganovich noted that criminal elements on the far eastern lines had been dealt with by resort to 'the weapon of the proletarian dictatorship'.[111] The eastern lines successfully fulfilled their half-yearly plan targets in June.[112] He called for a more conciliatory policy towards the managerial stratum, and rejected mass repression:

> In all discipline, whilst the state exists, there will always be an element of repression: there is today and there will be tomorrow. But repression does not constitute the basis of correct organization and conscious discipline. The basis must be the coordination of parts, the force of Bolshevik organization and leadership, the force of the convinced conscious organized majority of the collective, plus specific, necessary measures of repression.[113]

The limiters had been disproved, Kaganovich asserted, and had, in Stalin's words, been given a 'slap in the teeth'. Most of the leading limiters had been retained in work on the railways, and had been simply demoted. Many of them were now working by Stakhanovite methods. Only a 'small minority' comprised 'malicious wreckers and spies'. The great majority of limiters were conservatives or sceptics who had already been won over or were being persuaded. Kaganovich also upbraided the line directors whose policy towards cadres fluctuated wildly between lax liberalism and savage repression. NKPS, he insisted, had resolved on a more courageous line for the promotion of young workers.[114]

G. M. Segal', the Transport Procurator, noted that in comparison with the first quarter of 1935, the number of cases referred to the courts for accidents was reduced more than fourfold.[115] The NKPS Soviet's resolution condemned the excessive use of repressive measures by line directors and heads of *politotdely* on the major lines.[116] However, restraining the advocates of repression remained an uphill struggle.

On 7 January 1936 NKPS issued an order condemning the Institute for the Reconstruction of Traction (rolling stock) for obstructing the implementation of NKPS's order of 7 August 1935 (No. 183/Ts) on improving locomotive utilization. The institute was also accused of blocking the XVII Party Congress decision to introduce the heavier FD locomotive and of holding back proposals to introduce locomotive condensers (which were designed to operate in desert conditions by converting steam back into water).[117] At the Central Committee plenum in December 1935, Kaganovich hailed the locomotive condensers as a technical revolution. At the NKPS Soviet in April 1936, he stressed Stalin's keen interest in this innovation.[118] On this basis, he scrapped the dieselization programme, which was well developed, a decision that in hindsight proved to be a mistake.

In 1936 Kaganovich led a sustained attack on the former specialists of NKPS's Central Scientific Research Institute of Railway Construction.[119] NKPS's journal *Sotsialisticheskii transport* and its daily *Gudok* were thrown open to the radical specialists. The Stakhanovite movement was vigorously promoted. The X Congress of the Komsomol, in April, was attended by Kaganovich who again stressed the need to improve the party's ideological work.[120]

In January 1936 an unpublished NKPS order blamed the diversionary work of hostile class elements – kulaks, White Guardists and Trotskyists – as the main cause of railway accidents. It called for these elements be identified and purged.[121] At the NKPS Soviet in April Kaganovich conceded that the accident problem remained. In the first quarter of 1936, there had been 454 collisions, 887 derailments and 328 accidents as a result of which 166 locomotives and over 5,000 freight wagons had been damaged. NKPS's orders, he complained, had been flouted and the technical rules of operation were badly enforced.[122]

Kaganovich warned that those who breached the rules of technical operation would be 'strictly punished'. Class enemies were particularly active in organizing accidents, thus necessitating greater vigilance. However, he asserted, 'Ninety per cent of people wish to work and to fight collisions, and they recognize the necessity of this struggle', but too many still adopted a fatalistic attitude. Those who obstructed measures to reduce the accident rate would be treated as saboteurs. By the end of 1936, NKPS should aim to achieve accident-free transport.[123]

On the basis of the Central Committee's resolution of December 1935, Kaganovich, in April 1936, authorized an ambitious programme of training for railway workers.[124] In June proposals were announced for on-the-job training for 670,000 workers in minimum technical skills in 1936.[125] A further 40,000 Krivonosite workers were to receive training in 'schools of masters of socialist labour'.[126] His speeches in July and August stressed the importance of advancing this new heroic generation of railway workers.[127]

The NKPS Soviet authorized new operational norms for the railways.[128] This, Kaganovich noted, would bring the USSR in line with the United States, where the commercial speed of freight trains was 25.7 kilometres per hour.[129] These targets testify to a growing lack of realism in policy making.

The Stakhanovite/Krivonosovite movement was pioneered by Ordzhonikidze and Kaganovich. It was intended to achieve a huge improvement in labour productivity, to maximize the use of the large investment made in the economy since 1928. It was aimed at overcoming managerial conservatism. It used bonuses as a means of boosting performance, and used competition between workers for that end. Safety margins were lowered and the norms within which equipment was used were advanced beyond the specifications for which they had been designed. The consequences of the Stakhanovite movement were ambiguous. While output performances did increase, Stakhanovism often had seriously detrimental effects – the damage to machinery and equipment, the rising of the accident rate, the creation of serious imbalances and distortions in the economy. The movement provoked strong managerial opposition. The growing differentials between Stakhanovite and non-Stakhanovite workers stoked great resentment.

For its architects, Stakhanovism had another objective; it was intended to demonstrate that through incentives and changes in managerial methods, a dramatic improvement in efficiency could be attained. This stood in opposition to those, such as Yezhov in the Commission of Party Control, who saw the main obstacle to improving efficiency in wrecking and sabotage by managers and engineers. While Ordzhonikidze and Kaganovich saw the movement as a way of breaking managerial resistance, they did not see this primarily as a problem of wrecking and sabotage. Stakhanovism was initially conceived as an alternative to outright police repression. In practice, this strategy failed. Resistance to Stakhanovism by managerial personnel from the start of 1936 was increasingly identified as another form of wrecking and sabotage. The tensions generated between Stakhanovite workers and managers provided justification for the increased resort to police measures to investigate and arrests those accused of obstructing the movement. Stakhanovism unwittingly became a tool that could be used to justify the intensification of repression.

Rising tension between the USSR and Germany and Japan highlighted the central importance of the railways for defence planning. The militarization of the railways, the preparation of the railways to operate in conditions of warfare and defence construction, became major priorities[130]

The 30th of July was declared 'All-Union Day of Transport for the Soviet Union', and was to become an annual event, a major holiday in the Soviet calendar.[131] The climax of the festival was Kaganovich's two-hour-long speech to 25,000 railway workers in Gorky Park, Moscow, which was broadcast nationwide.[132] He underlined the Soviet government policy of peace, as promoted by Litvinov, but stressed the interdependence of the army, industry and the railways.

In this he highlighted the dramatic advance of the railways. He asserted that the situation with regard to railway cadres was general healthy. Although enemies remained, 'they are few, they are less than they were, but they exist'. In the main, he offered these guidelines:

> Here the way is not in purging and repression. No, for ninety-nine per cent of railway employees are honest people, who are committed to their work, who love their motherland.[133]

The technical institutes and research institutes needed to be reorganized in order to prepare more highly qualified engineers 'grounded in the achievements of world railway technology'.[134] He struck a strong patriotic note, warning of the dangers of war, and heaped adulation on Stalin – the inspirer of the recovery of the railways. The speech struck an obsequious tone, calling on the railway workers to model themselves on 'the great locomotive driver of the revolution, comrade Stalin... our beloved, dear, own, first railway worker, comrade Stalin'. The railway workers were uniting around the Central Committee, the government and comrade Stalin to secure new victories

Kaganovich's speech echoed the sentiments expressed by Ordzhonikidze at this time. At the NKTyazhprom Soviet at the end of June Ordzhonikidze dismissed allegations of wrecking against his technical-managerial personnel as 'nonsense' and delivered a rousing defence of his cadres.[135] The pronouncements of Ordzhonikidze and Kaganovich were clearly a warning to the NKVD, CPC, CSC and the Procuracy. In 1933 Stalin had reacted strongly to attempts to limit the powers of the security agencies. He now moved to circumvent such constraints by reviving the issue of the 'Trotskyist' threat. The Zinoviev-Kamenev trial in August 1936 (see Chapter 10) abruptly changed the political climate.[136] Kaganovich was assigned a central part in organizing the trial.

Conclusion

In 1935 Kaganovich was appointed head of NKPS, and transferred from party work to economic work. He secured increased investment for NKPS, but relentlessly forced up the targets for efficiency. In the face of strong internal opposition, the Soviet railways achieved a dramatic improvement in performance, which greatly strengthened his reputation as one of the most effective administrators within the Stalinist leadership. Relations between NKPS and NKTyazhprom, which had been extremely fraught, improved, reflecting the warm relations between Ordzhonikidze and Kaganovich. They were the principal architects of the Stakhanovite movement in 1935 and they adopted a common position to protect their commissariats from excessive interference by the police and control agencies. Stakhanovism was driven both by the objective of promoting increased efficiency, but it was also intended to remould the consciousness of workers and technicians.

NKTyazhprom and NKPS were remarkably successful in meeting their production targets. Early in 1936 their achievements were celebrated. Notwithstanding the successes of NKPS and NKTyazhprom, a campaign against wrecking and sabotage on the railways and in industry was promoted by the Commission of Party Control, under Yezhov. This led to a growing wave of repression from the start of 1936. This campaign clearly enjoyed Stalin's support. It served to pressurize the NKVD, which was accused of a lack of vigilance in exposing wrecking. But it was also targeted at the powerful NKTazhprom and NKPS. The fact that the campaign was spearheaded by Yezhov, Kaganovich's former deputy in the Commission of Party Control, added a sharp irony to the situation. In July 1936 this was to assume an ominous direction, linking wrecking and sabotage with the campaign against the defeated oppositionists.

Kaganovich's success at NKPS provided evidence that even intractable problems could be solved without recourse to violence and repression, which offered the prospect of new vistas of future progress. In this role, he emerged as a spokesman not just of NKPS, but a spokesman within the Stalinist group symbolizing the possibility of a new reconciliation between the regime and society based on actual material progress. In 1933 Stalin had bridled against attempts by the economic managers to limit police control over their activities. In this period he was obliged to tolerate a degree of independence exercized by Kaganovich and Ordzhonikidze as heads of their respective commissariats, reflected in their role in promoting the Stakhanovite movement. By 1936 he saw the independence of NKTyazhprom and NKPS as incompatible with the further strengthening of his absolute power. The Central Committee that had so publicly endorsed Ordzhonikidze and Kaganovich in December 1935 now itself became a subject of Stalin's distrust. The attack on the two economic commissariats was to be a key part of a strategy to fundamentally restructure the party-state apparatus as a means of further strengthening the *vozhd"*s power.

Chapter 10

POLITICAL AND SOCIAL REVOLUTION THROUGH TERROR, 1936–1938

The Great Terror from 1936 to 1938 transformed the Soviet system. It erupted unexpectedly and with little warning. It developed through a series of steps acquiring momentum. In the first half of 1936 Kaganovich and Ordzhonikidze both spoke publicly against mass repression of their own cadres. In this they stood in clear opposition to Yezhov, the most vocal advocate of punitive measures against those deemed to be enemies of the state. Stalin's ability to use repression in the economy in 1933 had been thwarted by Ordzhonikidze and Kaganovich. By July 1936 he had decided to unleash a new witch-hunt. Kaganovich was required to change his stance on this issue. His shifting outlook and role sheds light on the way in which the Terror was initiated and on how the *vozhd'* managed his relations with his deputies. The rationalization for the Terror provided by Kaganovich at the time and subsequently provides a key to understanding the tortured logic of those involved in implementing these measures.

The mass repression of 1936 was shaped in part by the long shadow cast by collectivization, dekulakization and the famine, which remained issues of bitter recriminations. In industry and transport the problem of low labour efficiency and the disappointing return on investment generated conflicting viewpoints between those who saw the problems as stemming from obstruction and wrecking and those who saw the problems as rooted in the rigidities of the state-owned, planned economy. Stakhanovism in 1935 was an attempt to address these issues. But the Stalinist developmental model had its direct concomitants in the growth of state authoritarianism and the brutalization of society. These issues acquired a new urgency against the deteriorating international situation and the threat of war.

The Prelude to the Terror

In the first half of 1936 the attack on former oppositionists was intensified and in the summer, on Stalin's initiative, investigations were reopened into the circumstances of Kirov's assassination. Stalin's deputies shared a deep animus towards the former oppositionists. Nikolai Yezhov, head of the Commission of Party Control, who already in June 1935 had advanced the theory of a major conspiracy against the state, systematically worked to undermine Yagoda in NKVD.[1] Kaganovich, who was privy to these developments, reported to Stalin on 6 July 1936 on the dispositions extracted from two former oppositionists concerning the assassination, which implicated Trotsky, Zinoviev and Kamenev in the conspiracy. He proposed that they declare Trotsky an 'outlaw' and 'shoot the rest of the lowlifes we have in jail.'[2] Similarly, Voroshilov two days later wrote to Stalin concerning Trotsky, Kamenev and Zinoviev: 'This poisonous and miserable scum ought to be annihilated'.[3]

Stalin now committed himself to a thorough purge of the former oppositionists and suspected oppositionists. On 29 July a top secret circular was sent to all party committees on 'The Terrorist Activity of the Trotskyite, Zinovievite Counter-Revolutionary Bloc'.[4] This set the agenda for the Terror, linking the former oppositionists (Trotsky and Zinoviev) with the most implacable enemies of the Soviet regime in an enormous conspiracy that was well concealed and needed to be ruthlessly exposed.[5] Yezhov's assessment of the threat to the state was now made the official position of the party.

With Stalin on leave, Kaganovich settled the final details of the trial with V. V. Ul'rikh, president of the Military Collegium of the Supreme Court, and with Vyshinsky, the Procurator.[6] The trial of the 'Anti-Soviet Unified Trotskyite-Zinovievite Centre' opened on 24 August. The principal defendants were Zinoviev, Kamenev, G. E. Evdokimov, I. N. Smirnov, S. V. Mrachkovsky and I. P. Bakaev. They were accused of organizing a 'terrorist centre' from 1932 onward, under Trotsky's direction and guidance. It had engaged in wrecking and sabotage, and had plotted the assassination of Stalin, Voroshilov, Kaganovich, Ordzhonikidze and Zhdanov. Vyshinsky and Ul'rikh submitted the draft sentences to Kaganovich for his approval. He tightened up the accusation of terrorism against various individuals,[7] and added his own name and that of Ordzhonikidze to the list of persons against whom terrorist acts had allegedly been plotted.[8]

Molotov was an enthusiastic supporter of the trial, but the exclusion of his name from the list of targets suggests that he was out of favour with Stalin at this time.[9] Through crude intimidation, Stalin cowed his deputies. The disintegration of the Politburo as a collective decision-making body and the deep divisions within the ruling group, notably the animosity between Molotov and Kaganovich, precluded any concerted counteraction. Stalin's deputies lacked the political and moral courage to stand up to him and to halt the course of events.

Kaganovich oversaw the trial's organization.[10] He and Yezhov sent detailed joint reports of the proceedings to Stalin.[11] They monitored the coverage of the trial in the Soviet press, the reports of TASS the official Soviet news agency and their reception in the foreign press.[12] Orchestrated mass meetings of workers and party activists demanded the death penalty.[13] The accused were found guilty and executed.

A vigorous campaign was initiated against Trotskyist wreckers in the industries of Ukraine, especially in Donetsk.[14] Kaganovich reported to Stalin that alleged leaders of a 'Ukrainian terrorist centre' had implicated Ya. A. Lifshits and Pyatakov, both former Trotskyists.[15] At the end of August Yezhov and Kaganovich wrote to Stalin on the need to move against figures in Dnepropetrovsk and Krivoi Rog.[16]

In August–September 1936 Kaganovich presided at two confrontations in the Central Committee building between Bukharin and Sokolnikov, at which Sokolnikov accused Bukharin of involvement in a conspiracy against the party. Kaganovich is said to have expressed to Bukharin his disbelief in the accusations. On 9 September he wrote to Stalin that there was no evidence to warrant bringing Bukharin and Rykov to trial.[17] The Procuracy endorsed this judgement. Bukharin and his wife considered that Sokolnikov's accusations were inspired by Stalin and believed that Kaganovich at this stage had protected him.[18]

On 14 September Kaganovich reported to Stalin on the interrogation of Rykov, Bukharin and Sokolnikov. He believed that the Rightists had their own organization, and were in contact with the Trotskyist-Zinovievite bloc even if there was no organizational link between them. He reported that Pyatakov was not yet giving 'testimony', but concluded, 'It's good that we are completely smashing all of these Trotskyite-Zinovievite rats.'[19] How far the policy of repression was to go remained unclear.

In early September Mikoyan sent his close friend Kaganovich a letter from Chicago offering his observations on the Zinoviev-Kamenev trial. The letter was addressed 'Dear Lazar' and concluded, 'I give you a great hug'. Mikoyan welcomed the decision to extirpate 'the Trotskyist gang of Zinoviev and Kamenev' and expressed regret that Trotsky so far had escaped the same fate.[20] Kaganovich publicly endorsed this view on 31 January 1937 with the cry 'Death to Trotsky!'[21] This slogan articulated the Stalin group's real intent and was finally realized in 1940.

On 25 September Stalin and Zhdanov, on holiday on the Black Sea, sent a telegram to Kaganovich, Molotov and other members of the Politburo, demanding the appointment of Yezhov as head of the NKVD in place of Yagoda, who had 'definitely proved himself incapable of unmasking the Trotskyite-Zinovievite bloc'. The NKVD, Stalin asserted, was four years behind 'in this matter'.[22] Under Yezhov, the NKVD was purged and radically reorientated. His role in the Terror has been documented by J. Arch Getty and Oleg V. Naumov. But a rather obvious facet of Yezhov's character, his schizoid persona, is overlooked.[23] Stalin understood Yezhov better than his contemporaries. With this appointment, Stalin for the first time had a NKVD that was answerable to him and would do his bidding.

On 29 September, on Stalin's instructions, Kaganovich prepared a decision on dealing with the 'counter-revolutionary Trotskyite-Zinovievite elements' which proclaimed that these individuals had degenerated into 'intelligence agents, spies, saboteurs and wreckers of the fascist bourgeoisie in Europe.'[24] On 30 September Kaganovich wrote to Ordzhonikidze, welcoming Yezhov's appointment as head of NKVD as 'this momentous, wise decision of our father (*nashego roditel'ia*, i.e. Stalin)'. Yagoda had proved ineffectual for the grown-up task of uncovering in time political enemies.[25] On 12 October he again wrote to Ordzhonikidze:

> I can say that Yezhov is leading things well! He strongly tackles things, in a Stalinist way. We must deal with the bandit counter-revolutionary Trotskyists in a Bolshevik manner. History knows of no such villainous two-faced, deceitful provocateurs, and therefore revolutionary reprisal must be commensurate.[26]

Stalin by this time had access to the communications between his deputies and this may well have influenced their exchanges with each other. Ordzhonikidze's fiftieth birthday on 28 October was extensively covered in the press.[27] Kaganovich sent warm greetings to his friend.[28]

On 16 September Lifshits, Kaganovich's deputy at NKPS, wrote a long letter to Stalin defending his past record, claiming that the NKVD had falsified a confession in which he admitted to having participated in a 'terrorist Trotskyite centre'.[29] On 5 October Kaganovich asked Stalin's permission to remove Lifshits from his duties because his position had become untenable.[30] He was shortly thereafter arrested by the NKVD. The new wave of repression created its own dynamics. On 27 September Kaganovich informed Stalin of denunciations levelled at him by I. D. Balashov, head of freight management on the Yaroslavsky line, for alleged errors in policy and cadre appointments.[31] But Balashov may well have been trying to defend himself from criticism by Kaganovich.

Kaganovich and Ordzhonikidze still attempted to build some defences to protect their agencies. On 8 September Kaganovich ordered the heads of the *politotdely* of the railways to familiarize themselves with the recent Politburo directive that leading economic officials could only be removed with the express approval of the Central Committee.[32] The heads of the two principal economic commissariats, must have shared a clear understanding of the growing threat that faced them.

In August and September Kaganovich issued a stream of orders to line administrations and *politotdely* demanding immediate improvements in their work.[33] On 14 September he informed Stalin that the NKVD's Transport Department had uncovered a Trotskyist group on the railways in Moscow. Some of these had worked in Moscow under Uglanov, which implied, he argued, the existence of a Trotskyist-Rightist conspiracy.[34]

At a meeting of workers of the Moscow depot at the end of September, Kaganovich, albeit more circumspectly, continued to hold the line against mass repression. Enemies on the railways were still active and the problem of accidents and disruption remained, but the two issues which he stressed were stricter enforcement of policy and improvements in the education of workers.[35] On 1 October new technical rules of operation for the railways were introduced with the aim of boosting performance.[36]

From 9 September to 16 October, five line directors were dismissed.[37] A virulent attack was launched on those branded as wreckers, counter-revolutionary Trotskyists, saboteurs, fascists and White Guardists.[38] In December the Supreme Court's Transport Collegium tried a number of top officials of the Orenburg line, but the relative leniency of the sentences indicates that the shift to mass repression was still uncertain.[39]

Severe weather conditions during the winter of 1936–37 caused acute disruption in shipments of coal from the Donbass and of iron ore from Krivoi Rog. At the end of November Kaganovich undertook an inspection tour of the Donetsk and Stalin lines, urging all efforts to ensure the realization of the traffic plan.[40] Nevertheless, in January 1937 NKPS reported to Stalin and Molotov that it had fulfilled its annual freight plan ahead of schedule.[41] For 1936 the Soviet railways carried 483 million tons of freight compared to 317 million tons for 1934, a staggering 52 per cent increase.[42] Notwithstanding a sharp rise in the accident rate, Kaganovich achieved a dramatic improvement in performance through increased use of spare capacity.

Heavy industry was badly hit by the new wave of repression. Ordzhonikidze's position was shaken by the arrest of his deputies, Pyatakov, N. I. Muralov and Ya. N. Drobnis, all former oppositionists who were accused of leading the sabotage campaign in industry. These arrests were part of a wider pattern whereby deputies were arrested in order to intimidate their superiors and in many cases, as a preliminary to their own arrest. The Kemerovo trial in November, at which administrators at the Kuzbass coalfield were charged with wrecking and sabotage, gave new impetus to the repression.[43] Ordzhonikidze, however, continued to argue that the problems of the Kuzbass coalfield stemmed from mismanagement, not wrecking.[44]

Control over the railways was tightened. A. M. Shanin, head of the NKVD's Transport Department, was ousted and arrested and replaced by

L. N. Bel'sky.⁴⁵ The Supreme Court and its Military and Transport Collegiums, the USSR Procuracy and the Chief Procuracy of the Railways began organizing cases against wreckers and spies. The Commission of Party Control, headed by Yezhov, was also put on alert. NKPS's Political Administration, headed by N. N. Zimin, was required to strengthen control.⁴⁶

Kaganovich's attitude to the Terror reflected his dual responsibility as a Politburo member and as departmental head of NKPS. As a Politburo member, he supported the execution of the former oppositionists. As head of NKPS, his position was more nuanced: while determined to root out so-called enemies, he opposed mass repression on the railways. On 6 January 1937 addressing railway employees, he denounced 'Trotskyist-fascist wreckers' in the locomotive and wagon works.⁴⁷

Initiating the Great Terror

Yezhov's report on the 'Anti-Soviet Trotskyist and Rightist Organizations' to the Central Committee plenum in early December 1936 extended the scope of the purge. He identified Pyatakov, Sokolnikov, Radek and Serebryakov as the reserve centre of a Trotskyist-Zinovievist terrorist centre. On rail transport, he identified Lifshits as the organizer of the conspiracy. At the plenum, Bukharin and Radek were accused of collusion with the Trotskyists.⁴⁸

Kaganovich, who held the followers of Trotsky and Zinoviev in contempt, had appeared to offer some protection to Bukharin. By December this had completely changed. He now led the attack on Bukharin and Rykov, claiming that they were linked to the Trotskyists-Zinovievist groups.⁴⁹ Moreover, this block had its own 'army' ready to carry out planned terrorist acts. Bukharin responded incredulously: 'What? You have taken leave of your senses, comrade Kaganovich'.⁵⁰ Kaganovich's strategy of a selective endorsement of the Terror was already in disarray.

The Terror was developed against a background of economic stability and steady advance. Although the 1936 harvest was poor and various economic sectors at the end of the year encountered difficulties, there was no crisis. The two economic commissariats that had registered the greatest advances during the Second Five-Year Plan were now set up as the principal targets for investigation: Ordzhonikidze's NKTyazhprom and Kaganovich's NKPS.

The trial of the 'Anti-Soviet Trotskyite Centre' opened before the Supreme Court's Military Collegium on 23 January 1937 in the October Hall in Moscow. Seventeen defendants were tried, the chief of which were Pyatakov, Radek, Sokolnikov, Serebryakov and Lifshits.⁵¹ Serebryakov, a former deputy narkom of NKPS in the twenties, was accused of directing the wrecking campaign on the railways. Leading NKPS officials such as Lifshits and I. A. Knyazev

Figure 6. I. V. Stalin, A. A. Zhdanov, L. M. Kaganovich, A. I. Mikoyan and K. E. Voroshilov stand beside the body of G. K. Ordzhonikidze, February 1937

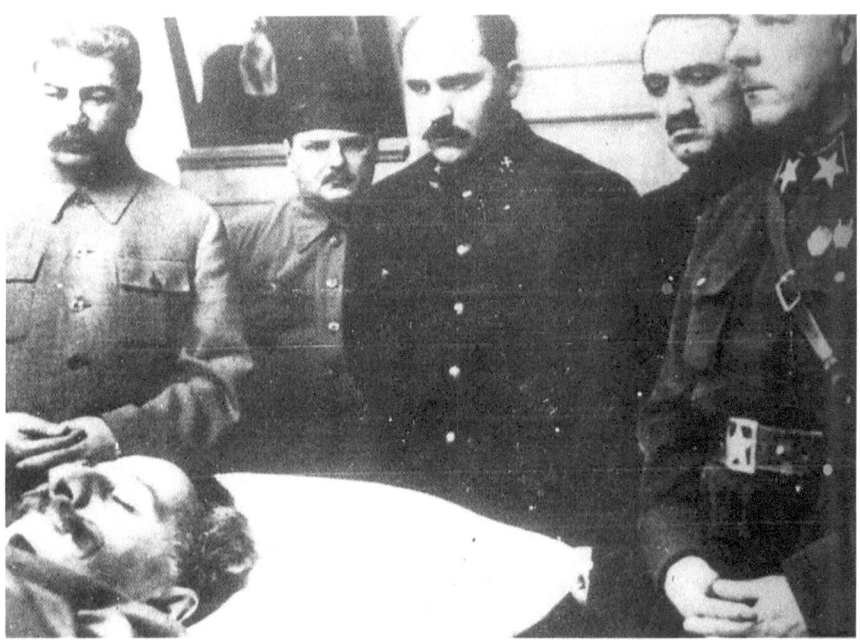

were implicated, alongside many directors and heads of the line *politotdely*. The Military Collegium sentenced 14 of the accused to death. A meeting of workers on Red Square on 30 January 1937 passed a resolution welcoming the sentences.[52]

On 9 February the Politburo instructed Ordzhonikidze and Kaganovich to prepare reports for the Central Committee plenum on wrecking, diversion and espionage in NKTyazhprom and NKPS. A draft resolution entitled 'Lessons of Wrecking, diversion and espionage of Japanese-German Trotskyist Agents' was drawn up.[53] Yezhov was to report on the NKVD's work in industry and transport and also on the cases against Bukharin and Rykov. Zhdanov was to report on the party's role in the elections to the Supreme Soviet. Stalin was to report on the education of party cadres and the measures adopted to combat Trotskyist influences.[54]

On 18 February the Politburo discussed the reports for the plenum. Ordzhonikidze's report drew Stalin's ire for failing to expose the extent of the wrecking within NKTyazhprom. Kaganovich and Ordzhonikidze discussed the proposed resolutions with A. N. Poskrebyshev. It was against this background, and heated exchanges with Stalin, that Ordzhonikidze shot himself.[55] In these final days, Ordzhonikidze had had long discussions with Kaganovich and with Mikoyan, during which he had spoken of suicide. Mikoyan, much later, imputed responsibility for his death to L. P. Beria, party and security chief of the Trans-Caucasus.[56]

A strong, independent figure with a broad following in the party, Ordzhonikidze was a staunch defender of his managers and executives, who included several prominent ex-oppositionists. He had transformed NKTyazhprom into a powerful organization. His health was poor and he was highly temperamental. The arrest of his brother Papulia in 1936, the trial of his deputy Pyatakov and the searching of his apartment by the NKVD had gravely undermined his position.[57] The persecution of Papulia was attributed to Beria, who then led a campaign against Ordzhonikidze's supporters in Trans-Caucasus.

In his retirement, Kaganovich refused to blame Stalin for Ordzhonikidze's suicide, asserting that 'We not once heard any cursing between Stalin and Sergo.'[58] In fact, Stalin's favoured tactic was that of relentless political and psychological attrition. Nevertheless, Ordzhonikidze's death was a great shock and removed his closest ally from the Politburo. NKPS's leadership in a tribute to Ordzhonikidze hailed him as a 'great friend of the railway workers'.[59] The common front between Ordzhonikidze and Kaganovich to protect their own cadres fell apart. Ordzhonikidze was not squeamish as regards the use of force for political ends, but he possessed a strong sense of integrity as regards party ethics.[60] His suicide testifies to the acute tensions within the ruling group at this time and signalled the end of the relatively open relationship of mutual trust between Stalin and his deputies that had characterized his dictatorship since 1933.

The Central Committee plenum, delayed on account of Ordzhonikidze's death, met on 23 February. The presence of a large number of NKVD personnel from all regions of the country was intended to intimidate and to secure acceptance of Stalin's line. It lasted 11 days, but its deliberations were not reported, and the only published resolution concerned the party's role in the elections to the Supreme Soviet.

Molotov's report dealt with wrecking in NKTyazhprom and NKPS.[61] Yezhov's report, entitled 'The results of wrecking, diversion and espionage by Japanese-German Trotskyite agents' concerning the lessons of the January trial was also discussed.[62] In this frenzied atmosphere, delegates sought to demonstrate their vigilance in identifying whole categories of different enemies of the state: defeated oppositionists, members of other parties, former people, dispossessed kulak", ex-party members, religious believers, criminal elements and others. Voroshilov, however, in a meek show of independence, confidently asserted that the Red Army was untainted by wrecking.

Kaganovich's report on the railways reflected a marked shift in his position. He acknowledged that the liquidation of the consequences of wrecking on railways had proceeded slower than in heavy industry.⁶³ 'Trotskyists' activities on the railways were traced back to 1931. After 1935 the Trotskyists had made common cause with the 'limiters'. Wrecking-espionage organizations had been uncovered on the Donetsk line and at the Krasnoyarsk locomotive depot. Nevertheless, Kaganovich continued to warn against the indiscriminate use of the term wrecking, stressing that railway employees who had worked badly, began to work better after 1935; they were not all Trotskyists. Surprisingly, he also noted that Lifshits in 1935 had been one of the first to denounce the limiters and had been one of the keenest advocates of the new methods. It was essential, he argued, to show faith in workers and to reduce the high rate of cadre turnover through incentives, better training and tighter control. Since 1933 NKPS had received a large number of engineers and technicians, many of them party members. However, of the top 5,000 commanders of NKPS, only 17 per cent had been appointed since the Shakhty affair, compared to 50 per cent in heavy industry. Since January 1935 NKPS's leadership had been purged of former oppositionists. Out of 39 line directors, 27 were recent appointees.

Kaganovich now claimed that wrecking had assumed fantastic proportions in NKPS. There was not a single network, not a single branch of railway administration, in which Trotskyist-Japanese wreckers had not been active. Those unmasked as wreckers included three former narkoms of NKPS – A. I. Emshanov, V. I. Nevsky and Trotsky; 7 deputy narkoms and 17 out of 59 collegium members. Following the order of January 1936 concerning accidents caused by class enemies, they had expelled from transport 485 gendarmes, 220 SRs and Mensheviks, 3,800 Trotskyists, 1,415 White Guard officers, 282 wreckers, 440 spies, as well as large number of ex-kulaks.⁶⁴ The 6,000 repatriated workers from Harbin and 6,000 former employees of the Chinese Eastern Railway were heavily purged as enemy agents and wreckers.

The wreckers, Kaganovich claimed, had concentrated on NKTyazhprom and NKPS, because of their defence and economic significance, but other narkoms should not think their commissariats immune. The wrecking campaign, from the Shakhty case onward, reflected the problem of internal enemies in the context of capitalist encirclement and highlighted the need to advance the new cadres. He added: 'It is good that this wrecking was uncovered now, before our country is subject to military attack.' Their task was 'root out the wreckers, to expose, to destroy them to the last', without being swayed by concerns that they might arrest innocent individuals.⁶⁵

Kaganovich also attacked Pavel Postyshev, party secretary of Ukraine, and a former protégé. In January 1937 he had been sent to Kiev to remove Postyshev as secretary of the Kiev province party committee. He accused him of violating the party's orders and of showing blindness towards enemies of the people. He encouraged the denunciation of the party leaders by rank and file activists, such as the mentally unstable Nikolaenko.[66]

Stalin did not speak until the 3rd and 5th of March. This typified his strategy of directing events from behind the scenes, allowing his subordinates to develop the new line of policy while he looked on. The speeches reveal a paranoid mind, a man detached from reality who paraded his own delusions as truth. The basic theme was that the Soviet Union was threatened by a major conspiracy of wreckers and spies. The evidence for this conspiracy was provided by the reports of the delegates themselves, by the testimony of the show trials and the evidence drawn from the Shakhty affair and the Kirov assassination. The warnings issued by the Central Committee (i.e. by Stalin himself) in July 1936 were a signal that all was not well. Wrecking was now carried out by people with party cards who had wormed their way into the party's confidence. Now, 'new methods, uprooting and smashing methods' were needed to eliminate them.[67] The party had to be hardened and turned into an army of 'granite Bolsheviks' and needed 'several relays' of people to promote at the regional, republican and all-union levels.[68] This was a mere hint of the carnage that was about to be inflicted on the party-state elite.

Only Stalin had the perspicacity to recognize the true situation. In his speech he recalled the critical reaction to his article 'Dizzy with Success' of March 1930, when he had then also censured the cadres. It is clear that the criticisms directed at him still ranked with him seven years later. He denounced the complacency of those cadres who considered that problems were being invented by members of the Central Committee (i.e. by Stalin).[69] Here we have another example of him expressing the inexpressible so as to test and challenge his audience. The errors of the cadres, he insisted, should be ruthlessly exposed. Not to expose these defects was the metaphorical equivalent of 'killing the cadres.'[70] The metaphorical killing of cadres was about to give way to their literal killing.

Stalin's second speech on 5 March delivered a sharp criticism of Ordzhonikidze for his 'lordly' attitude in protecting his own cadres. This carried a clear warning. Kaganovich and Voroshilov could have been charged with precisely the same offence. Stalin concluded with a literary analogy comparing the party (and by implication, himself) to the Greek hero Antaeus, the son of Poseidon, the god of the seas, and Gaea, goddess of the earth. Antaeus was invincible in personal combat, but was killed by Hercules, who understood that once he was detached from the earth, he lost his strength. The Party, like Antaeus, should keep its links to the earth (the working class).[71] Stalin omitted to mention that in the legend, Antaeus killed his enemies and amassed their skulls in order to build a temple in honour of his father.

At the plenum no one dared contradict the line espoused by the leader. To do so would have been to reveal one's own political blindness and to place oneself in the camp of the enemies. The whole Central Committee was required to subscribe to and to elaborate on his paranoid conception of the world. While some expressed scepticism regarding the alleged scale of the wrecking campaign, the resistance offered by party officials to the repression was pitifully small.[72] Thus, Stalin secured the formal backing of the Central Committee for an open-ended extension of the Terror. This was the prelude to the Central Committee's own destruction.

In March 1937 a Central Committee commission, on Stalin's proposal, expelled Bukharin and Rykov from its ranks. The commission, comprising Stalin, Molotov, Kaganovich, Voroshilov, Mikoyan, Yezhov and Kosarev, was established to decide their fate. While the majority expressed their terse judgement, 'Arrest, try, shoot', Stalin proposed handing the matter over to the NKVD to investigate and presumably, to extract confessions.[73]

The Course of the Purge, March–July 1937

Kaganovich now committed himself fully to the purge. He was under intense pressure to accede to the new policy and was neither politically nor temperamentally disposed to resist. With Ordzhonikidze dead, and Molotov and Kaganovich committed to the purge, there was no scope for any effective resistance. Following the plenum, meetings of the party activists in the commissariats, central institutions and local party organizations discussed the new line and adopted supportive resolutions.[74] In March Kaganovich addressed a mass meeting of executives, engineers, trade unionists, Stakhanovites and activists on the scale of wrecking on the railways.[75] Early in April, a three day meeting of NKPS's party organization was held at which a new leadership was elected.[76]

In April–May 1937 Kaganovich and A. A. Andreev, both old trade unionists and both party secretaries attended the All-Union Central Council of the Trade Union (VTsSPS) plenum. They delivered stinging attacks on the trade union leadership and oversaw the election of a new presidium and secretariat. In his report, N. M. Shvernik, chairman of VTsSPS, engaged in self-criticism, asserting that the unions had been penetrated by 'class enemy elements'. The NKVD had arrested leading officials as 'enemies of the people'. Kaganovich, in his report, criticized VTsSPS secretaries and accused the trade unions of failing to show proper vigilance, allowing saboteurs, Trotskyists and Rightists to gain influence.[77] Kaganovich met Stalin seven times during the session of the plenum to keep him apprised of developments. On 10 May VTsSPS's secretaries met with Stalin and Kaganovich. On 15 May the new secretariat of

VTsSPS was approved; Shvernik remained as first secretary, but Kaganovich's nominees were elected.[78]

The Komsomol Central Committee, which met in closed session in August 1937, in a highly critical resolution, drafted by Kaganovich, Andreev and Zhdanov, condemned the failure of Kosarev and his leadership to expose the wreckers in their midst.[79] After this meeting many leading Komsomol officials were arrested, but Kosarev was spared until 1939.

On 14 April 1937 the Politburo, on Stalin's initiative, determined that in the future, decisions requiring speedy resolution should be resolved in its name by two commissions. Foreign policy matters were entrusted to a commission comprising Stalin, Molotov, Voroshilov, Kaganovich and Yezhov, and economic policy matters was assigned to a commission made up of Molotov, Stalin, V. Ya. Chubar', Mikoyan and Kaganovich.[80] This removed the need for formal meetings of the Politburo. Stalin rationalized this decision with regard to the overburdening of his deputies with departmental responsibilities.[81] On 27 April the Politburo set up a Commission of Defence attached to Sovnarkom, which replaced the old STO. It was to be chaired by Molotov and included as members Stalin, Kaganovich, Voroshilov, Chubar', M. L. Rukhimovich, V. I. Mezhlauk and four candidate members.[82]

This was a final nail in the coffin of the Politburo.[83] In the first half of 1937 there were six meetings of the Politburo; in the second half, there were none. The Politburo was now supplanted by Stalin's inner circle of 'trusted' subordinates that made up the 'leading group'.

After the assault on heavy industry and the railways, Stalin directed his attention at the Red Army. In June 1937 the arrest, trial and execution of Marshall Tukhachevsky, Yan Gamarnik, I. E. Yakir and I. P. Uborevich and other military commanders was the signal for a wholesale purge of the officer corps. Stalin, Molotov, Voroshilov and Kaganovich approved lists, compiled by Yezhov, of military personnel to be arrested and shot.[84]

In July Kaganovich was summoned and questioned by Stalin, Molotov, Voroshilov and Kalinin regarding his friendship with Yakir, a close associate of Trotsky in the twenties. This again provides an example of Stalin's methods. Kaganovich recalled that in 1925, he had accepted Yakir as commander of the Ukrainian Military District on Stalin's recommendation. He came to regard Yakir as a personal friend.[85] On Yakir's letter of appeal Stalin wrote, 'Scoundrel and prostitute'; Voroshilov added, 'A perfectly accurate description'. Molotov put his name to this, and Kaganovich appended, 'For the traitor, scum and [scurrilous obscene term] one punishment – the death sentence'.[86]

In his memoirs, Kaganovich justified the purge of the military high command, claiming that the military was subject to Rightist and Trotskyist influences and that Tukhachevsky had harboured Bonapartist ambitions.[87] Molotov and

Georgi Dimitrov, in their accounts, refer to Stalin's fear of a military coup in the summer of 1937.[88] Evidence of alleged links between the Soviet military high command and the leaders of the Wehrmacht were supplied to the Soviet leadership by President Benes of Czechoslovakia. It is possible that this evidence was fabricated by the German Gestapo, which suggests a sound understanding of Stalin's paranoid sensibilities. The purge of the army was a necessary precondition for the development of the purge on a mass scale. The army was the one institution that might have stopped the carnage.

The purge now entered a new, more frenzied phase, with the initiation of mass operations. NKVD's Order No.00447, based on Stalin's secret order of 9 July, set quotas for the arrest and execution of former kulaks who had returned from exile. The quotas were invariably revised upwards by local party secretaries and then approved by the Politburo. Between July 1937 and August 1938 Kaganovich, alongside other Politburo members, signed 38 decisions confirming these upward revisions. Collective responsibility became a cover for collective complicity.[89]

The issuing of the order on the 'Polish Operation' initiated action against 'national contingents' and resulted in the arrest and execution of large numbers of Poles, Germans, Finns and other nationalities. Other social groups, including criminals and religious believers, were now also targeted. The system of quotas allowed local party and NKVD bodies to revise the targets upwards in a demonstration of zeal and vigilance.

The Purge in the Provinces

Kaganovich was involved in the moves to restrict the cultural rights of the non Russian peoples.[90] Stalin's Politburo colleagues were sent out to direct the purge in the republics and provinces. Kaganovich was sent to Ivanovo, Yaroslavl, Smolensk and Chelyabinsk; Malenkov to Byelorussia and Armenia; A. A. Andreev visited Voronezh, Chelyabinsk, Sverdlovsk, Kursk, Saratov, Kuibyshev, Rostov and Krasnodar. Zhdanov went to Leningrad, Orenburg, Bashkirya, and Tatary; Mikoyan visited Armenia and Shkiryatov went to North Caucasus.[91] Khrushchev was assigned to Ukraine in 1938. Everywhere, they destroyed the old leadership.

From 18–20 June an extraordinary plenum of the Western province party committee in Smolensk was held, which was addressed by Kaganovich. The resolution announced that the first secretary I. P. Rymyantsev and a large group of leading officials were 'traitors, spies of German and Japanese fascism and members of the Rightist-Trotskyite gang'. They were allegedly connected to the military high command via Uborevich as part of a 'military-fascist organization'. Under a new secretary, the province experienced the extremes of the Terror.[92]

In June Kaganovich and Malenkov attended the Yaroslavl province committee conference, where they denounced the local party leadership and the management of the local Rubber-Asbestos Combine.[93] I. A. Nefedov, the second secretary of Yaroslavl province party committee, branded by Kaganovich as an enemy of the people, was arrested and was soon after executed.

In August Kaganovich and Shkiryatov visited the great textile centre of Ivanovo. This became known as 'the black tornado'.[94] Early on the morning of 7 August, the two arrived unannounced in Ivanovo by special train from Yaroslavl, accompanied by a 35-man security detail, following a purported attempt on Kaganovich's life. They consulted with the local NKVD. At the Ivanovo party province party committee plenum, Kaganovich and Shkiryatov denounced the influence of wreckers and Trotskyists in the party, soviet and economic organs.[95] On Kaganovich's orders, the first secretary of the province party committee was denounced.[96]

The stenographic versions of Kaganovich's speeches in Ivanovo and other centres during the Great Terror, which are preserved in the archives, are often anodyne and were clearly edited to conceal the rawness of these encounters. An official of the Ivanovo party committee recounted in 1963 to the Party Control Committee how Kaganovich had summoned A. A. Vasilev, secretary of the Ivanovo city party committee, three times to the podium to admit his membership in a counter-revolutionary organization, and had torn his party card from his hands. After Vasilev was arrested, Kaganovich read out his confession and declared, 'You see how this filth wriggles. Thus at the plenum he was pregnant, but he was unwilling bravely to deliver, but in the NKVD after half an hour he happily delivered and admits everything'.[97] This account probably provides a truer representation of the tenor of these meetings. The crudity of the language, the comparison between the pain of torture and labour pains, done as a joke, still has the power to shock.

During his stay in Ivanovo, Kaganovich telephoned Stalin several times a day to report on progress. This served as the prelude to the unleashing of the purge in its most dramatic form. From July 1937 to January 1938 the province leadership of the party and soviet bodies was decimated: former SRs, party members with a record of dissent, former Anarchists, Monarchist, former employees of the Chinese Eastern Railway and 'former people' were shot.[98]

The Purge in NKTyazhprom

The All-Union Day of Railway Workers, on 31 July, was a day of nationwide celebrations. Kaganovich attended the main celebrations at Gorky Park in Moscow and his address, broadcast nationwide, celebrated the year's achievements and paid tribute to Stalin as the author of these triumphs.[99]

The railways were still performing well in spite of the purges. On 22 August Kaganovich was appointed narkom of NKTyazhprom in place of Mezhlauk, and was replaced as head of NKPS by his deputy, the relatively unknown Aleksei Bakulin.[100] Kaganovich retained responsibility for the railways in the Politburo.

Kaganovich was transferred to NKTyazhprom to oversee the purge in industry and to tighten up management. At the end of August, in *Trud* he scathingly criticized the party committee of NKTyazhprom, as a result of which the committee was destroyed.[101] Stalin, at a meeting with executives on 29 October, warned of the continuing influence of spies and wreckers at the top level of industry.[102]

The direction in which the purge might develop remained uncertain. In August 1937 I. E. Lyubimov, head of the People's Commissariat of Light Industry, at an open meeting blamed defects in the work of the shoemakers *glavk* on the influence of Jews. This was reported to Kaganovich. Some days later, Sovnarkom rebuked Lyubimov for this 'anti-Semitic outburst' and instructed him to correct his error at the next meeting of the *glavk*.[103]

In October Kaganovich visited the Donbass coalfield with the first secretary of the province committee, A. S. Shcherbakov.[104] He delivered a report, 'On Sabotage', to the local party; alleging that there were not a few 'enemies' and 'saboteurs' among the engineers and party cadres.[105] On 7 October Kaganovich addressed a rally of Stakhanovites and shock-workers in Donetsk.[106] The speech, in the version preserved in the archives, was full of jokes and avoided abrasive attacks on wreckers. In these days, the NKVD, with Kaganovich's authorization, arrested some 140 leading officials in the Donbass.[107] In January 1938 he issued a new Central Committee order aimed at turning Stakhanovism in the coal industry into a mass movement by overcoming the resistance of managers and engineers.[108]

From 25 to 29 October 1937 NKTyazhprom convened a meeting of the workers of the metallurgical industry, which was held in the Kremlin, to discuss the campaign against spies, wreckers and saboteurs.[109] In his speech, Kaganovich offered a lengthy and elaborate toast to Stalin, 'the great steel founder of our socialist construction.'[110] Stalin, in editing the report for publication, eliminated this panegyric entirely. On 23–25 November Kaganovich, at an all-union meeting of workers in the copper industry in Sverdlovsk, criticized the poor leadership of the industry.[111]

On 9 December Kaganovich addressed the electors of Tashkent, who had nominated him as their representative to the Supreme Soviet. This was the first time he had visited the city since 1922. He lauded the Bolshevik party as 'flesh of the flesh, blood of the blood of the toiling people'; it was the party of the working class from which he himself hailed.[112] Now, a great many outstanding new people were being advanced into leading positions. The 'glorious officers of the NKVD' had dealt a crushing blow to the fascists, their Trotskyist-Zinovievist agents and the Rykov-Bukharin spies.[113] In the nominations for election to the Supreme Soviet at the end of 1937, Kaganovich now ranked in sixth place after Stalin, Voroshilov, Yezhov, Kalinin (whose ranking was purely symbolic) and Molotov, reflecting the priority now accorded to the Red Army and the NKVD.[114]

On 21 December 1937 the twentieth anniversary of NKVD, there was a grand celebration in the Bolshoi Theatre attended by Stalin, Kaganovich, Molotov, Voroshilov, Mikoyan and Khrushchev. Mikoyan delivered the main address, lavishing praise on Yezhov as a worthy successor of Dzerzhinsky. He compared Yezhov's success in galvanizing the NKVD into action to Kaganovich's 'Stalinist style' of work in turning around NKPS. Mikoyan's relations with Kaganovich at this stage evidently remained good.[115]

Supremo of Rail Transport and Heavy Industry, 1938

In 1938 Kaganovich continued with purging NKTyazhprom. In February he attended a meeting of oil industry workers in Baku, which approved the plan to develop the 'Second Baku of the East'.[116] He later stressed his role in promoting younger personnel into leading positions with the support of the Azerbaidzhan and Transcaucasus party committees, headed by M. D. Bagirov and Beria.[117] In March he attended meeting of workers of the gold and cement industries.[118] Thereafter, he turned his attention to purging the chemical, aluminium and rubber industries.[119] On 29 October he censured the administration of the Krivoi Rog iron ore basin for failing to liquidate the consequences of wrecking.[120]

The Central Committee plenum in January 1938 criticized mistakes by local party organizations in expelling members from the party.[121] This heralded a temporary let up in the purge. Kaganovich assumed a central role at the plenum in leading the interrogation of his former friend and protégé Postyshev. In the name of principle, sincerity and honesty, colleagues were denounced in the most underhanded manner. He praised the educative role of the purges:

> I think that it can be said without exaggeration that the last year, the extirpation of the enemies of the party and the enemies of the people, for honourable Bolsheviks, despite naivety and blindness in their work, was a year of such education and such tempering which we, in ordinary times, would not have received in decades.[122]

But he accepted that mistakes had been committed which sincere and honest party members would wish to rectify.

In March the Military Collegium tried the case of the 'Anti-Soviet Bloc of Rights and Trotskyites', headed by N. I. Bukharin, A. I. Rykov, G. G. Yagoda, N. N. Krestinsky and seventeen other defendants. They were accused of forming a terrorist group, headed by a former Socialist Revolutionary, and plotting to assassinate Stalin and Kaganovich.[123]

In the winter of 1937–38 the railways encountered serious hold-ups in the Donbass and Kuzbass. On 7 January the Politburo assigned Kaganovich as a Central Committee–Sovnarkom plenipotentiary to NKPS until 1 April. NKPS orders were all to be jointly signed by Bakulin and Kaganovich.[124] *Pravda*, in its editorials, scathingly criticized Bakulin's leadership of NKPS.[125] On 5 April the Politburo reappointed Kaganovich as narkom of NKPS and blamed Bakulin for the deterioration in rail performance and the sharp rise in the number of accidents and collisions during the winter season.[126] Now, Kaganovich combined the leadership of NKPS with his post as head of NKTyazhprom.[127]

The new re-established NKPS collegium, approved by the Politburo on 8 April, had a strong NKVD presence, including its deputy narkoms M. A. Volkov and P. V. Zhuravlev. NKVD's Transport Department, headed by V. V. Yartsev, maintained close oversight of NKPS.[128] Kaganovich took charge of NKPS's main planning, financial and cadres departments.

The commissariat's administration returned to a semblance of normality. Between 9 April and 30 December 1938 there were 66 meetings of the NKPS collegium, with Kaganovich chairing every session. The protocols of these meetings indicate a disciplined and businesslike management.[129] On 27–28 April, he convened a meeting of NKPS's activists and line commanders, which examined the mistakes of the old leadership in a mood of 'deep self-criticism'.[130] *Pravda* in August 1938 published a list of the 40 line directors, the first such listing to appear since January 1937, indicating a new stress on cadre stability.[131]

With Kaganovich's recall, railway investment, which had been cut under Bakulin, was partly restored. On 22 May an investment of 5,030 million rubles in the railways in 1938 was approved.[132] In June, he visited the key coal-carrying South and North Donetsk lines.[133] In July NKPS's party organization welcomed the immediate improvements in the railways' performance following his appointment as narkom.[134] On 20 May he issued NKPS's order on preparing the railways for the winter 1938–39, which blamed past failure on leadership. It called for the extension of Stakhanovism to all professions, but also stressed the need to create stability of cadres, to reduce labour turnover, to halt the unwarranted 'harassing' of workers and to end 'mass rebukes and punishments'.[135] On 15–17 November a meeting of 1,200 NKPS's activists, addressed by Kaganovich, discussed winter preparations.[136]

In November–December, as a result of severe weather, performance faltered badly. NKPS was placed on emergency footing, with collegium members instructed to be at their posts from 5 a.m. to 12 midnight daily to oversee operations.[137]

In 1937–38 several former leaders of NKPS – Rudzutak, Rukhimovich, D. E. Sulimov and G. I. Blagonravov – were executed. Amongst those executed included 13 deputy narkoms of NKPS, 64 line directors, 63 heads of the *politotdely* and deputy line directors. From April to October 1938 Kaganovich oversaw a major renewal of NKPS's leading personnel. Over 40 per cent of the 3,300 heads of sections, heads of departments, line directors, deputy directors, heads of traffic sections, stations, locomotive sections, locomotive depots and line sections were replaced.[138] Several Stakhanovites, including P. F. Krivonos, became line directors. Between 22 August 1937 and 9 April 1938 a total of 46,278 railway men were dismissed from their posts.[139] NKPS's central administration on 13 November 1938 had 2,968 personnel, of whom just 24 per cent had been in office prior to 1 November 1937.[140]

Yezhov, Kaganovich's erstwhile subordinate, now eclipsed his former master in power and status. NKVD personnel, by the summer of 1938, controlled the commissariats of the timber industry, post and telegraph, and water transport and had a major presence in NKPS. One NKVD informant suggests that Yezhov attempted to construct a case against Kaganovich and secured statements compromising him from I. M. Bondarenko, head of the Kharkov Tractor Works. However, Beria's appointment as deputy narkom of the NKVD on 20 July significantly weakened Yezhov's position. In December Beria replaced him as head of the NKVD. Many of Yezhov's appointees were purged. S. R. Milshtein, one of Beria's men, was appointed head of the Transport Department.[141]

Kaganovich and the Terror

The Terror directed at leading cadres was organized on the basis of lists of those to be arrested and executed, which the NKVD submitted to Stalin and his colleagues for approval. In 1987 a Politburo commission reported that from 27 February 1937 until 29 September 1938 a total of 383 lists, with 44,161 names, were examined and approved. Of these, 38,627 were sentenced to be shot and the rest were to be interned in labour camps from 8 to 10 years. Molotov signed 373 lists with 43,569 names, Stalin 361 lists with 41,391 names, Zhdanov 175 lists with 20,985 names, Kaganovich 189 lists with 19,110 names, Voroshilov 186 lists with 18,474 names.[142] In 1937 and 1938, according to official figures, a total of 1,372,292 people were arrested, of whom 681,692 were sentenced to death.¹⁴³ This must be regarded as a minimum figure.

At the XXII Party Congress in 1961, N. M. Shvernik revealed that the Commission of Party Control, in investigating the Stalinist repression, had found 32 letters from Kaganovich to the NKVD demanding the arrest of 83 leading transport workers.¹⁴⁴ These included letters calling for the arrest of wreckers at the Proletarsky locomotive repair workshop in Leningrad and at the Voronezh locomotive repair works.

Historian Oleg Khlevniuk advances the notion of the purge as a 'prophylactic purge' aimed at eradicating a potential fifth column in anticipation of war, drawing a lesson from the Spanish Civil War.¹⁴⁵ This idea was current at the time. Even Bukharin, in his final letter to Stalin in December 1937, spoke of the 'great and courageous idea of a general purge' of society in anticipation of war.¹⁴⁶ In June 1938 Kaganovich, addressing a party conference in the Donbass, deployed the 'fifth column' thesis to justify the purge.¹⁴⁷ Stalin, the party and the NKVD had eliminated the enemies without fearing what would be said about it, thereby delaying war.¹⁴⁸

Undoubtedly the war threat was a factor in the decision to unleash the Terror, but the 'fifth column' argument needs to be treated with great care. This was the argument deployed by its perpetrators to rationalize the Terror.¹⁴⁹ Up to February 1937 Ordzhonikidze, Kaganovich and Voroshilov were openly sceptical of this argument as applied to their own cadres. Stalin's colleagues accepted the idea of a massive conspiracy under duress. The singular idea that almost the whole of the pre-1937 Soviet political elite were part of a potential 'fifth column' suggests that the purge had a different purpose. The failure of Kaganovich, Molotov, Khrushchev and Mikoyan in the post-Stalin era to provide a coherent or convincing explanation for the Terror is an issue we shall return to (see Chapter 13). The designation of the Great Terror as the *Yezhovshchina* is a misnomer and conceals the true architect of these events.

Conclusion

The Great Terror was initiated and directed by Stalin. It was not, as some historians have argued, an eruption of conflicts within the party state-apparatus or the result of pressures from other party officials.¹⁵⁰ Neither was it a response to an economic crisis or a law-and-order crisis in the society in 1936.¹⁵¹ Nor was it a response to the growing threat of war. The relative calm of 1936 was a necessary precondition for the initiation of this policy. Causal connections between the domestic and international situation and the Terror remain unproven. The Terror can only be explained in terms of Stalin's motives, his threat perception, and his psychological state. But this has to be seen against the background of the culture of the Stalinist regime, its obsessive concern with enemies and its glorification of the state. Stalin resolved to turn terror into a permanent tool in a system of despotic rule.[152] The Great Terror marked a turning point in the criminalization of the regime. Through intimidation, Stalin cowed his own deputies into submission, requiring them to subscribe to his own delusional conception of the enemy threat.

The Terror was consciously planned and directed with the purpose of achieving very specific ends. It aimed to annihilate Stalin's many critics, to remove those who might possibly pose a threat to the regime, including 'unconscious enemies'.[153] The objective of the Terror was to strengthen the *vozhd"*'s power, through a fundamental restructuring of the Soviet party-state. The mighty economic commissariats – NKTyazhprom and NKPS – had their power clipped. The NKVD's power was greatly enhanced and was turned into an obedient instrument of Stalin's will. The military was ruthlessly purged and its potential as a counterweight to the party and security apparatus removed. The power of the party Politburo and Central Committee was further drastically diminished. The republican and regional party committees were purged, asserting the centre's control over the periphery. This gave Stalin unprecedented freedom to shape the domestic, security, foreign and defence policies of the state. The generation trained during the period of the First Five-Year Plan were the people who were promoted in 1937–38. The Terror was also a social cleansing operation that was intended to consolidate the 'revolution from above.' It aimed to close the great gulf that separated the hypertrophied party-state apparatus from society by sacrificing a large proportion of officialdom, now dispatched as scapegoats for the regime's own failings, and by heightening vigilance.

During collectivization, Stalin's deputies were united by shared convictions; in 1936–38 they were held together by duress, by the need to display allegiance to the *vozhd'* through their commitment to the uprooting of all potential dissent.[154] Kaganovich, like all other deputies, was compromised by his past association with those arrested and executed. Stalin's subordinates were complicit in the Terror, and thereafter bound together by mutual guilt. They were required to purge their own institutions, to authorize the arrest and execution of former friends and colleagues. This involved not only a brutalization of these men, but, in a sense, their destruction as morally autonomous beings. Having publicly opposed mass repression in 1936, Kaganovich was required to demonstrate his zealous commitment to the purge, and thus became one of its main exponents.

Chapter 11

THE MAN

Up to 1936 Stalin and his deputies were bound together by shared ideology, common experiences and aspiration. Stalin was not omnipotent or omniscient and had to depend on his lieutenants, but during the Great Terror he compelled his deputies to carry out his will. Collective responsibility, but not collective decision making, operated in the most binding way. This marked a profound transformation of the Soviet party-state. This involved huge institutional changes, and the transition of a system of dictatorship into something qualitatively different, which we might label a despotism or tyranny. Terror became a permanent part of the system of rule. This changed Stalin's relations with his deputies and wrought a huge change in the mental and moral outlook of these people. Kaganovich's biography provides an insight into this transformation. It offers an insight into the way Stalin's deputies become his accomplices in mass murder, how they rationalized their actions, and how they reflected on their role in these events, insofar as they were capable of undertaking such reflective assessment and possessed sufficient self-knowledge to do this.

The Culture of Stalinism

The 'revolution from above' profoundly changed the Soviet state and its relations with society. It saw the consolidation of the Stalin's group's power. The culture of Bolshevism underwent a profound change whilst the cultic, messianic, quasi-religious aspect of the Stalinist political system became pronounced.[1] The state came to rely ever more on coercion to maintain its position and enforce its policies. Legal norms and restraints were swept aside. Kaganovich himself was at the centre of the drive to promote and justify state authoritarianism. In 1929–36 this enjoyed the general consent of the ruling group.

Lenin's attempts in 1923 to set up a self-governing dictatorship had failed. In the 'revolution from above' the state exercised unconstrained power to force the peasants into the collective farms. The power of the coercive institutions of the state grew. The state assumed growing power over the economy and over society, seeking to mould them in accordance with its ideals of what a socialist system should be. The dismantling of civil society and the destruction of the public sphere produced a bludgeoned and infantilized society.

This affected a significant change within the party. It reinforced a culture of conformity or party idolatry. Already in the 1920s Trotsky voiced the view, 'It is impossible to be right against the party.'[2] Similarly, Pyatakov described the Bolshevik party as bound by no laws: 'Nothing is inadmissible for it, nothing unrealizable.' The true Bolshevik submerged his individuality into the party; he would swear that black was white and white was black, even abandon his own personality for the party's sake.[3] A life of amoral political intrigue and duplicity subverted the individual's own sense of self. Bukharin gave this assessment of Pyatakov to Ordzhonikidze: 'My impression of him is that he is the sort of person who is so thoroughly ruined by his tactical approach to things that he doesn't know when he is speaking the truth and when he is speaking from tactical considerations.'[4]

In this growing climate of authoritarianism, suspiciousness and distrust became endemic. Protestations of loyalty could no longer be taken at face value. In studying the pronouncement of Stalin's deputies it becomes difficult to determine what they really thought, what they thought it expedient to think, and what with hindsight they claimed to have thought at the time. Marxism-Leninism, with its distinction between objective reality and its subjective perception, its focus on law-governed historical processes, its amoralism as regards to means, its doctrine of class hatred, its requirement on its adherents to refashion themselves, fostered a paranoid conception of politics of which Stalin was the arch exponent.

Stalinism represented an important departure, but in a sense, was an emanation of certain strands within Leninism. The departure has been documented already by Trotsky, Timasheff and Stites in their different ways:[5] the rejection of experimentation; the turn towards a state-centred model of administration, the abandonment of democratic principles, the repudiation of egalitarianism and the reaction against the more libertarian policies on education and on women's rights. It reflected a turn away from the ideological agenda of 1917 to more pragmatic policies of state management and a pronounced concern with realpolitik. It showed a growing disregard, even contempt, for popular opinion with the focus on the reshaping of popular consciousness. With this, the working class lost the privileged position they had been accorded and became the subject of state management and direction.

Stalinism conforms more to what A. James Gregor defines as 'developmental dictatorship'.[6] In this, Stalinism shared many common characteristics with

Italian Fascism and Nazism: the emphasis on state regulation of the economy; direction and management of labour; the orchestration of consensus; the development of social policies aimed at appeasing social groups, but prioritizing the controlling role of the state; and the repudiation of the rule of law. Stalinism as a 'charismatic' regime aspired to the creation of an orchestrated social consensus and the formation of an organic social unity through the exclusion of particular groups. Stalinism itself, as a police and propaganda state in the 1930s, increasingly approximated the model of the Nazi and fascist regimes with a similar apotheosis of the state and patriotic values.

Ideologically, Stalinism retained its Marxist-Leninist commitment in opposition to the corporatism of Mussolini's Italy and the racist ideology of Hitler's Nazism. But these ideologies, based on class and racial discrimination, also shared common areas of agreement: they were revolutionary, atheistic, anticapitalist in varying degrees; antiliberal; authoritarian, militaristic, and driven by a similar consequentialist view of ethics. The aesthetic ideals of these states showed the same taste for the epic, the monumental and the heroic. The cosy relationship between the USSR and Fascist Italy from 1924 to 1936 and the desire of the Soviet leadership to find an accommodation with Hitler's Germany in 1933–34 reflected a degree of shared assumptions between these regimes. Mussolini and his supporters often referred complimentarily to Stalinism as a form of 'slav fascism.'[7] Anticapitalism was a current of varying influence with the Nazi party.[8]

This ideological transformation of Stalinism highlights the ideological tensions within the party. Trotsky in the 1930s referred to the Soviet regime under Stalin as a form of Bonapartism, a counter-revolution, a form of 'totalitarianism'.[9] Souvarine, the leading French Trotskyist, used the same terminology.[10] A whole group of left-leaning intellectuals of the 1930s saw a clear affinity between the USSR, Germany and Italy as 'totalitarian states.'[11] These controversies reflected the depth of the divisions created as a result of the triumph of the Stalin group. The defeated oppositionists saw the Stalinists as subverting the revolution, as betraying socialism, as bringing the revolutionary project of 1917 to ruins. They saw themselves as the conscience of the revolution, the remnants of the true believers of 1917. This explains the depth of hatred of Stalin and his deputies for the oppositionists.

Stalinism after 1936 acquired a new meaning. The Great Terror transformed the Soviet party-state into a qualitatively different form of rule; a transition from dictatorial to despotic rule. Terror became a permanent and central instrument whereby the political realm and the wider society was governed. Terror and state repressive measures were applied in an arbitrary and unpredictable way and heightened aspects of Stalinist culture that were already well advanced – the culture of conspiracy, of blame, of scapegoating, of informing, of thought control, of the demonization of opponents and of the dehumanization of enemies. The creation of a closed society, isolated from the outside world, reinforced the paranoid *weltanschaung* of Bolshevism. The growth of terror turned the security police into a state within the state.

Kaganovich up to 1936

The Communist Party leadership after October 1917 was made up of two distinct elements: those from the émigré circles in the West (the *intelligenty* or *teoretiki*, the theoreticians) and the *praktiki*,[12] primarily the underground party activists of the pre-1917 era, sometimes referred to as the committeemen (the *komitchetki*). Under Stalin it was the *praktiki*, especially those who had made reputations for themselves as commissars and organizers during the Civil War, who gained control of the Bolshevik party. In almost all particulars Kaganovich corresponded with the *praktiki*.

Trotsky saw Stalin's rise to power as reflecting certain group and social dynamics:

> There is no doubt that Stalin, like many others, was moulded by the environment and circumstances of the Civil War, along with the entire group that later helped him to establish his personal dictatorship – Ordzhonikidze, Voroshilov, Kaganovich – and a whole layer of workers and peasants raised to the status of commanders and administrators.[13]

Victor Serge writes:

> In the party, yesterday's subalterns were coming to the fore. Men like Kirov, Kuibyshev, Mikoyan – passable second-raters – or persons entirely unknown during the great years, such as Kaganovich.[14]

Kaganovich was promoted very rapidly after 1922. He did not merit an entry in a bibliography of the top 240 leading political figures of the USSR and the October Revolution, published in 1925.[15]

In his memoirs, the well-informed Mikoyan mistakenly included Kaganovich in Stalin's Tsaritsyn group from the Civil War period.[16] In fact, as we have seen, he was associated with the Eastern Front, where Trotsky's supporters were in command.

In 1937, following the October Revolution anniversary celebrations, at a reception in Dimitrov's flat, Stalin asserted that after Lenin's death, the opposition had failed because it did not take account of the will of the 'average masses', the backbone of the party, but instead tried to secure a majority in the Central Committee. In a display of self-deprecating mock modesty, Stalin downplayed his own significance after Lenin's death: 'What was I compared with Il'ich? A poor specimen'. Molotov, Kalinin, Kaganovich, and Voroshilov were all unknowns.[17] Stalin's depiction of the triumph of his group as a reflection of the party's democratic will should be taken with a pinch of salt. In 1946 he again proudly proclaimed his affinity with the *praktiki*.[18]

Within the leadership Stalin, Voroshilov, Andreev, Kirov and Kaganovich were genuine proletarians, Kalinin was of poor peasant background, while Molotov, Kuibyshev, Ordzhonikidze, Mikoyan and Zhdanov were of provincial, middle-class background. Alongside the Caucasians – Stalin, Ordzhonikidze, and Mikoyan – Kaganovich belonged to the non-Russians in the leadership. He was one of that cohort of autodidacts, self-educated workers, lacking the refinement and range of experience of the earlier cosmopolitan generation of leaders. Kaganovich drafted his notes to Stalin himself. They were marked by errors of punctuation and spelling, and on occasion he offered his apologies for these defects.[19] He would draft successive versions of the text in order to eradicate as many errors as possible. He visited the West on two brief visits, to see housing projects in Vienna and the metro system in Berlin in the early 1930s.

Kaganovich's formative experience was during the Civil War, when he was given charge of Nizhnyi Novgorod and oversaw the Red Terror in the city in 1918. His career really only took off after 1922 as one of Stalin's deputies in the Secretariat. Molotov, Kuibyshev and Kaganovich were the core members of the Stalin faction. Kaganovich was the youngest member of this group. He emerged into prominence a decade earlier than the group of young Stalinists, to which he belonged by age, who were promoted after 1938.[20] His career was made by Stalin. His rapid advancement stemmed from both his organizational talents and his role as a policy innovator. He was an energetic and forceful administrator, but often abrasive in handling subordinates. A workaholic, he was the party's top troubleshooter, and one always ready to show his mettle. An autodidact, he retained a distrust of bourgeois specialists, but showed himself able to work with experts in NKPS and on the great construction projects in Moscow. He possessed great self-confidence and did not suffer fools gladly.

Boris Bazhanov, who from 1922 onward worked in the party Secretariat and Orgburo and had close contacts with Stalin, Molotov and Kaganovich, defected in 1928.[21] In his memoirs, published in 1930, he offered the following assessment:

> If Molotov is, at present, the number two figure in Russia, Kaganovich is the number three. He is a lively lad, no fool, young and energetic.

He has advanced in his career by leaps and bounds. He thus implicitly obeys Molotov, what Molotov directs from Stalin. But, in the main, he is more indifferent to the theoretical work of Bolshevism than Stalin, Molotov and all their camarilla. The essential thing for him is the right to power.[22]

Bazhanov's assessment of Kaganovich's disinterest in theory is overstated. Within the Stalin group he was undoubtedly one of the most intellectually gifted. He produced a not inconsiderable body of work in articles and pamphlets, which provide an insight into the thinking behind the development of the Soviet party-state and show a degree of intellectual reflection far ahead of most of the other members of the Stalinist group.

Pyatakov, Trotsky's leading supporter until he capitulated to Stalin in 1928, held Kaganovich in contempt. In 1929 he wrote, 'Stalin is the only man we must obey, for fear of getting worse. Bukharin and Rykov deceive themselves in thinking that they would govern in Stalin's place. Kaganovich and such would succeed him, and I cannot and will not obey a Kaganovich.'[23] For Trotsky, Kaganovich was a particular *bête noir* and the butt of his many sarcastic observations on the Stalinist leadership.[24] In March 1932 he described the transformation of Soviet communism into a kind of political religion based on 'supermonarchical authority' in which 'Kaganovich, in the role of high priest, burns incense to the idol of eternal perfection'.[25] His dislike of Kaganovich was strongly reciprocated. Trotsky, in general, underestimated Stalin's personal role within the Soviet system and anticipated that he could easily be replaced by Molotov or Kaganovich.

Bukharin, who dismissed Molotov as obtuse with a low understanding of Marxism, rated Kaganovich as a 'capable and great organizer', although his wife added that he failed to anticipate that he would turn out so treacherous.[26] Bukharin's judgement on individuals was not always sound; he had a positive view of Yezhov and considered him an honourable man.

Grigory Bessedovsky, a Soviet diplomat who defected in 1929, confirms the rumours of intense rivalry between the two deputies. Kaganovich and Molotov were the two side horses, alongside Stalin, the lead horse, in the troika.[27] The journalist Essad-Bey depicted the relationship between Stalin, Molotov and Kaganovich as essentially an instrumental one, which would survive only as long as Stalin thought it advantageous. He dismissed speculation that Kaganovich might succeed Stalin, noting that 'Kaganovich is not enough of a personality for the position', and if Stalin should disappear, his place would be taken by a collective leadership.[28]

Like all top leaders, Kaganovich had his own staff of aides and secretaries.[29] Aides were shuffled between different leaders. Boris Bazhanov asserts that in the mid-1920s he was his principal aide in the Orgburo, but Kaganovich denied this.[30]

Kaganovich took pride in his proletarian character, his toughness and willpower. From his early appointment in Nizhnyi Novgorod, he demonstrated a ruthless and manipulative approach to politics. His conception of socialism was 'statist', showing little faith in the creativity of the masses, and was informed by the notion of progress as measured in practical achievements. He was impatient of ethical questions in politics, seeing socialism as the ultimate good to which all should be sacrificed. He was contemptuously dismissive of democracy in the party and in the mass organizations. He adopted a belligerent stance against the regime's so-called class enemies.

It was in the context of collectivization and dekulakization that Stalin (the Man of Steel) applied to him the appellation 'Iron Lazar'. Kaganovich's meteoric rise was well recognized. In 1931, Yan Larri published *The Land of the Happy*, the last science fiction utopian novel to appear under Stalin. It is set in the USSR in the 1980s. The country is led by authoritarian leaders, headed by Molybdenum and Kogan. Molybdenum (Stalin) is hard, direct, 'simple' and unyielding. His crony Kogan (Kaganovich) is mettlesome, obviously Jewish, brash and short-tempered. They are overthrown by a group of young, adventurous heroes.[31]

The historian Richard Stites characterized Kaganovich as the archrepresentative of the antiutopian element in Stalinism, one of the leaders of the 'War on the Dreamers':

> Kaganovich was the main voice in the war against many experiments in the 1920s; the woman's movement, the visionary town-planners, communist moral teaching, communes, equality and virtually everything else that smacked of autonomous culture building, independent social experimentation and 'useless' speculation about the future.[32]

Kaganovich reflected the turn to hard-nosed *realpolitik*, cultural conservatism and coercive authoritarianism associated with Stalin's personal dictatorship.

It was inevitable that Stalin's two deputies should be rivals. Molotov, the careful, ponderous, methodical, self-effacing executive stood in contrast to Kaganovich, the quick-witted, dynamic administrator, the showman and orator. The rivalry might be concealed by a veneer of bonhomie. In the summer of 1931 Molotov spent time with Stalin on vacation, and Kaganovich, in his letters to Stalin at this time, frequently concluded by sending 'Greetings to comrade Molotov'.[33] In his conversations with Feliks Chuev, Kaganovich argued that in the Central Committee apparatus they had worked together harmoniously. Differences between them had stemmed essentially from differences of policy.

As head of NKPS, he clashed with Molotov over questions of investment and resource supplies to the railways. Similarly, Ordzhonikidze had clashed with Molotov over investment in NKTyazhprom.[34] Molotov had a rather different recollection of their relationship, saying of Kaganovich, 'He was generally always personally against me. Everybody knew this. He would say "You are soft, you are an *intelligent*, and I am from the workers."' Molotov added, 'Kaganovich – he is an administrator, but crude, therefore not all can stand him. He not only pressurizes, but is somewhat personally self-regarding. He is strong and direct. A strong organizer and quite a good orator.'[35]

The social origins of the new Soviet elite in part coloured their attitudes and outlooks. But just as Kaganovich distanced himself from his Jewish origins, so his proletarian roots became increasingly remote. In his speech and manners, he remained stamped by this background. At 24 years of age he became a full time party functionary and for the next forty years occupied senior positions within the Soviet elite, with all that entailed in terms of power, status and material benefits. He was fond of evoking his proletarian roots. But such roots provided no basis for predicting the outlook or conduct of such functionaries. It provided no guarantee that they were more considerate of the opinions or interests of the ordinary man.

The outlook of the de-proletarianized party functionary was shaped by the requirements placed on him by his post, by the exigencies of political survival and by careerist considerations of self-advancement and survival. The obligation of a Bolshevik revolutionary was to remake, reforge himself into a worthy member of the party. The play on his proletarian roots was politically useful, but as part of the mobile elite of functionaries, assigned to posts across the USSR, required to enforce the changing dictates of official policy, driven by the need to act as a defender of the official line, the proletarian functionary became shaped more by his functions than his background.

The way in which the elite were perceived was a matter of great sensitivity. The ideology sought to legitimize the elite as the builders of the communist future. In 1934 Stalin, in a note to the Politburo, insisted that an article by Engels on Russian foreign policy in the nineteenth century should not be published. The Russian autocratic state, Engels argued, was guided not by a particular class interest, but was controlled by a gang of adventurers, predominantly non-Russian, who promoted a policy of Russian expansionism according to their own whims and interests. Stalin argued that the article should not be published as it was insufficiently Marxist.[36] The real reason for withholding publication was the obvious parallels that would be drawn with the Soviet elite.

What held the elite together was their common fate, which nurtured a degree of opportunism. Their shared identity and self-rationalization was rooted in Marxism-Leninism. But the official ideology was something that was to undergo profound transformation. Underlying the official ideology was a deeper set of attitudes that held the elite together, attitudes which were deeply rooted in the revolutionary movement, and dating back to the 'Nihilism' of the 1850s and 1860s. Nihilism was distinguished by an iconoclastic rejection of existing authority, secular and religious. It was guided by a notion of progress and an idea of service to mankind, in which the liberation of the ordinary people and the liberation of women, occupied a central place. To this higher end all moral and legal considerations had to be subordinated. It was informed by a faith in science and technology. It adopted an ascetic attitude toward life and a utilitarian attitude toward art. It was driven by Nikolai Chernyshevsky's idea of 'rational egoism' (rational self-interests) whereby the individual was perceived as pursuing his/her own self-interests, but could only realize that as part of a project for realizing the common good, based on collective endeavour and collectivist values.[37] Kaganovich, like other members of the Soviet elite, embodied that synthesis of individual self-interest and collective values.

A Portrait of Kaganovich

In November 1933 the Menshevik journal *Sotsialisticheskii vestnik* carried an anonymous article entitled 'The Dictator's Closest Associates'. Stalin's position, it argued, was bolstered by the support of associates who were not without talent, such as Kaganovich, Postyshev, Yezhov and Stetsky.[38] It offered an analysis of Kaganovich's character and of his relationship with Stalin. He was a man 'of quite exceptional abilities' with an amazing capacity for work: attending meeting and conferences, presenting reports, editing and drafting documents. Although an autodidact, he was widely read and was exceptionally quick-witted, able to seize new ideas on the wing, and willing to adopt ideas and suggestions.

Kaganovich was also said to possess 'a quite exceptional ability to deal with people'. He could remember faces and names and was a 'biographical dictionary', and in this, surpassed all other party leaders. He was reputed as a 'combiner who knew which individuals could be put to work with others, a talent that was considered important at a time when oppositionist views were widespread. He could be charming but could also show his claws. He sought to make himself indispensable for Stalin. He presented himself as Stalin's loyal supporter, his shadow, and was careful not to steal his thunder. This was 'devotion by calculation'. But Stalin was also more primitive, less original, more ponderous, although possessing great willpower ('the power of a car hurtling into a wall'). Kaganovich's influence stemmed from his ability to insinuate his idea to the *vozhd'*, who took them on as his own.

The judgements offered of Kaganovich in this portrait are perceptive, but they might also be seen as a piece of mischief making. The publication of this piece before the XVII Party Congress was well timed. *Sotsialisticheskii vestnik* depicts Stalin as a dictator whose responsibility for the famine had evoked widespread hatred of him in party circles. Stalin was reputed to avidly read oppositionist publications. The charge that Stalin unconsciously adopted the ideas of others, notably those of Lenin, had been advanced earlier by Krupskaya in 'Memoirs of Lenin' and was later repeated by Trotsky.[39] If this exaggerated Stalin's reliance on Kaganovich, this was something that Stalin was to put right in 1935.

Kaganovich and Stalin

Kaganovich was instrumental in downgrading the Politburo in 1932–33 as a decision-making forum. While Stalin's deputies retained their own areas of competence, the Politburo was sidelined and Stalin's private office became the key centre of decision making. The transition from an oligarchic leadership into one of personal dictatorship profoundly transformed the dynamics between Stalin and his deputies, with the deputies striving to win the *vozhd*'s support and to avoid incurring his disapproval. Having elevated Stalin into a dictator, his deputies thought they could still restrain his darker impulses. In 1936 they lost the means to control or restrain him.

Kaganovich's attitude toward Stalin was always formal and deferential. He was never able to address Stalin with the familiar *ty* (thou), unlike the majority of Stalin's colleagues, keeping to the more formal *vy* (you). Stalin had sought to use *ty* in conversation with Kaganovich, but had reverted to *vy*. Molotov and Kaganovich addressed each other as *ty*.[40] In his letters, Stalin addressed Molotov as Vyacheslav, but addressed Kaganovich simply as 'comrade Kaganovich'. Voroshilov would address Stalin as 'Koba', his prerevolutionary Georgian pseudonym, and Ordzhonikidze would sometimes address him as 'Soso', the familiar form of Joseph.[41]

The Stalin group was distinguished by strong male camaraderie, strong friendships and intense rivalries. Stalin always occupied a more distant, aloof stance in relation to his deputies. Molotov and Kuibyshev in the 1930s formed an alliance within the ruling group based on the shared interests of Sovnarkom and Gosplan in opposition to the high spending economic commissariats. Kaganovich was close friends with Voroshilov, Mikoyan, Kirov and Kosior. But his closest friend was 'Sergo' Ordzhonikidze: 'Our relationship was loving.'[42] In 1932, in a letter to his temperamental friend aimed at reconciling him to a cut in investment in his commissariat, he concluded with warm greetings from his wife and daughter to Ordzhonikidze's wife and daughter and with the

Figure 7. Stalin and Kaganovich. Sculpture by Rakitina and Eletskaya, probably 1933 or 1934

words 'I kiss you, Yours, Lazar'.⁴³ Stalin and Kaganovich would sign off their letters to each other with the more formal 'I shake your hand' or the simple 'Greetings'. On rare occasions Kaganovich might be more effusive and sign off 'Hearty greeting', and on one exceptional case in September 1933, when it was thought that Stalin's life had been in danger during an air flight, 'I firmly shake your hand and kiss you, Yours, Lazar'.⁴⁴ With the rise of Zhdanov to prominence after 1934, Kaganovich recalled that their relations were cordial: 'He [Zhdanov] and I were close to Stalin and in this we were like relatives.... I admired him as an amazing orator.'⁴⁵ Molotov argues that only Zhdanov after Kirov enjoyed such warm relations with Stalin.

Kaganovich's need for a mentor was initially focussed on Lenin. He modelled himself on Lenin, and even the beard he wore hints at emulation. In 1932 Stalin jestingly drew attention to this and threatened to cut it off. Kaganovich himself decided to shave it off, while retaining a Stalin-style moustache.⁴⁶ This trivial incident, which Kaganovich later recounted, tells us much about his need to identify with and gain the approval of significant and dominant figures. No one was to upstage Stalin as Lenin's chief disciple.

In 1934–35 Kaganovich was at the height of his career. The reception that he received at the Moscow party conference in January 1934, his triumph associated with the opening of the Metro in 1935, the ovations that he received at the Central Committee plenum in December 1935 indicate that in the party he was the most popular of the Stalinist leadership. Various towns, districts, villages, factories and collective farms were named after him.⁴⁷ The life-size sculpture of Stalin and Kaganovich by Rakitina and Eletskaya dates from the mid-1930s and recalls earlier works that depict Lenin and Stalin as master and pupil.⁴⁸ His transfer from the leadership of the Moscow party organization to NKPS in 1935 suggests that Stalin intended to cut his wings.

Kaganovich retained connections with the places where he had served. Local histories of Nizhnyi Novgorod in the 1920s and 1930s recounted his role there during the Civil War. In Voronezh, a square and a street were named in his honour. A Soviet history of the Civil War, published in 1942, gives a stirring account of his role in rallying the soldiers of Gomel' in October 1917, and a painting on this theme was done by B. E. Vladimirsky.⁴⁹ In 1937 he was elected as the representative for the Lenin district of Tashkent to the Supreme Soviet, and reelected in 1946, 1950 and 1954. A biographical sketch of his career in Turkestan in 1920–22 was published in Tashkent in 1946.⁵⁰

However, Kaganovich, unlike Molotov, was never honoured with an official biography and no edition of his collected works was ever published. Nevertheless, from 1930 onward, his words carried the weight of official pronouncements, his speeches were regularly republished in *Bol'shevik*, *Partiinoe stroitel'stvo* and *Izvestitya TsK RKP(b)* and some were translated into English, French, German and Chinese. His speeches and articles were often strongly argued and enlivened with literary references, comments on current affairs and historical analogies. His speeches were peppered with jokes: Sten, the party philosopher close to Bukharin, was dismissed as 'Hegel's representative on earth';[51] the automated machines installed at the Nizhnyi Novgorod car plant were 'machines with higher education'.[52] He retained close links with the Komsomol, the trade unions and the voluntary organizations. His speeches on the annual Railway Workers Day were set pieces. Newsreel films of his speeches in December 1934 at the Trekhgorka and Sharikopodshipnik factories, which *Izvestiya* reported had been greeted with stormy applause, were viewed in the Kremlin cinema.[53]

Galina Shtange, the wife of a prominent railway engineer and a leading activist in the association of the wives of economic executives, confided to her diary her impressions of Kaganovich, who presided at a banquet for the wives in December 1936. She records his simple manner, joining in the dancing, asking how he had done. He was rather handsome, with very expressive eyes; 'Above all, enormous serenity and intelligence, then firmness of purpose and an unyielding will; but when he smiles, his basic goodness shows through.'[54]

Kaganovich effected the image of himself as the simple worker. On his visit to Ivanovo in 1937 to purge the provincial party, he sought to stress his simplicity and democratic character, talking with the cook and service workers and giving them generous tips.[55] A leading planning official, S. I. Semin, recounted how Kaganovich, as head of the war industries commission before the war, had ordered him to remove his boots for him to pass his expert eye over them.[56]

The deracinated Jewish political activist was often contemptuous and dismissive of Jewish culture and hostile to any manifestations of Jewish nationalism or Zionism. Kaganovich fits this model. Kaganovich, Molotov claimed, was no lover of the Jews.[57] As the most prominent Jew in Soviet political life, he was caricatured by Nazi propagandists as the embodiment of the Jewish–Bolshevik conspiracy.[58] In February 1936 he visited the Jewish autonomous region of Birobidzhan and addressing a meeting of activists, highlighted the need to counteract the growth of Jewish nationalism.[59]

Family

Kaganovich, as one of the top members of the Soviet elite, enjoyed the power, status and material comforts which such a post afforded. The elite were a

Figure 8. L. M. Kaganovich with his wife Maria and their daughter Maia in 1934

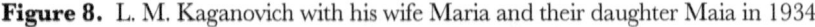

self-conscious entity who saw themselves as the builders of socialism. They lived together in the Kremlin apartments. They had access to special shops, sanatoria, medical facilities, apartments, servants and cars. As public figures, they were visible as the theatre, the opera, the concert hall, public events and social festivities. The tastes and lifestyles of the elite underwent a certain embourgeoisement, but as functionaries, they were also highly conscious that their privileges were dependent on them retaining their posts. While assertive in dealing with those subject to their authority, they were deferential – even craven – to those with power over them and highly sensitive to any sign of declining favour.

Through the second half of the 1920s and the early 1930s, those around Stalin frequently socialized with one another. Kaganovich's wife, Maria, was friends with the wives of Stalin, Ordzhonikidze, Mikoyan and Yezhov. Maria Svanidze in her memoirs recalled the easy informality in Stalin's apartment in 1934, when Stalin and Kaganovich and others would discuss business.[60] Gradually, the socialization became confined to the *vozhd'* and his most trusted deputies.

Like all Bolshevik leaders, Kaganovich kept the political and private sides of his life separate, declaring 'the personal has no social significance'.[61] His family life, like that of most of the top elite, offers little in terms on insight into his character or role as leader. More than any other figure, Kaganovich was a workaholic. He lived modestly. He drank moderately, prompting Stalin's remark, 'Jews generally cannot drink.'[62] He was a keen player of chess and bridge. He was also an enthusiastic skier and, like other members of the Kremlin elite in the thirties, played tennis. He enjoyed robust health, although in 1922 he contracted malaria; in February 1932 he was given a six-week break on account of headaches and dizziness and confined to his bed; and in July 1934 he underwent an operation for tonsillitis.[63]

After the Civil War, Maria Markovna Kaganovich worked on party soviet assignments wherever her husband's work took him. From 1931 until she retired 27 years later, she occupied senior positions in the trade unions and was a member of the Revision Commission of All-Union Central Council of the Trade Unions. She was a long-serving member of the editorial board of the women's journal *Rabotnitsa*, and published several pamphlets on labour issues.[64] She served for many years as a deputy of Moscow city soviet, and was a member of various Moscow party district committees. She received state awards for her services, including the Order of Lenin.

They had one daughter, Maia, and they later adopted a son, Yuli, from a children's home. Other leaders, Stalin, Molotov and Voroshilov, also adopted children.[65] Maia became an architect. Yuli studied at the Zhukov institute and later at the Chkvalov institute. They lived quite modestly. Both were fully employed in their work, but Sunday was a day for the family in the dacha. They lived in a Kremlin apartment, near the Spassky tower. The Politburo in April 1937 ruled that a fire in the apartment should be investigated as the work of enemies.[66]

The story that Kaganovich's 'sister' Roza became Stalin's lover following the suicide of Nadezhda Alliliueva has no foundation.[67] Kaganovich's daughter, Maia, insisted that Roza Kaganovich did not exist. She also recounted that rumours linking herself with Stalin emerged when she was only a young girl, a member of the Pioneers, and the family were much concerned that the rumour might reach Stalin.[68]

Lazar Kaganovich's elder brother Mikhail, in the 1920s and 1930s, forged his own political career (see Chapter 12). His brother Yuli attained positions of moderate significance. In 1937–39 he served as first secretary of Nizhnyi Novgorod (Gorky) and was heavily implicated in purging the province.[69] In January 1936 he joined the Budget Commission. In January 1938, like his brothers Lazar and Mikhail, he became a member of the presidium of the Supreme Soviet.[70] From 1938 until 1941 he served as deputy head of the People's Commissariat of Foreign Trade.[71] The two older brothers, Aron and Izrail, did not make any political career. One, it is reported, became the manager of the main department store in Kiev and later head of the city department of trade. Only a Kaganovich cousin suffered in the purges.

Kaganovich's personal and family life, like most of the other deputies, was conventional and respectable. He was a faithful husband and a devoted father. Within the Stalin group, the individuals with more troubled personal and family lives were Stalin, Yezhov and Beria. It is notable that Stalin's deputies were pressurized often through their close family members – Ordzhonikidze and Kaganovich though attacks on their brothers, Kalinin and Molotov through attacks on their wives. Several members of Stalin's own family and near relatives fell victim of his regime.

The Master

The role of Kaganovich's career cannot be understood outside of his relationship with Stalin. The horrors of the Stalin era – collectivization, dekulakization, the Gulag, the show trials of bourgeois intellectuals, the Great Terror – were not misfortunes that befell an unlucky leader. These events stemmed from choices made by Stalin. He has been variously viewed as a form of oriental despot, as a kind of political gangster.[72] Historians who favour social and political explanations see his conduct as shaped by circumstances which evolved over time. An alternative explanation highlights the nature of Stalin's psychology as a crucial factor in shaping developments in this era.

Stalin's behaviour and conduct conforms to what psychologists define as malignant antisocial personality disorder (sociopath).[73] This corresponds to four main psychological categories: the 'successful' high-functioning psychopath, the Machiavellian personality, the paranoid personality and the malignant narcissist.[74] The extreme concentration of power carries with it the danger of a lapse into psychopathic behaviour; paranoia is the illness of autocratic rulers. It might be argued that tyranny breeds psychopathy, but in the case of Stalin there is a strong argument to be made that it was psychopathy that bred tyranny.

Robert C. Tucker in *Stalin as Revolutionary* presents a convincing picture of Stalin as a psychopath.[75] Raymond Birt characterizes Stalin as a paranoid personality.[76] Daniel Rancour-Lafferiere analyses Stalin's 'paranoia', 'megalomania', 'narcissism' and 'sadism', with its psychosexual roots, and entertains the possibility that he was clinically psychopathic.[77] He notes that in 1927 the neuropathologist V. M. Bekhterev, after speaking with Stalin, diagnosed him as 'typical case of severe paranoia' and that in 1936 Kremlin physicians D. D. Pletnev and L. G. Levin came to similar conclusions.[78] Stalin's mental state was a recurrent subject of rumour and speculation.

Psychopaths are not psychotic nor are they irrational. The defining features of the classic psychopathic personality are the absence of conscience or moral restraint and the inability to feel empathy or to experience emotion except at a superficial level. The high-functioning psychopath has to be distinguished from ordinary criminal psychopaths who indulge in reckless, impulsive acts. They are often intelligent and have organizing ability and are capable of great single-mindedness in pursuit of their goals. They often display great personal self-confidence. They can be highly successful and often ascend to the top in the organizations in which they work. They are often self-satisfied, untroubled by self-questioning or self-doubt, and are characterized by an exaggerated sense of their own abilities, reflected in the narcissistic aspect of their personality. They possess a rock-solid personality structure that is extremely resistant to outside influence. Psychopaths may function normally, can be socially adept, can be brilliant, very efficient survival machines. They are capable of providing fearless, audacious leadership and to function in highly competitive environments.

Psychopaths are distinguished by a cold, calculating predatory character. They adopt an instrumental attitude towards others, and are able to effect an elaborate camouflage of words and appearances – lies and manipulation – in order to 'assimilate' their prey. They are able to plan ahead, to scheme in the long term. They seek to ensure maximum benefits for themselves in all situations and to isolate and destroy potential enemies. They consume others as a form of cannibalism, draining them of energy, subverting their sense of autonomy. They might be described as soul eaters ('psychophagic'). Lacking an inner conscience, they assume that others are like them and function in the same instrumental way. Being unimpeded by conscience, they have an enormous advantage over those who are. But the psychopath has the capacity to simulate normal moral concerns and to imitate or feign normal emotional behaviour. Their conception of the world is of necessity paranoid. But whereas neurotic personalities are timid, fearful figures, the psychopath is assertive and seeks to dominate.

Psychopathic behaviour is driven by the need to control and to have mastery over others and to secure recognition by others. This reflects a degree of insecurity, inferiority or inadequacy. Psychopaths can be socially adept in cultivating friends and colleagues and may also inspire great loyalty in their subordinates. They have a talent to charm, deceive and manipulate, but they require people who are amenable to manipulation. They may be good judges of people, with a clear sense of individual needs and weaknesses. They are distinguished by a great talent for deception and dissimulation, and are good liars. They derive satisfaction from their ability to dominate and outsmart opponents and from inflicting humiliation and making others suffer. This style of leadership is confrontational and the psychopath seeks new challenges to demonstrate his mastery and prowess.

The psychopath requires a social environment in which the narcissistic side of his personality receives gratification. He is unscrupulous in establishing his dominance and ruthless in its maintenance. He may display a pervasive, obsessive-compulsive desire to force his delusions on others. The inner world of the psychopath is commonly banal, sophomoric and devoid of colour. Such personalities may be especially attracted to small religious or political sects. These behavioural traits are related to other psychological states, notably paranoia, 'malignant narcissism'– the desire for praise, adulation and respect, hypersensitivity to criticism – and Machiavellianism, the ability to engage in amoral conduct driven by egotistical self-interest.

Stalin conforms closely to the image of the high-functioning psychopath. His prickliness, his sensitivity towards slights, his distrust of individuals meant that his deputies had to deal with him with greatest care, had to anticipate his thinking, bolster his self-esteem, be sensitive to his narcissistic needs and to manage his paranoid delusions. He possessed rare self-control: he was undemonstrative; he did not raise his voice or engage in bruising arguments with his colleagues. He expected to be obeyed, and he expected deference.

Stalin was not psychotic, although aspects of his behaviour in 1936–38, and 1949–53 suggest psychotic traits. His plans were carefully laid and he acted with great deliberation. He was able to manage the party-state apparatus to realize his aims, and to delegate powers to his deputies so as not to overburden himself with the micromanagement of affairs. But features of his behaviour stand out. He engaged compulsively and obsessively in intrigue. Volkogonov noted 'maniacal suspiciousness' as 'a dominant feature of his personality.'[79] Those who crossed him were never able to regain his confidence. He found difficulty in distinguishing between reality and his own delusions. He identified himself with the interests of the party, the state and the revolution and saw criticism of himself as an attack on these ideals. He concealed his personal actions and motives as decisions of the party. Modesty, courage and principledness were the virtues which he ascribed to himself, while branding his adversaries as deceitful and cowardly. His notion of truth was contingent; he was an inveterate liar. He sought to dominate and gain the submission of others to his will. He derived pleasure from humiliating and inflicting pain on his enemies. He took delight in the loss of control of bodily functions by his enemies under stress and interrogation as proof of their cowardice. Untroubled by conscience, he perpetrated acts of extreme inhumanity. His intellectual world, as reflected in his language, was constructed of simple dichotomies and opposites, of friends and enemies.

The psychological state of leaders impact the psychology of the organizations they lead.[80] This does not mean that the leader's psychology is the sole causal factor. In the case of Stalin, the context, both in terms of domestic and international situational factors, were of crucial importance, as was the general culture of Bolshevism. The high-functioning psychopath is a highly calculating individual, very conscious of his environment and very conscious of the need to proceed in ways that do not jeopardize his own interests or his own reputation.

Historians have attempted to trace Stalin's pathological persona to his early childhood. While environmental factor are undoubtedly important, psychologists lean toward the view that psychopaths are born, not made. The psychopathic aspects of his personality were evident in the 1920s. In 1936 they became more pronounced, when he was able to act according to his own will, unconstrained by the opinion of his colleagues. The question of whether Stalin was sincere in his campaign to root out enemies is the wrong question. As a paranoid personality, Stalin was no doubt convinced that he was engaged in a struggle with real enemies. The identification of his own self-interest with that of the interests of the state, the party and the revolution, similarly should be seen as an aspect of his narcissism.

In 1929 F. F. Raskol'nikov, in a highly perceptive judgement, wrote in his diary of Stalin's 'superhuman strength of will', noting the psychopathic side of his persona:

> Stalin's strength of will suffocates, destroys the individuality of people who come under his influence. He easily succeeded in crushing not only the soft and weak-willed M.I. Kalinin but even such wilful people as L.M. Kaganovich. Stalin does not need advisers, he needs only executors.

Therefore, he demands from his closest aides complete submission, obedience, subjection- unprotesting, slavish discipline. He does not like people who have their own opinion, and with his usual nastiness drives them away.[81]

This highlights the question of Stalin's relationship with his deputies; the kind of deputies he chose; the kind of people who chose to work under him. The year 1936 marked a crucial turning point, by which Stalin became the undisputed leader who was no longer constrained by his deputies and who was able to require his subordinates to share his paranoid conception of the world and to act in accordance with his will. This derived not simply from his strength of will, but from the pliant nature of his deputies and their lack of political and moral courage to stand up to him.

Kaganovich after 1936

Stalin's dictatorial rule from 1933 to 1936 was based on a system of coercive rule, the central principles and justification for which were accepted by the dictator and his lieutenants in a rather frank, even open-hearted manner. By contrast, Stalin's despotic rule from 1936 onward removed the constraints on the psychopathic aspects of his character. The Terror of 1936–38 transformed state–societal relations, further criminalized the regime and destroyed its claim to moral authority. The Terror also profoundly changed Stalin's relations with his deputies, marked by a pathological distrust, with the *vozhd'* wielding the power of life and death. Driven by the imperatives of survival, his deputies were required to carry out the leader's will.

The Soviet leadership of these decades has been termed 'team Stalin'.[82] The 'team' is a retrospective construct made up of the survivors. Out of 36 members and candidate members of the Politburo between 1924 and 1953 – excluding Stalin – 14 (38 per cent) were executed after 1936.[83] The Central Committee in this period was devastated. The Terror profoundly transformed the dynamics of the ruling group. Held together by the discipline of the group, and of the group mind, this was now reinforced by intense insecurity. The leadership underwent a pathological regression. Under 'high Stalinism', the need to placate the leader together with murderous factional rivalries became an intrinsic part of the dynamics of the leading group.

While the term 'team' does not adequately characterize Stalin's relations with his deputies, there are aspects of his methods of managing the party-state machine that, in part, correspond to this designation. The party-state apparatus retained important polycratic features, with power delegated to institutions. Stalin expected his deputies to manage their own fiefdoms. He retained his deputies in post often over long periods of time. Personal loyalty was the basis on which he managed his deputies. He preferred to deal with people with whom he had an established relationship, those whom he trusted. But these individuals were highly conscious that they had to retain the *vozhd*'s confidence.

In 1937 Stalin required his 'clients' to purge their own institutions and to destroy 'family circles'. Kaganovich abandoned his colleagues in NKPS as well as others who had been close to him, such as Yakir, Lifshits and Zimin. The network of political associates that had developed around Kaganovich and Ordzhonikidze was scattered. The murder of Kirov in 1934 removed one key connection. Ordzhonikidze's suicide in 1937 removed its principal pillar. The execution of Kosior, Chubar' and Postyshev in 1939 removed the remaining supports.

Psychologically, the Terror had a deeper brutalizing effect than the experience of the Civil War, collectivization or the Great Patriotic War. The ruling group were all complicit in the judicial murder of former friends and colleagues. The émigré Victor Kravchenko related how Ordzhonikidze's death led to an acceleration of the purge in heavy industry: 'His successor, Kaganovich, had none of Ordzhonikidze's scruples and squeamishness. He 'cooperated' and arrests of technical and industrial personnel increased sharply.'[84] Kravchenko saw him as a man transformed from an intellectual into a brutal bureaucrat. If in the mid-1920s the Soviet leaders could wander through the streets of Moscow at night, by the late 1930s they travelled in bulletproof Packard cars with security escorts.[85]

A. E. Kolman, who worked in the scientific department of the Moscow city party committee in the mid-1930s, describes the close relationship between Kaganovich and Khrushchev:

> I remember them both very well. They both bubbled with vitality and energy, and, different from each other as they may have been, they were also a lot alike. Kaganovich, in particular, possessed a superhuman capacity for work. They both compensated (not always successfully) for their lack of education and general culture by intuition, improvisation, native wit and great natural gifts. Kaganovich had a bent for systematizing and even theorizing the work, while Khrushchev's penchant was for pragmatism and technique...[86]

They were both 'easy-going, straightforward, slap-on-the-back types, open-hearted in the 'Russian style', willing to learn from their subordinates – before they were corrupted by power.

Kaganovich, more than most other leaders, was immersed in a daily routine of endless meetings. Khrushchev wrote:

> Kaganovich was a less engaging man than Voroshilov, but, in terms of industriousness, Kaganovich was a whirlwind. He worked as hard as he possibly could. He drove himself mercilessly and never kept track of time. All his time, he devoted to the party. He was a careerist, but that's another matter. I'm talking now about his style of work.[87]

Volkogonov recounts how the Central Committee during the war issued a directive ordering the heads of institutions, enterprises and agencies to conduct Marxist-Leninist studies with their staffs. I. V. Kovalev, who replaced Kaganovich as head of NKPS, recounted a sharp disagreement with Kaganovich, with the latter evidently unfamiliar with Lenin's proposition that the working class was capable of developing only trade union consciousness and that scientific theory had to be brought to them by intellectuals.[88]

Kaganovich: The Administrator and the Man

Kaganovich was one of the generation of revolutionaries-turned-administrators. His life during these decades was an almost endless round of meetings, conferences, interviews and tours of inspection. He was generally considered extremely able, a man of considerable intellect. He could be charming and had a lively sense of humour. He was adept at ingratiating himself with the *vozhd'*. More than any other of Stalin's deputies, he was instrumental in the destruction of internal party democracy, in promoting the fusion of the party and state apparatus, in subordinating the mass organizations to party dictates and in justifying repressive measures. He promoted the Communist regime's obsessive preoccupation with control and regulation; the crudity of this militarized model of administration stood at variance with the regime's protestations of its modernity.[89]

Kaganovich's career was dependent on Stalin. He sought to make himself indispensable and to place himself, in the *vozhd'*'s eyes, as beyond reproach. All of Stalin's subordinates adopted similar strategies, which compromised the Politburo's collective leadership and paved the way for a system of personalized power in which cliques within the ruling group were held in tension with one another and sought the ear and favour of the boss. Kaganovich was a Stalinist by conviction, but his relationship with the *vozhd'* was not conflict free. His demotion in 1935 shows that Stalin was not prepared to countenance a situation where any one deputy became too powerful. Kaganovich was a powerful patron within a highly clientele system. In 1930–35, as party secretary and Moscow party chief, he built up a formidable team of administrators whose careers he advanced. Once his power declined, his clients – Khrushchev, Malenkov and Bulganin – distanced themselves from their mentor.

Trotsky alludes to Stalin's psychopathic nature: 'Stalin is a past master of the art of tying a man to him not by winning his admiration, but by forcing him into complicity in heinous and unforgiveable crimes.'[90] For this, Kaganovich was prepared in 1936–39 to trample on those whom he had earlier advanced, whom he had previously considered friends. Stalin's deputies were held together by a collective guilt. But with no prospect of being held accountable for these crimes, the notion of guilt seems to have troubled them little, and, justifying their actions by reference to historical necessity, their state of denial was reinforced.

Kaganovich had a clinical, unsentimental view of politics, derived as much from Lenin as from Stalin. He was noted for his intemperate attacks on those construed as enemies of the regime. As the regime's chief troubleshooter, he was brought into abrasive confrontations, which fostered his reputation for bullying and abusing subordinates and for foul language. Roy Medvedev in his work, *Let History Judge*, wrote of Kaganovich already in the early twenties as 'distinguished by his vicious, underhanded way with people. By the early thirties he was a finished Stalinist, ready to commit any crime for the sake of his career.'[91] However, in his work *All Stalin's Men*, Medvedev offers a more nuanced, more complex picture of the man, which also acknowledges the way in which he was transformed over time:

> Of course, Kaganovich's transformation took some time, but under Stalin's influence and given the corrupting effects of unlimited power, he gradually became coarser and harsher. Moreover, as he was afraid of becoming a victim himself of the savage time in which he was living, he took refuge in destroying the lives of others.[92]

While he grovelled before Stalin, he was tyrannical in his dealing with subordinates, even on occasion resorting to physical violence.

Dimitri Volkogonov, who had a particular dislike of Kaganovich, wrote that Stalin liked Kaganovich for his 'superhuman capacity for work', his absolute lack of opinion on political matters and his uncomplaining willingness to carry out instructions, especially those of the boss. 'Cruel and extremely crude by nature, Kaganovich was the classic man of the system, the bureaucrat who would wade straight into any job without ceremony.'[93]

Robert Conquest provides a more dispassionate assessment of Kaganovich:

> Kaganovich, though to some degree shallow in his appreciation of problems, was a brilliant administrator. A clear mind and a powerful will

went with a total lack of the restraints of humanity. If we have used the word ruthless as general description of Kirov, for Kaganovich, it must be taken quite literally— there was no ruth, no pity, at all in his make-up.[94]

But Kaganovich's transformation can be understood in psychological terms. In response to the pressures placed upon them, Stalin's lieutenants were left with a choice, either to capitulate or to resist. But resistance was hopeless. The despair this bred led to Ordzhonikidze's suicide. The other deputies capitulated. These individuals were brutalized and desensitized, and required to act as Stalin's agents in the terror. It involved, in a sense, their destruction as morally autonomous beings. They adopted various defence mechanisms to rationalize their actions: denial, repression, depersonalization, reduction of affect and compartmentalization. Associated with this we see an identification with the aggressor. Above all we see the process of dissociation, whereby the individual is disconnected from the world and from others, and sees his actions as purely instrumental. Dissociation is associated with a kind of deadness, emotional and moral numbness, disregard for others – a kind of internal disintegration.[95]

Kaganovich conforms to the type of subordinate leader that we might characterize as the acolyte. The acolyte can only emerge in organizations where there is a strong leader who is intolerant of dissent. The relationship between the authoritarian leader and the acolyte is symbiotic. They need each other. The acolyte may be able and intelligent, but he accepts a subordinate role. He is bound to the leader not so much by shared ideas or ideology, but by bonds of personal loyalty. He lacks something in his personal makeup – in terms of resolve, will power, ruthlessness – that the leader possesses. His identification with the leader might be seen as a way of identifying with those leadership qualities of which he is deficient. He basks in the reflected glory of the leader, identifies himself wholly with his achievements, and justifies his every tergiversation of ideas and policy.

Kaganovich, more than any other of Stalin's deputies, conforms to this type, although all of the deputies to some degree shared some of these features. He was distinguished by his effusive protestations of loyalty to the *vozhd'*, by his central role in promoting his cult and by his part in defending and justifying the leaders' policies. He scathing attacks on the leaders' enemies won him the hatred and contempt of the oppositionists. The acolyte has to modulate his speech and actions so that he does not appear simply as a sycophant. Thus, Kaganovich's justifications of policies were often more creative and ingenious than those of Stalin himself. His attacks on the leaders' enemies were more destructive and piercing. His role was to bolster, sustain and promote the leader. He was careful not to pose any threat to the leader and acted as a watchdog against others who were deemed insufficiently loyal to him.

The role of the acolyte is to protect the leader politically, and psychologically to bolster his self-esteem. The acolyte attracts more of the venom of the leader's critics. The leader is seen as somehow distanced from the opinions of his more extreme supporters. The subordinate role of acolytes undermines their own claims to succeed as supreme leader. Without the leader they are adrift, lacking a compass by which to orientate themselves. They lack their own vision. They are not trusted. They are dependent on the support they receive, and are highly sensitive to the leader's changing opinions and moods. They are required to be pliable and can be induced to undertake tasks that others might shy away from. They are required to prove their loyalty not only in words, but in deeds. The acolyte is conscious of the threat posed to his status, dignity and reputation by the role he has assumed as the leader's alter ego. The danger to the figure who assumes the role of alter ego is the threat of a loss of self. The plight of the acolyte who loses the confidence or respect of the supreme leader is wretched.

Conclusion

The Soviet regime underwent a peculiar involution in the 1930s, whereby basic core aspects of the ideology were jettisoned, organizational practices transformed and the regime's reliance on coercion greatly extended. Stalin's drive to create a system of dictatorial and then despotic rule was central to this process. These trends were shaped by domestic and international factors and by the culture of Bolshevism and Russian authoritarianism, but a decisive factor was Stalin's own personality and his own psychological needs, which set him apart from all the other members of the ruling group. Under the pressure of the radicalization of policies after 1928–30, the Bolshevik party-state evolved through a series of cycles of repression, culminating in the Terror of 1937–38. But Stalin managed the terror and was prescient enough to check these processes when they jeopardized the regime's survival.

Kaganovich was Stalin's willing accomplice. He played a key role in promoting the Stalin cult and in developing the Stalinist political system He liked to present himself as a man, like Stalin, of strong, fixed principles. This commitment to the cause had deep roots. Like other deputies, he was caught up in developments which he could not control and of which he was also, in a sense, a victim. Accused by some of being cruel, he was not a sadist. He was not paranoid and he was not a psychopath. He displayed the psychological characteristics of Machiavellianism, being able to enforce repressive measures with a 'good conscience', willing to override moral qualms in carrying out the party's policy as a demonstration of his loyalty and ideological resolve. After 1936 Kaganovich deliberately blurred his commitment to Marxism-Leninism as an ideology and his adherence to the *vozhd*'s idiosyncratic conception of politics. For careeristic reasons and then for reasons of his own survival, he preferred to stifle any doubts.

In rationalizing the policy choices which they made, the Stalin group resorted to a whole armoury of arguments. They presented the achievement of the Soviet government in the most positive light. Harsh policy choices were justified by recourse to the argument that events had been outside of their control; that the policies pursued had been reactive, shaped by circumstances; that policies were dictated by historical necessity or that the course adopted was the 'lesser evil'. The construction of a virtuous image of the self was combined with the construction of the image of the 'enemy'. They saw Stalin as a strong leader, driven by his ideological beliefs and his ruthless understanding of *raison d'état*. Only some comprehended or could admit that this was the manifestation of a psychopathic personality.

Chapter 12

THE DESPOT'S CREATURE, 1939–1953

From 1939 to 1953 Kaganovich's influence in policy making declined dramatically, although for periods he remained a member of Stalin's leading group. These momentous years of war and postwar reconstruction, therefore, will be more cursorily examined than the preceding hectic decade. The Stalinist developmental programme became transformed with the priority of rearmament, the management of the war and the tasks of postwar reconstruction. The Stalinist regime was shaped by these changing priorities. Kaganovich's career in this period sheds light on these shifting priorities. It also illustrates his role under Stalin's personalized rule. It illustrates the survival strategies adopted by the leader's deputies, the impact that the stress of operating under these conditions of intense personal insecurity had on individuals and the way it influenced intergroup dynamics with the shift from dictatorial to despotic rule. The Terror transformed the lieutenants' relations with the *vozhd'* and their relations with one another. Terror became a central instrument of rule, but after 1939 was more carefully managed so as not to endanger the regime and to foster a sense of dependency on the leader who alone could offer protection.

In the Shadow of War, 1939–1941

Kaganovich weathered the Terror and retained his post as head of NKTyazhprom and NKPS. On 16 June 1938 Kaganovich was appointed deputy chair of Sovnarkom in place of Vlas Chubar', who had been arrested and thereafter executed.[1] This placed him among the top four leading figures. It testified to the lack of leading cadres at Stalin's disposal in 1938. Kaganovich's control of the top industrial and transport commissariats compromised the ability of Sovnarkom and Gosplan to effectively coordinate and plan the economy. This situation could not be sustained for long.

To correct this imbalance, urgent steps had to be taken to reassert the power of Sovnarkom and Gosplan over the economic and transport commissariats. On 19 January 1938 N. A. Voznesensky, a protégé of A. A. Zhdanov, became chairman of Gosplan. Sovnarkom approved a new Gosplan statute. One of Gosplan's tasks was to reduce the burden on the railways.[2] A Sovnarkom decree of 26 February 1939 condemned 'gigantomania' in planning and construction, which had also added to the burden on the railways.[3] These issues had been raised in the specialist planning journal since 1937.[4] Over-concentration of production in giant enterprises made them vulnerable in the event of war.

In a move to strengthen central control over the economy, in January 1939 the economic commissariats were subdivided. The mighty NKTyazhprom was broken up into six branch commissariats. Kaganovich at a stroke lost his position as overlord of heavy industry.[5] He was appointed head of the People's Commissariat for the Fuel Industries in charge of coal, oil and peat production. At the same time, he remained head of NKPS.

In 1938 the Soviet economy was gripped by a major fuel crisis. In October a joint Central Committee–Sovnarkom resolution, based on the report of a commission headed by Kaganovich, criticized the failure of the major coal combines and trusts to meet the planned targets and their failure to bring down the high accident rate in the mines.[6] In November, he issued orders on increasing coal output in the Donbass, improving material-technical supplies and speeding up mine construction.[7] The problems persisted and on 16 May 1939 he issued an order censuring the coal mining *glavki* and combines, demanding an increase of output in the backward mines' in the Donbass, Moscow province and the Kuzbass.[8]

On 28 December 1938 a joint Central Committee, Sovnarkom and VTsSPS resolution was directed at tightening labour discipline and reducing the high labour turnover in all sectors of industry and transport.[9] Kaganovich, as head of NKPS and NKTyazhprom, issued orders to ensure strict implementation of this resolution.[10] In June 1939 he launched a drive to recruit the wives of miners for work on the surface and underground.[11] The law prohibiting the employment of women underground was only waived several months later.

The XVIII Party Congress

Stalin's speech to the XVIII Party Congress in March 1939 stands in marked contrast to the speech he delivered to the Central Committee plenum in March 1937. He warned that the USSR would seek peace, but not at all costs. The USSR now occupied first place in terms of the 'saturation of industry with modern machinery'.[12] Contrary to the assertion of Western commentators that the purges had 'shaken' the Soviet system, he claimed they had strengthened the party-state and its links with society. The new Soviet intelligentsia constituted a major force that underlined the 'moral and political unity of Soviet society'.[13] Since 1934 some 500,000 people had been promoted to responsible party and government posts. On the concept of the 'withering away' of the state, the Red Army and Navy and the punitive organs and the intelligence service remained indispensable to secure the country's internal and external security.[14] These figures provide some measure of the generational change, a veritable sociological revolution in the composition of the Soviet party-state wrought by the Great Terror.

In his report to the congress, Kaganovich declared that socialism in the USSR had 'triumphed irreversibly', the threat of internal counter-revolution had been defeated and the country's defences had been strengthened. Stalin's call in 1931 to catch up with the advanced capitalist states in ten years had been realized.[15] He struck a light-hearted tone, joking about the division of the heavy (pregnant) NKTyazhprom, and noting how miners were achieving *komplektnost* and cyclical rhythms in their private lives as reflected in marriage rates and children born.

His report focused on the fuel crisis and measures to overcome it. The People's Commissariat of the Fuel Industry had prepared plans to develop regional coalfields, to speed up mine construction work and to accelerate measures to mechanize the industry. The expansion of the oil industry was to be based on developing the 'Second Baku' of the East between the Volga and the Urals.[16] He also highlighted the need to develop the gas industry, 'the industry of communist society'.[17]

Kaganovich hailed the fulfilment of the Second Five-Year Plan for rail freight traffic ahead of schedule as a 'Stalinist triumph.' The Soviet railways, he claimed, were operating more efficiently than those of the United States and Europe. The top priority was to strengthen the rails and rail bed in order to cope with much heavier and faster trains. He advanced ambitious plans for railway construction, including the building of the Baikal–Amur line. It was necessary to develop defence constructions and to eradicate disproportions in the network and to search out hidden reserves. The wages and conditions of railway workers had significantly improved and the number of Stakhanovites and party members on the railways was growing.[18] But the carriage of freight stagnated in 1938 and fell below plan target.[19]

He reported a huge renewal of the leading cadres of heavy industry, in particular the fuel industry and railway transport, in 1937–38, creating a new production-technical intelligentsia.[20] Of over 70,000 specialists with higher education in heavy industry, 76 per cent were 40 years of age and younger, and 80 per cent had graduated from the technical institutes since 1929.[21] They had smashed the spies and diversionists and had delivered a crushing blow to capitalist encirclement. The XVIII Party Congress, Kaganovich asserted, should be doubly named the congress of victors, marking the triumph of socialism and the adoption of the Stalin Constitution.

Molotov, in outlining the targets of the Third Five-Year Plan, demanded 'an all-round development' of the main economic regions and denounced 'gigantomania' in planning.[22] Voznesensky proposed a long-term, fifteen-year plan for the economy, based on greater regional balance, in part to reduce the burden on the railways. The congress elected a sixty-man commission, including Stalin, Molotov and Kaganovich, to revise Molotov's thesis.[23] Investment in transport as a whole during the Third Five-Year Plan was modestly raised, aimed at building up reserves to deal with the threat of war.[24] The official attack on 'gigantomania' emboldened others to speak out. The distinguished specialist T. S. Khachaturov urged large-scale investment in order to surmount the heritage of past neglect.[25]

The Politburo had already lost its role as a collective decision-making body, and membership of the Politburo provided only an indication of the ranking of the leading figures within the party-state. Kaganovich retained his Politburo and Orgburo seats, but lost his post as party secretary. A significant development was the elevation of the younger Stalinist leaders – Zhdanov, Khrushchev and Beria – as Politburo members.[26]

After the Terror, Stalin and the other leaders became more publicly visible as a display of normality. In October 1938 Kaganovich delivered an address on behalf of the party and government at the Byelorussian station to commemorate the record-breaking non-stop flight of Polina Osipenko, Valentina Grizodubova and Maria Raskova from Moscow to the Far East. He hailed the three fliers as heroines of the USSR, declaring, 'Aviation is the highest expression of our achievements. Our aviation is a child of Stalinist industrialization; the fliers are our proud falcons, brought up lovingly and with care by Stalin.'[27] In May 1939 he delivered the oration at Krupskaya's funeral,[28] a bitter irony, considering the dressing down he had administered to her in 1930. On 30 July 1939, All-Union Railway Workers Day, he addressed mass meetings in Gorky Park and in Sokol'niki Park.[29] At the celebrations of the leader's 60th birthday, in December 1939, Kaganovich hailed Stalin's role in the reconstruction of Moscow, a reference to his own past achievements and his past close association with the *vozhd'*.[30]

War Preparations

The mobilization of industry for war became the political leadership's overriding concern, prompting a struggle for precedence among leaders and the institutions they headed. In October 1937 Mikhail Kaganovich was appointed narkom of the People's Commissariat of the Defence Industry following the arrest of Rukhimovich. Molotov, as chairman of Sovnarkom's Defence Committee, proposed that the commissariat should prepare a mobilization plan. The procedure of drafting this plan provoked a sharp clash between Lazar and Mikhail Kaganovich, with the former complaining that the coordinating role of the People's Commissariat of Heavy Industry was being bypassed. His objections were rejected.[31]

In June 1938 Mikhail Kaganovich replaced Chubar' as head of the Defence Committee's Military Industrial Commission. On his fiftieth birthday in October 1938, he was awarded the Red Banner of Labour and received a congratulatory telegram from Stalin and Molotov.[32] In January 1939 the People's Commissariat of the Defence Industries was subdivided and Mikhail Kaganovich became head of the People's Commissariat for the Aviation Industry. From 1937 to 1940 he ranked among the top dozen officials who had direct access to Stalin.[33] Lazar Kaganovich and Mikhail Kaganovich exercised great influence over the defence industries. This brought them into conflict with Voznesensky, who sought to extend his control in this field.[34]

In May 1939 Molotov replaced Litvinov as commissar for Foreign Affairs, declaring that his orders were to purge the commissariat of Jews. In August Stalin and Molotov negotiated the non-aggression pact with the German foreign minister Joachim von Ribbentrop, with the other Politburo members as onlookers. Kaganovich in the 1930s was the subject of a bitter anti-Semitic campaign by leading Nazi propagandists. At the banquet in honour of Ribbentrop Kaganovich recalled that Stalin proposed a toast to Lazar Kaganovich as a means of demonstrating the differences between the two regimes on the issue of anti-Semitism.[35] Nevertheless, the signing of the Nazi–Soviet Pact unleashed an upsurge of popular anti-Semitism in the USSR.

Kaganovich's own position was not secure. On 13 September, at a meeting of the Defence Committee, Stalin scathingly rebuked Kaganovich for shortcomings in the coal industry and on the railways, which he blamed on the constant reshuffling of personnel and the appointment of unqualified Stakhanovite workers as directors of coalmine combines. The Central Committee (i.e. Stalin himself), he reported, had instructed Kaganovich to curb the high turnover of cadres.[36] In October the Fuel Commissariat was split in two. Kaganovich headed the People's Commissariat of the Oil Industry, while V. V. Vakhrushev took over the more important Commissariat for the Coal Industry.

The battles between the Red Army and Japanese forces at Lake Khasan in Manchuria in the summer of 1938 and at Khalkhin Gol in the summer of 1939 placed new demands on the railways.[37] The Winter War with Finland in 1939–40 seriously disrupted the rail transport network of the industries of Moscow and Leningrad. The integration of the rail systems of the Baltic states, eastern Poland, northern Bukovina and Bessarabia (with their European standard gauge) into the Soviet network under the terms of the Nazi–Soviet Pact, posed new problems.[38]

The construction of the Baikal–Amur line was halted in 1941 and this ambitious scheme was not resumed again until the 1970s and only completed in 1991.

Following the partition of Poland between Nazi Germany and the USSR, some 25,700 Polish army and police officers were apprehended by the Soviet authorities. Beria's recommendation, dated 5 March 1940, that they be executed was endorsed by Stalin, Voroshilov, Molotov and Mikoyan, with Kalinin and Kaganovich giving their consent.[39] On 21 March Beria sent Kaganovich a request that NKPS provide the NKVD with railway wagons to transport16,000 prisoners, evidently part of the contingent of Polish officers consigned to be executed.[40] When the German forces unearthed the mass graves at Katyn in 1943, the Soviet authorities placed the blame on the Nazi regime. Only in 1990 did the Soviet authorities finally admit the truth.

In 1940 investment in the railways was raised by 20 per cent to over 6000 million rubles, substantially above the target for the Third Five-Year Plan.[41] Priority was accorded to defence construction projects and to the development of the rail network in the eastern part of the country.[42] The freight targets were relentlessly pushed upwards. The Supreme Soviet on 26 June 1940 introduced new draconian rules on labour discipline.[43] This law was widely applied and infractions of timekeeping and labour regulations were punished with periods in labour camps.[44]

On 4 April 1940 Mikhail Kaganovich was replaced as head of the People's Commissariat of the Aviation Industry by A. I. Shakhurin.[45] He was appointed manager of an aircraft works. The same month, Voznesensky was appointed chairman of Sovnarkom's Council for the Defence Industries. On 24 July the Politburo's Defence Commission was reorganized, with Voroshilov (chairman), Voznesensky (vice chairman), Stalin, S. K. Timoshenko, Beria, Kaganovich, N. G. Kuznetsov and B. M. Shaposhnikov as members.[46]

Lazar Kaganovich's own position was also weakened. The commissariat for the oil industry was placed under Sovnarkom's Council for the Fuel and Electricity Industry, chaired by M. G. Pervukhin.[47] With difficulties in fuel supply persisting, on 7 August Kaganovich was replaced as head of the commissariat by his deputy, I. K. Sedin. He thus lost his last post in industrial administration. Kaganovich's leadership of NKPS was now also subjected to searching criticism. On 17 January 1941 a NKVD memorandum signed by Beria and S. R. Mil'shtein, head of NKVD's Main Transport Administration, identified a 'number of serious abnormalities' in NKPS's war preparation, including the failure to draft a mobilization plan.[48]

The XVIII Party Conference in February 1941 was devoted to industrial and transport mobilization. Voznesensky, chairman of Gosplan, criticized the country's excessive dependence on the railways and demanded that NKPS eliminate irrationalities and bottlenecks in freight shipments.[49] Kaganovich's absence from the conference may reflect his preoccupation with the problems of supplying the front in the Finnish War.

At the conference, Mikhail Kaganovich was threatened with dismissal and loss of his Central Committee seat if he failed to implement party and government assignments.[50] In the following weeks, he was accused of organizing a 'fascist centre', with the aim that he was to become vice-president in the event of the Nazis seizing Moscow. A Politburo committee comprising Malenkov, Beria and Mikoyan was charged with investigating the matter. Boris Vannikov, narkom of the People's Commissariats of Armaments and Mikhail Kaganovich's former deputy, testified against him. As a result, Mikhail Kaganovich committed suicide. Lazar Kaganovich insisted that his brother was never placed under arrest and had shot himself in the Sovnarkom building. He described him as a hot-blooded, temperamental but resolute man who preferred suicide rather than imprisonment, and, what he does not say, torture, whose use he had himself endorsed in 1937.[51]

Khrushchev, in his memoirs, indignantly condemned Kaganovich for his failure to defend his brother, and for his silence following his suicide: 'And all the while, Lazar Moiseyevich never stopped grovelling before Stalin.'[52] Roy Medvedev asserts that at a Politburo session, Stalin had praised Lazar Kaganovich's 'principled' stance on the matter.[53] In conversation with Chuev, Kaganovich vehemently denied Khrushchev's charges:

> I defended my brother. But not as a brother, as a worker, as a man whom I knew. Not as a brother. I staunchly, resolutely defended him. I defended many. On some cases, Stalin obstructed me.[54]

He dismissed the charge that Mikhail Kaganovich was to head a pro-Nazi government as 'idiocy'.[55]

This affair underlined the vicious intrigues at the top, which Stalin nurtured and exploited. Beria used the same line of attack against Kaganovich as he had with Ordzhonikidze, namely, by attacking their brothers.[56] It exposed Kaganovich's weakened position, and stoked bitter personal enmity between him and Beria.

The War Years, 1941–1945

With war looming, Sovnarkom was strengthened as the coordinating and directing centre. On 21 March 1941 a new Sovnarkom Bureau assumed most of the functions of Sovnarkom's Defence Committee and Economic Council. On 4 May Stalin became chairman of Sovnarkom, with Molotov as his deputy.[57] On 7 May the Politburo approved the Bureau of Sovnarkom, with

Stalin as chairman and Voznesensky as first deputy chairman.[58] Kaganovich was listed as one of 15 deputy chairmen.[59]

On 22 June 1941 the German forces invaded the USSR. In the following six days, Stalin held high-level meetings of military, security, party and government chiefs. Kaganovich was in attendance at all of these meetings. Khrushchev, Molotov and Mikoyan concur that Stalin, taken aback by the rapid German advance, at one point withdrew from active work for a number of days until a delegation of Politburo members persuaded him to return.[60] Kaganovich dismissed this as simply a legend, refusing to acknowledge that the political colossus had feet of clay.[61] Stalin was for a moment vulnerable, but as in earlier crises, his lieutenants rallied around him. He had chosen his deputies for their compliance to his will and had chosen well.

On 23 June the main command (Stavka) of the Soviet armed forces was formed with Stalin as supreme commander. It was dominated by senior military and government figures. Kaganovich was one of 13 figures listed as counsellors. On 30 July the State Defence Committee (GKO) was established, headed by Stalin, with Molotov as deputy head. Other members were NKVD chief Beria, Central Committee secretary Malenkov, and Marshall Voroshilov. In February 1942 Mikoyan, Voznesensky and Kaganovich were added. Voznesensky oversaw the war economy and other members had charge of key sectors: Molotov (tank industry); Malenkov (aircraft and aero-engines), Mikoyan (consumer goods), Voznesensky then Beria (armaments and ammunition) and Kaganovich (rail transport).[62]

On 27 June the Evacuation Council was set up, with Kaganovich as chairman. On 16 July, as problems with evacuation mounted, N. M. Shvernik replaced Kaganovich as chairman. His place on the Council was taken by his deputy at NKPS, B. N. Arutyunov.[63] The Herculean tasks of wartime management of NKPS and of the Evacuation Council was beyond the ability of even Kaganovich. In 1941 some 2,593 factories were evacuated to the rear by the Soviet railways. In an interview in 1990, Kaganovich emphasized his role as head of NKPS in the evacuation of factories from particular centres such as Zaporozhe.[64]

On 17 or 18 October Stalin convened a meeting of senior leaders in the Kremlin to approve the evacuation of key ministries from the capital.[65] In his memoirs, Mikoyan recalled how Kaganovich turned to him in the lift and said, 'Listen, when the night comes to leave, please tell me, so that I am not left here.'[66] This is presented as evidence of Kaganovich's loss of nerve. Before 1938 Kaganovich and Mikoyan had been close friends. In confiding his vulnerability, Kaganovich may have been seeking to re-establish a bond between them. Mikoyan's memoirs, which seek to elevate his own role in the wartime evacuation, indicate that during the war, relations between the two further deteriorated.

Kaganovich was evacuated with the commissariat NKPS to Kuibyshev. In the winter of 1941–42 the railways encountered serious difficulties. At one stage, Beria was given oversight of the railways. In February 1942 Stalin, at a meeting of GKO, announced a decision to create a Transport Commission, appointing himself its chairman and warning that anyone failing to carry out its orders would be referred to the military tribunal.[67] A GKO resolution dated 25 March complained that NKPS had disintegrated into a 'federation' of semiautonomous administrations.[68] The militarization of the railways also served to create parallel lines of authority that weakened the narkom's power. The next day, Kaganovich was replaced as narkom of NKPS by General A. V. Khrulev. This was a devastating blow to his standing. Under Khrulev's leadership, the transport bottleneck was solved and capacity utilization improved, but the rail system continued to be dogged by problems.[69]

Kaganovich requested that Stalin assign him to the front.[70] On 28 July 1942 Stavka created the Military Council of the North Caucasus headed by M. Budyennyi. On Stalin's proposal, Kaganovich was appointed a member of the council. He flew immediately to Krasnodar to take up his duties. The Council coordinated its work with the military commander of the front, I. V. Tyulenev, the Krasnodar province party committee, headed by its first secretary P. I. Seleznev, the Stavropol territorial party committee, headed by its first secretary M. A. Suslov, and with the Ministry of Oil Industry, headed by Nikolai Baibakov.[71] In the summer of 1942 the Wehrmacht staged a successful offensive on the southwestern front but in the autumn, a fierce Soviet counteroffensive was mounted, aimed at halting the German drive to seize the oil wells of the Caucasus.

Kaganovich was involved in selecting commanders and political workers and had charge of the military tribunals that dealt with infractions of discipline.[72] He kept up his correspondence with Stalin.[73] In October 1942 he was wounded in the arm by enemy bombing while on a mission to improve supply lines. In November, Kaganovich, Tyulenev, commander of the North Caucasus front, and General I. E. Petrov, head of the Black Sea group, were summoned to Moscow to report to the GKO.[74] Kaganovich had discussion with Stalin about the situation and after two days in Moscow, flew back via Tiblisi to the front. L. I. Brezhnev, deputy head of the Political Administration and Tyulenev provided him letters testifying to his role in organizing the front.[75]

N. I. Strakhov, who oversaw road transport in Caucasus in these years, recounted Kaganovich's arrival to investigate affairs accompanied by his personal bodyguards, aides and consultants. Around him there developed a 'double-dyed cult of personality', and within the organization there ruled 'an oppressive atmosphere of intrigue, suspiciousness and distrust'. His recall was met with a sigh of relief.[76]

The winter of 1942–43 marked a turning point in the war with the major Soviet victory at Stalingrad. But this coincided with major difficulties on the railways. In February 1943 Kaganovich was reappointed head of NKPS. After a twelve-month absence, his recall might be seen as recognition that he possessed certain administrative qualities of drive and great attention to detail. On 15 April martial law was imposed on the railways. On 31 May the railway *politotdely*, established in 1933, was abolished in the name of strengthening individual managerial authority and responsibility.[77] In the summer, the situation on the railways improved. Stalin, in his speech on 6 November, paid tribute to the achievements of the railways.[78] On 5 November the Supreme Soviet honoured Kaganovich, his deputies, leading officials and prominent Stakhanovites as Heroes of Socialist Labour.[79] On 21 November, on his fiftieth birthday, Kaganovich was awarded the Order of Lenin. Stalin sent him his signed greetings on behalf of the Central Committee and Sovnarkom.[80] He appeared to have returned to the inner circle. In February 1944 Kaganovich, in an ebullient mood, together with other leaders attended a reception for the American, British and Czechoslovakian ambassadors.[81]

GKO's Operative Bureau, headed by Beria, Malenkov, Mikoyan and Voznesensky, organized the war economy. From 23 May to 29 December 1944 Kaganovich, as head of NKPS, attended 37 sessions out of 46. From 26 December 1944 until 28 August 1945, he attended 38 out of 48 meetings of the Operative Bureau.[82] By the summer of 1943 Soviet and allied victory over Nazi Germany was seen as a matter of time. The immense strain placed on the Soviet economy in 1941 and 1942 was eased. But GKO's Operative Bureau in July–August and again in November–December 1943, held extensive discussions on the problems of the railways. According to Roy Medvedev, on 16 March 1944 the People's Commissariat of State Security (NKGB), on the authorization of Stalin and Kaganovich, purged NKPS's management.[83] On 12 December 1944 GKO's Operative Bureau dismissed Kaganovich as head of NKPS and censured NKPS's failure to meet its freight targets, particularly regarding the supply of coal to the major factories. He was replaced by General I.V. Kovalev as narkom of NKPS.[84] He remained a member of the Operative Bureau, but was thereafter listed as a deputy chairman of Sovnarkom.[85]

Kaganovich's diminished standing within Stalin's council is clearly reflected in his declining attendance at the meetings in the latter's office. In 1939 he attended 89 meetings and in 1940 he attended 43 meetings. In the first six months of 1941 he attended 25 out of 104 meetings.[86] With his dismissal as head of NKPS in 1942, he ceased to attend the meetings in Stalin's private office. Even with his recall in March 1943, his attendance at these meetings was sporadic.[87] This highly significant fall from favour is absent from Kaganovich's memoirs.

Estimates of Kaganovich's role vary widely. Soviet historiography, following his disgrace in 1957, portrayed him as a leader who covered up his lack of expertise and competence with force of will and dictatorial methods.[88] He was sacked twice as head of NKPS.[89] But Kaganovich led the railways during 30 of the 48 months that the war lasted. Kovalev, his successor at NKPS, held his technical competence in high regard.[90] He recounted that Kaganovich was immersed in managing the affairs of NKPS; rarely was he seen at the meetings in Stalin's office, where Molotov, Beria and Malenkov were in regular attendance.[91] A proper objective assessment of his role as head of NKPS during the war remains to be written.

Marshall Zhukov held Kovalev in high regard as one of the principal architects of military victory.[92] He remained as head of the ministry of rail transport until he was replaced in June 1948 by B. P. Beshchev, who led the ministry for the next decade and a half. Much later, Kaganovich sought to claim some of the credit, stressing that NKPS's wartime performance had been made possible only because of the accumulation of reserves which had been undertaken in peacetime.[93]

Stalin failed to anticipate the German invasion in 1941 and he presided over the disastrous conduct of the war in 1941 and 1942. Only with the delegation of greater military control to Zhukov was the tide of war gradually turned. Typically, Stalin was jealous of sharing credit for the victory. In 1945 he convened a special session, attended by Beria, Kaganovich and other top party officials and military commanders, and, on the basis of the evidence from some arrested generals, Zhukov was accused of 'awarding himself the laurels of the chief victor'. Some of the generals spoke in Zhukov's defence. Stalin, instead of arresting him, demoted him to command post, first in Odessa and then in the Urals.[94] Even the despot's powers were not unlimited.

Postwar Recovery, 1946–1953

The years 1946 to 1953 were dominated by the task of post war reconstruction. But this was also the era of 'High Stalinism'. Stalin, in his toast to the 'Great Russian people' at a Kremlin reception in June 1945 and his speech on the defeat of Japan, which stressed the removal of the blot on Russian history caused by the defeat of imperial forces in 1904–5, underlined the new theme of Soviet and Russian patriotism. The transformation of the USSR into a superpower and the head of the world communist movement reflected the development of the new communist empire.

The victory provided the basis for relegitimizing the Soviet regime, based on cultural regimentation and the construction of an orchestrated consensus. The Cold War heightened international tensions. The process of relegitimation saw the emergence of new currents. First was the attack on western cosmopolitanism, spearheaded by Zhdanov in 1945–46, which fostered the mood of cultural chauvinism and transformed the intellectual climate, with attacks on the journals *Zvezda* and *Leningrad*. Stalin closely directed the campaign, with Zhdanov acting as his master's mouthpiece.[95] The second was the growth of official anti-Semitism from 1947 onward.

Politically, this period was marked by the reconsolidation of the Stalinist regime and the flourishing of the leader cult. In 1945–46, for a brief period, formal meetings of the Politburo were convened, but this was quickly abandoned. Stalin controlled decision making at the highest level through Politburo commissions – 'quintets', 'sextets', 'septets' and 'novenaries'.[96] Volkogonov asserts that it was during the war that the 'night watch', whereby Stalin invited select Politburo members to dine at his dacha at Kuntsevo, became established.[97] These years were marked by acute struggles within the ruling circle, between the Zhdanov-Voznesensky group and the Malenkov-Beria group.

At the end of 1944 Sovnarkom set up a committee, chaired by Malenkov, to deal with the dismantling of German industry in payment of reparations to the USSR. This policy may have been supported by Beria and Kaganovich, both of whom were interested in securing equipment for the enterprises they controlled.[98] It was criticized by Zhdanov and Voznesensky. The policy was abandoned following a report from a commission headed by Mikoyan, which instead established Soviet-owned corporations in Germany to produce goods for the USSR.

From December 1944 until March 1947 Kaganovich headed the People's Commissariat for Construction Materials.[99] In 1945 production of construction materials was only a fraction of pre-war levels. Kaganovich visited the main works, and summoned an all-union meeting of workers of the industry to discuss their role in the Fourth Five-Year Plan.[100]

At the end of the war Sovnarkom was renamed the Council of Ministers. According to Molotov, sometime in 1946 Stalin proposed that they should find someone younger to take his place as chairman of the Council of Ministers and proposed Molotov. Kaganovich, Molotov recalls, was reduced to tears at this.[101] Kaganovich denied any recollection of the incident. On various occasions, Stalin, in reviewing the question of his successor, ruled out Kaganovich along with other figures.[102] In reality, Kaganovich had already lost out in this contest in 1939. Stalin remained head of government and of the party until his death.

Ukrainian Interlude, 1947

In 1946 Ukraine was afflicted by famine. A great many chairmen of collective farm, state farm and MTS were dismissed. The restoration of the coal and metallurgical industry from the devastation of war also encountered difficulties. On 27 February 1947 Stalin assigned Kaganovich as first secretary of the republic.[103] He replaced Khrushchev, although the latter retained the post of chairman of the Council of Ministers in Ukraine.[104] But for much of this period, Khrushchev was incapacitated by pneumonia.

On 12 March Kaganovich addressed the Ukrainian Central Committee plenum on the problems of Ukrainian agriculture. His speech was a long-winded, tiresome litany of slogans and clichés. He was no longer the volcanic force which he had been. He blamed the shortcomings of agriculture on the Ukrainian Ministry of Agriculture. Members of the Ukrainian Politburo were sent out to the regions to enforce directives on harvesting and grain collection. He clashed with N. S. Patolichev, a Malenkov protégé, who was Central Committee secretary in charge of Agriculture, as a result of which the latter was transferred to Rostov.

Kaganovich maintained close contact with Stalin, informing him of developments and submitting demands for technical assistance. In July he ordered the Ukrainian MVD (Ukranian Ministry of Internal Affairs) and the Procuracy to wage a campaign against thefts of state property, sabotage and terroristic acts against the Soviet authorities. These measures recall Stalin's response to the grain crisis in August 1932. The grain collection target was attained in October 1947, but efforts were made to overfulfil the target.[105] Kaganovich was subsequently charged with grave errors in agricultural policy, including reducing the acreage of winter wheat in favour of spring-sown wheat.[106]

Kaganovich also intervened in industrial policy, investigating the building of the steel works of 'Azovstal' and 'Zaporozhstal', the reconstruction of the coal industry of the Donbass and the problems of the electrical power industry.[107] He had contact with Brezhnev, first secretary of Zaporozhe, and from their war time work, Kaganovich held him in high regard.[108]

Khrushchev's relations with Kaganovich also deteriorated:

> He became simply unbearable. He developed his intensive activities in two directions: against the so-called Ukrainian nationalists and against the Jews. A Jew himself, Kaganovich was against the Jews! His anti-Semitism was directed mainly against the Jews who happened to be on friendly terms with me.[109]

Kaganovich initiated an ideological campaign against bourgeois nationalism in the Ukrainian Academy of Science and the Ukrainian Institute of Marxism-Leninism.[110] Leading historians and writers were censured. Kaganovich denounced the Jewish writer I. Kipnis for 'Jewish chauvinistic

Zionism'.[111] Maksim Rylsky was dismissed as chairman of the Ukrainian Writers Union.[112] Pavel Sudoplatov, a leading security agent, claims that he organized the assassination of A. Ya. Shumsky in September 1946 and other Ukrainian figures on the orders of Khrushchev and Kaganovich.[113] This testimony needs to be treated with great scepticism. The assassination predated Kaganovich's assignment to Ukraine, and decisions of this kind were decided at the very top.

Kaganovich continued to stress the achievements of Soviet power which had given Ukraine a state, had unified the historic ethnic lands of Ukraine and created the basis for the cultural and economic development of the republic.[114]

Following the successful harvest of 1947, Kaganovich was recalled to Moscow, and Khrushchev again took up the post as first party secretary of Ukraine. This episode poisoned relations between the two, but Kaganovich in his memoirs claimed they had worked on a friendly basis.[115]

The Postwar Leadership

In the postwar period Stalin, while dominating internal security, foreign and defence policy, delegated the details of economic management to his deputies. The Bureau of the Council of Ministers oversaw postwar reconstruction. Its weekly sessions were chaired in turn by Beria, Mikoyan and Voznesensky. It provided for a more formal, predictable system of rule. Stalin rarely (if ever) attended its meetings. Kaganovich regularly attended the bureau's sessions from 1946 to 1953, except for 1947, when he was in Ukraine, and from July to September 1950, when he was again absent.[116] Stalin controlled the Council of Ministers through his deputies. The Council was headed by a bureau, which from February 1947 was chaired by Molotov. There were eight new sectoral bureaus for different branches of the economy, with Kaganovich in charge of Transport and Communication.[117]

Kaganovich from 1941 to 1947 was largely excluded from attending the meetings in Stalin's office. In 1948 Stalin capriciously returned him to favour as one of the inner circle.[118] This did not reflect the assumption of any new posts by Kaganovich that would have justified such a recall. Instead, Stalin needed someone he could rely on in controlling his deputies, and in managing the rivalries between the Malenkov-Beria and the Zhdanov-Voznesensky groups, and who could lend him political and psychological support.

On his recall from Ukraine in December 1947, Kaganovich was reappointed deputy chairman of the Council of Ministers.[119] He had oversight of the Ministry of Heavy Industry Construction, the Ministry of Construction

Material Industry and the Committee for Architecture. On Stalin's initiative, he was appointed chairman of the State Committee for Material Technical Supplies of the National Economy of the USSR – Gossnab – which, on Stalin's initiative, was created out of Gosplan with the task to plan the distribution of all material resources of the state. He also had oversight over all branches of transport.[120] Stalin saw Kaganovich as his eyes and ears in the Council of Ministers.[121]

On 31 August 1948 Zhdanov died of a heart attack and soon after, many of his supporters were purged. Voznesensky was arrested and executed in 1949. A. A. Kuznetsov and other leading figures from Leningrad suffered the same fate.[122] The 'Leningrad Affair' marked a return, on a local level, to the methods of 1936–38. Kaganovich's loss of political influence from 1940 onward was associated with the rise of Voznesensky. His return to favour in 1948 was associated with the fall of Voznesensky. Kaganovich no doubt welcomed his rival's demise, but played no role in it. His loss of power had also been associated with the rise of Beria, and his return to favour was associated with moves to weaken the Malenkov-Beria group. In December 1949 Stalin appointed Khrushchev, for whom he had a particular fondness, to replace G. M. Popov, secretary of the Moscow Party committee, as part of a scheme to build up a group to counterbalance the Malenkov-Beria group.[123]

Stalin became increasingly distrustful of his deputies. For a time he suspected Voroshilov of being a British agent. In March 1949 Molotov was sacked as foreign minister and replaced by Vyshinsky. Molotov's wife, Polina Zhemchuzhina, was accused of Zionism and he was obliged to divorce her. At this time, Mikoyan was sacked as minister of foreign trade and Kaganovich lost his post as chairman of Gossnab.[124] Khrushchev later decried Kaganovich's administrative skills, asserting that as chairman of Gossnab this 'genius' had devised a mathematical formula to reduce the stocks of materials and goods held in the factories.[125] In fact, no solution was ever found to the persistent and endemic problem of excessive stockpiling within the planned economy.

On 1 September 1949 the chairmanship of the Council of Ministers' bureau passed to five deputy chairmen – Beria, Bulganin, Malenkov, Kaganovich and M. Z. Saburov – who chaired the sessions in turn[126] On 18 October 1951 Molotov, Mikoyan and Kaganovich were freed from duties at the Council of Ministers and assigned to new commissions established by the party Politburo.

Kaganovich and Stalin

Khrushchev, whose relations with Kaganovich had been poisoned after 1947, depicts him as an obsequious lackey and flatterer of Stalin.[127] At private gatherings of the leadership, he would frequently expostulate on the need to substitute 'Stalinism' for 'Leninism' as the party credo. Molotov recalls that in this period Khrushchev would support Kaganovich's proposal.[128] Stalin, according to Khrushchev, would rebuke Kaganovich for daring to make such a suggestion, while, evidently, also flattered by it. Khrushchev adds, 'Kaganovich was unsurpassed in his viciousness. Stalin used to hold him up as an example of a man "resolute in his class consciousness" and "implacable towards his class enemies."'[129] Kaganovich had early learnt how to cater to Stalin's narcissism, but also, like his master, to dress up lack of scruples as the highest form of principledness. Khrushchev recounts that Kaganovich was treacherous towards his colleagues and that he used Molotov's fall from grace in 1949 as a means to ingratiate himself with Stalin:

> Kaganovich's maliciousness was a particularly good barometer of Molotov's precarious position. Incited by Stalin, Kaganovich played the part of a vicious cur who was unleashed to tear limb from limb any member of the Politburo toward whom he sensed Stalin's coolness, and Kaganovich was turned loose on Molotov.[130]

But Kaganovich, Khrushchev asserted, was a cowardly figure who would back down if enough Politburo members stood up against him. Kaganovich's obsequious attitude to Stalin was by no means unique. Khrushchev, who was close to Stalin, showed himself desirous to anticipate and gratify his master's every whim.

The celebration of Stalin's seventieth birthday in 1949 saw an phenomenal elaboration of his cult. At this time, Kaganovich even proposed that Moscow be renamed Stalinodar in his honour, a proposal that Stalin himself indignantly rejected.[131]

Kaganovich cultivated the role of the ultraloyalist executive, distinguished by his obsequiousness and his flattery of Stalin, and his ruthless treatment of subordinates became most pronounced. By ingratiation, Kaganovich sought to re-establish himself with the *vozhd'*, a reflection of his own personal weaknesses and his vulnerability. His involvement in Stalin's crimes drained him of autonomy as a moral being with his own conscience and will. It was deeply rooted in his conception of Stalin and of himself, reflecting his need to identify himself with the boss, to rationalize his own actions and to anchor himself as a historic actor as a means to salve his conscience. This represented a particular psychological adaptation by which his sense of self became subjugated to an idealized image of the dominant *vozhd'*.[132] This was not merely an expedient survival strategy; it long survived Stalin's death in 1953.

Anti-Semitism and the Doctors' Plot

The Nazis massacred about half of the 5 million Jews in the USSR who were concentrated in Byelorussia, Western Ukraine and the Baltic republics. In December 1941 the Jewish Anti-Fascist Committee (JAFC) was established, aimed at mobilizing international support for the war effort. Kaganovich kept himself aloof from this body.[133] Anti-Semitism remained a powerful force. In August 1942 G. E. Aleksandrov, head of the Department of Agitation, and a Zhdanov protégé, advocated removing Jews from leading positions in the administration of culture, but this was not acted on.[134] In September 1945 in west Ukraine, newly incorporated into the USSR, one local party committee refused to display Kaganovich's portrait alongside those of other Politburo members.[135]

Strangely, we know nothing of Kaganovich's response to the Holocaust. At the end of the war, the matter of a Jewish homeland was raised. In 1945 leading Jewish activists solicited his support for various projects for such a homeland in the Crimea, Birobidzhan and in Palestine.[136] Given his attitude to things Jewish, it is unlikely that he took any initiative.

Stalin's anti-Semitism became more pronounced. A report compiled by Mikhail Suslov in November 1946 accused the JAFC of nationalism and Zionism, and in the following summer, its leadership was changed.[137] The writer Viktor Nekrasov recounts a meeting with Stalin in 1947 at which the latter expressed admiration for Hitler's solution 'of genius' to the Jewish problem, posing to Khrushchev, in a typically provocative way, the question of whether Kaganovich himself was not a 'thief'.[138] In 1948, on Stalin's orders, the famous Jewish actor Solomon Mikhoels was killed in Minsk.[139] Itshak Fefer, on behalf of JAFC, passed on letters of condolences from abroad on the death of Mikhoels to Kaganovich.[140]

Within the leading circle, anti-Semitic views were current but not openly expressed. According to Khrushchev, Stalin did not voice anti-Semitic views in Kaganovich's presence.[141] Relations between Beria and Kaganovich were bad. Beria in private referred to him as 'Lazar the Israelite'.[142] Kaganovich returned as a regular attendee of the meetings in Stalin's Kremlin office in 1948. Stalin could thus use Kaganovich as a cover, allowing himself to promote anti-Semitism while absolving himself of the charge of being an anti-Semite. This conforms to what we know of the instrumental way Stalin used people.

Following the foundation of the Israeli state in 1948, anti-Semitism in the USSR received official encouragement. Jewish culture thereafter was severely repressed: all publications in Yiddish ended and the Yiddish theatres were closed down. In 1952 the leaders of the JAFC and prominent figures in Jewish culture were arrested, tried and executed. Stalin may have contemplated the mass deportation of all Soviet Jews, but archival evidence of this has proved elusive.[143]

Kaganovich stood by as the anti-Semitic campaign mounted. His position within the leadership was shielded by his past close relationship with Stalin and, paradoxically, by his standing as the most prominent Jew in Soviet public life. When N. M. Mikhailov, secretary of the Central Committee, presented him with a document signed by some prominent Jewish citizens charging Jewish Kremlin doctors with plotting against the lives of the party leaders, he informed Stalin that he would not sign as a Jewish social activist, but would sign the document as a Politburo member. In his memoirs, he rejected the charge that Stalin was an anti-Semite and denied that there had ever been any plans for the wholesale resettlement of Jews in the USSR.[144] But Kaganovich must have known that Stalin had used him as a cover to promote his anti-Semitic policies.

The XIX Party Congress

At the XIX Party Congress in October 1952, Stalin, who was obviously frail, delivered only a short report on the prospects for socialist development, particularly in the developing world. His criticisms of Molotov and Mikoyan underlined the precariousness of their positions. The congress was dominated by Malenkov as the obvious heir-apparent, and by Beria and Khrushchev. Kaganovich chaired one of the congress sessions and delivered a brief speech largely devoted to praising Stalin's 'theoretical genius' as the author of *The Economic Problems of Socialism in the USSR*. He proposed revising the 1919 Party Programme to take account of the *vozhd*'s latest pronouncements and became one of the members of the commission, chaired by Stalin, to undertake this work.[145]

On Stalin's command, the congress established the new party Presidium of twenty-five members and eleven candidates to replace the Politburo.[146] Khrushchev asserts that Stalin selected the members in consultation with Kaganovich. For more effective decision making, Stalin proposed a bureau of nine men and immediately appointed them himself: Malenkov, Beria, Khrushchev, Voroshilov, Kaganovich, Saburov, Pervukhin and Bulganin. The Presidium never met, and all matters were nominally decided by a camarilla of five, namely, Stalin, Malenkov, Beria, Bulganin and Khrushchev.[147] Kaganovich and Voroshilov rarely attended these meetings. Molotov and Mikoyan were excluded from the bureau and remained out of favour to the end.

Stalin may have intended the establishment of the Presidium as a step towards a thorough renewal of the leadership. He maintained his control by concentrating power within a small but changing core of deputies. He capriciously favoured, intimidated and humiliated his lieutenants. The politics of the late Stalin era acquired a venomous, surreal, psychotic quality. With his physical and mental powers in decline, Stalin became reliant in his final years on Malenkov, Beria and Khrushchev. His inconclusive manoeuvres against Beria in 1952–53 indicate that he could no longer dominate his subordinates as in the past. But he continued to exercise an absolute veto on any policy innovations. From 1945 to 1953 the population of the Gulag and forced labour settlements ballooned to over 5 million.

Conclusion

From 1941 until 1948 Kaganovich was conspicuously excluded from Stalin's inner circle. The suicide of his brother indicated his loss of influence. He lost his place in industrial administration. His demise was associated with the rise of Voznesensky and Beria. In 1942 and 1944 he was dismissed as head of NKPS, in both cases being replaced by his own deputy. Through his ruthless policies in Ukraine in 1947 he succeeded in re-establishing himself in Stalin's standing. In 1948 he returned as a member of the ruling group, in his self-ascribed role as the *vozhd*'s eyes and ears, as a prop and support for the leader and as an adviser on personnel matters. His return to favour was associated with Stalin's moves against Voznesensky and his move to check the power of the Beria-Malenkov group, although Kaganovich does not appear to have played a key role in these manoeuvres. Stalin's moves against Molotov and Mikoyan in 1949 were also instrumental in his return to favour.

But Kaganovich was no longer indispensable to Stalin as he had been in the 1930s. He no longer held key positions in the party or state apparatus, and his standing was based on his role as the despot's creature, and as a dependable political prop. In the post war era he assumed the role of one of the party's elder statesmen, an adviser and a troubleshooter. With the demise of his rivals he no doubt entertained the hope of regaining the position of influence that he had had in the 1930s. The anti-Semitic campaign of the late Stalin era made him conspicuously vulnerable.

Chapter 13

DE-STALINIZATION AND NEMESIS, 1953–1991

Stalin died on 5 March 1953. The ensuing succession struggle was bound up with questions of policy and ideology, and with questions regarding the restructuring the party-state and reordering state–societal relations as part of the general issue of coping with dismantling Stalin's tyrannical regime. The process of 'de-Stalinization' that ensued represented represented an attempt, within strictly controlled limits, to come to terms with the legacy of the Stalin era. In this power struggle, Molotov and Kaganovich, the leading figures of the Stalinist old guard, sought to re-establish their authority. But the reappraisal of the Stalin era posed serious dangers for them, which they were slow to recognize. The *vozhd*'s despotic rule, the regime of terror, the Gulag, all that had been considered necessary to the survival of the state were now to be reinterpreted as an incubus that had inhibited the state's development and had imposed a crippling cost on society. The developmental priorities of the regime after 1953 were driven by the task of dismantling the Stalinist regime, reorientating the state's relationship with society, and shifting the economic priorities of the regime to take greater account of consumer expectations.

Stalin's death remains shrouded in mystery. Molotov and Khrushchev both later hinted that his death was not natural. Molotov reports that Beria even claimed responsibility for the death, asserting that he had saved his colleagues by his action. For those under the despot's suspicions – Beria, Molotov and Mikoyan – his death must have been a relief.[1] For others, it was a loss. Svetlana Alliluyeva records that she saw Voroshilov, Kaganovich, Malenkov, Bulganin and Khrushchev in tears. They were bound to Stalin by a 'common cause', and were 'under the spell of his extraordinary personality'.[2] Extraordinary might be here translated as pathological.

Kaganovich later acknowledged that he had shed tears on Stalin's death.[3] Khrushchev and Kaganovich were in the commission for the funeral. According to Kaganovich, Khrushchev asked him, 'How, Lazar, will we live and work without Stalin?'[4] But Khrushchev was the only leader to acknowledge the enormity of Stalin's crimes. At a meeting of the Presidium on 10 March 1953, he addressed his colleagues, 'I, Khrushchev, you, Klim [Voroshilov], you, Lazar [Kaganovich], you, Vyacheslav Mikhailovich [Molotov] – we should all offer repentance to the people for 1937.'[5]

During the night of 4 March 1953, a meeting of the Presidium bureau decided to abolish the enlarged Presidium and to establish a small Presidium of ten members.[6] Molotov and Mikoyan, who had been excluded from the bureau in 1951 were now included. Malenkov assumed the posts of party secretary and chairman of the Council of Ministers. Beria, Molotov, Bulganin and Kaganovich were designated as vice chairmen of the Council of Ministers. Beria became head of the single Ministry of Internal Affairs, with the merger of the MVD and the MGB.[7] Molotov again became foreign minister, and Bulganin became minister of defence.

The political leadership of the country was dominated by a triumvirate made up of Beria, Malenkov and Khrushchev. In the days and weeks following Stalin's death, Beria initiated a whole series of reforms: drastically reducing the size of the labour camps, transferring economic activities from the Gulag to the economic ministries, decentralizing administration and transferring greater powers to the republics and provinces, He also sought to place the USSR's relations with its sister parties in Eastern Europe on a new footing and to reunify Germany as a demilitarized state. At the time, Presidium members, including Kaganovich, supported Beria's line.[8]

They became alarmed, however, at Beria's radical proposals and feared that he would use the MVD to consolidate his position. Khrushchev assumed the lead role in the campaign against Beria and secured the backing of Malenkov, Bulganin, Molotov and Saburov. Khrushchev broached the plan to Kaganovich, who immediately agreed and undertook to sound out Voroshilov, who was a close friend, on the matter. Beria was arrested at a meeting of the Presidium.[9] Kaganovich committed himself to the campaign when a majority of the Presidium – had already committed themselves.[10]

At the Central Committee plenum in July Kaganovich denounced Beria as an 'antiparty, anti-state criminal' who had plotted to seize power and carry out a 'fascist revolution'.[11] This was the first indication that he was to be charged with treason, a capital offence. Beria, Kaganovich asserted, had wormed his way into Stalin's confidence and had 'trampled underfoot all that was sacred in the party'. He contrasted the character of Beria with that of the honourable Ordzhonikidze, which hinted at Beria's role in Ordzhonikidze's death and in that of his brother Mikhail Kaganovich. Yagoda, Yezhov, Beria and V. Abakumov had corrupted the internal security apparatus. Beria had sought to reduce the Central Committee to the role of propaganda and personnel appointments. Kaganovich insisted on preserving the party's leading role as the 'holy of holies.' Moreover, Beria was scathing of Stalin's leadership talents and derided the claims that he was the great continuer of the work of Lenin, Marx and Engels.

Marshall K. S. Moskalenko informed Volkogonov that the trial of Beria took place in the offices of the Moscow Military District, while Malenkov, Khrushchev, Molotov, Voroshilov, Bulganin, Kaganovich, Mikoyan, Shvernik and some others sat in the Kremlin and listened to it on a specially installed link.[12] Beria was sentenced and executed.

The new emphasis on 'socialist legality' did not impinge on the party's power and was still far from the creation of a law-governed state. The reliance on terror was abandoned, the secret police was brought under party control and the Gulag system was run down. The Soviet system came to rely less on coercion and sought to develop policies that would ensure a greater degree of popular consent. The Presidium, Kaganovich asserted, withdrew all charges against his brother and he received permission that his headstone at Novodevichy should bare the legend 'Member of the CC'.[13]

Domestic and Foreign Policy

In September 1953 Malenkov surrendered the post of first party secretary to Khrushchev, while retaining the chairmanship of the Council of Ministers.[14] This marked an important step in reasserting collective leadership. The planned switch of resources under Malenkov's 'New Course' from the military into the civilian sector was reversed, as a concession to the conservatives in the party leadership. However, in 1954 Khrushchev launched the Virgin Lands policy, which again placed a priority on boosting civilian consumption and living standards,

In November 1953, to commemorate his sixtieth birthday, Kaganovich was sent greetings from the Council of Ministers and the Central Committee and the presidium of the Supreme Soviet awarded him a third Order of Lenin.[15] In April 1954 he was re-elected to the Council of Ministers as one of the three first deputy chairmen, together with Molotov and Bulganin.[16]

Kaganovich attempted to regain influence and sought to replace B. P. Beshchev as minister of transport. In December 1953 the Council of Ministers established a Bureau of Transport and Communications, chaired by Kaganovich. From January 1954 until February 1955, when it was dissolved, the bureau met on 42 occasions.[17] Kaganovich's secretariat oversaw the work of the bureau and examined in detail all aspects of transport policy. Beshchev endeavoured to limit the bureau's influence, barely acknowledging its existence.[18] Addressing the Supreme Soviet in April 1954, Kaganovich criticized the Ministry of Transport for failing to tackle the problem of irrational hauls and the country's excessive dependency on rail transport. He called for a new general plan for transport modernization.[19]

On 4 May 1954 the Bureau of Transport convened an all-union conference of over 2,000 railway activists in the Great Kremlin Palace.[20] It produced a sharp exchange between Beshchev and Kaganovich. In a barely disguised criticism of Kaganovich and his bureau, Beshchev deplored the system of 'petty tutelage and endless check-ups, which prevent officials from attending to business'.[21] Kaganovich acknowledged the achievements of the railways, but warned of complacency. He called for a general plan for the full completion of railway reconstruction as soon as possible and to speed up the deployment of new diesel-electric and electric locomotives.[22] He stressed that steam locomotives would continue to play a major role on Soviet railways, an assertion that later was turned into an accusation that he had opposed dieselization and electrification.[23] Beshchev got the better of the exchange.

In February 1955 Bulganin replaced Malenkov as chairman of the Council of Ministers.[24] Kaganovich became chairman of the Council of Ministers' Committee on Labour and Wages with Shvernik as vice chairman. Kaganovich later claimed that plans advanced by the committee to increase pensions received the backing of Bulganin, but were opposed by Khrushchev.[25]

In 1955 Bulganin, Khrushchev and Molotov dominated the political scene. Kaganovich was sidetracked into the role of elder statesman. In April 1955 he delivered a speech in Prague on the tenth anniversary of Czechoslovakia's liberation,[26] and in November he addressed the Moscow Soviet on the anniversary of the October Revolution.[27] Three members of the Presidium – Khrushchev, Bulganin and Malenkov – had enjoyed Kaganovich's patronage, but there was no Kaganovich group. Kaganovich's closest colleague was Voroshilov. In February 1955 his old comrade Budennyi sent him hearty greetings on the anniversary of the founding of the Soviet army and navy.[28]

The post-Stalin leadership increasingly found itself at loggerheads on defence and foreign policy. While Khrushchev and Mikoyan stressed the dangers posed by nuclear weapons to humanity in general, Molotov, Kaganovich and Voroshilov continued to uphold the Leninist view of the inevitability of war while imperialism survived. In March 1954 Kaganovich still advocated a policy of 'active defence'.[29] In May 1955 he spoke of the imperialists as having 'lost their heads', hinting at the dangers of war.[30]

The XX Party Congress

In public, the leadership continued to pay tribute to the dead leader. In April 1954 Malenkov, addressing the Supreme Soviet, spoke of the party leadership continuing the work of the 'immortal Lenin, and his comrade-in-arms, the great Stalin'.[31] Kaganovich similarly paid homage to Stalin as 'the great continuer of the cause' of the great Lenin.[32] Molotov and Kaganovich strongly resisted Khrushchev's attempts to raise the issue of Stalin's historical role. As part of the restoration of the authority of Lenin, the Presidium, in November 1955, on the recommendation of I. V. Kapitonov, secretary of the Moscow city party committee, renamed the Moscow metro system after Lenin, thus dropping the name of Kaganovich, which it had carried since 1935. Kaganovich endorsed the decision.[33]

At the Presidium on 21 December 1955 there was a sharp exchange between Kaganovich and Khrushchev on the Stalin cult. Kaganovich claimed that he had sincerely supported the Central Committee's line on the 'cult of the individual'.[34] In the discussion of the draft report on the CPSU to the XX Party Congress in January 1956, he emphasized opposition to revisionism and a Leninist commitment to revolutionary strategy.[35] At a meeting of the Presidium on 9 February he argued that the whole leadership bore responsibility for the decisions of the Stalin era, but that circumstances had to be taken into account. The victims, such as his own brother Mikhail, could not be bought back to life.[36]

Molotov, Kaganovich and Voroshilov strongly opposed the establishment of a commission to investigate the crimes of the Stalin era, but Khrushchev was supported by Bulganin, Mikoyan, Saburov, Pervukhin and the wavering Malenkov. A commission, chaired by P. N. Pospelov, editor of *Pravda* and director of the Marx-Engels-Lenin Institute, using material from the MGB (Ministry of State Security) and KGB (Committee of State Security) archives, wrote a report on the Stalinist repressions.[37] Khrushchev proposed that the findings be presented to the party congress. According to Kaganovich, he, Molotov and Voroshilov spoke against the proposal, but he was the most insistent; but they did not press the issue so as not to split the congress.[38] At the last moment, the Presidium authorized Khrushchev to deliver the report.[39]

At the XX Party Congress of February 1956, Khrushchev delivered his famous 'Secret Speech' attacking Stalin's 'cult of the individual'. Initially, Khrushchev argued, Stalin operated as part of a collective leadership. The defeat of the various opposition groupings of the 1920s, the First Five-Year Plan and the collectivization of agriculture were positive achievements. After 1934 he created a system of personal rule based on lawlessness and terror. Thereafter, Stalin committed serious mistakes: he failed to anticipate the German invasion in 1941 and was guilty of major errors in the management of the war. His megalomania, his desire for adulation and his 'sickly suspicious' personality influenced all aspects of the regime. From Khrushchev's account, we might conclude that the term 'cult of the individual' should be understood as a euphemism for despotic/tyrannical rule.

Kaganovich's speech to the congress avoided controversy. He endorsed the official position of 'peaceful coexistence', while insisting that the Leninist theory of world imperialism remained valid, stressing the aggressive nature of imperialism and the importance of it being restrained by social and revolutionary forces.[40] On the economic front, he emphasized the importance of technological innovation and the raising of labour productivity to the level of that of the United States. He referred to the struggle with the consequences of the 'cult of the individual', but offered no hint of his opposition to any searching inquiry.

Following the XX Party Congress, discussion in party organizations on the Stalin cult produced heated debates. In the railway party organizations, Kaganovich's role in the repression of 1936–38 was aired. At one such meeting, he was described as one of the inspirers of the Stalin cult and as 'Stalin's troubadour'.[41]

In April 1956 the Central Committee established a commission, chaired by Molotov, to examine the political trials and mass repression of the 1930s. The commission was deeply divided. Molotov and Kaganovich insisted that the show trials of the 1930s had been correct. Under pressure, Kaganovich conceded that excesses had been committed, while Molotov spoke of 'political expediency'.[42] The commission attributed the mass repression to the 'abuse of power by I. V. Stalin' which was facilitated by the rise to power in the NKVD of careerists and provocateurs.[43]

Molotov and Kaganovich sought to minimize the ideological dimension of de-Stalinization. In April 1956, in the Presidium, Kagnovich declared that the *Short Course* was in the main correct and that the importance of the class struggle and the struggle with opportunism should not be downplayed. On 7 June 1956 he delivered a critical report on a proposed article on Stalin in the *Great Soviet Encyclopaedia*, demanding 'greater objectivity'.[44] Molotov and Kaganovich also appear to have protected M. D. Bagirov, one of Beria's chief deputies, who was executed in 1956 for repressions conducted in Azerbaidzhan.[45]

After discussion with other communist leaders, including Maurice Thorez, Walter Ulbricht and Mátyás Rákosi, the Central Committee on 30 June 1956 adopted its resolution 'Concerning the overcoming of the cult of the individual and its consequences'.[46] Following the party congress, the Presidium became deeply divided over a broad range of economic questions, foreign policy issues and the attitude toward de-Stalinization. In these policy disputes, Molotov and Kaganovich emerged as the Stalinist diehards.

The Hungarian Uprising of 1956 brought divisions within the Soviet Presidium to the surface. Molotov and Kaganovich took the most hard line positions. In the Presidium in October–November 1956, Kaganovich counselled speedy action to put down the rising and to suppress the threat posed by 'counter-revolution' and 'reaction'. The policies of the Hungarian leader, Janos Kadar, he argued, should be closely controlled; there should be no change in the name of the Hungarian Communist Party and friendship with the USSR should remain a cardinal principle of Hungarian foreign policy.[47]

In November 1956 Israel, militarily supported by France and Britain, launched its assault on Egypt. Kaganovich, at the party Presidium, proposed mobilizing Soviet Jews in protest against Israeli policy.[48] His well-established hostility to Zionism was also reflected in May 1956 when he criticized the Polish government's weakness in combating Jewish nationalism.[49] In October a delegation made up of Khrushchev, Mikoyan, Molotov and Kaganovich visited Warsaw, unannounced, for the plenum of the Central Committee of the Polish United Workers Party for 'consultations' regarding the domestic crisis in Poland.[50]

On 3 September 1956 Kaganovich was again appointed minister of the construction materials industry. He had been involved within this industry in various capacities since the end of the war. From 1945 to 1957 the construction materials industry was one of the great success stories of postwar reconstruction.[51] Khrushchev carpingly noted that production growth often concealed a deterioration in quality.[52] In December 1956 a new State Economic Commission, chaired by Pervukhin, was established to oversee economic planning, but from which Molotov, Kaganovich and Malenkov were excluded.[53]

In 1957 Khrushchev's plans to create regional economic councils (*sovnarkhozy*) and to abolish the central economic ministries drew the opposition of Molotov and Kaganovich. Moreover, they accused Khrushchev of concentrating excessive power in his hands. They proposed scrapping the post of first secretary in favour of a more collegial system of rule, although Kaganovich denied that he had argued for removing Khrushchev from the Secretariat and appointing him as minister of agriculture.[54]

At the Central Committee plenum in December 1958, Molotov, Kaganovich and D. T. Shepilov were accused of leading the campaign against the abolition of the Machine Tractor Stations. V. V. Matskevich, minister of agriculture, accused them of attempting to 'terrorize' the ministry to gain hold of materials to discredit the reform.[55] In his memoirs, Kaganovich accused Khrushchev of serious errors in agriculture: his support of the charlatan T. D. Lysenko, his obsessive promotion of maize cultivation, his plans for large *kolkhozy* and the destruction of thousands of villages.[56]

Velko Mićunović, the Yugoslav ambassador to Moscow in the fifties, who was well disposed to Khrushchev, depicts Kaganovich as a spent force, a man out of touch with developments.[57] This may be overstated. The accounts of the Presidium meetings from 1953 to 1957 indicate that he was a regular attendee and a very active participant in debates.

The 'Anti-Party' Group

At the meeting of the Presidium in the second half of June 1957, Khrushchev's leadership style was strongly criticized, with seven members of the Presidium – Bulganin, Malenkov, Voroshilov, Kaganovich, Molotov, Pervukhin and Saburov – demanding his removal. Mikoyan merely called on him to correct his method of leadership. At this meeting, Kaganovich brought up the fact that Khrushchev had been a Trotskyist in 1923–24. Outvoted in the Presidium, Khrushchev took the matter to the Central Committee. He was supported by Marshall Zhukov and Colonel I. A. Serov, chairman of the KGB, who flew in sympathetic members for the meeting in Moscow. This, Kaganovich describes as an act of 'usurpation'. Malenkov and Kaganovich appear to have tried to neutralize Zhukov, and had mooted the possibility of elevating him as a full member of the Presidium.[58]

The Central Committee plenum met in Sverdlov Hall. The main question on the agenda was what was now termed the 'Anti-Party group' headed by Malenkov, Kaganovich and Molotov. In his memoirs, Kaganovich depicts this move as a tactic by Khrushchev to split his opponents.[59] At the plenum, Kaganovich came under a hail of fire. He challenged Khrushchev, asserting that as late as October 1955, he had been fulsome in his praise of Stalin. Kaganovich declared:

> I loved Stalin, and I loved him because he was a great Marxist. He did much that was not good, and for this we judge him.[60]

Mao Tse-tung, Kaganovich added, judged Stalin's achievements as 70 per cent good and 30 per cent bad. While this could not be reduced to a percentage, he argued that a balanced appraisal was necessary.

Zhukov led the attack on Kaganovich, accusing him of sending 300 railway workers to their graves in 1937. This, he insisted, was not a political issue but a criminal one.[61] The events of 1937, Kaganovich insisted, had to be judged in their context: there were enemies and there was intense class struggle, although he conceded that mistakes and crimes had been committed. He claimed that he had supported Khrushchev's report on Stalin to the party congress, although this had caused him much pain.[62] He sought to minimize his role in the repression, arguing that after 1934 he was assigned to economic work. He questioned whether Khrushchev or Zhukov had not themselves signed orders authorizing executions. Khrushchev intervened to declare that they had all signed such declarations. In response to Kaganovich's evasive replies to questions concerning his own culpability, Khrushchev interjected that he was 'cringing'.[63]

Khrushchev raised the question of the destruction of the military cadres in 1937, specifically, the case of Yakir. After Yakir confessed, Kaganovich had denounced him. Fabricated testimony had implicated Kaganovich in a conspiratorial group with Yakir and Gamarnik.[64] A major issue concerned the authorization of the use of torture against so-called spies in 1937 which had emanated from Stalin, but had been signed by members of the Politburo. Prior to the XX Party Congress, Khrushchev reported, Kaganovich had proposed that this incriminating document be destroyed.[65]

Leonid Brezhnev recalled that sometime after 1953, Malenkov and Kaganovich had called for the removal of Serov, chairman of the KGB. They had argued that the KGB be made accountable to the Presidium rather than to Khrushchev directly. Brezhnev accused Kaganovich of having been the most fervent advocate of repression in the 1930s and of turning NKPS into a 'model' for how the destruction of enemies should be carried out.[66]

A. B. Aristov, a member of the Presidium, asserted that at a Central Committee meeting discussing the 'cult of the individual', Kaganovich, responding to the charge that thousands of innocent party, state and military officials had been killed, acknowledged that indeed the 'superfluous' (*izlishestva*) had been got rid of.[67] Kaganovich angrily denied this. Khrushchev accused him of destroying the Ukrainian leaders – Postyshev, Kosior and Chubar'. In 1937 Stalin and Kaganovich had used denunciations by ordinary party members, such as those made by the 'crazy' Nikolaenko, to destroy leading cadres. Kaganovich conceded that Nikolaenko was 'not normal'.[68] N. V. Podgorny, head of the Ukrainian Communist Party, described Kaganovich's role in 1947 as 'the black days of Ukraine', a return to the methods of 1937.[69]

Khrushchev recounted how Beshchev had implored him not to send Kaganovich to the railways to carry out a reorganization, which he feared would lead to its destruction. D. S. Polyansky, first secretary of Orenburg province, denounced Kaganovich as an 'intriguer, careerist, executioner' whose hands were soaked in innocent blood and who had had 'tens of thousands of people executed'.[70]

According to Khrushchev's assessment, Stalin, Molotov and Voroshilov played a more prominent role in the terror than Kaganovich.[71] However, with Beria and Abakumov executed, Kaganovich was now assigned the role of the main villain after Stalin. He was a target because he had distinguished himself as the most intransigent defender of Stalin and his most sycophantic deputy. It was easier to attack a spent force. This also pandered to the latent anti-Semitism in the party and society.

On 28 June Molotov, Malenkov and Kaganovich capitulated, with each engaging in self-criticism before the Central Committee. Kaganovich, a beaten man, admitted to his errors and even 'crimes'. He confessed to having been part of a conspiracy to oust Khrushchev as first secretary. He denied that his actions had an 'anti-party character', and recalled his past services, including at the front, and appealed to the Central Committee to forgive his mistakes.[72]

Each of the three submitted letters to the Central Committee, admitting past errors. On 29 June 1957 the party issued a communiqué which denounced the 'Anti-Party group', headed by Malenkov, Kaganovich and Molotov. They Central Committee expelled them from its ranks.[73] Molotov, Kaganovich, Malenkov, Saburov and Pervukhin were then expelled from the Presidium. Khrushchev then advanced his own people from the Secretariat into the Presidium.

In the organization of the Anti-Party group, Khrushchev asserted, Molotov had been the 'ideological leader', Kaganovich the 'knife sharpener' and Malenkov the 'main organizer'.[74] According to Khrushchev's account, at this time, Kaganovich telephoned him and begged him 'not to allow them to deal with me as they dealt with people under Stalin'.[75] Other examples of Kaganovich's cowardice – his failure to defend his brother Mikhail, Mikoyan's claim of his loss of nerve in 1941, his failure to resist the anti-Semitic course of Stalin in the later years – fit the stereotyped image of the ambitious but cowardly, self-serving Jew.

At the Central Committee plenum in July 1957, Alexander Shelepin criticized Kaganovich's aides, branding M. F. Chernyak, his assistant of twenty years, as a true sadist.[76] As Kaganovich's star fell, so even some of his long serving assistants turned against him. At this time the party Control Committee examined the complaints of Yu. V. Klement'ev and A. M. Nabatchikov, and issued a sharp reprimand to Kaganovich concerning his attitude toward his assistants.[77]

Kaganovich later argued that the mistake of the 'Anti-Party group' was its failure to organize, to form a faction; they had a majority in the Presidium and they could have taken power.[78] However, Khrushchev quickly consolidated his position, replacing Marshall Zhukov with Marshall R. Ya. Malinovsky as minister of defence. In March 1958 Khrushchev replaced Bulganin as chairman of the Council of Ministers, combining this post with the post of first secretary of the party.

In 1957 Kaganovich was relieved of his post as minister for the construction materials industry. He and his wife moved out of their Kremlin apartment to one on the Lenin Hills. He was assigned as manager of the Urals Potash Works in Solikamsk, Perm province, the largest of its kind in the country, where, according to Roy Medvedev, 'he was, in all respects, the model of a fair-minded boss.'[79]

The XXII Party Congress: Judgement

De-Stalinization opened up a major dilemma for the regime. Regime legitimacy since 1917 was based less on Max Weber's conception of charismatic authority, rational legal authority or traditional authority. It was based essentially on self-legitimation – the claim of the regime to a special status, guided by a special ideology and led by outstanding individuals.[80] This was buttressed by the claim to past, present and promised future achievements. Khrushchev's revelations showed that the regime had engaged in criminal acts against its own populace and that many of its claimed achievements were open to question. The regime's leaders were exposed as all too human and all too fallible. Even the re-legitimization of the regime based on victory over Nazi Germany was laid open to debate. De-Stalinization exposed the hollowness of many of these claims. It allowed for a partial recovery of the public sphere, and the slow re-emergence of real public opinion which carried the potential for the regime's claims to be challenged.

At the XXII Party Congress in October 1961, Khrushchev renewed his denunciation of Stalin, extending it to criticize Molotov, Malenkov and Kaganovich as the main supporters of the Stalin cult, perpetrators of mass repression and ideological dogmatists.[81] Nikolai Podgorny depicted Kaganovich as a master of intrigue and provocation, and one who had grovelled before Stalin while exploiting his 'weak side'. In promoting Stalin's cult he had promoted his own cult as '*vozhd*' of the Ukrainian people. He had conspired to discredit Khrushchev as leader of the Ukrainian Communist Party.[82] E. A. Furtseva declared that Kaganovich had on his conscience hundreds of repressed and executed railway personnel.[83] D. S. Polyansky censured Voroshilov for having defended Kaganovich in June 1957 for his role in the repression of the Kuban peasants in 1932.[84]

Shvernik charged Kaganovich with initiating a policy of 'mass arrests' in NKPS, NKTyazhprom and in the provinces. In the trials of the 1930s, he had personally edited drafts of the verdicts and arbitrarily modified the charges, inserting alleged planned terrorist acts against his person.[85] Beshchev, minister of transport USSR, denounced Kaganovich's bullying, intimidating and hectoring methods and his technical lack of competence as head of NKPS. In addition, he had used the so-called 'counter-revolutionary limit theory' to organize 'mass slaughter' of the engineering-technical cadres.[86]

Pospelov demanded that these 'renegades and dissenters' be expelled from the party and be brought to account for their crimes.[87] N. Rodionov denounced the three as mercenary careerists and adventurers whose hands were 'stained with the sacred blood of the best sons of the people.'[88] Z. T. Serdiuk, first deputy chairman of the Party Control Committee, demanded their expulsion

Figure 9. L. M. Kaganovich before his expulsion from the Presidium in 1957

from the party.[89] In response to such demands, the congress resolved to expel Kaganovich and Molotov from the party.

Molotov and Kaganovich were the Presidium members most critical of Khrushchev's policy innovations. They criticized his campaign approach to economic problems, especially the *sovnarkhoz* (the regional economic council) reform of 1957 and the decision to divide the party into industrial and agricultural wings. They criticized Khrushchev's boastful claim that the Soviet economy would soon overtake that of the United States, a criticism that rankled with him.[90] By 1964 the Presidium itself had had enough of his methods and 'hare-brained schemes' and decided to remove him. Notwithstanding Khrushchev's reputation as a de-Stalinizer and a reformer, he often pursued policies that were wrong-headed and economically destructive, and on many matters, Molotov and Kaganovich showed a greater sense of realism.

In his memoirs, Kaganovich accused Khrushchev of announcing policy without prior consultation of the Presidium. He had supported his election as party secretary despite misgivings regarding his 'insufficient cultural-theoretical level', his 'eccentric' personality and his tendency towards autocratic behaviour.[91] Khrushchev had publicly rebuked Bulganin, chairman of Council of Ministers, and had tried to oust Molotov from the post of foreign minister.[92] After 1956 Khrushchev increasingly personally decided matters of foreign policy. This, Kaganovich claimed, was in contrast to the situation under Stalin, when foreign policy was discussed in the Politburo.⁹³ This was an example of extremely selective recall.

Following the XXII Congress in 1961, Kaganovich was dismissed as manager of the Urals Potash Works. On his return to Moscow, the Krasnaya Presnaya district party committee expelled him from the party. His wife, Maria, died the same year. He recalled his 'great sorrow' at the loss of his wife and 'comrade-in-arms', but had overcome these misfortunes 'as a Bolshevik'. Characteristically, he fused the personal and the political. He busied himself in his neighbourhood, recounting his experiences and beliefs to his neighbours, 'feeling myself as an old propagandist-agitator for the party, for Marxism-Leninism, for socialism-communism'. He devoted himself to reading newspapers and journals, writing his own comments on the resolutions passed by the Presidium and the Council of Ministers, which he would have made had he attended these sessions.⁹⁴ And, above all, he began writing his memoirs.

In early 1963 the Commission of the Presidium investigating the mass repression of the 1930s concluded that the repression of the period had no foundation in law, was unwarranted by the political situation and that 'Stalin, Molotov, Kaganovich and Yezhov orientated the party and the organs of the NKVD to a wide development of repression, to mass terror.'⁹⁵

Kaganovich on Stalin

Kaganovich's memoirs, *Pamyatnye zapiski rabochego, kommunista-bol'shevika, profsoyuznogo, partiinogo i sovetskogo rabotnika* (The Memoir Notes of a Worker, Communist-Bolshevik, Trade Union, Party and Soviet Worker), provide a clear picture of his idealized self-image as the resolute, stalwart, proletarian revolutionary, the committed Marxist-Leninist-Stalinist who had loyally and selflessly served the party throughout his life. It was the party and the cause that had given his life meaning and purpose. The achievements of the Soviet system were vindicated, and this absolved its agents of the measures they had taken.

Kaganovich's published memoirs were edited from 14,000 pages of handwritten notes. They were intended, he claimed, primarily as an ideological inspiration for youth and to depict a revolutionary who remained faithful to Lenin and Stalin throughout his whole life and did not crack; 'Did not crack to the very end.'⁹⁶ Notwithstanding this protestation of ideological steadfastness, Kaganovich was a man morally pliant who was corrupted by the system he chose to serve.

In the years of defeat and disgrace after 1961, relations between Kaganovich and Molotov were cordial, but never close. They were on first-name terms and exchanged greetings on special occasions. But Molotov preferred to let Kaganovich take the initiative in such contacts. Molotov presented Feliks Chuev's book '*Sto sorok besed c Molotvym*' (One Hundred and Forty Discussions with Molotov) to Kaganovich with the dedication, 'To a fighter of the Leninist-Stalinist epoch, in memory, from his friend and co-worker in the struggle to build the first socialist state in the world'.[97]

Kaganovich, who never gave interviews, on Molotov's recommendation agreed to be interviewed by the poet and writer Feliks Chuev. Chuev first met Kaganovich in 1986, when he was already 93 years of age. He was physically frail, but remained alert with a sound, if selective, recall of past events. He rejected the accusation that he was crude (*grubyi*), but accepted that his manner was sharp (*rezkyi*).[98]

On basic questions, Molotov and Kaganovich were united. Molotov's view of Kaganovich was that the former did not much like him, but that 'Lazar was, of course, on a great scale, extremely energetic, a good organizer and agitator, but, in theoretical matters, he was lost'. Kaganovich responded that he did not rate Molotov as a theoretician, either.[99] Undoubtedly, Kaganovich was the more original thinker and the more creative and dynamic administrator. According to Molotov, Kaganovich remained a '200 per cent Stalinist' who would hear no criticisms of the *vozhd*'.[100]

Molotov noted the deep generational divide within the Stalinist leadership, between the older and younger cohort, branding Khrushchev, Beria and Malenkov as Rightists, who by duplicitous means had won Stalin's support. Stalin's deputies, he acknowledged, feared him, and some – Khrushchev and Beria – lived lives beset by insecurity.[101]

For Kaganovich, Stalin was a great man: 'Stalin needs no defence'.[102] In his retirement, he declared, 'Stalin is a phenomenon of world order, a politician of world rank, and the leader of the unified economy of the country. Stalin is also a military leader, the type of commander that the world has never seen, not only in his ability, but also in his whole scale.'[103] He rejected the view that Stalin was cruel from childhood. In the early twenties Stalin followed a simple lifestyle and was modest in his dealings with others. He became more severe only as a result of the intensity of the political struggle and the hatred that he attracted. He was a man of remarkable self-control, who 'never shouted'.[104] According to Kaganovich, Stalin's was not a fixed character, but changed over time.

> This is an original man, by the way. Thus, he took on different aspects according to the time and period. After the war, there was another Stalin. Pre-war, another. Between 1932 and 1940, another. Up to 1932, a quite different one. He changed. I saw no less than 5-6 different Stalin's.[105]

This corresponds to the chameleon-like character of an efficient survival machine.

Stalin, Kaganovich argued, was a theoretician of note, not in the class of Lenin, but he had the ability to synthesize Lenin's ideas; his *Questions of Leninism* and *Foundations of Leninism* were classics of Marxism-Leninism.[106] Stalin, he claimed, was a dictator, but 'a dictator from the party'.[107] This implies that the party had some mechanism of appointing and removing the dictator. The dictator who is immoveable becomes a tyrant.

Kaganovich always insisted that the mistakes of the Stalin era were the responsibility of the entire leadership.[108] Collective responsibility was to be maintained even where collective decision making was a fiction. Although he hints at a pathological side to Stalin's nature, he confused it with ideological steadfastness.

> Stalin did not recognize any personal relationship. For him, love did not exist, so to speak, towards a person as a person. For him, there was love towards the figure in politics.[109]

Stalin, he claimed, was not driven by a lust for personal power, but was, above all else, a man of ideas, 'He did everything for the idea of socialism!'[110] Chuev argues that Kaganovich, Molotov and other Soviet leaders of this era were similarly driven by the same all-consuming ideal.[111] This certainly corresponds with Kaganovich's self-image.

Stalinism, for Kaganovich, was 'Marxism-Leninism of the epoch of the construction of socialism'.[112] Allowances had to be made for this 'complicated epoch'. Stalin had to employ guile, as all statesmen employ guile, to secure the triumph of socialism in the USSR. Without him, capitalism would have been restored in Russia. The Nazi–Soviet Pact of 1939 had been necessary to avert the danger of the USSR being turned into a colony. 'The greatness of Stalin was that he understood historical necessity. This influenced the will of the leadership, the will of the party, the will of the people.'[113]

However, he offered a qualification, by a resort to special pleading:

> Of course, it is impossible to justify much that was done. And I am convinced that Stalin himself would have recognized the errors. At the XX Party Congress, addressing the communist and workers parties from around the world, he said that he hoped that they would not repeat our mistakes.[114]

Kaganovich resorted to the scholastic defence of Stalinism, as having been the lesser evil. The purges in 1937–38, he insisted, had been historically necessary, although many innocent people had suffered. Matters could not be viewed simply from a narrow juridical standpoint.[115]

Kaganovich's stance on the terror was not dissimilar to that of Molotov. And yet Kaganovich had initially resisted it. Molotov was more implicated in the Terror, and by his own admission had signed most of the death lists in 1937–38.[116] He was also more categorical in justifying the Terror as necessary to safeguard Soviet power in Russia and the international communist movement.[117] He showed no remorse for the arrest and imprisonment of the wives and children of 'enemies'.[118] Kaganovich in retirement claimed to have tried to save his friend Kosior by appealing directly to Stalin ('I was almost in tears'), and claimed that he had defended Chubar', but when he was shown his deposition, gave up. His claim to have tried to defend Postyshev is difficult to square with his role in denouncing his former protégé.[119] This was the closest that Kaganovich ever came to expressing contrition for the Great Terror.

Kaganovich judged Yezhov to be worse than Yagoda, This is an unsurprising judgement, but obscures the fact that he had strongly endorsed Yezhov's appointment as head of NKVD.[120] He depicted the purged former leaders as a threat to the state. Zinoviev and Kamenev had opposed the October Revolution. Trotsky was a former Menshevik. The eminent economists Chayanov and Kondrat'ev had been the spokesmen of kulak interests.[121] Tukhachevsky had been a potential Bonapartist. His one-time friends Antonov-Ovseenko and Bukharin had been counter-revolutionaries.[122] This stands in contrast to the evidence that Kaganovich initially tried to shield Bukharin.

Kaganovich saw Stalin as a political genius, as a Soviet Robespierre, whose firmness and resolve had ensured the Revolution's survival.[123] Stalin, like Lenin, displayed great historical will. Kaganovich noted that in 1907 the Bolsheviks had shared a congress with the Mensheviks at Stockholm, but in 1918 the Bolsheviks had been ready to arrest and shoot them.[124] Kaganovich, like other deputies, rationalized his actions as those of a true believer who had acted in all sincerity 'for the good of the cause'. For this, they had sacrificed everything, including their moral conscience, transforming themselves into instruments of history.

Kaganovich's recollection of events are selective and one-sided; in 1927–28 the kulaks had threatened the proletariat with famine; collectivization had won support from below. He never acknowledged the famine of 1932–33, and he had forgotten that the peasants had been deprived of internal passports in 1932.[125] He passed over the Terror of 1936–38, the Gulag and the massacre of the Polish officers in 1940. Kaganovich, like Molotov, knew they had signed death warrants for innocent people, including colleagues and former friends. He was clearly affected by the suicide of Ordzhonikidze and of his brother Mikhail. But in these and other cases, he steadfastly refused to ascribe any blame to Stalin.

Kaganovich and Molotov sought to rationalize the Terror as dictated by necessity: the war threat, the existence of real enemies and the pressure of public attitudes. According to Kaganovich:

> There was such a situation in the country and in the CC, such a mood amongst the masses that it was not possible to think of any other way out.[126]

That this psychosis had been whipped up by the leadership could not be admitted. Nor could Kaganovich admit that initially he had opposed the Terror, but had capitulated under duress and thereafter became one of its most energetic exponents. Thus he and Molotov sought to absolve themselves of moral responsibility for their actions. They could never quite comprehend the obloquy that was directed at them. They were inclined to see this purely as past history that was being used opportunistically by their enemies in the struggle for power.

Apart from his contacts with Molotov, Kaganovich's relations with other senior colleagues seem to have ceased. Voroshilov died in 1969 and, notwithstanding his role in the Terror, was buried with full state honours. Khrushchev died in 1971 in disgrace. Bulganin died in 1975. Mikoyan, who had been a close friend, but then became a bitter critic of Kaganovich, died in 1978. Molotov died in 1986, having been restored to party membership. Malenkov, although a near neighbour, never had contact with Kaganovich and only rarely met with Molotov, died in 1988.[127]

The Nature of the Stalin Leadership

Khrushchev's comments on Stalin's leadership, while sanitizing his own role, nevertheless provide the most penetrating analysis by a participant of how the leadership worked. With 'the accumulation of immense and limitless powers in the hands of one person', party democracy and revolutionary legality were violated.[128] After 1934 Stalin ceased to heed the opinion of the Central Committee or the Politburo: 'Stalin's arbitrary rule' operated in 'the absolute absence of any restraints on his authority.'[129] He discarded Lenin's 'collegial' methods of rule, and his 'despotic character' brooked no opposition.[130] In time, the cult turned him into an infallible god-like being. After 1937 he had surrounded himself with people with no conscience and no scruples, such as Beria, A. S. Shcherbakov and L. Z. Mekhlis. His behaviour became coarser, with decisions being taken at long, drunken dinner parties. His subordinates sought to ingratiate themselves with him by informing on each other.

Khrushchev offered a stinging criticism of Kaganovich's responsibility for the crimes of the Stalin era:

> As for Kaganovich, I don't think he knew all the details of what happened. Stalin hardly needed to confide in him. Kaganovich was such a yes-man that he would have cut his own father's throat if Stalin had winked and said it was in the interests of the cause – the Stalinist cause, that is. Stalin never needed to keep Kaganovich reined in. Kaganovich had always been a detestable sycophant, exposing enemies and having people arrested right and left.[131]

At the same time, he acknowledged that most of the party leaders had actively backed Stalin 'because Stalin was one of the strongest Marxists, and his logic, his strength and his will greatly influenced the cadres and party work'.[132]

The Soviet leadership's room for manoeuvre in domestic and foreign policy, Khrushchev argued, was limited. They were also held together by shared values and outlook, by the self-imposed discipline of the group and by a pervasive insecurity. But the central influence was Stalin. After the war, he separated himself from the collective even more. Referring to Stalin's wilfulness and monomania, Khrushchev declared, 'He had completely lost consciousness of reality'.[133] Khrushchev noted, 'All of us around Stalin were temporary people. As long as he trusted us to a certain degree, we were allowed to go on living and working.'[134]

Khrushchev notes Stalin's rare self-control and his 'overpowering personality'.[135] He was able to formulate his conceptions clearly and persuasively, but could also bludgeon his colleagues into accepting his views.[136] 'Stalin's character was brutish and his temper was harsh, but his brutishness didn't always imply malice towards the people to whom he acted so rudely.'[137] He could, in some instances, be persuaded to change his mind, but this required tact and calculation. With the Politburo's demise, it was difficult for lone individuals to take a stand.[138] It was enough for Stalin to declare people to be enemies.[139] Stalin signed sentencing orders and passed them on to his colleagues to sign. In the case of the Doctors' Plot, the Presidium members only saw the confessions. Thus, Khrushchev sought to explain the failure of Stalin's deputies to halt the drift towards despotic power. Similarly, Mikoyan placed stress on Stalin's vindictiveness, his persecution of his deputies and the frequent adoption of decisions that were 'incomprehensible', even to his immediate subordinates.[140]

Khrushchev characterized Stalin as a 'despot', but not a 'giddy despot'; instead, he saw himself as safeguarding the party and the gains of the Revolution.[141] In a radio broadcast in 1964 Khrushchev, in an apparent reference to Stalin's death, noted, 'Throughout human history there have been a number of cruel tyrants, All died by the very ax with which they had maintained power.'[142] Kaganovich and Molotov, by contrast, present Stalin as at most a dictator, but a dictator for the party; they denied his engagement in criminal acts, but acknowledged that errors were committed under his rule. They apparently saw nothing abnormal in Stalin's psychological make-up. They sought to redeem his reputation, and to disparage the veracity of Khrushchev's testimony.

While Khrushchev and Mikoyan acknowledged some share of moral responsibility for the crimes of the Stalin era, Kaganovich and Molotov, who were more heavily implicated in Stalin's crimes, remained in a state of denial. They continued to justify their actions under the notion of moral relativism and historical necessity.[143] In one of his final interviews, Kaganovich asserted that the arrests and executions of 1937–38 had been done according to Soviet law.[144] He thus ignored his own role as a leading advocate of Soviet state lawlessness.

Pensioner

When Kaganovich was ousted from power in 1957 he was 64 years old. His political demise, however, dates from much earlier. In his retirement after 1961, he was a political non-person, ignored by the regime, isolated, a political pariah. At the same time, he was protected from prosecution by a regime which chose to draw a veil over the crimes of the past. His attitude to de-Stalinization was 'negative'.[145]

Kaganovich welcomed Khrushchev's ouster from power in October 1964 and held out hopes for the new collective leadership under Brezhnev and Kosygin. He appealed to the Presidium to have his party membership restored, but was declined.[146] Molotov continued to hope that the party would reappraise Stalin's role and condemn Khrushchev's errors.[147] On 12 July 1984 the Presidium, again renamed the Politburo and chaired by Konstantin Chernenko, discussed the question of readmitting Molotov, Malenkov, and Kaganovich into the party. In the discussion, several members directed their most venomous criticisms at the deceased Khrushchev, who had been responsible for their expulsion. Even the reformist Mikhail Gorbachev proposed that these individuals might be restored to party membership, but that no public announcement of this decision be made.[148] Soviet Communism, with its elevation of realpolitik and its lack of legal culture, failed to comprehend that a loss of moral authority might produce a crisis of regime legitimacy.

On the intermediation of Andrei Gromyko, minister of foreign affairs, Molotov was restored to party membership. Kaganovich and Malenkov were not readmitted, although it is difficult to see how their crimes were more heinous than those of Molotov.[149] On 5 August 1985 Kaganovich petitioned Gorbachev, the new general secretary of the CPSU, for readmission into what he described 'as my very own (*rodnoi*) Communist Party'. He received no reply.[150] Molotov expressed surprise that Kaganovich had not been readmitted.[151] Molotov, although more deeply implicated than Kaganovich in the Terror of 1936–38, had institutional support and was a Russian.

Kaganovich was critical of Gorbachev's reforms, defending the primacy of state ownership and planning of the economy and opposing the abandonment of the party's monopoly of power. He disapproved of the strongly reformist policies adopted by the XXVIII Party Congress in July 1990.[152] As a 'scientific optimist', he expressed confidence in the triumph of communism, but 'humane socialism', he asserted, was 'sweet sugar'.[153]

After 1988 Kaganovich's Jewish identity was on several occasions broached; the notion of the deracinated Jewish revolutionary who transformed himself into an instrument of despotic power. He denied that he was anti-Semitic, but admitted that he had always fought resolutely against Zionism. The charge of anti-Semitism, he noted, had also been levelled at Lenin and Stalin. Most of Stalin's opponents in the 1920s were Jews, but for many years thereafter, he had promoted Jews into important positions.[154] Attacks on Kaganovich's role under Stalin often played on the anti-Semitic theme; the most blatant of these is Evgenyi Evseev's *Satrap*.[155]

In 1990 the journal *Argumenty i fakty* published what purported to be an interview with Kaganovich in which he allegedly expressed anti-Semitic views. In its following number, a letter from him upbraided the journal for publishing scurrilous and unsubstantiated allegations.[156] The same year, the journal *Sovetskaya kultura* published extracts from the Italian journal *Repubblica* which purported to be an interview with Kaganovich in which he defended the achievements of the Stalinist era. In an indignant letter to the journal, he protested that what was published as an interview was in fact a secret recording of a private conversation.[157] In 1991 the hard-line communist Nina Andreeva attempted to use Kaganovich in her attack on the Gorbachev leadership.

Kaganovich lived out his final years alone on Frunze Embankment, block 50, flat 384, on the sixth floor.[158] He survived on a modest pension of 120 rubles per month, the same as Molotov received. Chuev describes his flat as poor, with old furniture, and more spartan than Molotov's flat. He had no dacha and no car.[159] His only immediate relative was his daughter Maia, who devotedly looked after him, visiting him daily.[160] Strangers were kept away. His robust health began to give way. In 1985 he suffered a broken right hip and thereafter could move only with the help of crutches. His eyesight deteriorated and at end of his life he was almost blind. He suffered a first heart attack in May 1990. He died suddenly, sitting in his armchair, from a second seizure, on 30 July 1991, aged 98.

The funeral at Donskoi Monastery was attended by family members and about a hundred admirers. It was a simple ceremony. The ribbon-covered coffin, as in common funerals, was transported in a dilapidated bus which served as a hearse. A brief eulogy was delivered. His body was cremated and his ashes buried in the Novodevichy cemetery alongside those of his wife.[161] A broad obelisk of dark red Finnish stone marks his grave, bearing the simple legend 'Kaganovich, Lazar Moiseevich' with his dates. His wish that the words 'Bolshevik-Leninist' be added was not respected.[162]

Conclusion

After 1953 Kaganovich attempted to claw back some of his lost power. But as the attack on the Stalin era developed, his position was progressively undermined. Ousted from the Presidium in 1957 and expelled from the party in 1961, he, like the other Stalinist leaders, escaped any prosecution. He rationalized his role under Stalin, highlighting the achievements of the regime, the constraints with in which they had operated and their commitment to the lofty ideals of socialism. But these goals under Stalin were subsumed under the demands of reasons of state. The notion that Stalinism had perverted or morally compromised the whole socialist project could never be admitted. Kaganovich's conduct was shaped not only by ideology, which itself underwent a profound transformation, but also by the self-discipline of the ruling group, personal ambition and the instinct of survival.

Khrushchev's 'Secret Speech' exposed the criminalization of the state under Stalin, but stopped far short of launching a full inquiry, let alone initiating the prosecution of those implicated. The limited revelations regarding the crimes of the era meant that the USSR remained in a 'state of denial' in which the past was shrouded in a veil of secrecy and misrepresentation. New strategies for re-legitimizing the state were attempted, in which the cult of the individual served as a convenient scapegoat for past errors. However, Gorbachev's *glasnost* after 1988, by its revelations of the crimes of the Stalin era, precipitated a crisis of legitimacy for the party-state which proved terminal.

Kaganovich lived to see the work of the Politburo Commission on the repression of the Stalin era, which ruled that the show trials of that epoch had been a travesty of justice and rehabilitated those sentenced. He survived to witness the USSR collapse in ruins and the outlawing of the Communist Party. His death marked the last of a generation of revolutionaries who had been at the very centre of political life and who, trapped in their own conceptions of the world, were increasingly disconnected from their own society.

CONCLUSION

The life and career of Lazar Kaganovich was crucially shaped by his relationship with Stalin. He was Stalin's deputy for a period and most of his life was lived in his shadow. As a key member of the leading group he, alongside Stalin, contributed more than any other individual to shaping the regime in its formative years. He was an executive who was closely involved in designing and implementing the regime's developmental programme. He was an administrator and practical problem solver who was required to deal with planners, managers and engineers. His range of experience, and accomplishments – agricultural policy, urban development, railway management, industrial administration – was far greater than any of Stalin's other deputies. In this, he showed an ability to be guided both by ideological demands and more pragmatic, practical considerations. His long-term survival depended on his ability to not only make himself indispensable to Stalin, but also to deliver results as an executive charged with key tasks in implementing the regime's policies.

Kaganovich was one of the proletarian, political activists who made his mark before 1917 as a trade unionist. In 1917 he was drawn into the Bolshevik Military Organization and was one of that legion of political leaders who made his career as a political commissar during the Civil War. He possessed great intellectual self-confidence. A formative stage in his career was his role in enforcing the Red Terror in Nizhnyi Novgorod and his role in establishing Soviet power in Voronezh and Tashkent. In 1919 he was the first Bolshevik to theorize the nature of the monolithic party as one of the ideological cornerstones of the regime. He was also one of the first Bolsheviks to promote the idea of using the soviets as a crucial link with society. He was dismissive of the more democratic and libertarian currents in Bolshevism.

From 1922 onward he was drawn into the administration of the central party Secretariat, and from this point developed his links with Stalin. Kaganovich, together with Molotov and Kuibyshev, werethe core members of the Stalin group. He played a not insignificant role in the defeat of the Trotskyist opposition. He was closely involved in the drive to define Leninism in a strict sense, based on the principles expounded in 'What is to Be Done?' In this, he promoted Stalin's vision of Leninism, castigating Trotskyism as a deviation, and was a key figure in inculcating this new interpretation in the new generation of recruits via the Lenin enrolment. In 1925 Stalin assigned Kaganovich to take charge of the Ukrainian Communist party. In this post, he employed the manipulative, domineering methods for which the Stalinist regime became notorious. But he promoted policies on language and culture that were intended to appease Ukrainian nationalists, which offended the more Russocentric elements. From 1926 onward he became a strong advocate of industrialization. He and Kuibyshev were instrumental in persuading Stalin of the need for such a change of course. In 1928 Stalin withdrew him from Ukraine as a gesture to the Ukrainian leaders.

The Stalin group which emerged from 1928 onward was united by its commitment to industrialization and to the collectivization of agriculture. Kaganovich was pitched into the struggle with the Rightists in the Moscow party organization and in the trade unions. He was the principal author of the Urals-Siberian method of grain procurement of 1929–30 that acted as a prelude to forcible collectivization. He facilitated the mass deportation of the kulaks and played a key role in the expulsion of Kuban peasants in 1932. In the years of famine he was the most vocal supporter of Stalin's draconian law of 7 August 1932, and was the principal architect of the militarization of party organization in the countryside via the *politotdely*. The policy choices made by the Stalin group in agriculture carried profound implications for the development of the regime and set the course for the growth of state repression and the expansion of the Gulag that culminated in the Great Terror.

Kaganovich, like the other members of the Stalin group, embraced the 'revolution from above' out of conviction. They were not victims of circumstances, but very much masters of their own destiny. He played a central role in reorientating the central party apparatus as an instrument for overseeing the economy. He, more than anyone, promoted and theorized the role of the party instructors. He headed the party's drive to proletarianize its ranks and to train and advance a new cohort of proletarian administrators during the First Five-Year Plan. He played a role alongside Stalin in redefining Marxism-Leninism in accordance with these new priorities and in transforming the culture of Bolshevism into the culture of the Stalin era. He was also one of the most articulate defenders of official policy, justifying the erosion of party democracy, the rejection of egalitarianism, the retreat on women's rights, the abandonment of experimentation in education and the adoption of more utilitarian notions of culture and of urban development. In the early 1930s the deep transformation of the regime in its ideology, its policies, its structures and practices, marked the end of utopian aspirations and the rise of a new realpolitik that imposed stringent demands on its members. The Stalinist state adopted repression and coercion as an instrument of rule.

For a brief period, Kaganovich sought to advance himself as a party theoretician in succession to the defeated Bukharin, as an unabashed defender of the proletarian dictatorship as a state unconstrained by law and as one who adopted a dismissive attitude toward democracy in the party, the trade unions and mass organizations. From 1930 to 1935 he was at the height of his influence and a figure of enormous power. He emerged as the party's chief troubleshooter and policy enforcer. His career entered a much more significant phase as a full member of the Politburo, party secretary and, in effect, Stalin's number two in the party. For a period, he appeared to be a possible successor to Stalin. He enjoyed a very close relationship with Stalin, but always presented himself as the *vozhd'*s agent, never as a rival, although this relationship was not without its stresses and strains. He was the chief promoter of the Stalin cult and of his personal dictatorship.

He played a leading role in the drive to reconstruct Moscow. His lasting achievement was the building of the Moscow Metro. He also oversaw the Moscow–Volga canal project that was built with Gulag labour. The prominence of Kaganovich as head of the Moscow party organization and his evident popularity drew Stalin's suspicions. In 1935 he lost his Moscow party post and his chairmanship of the Commission of Party Control. He was transferred from party work into economic administration in what was clearly a demotion. As head of NKPS in 1935–36, he achieved a dramatic turnabout in the performance of the Soviet railways. In 1935 Kaganovich and Ordzhonikidze were the authors of Stakhanovism as a means of boosting labour productivity in heavy industry and on the railways. But an alternative policy agenda was already being formulated, with Stalin's connivance, by Yezhov, head of the Commission of Party Control, aimed at delivering a decisive blow against those defined as enemies of the regime. In 1936 Kaganovich and Ordzhonikidze attempted to defend their cadres from mass purging and became associated with an attempt to soften and humanize the image of the regime, to direct it away from mass repression and to return it to a degree of normality.

From July 1936 onward Stalin relentlessly pursued his agenda of a deep-seated purge of the party, state and society. His deputies lacked the political and moral courage to stand up to him. Following the suicide of Ordzhonikidze, Kaganovich fell into line and became one of the main organizers of the purge. The Great Terror effected a veritable political revolution: the diminution of the party's role, the purge of the military, the promotion of the secret police apparatus, the downgrading of the powerful economic commissariats and of the republican and regional party organizations. It also constituted in part a social revolution. It marked a major watershed in the development of the

Stalinist state, politically, morally and psychologically, a transformation that was reflected in individual leaders as well. From 1936 onward, despotic/tyrannical rule based on terror marked a regression to a more primitive, cruder, more brutal, atavistic conception of politics. The terror was not produced by domestic or international circumstances. Its causes are to be found not in objective circumstances, but rather in Stalin's motivations and in his subjective evaluation of reality. It was initiated by Stalin cold-bloodedly, with the aim of consolidating his power and elevating terror into an intrinsic part of his method of rule. He required his subordinates to act in accordance with his will, and required them to accept his conception of the threat posed to the state as he interpreted it.

Kaganovich's role in the Great Terror and his role in authorizing the murder of the Polish officers are among the most heinous of his crimes. For a brief period, he had charge of the railways and of heavy industry. His role as head of the railways during the war was marked by two dismissals, and his career after 1941 faltered. Thereafter, he occupied a number of lesser positions and fell in the leadership ranking. After Stalin's death in 1953, he re-emerged with Molotov as a representative of the hardliners within the Politburo, a critic of de-Stalinization, and, as one of the leaders of the 'Anti-Party Group', in 1957 was defeated. His career from 1941 was a prolonged denouement. Expelled from the party in 1961, he was never readmitted, but remained a convinced Stalinist to the end.

Kaganovich was not a great intellectual or original theorist; it was as an administrator that he contributed to shaping the Stalinist system. He possessed a charismatic quality, and from 1930 to 1936 he was probably the most popular member of the Stalin leadership. He possessed great energy, willpower, intellectual self-confidence and a phenomenal capacity for work, although assessments of his achievements vary. He could be creative and innovative, but he often relied on high-handed methods. He was a talented spotter of ability and advanced a number of administrators by his patronage. Like other members of the Stalin leadership, his hostility towards the defeated oppositionists was intense. He did not share the *vozhd"*s paranoid assessment of the threat posed to the state by wreckers, saboteurs, class enemies and spies until compelled to do so in 1937.

The Bolsheviks sought to 'refashion' themselves and to reshape the world. They were expected to turn themselves into instruments of history, subordinating individual conscience to the needs of the cause. Political crises were conceived as a process whereby the cadres were tempered and renewed. After 1928 the Soviet regime underwent a kind of involution. This was not dictated by circumstances but was self-imposed. The basic political questions for the Stalin leadership had already been resolved by 1931. The Stalin regime was marked by its restricted political and intellectual horizons and by its unreflective approach to politics. But narrowness did not mean limited ambition. Kaganovich, as one of the Stalin's leading deputies, imparted great energy and purpose to the system.

In this process, the pressures imposed on individual party members to be in accord with the new realities dictated by the party imposed huge strains. Those who were deemed to be unable to meet this challenge, who continued to hanker after the lost ideals of the revolution were demonised as deviationists, enemies, faint hearts, saboteurs, traitors and spies. The Stalinists projected themselves as heroic figures, the defiant enemies of the old order and the builders of the new socialist world. The idealized cult of the individual Bolshevik leader was counterposed to the demonization of their enemies.

Stalin corresponds to the paranoid personality, the 'high-functioning psychopath', with its malignant 'narcissistic' and Machiavellian aspects. His personality bore a murderous, sadistic dimension. He nurtured a political culture based on intimidation, fear and terror. The central role played by Stalin's personality in the development of the Soviet state can be measured in part by the impact of his death in 1953. Both Khrushchev and Mikoyan depict Stalin as a high-functioning psychopath, although they lacked the terminology to properly describe him. The ideological principles and practices of Bolshevism provided a cover for Stalin as a leader driven by his own inner compulsions. In 1936 the controls imposed on Stalin by his deputies collapsed, allowing him to pursue untrammelled his drive to destroy his enemies.

Kaganovich, like most of his Politburo colleagues, was not a psychopath. Like them, he conforms much more to the type of Machiavellian personality who willingly engages in amoral actions, and who regards such acts as necessary, even laudable. This behaviour was rationalized with reference to ideology, reasons of state, and difficulties of policy choices as dictated by domestic and international circumstances. Kaganovich already in 1919 advanced a Machiavellian conception of how Bolshevik state power should be organized. He displayed a disregard for democracy. He was strongly committed to the fight against the various opposition groups. His conception of socialism was statist. He did not flinch from the resort to violence for state ends.

Kaganovich was one of the generation of Civil War commissars and activists, the generation of workers turned functionaries who came to dominate the Stalinist system. He personified the deracinated Jewish, de-proletarianized, self-educated party functionary whose whole being was wrapped up with the life of the state he served. He belonged to that type of tough, ruthless, driving administrators. He saw Stalin as an adept, principled, committed politician and revolutionary, and was unable to see, or chose not to see, the paranoid and psychopathic aspects of his persona, or thought that this side of his character could be contained and channelled in less destructive directions. In this, he proved to be deluded. Kaganovich and Molotov, who had made their careers as Stalin's aides in the party Secretariat, never succeeded in shaking off this relationship of subordination to their chief, and always remained in his shadow.

The terrible demands which Stalin made on his deputies in carrying out the Terror profoundly changed them. It marked a turning point in Kaganovich's career and marked a step in his transformation. He became more ruthless, more brutal, more treacherous in his relations with colleagues, more preoccupied with his own survival, more inclined to fawn on Stalin. Issues of personal conscience were suppressed to perform the tasks that were assigned him. This required individuals to adopt a chameleon-like approach, and a cold-blooded calculation of what was needed to guarantee their own survival.

Kaganovich, like other members of the Stalin group, combined ideological flexibility with a ruthless understanding of realpolitik. In his writings and speeches, he fully articulated this aspect of Bolshevism: his contemptuous attitude to party and soviet democracy, his advocacy of arbitrary state power, his dismissive attitude to the idealistic strand in Bolshevik thinking. Stalin's lieutenants were delegated considerable powers in their own spheres. The party-state retained significant polycratic aspects. This was fully compatible with a system of personal dictatorship and of despotic rule and, indeed, was a central component of that system. Ultimately, Stalin had the final say. Suggestions that Kaganovich was part of a hardline current in the Politburo that pushed Stalin in the direction of ever more repressive measures is an oversimplification.

The Stalinist system was shaped by its own inner logic, one that was derived from Bolshevik ideology, but one that also radically reinterpreted that ideology. It was shaped by objective domestic and international circumstances. But policies were shaped by a particular mind set: the demonization of enemies coexisted with a heroic utopian conception of the future order. The Stalinist leadership justified policies by making a virtue out of necessity. But policies often followed a kind of self-fulfilling logic, whereby policies were justified in terms of necessity, by the dictates of the building of socialism or the exigencies of the domestic and international class struggle.

His role was that of the acolyte to the dominant leader who was intolerant of dissent. He appears often to have anticipated Stalin's thinking and often provided a more coherent justification of official policy. He was tied to the *vozhd'* by bonds of personal loyalty, and only secondarily of intellectual or ideological conviction. Kaganovich's testimony reveals that his relationship with Stalin became the central point of reference in his life. But this was an asymmetric relationship; the loyalty that was given was not necessarily reciprocated. The despot as supreme decision maker and supreme arbiter effected a transformation in his relationship with his deputies. This undermined their sense of themselves as autonomous agents and required them to think of themselves as an extensions of Stalin's own persona, or as multiple parts of that persona, an extension of Stalin's will.

For most of Stalin's deputies, this was a part they played. Individuals such as Khrushchev, Beria, Molotov and Mikoyan remained more critical of Stalin. In Kaganovich's case, identification with Stalin was so strong that it requires some explanation. His slavish attitude towards Stalin, already evident in the early 1930s, became more pronounced in the 1940s and remained a central aspect of his worldview after Stalin's death. He was no more deeply implicated in the Terror than colleagues such as Molotov, Zhdanov, Voroshilov or Beria. The explanation, in part, relates to Kaganovich's character and his willingness to see himself as Stalin's agent, based on his close identification with the *vozhd'*, his mentor and protector. It is also related to the great insecurity and psychological stress that he was subject to from 1939 onward. No other of Stalin's deputies was placed in such a position over such a sustained period of time. The rise of official anti-Semitism, promoted by Stalin after 1948, placed Kaganovich, as a Jew, in a very precarious position. But his close identification with Stalin was related to his need to justify his role and to salve his conscience.

Kaganovich was as culpable as any of the other lieutenants in the crimes of the Stalin era. He defended, promoted and rationalized the key policies of the Stalinist leadership. In this, he showed a degree of political myopia as to where these policies might lead for the country and for the regime itself. Opportunism became a condition of survival. At the same time, there was a strong element of continuity in his thought throughout his career: his belief in the efficacy of state socialist construction, his preoccupation with administration of a particularly centralized, hierarchical kind, his contemptuous attitude toward democracy, his willingness to defend the Soviet state as a state guided by revolutionary expediency rather than by law, his consequentialist view of ethics and his faith in the promotion of new cadres from the proletariat.

Kaganovich, as we have noted, was, to all appearances, a normal, well-adjusted individual. He was intelligent, quick-witted and had considerable social skills; he could be charming. He was strong-willed and had a stormy temperament that was reflected often in relations with subordinates. Stalin had recognized his ability and promoted him, and in return, Kaganovich was to repay him with obedience and devotion. Stalin may have demoted him on several occasions, but he knew that he had to handle him with care and that he could not afford to humiliate him. Kaganovich, who had always been distinguished by his role in praising Stalin, became known for his slavish sycophancy.

He was both an agent in constructing the Stalinist system and was, in a sense, also a victim of that system. In joining the ruling coterie, its members entered into a kind of Faustian pact. Stalin had the will to break even the most wilful of his deputies. Identification with the dominant partner became a central mechanism of self-rationalization and self-evaluation. An attack on the dominant partner becomes an attack on the subordinate partner's own self-esteem. Kaganovich's identification with Stalin served as a means to protect himself from the bad conscience associated with the crimes in which he was implicated. The extraordinary demands that Stalin made on Kaganovich amounted to a form of psychological cannibalism (psychophagy). In the later Stalin years, Kaganovich assumed the craven role of the despot's creature.

Notwithstanding his great talents, Kaganovich lacked Stalin's self-possession. He needed a leader from whom he could take his cue. The boldness he displayed was the boldness of one who knew that his judgement could be questioned only by the *vozhd'*. He adjusted himself to whatever shift in policy Stalin undertook. Once Stalin was gone, he lost his political mainstay. Unlike Beria or Khrushchev, he lacked the boldness of vision to rethink the basic aspects of the system and was too implicated by his past to undertake such an exercise. But Kaganovich also lacked a base of institutional support and he lacked the authority of a figure like Molotov. In the de-Stalinization process, he became the most reviled of Stalin's deputies, the embodiment of the unprincipled careerist, and one of the main props of Stalin's despotism. He served as a scapegoat for the Stalin era that was in part coloured by latent anti-Semitism. Undoubtedly, he was the Politburo member least willing to countenance the dismantling of the Stalin myth. At the same time, his criticisms of Khrushchev's policies and methods were often sharp and to the point.

Kaganovich lent his formidable talents to realizing the great historical project which Stalin himself embodied. He identified himself wholly with that undertaking and held Stalin in awe. Through his work in enforcing the leader's will, he made a great many enemies. Thus he was seen as Stalin's creature, a sycophant who slavishly pandered to Stalin. But Kaganovich was a ruthless politician and not one to make an enemy of lightly. His role as Stalin's alter ego fitted him badly as a potential successor. He was seen as an executor of Stalin's will, not as a politician or statesman in his own right. He was not trusted and even as a patron, his clients quickly deserted him. While Molotov, Voroshilov and Zhdanov were equally if not more heavily implicated in the mass terror of 1936–39, they escaped the obloquy directed at Kaganovich.

Alongside this transformation, we also see the operation of the 'state of denial', an unwillingness to confront or come to terms with past experiences, or to face up to his own personal moral responsibility. For Kaganovich, the actions of the Stalinist regime and his own part in it was rationalized as being shaped by necessity, or as the lesser evil, which closed off any need to reflect on the criminalization of the regime or on his own personal guilt. Any self-reflection by Kaganovich or any of the other deputies, of the personal costs incurred by this process would have been construed as the most abject sign of weakness. In this, Bolshevik ideology created a closed system, where the actions of the party-state and the role of individuals within it, were not open to critical reflection or challenge. In the case of Kaganovich, this was more pronounced than with any other of Stalin's deputies.

The rationalization offered by Stalin's supporters was that the achievements of the era outweighed the costs; that forced development corresponded to a necessary stage in the transition from backwardness to modernity, that choices were dictated by historical necessity. The argument that Stalin was necessary has largely been abandoned by scholars in relation to the 'revolution from above'. Similarly, the Terror stemmed not from some objective need of the state or society, but derived largely from Stalin's own threat perception and his own psychological needs. Alternatives to the Stalinist path of development existed; not only non-Stalinist paths, but even alternative paths within the Stalinist model. Stalin's path imposed enormous costs, and the system he created proved unable in the long term, to adapt itself to the needs of a modernizing society.

NOTES

Introduction

1 Erik van Ree, *The Political Thought of Joseph Stalin: A study in twentieth century revolutionary patriotism* (London and New York, 2002). E. A. Rees, *Political Thought from Machiavelli to Stalin: Revolutionary Machiavellism* (Basingstoke, 2004).
2 Manfred F. R. Kets de Vries, *Reflections on Character and Leadership* (Chichester, 2009).
3 J. Hellbeck, 'Working, Struggling, Becoming: Stalin-Era Autobiographical Texts', in David L. Hoffmann (ed.), *Stalinism: The Essential Readings* (Oxford, 2003), 181–210. Igal Halfin (ed.), *Language and Revolution: Making of Modern Political Identities* (London, 2002).
4 Orlando Figes and Boris Kolonitsky, *Interpreting the Russian Revolution: The Language and Symbols of 1917* (Yale University Press, 1999).
5 Carl A. Linden, *The Soviet-Party State: The Politics of Ideocratic Despotism* (New York, 1983).
6 The strongest case for Stalin as a weak ruler is made by J. Arch Getty, *The Origins of the Great Terror: The Soviet Communist Party Reconsidered, 1933–1938* (Cambridge, 1985) and J. Arch Getty, 'Stalin as Prime Minister: Power and the Politburo', in Sarah Davies and James Harris (eds), *Stalin: A New History* (Cambridge, 2005).
7 Markku Kangaspuro and Jeremy Smith (eds), *Modernisation in Russia since 1900* (Helsinki, 2006), 38–51.
8 Bertrand Russell, *Bolshevism: Practice and Theory* (New York, 1972; first published 1920 as *The Practice and Theory of Bolshevism*).
9 For an illuminating comparison between Stalinism and Italian Fascism see A. James Gregor, *Italian Fascism and Developmental Dictatorship* (Princeton, 1979).
10 See the discussion of 'neo-patrimonialism' in Yoram Golizki and O. V. Khlevniuk, *Cold Peace: Stalin and the Soviet Ruling Circle, 1945–1953* (Oxford, 2004).
11 O. V. Khlevniuk, *Master of the House: Stalin and his Inner Circle* (Yale University Press, 2009).
12 Stephen G. Wheatcroft, 'From Team-Stalin to Degenerate Tyranny', in E. A. Rees (ed.), *The Nature of Stalin's Dictatorship: The Politburo, 1924–1953* (Basingstoke, 2004), ch. 3.
13 T. H. Rigby, 'Was Stalin a Disloyal Patron?' *Soviet Studies* 38, no. 3 (1986): 311–24.
14 Andrea Graziosi, *The Great Soviet Peasant War: Bolsheviks and Peasants 1917–1933* (Cambridge, MA, 1996), 28.
15 E. A. Rees (ed.), *The Nature of Stalin's Dictatorship: The Politburo 1924–1953* (Basingstoke, 2004): ch. 1, E. A. Rees, 'Stalin as Leader 1924–1937: From Oligarch to Dictator'; ch. 7, 'Stalin as Leader, 1937–1953: From Dictator to Despot'.

16 A. J. Polan, *Lenin and the End of Politics* (London, 1984); Ronald Tiersky, *Ordinary Stalinism: Democratic Centralism and the Question of Communist Political Development* (London and Sydney, 1985); Michael Waller, *Democratic Centralism: An Historical Commentary* (Manchester, 1981).
17 Jürgen Habermas, *The Structural Transformation of the Public Sphere: Inquiry into a Category of Bourgeois Society*, trans. Thomas Berger (London, 1992). Gábor T Rittersporn, Malte Rolf and Jan C. Behrends (eds), *Public Spheres in Soviet Type Societies* (Frankfurt, 2003).
18 Frances Nethercott, *Russian Legal Culture Before and After Communism: Criminal Justice, Politics and the Public Sphere* (London, 2007); Robert Sharlet, 'Stalinism and Soviet Legal Culture', in Robert C. Tucker (ed.) *Stalinism: Essays in Historical Interpretation* (New York and London, 1977).
19 S. Kotkin, *Magnetic Mountain: Stalinism as Civilization* (Berkeley, Los Angeles and London, 1995), ch. 5 'Speaking Bolshevik'; J. Arch Getty and Oleg V. Naumov, *The Road to Terror: Stalin and the Self-Destruction of the Bolsheviks, 1932–1939*, trans. Benjamin Sher (New Haven and London, 1999), introduction 'Party Documents and Bolshevik Mentality', 1–29.
20 Sarah Davies, *Popular Opinion in Stalin's Russia: Terror, Propaganda and Dissent, 1934–1941* (Cambridge, 1997).
21 Jürgen Habermas, *Legitimation Crisis*, trans. Thomas McCarthy (London, 1992). Jan Pakulski, 'Legitimation and Mass Compliance. Reflections on Max Weber and Soviet Type Societies', *British Journal of Political Science* 16, no. 1 (1986): 35–56. See also E. A. Rees, 'Leader Cults: Varieties, Preconditions and Functions', in B. Apor, J. Behrens, P. Jones and E. A. Rees, *The Leader Cult in Communist Dictatorship* (Basingstoke, 2004), 3–28.
22 Hans Buchheim, 'Despotism, ersatz religion, religious erzats', in Hans Meier (ed.), *Totalitarianism and Political Religions, Vol.1 Concepts for the Comparison of Dictatorship*, trans. Jodi Bruhn (London, 2004), 224–7; Christel Lane, *The Rites of Rulers: Ritual in Industrial Society – the Soviet Case* (Cambridge, 1981), ch. 3.
23 O. Khakhordin, *The Collective and the Individual in Russia: A Study of Practices* (Berkeley, 1999); Sheila Fitzpatrick, 'Ascribing class: The construction of social identity in Soviet Russia', in Sheila Fitzpatrick (ed.) *Stalinism: New Directions* (London and New York, 2000).
24 On the Leninist view of ethics, see P. Boobbyer, *Conscience Dissent and Reform in Soviet Russia* (London, 2009).
25 Loris Marcucci, *Il Commissario Di Ferro Di Stalin* (Turin, 1997).
26 R. Medvedev, *All Stalin's Men* (Oxford, 1983).
27 R. Medvedev, Sergei Parofenov and Petr Khmelinsky, *Zheleznyi yastreb* (Ekaterinburg, 1992).
28 Yuri Shapoval, *Lazar Kaganovich* (Kiev, 1994).
29 Stuart Kahan, *The Wolf in the Kremlin* (London, 1989).
30 See the scathing review by R. Medvedev, 'Stalin i Kaganovich', in *Moskovskie novosti* 52 (25 December 1988): 16.
31 F. Chuev, *Tak govoril Kaganovich: Ispoved' stalinskogo apostola* (Moscow, 1992), 49; 'Dve besedy s L.M. Kaganovichem', *Novaya i noveishaya istoriya* (1999) no. 2: 121.
32 See Kaganovich's biography in *Bol'shaya Sovetskaya Entsiklopaediya* 30 (1937): 514–18.
33 L. M. Kaganovich, *Pamyatnye zapiski rabochego, kommunista-bol'shevika, profsoyuznogo, partiinogo i sovetskogo rabotnika* (Moscow, 1996).
34 *Moskovskie novosti* 30 (28 July 1996): 11.
35 F. Chuev, *Tak govoril Kaganovich*.
36 'Dve besedy s L.M. Kaganovichem', *Novaya i noveishaya istoriya* (1999) no. 2: 101–22.

37 O. V. Khlevniuk, R. W. Davies, L. P. Kosheleva, E. A. Rees and L. A. Rogovaya (eds), *Stalin i Kaganovich. Perepiska. 1931–1936gg* (Moscow, 2001); R. W. Davies, E. A. Rees, O. V. Khlevniuk, L. P. Kosheleva and L. A. Rogovaya (eds), *The Stalin-Kaganovich Correspondence, 1931–1936* (New Haven, CT and London, 2003). See also Yves Cohen, 'Des lettres comme action. Stalin au début des années 1930 vu depuis le fonds Kaganovich', *Cahiers du monde russe* 38, no. 3 (1997): 307–46.

Chapter 1: The Making of a Bolshevik, 1893–1917

1 L. M. Kaganovich, *Pamyatnye zapiski rabochego, kommunista-bol'shevika, profsoyuznogo, partiinogo i sovetskogo rabotnika* (Moscow, 1996), 19; henceforth *PZ*.
2 *PZ*, 22.
3 *PZ*, 25.
4 F. Chuev, *Tak govoril Kaganovich: Ispoved' stalinskogo apostola* (Moscow, 1992), 106–7.
5 *PZ*, 26.
6 *PZ*, 28–9.
7 Jonathan Frankel, *Prophecy and Politics: Socialism, Nationalism and the Russian Jews, 1862–1917* (Cambridge, 1991); John D. Klier and Shlomo Lambroza (eds), *Pogroms: Anti-Jewish Violence in Modern Russian History* (Cambridge, 1992).
8 *PZ*, 33.
9 Chuev, *Tak govoril Kaganovich*, 29, 106–7, 49–50.
10 RGASPI, 81/3/413, 7, 77.
11 *PZ*, 37.
12 *PZ*, 39.
13 *PZ*, 44–5.
14 *PZ*, 50–1.
15 RGASPI, 81/3/413, 74.
16 *PZ*, 41.
17 Mary Louise Loe, 'Gorky and Nietzsche', in Bernice Glatzer Rozental (ed.), *Nietzsche in Russia* (Princeton, 1986), 251–74.
18 RGASPI, 81/3/413, 74.
19 Ibid.
20 *Sovetskaya kultura*, 6 October 1990, 8.
21 *PZ*, 42.
22 *PZ*, 29.
23 *PZ*, 76.
24 RGASPI, 81/3/413, 75.
25 Henry Jack Tobias, *The Jewish Bund in Russia from its Origins to 1905* (Stanford, 1972).
26 *PZ*, 36.
27 D. Lane, *The Roots of Russian Communism: A Social and Historical Study of Russian Social-Democracy 1898–1907* (London, 1968), 37, 41, 51.
28 See Boris Shragin and Albert Todd (eds), *Landmarks: A Collection of Essays on the Russian Intelligentsia* (New York, 1977).
29 V. I. Lenin, *Collected Works*, vol. 17 (Moscow, 1974), 247–9.
30 *Entsiklopedichesky Slovar' Russkogo Bibliograficheskogo Instituta Granat: Deyateli Soyuza Sovetskikh Sotsialisaticheskikh Respublik i Oktyabr'skoi Revolyutsii*, (Moscow, 1925), ch. 11, 134.
31 TsGAOOU (Tsentral'noi gosudarstvennyi arkhiv obshchestvennykh organizatsii Ukrainy), 59/1/220, 1–3.

32 Chuev, *Tak govoril Kaganovich*, 108.
33 TsGAOOU, 59/1/220, 1–3.
34 L. Trotsky, *My Life* (New York, 1970), 168–9, 226–30.
35 'Dve besedy s L.M. Kaganovichem', in *Novoe i Noveishaya istoryia* (1999) no. 2: 116. The Kiev committee included Kosior, Gavril Veinberg, Degtyarev, Lazar Kaganovich, Maior (Maiorov) and Dora Itkin.
36 TsGAOOU, 59/1/290, 7.
37 Chuev, *Tak govoril Kaganovich*, 118.
38 TsGAOOU, 59/1/124, 12–13 (testimony of Zaitsev).
39 N. S. Khrushchev, *Khrushchev Remembers* (London, 1971), 31. Khrushchev recounts that Kaganovich at this time used the pseudonym Zhirovich (Greasy One), not Kosherovich. Khrushchev knew it was an amusing pseudonym, but got it wrong.
40 *PZ*, 96.
41 TsGAOOU, 59/1/436, 17.
42 *PZ*, 100.
43 *PZ*, 100–1.
44 *PZ*, 101.
45 *PZ*, 105.
46 Donald J. Raleigh, *Revolution on the Volga, 1917 in Saratov* (Ithaca, NY and London, 1986), 133; E. Rabinovich, 'Vserossiskaya konferentsiya bol'shevistskikh organizatsii 1917g', *Krasnaya letopis* 5/38 (1930): 109.
47 *PZ*, 107–8.
48 Chuev, *Tak govoril Kaganovich*, 24–5, 67–8.
49 Alexander Rabinowitch, *Prelude to Revolution: The Petrograd Bolsheviks and the July 1917 Uprising* (Bloomington, IN and Indianapolis, 1991), 123.
50 *PZ*, 111–12.
51 Chuev, *Tak govoril Kaganovich*, 21.
52 Rabinowitch, *Prelude to Revolution*, 272n69, cites E. Rabinovich, 'Vserossiskaya konferentsiya bol'shevistskikh organizatsii 1917g', *Krasnaya letopis* 5/38 (1930): 124. The membership of the bureau included: N. I. Podvoisky (chairman), V. I. Nevsky, E. F. Rozmirovich, K. A. Mekhonoshin, I. Ya. Arosev, F. P. Khaustov, I. I. Dzevaltovsky, N. K. Belyakov, A. Ya. Semashko, V. V. Sakharov, N. V. Krylenko and L. M. Kaganovich.
53 Rabinowitch, *Prelude to Revolution*, 137–8, cites V. I. Nevsky, 'V oktyabre: beglye zametki pamyati', *Katorga i ssylka* (1932) nos. 11–12 (96–7): 20–30.
54 *PZ*, 116.
55 Chuev, *Tak govoril Kaganovich*, 74–5.
56 *PZ*, 119–26.
57 *PZ*, 127–8.
58 *PZ*, 135–6.
59 *PZ*, 141–2.
60 *PZ*, 143.
61 *PZ*, 145–8.
62 *PZ*, 154–5.
63 *PZ*, 156.
64 *PZ*, 157.
65 *PZ*, 160.
66 *PZ*, 163.
67 Oliver H. Radkey, *Russia Goes to the Polls: The Elections to the All-Russian Constituent Assembly, 1917* (Ithaca, NY and London, 1977; first published 1950), 148–51.

68 A. J. Polan, *Lenin and the End of Politics* (London, 1984).
69 *PZ*, 167.
70 *PZ*, 177.
71 *PZ*, 183. The drafting committee comprised Nikolai Podvoisky, Nikolai Krylenko, Konstantin Mekhonoshkin, and the representatives of the Red Guards Valentin Trifonov and K. K. Yurenev.
72 *PZ*, 185–6.
73 *PZ*, 189–90.
74 *PZ*, 204–5.
75 *PZ*, 199–200.
76 *PZ*, 194.
77 *PZ*, 411.
78 *PZ*, 202–3.
79 RGASPI, 81/3/413, 1.
80 *PZ*, 209.
81 RGASPI, 81/3/413, 76.
82 *Sotsialisticheskii vestnik* 23 (308), 10 November 1933: 3–10.
83 R. Terekhov, *Stranitsy geroicheskoi bor'by: Vospominaniya starogo bol'shevika*, (Kiev, 1963), 112. TsGAOOU, 57/1/135, 4.
84 TsGAOOU, 59/1/124, 12–13 (testimony of Zaitsev).
85 Yu. Ivanov, *Ostorozhno: sionism* (Moscow, 1971); Chuev, *Tak govoril Kaganovich*, 96–8.
86 See the photographs in *PZ*, between pages 160–1; Orlando Figes and Boris Kolonitsky, *Interpreting the Russian Revolution: The Language and Symbols of 1917* (New Haven, CT and London, 1999), 115–16.
87 *PZ*, 305.
88 F. M. Dostoevsky, *The Diary of a Writer* (Salt Lake City, 1985), 151.

Chapter 2: Red Terror and Civil War, 1918–1921

1 Kaganovich's autobiographical account of his political career in his party file: RGASPI, 81/3/413, 76–7.
2 E. A. Preobrazhensky (ed.), *1917–1920, Khronika revolyutsionykh sobitii v Gorkov'skom krae* (Gorky, 1932), 144. Henceforth *Khronika*.
3 L. M. Kaganovich, *Pamyatnye zapiski* (Moscow, 1996), 167. Henceforth *PZ*. F. Chuev, *Tak govoril Kaganovich: Ispoved' stalinskogo apostola* (Moscow 1992), 25–6.
4 *PZ*, 216.
5 John L. H. Keep, *The Russian Revolution: A Study in Mass Mobilization* (London, 1976), 369.
6 D. I. Chesnokov (ed.), *Nizhegorodskaya organizatsiya RKP(b) v gody inostranykh interventsiya i grazhdanskaya voina 1918–1920* (Gorky, 1957), 68. When Chesnokov wrote to Kaganovich in 1956 about the possibility of including extracts from his speeches and articles in this work, he received no reply – GARF, 5446/83/137, 5–6.
7 Vladimir N. Brovkin, *Behind the Front Lines of the Civil War: Political Parties and Social Movements in Russia, 1918–1921* (Princeton, 1994), 202; W. H. Chamberlin, *The Russian Revolution 1917–1921*, vol. 1 (London, 1935), 419.
8 Victor M. Fic, *The Bolsheviks and the Czechoslovak Legion* (New Delhi, 1978), 116.
9 *Dokumenty velikoi oktyabr'skoi sotsialisticheskoi revolyutsii v nizhegorodskoi gubernii* (Gorky, 1945),154.

10 *Desyat' let sovetskoi vlasti v nizhegorodskoi gubernii 1917–1927* (Nizhnyi Novgorod, 1927), 24; D. I. Chesnokov (ed.), *Nizhegorodskaya organizatsiya*, 71–3; *Perepiska Sekretariat TsK RKP(b) c mestnymi partiinymi organizatsiyami (yanvarya-mart 1919g)*, vol. 4 (Moscow, 1971), 13–14.
11 *Raboche-krest'yanskii nizhegorodskii listok*, 20 June 1918.
12 *Khronika*, 148.
13 Vladimir N. Brovkin, *Dear Comrades: Menshevik Reports on the Bolshevik Revolution and the Civil War* (Stanford, 1991), 98, 101, 133.
14 Orlando Figes, *A People's Tragedy: The Russian Revolution 1891–1924* (London, 1996), 527.
15 *Desyat' let sovetskoi vlasti*, 22. For Cheka orders on the strike and its aftermath see *Raboche-krest'yanskii nizhegorodskii listok*, 16 June and 18–20 June 1918.
16 Silvana Malle, *The Economic Organisation of War Communism, 1918–1921* (Cambridge, 1985); Samuel Barber, *Before Stalinism* (Cambridge, 1990).
17 *Raboche-krest'yanskii nizhegorodskii listok*, 21 June 1918.
18 *Desyat' let sovetskoi vlasti*, 20.
19 Ibid., 23–4.
20 *Raboche-krest'yanskii nizhegorodskii listok*, 27 June 1918.
21 *Dokumenty velikoi oktyabr'skoi*, 132.
22 G. Leggett, *The Cheka: Lenin's Political Police* (London, 1981), 104.
23 R. Pipes (ed.), *The Unknown Lenin: From the Secret Archives* (New Haven, CT and London, 1996), 43–53; R. J. Service, *Lenin: A Political Life: The Iron Ring*, vol. 3 (London, 1995), 40, 43.
24 L. Trotsky, *My Life: An Attempt at an Autobiography* (New York, 1970), 397; *The Trotsky Papers 1917–1922*, vol. 1, ed. Jan. M. Meiver (The Hague, 1964), 70–5.
25 V. I. Lenin, *Polnoe sobranie sochinenii* (5th ed.), vol. 37 (Moscow, 1963), 691. Henceforth *PSS*.
26 *PSS*, vol. 50, 142–3. The letter was first published at the height of the Great Terror, in *Bol'shevik* (1938), no. 2.
27 *Khronika*, 155, cites *Protokol Nizhniinovgorodskoi oblastnoi partinnoi komitet RKP(b) za 1918*, no. 31: 91. *Desyat' let sovetskoi vlasti*, 25. The members of the MRC were: G. F. Fedorov (Province Soviet Executive Committee) chairman, Ya. Z. Vorob'ev (also known as Kats) (Province Cheka), Kraevsky (Province Military Committee), S. A. Akimov (Province Soviet Executive Committee), Kaganovich (Province Party Committee) and I. S. Shelekhes, secretary.
28 *Zabveniyu ne Podlezhit: Neizvestnye stranitsy nizhegorodskoi istorii (1918–1984 gody)* (Nizhnyi Novgorod, 1994), 72–6.
29 Chesnokov, *Nizhegorodskaya organizatsiya*, 70.
30 *PSS*, vol. 50, 155.
31 *Zabveniyu ne Podlezhit*, 78–9.
32 *Raboche-krest'yanskii nizhegorodskii listok*, no. 183, 23 August 1918.
33 Chesnokov, *Nizhegorodskaya organizatsiya*, 66.
34 *Perepiska Sekretariat*, vol. 3, 283; vol. 4, 13–14.
35 *Khronika*, 160, cites *Raboche-krest'yanskii nizhegorodskii listok*, no. 189, 31 September 1918.
36 *Perepiska Sekretariat*, vol. 4, 202–3.
37 Leggett, *The Cheka*, 113–14.
38 W. H. Chamberlin, *The Russian Revolution 1917–1921*, vol. 2 (London, 1935), 66.
39 D. Volkogonov, *Stalin: Triumph and Tragedy* (London, 1991), 234.
40 *Khronika*, 161, cites *Nizghegorodskii listok*, 1 September 1918.

41 Leggett, *The Cheka*, 112, 148, cites *Ezhenedelnik VChK*, no. 1, 22 September 1918, 22; no. 6, 27 October, 27–8. S. P. Mel'gunov, *Krasnii terror v rossii* (Simferopol, 1991), 28.
42 *Khronika*, 164. *Dokumenty po istorii grazhdanskoi voiny v SSSR* (Moscow, 1940) vol. 1, 215.
43 *Zabveniyu ne Podlezhit*, 83–4, 87–88, 89.
44 *Khronika*, 166.
45 I. Deutscher, *The Prophet Armed* (Oxford, 1970), 423.
46 *Zabveniyu ne Podlezhit*, 89–91.
47 *Stenograficheskii otchet 5-i Nizhegorodskoi gubernskoi konferentsii RKP(bol'shevikov)* (Nizhnyi Novgorod, 1918), 62.
48 Ibid., 62, 88, 92.
49 Ibid., 68.
50 Ibid., 156.
51 *Nizhegorodskaya kommuna*, 4 December 1918, 2. Sergei Malashkin, *Muskuly: Poemy* (2nd ed.) (Nizhnyi Novgorod, 1919).
52 *Nizhegorodskaya kommuna*, 7, 8 and 18 December 1918; 3 January 1919.
53 *Stenograficheskii otchet 5-i Nizhegorodskoi gubernskoi konferentsii RKP (bol'shevikov)*, 2.
54 *Nizhegorodskaya kommuna*, 12, 13 November 1918.
55 *Nizhegorodskaya kommuna*, 31 December 1918; 1–2 January 1919.
56 Deutscher, *The Prophet Armed*, 427.
57 Service, *The Iron Ring*, 26–7.
58 *Protokol Nizhniinovgorod guberniya ispolkom za 1919*, 4–5.
59 Boris I. Nicolaevskii, *Power and the Soviet Elite*, ed. Janet D. Zagorina (London, 1966), 229–33.
60 *Protokol Nizhniinovgorod guberniya ispolkom za 1919*, 7.
61 *Perepiska Sekretariat*, vol. 7, 331, 216–17, 248, 281, 331.
62 *Protokol Nizhniinovgorod guberniya partii komitet za 1918*, 86.
63 *Nizhegorodskaya kommuna*, 6, 12 and 14 January 1919.
64 Trotsky, *My Life*, 436–50; Service, *The Iron Ring*, 72–5.
65 *Pravda*, 4 March 1919.
66 *Perepiska sekretariata*, vol. 6, 63, 127, 200–7.
67 *Nizhegorodskaya kommuna*, 8 March 1919.
68 *Nizhegorodskaya kommuna*, 11 March 1919.
69 R. J. Service, *The Bolshevik Party in Revolution: A Study in Organisational Change 1917–1923*, (London and Basingstoke, 1979), 106–10.
70 *Vos'moi s"ezd RKP(b), mart 1919 goda: Protokoly* (Moscow, 1959), 160–2, 219–25, 277–96, 11–26.
71 *Pravda*, 12 March 1919.
72 *Vos'moi s"ezd RKP(b)*, 178–9.
73 Ibid., 179.
74 *KPSS v rezolyutsiyakh i resheniyakh s"ezdov, konferentsii i plenumov TsK*, vol. 2 (Moscow, 1983), 105.
75 E. H. Carr, *The Bolshevik Revolution 1917–1923*, vol. 1 (Harmondsworth, 1969), 201.
76 Ibid., 447.
77 *Perepiska Sekretariat*, vol. 7, 51, 218; V. I. Lenin, *PSS*, vol. 38, 196–7.
78 Trotsky, *My Life* , 436.
79 *Nizhegorodskaya kommuna*, 28 March 1919, 1.
80 *Khronika*, 204, 218, 221.
81 *Pravda*, 4 April 1919, cited in Brovkin, *Dear Comrades*, 14.
82 Brovkin, *Behind the Front Lines of the Civil War*, 73.

83 *Khronika*, , 219, cites *Protokol Nizh RKP(b) za 1919*, no. 691, 50.
84 *Perepiska Sekretariat*, vol. 4, 29; vol. 6, 207; vol. 5, 69, 74, 270; vol. 6, 81; vol. 7, 31.
85 'Dve besedy s L.M. Kaganovichem', in *Novaya i noveishaya istoriya* (1999) no. 2: 116.
86 Brovkin, *Behind the Front Lines of the Civil War* , 147.
87 *Nizhegorodskaya kommuna*, 5 August 1919.
88 *Nizhegorodskaya kommuna*, 13 April 1919.
89 *Protokol Nizhegorodskoi ispolkom za 1919*, 15–16.
90 *Perepiska Sekretariat*, vol. 7, 247–48, 255–7, 307.
91 *Khronika*, 228–30, 241, 246.
92 *Khronika*, 247.
93 *Nizhegorodskaya kommuna*, 3 July 1919; *Khronika*, 246.
94 Chuev, *Tak govoril Kaganovich*, 26.
95 *Nizhegorodskaya kommuna*, 4 July 1919.
96 *Nizhegorodskaya kommuna*, 22 July 1919.
97 *Khronika*, 252–3. *Perepiska Sekretariat*, vol. 8, 568.
98 L. Trotsky, *Stalin: An Appraisal of the Man and his Influence*, ed. and trans. Charles Malamuth (London, 1968), 322–4.
99 *Khronika*, 258.
100 *PZ*, 217–8.
101 RGASPI, 81/3/413, 8.
102 S. M. Budennyi, *The Path of Valour* (Moscow, 1972).
103 *PZ*, 225–6; *Sovetskaya kultura*, 6 October 1990, 8. Interview with Kaganovich.
104 *PZ*, 230. On P. K. Kaganovich, see Lars T. Lih, *Bread and Authority in Russia, 1914–1921* (Berkeley, 1990), passim.
105 *7-i Vserossiskii s"ezd sovetov rabochikh, krestyanskikh, krasnoarmeiskikh i kazach'ikh deputatov: stenograficheskii otchet, 5–9 dekabrya 1919* (Moscow, 1920), 225–7.
106 Chuev, *Tak govoril Kaganovich*, 25.
107 L. M. Kaganovich, *Kak stroitsia sovetskaya vlast': Polozhenie ob organizatsionnom stroitel'stva gubernskoi sovetskom vlasti* (Voronezh, 1920).
108 *PSS*, vol. 41, 309–10.
109 See Martha B. Olcott, 'The Basmachi or Freeman's Revolt in Turkestan 1918–24', *Soviet Studies* 23, no. 3 (1981): 352–69.
110 *Bolshaya Sovetskaya Entsiklopediya*, vol. 26 (Moscow, 1977), 339. The Turkkommision comprised of: G. I. Boky, F. I. Golosheikin, V. V. Kuibyshev, Ya. E. Rudzutak, M. V. Frunze, and Sh. Z. Eliava.
111 K. Khasanov, *V.I. Lenin i Turkburo TsK RKP(b)* (Tashkent, 1969), 29.
112 Chuev, *Tak govoril Kaganovich*, 27. *PZ*, 235.
113 *Pravda Vostoka*, 9 December 1937.
114 *PZ*, 235.
115 *PZ*, 238. On 22 November 1920, Kaganovich addressed a conference of trade union and RKI cells, and in December a conference on work amongst women: RGASPI, 81/3/102, 74.
116 RGASPI, 81/3/413, 76.
117 RGASPI, 81/3/102, 1–12.
118 G. Safarov, *Kolonial'nya Revolyutstiya: Opyt' Turkestana* (Moscow, 1921).
119 RGASPI, 81/3/101, 13–41.
120 Radzhapov, 'Etapy razvitiya sovetskogo gosudarstennogo stroia v Srednei Azii', *Sovetskoe gosudarstvo i pravo* 11 (1948): 65.

121 *PZ*, 240.
122 L. M. Kaganovich, *Pamyatnaya knizhka sovetskogo stroitelya* (Tashkent, 1920).
123 *PZ*, 242.
124 Khasanov, *V.I. Lenin i Turkbyuro TsK RKP(b)*, 40.
125 *PZ*, 243–5, 248.
126 RGASPI, 81/3/102, 164–99. Khasanov, *V.I. Lenin i Turkbyuro TsK RKP(b)*, 41–5, asserts that the votes were cast as follows: Lenin – 97, Trotsky – 14, Workers' Opposition – 7.
127 *Desiatnyi s"ezd RKP(b), mart 1921 goda: stenograficheskii otchet* (Moscow, 1963), 770, 775.
128 Ibid., 189–201.
129 E. Voskoboinikov and A. Zevelev, *Turkkomissiya VTsIK i Sovnarkoma RSFSR i Turkbyuro TsK RKP(b) v bor'be za ukreplenie sovetskoi vlasti v Turkestane (M. V. Frunze, V. V. Kuibyshev, L. M. Kaganovich v Turkestane)* (Tashkent, 1951).
130 *PZ*, 412.
131 *PZ*, 303–4.
132 V. P. Nikolaeva, 'Turkkomissiya kak polnomochnyi organ TsK RKP(b)', *Voprosy istorii KPSS* 2 (1958): 73–88.
133 Khasanov, *V.I. Lenin i Turkbyuro TsK RKP(b)*, 76–7.
134 Ibid., 62–5.
135 *PSS*, vol. 44, 673–4; vol. 53, 189–90; vol. 54, 109.
136 *Leninskii sbornik*, vol. 35, 312.
137 *Odinnadtsatyi s"ezd RKP(b); mart-aprelia 1922 goda: stenograficheskii otchet* (Moscow, 1961), 178, 365, 269; *PZ*, 314–17.
138 Khasanov, *V.I. Lenin i Turkbyuro TsK RKP(b)*, 93.
139 *PZ*, 413.
140 R. Medvedev, *All Stalin's Men* (Oxford, 1983), 116; Chuev, *Tak govoril Kaganovich*, 105.
141 'Dve besedy s L.M. Kaganovichem', 114.

Chapter 3: Building the Monolithic Party, 1922–1927

1 A. I. Mikoyan, *Tak bylo: razmyshleniya o minuvshem* (Moscow, 1999), 350–1.
2 L. M. Kaganovich, *Pamyatnye zapiski* (Moscow, 1996). Henceforth *PZ*, 259.
3 *PZ*, 251–2.
4 L. Schapiro, *The Communist Party of the Soviet Union* (London, 1978), 252–5; R. V. Daniels, *The Conscience of the Revolution* (Cambridge, MA, 1965), 242.
5 *PZ*, 255.
6 *PZ*, 262–3.
7 *PZ*, 269.
8 L. M. Kaganovich, 'Blizhaishie zadachi paboty orgotdelov', *Izvestiya TsK RKP(b)* (1923) no. 1: 1–10.
9 See Lenin's note to Kamenev on 3 March 1922, Lenin, *Polnoe sobranie sochinenii* (5th ed.), vol. 44 (Moscow, 1963), 428. Henceforth *PSS*.
10 N. N. Pokrovsky and S. G. Petrov, *Arkhivy Kremlya: Politbyuro i tserkov 1922–1925gg* (Moscow, 1997), 113–98.
11 Lenin, *PSS*, vol. 54, 189–90.
12 Marc Jansen, *A Show Trial Under Lenin: The Trial of the Socialist Revolutionaries, Moscow, 1922*, trans. Jean Saunders (The Hague and London, 1982); I. V. Stalin, *Works*, vol. 5 (Moscow, 1953), 420.

13 For an exposition of communist ethics see E. A. Preobrazhensky, *Morali i klassovykh normakh* (Moscow, 1923). These issues are discussed more fully in E. A. Rees, *Political Thought from Machiavelli to Stalin: Revolutionary Machiavellism* (Basingstoke, 2004), ch. 6.
14 E. H. Carr, *Socialism in One Country 1924–1926*, vol. 2 (Harmondsworth, 1970), ch. 19 'The Monolithic Party'.
15 *PZ*, 319.
16 *PZ*, 321.
17 E. A. Rees, *State Control in Soviet Russia: The Rise and the Fall of the Workers' and Peasants' Inspection 1920–1934* (London, 1987), ch. 2.
18 *PZ*, 333.
19 Carr, *Socialism in One Country 1924–1926*, vol. 2, 220–1.
20 *PZ*, 335.
21 The signatories included Yu. L. Pyatakov, E. A. Preobrazhensky, V. Antonov-Ovseenko, V. V. Osinsky, V. Smirnov, T. V. Sapronov, L. P. Serebryakov, and A. P. Rozengolts.
22 *PZ*, 339.
23 B. Souvarine, *Stalin*, (London, n.d.), 430. Souvarine suggests that Kaganovich had some 'temporary "Trotskyist" aberration' to atone for. E. H. Carr, *The Interregnum 1923–1924* (Harmondsworth, 1969), 115, 380. Carr simply gives the name Kaganovich, without initials. On P. K. Kaganovich, see *Deviatye s"ezd RKP(b) mart-aprel'1920 goda: Protokoly*, (Moscow, 1960), 620. *Izvestiya TsK KPSS* (1990) no. 6: 189–95.
24 *PZ*, 342.
25 *PZ*, 412.
26 *PZ*, 343.
27 *PZ*, 345.
28 *PZ*, 340–1.
29 D. Hincks, 'Support for the Opposition in Moscow in the Party Discussion of 1923–24', *Soviet Studies* 44, no. 1 (1992): 137–51.
30 Stalin, *Works*, vol. 6, 7–8, 23.
31 F. Chuev, *Tak govoril Kaganovich: Ispoved' stalinskogo apostola* (Moscow, 1992), 191.
32 *Trinadtsatyi s"ezd RKP(b), mai 1924 goda: stenograficheskii otchet* (Moscow, 1963), 5, 528, 529–31, 591; *PZ* 357.
33 Ibid., 131.
34 Ibid., 749–66.
35 Schapiro, *The Communist Party of the Soviet Union*, 288.
36 *PZ*, 311. From 1924 onward, the Secretariat had 9 departments: Orgraspred, Agitation and Propaganda, Press, Work among Women, Work in the Villages, Accounting, Statistics, Information, and Administration of Affairs. L. Schapiro, *The Communist Party of the Soviet Union*, 652.
37 James Hughes, 'Patrimonialism and the Stalinist System: The Case of S. I. Syrtsov', *Europe-Asia Studies* 48, no. 4 (1996): 555.
38 This exchange was recalled by Kaganovich in 1953: *Izvestiya TsK KPSS* (1991) no. 1: 187–8. Vera Tolz, 'The Death and "Second Life" of Lavrentii Beria', *Radio Liberty Research*, 23 December 1993.
39 A. V. Kvashonkin, O. V. Khlevniuk, L. P. Kosheleva and L. A. Rogovaya (eds), *Bol'shevistskoe rukovodstvo. Perepiska. 1912–1917* (Moscow, 1996), 295.
40 *Pravda*, 12 July 1922.
41 *PZ*, 330–1, 361–2.
42 M. Fainsod, *Smolensk under Soviet Rule* (London, 1958), 335.

43 *Pyatnadtsatyi s"ezd VKP(b), dekabr' 1927 goda: stenograficheskii otchet* (Moscow, 1961), vol. 1, 126–7.
44 *Bol'shevistskoe rukovodstvo. Perepiska. 1912–1917*, 297.
45 John Hatch, 'The "Lenin levy" and the social origins of Stalinism: workers and the Communist Party in Moscow, 1921–1928', *Slavic Review* 48, no. 4 (1989): 558–77. In his memoirs, Kaganovich wryly noted that Zinoviev's figures did not add up. With an existing membership of 700,000, of whom just 300,000 were workers from the bench, this would require a recruitment of 600,000 workers from the bench and a reduction of the non-worker contingent by 300,000 – *PZ*, 253.
46 *PZ*, 354. The commission's members included Stalin, Molotov, Kaganovich, Kuibyshev, Kalinin, Uglanov, Dogadov, Bubnov and Syrtsov.
47 L. M. Kaganovich, 'O rabote sredi kandidatov i novykh chlenov partii', *Izvestiya TsK RKP(b)* no. 7 (12), 17 November 1924, 1; L. M. Kaganovich, 'O vospitanii leninskogo prizyva', *Izvestiya TsK RKP(b)* no. 12 (17), 22 December 1924, 1–3; L. M. Kaganovich, 'O vydvizhenii i vovlechenii v prakticheskuyu raboty vnov' vstypivshikh v partiyu rabochikh', *Izvestiya TsK RKP(b)* no. 7 (82), 16 February 1925, 1–2.
48 *Pravda*, 7 May 1925. M. Gorlov, *Leninskii priziv* (Moscow, 1962) provides some useful figures on recruitment during the Lenin enrolment.
49 R. J. Service, *The Bolshevik Party in Revolution* (London, 1979): 199, 238n45.
50 *PZ*, 255.
51 L. M. Kaganovich, *Kak postroena RKP (Bol'shevikov); Ob ustave partii* (Moscow, 1924). It was republished in Ekaterinoslav' (1924), Tula (1924), Samara (1924), Nizhnyi Novgorod (1924), Viatka (1925), Krasnoyarsk (1925), Pskov (1925), Tiflis (1925), Kharkov (1925) and Moscow-Leningrad (1925, 1926).
52 L. M. Kaganovich, *Kak postroena VKP(b)* (Moscow-Leningrad, 1927 and 1929).
53 *PZ*, 413.
54 Carr, *Socialism in One Country 1924–1926*, vol. 2, 339. Similar figures were cited by Kaganovich for just 122 provinces, in *Soveshchanie po voprosam sovetskogo stroitel'stva 1925 g. Ianvar'* (Moscow 1925), 11.
55 Carr, *Socialism in One Country 1924–1926*, vol. 1 (Harmondsworth, 1970), 215–16. On the actions of the Georgian Cheka against the Mensheviks, see Amy Knight, *Beria: Stalin's First Lieutenant* (Princeton, 1993), 33–4.
56 L. M. Kaganovich, *Mestnoe sovetskoe samoupravlenie. Stroitel'stva Sovetskoe vlast na mestakh* (Moscow, 1923).
57 L. M. Kaganovich, 'Ob ulushenii raboty sovetov', *Izvestiya TsK RKP(b)* no. 11, 15 December 1924, 1–2. A pamphlet by Kaganovich, *Ulushenie raboty sovetov v derevne* (Moscow, 1924) outlined a report which he presented to a meeting of the secretaries of rural party cells, organised by the Central Committee. *Izvestiya TsK RKP(b)* no. 10, 8 December 1924.
58 L. M. Kaganovich, *Kak ulushit' rabotu sovetov v derevne*, (Moscow, 1924).
59 *Soveshchanie po voprosam sovetskogo stroitel'stva 1925 g. Ianvar'*, 97–117; Carr, *Socialism in One Country 1924–1926*, vol. 2, 348.
60 *Soveshchanie po voprosam sovetskogo stroitel'stva 1925 g. Ianvar'*, 115; Carr, *Socialism in One Country 1924–1926*, vol. 2, 499.
61 *Soveshchanie po voprosam sovetskogo stroitel'stva 1925 g, Aprel'*, 11–12; Carr, *Socialism in One Country 1924–1926*, vol. 2, 354.
62 *Chetyrnadtsataya konferentsiya Rossiiskoi kommunisticheskoi partii (Bolshevikov): stenograficheskii otchet* (Moscow-Leningrad, 1925), 37–41; *Pravda*, 29 April 1925.

63 The event was advertised in *Pravda*, 26 April 1925.
64 L. Trotsky, *The Challenge of the Left Opposition 1926–27* (New York, 1980), 98.
65 L. M. Kaganovich, *Itogi plenuma TsK i TsKK VKP(b) (iyul' 1926 goda)* (Moscow, 1926).
66 Stalin, *Works*, vol. 10, 203.
67 *Odinnadtsatsyi s"ezd RKP(b); mart-aprelia 1922 goda: stenograficheskii otchet* (Moscow, 1961), 178, 365, 269.
68 Chuev, *Tak govoril Kaganovich*, 155.
69 Carr, *Socialism in One Country 1924–1926*, vol. 2, 110.
70 *PZ*, 396.
71 Carr, *Socialism in One Country 1924–1926*, vol. 2, 144.
72 L. M. Kaganovich, *Na putiakh strotel'stva sotsializm* (Kharkov, 1926). See, also, Kaganovich's report to the Kharkov activists on the results of the XIV Party Congress VKP(b): L. M. Kaganovich, *Itogi XIV s"ezda VKP(b)* (Kharkov, 1926).
73 *XIV s"ezd Vsesoyuznoi kommunisticheskoi partii (b); 18–31 dekabrya 1925g.; stenograficheskii otchet* (Moscow, 1926), 274 (Kamenev), 468 (Zinoviev), 335 (Sokolnikov), 484 (Molotov).
74 Ibid., 234.
75 Ibid., 238.
76 Ibid., 291.
77 L. M. Kaganovich, *Itogi XIV s"ezda VKP(b)*.
78 Alexander Vatlin, '"Class Brothers Unite!" The British General Strike and the Formation of the "United Opposition"', in Paul R. Gregory and Norman Naimark (eds), *The Lost Politburo Transcripts: From Collective Rule to Stalin's Dictatorship* (Standford, CA, New Haven, CT and London, 2008), 57–77.
79 George Breitman and Sarah Lovell (eds), *Writings of Leon Trotsky, 1932–33* (New York, 1973), 82.
80 RGASPI, 17/2/327, 409, 411.
81 L. M. Kaganovich, *Itogi plenuma TsK i TsKK VKP(b) (iyul'1926 goda)* (Kharkov, 1926).
82 Schapiro, *The Communist Party of the Soviet Union*, 304–5; *PZ*, 381.
83 Tsentral'noi gosudarstvennyi arkhiv obshchestvennykh organizatsii Ukrainy (TsGAOOU), 1/1/214, 16.
84 Trotsky, *The Challenge of the Left Opposition 1926–27*, 116–17.
85 *XV party konferentsiya: stenograficheskii otchet* (Moscow, 1926), 637–8.
86 RGASPI, 17/2(P1)/276, 50.
87 Trotsky, *The Challenge of the Left Opposition, 1926–27*, 270–90.
88 Ibid., 356.
89 Chuev, *Tak govoril Kaganovich*, 75.
90 Ibid., 190–1.

Chapter 4: Ukrainian Party Boss, 1925–1928

1 'Vokrug stat'i L. D. Trotskogo "Uroki Oktyabra"', *Izvestiya TsK KPSS* (1991) no. 8: 180.
2 P. Bachinsky, 'Emmanuel Ivanovich Kviring', *Politicheskoe obrazovanie* (1988) no. 17: 46–50.
3 'Vokrug stat'i L. D. Trotskogo "Uroki Oktiabria"', 190.
4 TsGAOOU (Tsentral'noi gosudarstvennyi arkhiv obshchestvennykh organizatsii Ukrainy), 1/6/60, 39.
5 Yuri Shapoval, *Lazar Kaganovich* (Kiev, 1994), 5.

6 L. M. Kaganovich, *Pamyatnye zapiski Lazar' Kaganovich* (Moscow, 1996), 373. Henceforth *PZ*.
7 G. Bessedovsky, *Revelations of a Soviet Diplomat* (London, 1931), 221–2.
8 RGASPI, 17/16/1396, 164.
9 *Pravda*, 7 May 1925.
10 *PZ*, 377.
11 F. Chuev, *Tak govoril Kaganovich: Ispoved' staklinskogo apostola* (Moscow, 1992), 42, 46.
12 R. J. Service, *The Bolshevik Party in Revolution* (London and Basingstoke, 1979), 128.
13 James E. Mace, *Communism and the Dilemmas of National Liberation: National Communism in Soviet Ukraine, 1918–1933* (Cambridge, MA, 1983).
14 *Izvestiya*, 5 May 1925.
15 *PZ*, 379.
16 Mace, *Communism and the Dilemmas of National Liberation*, 201–3.
17 *PZ*, 377.
18 RGASPI, 17/16/1405.
19 RGASPI, 81/3/127, 3–4.
20 *Izvestiya*, 5 May 1925.
21 E. H. Carr, *Socialism in One Country*, vol. 1 (Harmondsworth, 1970), 290.
22 Ibid., 546–7.
23 Mace, *Communism and the Dilemmas of National Liberation*, 281. See also TsGAOOU, 1/6/61, 43ob–44ob.
24 TsGAOOU, 1/1/165, 19.
25 Carr, *Socialism in One Country*, vol. 1, 291n1.
26 *XIV s"ezd Vsesoyuznoi kommunisticheskoi partii(b), 18–31 dekabria 1925g: stenograficheskii otchet* (Moscow, 1926), 234.
27 TsGAOOU, 1/6/59, 26.
28 *Komunistichna partiya Ukraini z izdi i konferentsii* (Kiev, 1991), 93.
29 RGASPI, 17/16/1396, 164.
30 Ibid., 158, 151.
31 Mace, *Communism and the Dilemmas of National Liberation*, 95–106.
32 TsGAOOU, 1/1/158, 147; 1/1/160, 70ob–71ob.
33 On the rise and fall of Ukranization, see Terry Martin, *Affirmative Action Empire* (Ithaca, NY and London, 2001), 83–101.
34 L. M. Kaganovich, *Dva goda ot IX do X s"ezda KP(b)U* (Moscow and Kharkov, 1927).
35 L. M. Kaganovich, *Rabota partii i oppozitsiya* (Kharkov, 1926).
36 TsGAOOU, 1/1/229, 195.
37 Kaganovich, *Rabota partii i oppozitsiya*. The membership of the Ukrainian Communist Party (members and candidates) grew from 57,016 on 1 January 1924 to 167,787 on 1 July 1926. The proportion of workers as members of the party grew from 56 per cent to 67.2 per cent.
38 RGASPI, 17/26/10, 9.
39 M. I. Panchuk, 'Natsional-ukhil'nitsvo', *Anatomiya problemi: Marshrutami istorii* (Kiev, 1990), 221–2. Cites the testimony of M. Tselyuk, former secretary of the Communist Party of Western Ukraine.
40 L. M. Kaganovich, *Na putiakh stroitel'stva sotsializm* (Kharkov, 1926).
41 TsGAOOU, 1/1/135, 244, 255.
42 *PZ*, 375, 377.
43 *PZ*, 379.

44 *XIV s"ezd Vsesoyuznoi kommunisticheskoi partii(b), 18–31 dekabrya 1925g.: stenograficheskiiotchet* (Moscow, 1926), 234.
45 TsGAOOU, 1/1/205, 201; 1/16/2, 168.
46 I. V. Stalin, *Works*, vol. 8 (Moscow, 1954), 157–63.
47 Panchuk, 'Natsional-ukhil'nitsvo', 224. See also Stalin, *Works*, vol. 8, 157–63.
48 TsGAOOU, 1/6/88, 134.
49 TsGAOOU, 1/1/88, 129ob.
50 Panchuk, 'Natsional-ukhil'nitsvo', 224.
51 Mace, *Communism and the Dilemmas of National Liberation*, 106–8.
52 Ibid., 107.
53 TsGAAOU, 1/1/205, 179, 195, 199, 201, 205, 208–210, 212, 217, 308; 1/1/209, 1.
54 RGASPI, 17/26/3, 103.
55 Mace, *Communism and the Dilemmas of National Liberation*, 95–106.
56 Ibid., 109. See also TsGAOOU, 1/6/93, 71.
57 RGASPI, 81/3/130, 47.
58 Stalin, *Works*, vol. 9, 328–69.
59 RGASPI, 81/3/127, 205–66.
60 RGASPI, 17/2/375, 60.
61 RGASPI, 81/3/124, 27–82. See also Kaganovich's report to the Central Committee plenum, in July 1928 –RGASPI, 17/2/375, 60.
62 Yu. Larin, 'Ob izvrashcheniyakh pri providenii natsional'noi politiki', *Bol'shevik* (1926) nos. 23–4: 50–58; and (1927) no. 1: 59–69.
63 V. Vaganyan, *O natsional'noi kulture* (Moscow, 1927), 120–7, 175.
64 RGASPI, 81/3/107, 170–5.
65 K. Tabolov, 'O natsional'noi culture, ob ukrainzatsii, o literaturnoi isterike Vaganyana i Larina', *Bol'shevik* (1927) nos. 11–12: 69–77.
66 L. M. Kaganovich, *Dva goda ot IX do X s"ezda KP(b)U* (Moscow and Kharkov, 1927).
67 H. Kostiuk, *Stalinist Rule in the Ukraine: A Study of the Decade of Mass Terror (1929–39)* (London, 1960), 145.
68 TsGAOOU, 1/1/229, 195.
69 L. M. Kaganovich, *Itogi XIV s"ezda VKP(b)* (Kharkov, 1926).
70 TsGAOOU, 1/6/88, 79, 107.
71 TsGAOOU, 1/1/196, 61.
72 RGASPI, 17/26/3 72.
73 L. M. Kaganovich, *Itogi plenuma TsK i TsKK VKP(b) (iyul'1926 goda)* (Kharkov, 1926).
74 Carr, *Socialism in One Country*, vol. 1, 389; L. Kosheleva, V. Lelchuk, V. Naumov, O. Naumov, I. Rogovaya and O. Khlevniuk. (eds), *Pis'ma I.V. Stalina V.M. Molotovu, 1925–1936 gg.: Sbornik dokumentov* (Moscow, 1995), 11.
75 TsGAOOU, 1/6/134, 108–10.
76 RGASPI, 17/26/3, 120, 169.
77 TsGAOOU, 1/1/253, 13.
78 *XV Vsesoyuznaya konferentsiya VKP(b): stenograficheskiiotchet* (Moscow-Leningrad, 1927), 150.
79 RGASPI, 17/26/3 181, 187.
80 TsGAOOU, 1/6/93, 71.
81 L. M. Kaganovich, *Rabota partii i oppozitsiya* (Kharkov, 1926).
82 RGASPI, 17/2(P1)/276, 22–3.
83 TsGAOOU, 1/6/ 121, 82. In 1928 the Ukrainian Politburo rejected Kuibyshev's proposal that Russian should be the exclusive language of communication in institutions of all-union significance in Ukraine, TsGAOOU, 1/6/142, 63.

84 L .M. Kaganovich, *Dva goda ot IX do X s"ezda KP(b)U* (Moscow and Kharkov, 1927).
85 *XV s"ezd VKP(b) dekabr' 1927 goda; stenograficheskii otchet* (Moscow, 1961), vol. 1, 154.
86 James R. Harris, *The Great Urals: Regionalism and the Evolution of the Soviet System* (Ithaca, NY, 1999).
87 TsGAOOU, 1/1/256, 407, 108.
88 TsGAOOU, 1/6/123, 134.
89 *PZ*, 387.
90 Ibid., 381.
91 *Pyatnadtsatyi s"ezd VKP(b) dekabr 1927 goda: stenograficheskii otchet*, vol. 1 (Moscow, 1961), 186.
92 *PZ*, 377.
93 RGASPI, 17/26/10, 4.
94 TsGAOOU, 1/6/144, 92.
95 TsGAOOU, 1/1/253, 140b; 1/6/123, 6, 7, 10.
96 E. H. Carr and R. W. Davies, *Foundations of a Planned Economy 1926–1929*, vol. 1 (London, 1969), 586–7.
97 TsGAOOU, 1/6/123, 132.
98 *Pravda*, 30 March 1928. See also RGASPI, 81/3/108, 2.
99 RGASPI, 17/3/666, 2, 19–21.
100 RGASPI, 17/26/15, 109.
101 G. Konyukhov, *KPSS v bor'be s khlebnymi zatrudneniyami* (Moscow, 1960), 151.
102 RGASPI, 81/3/102, 272–84.
103 *Pravda*, 30 March 1928. Carr and Davies, *Foundations of a Planned Economy, 1926–1929*, vol. 1, 59.
104 TsGAOOU, 1/1/284, 160b.
105 N. S. Khrushchev, *Khrushchev Remembers* (London, 1971), 31–2.
106 R. Medvedev, *All Stalin's Men* (Oxford, 1983), 117–18.
107 TsGAOOU, 1/1/144, 12.
108 Mace, *Communism and the Dilemmas of National Liberation*, 185.
109 TsGAOOU, 1/6/144, 60. Kaganovich, in his memoirs, refers to the wavering among certain Ukrainian members of the all-union Central Committee: *PZ*, 391
110 TsGAOOU, 1/1/144, 10.
111 TsGAOOU, 1/6/144, 83, 95.
112 TsGAOOU, 1/16/6, 59.
113 E. H. Carr, *Foundations of a Planned Economy*, vol. 2 (London, 1971) 71.
114 R. Medvedev, S. Parofenov and P. Khmelinskii, *Zheleznyi yastreb* (Ekaterinburg, 1992), 15.
115 Stephen F. Cohen, *Bukharin and the Bolshevik Revolution* (Oxford, 1989), 326.
116 James Hughes, 'Patrimonialism and the Stalinist System: The Case of S. I. Syrtsov', *Europe-Asia Studies* 48, no.4 (1996): 556–7.
117 Mace, *Communism and the Dilemmas of National Liberation*, 210–12.

Chapter 5: The Triumph of the Stalin Faction, 1928–1929

1 M. Harrison, 'Why did NEP fail?' *Economics of Planning* 16, no. 2 (1980): 57–67; J. R. Millar and A. Nove, "A debate on collectivization: was Stalin really necessary?" in Chris Ward (ed.), *The Stalinist Dictatorship* (London, 1998).
2 I. V. Stalin, *Works*, vol. 10 (Moscow, 1954), 303, 317.
3 *XV s"ezd VKP(b) dekabr' 1927 goda; stenograficheskii otchet* (Moscow, 1961), vol. 1, 148.
4 Ibid.
5 Ibid., 152.

6 Ibid., 154.
7 S. Cohen, *Bukharin and the Bolshevik Revolution* (Oxford, 1980), 278; L. M. Kaganovich, *Tseli i zadachi politicheskikh otdelov MTS i sovkhozov* (Moscow, 1933), 13.
8 *XV s"ezd VKP(b)*, 329–30.
9 RGASPI, 17/2/375, 60.
10 *XV s"ezd VKP(b)*, 329–30.
11 RGASPI, 17/2/375, 74.
12 *KPSS v rezolyutsiyakh i resheniyakh s"ezdov, konferentsii i plenumov TsK*, vol. 2 (Moscow, 1954), 516–17.
13 I. Deutscher, *Stalin* (Harmondsworth, 1968), 315.
14 L. M. Kaganovich, *Pamyatnye zapiski* (Moscow, 1996), 414. Henceforth *PZ*.
15 E. H. Carr, *Foundations of a Planned Economy*, vol. 2 (London, 1971), 71, cites Trotsky Archives T 1897.
16 *PZ*, 414.
17 *PZ*, 392, 395.
18 A. V. Kvashonkin, L. P. Kosheleva, L. A. Rogovaya and O. V. Khlevniuk (eds), *Sovetskoe rukovodstvo perepiska, 1928–1941* (Moscow, 1999), 40–1.
19 James Hughes, 'Patrimonialism and the Stalinist System: The Case of S. I. Syrtsov', *Europe-Asia Studies* 48, no. 4 (1996): 556–7.
20 L. M. Kaganovich, 'O rabote instruktorov', *Izvestiya Tsentral'nogo Komiteta VKP(b)* no. 4 (263), 15 February 1929, 1–2.
21 Stalin, *Works*, vol. 9, 333, 335–6; vol. 10, 48, 295 and 392.
22 S. A. Kislitsyn, *Shakhtinskoe delo: nachalo stalinskikh repressii protiv nauchno-technicheskoi inteligentsii v SSSR* (Rostov on Don, 1993), 52–3, 57–8.
23 RGASPI, 81/3/127, 20–172.
24 *PZ*, 391–2.
25 Shelia Fitzpatrick, 'Stalin and the Making of a New Elite 1928–1939', *Slavic Review* 38, no. 3 (1979): 377–402.
26 RGASPI, 17/2/441, 94. L. M. Kaganovich, 'Problem kadrov', *Bol'shevik* (1929), nos. 23–4: 50–68. N. Werth and Gael Moullenc (eds), *Rapports Secrets Soviétiques: La Société Russe dans les Documents Confidentiels 1921–1991* (Paris, 1994) 490, document 9.
27 L. M. Kaganovich, 'Problem kadrov'. See also Robert Lewis, 'Bukharin and Science Policy', in Anthony Kemp-Welch, *The Ideas of Nikolai Bukharin* (Oxford, 1992), 166.
28 *Pravda*, 26 November 1929.
29 Kaganovich, 'Problem kadrov', 50–68.
30 *KPSS v rezoliutsiyakh*, vol. 2, 632–42.
31 Shelia Fitzpatrick (ed.), *Cultural Revolution in Russia, 1928–1931* (Bloomington, IN and London, 1978).
32 L. Kosheleva, V. Lelchuk, V. Naumov, O. Naumov, I. Rogovaya and O. Khlevniuk. (eds), *Pis'ma I.V. Stalina V.M. Molotovu, 1925–1936gg.: Sbornik dokumentov* (Moscow, 1995), 194, 198, 211.
33 Yaglom quoted at the XVI Party Congress – *XVI s"ezd Vesesoyuznoi Kommunisticheskoi partii (b). Stenograficheskii otchet* (Moscow, 1930) II, 1194. For the attack by the Komsomol newspaper, see *Shestnadtsataya konferentsiya*, 783n78. For Tomsky's fall, see R. V. Daniels, *The Conscience of the Revolution* (Cambridge, MA, 1965), 344–8.
34 *Vos'moi s"ezd profesionalnykh soyuzov SSSR (10–24 dekabriya 1928 g.) polnyi stenograficheskii otchet* (Moscow, 1929), 3–6, 24–5, 186–207.
35 E. H. Carr and R. W. Davies, *Foundations of a Planned Economy*, vol. 1 (London, 1969), 594–5.

36 RGASPI, 17/2/401, 31–5. Bukharin's report to the Central Committee on 17 April 1929. I am indebted to Dr David Priestland (Oxford) for this reference.
37 *Pravda*, 25 December 1928. The North Caucasus delegation voted against Kaganovich's election to the presidium, see S. A. Kislitsyn, *Shakhtinskoe delo: nachalo stalinskikh repressi protiv nauchno-technikeskogo intelligentsia v SSSR* (Rostov on Don, 1993).
38 Daniels, *The Conscience of the Revolution*, 347–8.
39 *Sotsialisticheskii vestnik* (Berlin) nos. 7–8, 12 April 1929, 20.
40 Daniels, *The Conscience of the Revolution*, 347–8.
41 *Pravda*, 26 November 1929.
42 *Pravda*, 21 January 1930.
43 *XVI s"ezd Vesesoyuznoi Kommunisticheskoi partii (b): stenograficheskii otchet*, I, 122. *Pravda*, 1 June 1930.
44 *XVI s"ezd Vesesoyuznoi Kommunisticheskoi partii (b). Stenograficheskii otchet*, I, 62, 65.
45 R. W. Davies, *The Soviet Economy in Turmoil* (Basingstoke, 1989), 276.
46 N. Werth, and Gael Moullenc (eds), *Rapports Secrets Soviétiques: La Société Russe dans les Documents Confidentiels 1921–1991* (Paris, 1994), 211, 217–18.
47 Carr, *Foundations of a Planned Economy*, vol. 2, 184–7.
48 *Pravda*, 1 November 1929.
49 L. M. Kaganovich, *O zadachakh Komsomola* (Moscow, 1929).
50 L. M. Kaganovich, *Partiya i sovety* (Moscow, 1926; republished in 1928), 60–1. See also Carr, *Foundations of a Planned Economy*, vol. 2, 264, 270, 298–9, 300–1, 304, 453.
51 Daniel R. Brower, 'The Smolensk Scandal and the End of NEP', *Slavic Review* 4 (1986): 689–706.
52 *Vsesoyuznoe soveshchanie po perevyboram sovetov v 1929g.* (Moscow, 1928), 10, 12, 17–18, 19, 26–8, 103.
53 L. M. Kaganovich. 'Politicheskie zadachi kampanii perevyborov v sovety', *Bol'shevik* (1928) no. 19: 8–23.
54 Ibid., 20–26. M. Lewin, *Russian Peasants and Soviet Power* (London, 1968), 285–6.
55 Iuzuru Taniuchi, 'Decision-making on the Ural-Siberian Method', in J. Cooper M. Perrie and E. A. Rees (eds), *Soviet History 1917–1953* (Basingstoke, 1995), 78–103. Y. Taniuchi, 'A Note on the Ural-Siberian Method', *Soviet Studies* 33, no. 4 (1981): 518–47.
56 Kaganovich, 'Politicheskie zadachi kampanii perevyborov v sovety'.
57 RGASPI, 17/3/714, 1–12.
58 *Izvestiya*, 7, 19 and 22 February 1929.
59 RGASPI, 17/3/722, 1–2, 10–13. *Pravda*, 5 December 1928, 10 and 26 January 1929.
60 RGASPI, 17/2/417, 110–11; 17/3/722, 1–2, 10–12.
61 Cohen, *Bukharin*, 306.
62 RGASPI, 17/3/729, 7. RGASPI, 17/2/417, 150. RGASPI, 17/21/3898, 83–4.
63 RGASPI, 17/3/7301, 1.
64 RGASPI, 17/2/417, 171.
65 RGASPI, 17/21/3188, 36, 39–40.
66 RGASPI, 17/21/3188, 95.
67 J. Hughes, *Stalinism in a Russian Province: Collectivization and Dekulakization in Siberia* (Basingstoke, 1996), 153–5.
68 L. M. Kaganovich, *Sotsialisticheskaya rekonstruktsiya i zadachiya partii, doklad na IX Uralskaya oblastnaya konferentsiya VKP(b)* (Sverdlovsk, 1929). RGASPI 81/3/209, 1–131.
69 Hughes, *Stalinism in a Russian Province*, ch. 3 argues that it emanated from the Urals and Siberia. Y. Taniuchi, *The Village Gathering in Russia in the Mid-1920s* (Birmingham, 1968) argues that it emanated from the centre.

70 RGASPI, 17/2/417, 35–6 (Bukharin), 163–86 (Rykov).
71 N. Bukharin, *Problemy teorii i praktiki sotsializma* (Moscow, 1989), 253–90. RGASPI, 17/2/417, 73–88.
72 RGASPI, 17/2/375, vol. 2, 115–16.
73 RGASPI, 17/2/417, 57–8, 291–3.
74 RGASPI, 17/2/417, 51–3.
75 RGASPI, 17/2/417, 129, 148–55.
76 RGASPI, 17/2/417, 227.
77 RGASPI, 17/3/746, 1, 2, 7–9.
78 *Pravda*, 21 January 1930. 'Reorganizatsiya partapparata i ocherednye zadachi partraboty: mobilizatsiya aktivnosti mass'.
79 L. M. Kaganovich, 'Dvenadtsatyi let stroitel'stva sovetskogo gosudarstva', *Sovetskoe gosudarstvo i revolyutsiya prava* (1930) no. 1: 15, 29–30.
80 Ibid., 38.
81 Ibid., 39–41.
82 *Pravda*, 26 November 1929. Kaganovich's report to Moscow activists on 21 November 1929.
83 O. V. Khlevniuk, *Master of the House: Stalin and His Inner Circle*, trans. Nora Seligman Favorov (New Haven, CT and London, 2009), 3.
84 *PZ*, 400.
85 *Sovetskoe rukovodstvo perepiska 1928–1941*, 50–2.
86 E. A. Rees, *State Control in Soviet Russia: The Rise and Fall of the Workers' and Peasants' Inspectorate, 1920–1934* (Basingstoke, 1987), ch. 6.
87 *PZ*, 333.
88 Anna Larina, *Nezabyvaemoe* (Moscow, 1989), 314.
89 Ibid., 88.
90 I. Deutscher, *The Prophet Unarmed* (Oxford, 1970), 246.

Chapter 6: Revolution from Above, 1928–1935

1 E. A. Rees, *State Control in Soviet Russia: The Rise and the Fall of the Workers' and Peasants' Inspectorate, 1920–1934* (London, 1987), chs 2 and 3. David R. Shearer, *Industry, State and Society in Stalin's Russia, 1926–1934* (Ithaca, NY and London, 1996). Sheila Fitzpatrick, 'Ordzhonikidze's Takeover of Vesenkha: A Case Study in Soviet Bureaucratic Politics', *Soviet Studies* 37, no. 2 (1985): 153–72.
2 James W. Heinzen, *Inventing A Soviet Countryside: State Power and the Transformation of Rural Russia, 1917–1929* (Pittsburgh, 2004).
3 James R. Harris, *The Great Urals: Regionalism and the Evolution of the Soviet System* (Ithaca, NY, 1999).
4 I. V. Stalin, *Works*, vol. 12 (Moscow, 1955), 359–60.
5 R. W. Davies, *The Socialist Offensive: The Collectivisation of Soviet Agriculture, 1929–1930* (London, 1980), 157.
6 *KPSS v rezolyutsiyakh i resheniyakh, s"ezdov, konferentsii i plenumov TsK*, vol. 2 (Moscow, 1954), 629.
7 *Pravda*, 26 November 1929.
8 Ibid.
9 A. V. Kvashonkin, L. P. Kosheleva, L. A. Rogovaya and O. V. Khlevniuk (eds), *Sovetskoe rukovodstvo perepiska 1928–1941*(Moscow, 1999), 106.

10 *Pravda*, 17 January 1930. See ch. 6.
11 *Pravda*, 20 January 1930.
12 Quoted by Y. Taniuchi, 'A Note on the Ural-Siberian Method', *Soviet Studies* 33, no. 4 (1981): 542.
13 L. M. Kaganovich, *Ocherednye zadachi partraboty i reorganizatsiya partapparata* (Moscow-Leningrad, 1930), 51.
14 *Pravda*, 8 June 1930.
15 Lynne Viola, *The Best Sons of the Fatherland: Workers in the Vanguard of Soviet Collectivization* (New York and Oxford, 1987).
16 N. Yezhov, 'Sel'sko khoziaistvennye kadry', *Na agrarnom fronte* (1930) no. 2: 22–33.
17 Davies, *The Socialist Offensive*, 267.
18 *Rabochaya gazeta*, 28 Jan 1930, 3, and *Litsom k derevne* (1930) no. 4: 3, cited in Viola, *The Best Sons of the Fatherland*, 65.
19 Lynne Viola, *The Unknown Gulag: The Lost World of Stalin's Special Settlements* (Oxford, 2007), 205n54.
20 O. V. Khlevniuk, *Politbyuro: mekhanizmy politicheskoi vlasti v 1930-e gody* (Moscow, 1996), 18. Lynne Viola, *Peasant Rebels under Stalin: Collectivization and the Culture of Peasant Resistance* (New York and Oxford, 1996).
21 Stalin, *Works*, vol. 12, 197–205, 207–34.
22 Davies, *The Socialist Offensive*, 275.
23 James Hughes, *Stalin, Siberia and the Crisis of the New Economic Policy* (Cambridge, 1991), 370.
24 Stalin, *Works*, vol. 12, 214.
25 Ibid., 314.
26 *Shestnadtsatyi s"ezd VKP(b)* (Moscow, 1930), 71.
27 Ibid., 82.
28 F. Chuev, *Molotov Remembers*, ed. Albert Resis (Chicago, 1993), 248. Molotov admitted responsibility for the deportation of 400,000 kulaks.
29 RGASPI, 17/ 3/ 883, 1.
30 R. W. Davies, E. A. Rees, O. V. Khlevniuk, L. P. Kosheleva and L. A. Rogovaya (eds), *The Stalin-Kaganovich Correspondence, 1931–1936* (New Haven, 2003), 127–8, 134, 237.
31 I. Zelenin (ed.), *Tragediya sovetskoi derevni; kollektivizatsiya i raskulachivanie; Dokumenty i materialy; Tom. 3, Konets 1930–1933* (Moscow, 2001), 391.
32 *Bol'shevik* (1933) nos. 1–2: 23.
33 O. V. Khlevniuk (ed.), *Stalin i Kaganovich, Perepiska, 1931–1936gg* (Moscow, 2001), 210, document 174. Henceforth *SKP*.
34 *Pravda*, 9 July 1932.
35 *Visti*, 17 July 1932, cited in H. Kostiuk, *Stalinist Rule in the Ukraine* (London, 1960), 19.
36 L. M. Kaganovich, 'Zadachi ukrainskikh bol'shevikov v rabote na sele', *Partiinoe stroitel'stvo*, 14 July 1932, 1–8.
37 *SKP*, 273–4, document 248.
38 *SKP*, 283, document 263.
39 *Tragediya Sovetskoi Derevni*, 418–19.
40 *SKP*, 256–7, document 232.
41 *SKP*, 273, document 248.
42 Alter Litvin and John Keep, *Stalinism: Russian and Western Views at the Turn of the Millennium* (London and New York, 2005), 24.
43 *Tragediya Sovetskoi Derevni*, 460.

44 George Breitman and Sarah Lovell (eds), *Writings of Leon Trotsky, 1932* (New York, 1973), 266, 273.
45 Valery Vasiliev and Yuri Shapoval, *Komandiry Bol'shogo Goloda: Poezdki V. Molotova i L. Kaganovicha v Ukrainu i na Severnyi Kavkaz 1932–1933gg.* (Kiev, 2001).
46 *Tragediya Sovetskoi Derevni*, 28.
47 Ibid., 520–1.
48 Ibid., 30.
49 *O kolkhoznom stroitel'stve: sbornik rukovodyashchikh materialov*, 279.
50 R. Medvedev, *Let History Judge* (London, 1976), 93.
51 *O kolkhoznom stroitel'stve* (Moscow, 1932), 281.
52 *Tragediya Sovetskoi Derevni*, 540–1.
53 Andrea Graziosi, *The Great Soviet Peasant War: Bolsheviks and Peasants 1917–1933* (Cambridge, MA, 1996), 67–8.
54 *Tragediya Sovetskoi Derevni*, 547–55.
55 *O kolkhoznom stroitel'stve* (Moscow, 1932), 284.
56 *Semnadtsatyi s"ezd VKP(b)* (Moscow, 1934), 148.
57 Medvedev, *Let History Judge*, 93.
58 *Pravda*, 30 November 1932.
59 *Tragediya Sovetskoi Derevni*, 581.
60 *Tragediya Sovetskoi Derevni*, 603–4, 609.
61 Stalin, *Works*, vol. 13, 220–39.
62 L. M. Kaganovich, 'Tseli i zadachi politicheskikh otdelov MTS i sovkhozov', *Bol'shevik* (1933) nos.1–2: 12–37.
63 *Materialy ob"edinennogo plenuma TsK i TsKK VKP(b)* (Moscow, 1933), 144.
64 One rumour current at the time was that, at a Central Committee plenum early in 1933, Yakir and Postyshev had called for aid to the famine striken areas of Ukraine where cases of cannibalism had been reported. Kaganovich is supposed to have interjected: 'It is better that they eat themselves than us.' See Erich Wollenberg, *The Red Army* (London, 1940; reprint University of Illinois, 1973), 250.
65 *Partiinoe stroitel'stvo* (1934) no. 12: 1–3.
66 D. Thorniley, The *Rise and the Fall of the Soviet Rural Communist Party, 1927–39* (Basingstoke, 1988), 130.
67 R. W. Davies and Stephen G. Wheatcroft, *The Years of Hunger: Soviet Agriculture, 1931–1933* (Basingstoke, 2004), xv.
68 *Tragediya Sovetskoi Derevni*, 639.
69 Ibid., 644–5.
70 Stalin, *Works*, vol. 13, 256.
71 *Pravda*, 18 February 1933; *Tragediya Sovetskoi Derevni*, 21; L. M. Kaganovich, *Ukreplenie kolkhozov i zadachi vesennogo seva* (Novosibirsk, 1933).
72 O. V. Khlevniuk, V. Kvashonkin, L. P. Kosheleva and L. A. Rogovaya (eds), *Stalinskoe Politbyuro v 30-e gody: Sbornik dokumentov* (Moscow, 1995), 63.
73 RGASPI, 17/ 3/ 922, 58, 58ob. M. Fainsod, *Smolensk under Soviet Rule* (Boston, 1989; first published 1958), 185–8.
74 *Tragediya Sovetskoi Derevni*, 789–90, 791–2, 644–5, 687, 695–6, 802–6.
75 *Bol'shaya Sovetskaya Entsiklopaediya* (Moscow, 1975), vol. 20, 423.
76 *Pravda*, 10 February 1933.
77 L. S. Gatalova, L. P. Kozheleva, L. A. Rogovaya and Dzh. Kaio (eds), *TsK VKP(b) i Natsional'nyi Vopros, Kniga 2, 1933–1945* (Moscow, 2009), 19, 35, 50.

78 *Sovetskoe rukovodstvo perepiska, 1928–1941*, 244.
79 L. S. Gatalova et al. (eds), *TsK VKP(b) i Natsional'nyi Vopros, Kniga 2, 1933–1945*, 40.
80 Kostiuk, *Stalinist Rule in the Ukraine*, 73n22.
81 *Chervony shliakh* (1932) nos. 1–2: 92.
82 R. W. Davies, Mark Harrison and S. G. Wheatcroft, *The Economic Transformation of the Soviet Union, 1913–1945* (Cambridge, 1995), 67–77.
83 R. Conquest, *The Harvest of Sorrow* (London, 1988); J. E. Mace, *Famine in the Soviet Ukraine 1932–33* (Cambridge, MA, 1986).
84 'Dve besedy s L.M. Kaganovichem', *Novaya i noveishaya istoriya* (1999) no. 2: 101–22.
85 M. Fainsod, *Smolensk under Soviet Rule* (London, 1958), 74–5.
86 L. M. Kaganovich, 'O chistke partii', *Partiinoe stroitel'stvo* (1933) no. 11: 10.
87 *XVII S"ezd Vsesoyuznoi Kommunisticheskoi Partii (b): stenograficheskii otchet* (Moscow, 1934), 525.
88 Ibid., 525–6.
89 Ibid., 560.
90 Ibid., 562.
91 RGAPSI, 17/2/536.
92 *SKP*, 455, document 490.
93 *SKP*, 479–80, document 522.
94 L. M. Kaganovich, 'Itogi noyabr'skogo plenuma TsK VKP(b)', *Partiinoe stroitel'stvo* (1934) nos. 1–2: 11.
95 *Stalinskoe Politbyuro v 30-e gody*, 146.
96 Stalin, *Works*, vol. 12, 359–60.
97 *Pravda*, 8 June 1930. The *New York Times* correspondent was Walter Duranty. A similar speech was made by Molotov to the Leningrad regional party conference – *Pravda*, 11 June 1930.
98 *Pravda*, 8 June 1930. Davies, *The Soviet Economy in Turmoil, 1929–30* (Basingstoke, 1989), 257.
99 *IV Moskovskaya oblastnaya i III gorodskaya konferentsii VKP(b)* (Moscow, 1934), 455–6 (Sevast'ianov).
100 Ibid., 403–4 (Koldobsky).
101 L. M. Kaganovich, 'O zadachakh profsoyuzov SSSR na dannom etape razvitiya', *Partiinoe stroitel'stvo* (1932) no. 10: 6.
102 L. M. Kaganovich, 'Ocherednye zadachi partiino-massovoi raboty yacheik", *Partiinoe stroitel'stvo*, (1932) nos. 11–12: 1–9.
103 E. H. Carr and R. W. Davies, *Foundations of a Planned Economy*, vol. 1 (London, 1969), 597–9.
104 *XVII s"ezd*, xx.
105 R. W. Davies et al., *Stalin-Kaganovich Correspondence*, 268–70.
106 *Stalinskoe Politbyuro v 30-e gody*, 125–6.
107 Chuev, *Molotov Remembers*, 130.
108 Hiroaki Kuromiya, 'The Commander and the Rank and File: Managing the Soviet Coal-Mining Industry, 1928–33' in William G. Rosenberg and Lewis H. Siegelbaum (eds), *Social Dimensions of Soviet Industrialization* (Bloomington, IN, 1993), 154–5.
109 *PZ*, 410–11.
110 *Za Industrializatsiyu*, 24 May 1933.
111 *XVII S"ezd VKP(b)*, 162–3.
112 O. V. Khlevniuk, *1931-i: Stalin, NKVD i Sovetskoe obshchestvo* (Moscow, 1992), 28–9.
113 *Stalinskoe Politbyuro v 30-e gody*, 133.
114 RGASPI, 54/1/100, 107–8.
115 Julian Bullard and Margaret Bullard (eds), *Inside Stain's Russia: The Diaries of Reader Bullard 1930–1934* (Chaelbury, 2000), 213.

Chapter 7: Stalin's Deputy, 1930–1935

1. E. A. Rees, *Political Thought from Machiavelli to Stalin: Revolutionary Machiavellism* (Basingstoke, 2004) ch. 8. See also V. N. Maksimovskii, 'Idea diktatury u Makiavelli,' *Istorik Marksist* (1929) no. 13: 19–58.
2. RGASPI, 17/85/531–5.
3. RGASPI, 17/3/769, 5, 22–4; 81/3/74, 210–28.
4. *Stalin: sbornik statei k pyatidesiatiletiyu so dnya rozhdeniya* (Moscow and Leningrad, 1929), 48.
5. M. Lewin, *Russian Peasants and Soviet Power* (London, 1968), 452–3.
6. D. Volkogonov, *Stalin: Triumph and Tragedy* (London, 1991), 159.
7. A. I. Mikoyan, *Tak bylo: razmysheniya o minuvshem* (Moscow, 1999), 318.
8. On Kaganovich's role in promoting Stalin's cult, see Benno Ennker, 'The Stalin Cult, Bolshevik Rule, and Kremlin Interaction in the 1930's', in Balázs Apor, Jan C. Behrends, Polly Jones and E. A. Rees (eds), *The Leader Cult in Communist Dictatorships: Stalin and the Eastern Bloc* (Basingstoke, 2004).
9. RGASPI, 74/2/37, 9–12.
10. O. V. Khlevniuk, A. V. Kvashonkin, L. P. Kosheleva and L. A. Rogovaya (eds), *Stalinskoe Politbyuro v 30 gody* (Moscow, 1995), 99, 101. Syrtsov reported that Kuibyshev, Rudzutak and Kalinin were excluded from this group. Molotov stated that there had 'always been a leading group in the Politburo' in the Stalin era and that it excluded Kalinin, Rudzutak, Kosior and Andreev. F. Chuev, *Sto sorok besed s Molotvym* (Moscow, 1991), 424.
11. R. W. Davies, E. A. Rees, O. V. Khlevniuk, L. P. Kosheleva and L. A. Rogovaya (eds), *The Stalin-Kaganovich Correspondence, 1931–1936* (New Haven, CT and London, 2003), 21–36, 'Lazar' Kaganovich: The career of a Stalinist Commissar'.
12. Ibid., 52.
13. O. V. Khlevniuk, R. W. Davies, L. P. Kosheleva, E. A. Rees and L. A. Rogovaya (eds), *Stalin i Kaganovich, Perepiska, 1931–1936gg.* (Moscow, 2001), 50–1, document 13. Henceforth *SKP*.
14. R. W. Davies et al., *Stalin-Kaganovich Correspondence*, 80–81.
15. *SKP*, 711.
16. *Stalinskoe Politbyuro v 30-e gody*, 90–1, 135–7.
17. A. V. Kvashonkin, L. P. Kosheleva, L. A. Rogovaya and O. V. Khlevniuk (eds), *Sovetskoe rukovodstvo perepiska, 1928–1941* (Moscow, 1999), 259–63.
18. For a biographical sketch of M. M. Kaganovich, see *Izvestiya TsK KPSS* (1990) no. 7: 98.
19. Jeremy R. Azrael, *Managerial Power and Soviet Politics* (Cambridge, MA, 1966), 247–8.
20. R. V. Daniels, *The Conscience of the Revolution* (Cambridge, MA, 1985), 381–2. R. Conquest, *The Great Terror* (Harmondsworth), 35–6. B. Nicolasevskii, The 'Letter of an Old Bolshevik', in *Power and the Soviet Elite*, trans. Douglas Smith (London, 1965).
21. RGASPI, 54/1/99, 35–6, 40–40ob, 42–3.
22. R. W. Davies et al., *Stalin-Kaganovich Correspondence*, 102–3.
23. *Bol'shaya Sovetskaya Entsiklopaediya* (Moscow, 1975), vol. 20, 423.
24. RGASPI, 54/1/99, 42–3.
25. Marc Jansen and Nikita Petrov, *Stalin's Loyal Executioner: People's Commissar Nikolai Ezhov, 1895–1940*, (Stanford, CA, 2002), 14.
26. *Stalinskoe Politbyuro v-30e gody*, 178.

27 Valentin Kovalev, *Dva stalinskikh narkoma* (Moscow, 1995), 178.
28 E. A. Rees, 'Stalin – From Oligarch to Dictator', in E. A. Rees (ed.), *The Nature of Stalin's Dictatorship: Politburo 1924–1953* (Basingstoke, 2002).
29 O. V. Khlevniuk, P. Gregory and A. Vatlin (eds), *Stenogrammy zasedanii Politbyuro TsK VKP(b), 1923–1938* (Moscow, 2007) and Paul R. Gregory and Norman Naimark (eds), *The Lost Politburo Transcripts: From Collective Rule to Stalin's Dictatorship* (Stanford, CA, New Haven, CT and London, 2008).
30 *Stalinskoe Politbyuro v 30-e gody*, 112–13.
31 L. M. Kaganovich, *Ocherednye zadachi partraboty i reorganizatsiya partapparata* (Moscow-Leningrad, 1930).
32 *Pravda*, 17 January 1930; *Partiinoe stroitel'stvo* (1930) no. 2: 10.
33 Adam Ulam, *Stalin, the Man and His Era* (New York, 1973), 321.
34 *Stalinskoe Politbyuro v 30-e gody*, 74–8.
35 Ibid., 26–7.
36 L. M. Kaganovich, *Ocherednye zadachi partraboty i reorganizatsiya partapparata*.
37 *IV Moskovskaya oblastnaya i III gorodskaya konferentsii VKP(b)* (Moscow, 1934), 213. On *funktsionalka* in light industry see also the report of Ivanov in the same volume (467). L. M. Kaganovich, 'Ob itogakh sentyab'kogo plenuma TsK i zadachakh moskovskoi organizatsii', *Partiinoe stroitel'stvo* (1932) nos. 19–20: 10–11.
38 RGASPI, 558/11/769, 55–62.
39 RGASPI, 558/11/778, 43.
40 RGASPI, 558/11/738, 110–11.
41 *Sovetskoe rukovodstvo perepiska 1928–1941*, 144.
42 L. M. Kaganovich, *Pamyatnye zapiski* (Moscow, 1996), 395.
43 N. S. Khrushchev, *Khrushchev Remembers* (London, 1971), 58.
44 Niels Erik Rosenfeldt, *The 'Special' World*, vol. 1 (Copenhagen, 2009), 510.
45 *Pravda*, 21 January 1930. 'Reorganizatsiya partapparata i ocherednye zadachi partraboty: mobilizatsiya aktivnosti mass'.
46 *XVII Vsesoyuznoi Kommunisticheskoi Partii (b): stenograficheskii Otchet* (Moscow, 1934), 83.
47 T. H. Rigby, *Communist Party Membership in the U.S.S.R., 1917–1967* (Princeton, 1968), 52, 162, 199.
48 *XVII S"ezd Vsesoyuznoi Kommunisticheskoi Partii (b)*, 553.
49 Daniel Thorniley, *The Rise and Fall of the Soviet Rural Communist Party, 1927–1939* (Basingstoke, 1988).
50 Ibid., 556–7.
51 *Pravda*, 21 January 1930.
52 *Shestnadtsatyi s"ezd VKP(b)* (Moscow, 1930), 63.
53 L. M. Kaganovich, *Mezhdunarodnoe i vnutrennoe polozhenie i zadachi komsomola* (Moscow, 1931).
54 *Ekonomicheskaya zhizn'*, 22 January 1931.
55 L. M. Kaganovich, 'Lenin i Stalin s iskliuchitel'noi zabotlivost'iu vypoestovali komsomol', *Partiinoe stroitel'stvo* (1933) no. 22: 1–6.
56 Lewis Siegelbaum and Andrei Sokolov, *Stalinism as a Way of Life: A Narrative in Documents* (New Haven, CT, 2000), 384.
57 *Stalinskoe Politbyuro v 30-e gody*, 138n9. The other commission members were Postyshev, Yan Rudzutak, N. K. Antipov, M. F. Shkiryatov and Yaroslavsky.
58 N. Werth and Gael Moullenc (eds), *Rapports Secrets Soviétiques: La Société Russe dans les Documents Confidentiels 1921–1991* (Paris, 1994), 494.
59 L. M. Kaganovich, 'O chistke partii', *Partiinoe stroitel'stvo* (1933) no. 11: 1–11.

60 Ibid., 9. Kaganovich repeated this point in his report to the XVII Party Congress, see *XVII s"ezd VKP (b)*, 553.
61 *Stalinskoe Politbyuro v 30-e gody*, 137.
62 *XVII S"ezd Vsesoyuznoi Kommunisticheskoi Partii (b)*, 552.
63 Stalin, *Works*, vol. 13, 69.
64 *XVII S"ezd Vsesoyuznoi Kommunisticheskoi Partii (b)*, 525.
65 Ibid., 528.
66 Shelia Fitzpatrick, 'Stalin and the Making of a New Elite 1928–1939', *Slavic Review* 38, no. 3 (1979): 377–402.
67 *Stalinskoe Politbyuro v 30-e gody*, 106. The commission included Ordzhonikidze, Stalin, Kosior, Kaganovich, Kuibyshev, Voroshilov, Rudzutak, Shkiryatov, Yaroslavsky, Kalinin, Molotov and Kirov.
68 Boris I. Nicolaevskii, *Power and the Soviet Elite*, trans. Douglas Smith (London, 1965), 30. The claim that the 'Letters of an Old Bolshevik' were based on Bukharin's testimony is rejected by Bukharin's widow, Anna Larina, *Nezabyvaemoe* (Moscow, 1989), 262–8.
69 O. V. Khlevniuk, P. Gregory and A. Vatlin (eds), *Stenogrammy zasedanii Politbyuro TsK VKP (b), 1923–1938*, passim.
70 R. W. Davies et al., *Stalin-Kaganovich Correspondence*, 183–4.
71 RGASPI, 17/3/667–1031.
72 RGASPI, 17/113/600 to 17/114/40.
73 Niels Erik Rosenfeldt, *Knowledge and Power: The Role of Stalin's Secret Chancellery in the Soviet System of Government* (Copenhagen, 1978).
74 The frequency of the meetings in Stalin's Kremlin office are given in *Istoricheskii arkhiv* (1994) no. 6; (1995) nos. 2, 3, 4, 5–6; (1996) nos. 2, 3, 4, 5–6; (1997) no. 1; and (1998) no. 4 (index).
75 For the attendance of senior figures at these meetings see O. V. Khlevniuk, *Politbyuro, mekhanizmy politicheskoi vlasti v 1930-e gody* (Moscow, 1996), 289–91. See also Stephen G. Wheatcroft, 'From Team-Stalin to Degenerate Tyranny', in E. A. Rees (ed.), *The Nature of Stalin's Dictatorship: The Politburo, 1924–1953* (Basingstoke, 2004).
76 E. A. Rees, 'Stalin as Leader, 1924–1937: From Oligarch to Dictator', in E. A. Rees (ed.), *The Nature of Stalin's Dictatorship: The Politburo, 1924–1953* (Basingstoke, 2004).
77 Chuev, *Sto sorok besed*, 73.
78 *Stalinskoe Politbyuro v 30-e gody*, 133.
79 Stalin, *Works*, vol. 13, 220–24.
80 'Po povodu smerti Lenina', 'Po zavetam Lenina', *Pravda*, 21 January 1933, 1.
81 *IV Moskovskaya oblastnaya i III gorodskaya konferentsii*, 58, 269.
82 A. I. Mikoyan, *Tak bylo: razmysheniya o minuvshem* (Moscow, 1999), 592–3. D. Volkogonov, *Stalin: Triumph and Tragedy (London, 1991)*, 199–200.
83 Chuev, *Sto sorok besed*, 68–71. 'Dve besedy s L.M. Kaganovichem', in *Novaya i noveishaya istoriya* (1999) no. 2: 113.
84 *XVII S"ezd Vsesoyuznoi Kommunisticheskoi Partii (b)*, 525.
85 Ibid., 564.
86 Ibid.
87 RGASPI, 17/3/941, 55/35.
88 RGASPI, 17/114/392, 78.
89 *Stalinskoe Politbyuro v 30-e gody*, 141–2.
90 Ibid., 156, 171, 473, 78.

91 G. A. Trukan, *Yan Rudzutak* (Moscow, 1963), 92.
92 RGASPI, 17/3/939, 69/49 and 17/3/940, 153/137.
93 L. M. Kaganovich, 'O zadachakh partiinogo kontrolya i kontrol'noi rabote profsoyuzov, komsomola i pechati', *Partiinoe stroitel'stvo* (1934) no. 13: 1–10.
94 Ibid., 5–6.
95 L. M. Kaganovich, 'O vnutripartiinoi rabote i otdelakh rykovodyashchikh partinykh organov', *Partiinoe stroitel'stvo* (1934) no. 22: 7.
96 George M. Enteen, *The Soviet Scholar Bureaucrat: M. N. Pokrovsky and the Society of Marxist Historians* (London, 1978), 121, 128.
97 John Barber, *Soviet Historians in Crisis* (London, 1981), 147n38.
98 Ibid., 124.
99 L. M. Kaganovich, *Za bol'shevistskoe izuchenie istorii partii* (Moscow, 1932), 9.
100 RGASPI, 89/1009/62, 1–9.
101 *Sovetskoe rukovodstvo perepiska, 1928–1941*, 146–7, 227–8, 233, 234–5, 243–4, 302–3, 189–90, 299–300, 285.
102 *SKP*, 450–1, 462–4. Chuev, *Sto sorok besed*, 172.
103 *Sovetskoe rukovodstvo perepiska, 1928–1941*, 232.
104 See the group letter to Kaganovich in *Izvestiya*, 19 July 1997, 6.
105 Kaganovich may have been party to the campaign directed at theatre director Meyerhold. See Solomon Volkov, *Testimony: The Memoirs of Dmitri Shostakovich*, ed. Solomon Volkov and trans. Antonina W. Bouis (London, 1979), 60.
106 *Istochnik* (1994) no. 1: 14, 15–16, 19, 20.
107 N. V. Kornienko and E .D. Shubinoi (eds), *Andrei Platonov: Vospominaniya Sovremennikov: Materialy k biografii* (Moscow, 1978), 327–47.
108 R. Medvedev, *All Stalin's Men* (Oxford, 1983), 129–30.
109 G. L. Bondareva (ed.), *Kremlevskii Kinoteatr 1928–1953 Dokumenty* (Moscow, 2005), 160, 185, 220, 221, 222, 325.
110 Ibid., 981, 974, 954, 986.
111 Ibid., 246–7, 250–2.
112 L. M. Kaganovich and L. O. Utesov, *Kak organizovat' zheleznodorozhnye ansambli pesni i pliaski i dzhaz-orkestr* (Moscow, 1939), 67–9. S. Frederick Starr, *Red and Hot* (New York and Oxford, 1983).
113 G. L. Bondareva (ed.), *Kremlevskii Kinoteatr 1928–1953 Dokumenty*, 1005.
114 Ibid., 143, 420.
115 V. Kovalev, *Dva Stalinskikh Narkoma* (Moscow, 1995), 135–6.
116 R. W. Davies et al. (eds), *Stalin-Kaganovich Correspondence*, 151, 178.
117 *SKP*, 421, 425, 429, 431, 432, 437, 459, 460.
118 RGASPI, 17/162/17, 87.
119 L. M. Kaganovich, 'Itogi noyabr'skogo plenuma TsK VKP(b)', *Partiinoe stroitel'stvo* (1934) nos. 1–2: 18.
120 A. A. Fursenko (ed.), *Prezidium TsK KPSS, 1954–1964*, vol. 1 (Moscow, 2004), 80.
121 Ibid., 72.
122 Ibid., 133.
123 A. Kirilina, *Rikoshet, ili skol'ko chelovek bylo ubito vystrelom v Smol'nom* (St Petersburg, 1993); M. E. Lenoe, *The Kirov Murder and Soviet History* (New Haven, CT, 2010).
124 Paul Hagenloh, *Stalin's Police: Public Order and Mass Repression in the USSR, 1926–1941* (Washington DC and Baltimore, 2009), 147–57.
125 Kovalev, *Dva stalinskikh narkoma*, 155–6.

126 J. Arch Getty and Oleg V. Naumov, *The Road to Terror: Stalin and the Self-Destruction of the Bolsheviks, 1932–1939*, (New Haven, CT and London, 1999).
127 Lennart Samuelson, *Plans for Stalin's War Machine: Tukhachevsky and Military-Economic Planning 1925–1941* (Basingstoke, 2000), 108–20, 141–3.
128 RGASPI, 17/162/15, 46.
129 *Stalinskoe Politbyuro v 30- gody*, 19.
130 R. W. Davies et al., *Stalin-Kaganovich Correspondence*, passim.
131 Ibid., 16.
132 Ibid., 93, 142, 147.
133 Ibid., 294.
134 R. Medvedev, *All Stalin's Men*, 121.
135 R. W. Davies et al., *Stalin-Kaganovich Correspondence*, 311–13.
136 Ibid., 351, 149.

Chapter 8: Moscow Party Boss, 1930–1935

1 Catherine Merridale, *Moscow Politics and the Rise of Stalin: The Communist Party in the Capital, 1925–32* (Basingstoke, 1990); Nobuo Shimotomai, *Moscow Under Stalinist Rule, 1931–34* (Basingstoke, 1991); Timothy J. Colton, *Moscow: Governing the Socialist Metropolis* (Cambridge, MA, 1995); David L. Hoffman, *Moscow: Peasant Metropolis* (Ithaca, NY, 1994).
2 O. V. Khlevniuk, A. V. Kvashonkin, L. P. Kosheleva and L. A. Rogovaya, *Stalinskoe Politbyuro v 30-e gody* (Moscow, 1995), 116–17.
3 *Shestnadtsatyi s"ezd VKP(b)* (Moscow, 1930), 214–16, 230, 351.
4 E. H. Carr, *Foundations of a Planned Economy*, vol. 2, (London, 1971), 71.
5 L. M. Kaganovich, *Pamyatnye zapiski* (Moscow, 1996), 416. Henceforth *PZ*.
6 N. S. Khrushchev, *Khrushchev Remembers* (London, 1971), 57.
7 Ibid., 36.
8 F. Chuev, *Tak govoril Kaganovich: Ispoved' staklinskogo apostola* (Moscow, 1992), 99.
9 Khrushchev, *Khrushchev Remembers*, 42–3. Khrushchev was later to attribute his elevation to Stalin's wife, Nadezhda Alliluyeva.
10 Larisa Vasil'eva, *Kremlevskie zheny* (Moscow, 1992), 307.
11 Merridale, *Moscow Politics*, 83–6.
12 *Izvestiya*, 12 June 1956, 4, cited in Colton, *Moscow: Governing the Socialist Metropolis*, 839.
13 David R. Shearer, *Policing Stalin's Socialism: Repression and Social Order in the Soviet Union, 1924–1953* (New Haven, CT and London, 2009), 345–6.
14 *Rabochaya Moskva*, 8 June 1933, p 2, cited in Colton, *Moscow: Governing the Socialist Metropolis*, 839–40.
15 *IV Moskovskaya oblastnaya i III gorodskaya konferentsii*, 470 (Tarasov), 363 (Kogan), 72 (Kul'kov), 202 (Ryndin).
16 Ibid., 463 (Enov).
17 Ibid., 328 (Shurov), 468 (Surin), 469 (Tarasov).
18 O. V. Khlevniuk, R. W. Davies, L. P. Kosheleva, E. A. Rees and L. A. Rogovaya (eds), *Stalin i Kaganovich. Perepiska. 1931–1936gg* (Moscow, 2001), 96, 97–8. Henceforth *SKP*.
19 R. Medvedev, *Let History Judge* (London, 1972), 88–9.
20 *IV Moskovskaya oblastnaya i III gorodskaya konferentsii*, 248 (Mikhailov).

21 L. M. Kaganovich, *Kontrol'nye tsifry tret'ego goda piatiletki i zadachi Moskovskoi organizatsii* (Moscow, 1931).
22 O. V. Khlevniuk, '30-e gody. Krizizy, Reformy, Nasilie', *Svobodnaya mysl'* (1991) no. 17: 78.
23 R. Medvedev, *All Stalin's Men* (Oxford, 1983), 120.
24 *Pravda*, 7 June 1932.
25 Paul Hagenloh, *Stalin's Police: Public Order and Mass Repression in the USSR, 1926–1941* (Washington DC and Baltimore, 2009), 89, 104.
26 L. M. Kaganovich, *Boevye zadachi Moskovskoi partiinoi organizatsii po pode'emu sel'skogo khoyaistva i ukrepleniyu kolkhozov* (Moscow, 1932).
27 *Pravda*, 6 August 1932.
28 L. M. Kaganovich, 'Ob itogakh sentyabr'skogo plenuma TsK i zadachakh moskovskoi organisatsii', *Partiinoe stroitel'stvo* (1932) nos. 19–20: 6–15.
29 L. M. Kaganovich, *Na putyakh k okonchatel'nomu prevrashcheniyu Moskovskoi oblasti iz potrebliayushchei v proizvodyashchiyu* (Moscow, 1933).
30 *SKP*, 338, 341, documents 330, 335.
31 Medvedev, *Let History Judge*, 347. R. Medvedev S. Parofenov and P. Khmelinskii, *Zheleznyi yastreb* (Ekaterinburg, 1992), 64.
32 Ibid., 285.
33 A. V. Kvashonkin, L. P. Kosheleva, L. A. Rogovaya and O. V. Khlevniuk (eds), *Sovetskoe rukovodstvo perepiska, 1928–1941* (Moscow, 1999), 302.
34 *IV Moskovskaya oblastnaya i III gorodskaya konferentsii*, 370 (Sedel'nikov), 87 (Titov), 133 (Andreev), 328 (Shurov), 314 (Baskaev).
35 Ibid., 242 (Alekseev).
36 Merridale, *Moscow Politics*, 173.
37 *XVIII s"ezd Vsesoyuznoi Kommunisticheskoi Partii (b), 10–21 marta 1939: stenograficheskii otchet* (Moscow, 1939), 69–70 (Shcherbakov).
38 Ibid., 203 (Ryndin).
39 R. W. Davies, *Crisis and Progress in the Soviet Economy, 1931–1933* (Basingstoke, 1996), 311.
40 Ibid., 112–15.
41 *IV Moskovskaya oblastnaya i III gorodskaya konferentsii*, 209 (Ryndin), 315 (Baskaev), 476 (Peters), 500–1 (Pankov).
42 Ibid., 205, 446–8 (Gaidul'), 205, 370 (Sedel'nikov).
43 Ibid., 108.
44 *XVIII s"ezd Vsesoyuznoi Kommunisticheskoi Partii (b)*, 139, 214; see also 133 (Andreev), 326 (Karandasheva), 329 (Shurov).
45 RGASPI, 17/21/3011, 87.
46 *IV Moskovskaya oblastnaya i III gorodskaya konferentsii*, 237.
47 Ibid., 82, 224.
48 Ibid., 91–2 (Dorofeev), 220 (Ryndin), 406 (Peskarev).
49 RGASPI, 17/21/3012, 209.
50 *Proekt vtorogo pyatiletnego plana razvitiya narodnogo khozyaistva SSSR (1933–1937), tom. 2 Plan razvitiya raionov* (Moscow 1934), 240.
51 Ibid., 509–10.
52 S. Frederick Starr, 'Visionary Town Planning during the Cultural Revolution' in Sheila Fitzpatrick (ed.), *Cultural Revolution in Russia, 1928–1931* (Bloomington, IN and London, 1978), 207–40.
53 *Pravda*, 29 May 1930, 5.
54 *PZ*, 424.

55 L. M. Kaganovich, *Za sotsialisticheskyio rekonstrukstiyu Moskvy i gorodov SSSR* (Moscow-Leningrad, 1931).
56 Sir E. D. Simon, Lady Simon, W. A. Robson and J. Jewkes Simon, *Moscow in the Making* (London, 1937), 165.
57 Starr, 'Visionary Town Planning', 238. See L. M. Kaganovich, *Socialist Reconstruction of Moscow and Other Cities in the USSR* (London, 1931).
58 *Pravda*, 4 July 1931, 4.
59 The resolution is in *Pravda*, 17 June 1931, 23. Local implementing measures are in *Pravda*, 21–25 June 1931.
60 *Moskovskie novosti*, 28 July 1996, 11.
61 Bulganin in *Vechernaya Moskva*, 11 July 1935, 1.
62 Simon et al., *Moscow in the Making*, 154, 165–7.
63 Khrushchev, *Khrushchev Remembers*, 63.
64 *Pravda*, 5 August 1932, 4.
65 A. A. Fursenko (ed.), *Prezidium TsK KPSS, 1954–1964*, vol. 1 (Moscow, 2004), 1125.
66 *PZ*, 282, 427.
67 *PZ*, 427.
68 Colton, *Moscow: Governing the Socialist Metropolis*, 341.
69 Ibid., 839n55.
70 Colton, *Moscow: Governing the Socialist Metropolis*, 280, cites Tsentralnyi gosudarstvenni arkhiv obshchestvennogo dvizhenii Moskvy (Central State Archive of Social Movements of Moscow) (TsGAODM), 4/5/71, 12; 3/49/79, 3.
71 R. Medvedev reviewing Stuart Kahan's biography of Kaganovich, *Wolf in the Kremlin* (New York, 1987), in *Moscow News* 52 (1988): 16.
72 *Sovetskoe rukovodstvo perepiska 1928–1941*, 158–9.
73 Chuev, *Tak govoril Kaganovich*, 47.
74 D. Volkogonov, *Stalin: Triumph and Tragedy* (London, 1991), 234–5.
75 Chuev, *Tak govoril Kaganovich*, 47.
76 Ibid., 48.
77 'K istorii snosa Sukharevoi bashni', *Izvestiya TsK KPSS* (1989) no. 9:109–16.
78 R. Conquest, *The Harvest of Sorrow* (London, 1988), 209.
79 Colton, *Moscow: Governing the Socialist Metropolis*, 265, 268–9.
80 R. Medvedev, *On Stalin and Stalinism* (Oxford, 1979), 71.
81 Chuev, *Tak govoril Kaganovich*, 51.
82 *PZ*, 430.
83 Ibid., 434.
84 Ibid., 432–34.
85 Khrushchev, *Khrushchev Remembers*, 65–70.
86 Medvedev, *All Stalin's Men*, 124–5.
87 L. M. Kaganovich, *Postroem pervuyu ochered' metro k XVII godovshchinee oktyabrya* (Moscow, 1934). The resolution of the Moscow *gorkom* and *obkom* is in *Rabochaya Moskva*, 7 January 1934.
88 L. M. Kaganovich, *O stroitel'stve metropolitena i plana goroda Moskvy* (Moscow, 1934).
89 Khrushchev, *Khrushchev Remembers*, 65.
90 Medvedev, *All Stalin's Men*, 124–5.
91 Ye. T. Abakumov, 'Kto stroil metro', in *Istoriya metro Moskvy* (Moscow, 1935), II, 5.
92 N. Shimotomai, *Moscow Under Stalinist Rule, 1931–34* (Basingstoke, 1991), 111–12.
93 *Rabochaya Moskva*, 10 December 1931.

94 *KPSS v rezolyutsiyakh i resheniyakh, s"ezdov, konferentsii i plenumov TsK,* vol. 4 (1971), 545.
95 *PZ,* 443.
96 *Rabochaya Moskva,* 27 March 1932.
97 L. S. Bykov and A. S. Matrosov, *Kanal imeni Moskvy. 50 let ekspluatatsii* (Moscow, 1987).
98 L. M. Kaganovich, *Ob itogakh o"edinennogo plenuma TsK i TsKK VKP(b)* (Moscow, 1933), 17.
99 *Kanal imeni Moskvy, 50 let ekspluatatsii,* 24.
100 *Rechnoi transport SSSR, 1917–1957* (Moscow, 1957), 308.
101 RGASPI, 17/3/935, topic 9.
102 *Vechernaya Moskva,* 17 September 1934. *Izvestiya,* 9 September 1935.
103 *PZ,* 444.
104 *Propagandist* (1934) no. 16: 30.
105 *PZ,* 444.
106 W. Citrine, *I Search for Truth in Russia* (London, 1936), 80. Simon et al., *Moscow in the Making,* 224–25.
107 *Sovetskoe rukovodstvo perepiska, 1928–1941* (Moscow, 1999), 270.
108 'Blizhaishee okruzhenie diktatora', *Sotialisticheskii vestnik,* 10 November 1933, 3–10.
109 *IV Moskovskaya oblastnaya i III gorodskaya konferentsii VKP(b)* (Moscow, 1934), 6, 345 (Voropaev), 202 (Ryndin).
110 Ibid., 43.
111 Ibid., 47.
112 Ibid., 192, 197.
113 Ibid., 311. V. Markovich, 'Derevnya poluchila moguchii otryad bol'shevikov', *Partiinoe stroitel'stvo* (1933) nos. 13–14: 63.
114 Ibid., 479, 475, 364.
115 Ibid., 169.
116 Ibid., 161–2.
117 Ibid., 192.
118 Ibid., 373 (Karpov).
119 Ibid., 233 (Ryndin).
120 Ibid., 401, 427, 72, 442, 448, 313, 332, 84.
121 Ibid., 319–20, 202 (Ryndin), 235.
122 Ibid., 561–2 and 79.
123 Ibid., 553, 554, 560.
124 Ibid., 427–30 (Kogan) 156–7 (Berman), 561–2 (Bulganin).
125 Ibid., 160. In his memoirs, Kaganovich stressed the attention paid to the working conditions, rehabilitation and training of prisoners – *PZ,* 445.
126 Ibid., 279.
127 Ibid., 422–3.
128 Ibid., 178.
129 Ibid., 120.
130 Ibid., 137.
131 Ibid., 411.
132 Ibid., 378 (Kirshon), 495–7 (Filatov), 146 (Stasova).
133 Ibid., 413.
134 *Stalinskoe Politbyuro v 30-e gody,* 143.
135 William Taubman, *Khrushchev: The Man and His Era* (London, 2003).
136 Colton, *Moscow: Governing the Socialist Metropolis,* 257.
137 L. M. Kaganovich, *Pobeda metropolitena-pobeda sotsializma* (Moscow, 1935).

138 *PZ*, 440.
139 G. L. Bondareva (ed.), *Kremlevskii Kinoteatr 1928–1953 Dokumenty* (Moscow, 2005), 227, 286–7, 982, 984.
140 *PZ*, 440. A meeting of Metrostroi workers passed a resolution proposing that the Metro be named in honour of Kaganovich – *Vechernaya Moskva*, 10 February 1935.
141 Stalin, *Works*, vol. 14 (London, 1978), 81–3.
142 RGASPI 17/3/963, III. RGASPI, 17/3/967, IV.
143 RGASPI, 17/3/985, VI.
144 RGASPI, 17/3/989, 117. RGASPI, 17/3/989, 238, 251, 280. *Pravda*, 15 July 1937.
145 *SKP*, 524, 527, documents 584, 591.

Chapter 9: Boss of Rail Transport, 1935–1937

1 On Kaganovich's role in rail transport policy see E. A. Rees, *Stalinism and Soviet Rail Transport 1928–1941* (Basingstoke, 1995); H. Hunter, *Soviet Transportation Policy* (Cambridge, MA, 1957); and J. N. Westwood, *Soviet Locomotive Technology during Industrialization 1928–1953* (London, 1982).
2 RGASPI, 17/3/924, 123/106.
3 *KPSS v rezolyutsiyakh i resheniyakh, s"ezdov, konferentsii i plenumov TsK*, vol. 6, 80–4. The resolution was prepared by Stalin, Molotov, Kaganovich and Andreev – RGASPI, 17/3/926, 56/47, 57/48.
4 A. A. Andreev, *Za bol'shevistskoe providenie reshenii SNK i TsK VKP(b) rabote zheleznodorozhnogo transporta* (Moscow, 1933), 3.
5 O. V. Khlevniuk, A. V. Kvashonkin, L. P. Kosheleva and L. A. Rogovaya (eds), *Stalinskoe Politbyuro v 30-e gody: Sbornik dokumentov* (Moscow, 1995), 69.
6 *XVII S"ezd VKP(b) stenograficheskii otchet* (Moscow, 1934), 27. Stalin in an interview with the American journalist Walter Duranty acknowledged the acute problems of transport – I. V. Stalin, *Works*, vol. 13 (Moscow, 1955), 282–7. *Gudok*, 3 February 1935 (editorial).
7 *PZ*, 393–4.
8 O. V. Khlevniuk et al. (eds), *Stalinskoe Politbyuro v 30-e gody*, 70.
9 The protocols of the Central Committee–Sovnarkom Commission on Transport from April 1934 to May 1935 are preserved in the Ordzhonikidze fond, RGASPI, 85/29/256–85/29/265.
10 *Sobranie zakonov* (1934), art. 98. RGASPI, 17/3/941, 42/25, 51–4; *Sobranie zakonov* (1934), art. 117.
11 RGASPI 85/29/282, 14.
12 RGASPI, 85/29/304, 1; 85/29/303, 1.
13 *Pravda*, 30 June 1934.
14 RGASPI, 17/3/948, 135/48, 139/122.
15 *Gudok*, 9 December 1934.
16 *Voprosy istorii* (1993) no. 9: 6.
17 *The Second Five Year Plan for the Development of the National Economy of the USSR (1933–1937)* (Moscow, 1935), 39–42, 348, 274, 277.
18 RGASPI, 17/3/955; 17/3/956, 35.
19 Hunter, *Soviet Transportation Policy*, 53.
20 RGASPI, 85/29/261.
21 RGASPI, 85/29/260, 1–4.

22 *Pravda*, 12 January 1935; *Plannovoe khozyaistvo* (1935) no. 1: 15–18.
23 *Sobranie zakonov* (1935), art. 28, 29.
24 *Stalinskoe Politbyuro v 30-e gody*, 142.
25 *Gudok*, 4 March 1935.
26 *Vechernaya Moskva*, 2 March 1935.
27 V. Kravchenko, *I Chose Freedom* (New York, 1946), 428.
28 *Stalinskoe Politbyuro v 30-e gody*, 143.
29 Valentin Kovalev, *Dva stalinskikh narkoma* (Moscow, 1995), 182.
30 *Stalinskoe Politbyuro v 30-e gody*, 143.
31 *Vechernaya Moskva*, 3 March 1935. A letter from the Moscow party and province committees referred to Kaganovich as the 'beloved leader of the Moscow Bolsheviks' – *Vechernaya Moskva*, 7 March 1935.
32 *Pravda*, 1–2 March 1935.
33 Foreign Office, N 1602/52/38.
34 RGASPI, 81/3/413, 53–6, 57.
35 Foreign Office, N 6033/54/38.
36 RGASPI, 17/3/970, 39; *Sobranie zakonov* (1935), art. 112, 113, 120.
37 *Sobranie zakonov*, 1935, art. 33–4; *Gudok*, 5 March 1935.
38 RGASPI, 17/3/961, 196, 197.
39 *Pravda*, 27 November 1935.
40 *Gudok*, 17 April 1935.
41 RGASPI, 17/3/962, 6, 67, 87.
42 E. A. Rees, 'Stalin, the Politburo and Rail Transport Policy', in Julian Cooper, Maureen Perrie and E. A. Rees (eds), *Soviet History, 1917–1953: Essays in Honour of R. W. Davies* (Basingstoke, 1995).
43 'Dve besedy s L. M. Kaganovichem', *Novaya i noveishaya istoriya* (1999) no. 2: 103.
44 *Pravda*, 6 March 1935.
45 *Gudok*, 20 March 1935. See also B. Souvarine, *Stalin* (London, n.d.), 566–7.
46 *Pravda*, 20 March 1935. See also Foreign Office, N 1602\52\38. In 1935 Kaganovich presented a report to Stalin on the weakness of NKPS's rolling stock and track, a cause of the high accident rate. This cast doubts on the subsequent policy of raising the speeds and weights of freight trains, a decision that produced a dramatic increase in the accident rate. A. Artizov, Yu. Sigachev, I. Shevchuk and B. Khlopov (eds), *Reabilitatsiya: Kak eto bylo: fevral' 1956-nachalo 80-x godov* (Moscow, 2003), 564.
47 RGASPI, 85/29/308, 1–46.
48 *Pravda*, 16 April 1935; Foreign Office, N 2107/52/38, Chilston to Sir John Simon, 20 April 1935.
49 RGASPI, 85/29/285, 1–7; RGASPI, 85/ 29/277, 1; RGASPI, 85/29/264, 3–36.
50 RGASPI, 17/3/959, 95, 117. The commission included Kaganovich (convener), Chubar', Andreev, Postnikov, Mezhlauk and Zimin.
51 *Pravda*, 15 March 1935.
52 Ibid.
53 *Pravda*, 24 April 1935.
54 *Pravda*, 28 December 1935.
55 *Pravda*, 15 April 1935.
56 *Pravda*, 16 April 1935.
57 *Pravda*, 11 May 1935.

58 *Gudok*, 30 June 1935.
59 *Gudok*, 27 June 1935.
60 *Plannovoe khoyaistvo* (1935) no. 3: 10, 17.
61 *Izvestiya*, 24 July 1935.
62 *Pravda*, 6 May 1935.
63 Stalin, *Works*, vol. 14, 98.
64 RGASPI, 17/2/547, 49–51.
65 *Pravda*, 16 August 1935.
66 Ibid.
67 *Pravda*, 2 August 1935.
68 *Sotsialisticheskii transport* (1936) no. 5: 3. Henceforth *ST*.
69 *Gudok*, 15 July 1935.
70 F. Chuev, *Tak govoril Kaganovich: Ispoved' stalinskogo apostola* (Moscow, 1992), 164.
71 *Pravda*, 11 August 1935; Kaganovich's report – *Pravda*, 16 August 1935. RGASPI, 17/3/970, 74.
72 *Zheleznodorozhnyi transport v gody industrializatsii SSSR (1926–1941)* (Moscow, 1970), 261–8. RGASPI, 17/3/970, 75, 76.
73 R. W. Davies and O. V. Khlevniuk, 'Stakhanovism and the Soviet Economy', *Europe-Asia Studies* 54, no. 6 (2002): 867–903.
74 N. A. Zakharchenko, 'Zarozhdenie stakhanovsko-krivonosovskogo dvizheniya na zheleznodorozhnom transporte Donbassa', in *Voprosy istorii SSSR*, vol. 33 (Kharkov, 1988), 62–8.
75 *Izvestiya*, 6 September 1935. Stalin's six conditions were delivered in his speech to economic executives on 23 June 1931, 'New Conditions – New Asks of Economic Construction', in Stalin, *Works*, vol. 13, 53–82.
76 *Pervoe Vsesoyuznoe Soveshchanie rabochikh i rabotnits Stakhanovtsev, 14–17 noyabrya 1935, stenograficheskii otchet* (Moscow, 1935).
77 *Pravda*, 11 November 1935.
78 *Pravda*, 22 November 1935.
79 RGASPI, 17/3/973, 36.
80 RGASPI, 17/2/561, 54, 82.
81 *Pravda*, 28 December 1935.
82 *Pravda*, 10 December 1935.
83 D. I. Chernomordik, *Ekonomicheskaya politika SSSR* (Moscow, 1936), 301.
84 *Zheleznodorozhnyi transport SSSR v dokumentakh Kommunisticheskoi partii i Sovetskogo pravitel'stva (1917–1957gg)* (Moscow 1957), 314–15.
85 Hunter, *Soviet Transportation Policy*, 74.
86 *Osnoye pokazateli upravleniya narodno-khozyaistvennogo plana za 1935g* (Moscow, 1936), 123. Compare these figures were those provided for the first six months of 1935 in *Plannovoe khoziaistvo* (1935) no. 8: 30.
87 Stalin, *Works*, vol. 14, 115. On 1 December 1935 to a conference of combine harvester operators, Stalin proposed a growth in grain output from 5.5 million poods in 1935 to 7–8 million poods in 1938–9.
88 *Izvestiya*, 20 December 1935.
89 *Pravda*, 28 December 1935.
90 *Izvestiya*, 28 December 1935. This point was reiterated by Kaganovich in an article – *ST* (1935) no. 3: 62.
91 *KPSS v rez*, vol. 6, 294–5.

92 S. Fitzpatrick, 'Stalin and the making of a New Elite', *Slavic Review* 38, no. 3 (1979).
93 *Pravda*, 18 January 1936.
94 *Pravda*, 28 April 1936.
95 *Pravda*, 18 February 1936; 8 May 1936.
96 *Gudok*, 14 January 1936 (editorial).
97 Foreign Office, N 289/289/38; *Gudok*, 16 January 1936.
98 *Pravda*, 2 August 1936.
99 *Izvestiya*, 28 December 1935.
100 *Pravda*, 15 January 1936.
101 *Pravda*, 20 February 1936.
102 *Pravda*, 3 April 1936.
103 *Pravda*, 1 January 1936.
104 *Pravda*, 16 and 17 April 1936 (editorial).
105 *Gudok*, 20 and 29 May 1936.
106 *Zheleznodorozhnyi transport v gody industrializatsii SSSR (1926–1941)* (Moscow, 1970), 278.
107 See the reports in *Pravda*, 20 and 22 January 1936; 20 February 1936 (editorial); 1 and 15 March 1936.
108 RGASPI, 17/3/974, 122.
109 R. W. Davies, E. A. Rees, O. V. Khlevniuk, L. P. Kosheleva and L. A. Rogovaya (eds), *The Stalin-Kaganovich Correspondence* (New Haven, CT and London, 2003), 322–3.
110 Foreign Office, N 2034/565/38, cites unpublished report by the Military Collegium.
111 *ST* (1936) no. 3: 17–18.
112 *Pravda*, 16 June 1936.
113 *ST* (1936) no. 3: 7.
114 *ST* (1936) no. 3: 9–10, 24, 61–62.
115 *Sovet pri narodnom komissare putei soobshcheniya (16–23 aprelya 1936 goda)* (Moscow, 1936), 97.
116 Ibid., 367–76.
117 *Gudok*, 9 January 1936 (editorial).
118 *ST* (1936) no. 3: 19.
119 *ST* (1936) no. 7: 9–17, 27–49.
120 *Gudok*, 1 April 1936 (editorial).
121 *Voprosy istorii* (1993) no. 3: 27.
122 *ST* (1936) no. 3: 27.
123 *ST* (1936) no. 3: 30–1.
124 *Gudok*, 17 April 1936.
125 *Gudok*, 1 and 8 June 1936.
126 *ST* (1936) no. 3: 11, 63.
127 *ST* (1936) no. 9: 44, 69. See *Gudok*, 21 August 1936 (Kaganovich).
128 Foreign Office, N 3196/197/38.
129 *ST* (1936) no. 3: 4, 35.
130 Rees, *Stalinism and Soviet Rail Transport, 1928–1941*, 134.
131 *Pravda*, 29 July 1936.
132 *Gudok*, 1 and 2 August 1936.
133 *ST* (1936) no. 5: 8; *Pravda*, 2 August 1936.
134 *ST* (1936) no. 5: 13.
135 O. V. Khlevniuk, *1937-i: Stalin, NKVD i sovetskoe obshchestvo* (Moscow, 1992), 122.
136 *Gudok*, 16 and 18 August 1936.

Chapter 10: Political and Social Revolution through Terror, 1936–1938

1. Marc Jansen and Nikita Petrov, *Stalin's Loyal Executioner: People's Commissar Nikolai Yezhov 1895–1940* (Stanford, California, 2002), 45–8.
2. O. V. Khlevniuk, R. W. Davies, L. P. Kosheleva, E. A. Rees and L. A. Rogovaya (eds), *Stalin i Kaganovich Perepiska. 1931–1936gg.* (Moscow, 2001), 627. Henceforth *SKP*.
3. A. V. Kvashonkin, L. P. Kosheleva, L. A. Rogovaya and O. V. Khlevniuk (eds), *Sovetskoe rukovodstvo perepiska 1928–1941* (Moscow, 1999), 334.
4. M. Fainsod, *Smolensk under Soviet Rule* (Cambridge, MA, 1958), 233.
5. The claim that Stalin informed Kaganovich of his plans for a mass purge already in 1935 has no foundation. R. Medvedev, S. Parofenov and P. Khmelinskii, *Zheleznyi yastreb* (Ekaterinburg, 1992) 56; Kendall E. Bailes, *Technology and Society under Lenin and Stalin* (Princeton, 1978), 281.
6. *SKP*, 631.
7. A. Artizov, Yu. Sigachev, I. Shevchuk and B. Khlopov (eds), *Reabilitatsiya: Kak eto bylo: fevral' 1956-nachalo 80-x godov* (Moscow, 2003), 561.
8. A. N. Yakovlev (ed.), *Reabilitatsiya: politicheskie protsessy 30–50-kh godov* (Moscow, 1991), 187–8.
9. D. Watson, *Molotov: A Biography* (Basingstoke, 2005), 133–5.
10. *SKP*, 637–43.
11. *SKP*, 630, 634–5, 636–8.
12. *SKP*, 664–5.
13. *Gudok*, 23 August 1936.
14. *Pravda*, 6, 8, 15 and 19 August 1936.
15. *SKP*, 631.
16. *SKP*, 654–6.
17. *SKP*, 671.
18. Anna Larina, *Nezabyvaemoe* (Moscow, 1989), 306–8.
19. R. W. Davies, E. A. Rees, O. V. Khlevniuk, L. P. Kosheleva and L. A. Rogovaya (eds), *The Stalin-Kaganovich Correspondence, 1931–1936* (New Haven, CT and London, 2003), 357.
20. *Sovetskoe rukovodstvo perepiska 1928–1941*, 346–48.
21. Naomi Allen and George Breitman (eds), *Writings of Leon Trotsky 1936–37* (New York, 1970), 184: 'Kaganovich Anticipates my End' dated 31 January 1937.
22. R. Conquest, *The Great Terror* (Harmondsworth, 1971), 218.
23. J. Arch Getty and Oleg V. Naumov, *Yezhov: The Rise of Stalin's "Iron Fist"* (New Haven, CT and London, 2008). Yezhov's character offers striking similarities with that of Heinrich Himmler as a schizoid personality. See Peter Padfield, *Himmler, Reichsfuhrer – SS* (London, 1990).
24. RGASPI, 17/3/981, 50.
25. O. V. Khlevniuk, A. V. Kvashonkin, L. P. Kosheleva and L. A. Rogovaya (eds), *Stalinskoe Politbyuro v 30-e gody: Sbornik dokumentov* (Moscow, 1995), 148–9.
26. Ibid., 152.
27. *Pravda*, 28 October, 1936. NKPS's leadership paid fulsome praise to Ordzhonikidze's aid in improving the railways – *Sotsialisticheskii transport* (1936) no. 7: 6–8.
28. RGASPI, 85/29/435, 1–12.
29. *Sovetskoe rukovodstvo perepiska 1928–1941*, 342–6.
30. R. W. Davies et al., *Stalin-Kaganovich Correspondence*, 365.

31 *Sovetskoe rukovodstvo: Perepiska 1928–1941*, 375–7.
32 *SKP*, 653–4, document 7812; APRF, 3/22/150, 128–9.
33 *Gudok*, 12, 14, 18, 26 and 28 August 1936; 1, 10, 15, 17, 24 and 28 September 1936; 23 October 1936; 5 November 1936.
34 *Istochnik* (1993) no. 2: 17–18.
35 L. M. Kaganovich, *Vvedenie novykh pravil tekhnicheskoi ekplutatsii i likvidatsiya krushenie i avarii* (Moscow, 1936).
36 *Izvestiya*, 30 July 1936 (Tverskoi).
37 *Pravda*, 11 and 26 September 1936.
38 *Sotsialisticheskii transport* (1936) no. 9: 19, 21–3 (Lednik), 58–68 (Danilov). Henceforth *ST*.
39 *Voprosy istorii* (1993) no. 3: 7.
40 RGASPI, 17/3/981, 216.
41 *Pravda*, 3 January 1937.
42 E. Zaleski, *Stalinist Planning for Economic Growth 1933–1952* (London, 1980), 558–61.
43 For the trial reports, see *Pravda*, 20–4 November 1936.
44 O. V. Khlevniuk, *Master of the House: Stalin and his inner circle*, trans. Nora Seligman Favorov (New Haven, CT and London, 2009), 156–7.
45 *Izvestiya*, 4 November 1936.
46 *Gudok*, 14 and 15 August 1936.
47 *Za bol'shevistskuyu zimu na zheleznodorozhnom transporte* (Moscow, 1937), 8–9.
48 RGASPI, 17/2.576, 10, 17.
49 RGASPI, 17/2/576, 105.
50 RGASPI, 17/2/576, 106.
51 *Report of the Court Proceedings of the 'Anti-Soviet Trotskyite Centre'* (Moscow, 1937). *Izvestiya TsK KPSS*. (1989) vol. 9: 30–50, 'O tak nazyvaemom 'parallel'nom' antisovetskom trotskistskom tsentre.'
52 *Gudok*, 1 February 1937.
53 RGASPI, 85/29/160, 1–28.
54 RGASPI, 17/3/983, 339.
55 O. V. Khlevniuk, *1937-i: Stalin, NKVD i sovetskoe obshchestvo* (Moscow, 1992), 138–9.
56 A. I. Mikoyan, *Tak bylo: razmyshleniya o minuvshem* (Moscow, 1999), 327–33, 582.
57 Kendall E. Bailes, *Technology and Society under Lenin and Stalin* (Princeton, 1978), 283–7; R. Medvedev, *Let History Judge* (London, 1976),195–6.
58 F. Chuev, *Tak govoril Kaganovich: Ispoved' staklinskogo apostola* (Moscow, 1992), 162–3.
59 *Izvestiya*, 20 February 1937.
60 See Francesco Benvenuti, 'A Stalinist Victim of Stalinism: "Sergo" Ordzhonikidze', in J. Cooper, M. Perrie and E. A. Rees (eds), *Soviet History 1917–53* (Basingstoke, 1995), 135–6.
61 *Sotsialisticheskii transport* (1937) no. 5: 19 (Molotov).
62 *KPSS v rezolyutsiyakh i resheniyakh, s"ezdov, konferentsii i plenumov TsK* vol. 6, 378–81; *Pravda*, 6 March 1937.
63 *Voprosy istorii* (1993) no. 9: 3–32. D. Volkogonov, *Stalin: Triumph and Tragedy* (London, 1991), 247.
64 Ibid.
65 Artizov et al., *Reabilitatsiya*, 571.
66 Ibid., 583.
67 Stalin, *Works*, vol. 14, 261.

68 Ibid., 272.
69 Ibid., 258–9.
70 Ibid., 287.
71 Ibid., 291–2.
72 O. V. Khlevniuk, *1937 god: Protivostoianie* (Moscow, 1991). On A. A. Solts' criticism of the repression see Mikoyan, *Tak bylo*, 318–20.
73 Medvedev, *Let History Judge*, 174; Volkogonov, *Stalin*, 285, 287.
74 *Pravda*, 19–28 March 1937.
75 *Gudok*, 18, 21 and 26 (editorial) March 1937.
76 *Gudok*, 6 and 27 April 1937.
77 GARF, 5451/21/6, 56, 154,157–63, 209–15, 255–7, 261–4, and 286–9. Junbae Jo, 'Soviet Trade Unions and the Great Terror' in M. Ilič (ed.), *Stalin's Terror Revisited* (Basingstoke, 2006)72–3.
78 GARF, 5451/21/6, 21–2, 183–4, 294, 300.
79 Artizov et al., *Reabilitatsiya*, 640.
80 *Stalinskoe Politbyuro v 30-e gody*, 55.
81 RGASPI, 17/163/1145, 63.
82 *Stalinskoe Politbyuro v 30 gody*, 33.
83 O. V. Khlevniuk, *1937 god: Protivostoianie*, 234.
84 Artizov et al., *Reabilitatsiya*, 687, 781–2.
85 Chuev, *Tak govoril Kaganovich*, 46.
86 Conquest, *The Great Terror*, 305.
87 L. M. Kaganovich, *Pamyatnye zapiski* (Moscow, 1996), 45, 100. Henceforth *PZ*.
88 Giorgi Dimitrov, *Diario: Gli anni di Mosca* (Turin, 2002), 45. F. Chuev, *Molotov Remembers* (ed. Albert Resis) (Chicago, 1993), 298.
89 Mark Junge, Gennadii Bordiugov and Rol'f Binner, *Vertikal' Bol'shogo Terrora: Istoriya operatsia po prikazy NKVD No.00447* (Moscow, 2008), passim. Stalin, Molotov and Kaganovich were the figures who signed most of these orders.
90 L. S. Gatalova, L. P. Kozheleva, L. A. Rogovaya and Dzh. Kaio (eds), *TsK VKP(b) i Natsional'nyi Vopros, Kniga 2, 1933–1945* (Moscow, 2009), 228, 232, 238, 260, 306, 308, 314, 317, 398, 438–40.
91 J. Arch Getty and Oleg V. Naumov, *The Road to Terror: Stalin and the Self-Destruction of the Bolsheviks, 1932–1939*, (New Haven, CT and London, 1999), 433.
92 RGASPI, 81/3/227, 81–2.
93 Artizov et al., *Reabilitatiya*, 584.
94 Conquest, *The Great Terror*, 331–2.
95 Mikhail Shreider, *NKVD iznutri: zapiski chekista* (Moscow, 1995), 64.
96 RGASPI, 81/3/229, 1–37.
97 Artizov et al., *Reabilitatsiya*, 585.
98 Mikhail Shreider, 'Ivanovo 1937. From the notes of a Chekist operative', *Moscow News*, 27 November 1988, 7.
99 *Pravda*, 31 July 1937; *Gudok*, 1 August 1937.
100 For Bakulin's biography see *Gudok*, June 14 1937.
101 *Trud*, 23 August 1937.
102 O. V. Khlevniuk, 'Economic Officials in the Great Terror, 1936–38' in M. Ilič (ed.), *Stalin's Terror Revisited* (Basingstoke, 2006), 46.
103 GARF, 5446/1/136. I am indebted to Dr Oleg Khlevniuk for this reference.
104 *PZ*, 451.

105 R. Medvedev, *All Stalin's Men* (Oxford, 1983), 128. Kendall E. Bailes, *Technology and Society under Lenin and Stalin*, (Princeton, 1978), 288.
106 L. M. Kaganovich, *Za pod'em ugol'nogo Donbassa* (Moscow, 1937). *Trud*, 8 and 9 October 1937.
107 R. Medvedev and O. Khmelin'sky, 'Ostannyi iz stalinskogo otocheniya. Lazar Kaganovich na tli epokhi', *Vitchizna* (1990) no. 5: 144–5.
108 *Industriya*, 5 January 1938.
109 *PZ*, 448. See also Medvedev, *Let History Judge*, 489.
110 RGASPI, 558/11/1086, 37–44.
111 *PZ*, 448; *Pravda*, 27 November 1937.
112 *Pravda*, 10 December, 1937.
113 'Rech' tovarishcha L.M. Kaganovicha', *Partiinoe stroitel'stvo* (1937) no. 4: 14–15.
114 *Pravda*, 22, 25 and 27 November 1937; 5 and 10 December 1937. The number of nominations were: Stalin (3,346), Voroshilov (1,693), Yezhov (1,355), Kalinin (1,272), Molotov (1,192), Kaganovich (896), Mikoyan (438), Andreev (379), Chubar' (269).
115 A. Mikoyan, 'Slavnoe dvadtsatiletie sovetskoe razvedki', *Partiinoe stroitel'stvo* (1938) no. 2: 23.
116 *Industriya*, 26 February 1938.
117 *PZ*, 455–6.
118 *PZ*, 449.
119 Pravda, 8 May 1938; Artizov et al., *Reabilitatsiya*, 582. Kaganovich was responsible for the arrest of P. I. Miroshnikov, director of the Chief Aluminium combine, and Lukashin, director of the Chief Rubber combine.
120 *Industriya*, 30 October 1938.
121 *KPSS v rez*, vol. 7, 8–17; *Pravda*, 19 January 1938.
122 *Stalinskoe Politbyuro v 30-e gody*, 165.
123 *Report of the Court Proceedings in the Case of the Anti-Soviet 'Bloc of Rights and Trotskyites'* (Moscow, 1938); Conquest, *The Great Terror*, 514.
124 RGASPI, 17/3/994, 249.
125 *Pravda*, 11 and 24 January 1938 (editorials).
126 GARF, 5446/221/402, 14–21.
127 RGASPI, 17/3/998, 64; *Pravda*, 5 April 1938.
128 R. Conquest, *Inside Stalin's Secret Police: NKVD Politics 1936–39* (London, 1986), 68–9.
129 RGAE, 1887/28/587–591.
130 *Gudok*, 6 and 8 May, 1938.
131 Compare the listing of line directors in *Pravda*, 28 January 1937 and *Pravda*, 9 September 1938.
132 RGASPI, 17/3/999, 230.
133 *Gudok*, 5 and 14 June, 1938.
134 *Gudok*, 10 June 1938.
135 L. Vol'fson, A. Korneev and N. Shil'nikov, *Razvitie zheleznykh dorog SSSR* (Moscow, 1939), 174.
136 *Gudok*, 21 November 1938.
137 RGAE, 1884/28/591.
138 *Zheleznodorozhnyi transport v gody industrializatsii SSSR (1926–1941)* (Moscow, 1970), 309–10.
139 GARF, 546/22a/408, 11–21.
140 Rees, *Stalinism and Soviet Rail Transport, 1928–1941*, 241.
141 Conquest, *Inside Stalin's Secret Police*, 68–9, 86.
142 Artizov et al., *Reabilitatsiya*, 592, 625, 633.

143 Ibid., 667.
144 Ibid., 359, 581.
145 O. V. Khlevniuk, *Master of the House*, ch. 5.
146 *Istochnik* (1993), no. 0 (zero): 23.
147 *PZ*, 451.
148 RGASPI, 81/3/231, 73, 79.
149 S. Pons, *Stalin and the Inevitable War, 1936–1941* (London, 2002), 78–9.
150 J. Arch Getty and Oleg V. Naumov, *The Road to Terror: Stalin and the Self Destruction of the Bolsheviks, 1932–1939* (New Haven, CT and London, 1999).
151 R. W. Davies, 'The Soviet Economy and the Launching of the Great Terror', in M. Ilič, *Stalin's Terror Revisited* (Basingstoke, 2006), 11–37; Roberta Manning, 'The Soviet Economic Crisis of 1936–1940 and the Great Purges', in J. Arch Getty and R. T. Manning (eds) *Stalinist Terror: New Perspectives* (Cambridge, 1993); D. R. Shearer, *Policing Stalin's Socialism: Repression and Social Order in the Soviet Union, 1924–1953* (New Haven, CT, 2009); P. Hagenloh, *Stalin's Police: Public Order and Mass Repression in the USSR, 1926–1941* (Washington DC, 2009).
152 E. A. Rees 'Stalin as Leader 1937–53: From Dictator to Despot', in E. A. Rees (ed.), *The Nature of Stalin's Dictatorship: The Politburo 1924–1953* (Basingstoke, 2004).
153 Mark Harrison (ed.), *Guns and Rubles: The Defense Industry in the Stalinist State* (New Haven, CT and London, 2008), 7–10.
154 Conquest, *The Great Terror*, 247, 607–8.

Chapter 11: The Man

1 J. Hellbeck, 'Working, Struggling, Becoming: Stalin-Era Autobiographical Texts', in David L. Hoffmann (ed.), *Stalinism: The Essential Readings* (Oxford, 2003), 181–210. Igal Halfin (ed.), *Language and revolution: Making of modern political identities* (London, 2002).
2 *Trinadtsatyi s"ezd RKP(b), stenograficheskii otchet* (Moscow, 1963), 167.
3 L. Schapiro, *The Communist Party of the Soviet Union* (London, 1978), 385, cites N. Valentinov, 'Sut' bolshevizma v izobrazhenii Iu. Piatakova', *Novyi zhurnal* 52 (New York, 1958): 140–61.
4 J. Arch Getty and O. V. Naumov, *The Road to Terror* (New Haven, CT and London, 1999), 311.
5 L. Trotsky, *The Revolution Betrayed: What is the Soviet Union and Where is it Going?* (London, 1967, first published in 1936); Nicholas S. Timasheff, *The Great Retreat: The Growth and Decliner of Bolshevism in Russia* (New York, 1972, first published 1946); Richard Stites, *Revolutionary Dreams: Utopian Vision and Experimental Life in the Russian Revolution* (New York and Oxford, 1989).
6 A. James Gregor, *Italian Fascism and Developmental Dictatorship* (Princeton, 1979).
7 Denis Mack Smith, *Mussolini* (London, 1981), 155, 161, 198, 211, 220.
8 See Otto Strasser, *Hitler and I*, trans. Gwenda David and Eric Mosbacher (Boston, 1940, republished 1982). Peter D. Stachura, *Gregor Strasser and the Rise of Nazism* (London, 1983).
9 Trotsky, *The Revolution Betrayed*.
10 Boris Souvarine, *Stalin: A Critical Survey of Bolshevism* (London,1972, first published in French in 1939), esp. 'Postscript: The Counter-Revolution'.
11 David William Jones, *The Lost Debate: German Socialist Intellectuals and Totalitarianism* (Urbana, IL, 1999); David R. Roberts, *The Totalitarian Experiment in the Twentieth Century:*

Understanding the Poverty of Great Politics (London, 2006); Franz Borkenau, *The Totalitarian Enemy* (London, 1939); Rudolf Hilferding, 'The Logic of Totalitarianism', in Robert V. Daniels (ed.), *The Stalin Revolution* (Boston, 1965).

12 See Francesco Benvenuti, 'A Stalinist Victim of Stalinism: "Sergo" Ordzhonikidze', in J. Cooper, M. Perrie and E. A. Rees (eds), *Soviet History 1917–53* (Basingstoke, 1995), 135–6.
13 L. Trotsky, *Stalin: An Appraisal of the Man and his influence*, ed. Charles Malamuth (London, 1968), 385.
14 Victor Serge, *From Lenin to Stalin* (New York, 1973), 53.
15 *Entsiklopedicheskii slovar' russkogo bibliograficheskogo instituta Granat*, ed. Yu. S. Gambarov, V. Ya. Zheleznov, M. M. Kovalevsky, S. A. Muromtsev and K. A. Timiryazev (Moscow, 1925).
16 A. I. Mikoyan, *Tak bylo: razmyshleniya o minuvshem* (Moscow, 1999), 384.
17 RGASPI, 558/11/1122/161.
18 I. V. Stalin, *Sochineniya*, ed. Robert H. McNeal, vol. 1 (Stanford, 1967), xiii.
19 O. V. Khlevniuk (ed.), *Stalin i Kaganovich, Perepiska, 1931–1936gg.* (Moscow, 2001), 40, document 3. Henceforth *SKP*.
20 The years of birth of the leading group were as follows: Krzhizhanovsky – 1872; Kalinin – 1875; Stalin – 1878/9; Yaroslavsky – 1878; Voroshilov – 1881; Ordzhonikidze – 1886; Kirov – 1886; Rudzutak – 1887; Kuibyshev – 1888; Kosior – 1889; Molotov – 1890; Chubar' – 1891; Kaganovich – 1893; Khrushchev – 1894; Andreev – 1895; Mikoyan – 1895; Zhdanov – 1896.
21 B. Bazhanov, *Bazhanov and the Damnation of Stalin*, trans. and with commentary by David W. Doyle (Athens, OH, 1990), 15–16. Bazhanov's assertion that Molotov was responsible for Kaganovich's promotion in the party is mistaken.
22 Boris Bajanov, *Avec Staline dans le Kremlin* (Paris, 1930), 58.
23 Quoted in B. Souvarine, *Stalin* (London, 1939), 489. Victor Serge, *From Lenin to Stalin* (New York, 1973), 98.
24 George Breitman and Sarah Lovell (eds), *Writings of Leon Trotsky, 1932* (New York, 1973), 22.
25 George Breitman (ed.), *Writings of Leon Trotsky, 1929–33* (New York, 1979), 168.
26 Anna Larina, *Nezabyvaemoe* (Moscow, 1989), 269, 314.
27 Grigory Bessedovsky, *Revelations of a Soviet Diplomat*, trans. Matthew Norgate (London, 1931), 219–23.
28 Essad-Bey, *Stalin: The Career of a Fanatic*, trans. Huntley Paterson (London, 1932), 121–2, 351–2.
29 Niels Erik Rosenfeldt, *The 'Special' World: Stalin's power apparatus and the Soviet system's secret structures of communication*, vol. 1 (Copenhagen, 2009), 165, 170. In 1922 Kaganovich's assistants were Yu. V. Klement'ev and A. I. Mar'in. In 1932 Kaganovich's secretariat included Dement'ev, Kaplan, T. K. Slovatinskaya, Solov'ev, Elena Stasova and V. S. Fedorov.
30 B. Bazhanov, *Bazhanov and the Damnation of Stalin*, 8.
31 Stites, *Revolutionary Dreams*, 177–9.
32 Ibid., 243.
33 *SKP*, 40, 42, 47, 75, 79, 86, 99.
34 F. Chuev, *Tak govoril Kaganovich: Ispoved' staklinskogo apostola* (Moscow, 1992), 61. See also 129.
35 Ibid., 53.
36 I. V. Stalin, *Works*, vol. 14 (London, 1978), 12–13.

37 Nikolai Chernyshevsky, *What is to Be Done?*, trans. Michael R. Katz, annotated by William G. Wagner (Ithaca, NY and London, 1989). See the introduction by Katz and Wagner.
38 'Blizhaishee okruzhenie diktatora', *Sotsialisticheskii vestnik* 23 (308), 10 November 1933, 3–10. The article wrongly claims that Kaganovich before 1917 was an intellectual of undetermined occupation. It also confuses L. M. Kaganovich with P. K. Kaganovich during the grain requisitioning campaigns of the Civil War. I am indebted to Professor R. W. Davies for this reference.
39 Trotsky, *Stalin*, 157.
40 Chuev, *Tak govoril Kaganovich*, 129.
41 Mikoyan, *Tak bylo*, 352.
42 Chuev, *Tak govoril Kaganovich*, 62, 163.
43 O. V. Khlevniuk, A. V. Kvashonkin, L. P. Kosheleva and L. A. Rogovaya (eds), *Stalinskoe Politbyuro v 30-e gody: Sbornik dokumentov* (Moscow, 1995), 125–6.
44 *SKP*, 357
45 Chuev, *Tak govoril Kaganovich*, 71–2.
46 Ibid., 59.
47 *Istochnik* (1994) no. 3: 128. 'Kak Moskva chut'ne stala Stalinodarom', *Izvestiya TsK KPSS* (1990) no. 12: 126–7. Ternovsk in Moscow province, Tovarkovo in Tul'sk province, Pashennaya in Chitinskaya province and Popasnaya in Lugansk province were all renamed Kaganovich. The town of Tugalan in Tadzhik SSR was renamed Kaganovichabad. By 1937, his home town of Kabany in the Ukraine had been renamed his honour. However, a proposal in the mid 1930s to rename Chelyabinsk as Kaganovichgrad came to nought.
48 *PZ*, opposite 289.
49 *Istoriya grazhdanskoi voiny v SSSR*, vol. 2 (Moscow, 1942), 82, 135, 137.
50 E. Voskoboinikov and A. Zebelev, *Turkkomissiya VTsIK i Sovnarkom RSFSR i Turkbyuro TsK RKP(b) v bor'be za ukreplenie Sovetskou vlasti v Turkestane (M.V. Frunze, V.V. Kuibyshev, L.M. Kaganovich v Turkestane)* (Tashkent, 1946 and 1951).
51 L. M. Kaganovich, *Mezhdunarodnoe i vnutrennoe polozhenie i zadachi komsomola* (Moscow, 1931), 56.
52 L. M. Kaganovich, *O zadachakh profsoyuzov SSSR na dannom etape razvitiya* (Baku, 1932).
53 G. L. Bondareva, (ed.), *Kremlevskii Kinoteatr 1928–1953 Dokumenty* (Moscow, 2005), 227, 286–7, 982, 984.
54 V. Garros, N. Korenevskaya and T. Lahusen (eds), *Intimacy and Terror: Soviet Diaries of the 1930s* (New York, 1995), 184.
55 Mikhail Shreider, *NKVD iznutri: zapiski cheskista* (Moscow, 1995), 70.
56 Ibid., 246.
57 Chuev, *Tak govoril Kaganovich*, 53.
58 A. Rosenberg, *The Final Fight between Europe and Bolshevism* (Munich, 1936), 9–19; Dr R. Kommoss, *Juden hinter Stalin* (Berlin, 1938), 37–52.
59 L. S. Gatalova, L. P. Kozheleva, L. A. Rogovaya and Dzh. Kaio (eds), *TsK VKP(b) i Natsional'nyi Vopros, Kniga 2, 1933–1945* (Moscow, 2009), 169–72.
60 Maria Anisimovna Svanidze, 'Iosif Beskonechno Dobr,' *Istochnik* (1993) no. 1: 4–34.
61 Chuev, *Tak govoril Kaganovich*, 131.
62 Ibid., 106.
63 RGASPI, 81/3/413, 88–90.
64 Maria Markovna Kaganovich, *Prodsoyuzy i kooperatsiya* (Moscow-Leningrad, 1927); *Krasnaya kniga peredovykh profgrup* (Stalingrad, 1932); *Shefstvo i sotssovmestitel'stvo v gosapparate*

(Moscow, 1934); *Proizvodstvennye soveshchaniya* (Moscow, 1943); *O rabote komissii zarabotnoi platy fabzavmestkomov* (Magadan, 1943); *Soyuz rabochikh shveinoi i trikotazhnoi promyshlennosti SSSR* (Moscow, 1949).
65 Chuev, *Tak govoril Kaganovich*, 95.
66 RGASPI, 17/162/21, 30.
67 A. Barmine, *One who Survived* (New York, 1945), 264 recounts this story as a rumour. N. Bassechus, *Stalin* (London and New York, 1952), 230 retells the story as fact. Roy Medvedev and Anatoli Rybakov, also leant credence to the story: *Moskovskie novosti*, 25 December 1988, 16.
68 Larisa Vasil'eva, *Kremlevskie zheny* (Moscow, 1992), 309–10. Chuev, *Tak govoril Kaganovich*, 48–51.
69 Mark Junge, Gennady Bordiugov and Rol'f Binner, *Vertikal' Bol'shogo Terrora: Istoriya operatsia po prikazy NKVD No.00447* (Moscow, 2008), 62, 214, 279, 297, 633.
70 *Industriya*, 18 January 1938. In connection with the elections to the Supreme Soviet, Yuli Kaganovich wrote three articles for the party's theoretical journal, *Partiinoe stroitel'stvo*: (1937) no. 22; (1937) no. 24; and (1938) no. 11. The content, not surprisingly, was highly conventional.
71 Medvedev, *All Stalin's Men* (Oxford 1983), 128. R. W. Davies, M. J. Ilič, H. P. Jenkins, C. Merridale and S. G. Wheatcroft (eds), *Soviet Government Officials, 1922–41: A Handlist* (Birmingham, 1989), 305. In the 1940s, Yuli Kaganovich served as a Soviet trade delegate to Mongolia. He died in the early 1950s after a long illness.
72 T. H. Rigby, 'Was Stalin a Disloyal Patron?' *Soviet Studies* 38, no. 3 (1988): 311–24.
73 Manfred F. R. Kets de Vries, *Reflections on Character and Leadership* (Chichester, 2009), chs 8 and 9.
74 The classic study of psychopathy is Hervey Cleckley, *The Mask of Sanity* (St Louis, MO, 1941). See also Jason R. Hall and Stephen D. Benning, 'The "Successful" Psychopath: Adaptive and Subclinical Manifestations of Psychopathy in the General Population' in Christopher J. Patrick (ed.), *Hanbdook of Psychopathy* (New York and London, 2006); D. L. Paulhus and K. M. Williams, 'The dark triad of personality: Narcissism, Machiavelliainism, and Psychopathy', *Journal of Research in Personality* 36 (2002): 556–63. J. W. McHoskey, W. Worzel and C. Szyarto, 'Machiavellianism and psychopathy,' *Journal of Personality and Social Psychology* 74 (1998): 192–210. Richard Christie and Florence L. Geis, *Studies in Machiavellianism* (New York and London, 1970).
75 Robert Tucker, *Stalin as Revolutionary, 1879–1929: A Study in History and Personality* (London, 1974).
For the view of a sceptic see Ronald Grigor Suny, 'Beyond Psychohistory: The Young Stalin in Georgia', *Slavic Review* 50, no. 1 (Spring 1991): 48–58.
76 Raymond Birt, 'Personality and Foreign Policy: The Case of Stalin,' *Political Psychology* 14, no. 4 (1993): 607–25.
77 D. Rancour-Lafferiere, *The Mind of Stalin: A Psychoanalytic Study* (Ann Arbor, 1988), 15. See also Rancour-Lafferiere's discussion on Stalin's 'paranoia' (ibid., 18–21, 108–9, 121–3), 'machiavellianism' (ibid., 73, 126, 131–2) and 'narcissism' (ibid., 17, 41–50, 118–19).
78 Ibid., 122.
79 D. Volkogonov, *Stalin: Triumph and Tragedy* (London, 1991), 318.
80 Kets De Vries, *Reflections on Character and Leadership*.
81 R. Medvedev, *Let History Judge* (London, 1976), 330.
82 Stephen G. Wheatcroft 'From Team Stalin to Degenerate Tyranny', in E. A. Rees (ed.) *The Nature of Stalin's Dictatorship: The Politburo 1924–1953* (Basingstoke, 2004).

83 Rees (ed.), *The Nature of Stalin's Dictatorship*, 243–4.
84 V. Kravchenko, *I Chose Freedom* (New York, 1946), 270, 275–6. The authorship of Kravchenko's work is a matter of uncertainty, with other writers, including Eugene Lyons, claiming a role in their writing.
85 Ibid., 399.
86 Medvedev, *All Stalin's Men*, 121–2.
87 N. S. Khrushchev, *Khrushchev Remembers* (London, 1971), 308.
88 Volkogonov, *Stalin: Triumph and Tragedy*, 248.
89 E. A. Rees, 'Politics, Administration and Decision-Making in the Soviet Union, 1917–1953', in *Yearbook of European Administrative History, JEV 16*, (Baden-Baden, 2004), 259–90.
90 Trotsky, *Stalin*, 421.
91 Medvedev, *Let History Judge*, 346.
92 Medvedev, *All Stalin's Men*, 123.
93 Volkogonov, *Stalin: Triumph and Tragedy*, 249 and 247.
94 R. Conquest, *The Great Terror* (Harmondsworth, 1971), 34–5.
95 Kets de Vries, *Reflections on Character and Leadership*, 187–9.

Chapter 12: The Despot's Creature, 1939–1953

1 *Industriya*, 21 August 1938.
2 *Upravlenie narodnym khozyaistvom SSSR 1917–1940gg. Sbornik dokumentov* (Moscow, 1968), 215.
3 H. Schwartz, *Russia's Soviet Economy* (New York, 1954), 225.
4 E. A. Rees, *Stalinism and Soviet Rail Transport* (Basingstoke, 1995), 202.
5 *Sobranie zakonov*, (1939) art. 45–52, 58–61; *Industriya*, 25 January 1939.
6 *Industriya*, 21 October 1938. L. M. Kaganovich, *Pamyatnye zapiski* (Moscow, 1996), 453.
7 *Industriya*, 12 and 23 November 1938.
8 *Industriya*, 21 May 1939.
9 *KPSS v rezolyutsiyakh i resheniyakh, s"ezdov, konferentsii i plenumov TsK*, vol. 5, 324–32. *Sotsialisticheskii transport* (1938) no. 12: 1–7.
10 *Pravda*, 18 January 1939. *Industriya*, 14 January 1939.
11 *Industriya*, 26 June 1939, 'Zhenshchiny prishli na shakhty'.
12 I. V. Stalin, *Works*, vol. 14 (London, 1978), 379.
13 Ibid., 394.
14 Ibid., 421.
15 *XVIII s"ezd VKP(b), stenograficheskii otchet* (Moscow, 1939), 242.
16 *Industriya*, 30 January 1939.
17 *XVIII s"ezd VKP(b)*, 250–6.
18 Ibid., 260.
19 Ibid., 23.
20 Ibid., 266–7.
21 Ibid., 257.
22 Ibid., 299–300, 499.
23 Ibid., 501–2.
24 Ibid., 658. Compare these figures with those approved by the Politburo on the basis of Molotov's report – *Pravda*, 30 January 1939.
25 T. S. Khachaturov, 'Osnovaya ekonomicheskaya zadacha SSSR i puti razvitiya zheleznodorozhnogo transporta', *Plannovoe khozyaistvo* (1940) no. 10: 30–43.

26 L. Schapiro, *The Communist Party of the Soviet Union* (London, 1978), 446–7, 493.
27 *Industriya*, 28 October 1938.
28 *Industriya*, 18 March 1939.
29 *Industriya*, 1 August, 1939.
30 *Pravda*, 21 December 1939, 5.
31 R. W. Davies, 'Planning for Mobilisation: The 1930s', in Mark Harrison (ed.), *Guns and Rubles: The Defense Industry in the Stalinist State* (New Haven, CT and London, 2008), 128–130.
32 *Industriya*, 28 October 1938.
33 *Istoricheskii arkhiv* (1995) nos. 5–6: 4–64.
34 V. Kravchenko, *I Chose Freedom* (New York, 1946), 428. See also A. I. Mikoyan, *Tak bylo: razmyshleniya o minuvshem* (Moscow, 1999), 421–3, 344.
35 F. Chuev, *Tak govoril Kaganovich: Ispoved' staklinskogo apostola* (Moscow, 1992), 89–90; Chuev, *Molotov Remembers*, ed. Albert Resis (Chicago, 1993), 12–13.
36 V. A. Malyshev, 'Proidet desiatok let, i eti vstrechi ne vosstanovish' uzhe v pamyati', *Istochnik* (1997) no. 5: 108.
37 J. Haslam, *The Soviet Union and the Threat from the East, 1933–1941* (London, 1992) ch. 5.
38 G. A. Kumanev, *Na sluzhbe fronta i tyla: zheleznodorozhnyi transport SSSR nakanune i vy gody velikoi otchestvennoi voiny 1938–1945gg.* (Moscow, 1976), 41–3, 49–50.
39 *Organy gosudarstvennoi bezopasnosti SSSR v velikoi otechestvennoi voine*, vol. 1 (Moscow, 1995), 153–5.
40 Ibid., 167.
41 H. Hunter, *Soviet Transportation Policy* (Cambridge, MA, 1957), 393.
42 Ibid., 44.
43 *Resheniya partii i pravitel'stva po khozyaistvennym voprosam*, t.2 (Moscow, 1967), 757–8. See, also, N. Voznesensky, *Economic Results of the USSR in 1940 and the Plan of National Economic Development for 1941* (Moscow, 1941), 11.
44 Kumanev, *Na sluzhbe fronta i tyla*, 56–7.
45 A. I. Shakhurin, *Kryl'ia pobedy* (Moscow, 1990).
46 O. V. Khlevniuk, A. V. Kvashonkin, L. P. Kosheleva and L. A. Rogovaya (eds), *Stalinskoe Politbyuro v 30-e gody: Sbornik dokumentov* (Moscow, 1995), 34.
47 'Posetiteli kremlevskogo kabineta I. V. Stalina: Zhurnaly (tetradi) zapisi lits, prinyatykh pervym gensekom 1924–1953gg', compiled by A. V. Korotkov and A. A. Chernobaev, *Istoricheskii arkhiv* (1996) nos. 1–6: 14.
48 *Istoricheskii arhkiv* (1995) nos. 5–6: 103–7.
49 Voznesensky, *Economic Results of the USSR in 1940*, 23–7. See also the conference resolution, ibid., 36–9.
50 *Izvestiya TsK KPSS* (1990) no. 7: 98.
51 'Dve besedy s L.M. Kaganovichem', in *Novaya i noveishaya istoriya* (1999) no. 2: 115–16.
52 N. S. Khrushchev, *Khrushchev Remembers* (London, 1971): 47–8. Kaganovich's alleged indifference to his brother's death was also mentioned by V. N. Malin at the Central Committee plenum June 1957. N. Kovaleva, A. Korotkov, S. Mel'chin, Yu. Sigachev and A. Stepnov (eds), *Molotov, Malenkov, Kaganovich, Stenogramma iionskogo plenuma TsK KPSS i drugie dokumenty* (Moscow, 1998), 430.
53 R. Medvedev, *Let History Judge* (London, 1976), 310. Medvedev, *All Stalin's Men* (Oxford, 1983), 132–3. Medvedev mistakenly asserts that Mikhail Kaganovich's death occurred after the war.

54 Chuev, *Tak govoril Kaganovich*, 155.
55 Ibid., 77–8, 79.
56 Amy Knight, *Beria: Stalin's First Lieutenant* (Princeton, 1993), 30, 49–50, 73–5.
57 O. V. Khlevniuk, *Politbyuro; mekhanizmy politicheskoi vlastti v 1930–3 gody* (Moscow, 1996), 253–4.
58 *Stalinskoe Politbyuro v 30e gody*, 35.
59 Khlevniuk, *Politbyuro*, 254–5.
60 N. S. Khrushchev, *The 'Secret' Speech*, ed. Zh. Medvedev and R. Medvedev (Nottingham, 1976), 53; Mikoyan, *Tak bylo*, 391; Chuev, *Molotov Remembers*, 38–9.
61 Chuev, *Tak govoril Kaganovich*, 33–4, 88.
62 M. Harrison, *Soviet Planning in Peace and War, 1938–1945* (Cambridge, 1985), 277.
63 Kumanev, *Na sluzhbe fronta i tyla*, 117. See, also, A. I. Mikoyan, 'V pervye mesyatsy velikoi otechestvennoi voiny', *Novaya i noveishaya istoriya* (1985) no. 6: 103–4.
64 'Dve besedy s L.M. Kaganovichem', 104–5.
65 D. Volkogonov, *Stalin: Triumph and Tragedy* (London, 1991), 434.
66 Mikoyan, *Tak bylo*, 419.
67 Volkogonov, *Stalin: Triumph and Tragedy*, 418–19. The other members were Andreev (deputy chairman), Kaganovich, Mikoyan, P. P. Shirshov (NKMaritime Fleet), Z.A. Shashko (NKRiver Transport), Lieutenant-General I. V. Kovalev (deputy narkom NKPS) G. B. Kovalev, A. G. Karponsov and A. V. Khrulev, see Kumanev, *Na sluzhbe fronta i tyla*, 156.
68 Ibid., 158–9.
69 Kumanev, *Na sluzhbe fronta i tyla*, 218–20. See also Mikoyan, *Tak bylo*, 394–400.
70 L. M. Kaganovich, *Pamyatnye zapiski* (Moscow, 1996), 463. Henceforth *PZ*.
71 *PZ*, 464.
72 Volkogonov, *Stalin: Triumph and Tragedy*, 415, 478–9.
73 *PZ*, 533–40.
74 *PZ*, 470. Chuev, *Tak govoril Kaganovich*, 90.
75 *PZ*, 476–7.
76 N. I. Strakhov, 'Na voenno-avtomobil'nykh dorogakh', *Voenno-istoricheskii zhurnal* (1964) no.11: 71.
77 Kumanev, *Na sluzhbe fronta i tyla*, 222–3, 225.
78 Stalin, *Works*, vol. 15, 209.
79 *Izvestiya*, 6 November 1943. See also the VTsSPS and NKPS order granting state awards to railway workers engaged in socialist emulation – *Izvestiya*, 27 November 1943.
80 *Izvestiya*, 23 November 1943.
81 A. Jacob, *A Window in Moscow* (London, 1946), 110–12.
82 'Khronika zasedanie operativnogo buro gosudarstvennogo komitet oboronoi'. Uncatalogued protokols at GARF.
83 Medvedev, *Let History Judge*, 467.
84 'Khronika zasedanie operativnogo buro gosudarstvennogo komitet oboronoi'. Kovalev's appointment was reported in *Pravda*, 21 December 1944.
85 William O. McCagg, *Stalin Embattled, 1945–1948* (Detroit, 1978), 108, 159 argues that Kaganovich was dismissed in December 1944 because he was too closely allied to Malenkov. There is little to support this assertion.
86 'Posetiteli kremlevskogo kabineta I. V. Stalina: Zhurnaly (tetradi) zapisi lits, priniatykh pervym gensekom 1924–1953gg', compiled by A. V. Korotkov and A. A. Chernobaev, *Istoricheskii arkhiv* (1994) no. 6; (1995) nos. 1–6; (1996) nos. 1–6; (1997) no. 1.

87 *Istoricheskii arkhiv* (1995) nos. 5–6: 5–64; (1996) nos. 1–2: 4–86; (1996) no. 3: 4–72; (1996) no. 4: 67–131; (1996) no. 5–6: 4–61; (1997) no. 1: 2–39. Kaganovich's attendance at the meetings in Stalin's office from 1938 to 1953 is outlined in the table below.

Year	Number of meetings	Number of meetings attended by Kaganovich	Kaganovich's attendance (%)
1938	183	77	42.1
1939	256	90	35.2
1940	123	52	42.3
1941	230	35	15.2
1942	240	16	6.7
1943	191	12	6.3
1944	151	4	2.6
1945	147	4	2.7
1946	105	1	1.0
1947	135	13	9.6
1948	124	83	66.9
1949	114	81	71.1
1950	73	46	63.0
1951	48	40	83.3
1952	52	25	48.1
1953	7	0	0

88 See *Istoriya Velikoi Otchestvennaya Voena Sovetskogo Soyuza*, vol. 6 (Moscow, 1965), 70.
89 Kumanev, *Na sluzhbe fronta i tyla*, 117.
90 Medvedev, *All Stalin's Men*, 130.
91 Volkogonov, *Stalin: Triumph and Tragedy*, 418–19.
92 R. Medvedev, S. Parofenov and P. Khmelinskii, *Zheleznyi yastreb* (Ekaterinburg, 1992), 72.
93 Chuev, *Tak govoril Kaganovich*, 52.
94 Volkogonov, *Stalin: Triumph and Tragedy*, 468.
95 Yoram Gorlizki and O. V. Khlevniuk, *Cold Peace: Stalin and the Soviet Ruling Circle, 1945–1953* (Oxford, 2004).
96 Khrushchev, *The 'Secret' Speech*, 76–7.
97 Volkogonov, *Stalin: Triumph and Tragedy*, 219.
98 Vladimir Rudolph, 'The Administrative Organisation of Soviet Control, 1945–48', in Robert Slusser (ed.), *Soviet Economic Policy in Postwar Germany* (New York, 1953), 42–9.
99 Harrison, *Soviet Planning*, 270, 276.
100 *PZ*, 482–5.
101 Chuev, *Molotov Remembers*, 52, 60.
102 Gorlizki and Khlevniuk, *Cold Peace*, 93–4, 149, 193n66.
103 Ibid., 181n60.
104 Tsentral'noi gosudarstvennyi arkhiv obshchestvennykh organizatsii Ukrainy (TsGAOOU), 1/1/740, 75.

105 David R. Marples, *Stalinism in the Ukraine in the 1940s* (London and New York, 1992), 9–13.
106 *Molotov, Malenkov, Kaganovich, Stenogramma iionskogo plenuma TsK KPSS i drugie dokumenty*, compiled by N. Kovaleva, A. Korotkov, S. Mel'chin, Iu. Sigachev and A. Stepnov (Moscow, 1998), 244.
107 *PZ*, 490–1.
108 'Dve besedy s L.M. Kaganovichem', 104–5.
109 N. S. Khrushchev, *Khrushchev Remembers*, 243.
110 Serhy Yekelchyk, *Stalin's Empire of Memory: Russian-Ukrainian Relations in the Soviet Historical Imagination* (Toronto, 2004) ch. 3.
111 Marples, *Stalinism in the Ukraine in the 1940s*, 24
112 McCagg, *Stalin Embattled*, 361n53; cites *Kommunist* (1957) no. 12: 26.
113 Pavel Sudoplatov and Anatoli Sudoplatov (with Jerrold L. and Leona P. Schecter), *Special Tasks: The Memoirs of an Unwanted Witness – A Soviet Spymaster* (London, 1994), 281.
114 Ibid., 29.
115 *PZ*, 489.
116 Khlevniuk, O. V., I. Gorlitskii, L. P. Kosheleva, A. I. Miniuk, M. Iu. Prozumeshchikov, L. A. Rogovaya and S. V. Somonova (eds), *Politbyuro TsK VKP(b) i Sovet Ministrov SSSR 1945–1953* (Moscow, 2002).
117 Yoram Gorlizki, 'The Council of Ministers and the Soviet Neo-Patrimonial State, 1945–1953', *Journal of Modern History* 74, no. 4 (2002): 699–736.
118 See endnote 88.
119 *Pravda*, 5 February 1948.
120 *PZ*, 494–5.
121 *PZ*, 482, 483, 498.
122 Gorlizki and Khlevniuk, *Cold Peace*, 79–89.
123 Ibid., 91, 250.
124 Gorlizki and Khlevniuk, *Cold Peace*, 215n55.
125 A. A. Fursenko (ed.), *Prezidium TsK KPSS, 1954–1964*, vol. 1 (Moscow, 2004), 627.
126 Gorlizki and Khlevniuk, *Cold Peace*, 193n66.
127 Khrushchev, *Khrushchev Remembers*, 102.
128 Chuev, *Molotov Remembers*, 362.
129 Khrushchev, *Khrushchev Remembers*, 46–67.
130 Ibid., 260–1.
131 'Kak Moskva chut'ne stala Stalinodarom', *Izvestiya TsK KPSS* (1990) no. 12: 126–7; Chuev, *Molotov Remembers*, 176.
132 This is referred to by psychologists as the 'Stockholm syndrome'. See Daniel Rancour-Lafferiere, *The Mind of Stalin*, 52–3.
133 Shimon Redlich, *War, Holocaust and Stalinism: A Documentary Study of the Jewish Anti-Fascist Committee in the USSR* (Newark, NJ,1995).
134 G. V. Kostyrchenko, *Tainaya politika Stalina. Vlast i anti-Semitism* (Moscow, 2001), 258–66.
135 L. S. Gatalova, L. P. Kozheleva, L. A. Rogovaya and Dzh. Kaio, *TsK VKP(b) i Natsional'nyi Vopros, Kniga 2, 1933–1945* (Moscow, 2009), 980.
136 Redlich, *War, Holocaust and Stalinism*, 49, 52–3, 271. Petitions to Kaganovich from A. A. Rabinovch, B. Girsh, Vitvitsky, Itshak Fefer and Solomon Mikhoels.
137 Redlich, *War, Holocaust and Stalinism*, 121, 123.
138 Viktor Nekrasov, *Saperlipolet ili Esli by da kaby, da vo rtu rosli griby* (London 1983), 106–7.
139 Medvedev, *Let History Judge*, 483.

140 Redlich, *War, Holocaust and Stalinism*, 131, 444.
141 Khrushchev, *Khrushchev Remembers*, 263.
142 Ibid., 315.
143 Schapiro, *The Communist Party of the Soviet Union*, 543.
144 Chuev, *Molotov Remembers*, 173–75.
145 RGASPI, 592/1/80, 1–9.
146 *Pravda*, 16 October 1952.
147 Khrushchev, *Khrushchev Remembers*, 280–1.

Chapter 13: De-Stalinization and Nemesis, 1953–1991

1 F. Chuev, *Molotov Remembers*, ed. by Albert Resis (Chicago, 1993), 235–7, 327.
2 Svetlana Alliliueva, *Twenty Letters to a Friend* (Harmondsworth, 1968), 18.
3 F. Chuev, *Tak govoril Kaganovich: Ispoved' staklinskogo apostola* (Moscow, 1992), 61, 73.
4 L. M. Kaganovich, *Pamyatnye zapiski* (Moscow, 1996), 500. Henceforth *PZ*.
5 *Istoriya KPSS* (1989) no. 2: 53. Cited in W. J. Tompson, *Khrushchev: A Political Life* (London, 1995), 116.
6 L. Schapiro, *The Communist Party of the Soviet Union* (London, 1978), 558. The Presidium comprised of Malenkov, Beria, Molotov, Voroshilov, Khrushchev, Bulganin, Kaganovich, Mikoyan, M. G. Pervukhin, and M. Z. Saburov; the candidates were N. M. Shvernik, P. K. Ponomarenko, L. G. Mel'nikov and M. D. Bagirov.
7 Amy Knight, *Beria: Stalin's First Lieutenant* (Princeton, 1993), 180–1.
8 Myron Rush, *How Communist States Change Their Rulers* (Ithaca, NY and London, 1974), 58.
9 Chuev, *Tak govoril Kaganovich*, 65–6.
10 Sergei Khrushchev (ed.), *Memoirs of Nikita Khrushchev: Vol. 2 Reformer (1945–1964)*, trans. George Shriver (Providence, RI, 2006), 193–4.
11 *Izvestiya TsK KPSS* (1991) no. 1: 187–8. Vera Tolz, 'The Death and "Second Life" of Lavrentii Beria', *Radio Liberty Research*, 23 December 1993.
12 D. Volkogonov, *Stalin: Triumph and Tragedy* (London, 1991), 333.
13 Ibid., 77–8, 79.
14 *PZ*, 503.
15 *Pravda*, 22 November 1953.
16 *Pravda*, 22 April 1954.
17 GARF, 5446/83/60–5446/83/108.
18 GARF, 5446/83/43, 47–8, 51–4, 81.
19 L. M. Kaganovich, *Rech' na pervoi sessi Verkhognogo Soveta SSSR* (Moscow, 1954), 6–24.
20 *Pravda*, 5 and 6 May 1954.
21 *Pravda*, 19 May 1954.
22 L. M. Kaganovich, *Uluchshit' rabotu i organizosat' novyi pod'em zheleznodorozhnogo transporta* (Moscow, 1954), 70.
23 'Tekhnicheskaya revolyutsiya', *Gudok*, 3 February 2006, 4. The charges directed at Kaganovich were made by P. M. Shilkin. I am grateful for this reference to John Westwood.
24 *Pravda*, 9 February 1955.
25 *PZ*, 517.
26 *Pravda*, 9 May 1955.

27 L. M. Kaganovich, *38-ya godovshchina velikoi Oktyabrskoi sotsialisticheskoi revolyutsi* (Moscow, 1955).
28 GARF, 5446/83/84, 43.
29 *Pravda*, 13 March 1954.
30 *Pravda*, 9 May 1955.
31 *Pravda*, 27 April, 1954.
32 L. M. Kaganovich, *Rech' na pervoi sessi Verkhognogo Soveta SSSR* (Moscow, 1954), 6–24.
33 A. A. Fursenko (ed.), *Prezidium TsK KPSS, 1954–1964*, vol. 1 (Moscow, 2004), 64, 903.
34 Ibid., 56–7.
35 Ibid., 88–9.
36 Ibid., 100, 925.
37 Volkogonov, *Stalin*, 578.
38 Chuev, *Tak govoril Kaganovich*, 44–5.
39 *PZ*, 508–9.
40 *XX s"ezd Kommunisticheskoi Partii Sovetskogo Soyuza: stenogragficheskii otchet*, vol. 1 (Moscow, 1956), 512.
41 A. Artizov, Yu. Sigachev, I. Shevchuk and B. Khlopov (eds), *Reabilitatsiya: Kak eto bylo: fevral' 1956-nachalo 80-x godov* (Moscow, 2003), 50.
42 Ibid., 385.
43 Ibid., 9, 19, 70, 71, 86, 101, 110, 122, 128, 132, 149, 198, 203, 204, 207, 209, 249, 251, 268.
44 Fursenko (ed.), *Prezidium TsK KPSS, 1954–1964*, vol. 1, 125, 139–40.
45 Knight, *Beria*, 223.
46 Fursenko (ed.), *Prezidium TsK KPSS, 1954–1964*, vol. 1, 9.
47 Ibid., 182–93; *Istoricheskii arkhiv* (1994) no. 7: 95, 115.
48 Ibid., 203, 980.
49 Ibid., 128.
50 Ibid., 809.
51 *Promyshlennost' SSSR: statisticheskii sbornik* (Moscow, 1964), 318, 329, 343.
52 Sergei Khrushchev (ed.), *Memoirs of Nikita Khrushchev: Vol. 2 Reformer*, 272.
53 Schapiro, *The Communist Party of the Soviet Union*, 563–4.
54 *Istoricheskii arkhiv* (1993) no. 3: 69.
55 *Stenograficheskii otchet, plenum Tsentralnogo Komiteta KPSS, 15–19 December 1958* (Moscow, 1958), 422. Cited in Carl A. Linden, *Khrushchev and the Soviet Leadership 1957–1964*, (Baltimore and London, 1976), 63.
56 *PZ*, 505.
57 Veljko Micunovic, *Moscow Diary* (London, 1980), 35, 66, 262.
58 Chuev, *Molotov Remembers*, 274.
59 *PZ*, 521–22.
60 *Molotov, Malenkov, Kaganovich, Stenogramma iionskogo plenuma TsK KPSS i drugie dokumenty*, compiled by N. Kovaleva, A. Korotkov, S. Mel'chin, Yu. Sigachev and A. Stepnov (Moscow, 1998), 70.
61 Ibid., 39–40.
62 Ibid., 67–8.
63 Ibid., 69.
64 Ibid., 69.
65 Ibid., 119–22.
66 Ibid., 247.

67 Ibid., 189.
68 Ibid., 247–8.
69 Ibid., 327.
70 Ibid., 353.
71 Sergei Khrushchev (ed.), *Memoirs of Nikita Khrushchev: Vol. 2 Reformer*, 124, 171.
72 Ibid., 395–9.
73 Ibid., 563–80.
74 D. Watson, *Molotov: A Biography* (Basingstoke, 2005), 262.
75 *The Road to Communism: Documents of the 22nd Congress of the Communist Party of the Soviet Union, October 17–31, 1961* (Moscow, 1961), 350–1.
76 *Molotov, Malenkov, Kaganovich, Stenogramma iionskogo plenuma TsK KPSS i drugie dokumenty*, 342.
77 Artizov et.al., *Reablilitatsiya*, 359
78 Chuev, *Tak govoril Kaganovich*, 193.
79 R. Medvedev, *All Stalin's Men* (Oxford, 1983), 130.
80 Jan Pakulski, 'Legitimation and Mass Compliance. Reflections on Max Weber and Soviet Type Societies', *British Journal of Political Science* 16, no. 1 (1986): 35–56.
81 *XX s"ezd Kommunisticheskoi Partii Sovetskogo Soyuza: stenograficheskii otchet*, vol. 1 (Moscow, 1961) 127, 253.
82 Ibid., 280.
83 Ibid., 394.
84 *XXII S"ezd KPSS*, vol. 2 (Moscow, 1961), p. 43.
85 Ibid., 215.
86 Ibid., 497.
87 Ibid., 464.
88 *XXII S"ezd KPSS*, vol. 3 (Moscow, 1961), 130.
89 Ibid., 153.
90 Fursenko, *Prezidium TsK KPSS, 1954–1964*, vol. 1, 488.
91 *PZ*, 503.
92 *PZ*, 507.
93 *PZ*, 511, 564–5.
94 *Moskovskie novosti*, 28 July 1996, 11.
95 Artizov et al., *Reablilitatsiya*, 575.
96 Chuev, *Tak govoril Kaganovich*, 186; *PZ*, 15–16.
97 Chuev, *Tak govoril Kaganovich*, 167.
98 Ibid., 152.
99 Ibid., 52.
100 F. Chuev, *Sto sorok besed s Molotvym* (Moscow, 1991), 319.
101 Ibid., 283, 364.
102 Chuev, *Tak govoril Kaganovich*, 67.
103 Ibid., 166.
104 Ibid., 35–6, 81, 191.
105 Ibid., 154.
106 Ibid., 27.
107 Ibid., 150.
108 Ibid., 38.
109 Ibid., 151.
110 Ibid., 126.

111 Ibid., 79.
112 Ibid., 82–3.
113 Ibid., 59.
114 Ibid., 101.
115 Ibid., 125–6, 141–3.
116 Ibid., 296.
117 Chuev, *Molotov Remembers*, 356.
118 Ibid., 254, 256, 258, 260, 263, 270, 275, 277–8, 279, 339.
119 'Dve besedy s L.M. Kaganovichem' in *Novaya i noveishaya istoriya* (1999) no. 2: 117.
120 Chuev, *Tak govoril Kaganovich*, 79, 88–9.
121 Ibid., 76.
122 Ibid., 138–9, 74–6.
123 Ibid., 56, 140.
124 Ibid., 141.
125 Ibid., 58, 101, 158.
126 Ibid., 105.
127 Ibid., 33.
128 N. S. Khrushchev, *The 'Secret' Speech*, ed. Zh. Medvedev and R. Medvedev (Nottingham, 1976), 20.
129 N. S. Khrushchev, *Khrushchev Remembers* (London, 1971), 262.
130 Ibid., 21, 27.
131 Ibid., 345.
132 Khrushchev, *The 'Secret' Speech*, 75.
133 Ibid., 59, 62.
134 Khrushchev, *Khrushchev Remembers*, 307.
135 Ibid., 210.
136 Ibid., 275.
137 Ibid., 289.
138 Khrushchev, *The 'Secret' Speech*, 76.
139 Khrushchev, *Khrushchev Remembers*, 133.
140 A. I. Mikoyan, *Tak bylo: razmyshleniya o minuvshem* (Moscow, 1999), 335–6, 358, 361, 589, 591.
141 Khrushchev, *The 'Secret' Speech*, 78.
142 Chuev, *Molotov Remembers*, 236.
143 Ibid., passim.
144 'Dve besedy s L.M. Kaganovichem' in *Novaya i noveishaya istoriya* (1999) no. 2: 116.
145 Chuev, *Tak govoril Kaganovich*, 54–5.
146 Medvedev, *All Stalin's Men*. 135–6.
147 Chuev, *Molotov Remembers*, 365.
148 Artizov et al., *Reablilitatsiya*, 538–9.
149 R. W. Davies, *Soviet History in the Yeltsin Era* (Basingstoke, 1997), 212–13.
150 Chuev, *Tak govoril Kaganovich*, 39.
151 Chuev, *Molotov Remembers*, 230–1.
152 Chuev, *Tak govoril Kaganovich*, 109, 146, 156, 182, 194.
153 Ibid., 93, 131, 147.
154 Ibid., 96, 127–8, 175.
155 Evgenyi Evseev, *Satrap* (Moscow, 1993), and his article 'Satrap', in *Kuban*, August 1989, 64–78. V. Rasputin in *Knizhnoe obozrenie* (1988, no. 14: 9), and Anatolyi Ivanov in *Nash sovremennik* (1988, no. 5: 175).

156 Ibid., 94–5.
157 *Sovetskaya kultura*, October 1990, 8 'Lazar' Kaganovich zagovoril...'
158 Chuev, *Tak govoril Kaganovich*, 19.
159 Ibid, 19, 90, 105.
160 Medvedev, *All Stalin's Men*, 113–14. David Remnick, *Lenin's Tomb* (Harmondsworth, 1995), 10–13, 34, 128, 441, 518.
161 Remnick, *Lenin's Tomb*, 442.
162 Chuev, *Tak govoril Kaganovich*, 91, 196.

BIBLIOGRAPHY

Russian Language Sources

Archival sources

GARF – Gosudarstvennyi arkhiv Rossisskoi Federatsii (State Archives of the Russian Federation)
RGASPI – Rossiskii gosudarstvennyi arkhiv sotsialno-politicheskoi istorii (Russian State Archives of Social-Political History)
TsGAOOU – Tsentral'noi gosudarstvennyi arkhiv obshchestvennykh organizatsii Ukrainy (Central State Archives of Social Organizations of the Ukraine)

Journals

Historical journals
Istochnik
Istoricheskii arkhiv
Istoriya KPSS
Leninskii sbornik
Novaya i noveishaya istoriya
Voenno-istoricheskii zhurnal
Voprosy istorii
Voprosy istorii KPSS

Party theoretical journals
Bol'shevik
Izvestiya TsK RKP(b)
Izvestiya TsK VKP(b)
Izvestiya TsK KPSS
Partiinoe stroitel'stvo
Sovetskoe gosudarstvo i pravo

Technical journals
Plannovoe khozyaistvo
Sotsialisticheskii transport

Other
Sotsialisticheskii vestnik

Newspapers

Ekonomicheskaya zhizn'
Gudok
Industriya
Izvestiya
Moskovskie novosti
Nizhegorodskaya kommuna
Raboche-krestyanskii nizhegorodskii listok
Pravda
Rabochaya Moskva
Vechernaya Moskva

Stenographic reports of Party Congresses and Conferences

Chetyrnadtsataya konferentsiya Rossiskoi kommunisticheskoi partii (Bolshevikov): Stenograficheskii otchet (Moscow-Leningrad, 1925)
Vos'moi s"ezd RKP(b), mart 1919 goda: Protokoly (Moscow, 1959)
Deviatyi s"ezd RKP(b): mart-aprel' 1920 goda: Protokoly (Moscow, 1960)
Desiatyi s"ezd RKP(b), mart 1921 goda: stenograficheskii otchet (Moscow, 1963)
Odinnadtsatsyi s"ezd RKP(b), mart-aprelya 1922 goda: stenograficheskii otchet (Moscow, 1961)
Trinatsatyi s"ezd RKP(b), mai 1924 goda: stenograficheskii otchet (Moscow, 1963)
XIV s"ezd Vsesoyuznoi kommunisticheskoi partii (b), 18–31 dekabrya 1925g: Stenograficheskii otchet (Moscow, 1926)
Piatnadtsatyi s"ezd VKP(b), dekabr' 1927 goda: stenograficheskii otchet, vols 1–2 (Moscow, 1961)
[Shestnadtsatyi] XVI s"ezd Vsesoyuznoi Kommunisticheskoi partii (b). Stenograficheskii otchet (Moscow, 1930)
[Semnadtsataya] XVII konferentsiya Vsesoyuznoi Kommunisticheskoi partii(b): stenograficheskii otchet (Moscow, 1932)
[Semnadtsatyi] XVII s"ezd Vsesoyuznoi Kommunisticheskoi partii (b). Stenograficheskii otchet (Moscow, 1934)
[Vosemnadtsatyi] XVIII S"ezd Vsesoyuznoi Kommunisticheskoi partii (b). Stenograficheskii otchet (Moscow, 1939)
XX S"ezda Kommunisticheskoi Partii Sovetskogo Soyuza: stenograficheskii otchet, vols 1–2 (Moscow, 1956)
Vneocherednoi XXI S"ezda Kommunisticheskoi Partii Sovetskogo Soyuza: stenograficheskii otchet, vols 1–2 (Moscow, 1959)
XXII S"ezda Kommunisticheskoi Partii Sovetskogo Soyuza: stenograficheskii otchet, vols 1–3 (Moscow, 1962)
IV Moskovskaya oblastnaya i III gorodskaya konferentsii Vsesoyuznoi Kommunisticheskoi Partii (b), 16–24 ianvaria 1934 g; Stenograficheskii otchet (Moscow, 1934)
Pervoe vsesoyuznoe soveshchanie rabochikh i rabotnits stakhanovtsev 14–17 noyabrya 1935: stenograficheskii otchet (Moscow, 1935)
The Road to Communism: Documents of the 22nd Congress of the Communist Party of the Soviet Union, October 17–31, 1961 (Moscow, 1961)

Document collections (Russian and Ukrainian)

Adibekov, G. M., K. M. Anderson and L. A. Rogovaya (eds), *Politbyuro TsK RKP(b)-VKP(b) Povestki dnia zasedanyi: Katalog*, vols 1–3: 1919–1929; 1930–39; 1940–52 (Moscow, 2000)

Anderson, K. M., P. Gregory, O. V. Khlevniuk, A. K. Sorokin, R. Sousa and A. Yu. Vatlin (eds), *Stenogrammy zasedanyi Politbyuro TsK RKP(b)-VKP(b) 1923-1939gg.*, vols 1–3 (Moscow, 2007)

Artizov, A., Yu. Sigachev, I. Shevchuk and B. Khlopov (eds), *Reabilitatsiya: Kak eto bylo: fevral' 1956-nachalo 80-x godov* (Moscow, 2003)

Bondareva, G. L. (ed.), *Kremlevskii Kinoteatr 1928–1953 Dokumenty* (Moscow, 2005)

Chesnokov, D. I. (ed.), *Nizhegorodskaya organizatsiya RKP(b) v gody inostranykh interventsiya i grazhdanskaya voina 1918–1920* (Gorky, 1957)

Dokumenty velikoi oktyabr'skoi sotsialisticheskoi revolyutsii v nizhegorodskoi gubernii (Gorky, 1945), 154

Desiat' let sovetskoi vlasti v nizhegorodskoi gubernii 1917–1927 (Nizhnyi Novgorod, 1927)

Fursenko, A. A. (ed.) *Prezidium TsK KPSS, 1954–1964*, vol. 1 (Moscow, 2004)

Gatalova, L. S., L.P. Kosheleva, L.A. Rogovaya and Dzh. Kaio (eds), *TsK VKP(b) i Natsional'nyi Vopros, Kniga 2, 1933–1945* (Moscow, 2009)

Golod 1932–1933 rokiv na Ukraini: ochima istorikiv, novoyu dokumentiv (Kiev, 1990)

Golodomor 1932–33 rr b Ukraini: prichini i naslidki. Mizhnarodna naukova konferentsiya (Kiev, 1993)

Junge, Mark, Gennadii Bordiugov and Rol'f Binner, *Vertikal' Bol'shogo Terrora: Istoria operatsia po prikazy NKVD No.00447* (Moscow, 2008)

Khlevniuk, O. V., R. W. Davies, L. P. Kosheleva, E. A. Rees and L. A. Rogovaya (eds), *Stalin i Kaganovich Perepiska. 1931–1936gg.* (Moscow, 2001)

Khlevniuk, O. V., A. V. Kvashonkin, L. P. Kosheleva and L. A. Rogovaya (eds), *Stalinskoe Politbyuro v 30-e gody: Sbornik dokumentov* (Moscow, 1995)

Khlevniuk, O. V., I. Gorlitskii, L. P. Kosheleva, A.I. Miniuk, M. Iu. Prozumeshchikov, L. A. Rogovaya and S. V. Somonova (compilers), *Politbyuro TsK VKP(b) i Sovet Ministrov SSSR 1945–1953: Sbornik dokumentov* (Moscow, 2002)

Khlevniuk, O. V., P. Gregory and A. Vatlin (eds), *Stenogrammy zasedanii Politbyuro TsK VKP(b), 1923–1938* (Moscow, 2007)

Kosheleva, L., V. Lelchuk, V. Naumov, O. Naumov, I. Rogovaya and O. V. Khlevniuk (eds), *Pis'ma, I.V. Stalina, V.M. Molotovu 1925–1936gg.: Sbornik dokumentov* (Moscow, 1995)

Kommunisticheskaya partiya Sovetskogo Soyuza v rezolyutsiyakh i resheniyakh s'ezdov, konferentsii i plenumov TsK (Moscow, 1984; 9th ed.)

Kovaleva, N., A. Korotkov, S. Mel'chin, Iu. Sigachev and A. Stepnov (compilers), *Molotov, Malenkov, Kaganovich. 1957: Stenogramma iiun'skogo plenuma TsK KPSS i drugie dokumenty* (Moscow, 1998)

KPSS v rezolyutsiyakh i resheniyakh, s"ezdov, konferentsii i plenumov TsK, 1898–1954, vols 1–4 (Moscow, 1953–1960; 7th ed.)

KPSS v rezolyutsiyakh i resheniyakh, s"ezdov, konferentsii i plenumov TsK, 1898–1981, vols 1–14 (Moscow, 1972–1984; 8th ed.)

Kvashonkin, A. V., O. V. Khlevniuk, L. P. Kosheleva and L. A. Rogovaya (eds), *Bol'shevistskoe rukovodstvo. Perepiska. 1912–1927* (Moscow, 1996)

Kvashonkin, A. V., L. P. Kosheleva, L. A. Rogovaya and O. V. Khlevniuk (eds), *Sovetskoe rukovodstvo. Perepiska. 1928–1941* (Moscow, 1999)

Livshin, A. Ia. and I. B. Orlov (eds), *Pis'ma vo vlast'. 1917–1927* (Moscow, 1998)

Perepiska Sekretariat TsK RKP(b) c mestnymi partiinymi organizatsiyami (yanvarya-mart 1919g) (Moscow 1971)

Pokrovsky, N. N. and S. G. Petrov, *Arkhivy Kremlya: Politbyuro i tserkov 1922–1925gg.* (Moscow, 1997)
Politbyuro, Orgbyuro, Sekretariat TsK RKP(b)-VKP(b)-KPSS: Spravochnik (Moscow, 1990)
Politbyuro (Prezidium) TsK Partii v 1917–1989gg: Personali spravochno (Moscow, 1990)
'Posetiteli kremlevskogo kabineta I. V. Stalina: Zhurnaly (tetradi) zapisi lits, priniatykh pervym gensekom 1924–1953gg' (compiled by A. V. Korotkov and A. A. Chernobaev), *Istoricheskii arkhiv* (1994) no. 6; (1995) nos. 1–6; (1996) nos. 1–6; (1997) no. 1
Resheniya partii i pravitel'stva po khoziaistvennym voprosam, vol. 2 (Moscow, 1967)
Preobrazhensky, E. A. (ed.), *1917–1920, Khronika revolyutsionykh sobitii v Gorkov'skom krae.* (Gorky, 1932)
Yakovlev, A. N. (ed), *Reabilitatsiya: politicheskie protsessy 30–50-kh godov* (Moscow, 1991)
Zabveniyu ne Podlezhit: Neizvestnye stranitsy nizhegorodskoi istorii (1918–1984 gody) (Nizhnyi Novgorod, 1994)
Zelenin, I. (chief ed.), *Tragediya sovetskoi derevni; kollektivizatsiya i raskulachivanie; Dokumenty i materialy; Tom. 3, Konets 1930–1933* (Moscow, 2001)

Books and articles (Russian and Ukrainian)

Aksenov, Iu. S., 'Apogei stalinizma: Poslevoennaya piramida vlasti', *Voprosy istorii KPSS* (1990) no. 11: 90–104
Chernev, A., *229 kremlevskikh vozhdei. Politbyuro, Orgbyuro, Sekretariat TsK Komunisticheskoi partii v litsakh i tsifrakh* (Moscow, 1996)
Chuev, F., *Sto sorok besed s Molotvym* (Moscow, 1991)
——— *Tak govoril Kaganovich: Ispoved' staklinskogo apostola* (Moscow, 1992)
Danilov, A. A., 'Stalinskoe politbyuro v poslevoennye gody', *Politicheskie partii Rossii: Stranitsy Istorii* (Moscow, 2000)
'Dve besedy s L. M. Kaganovichem', *Novaya i noveishaya istoriya* (1999) no. 2: 101–22
Evseev, Evgenyi, *Satrap* (Moscow, 1993)
Gambarov, Yu. S., V. Ya. Zheleznov, M. M. Kovalevsky, S. A. Muromtsev, K. A. Timiryazev (eds), *Entsiklopedicheskii Slovar': Russkogo Bibliograficheskogo Instituta Granat* (Moscow, 1989)
Ivkin, Vladimir, 'Rukovoditeli Sovetskogo pravitel'stva (1923–1991): Istoriko-biograficheskaya spravka', *Istochnik* (1996) no. 4: 152–92; (1996) no. 5: 135–60
Ivnitskii, N. A., *Kollektivizatysiya i raskulachivanie (nachalo 30-x godov)* (Moscow, 1994)
Khasanov, K., *V. I. Lenin i Turkbyuro TsK RKP(b)* (Tashkent, 1969)
Khlevniuk, O. V., *Stalin, NKVD i sovetskoe obshchestvo* (Moscow, 1992)
——— *Stalin i Ordzhonikidze. Konfl ikty v Politbyuro v 30-e gody* (Moscow, 1993)
——— *Politbyuro: mekhanizmy politicheskoi vlasti v 1930-e gody* (Moscow, 1996)
——— 'Stalin i Molotov: Edinolichnaya diktatura i predposylki 'kolletivnogo rukovodstva', in G. S. Sagatelian (ed.), *Stalin, Stalinism, Sovetskoe Obshchestvo: Sbornik statei k-70 letyu prof. V.S. Lel'chuk* (Moscow, 2000)
Kirilina, A., *Rikoshet, ili skol'ko chelovek bylo ubito vystrelom v Smol'nom* (St Petersburg, 1993)
Kislitsyn, S. A., *Shakhtinskoe delo: nachalo stalinskikh repressii protiv nauchno-tekhnicheskoi intelligentsii v SSSR* (Rostov on Don, 1993)
Kumanev, G. A., *Na sluzhbe fronta i tyla: zheleznodorozhnyi transport SSSR nakanune i v gody velikoi otchestvennoi voiny 1938–1945gg* (Moscow, 1976)
Larina, Anna, *Nezabyvaemoe* (Moscow, 1989)

Lenin, V. I., *Polnoe sobranie sochinenii V. I. Lenina*, vols 1–55 (Moscow, 1958–1965)
Malashkin, Sergei, *Muskuly: Poemy* (Nizhny Nogorod, 1919; 2nd ed.)
Medvedev, R., S. Parofenov and P. Khmelinskii, *Zhelezni yastreb* (Ekaterinburg, 1992)
Mikoyan, A. I., *Tak bylo: razmyshleniya o minuvshem* (Moscow, 1999)
Pikhoia, R. G., 'O vnutripoliticheskoi bor'be v Sovetskom rukovodstve 1945–1958 gg.', *Novaya i noveishaya istoriya* (1995) no. 6: 3–14
_____, *Sovetskii Soyuz: Istorii a Vlasti 1945–1991* (Moscow, 1998)
Shapoval, Yu., 'Kaganovich na Ukraine', *Ukrainskii istoricheskii zhurnal* (1990) no. 8: 62–74; (1990) no. 10: 117–29
_____, *Lazar Kaganovich* (Kiev, 1993)
Shreider, M., *NKVD iznutri: sapiski chekista* (Moscow, 1995)
Stalin, I. V. *Sochineniya*, vols 1–13 (Moscow, 1952–4)
Svanidze, Maria Anisimova, 'Iosif Beskonechno Dobr.' (extract from the diary of M. A. Svanidze 1933–7), *Istochnik* (1993) no. 1: 4–34
Vaganyan, V., *O natsional'noi kulture* (Moscow, 1927)
Vasiliev, Valery and Yuri Shapoval, *Komandiry Bol'shogo Goloda: Poezdki V. Molotova i L. Kaganovicha v Ukrainu i na Severnyi Kavkaz 1932–1933 gg* (Kiev, 2001)
Voskoboinikov, E., and A. Zevelev, *Turkkomissiya VTsIK i Sovnarkoma RSFSR i Turkbyuro TsK RKP(b) v bor'be za ukreplenie sovetskoi vlasti v Turkestane (M. V. Frunze, V. V. Kuibyshev, L. M. Kaganovich v Turkestane)* (Tashkent, 1951)
Zabveniyu ne Podlezhit: Neizvestnye stranitsy nizhegorodskoi istorii (1918–1984 gody) (Nizhnyi Novgorod, 1994)
Zhukov, Yu., 'Bor'ba za vlast' v rukovodstve SSSR v 1945–1952 godakh', *Voprosy istorii* (1995) no. 1: 23–39
_____, *Tainy Kremlina: Stalin, Molotov, Beria, Malenkov* (Moscow, 2000)

Works by Kaganovich (in Russian)

Kaganovich, L. M., 'Blizhaishie zadachi raboty orgotdelov', *Izvestiya TsK RKP(b)* (1923) no. 1: 3–10
_____, *Boevoi zadachi Moskovskoi partiinoi organizatsii po pod'emu sel'skogo khozyaistvo i ukreplenie kolkhozov* (Moscow, 1932)
_____, *Dva goda ot IX do X s"ezda KP(b) Ukraina* (Kharkov, 1927)
_____, 'Dvenadtsatyi let stroitel'stva sovetskogo gosudarstva i bor'ba c opportunismom', *Sovetskoe gosudarstvo i revolyutsiya prava* (1930) no. 1: 7–43
_____, 'God pod'ema i blizhaishie zadachi zheleznodorozhnogo transporta', *Partiinoe stroitel'stvo* (1936) no. 13: 10–55
_____, *Itogi XIV S"ezda VKP(b)* (Kharkov, 1926)
_____, 'Itogi noyabrs'kogo plenuma TsK VKP(b)', *Partiinoe stroitel'stvo* (1935) nos. 1–2: 11–18.
_____, *Itogi sentyabr'skogo plenuma TsK VKP(b)* (Moscow-Tashkent, 1932)
_____, *Kak postroena RKP (Bol'shevikov); Ob ustave partii* (Ekaterinoslav' and elsewhere, 1924, 1925, 1926)
_____, *Kak postroena VKP(b)* (Moscow-Leningrad, 1927, 1929)
_____, *Kak stroitsia sovetskaya vlast': Polozhenie ob organizatsionnom stroitel'stva gubernskoi sovetskom vlasti* (Voronezh, 1920)
_____, *Kak ulushit' rabotu sovetov v derevne* (Moscow, 1924)
_____, *Kontrol'nye tsifry tret'ego goda piatiletki i zadachi Moskovskoi organizatsii* (Moscow, 1931)

———, 'Lenin i Stalin s isklyuchitel'noi zabotlivost'yu vypestovali komsomol', *Partiinoe stroitel'stvo* (1933) no. 22: 1–6

———, *Mestnoe sovetskoe samoupravlenie. Stroitel'stva Sovetskoe vlast na mestakh* (Moscow, 1923)

———, *Mezhdunarodnoe i vnutrennoe polozhenie i zadachi komsomola* (Moscow, 1931)

———, *Na putyakh k okonchatel'nomu prevrashcheniya moskovskoi oblasti iz potrebliayushchei v proizvodyashchiyu* (Moscow, 1932). Also published in *Partiinoe stroitel'stvo* (1933) nos. 13–14: 1–7

———, *Na putiakh stroitel'stvo sotsializm* (Kharkov, 1926)

———, 'Ob apparate TsK VKP(b)', *Partinnoe stroitel'stvo* (1930) no. 2: 9–13

———, 'Ob itogakh sentyabr'skogo plenuma TsK i zadachakh moskovskoi organizatsii', *Partiinoe stroitel'stvo* (1932) nos. 19–20: 6–15

———, 'Ob uluchshenii raboty sovetov', *Izvestiya TsK RKP(b)*, no. 11, 15 December 1924

———, 'Ocherednye zadachi partiino-massovoi raboty yacheik', *Partiinoe stroitel'stvo* (1932) nos. 11–12: 1–9

———, 'Ocherednye zadachi partraboty i reorganizatsiya partapparata' (Moscow-Leningrad, 1930)

———, *O chistke partii* (Moscow, 1933). Also published in *Partiinoe stroitel'stvo* (1933) no. 11: 1–11.

———, 'O rabote instruktorov', *Izvestiya TsK VKP(b)*, no. 4 (263), 15 February 1929, 1–2.

———, 'O rabote sredi kandidatov i novykh chlenov partii', *Izvestiya TsK RKP(b)*, no. 7 (12), 17 November 1924, 1

———, *O stroitel'stve metropolitena i plana goroda Moskvy* (Moscow, 1934)

———, *Ot XV k XVI s"ezdu VKP(b)(doklad o rabote TsK VKP(b) na 2-i Moskovskoi oblastnoi konferentsii, 3 iyulia 1930)* (Moscow, 1930)

———, 'O vnutripartiinoi rabote o otdelakh rukovodyashchikh partinykh organov', *Partiinoe stroitel'stvo* (1934) no. 22: 1–12, and in *Bol'shevik* (1934) no. 21: 8–19

———, 'O vospitanii leninskogo prizyva', *Izvestiya TsK RKP(b)*, no. 12 (17), 22 December 1924, 1–3

———, 'O vydvizhenii i vovlechenii v prakticheskuyu raboty v nov' vstypivshikh v partiyu rabochikh', *Izvestiya TsK RKP(b)*, no. 7 (82), 16 February 1925, 1–2

———, *O zadachakh Komsomola* (Moscow, 1929)

———, *O zadachakh profsoyuzov SSSR na dannom etape razvitie* (Baku, 1932). Also published in *Partiinoe stroitel'stvo* (1932) no. 10: 1–12

———, *O zadachakh partiinoi kontrolia i kontrolnoi rabote profsoyuzov, komsomola i pechati* (Moscow, 1934). Also published in *Partiinoe stroitel'stvo* (1934) no. 13: 1–10

———, *Pamyatnye knizhka sovetskogo stroitelia* (Tashkent, 1920)

———, *Pamyatnye zapiski rabochego, kommunista-bol'shevika, profsoyuznogo, partiinogo i sovetskogo rabotnika* (Moscow, 1996)

———, *Pobeda metropolitena-pobeda sotsializma* (Moscow, 1935)

———, 'Po-bol'shevistski borot'sia za perevypolnenie plana zheleznodorozhnym transportom', *Partiinoe stroitel'stvo* (1935) no. 10: 4–9

———, 'Politicheskie zadachi kampanii perevyborov v sovety', *Bol'shevik* (1928) no. 19: 8–23

———, *Postroem pervuyu ochered' metro k XVII godovshchinee oktyabrya* (Moscow, 1934)

———, 'Problem kadrov', *Bol'shevik* (1929) nos. 23–24: 50–71

———, *Rabota partii i oppozitsiya* (Kharkov, 1926)

———, *Rech' na pervoi sessi Verkhognogo Soveta SSSR* (Moscow, 1954)

———, *Rech' na soveshanie po voprosam stroitel'stva* (Moscow, 1935)
———, *Sotsialisticheskaya rekonstruktsiya i zadachi partii* (Sverdlovsk, 1929)
———, 'Stakhanovsko-krivonosovskoe dvizhenie- zalog novogo moshchnogo sotsialisticheskogo khoyaistva', *Partiinoe stroitel'stvo* (1935) nos. 19–20: 14–26
———, 'Stalinskii god na zheleznodorozhnom transporte', *Partiinoe stroitel'stvo* (1936) no. 16: 24–34 (published as pamphlet by Partizdat)
———, *38-ya godovshchina velikoi Oktyasbrskoi sotsialisticheskoi revolutsii* (Moscow, 1955)
———, *Tseli i zadachi politicheskikh otdelov MTS i sovkhozov* (Moscow, 1933), also published as article in *Bol'shevik* (1933) nos. 1–2: 12–37 and *Partiinoe stroitel'stvo* (1933) nos. 3–4: 1–22
———, *Ukreplenie kolkhozov i zadachi vesennogo seva* (Novosibirsk, 1933)
———, *Uluchshit' rabotu i organizosat' novyi pod'em zheleznodorozhnogo transporta* (Moscow, 1954)
———, *Ulushenie raboty sovetov v derevne* (Moscow, 1924)
———, 'Velikyi machinist lokomotiva istorii', *Bol'shevik* (1940) no. 1: 33–40
———, *Voprosy zheleznodorozhnogo transporta v svyaz so stakhanovskim dvizheniem* (Moscow, 1936)
———, *Vvedenie novykh pravil tekhnicheskoi ekspluatatsii i likvidatsiya krushenie i avarii* (Moscow, 1936)
———, *Za bol'shevistskoe izuchenie istorii partii* (Moscow, 1932). Also published in *Partiinoe stroitel'stvo* (1931) no. 24: 1–12
———, *Za pod'em ugol'nogo Donbassa* (Moscow, 1937)
———, *Za sotsialisticheskuyu rekonstruktsiyu Moskvy i gorodov SSSR* (Moscow-Leningrad, 1931)
Kaganovich, L. M. and V. Chubar', *Itogi plenuma TsK i TsKK VKP(b) (iyul' 1926 goda)* (Kharkov, 1926)
Kaganovich, L. M. and V. M. Molotov, *Zadachi Ukrainskikh Bol'shevikov v rabote na sele* (Moscow-Leningrad, 1932). Kaganovich's report is published also in *Partiinoe stroitel'stvo* (1932) no. 14: 1–8
Kaganovich, L. M. and L. O. Utesov, *Kak organizovat zheleznodorozhnye ansambli pesni i pliaski i dzhaz orkestr* (Moscow, 1939)

Works by Kaganovich (in English translation)

Kaganovich, L. M., *Socialist Reconstruction of Moscow and Other Cities in the USSR* (London, 1931)
———, *Report on the Organizational Problems of Party and Social Construction* (Moscow, 1934)
———, *The Construction of the Subway and the Plan for the City of Moscow* (Moscow, 1934)
———, *Stalin Is Leading Us to the Victory of Communism* (Moscow, 1950)

English Language Sources

Books and articles

Agursky, Mikhail, *The Third Rome: National Bolshevism in the USSR* (Boulder, CO and London, 1987)
Apor, Balázs, Jan C. Behrends, Polly Jones and E. A. Rees (eds), *The Leader Cult in Communist Dictatorships: Stalin and the Eastern Bloc* (Basingstoke, 2004)
Bailes, Kendal E., *Technology and Society under Lenin and Stalin: Origins of the Soviet Technical Intelligentsia, 1917–1941* (Princeton, 1978)
Barber, John, *Soviet Historians in Crisis* (London, 1981)

Bazhanov, Boris, *Bazhanov and the Damnation of Stalin* (trans. and commentary David W. Doyle) (Athens, OH, 1990)
Benvenuti, Francesco, *The Bolsheviks and the Red Army, 1918–1922* (Cambridge, 1988)
Bessedovskii, G., *Revelations of a Soviet Diplomat* (trans. Matthew Norgate) (London, 1931)
Birt, Raymond, 'Personality and Foreign Policy: The Case of Stalin', *Political Psychology* 14, no. 4 (1993): 607–25
Boobbyer, P., *Conscience, Dissent and Reform in Soviet Russia* (London, 2009)
Brovkin, Vladimir N., *Behind the Front Lines of the Civil War: Political Parties and Social Movements in Russia, 1918–1921* (Princeton, 1994)
Brovkin, Vladimir N., *Dear Comrades: Menshevik Reports on the Bolshevik Revolution and the Civil War* (Stanford, 1991)
Brower, Daniel R., 'The Smolensk Scandal and the End of NEP', *Slavic Review* 4 (1986): 689–706
Carr, E. H., *The Bolshevik Revolution*, vol. 2 (London, 1966)
———, *The Interregnum, 1923–24* (Harmondsworth, 1969)
———, *Socialism in One Country 1924–1926*, vol. 1 (Harmondsworth, 1970)
———, *Socialism in One Country 1924–1926*, vol. 2 (Harmondsworth, 1970)
———, *Foundations of a Planned Economy 1926–29*, vol. 2 (London, 1971)
Carr, E. H. and Davies, R. W. *Foundations of a Planned Economy, 1926–1929*, vol. 1 (London, 1969)
Chamberlin, W. H., *The Russian Revolution 1917–1921*, vols 1–2 (London, 1935)
Checkley, Harvey, *The Mask of Sanity* (St Louis, MO, 1941)
Chuev, Felix, *Molotov Remembers: Inside Kremlin Politics* (ed. Albert Resis) (Chicago, 1993)
Cohen, Stanley, *States of Denial: Knowing about Atrocities and Suffering* (Cambridge, 2001)
Cohen, Stephen, *Bukharin and the Bolshevik Revolution: A Political Biography, 1888–1938* (Oxford, 1980)
Colton, Timothy J., *Moscow: Governing the Socialist Metropolis* (Cambridge, MA, 1995)
Conquest, R., *The Great Terror* (Harmondsworth, 1971)
———, *Inside Stalin's Secret Police: NKVD Politics 1936–39* (Basingstoke and London, 1986)
———, *The Harvest of Sorrow* (London, 1988)
Cooper, J. M., M. Perrie and E. A. Rees (eds), *Soviet History 1917–1953: Essays in Honour of R. W. Davies* (Basingstoke, 1995)
Crowfoot, John and Mark Harrison, 'The USSR Council of Ministers under Late Stalinism, 1945–1954: Its Production Branch Composition and the Requirements of National Economy and Policy', *Soviet Studies* 42, no. 1 (1990): 39–58.
Daniels, R. V., *The Conscience of the Revolution: Communist Opposition in Soviet Russia* (Cambridge, MA, 1965)
Davies, R. W., 'A Note on Defence Aspects of the Ural-Kuznetsk Combine', *Soviet Studies* 26, no. 2 (1974): 272–3
———, *The Industrialisation of Soviet Russia 1: The Socialist Offensive: The Collectivisation of Soviet Agriculture, 1929–1930* (London, 1980)
———, *The Industrialisation of Soviet Russia 2: The Soviet Collective Farm, 1929–1930* (Basingstoke and London, 1980)
———, 'The Syrtsov-Lominadze Affair', *Soviet Studies* 33, no. 1 (1981): 29–50
———, *The Industrialisation of Soviet Russia 3: The Soviet Economy in Turmoil, 1929–1930* (London, 1989)
———, *Soviet History in the Gorbachev Revolution* (Basingstoke and London, 1989)

———, *The Industrialisation of Soviet Russia 4: Crisis and Progress in the Soviet Economy, 1931–1933* (London 1996)
———, *Soviet History in the Yeltsin Era* (Basingstoke and London, 1997)
Davies, R. W. and O. V. Khlevniuk, 'Stakhanovism and the Soviet Economy', *Europe-Asia Studies* 54, no. 6 (2002): 867–903
Davies, R. W. and S. G. Wheatcroft, *The Industrialisation of Soviet Russia 5: The Years of Hunger: Soviet Agriculture, 1931–1933* (Basingstoke and London, 2003)
Davies, R. W., M. Harrison, and S. G. Wheatcroft, *The Economic Transformation of the Soviet Union, 1913–1945* (Cambridge, 1994)
Davies, R. W., M. J. Ilič, H. P. Jenkins, C. Merridale and S. G. Wheatcroft (eds), *Soviet Government Officials, 1922–41: A Handlist* (Birmingham, 1989)
Davies, R. W., E. A. Rees, O. V. Khlevniuk, L. P. Kosheleva and L. A. Rogovaya (eds), *The Stalin-Kaganovich Correspondence* (New Haven, CT and London, 2003)
Davies, Sarah, *Popular Opinion in Stalin's Russia: Terror, Propaganda and Dissent, 1934–1941* (Cambridge, 1997)
Davies, Sarah and James Harris, *Stalin: A New History* (Cambridge, 2005)
Deutscher, I., *Stalin: A Political Biography* (London, 1966)
———, *The Prophet Unarmed: Trotskii 1921–1929* (Oxford, 1970)
Duncan, Peter, *Russian Messianism: Third Rome, Revolution, Communism and After* (Routledge, 2000)
Ellman, Michael, 'The Role of Leadership Perceptions and of Intent in the Soviet Famine of 1931–1934', *Europe-Asia Studies* 57, no. 6 (2005): 823–41
Essad-Bey, *Stalin: The Career of a Fanatic* (trans. Huntley Paterson) (London, 1932)
Figes, Orlando, *A People's Tragedy: The Russian Revolution 1891–1924* (London, 1996)
———, *The Whisperers: Private Life in Stalin's Russia* (London, 2007)
Figes, Orlando and Boris Kolonitsky, *Interpreting the Russian Revolution: The Language and Symbols of 1917* (Yale University Press, 1999)
Fitzpatrick, Sheila, 'Stalin and the making of a new elite, 1928–1939', *Slavic Review* 38, no. 3 (1979): 377–402
———, 'Ordzhonikidze's Takeover of Vesenkha: A Case Study in Soviet Bureaucratic Politics', *Soviet Studies* 37, no. 2 (1985): 153–72
———, (ed.), *Stalinism: New Directions* (London and New York, 2000)
Garros, V., N. Korenevskaya and T. Lahusen (eds), *Intimacy and Terror: Soviet Diaries of the 1930s* (New York, 1995)
Getty, J. Arch, *Origins of the Great Purges: The Soviet Communist Party Reconsidered, 1933–1938* (Cambridge, 1985)
Getty, J. Arch and Oleg V. Naumov, *The Road to Terror: Stalin and the Self-Destruction of the Bolsheviks, 1932–1939* (New Haven, CT and London, 1999)
———, *Yezhov: The Rise of Stain's 'Iron Fist'* (New Haven, CT, 2008)
Getty, J. Arch and Roberta T. Manning (eds), *Stalinist Terror: New Perspectives* (Cambridge, 1993)
Gill, Graeme, *The Origins of the Stalinist Political System* (Cambridge, 1990)
Gorlizki, Yoram, 'Party Revivalism and the Death of Stalin,' *Slavic Review* 54, no.1 (1995): 1–22
———, 'Stalin's Cabinet: the Politburo and Decision Making in the Post-war Years', *Europe-Asia Studies* 53, no. 2 (2001): 291–312
———, 'Ordinary Stalinism: The Council of Ministers and the Soviet Neo-Patrimonial State, 1945–1953', *Journal of Modern History* 74, no. 4 (2002): 699–736
Gorlizki, Yoram and O. V. Khlevniuk, *Cold Peace: Stalin and the Soviet Ruling Circle 1945–1953* (Oxford, 2004)

Graziosi, Andrea, *The Great Soviet Peasant War: Bolsheviks and Peasants 1917–1933* (Cambridge, MA, 1996)
Gregor, A. James, *Italian Fascism and Developmental Dictatorship* (Princeton, 1979)
Gregory, Paul (ed.), *Behind the Façade of Stalin's Command Economy* (Stanford, CA, 2001)
Gregory, Paul R. and Norman Naimark (eds), *The Lost Politburo Transcripts: From Collective Rule to Stalin's Dictatorship* (New Haven, CT and London, 2008)
Habermas, Jürgen, *Legitimation Crisis* (trans. Thomas McCarthy) (London, 1992)
———, *The Structural Transformation of the Public Sphere: Inquiry into a Category of Bourgeois Society* (trans. Thomas Berger) (London, 1992)
Hagenloh, Paul, *Stalin's Police: Public Order and Mass Repression in the USSR, 1926–1941* (Washington DC and Baltimore, 2009)
Hahn, Werner G., *Postwar Soviet Politics: The Fall of Zhdanov and the Defeat of Moderation, 1948–1953* (Ithaca, NY and London, 1982)
Halfin, Igal (ed.), *Language and Revolution: Making of Modern Political Identities* (London, 2002)
Harris, James R., *The Great Urals: Regionalism and the Evolution of the Soviet System* (Ithaca, NY, 1999)
———, (ed.), *Anatomy of Terror* (Oxford, 2012)
Harris, Jonathan, 'The Origins of the Conflict between Malenkov and Zhdanov, 1939–41', *Slavic Review* 35, no. 2 (1976): 287–303
Hellbeck, J., *Revolution on My Mind: Writing a Diary under Stalin* (Cambridge, MA, 2006)
Hoffmann, David L. (ed.), *Stalinism: The Essential Readings* (Oxford, 2003)
Hughes, James, 'The Irkutsk Affair: Stalin, Siberian Politics and the End of NEP', *Soviet Studies* 41, no. 2 (1989): 228–53.
———, 'Patrimonialism and the Stalinist System: The Case of S. I. Syrtsov', *Europe-Asia Studies* 48, no. 4 (1996): 551–68.
———, *Stalinism in a Russian Province: Collectivisation and Dekulakisation in Siberia* (Basingstoke, 1996)
Hunter, H., *Soviet Transportation Policy*, (Cambridge, MA, 1957)
Ilič, Melanie (ed.), *Stalin's Terror Revisited* (Basingstoke, 2006)
Kahan, Stuart, *The Wolf in the Kremlin* (London, 1987)
Kangaspuro, Markku and Jeremy Smith (eds), *Modernisation in Russia since 1900* (Helsinki, 2006)
Kelly, Catriona, *Comrade Pavlik: The Rise and Fall of a Soviet Boy Hero* (London, 2005)
Kershaw, Ian, and Moshe Lewin (eds), *Stalinism and Nazism: Dictatorships in Comparison* (Cambridge, 1997)
Kets de Vries, Manfred F. R., *Reflections on Character and Leadership* (Chichester, 2009)
Khakhordin, Oleg, *The Collective and the Individual in Russia: A Study of Practices* (Berkeley, CA, 1999)
Khlevniuk, O. V., *In Stalin's Shadow. The Career of 'Sergo' Ordzhonikidze* (New York, London, 1995)
———, *The Master of the House: Stalin and his inner circle* (trans. Nora Seligman Favorov) (New Haven, CT and London, 2009)
Khlevniuk, O. V. and R. W. Davies, 'The End of Rationing in the Soviet Union, 1934–1935', *Europe-Asia Studies* 51, no. 4 (1999): 557–609
Khrushchev, N. S., *Khrushchev Remembers* (trans. Strobe Talbot, introduction and commentary by Edward Crankshaw) (London, 1971)
———, *The 'Secret' Speech* (introduction by Zhores A. Medvedev and Roy A. Medvedev) (Nottingham, 1976)
———, *Khrushchev Remembers: The Glasnost Tapes* (trans. and ed. Jerrold L. Schecter) (Boston, 1990)

Khrushchev, Sergei (ed.), *Memoirs of Nikita Khrushchev: Vol. 2 Reformer (1945–1964)* (trans. George Shriver) (Providence, RI, 2006)
Knight, Amy, *Beria: Stalin's First Lieutenant* (Princeton, 1993)
Kostiuk, Hryhory, *Stalinist Rule in the Ukraine: A Study of the Decade of Mass Terror (1929–39)* (London, 1960)
Kotkin, Stephen, *Magnetic Mountain: Stalinism as Civilization* (Berkeley, CA and London, 1995)
Kravchenko, V., *I Chose Freedom* (New York, 1946)
Lane, Christel, *The Rites of Rulers: Ritual in Industrial Society – The Soviet Case* (Cambridge, 1981)
Leggett, G., *The Cheka: Lenin's Political Police* (London, 1981)
Lenoe, M. E., *The Kirov Murder and Soviet History* (New Haven, CT, 2010)
Lewin, M., *Russian Peasants and Soviet Power* (London, 1968)
———, *The Making of the Soviet System* (London, 1985)
Lih, Lars T., O. V. Naumov and O. V. Khlevniuk (eds), *Stalin's Letters to Molotov* (New Haven, CT, 1995)
Linden, Carl A., *Khrushchev and the Soviet Leadership 1957–1964* (Baltimore and London, 1976)
———, *The Soviet-Party State: The Politics of Ideocratic Despotism* (New York, 1983)
Mace, James E., *Communism and the Dilemmas of National Liberation: National Communism in Soviet Ukraine, 1918–1933* (Cambridge, MA, 1983)
Marples, David R., *Stalinism in the Ukraine in the 1940s* (London and New York, 1992)
Martin, Terry, *The Affirmative Action Empire: Nations and Nationalism in the Soviet Union, 1923–1939* (Ithaca, NY and London, 2001)
McDermott, Kevin, *Stalin* (Basingstoke, 2006)
McLoughlin, Barry and Kevin McDermott (eds), *Stalin's Terror: High Politics and Mass Repression in the Soviet Union* (Basingstoke, 2003)
McNeal, Robert H., *Stalin: Man and Ruler* (New York, 1988)
Medvedev, R., *Let History Judge* (London, 1976)
———, *On Stalin and Stalinism* (Oxford, 1979)
———, *All Stalin's Men* (Oxford, 1983)
Medvedev, Zhores A. and R. Medvedev, *The Unknown Stalin* (trans. Ellen Dahrendorf) (London and New York, 2003)
Meier, Hans (ed.), *Totalitarianism and Political Religions: Vol.1 Concepts for the Comparison of Dictatorship* (trans. Jodi Bruhn) (London, 2004)
Merridale, Catherine, *Moscow Politics and the Rise of Stalin: The Communist Party in the Capital, 1925–1932* (Basingstoke and London, 1990)
Nethercott, Frances, *Russian Legal Culture Before and After Communism: Criminal Justice, Politics and the Public Sphere* (London, 2007)
Nicolaevskii, Boris I., *Power and the Soviet Elite* (trans. Douglas Smith) (London, 1965)
Pakulski, Jan, 'Legitimation and Mass Compliance: Reflections on Max Weber and Soviet Type Societies', *British Journal of Political Science* 16, no. 1 (1986): 35–56
Pipes, R. (ed.), *The Unknown Lenin: From the Secret Archives* (New Haven, CT and London, 1996)
Polan, A. J., *Lenin and the End of Politics* (London, 1984)
Pons, Silvio, *Stalin and the Inevitable War, 1936–1941* (London, 2002)
Rancour-Lafferiere, D., *The Mind of Stalin: A Psychoanalytic Study* (Ann Arbor, 1988)
Redlich, Shimon, *War, Holocaust and Stalinism: A Documentary History of the Jewish Anti-Fascist Committee in the USSR* (Newark, NJ,1995).
Ree, Erik van, *The Political Thought of Joseph Stalin: A study in twentieth century revolutionary patriotism* (London, 2002)
Rees, E. A., *State Control in Soviet Russia: The Rise and Fall of the Workers' and Peasants' Inspectorate, 1920–34* (London, 1987)

———, *Stalinism and Soviet Rail Transport 1928–1941* (Basingstoke, London and New York, 1995)
———, (ed.), *Decision-Making in the Stalinist Command Economy, 1932–1937* (Basingstoke, London and New York, 1997)
———, (ed.), *Centre-Local Relations in the Stalinist State, 1928–1941* (Basingstoke, London and New York, 2002)
———, *Political Thought from Machiavelli to Stalin: Revolutionary Machiavellism* (Basingstoke, 2004)
———, (ed.), *The Nature of Stalin's Dictatorship: The Politburo 1924–1953* (Basingstoke, 2004)
Remnick, David, *Lenin's Tomb* (Harmondsworth, 1994)
Rigby, T. H., *Communist Party Membership in the U.S.S.R., 1917–1967* (Princeton, 1968)
———, 'Was Stalin a Disloyal Patron?' *Soviet Studies* 38, no. 3 (1988): 311–24
Rittersporn, Gábor T., Malte Rolf and Jan C. Behrends (eds), *Public Spheres in Soviet Type Societies* (Frankfurt, 2003)
Rosenfeldt, N. S., *The 'Special' World: Stalin's Power Apparatus and the Soviet System's Secret Structures of Communication*, vol. 1 (Copenhagen, 2009)
Rossman, Jeffrey J., 'The Teikovo Cotton Workers Strike of April 1932: Class, Gender and Identity Politics in Stalin's Russia', *Russian Review* 56 (1997): 44–69.
Rosenfeldt, Niels Erik, *Knowledge and Power: The Role of Stalin's Secret Chancellery in the Soviet System of Government* (Copenhagen, 1978).
Russell, Bertrand, *Bolshevism: Practice and Theory* (New York, 1972; first published in 1920 as *The Practice and Theory of Bolshevism*)
Serge, Victor, *Memoirs of a Revolutionary* (London, 1963)
———, *From Lenin to Stalin* (New York, 1973)
Service, R. J., *The Bolshevik Party in Revolution: A Study in Organisational Change 1917–1923* (London and Basingstoke, 1979)
———, *Lenin: A Political Life*, vol. 3 (London, 1995)
Schapiro, L., *The Origins of the Communist Autocracy* (London, 1977)
———, *The Communist Party of the Soviet Union* (London, 1978)
Shearer, David R., *Industry, State and Society in Stalin's Russia, 1926–1934* (Ithaca, NY and London, 1996)
———, *Policing Stalin's Socialism: Repression and Social Order in the Soviet Union, 1923–1953* (New Haven, CT, 2009)
Shimotomai, Nobuo, 'A Note on the Kuban Affair (1932–1933)', *Acta Slavica Iaponica* 1, (1983): 39–56
———, *Moscow under Stalinist Rule, 1931–34* (Basingstoke and London, 1991)
Simon, Sir E. D., Lady Simon, W. A. Robson and J. Jewkes Simon, *Moscow in the Making* (London, 1937)
Souvarine, Boris, *Stalin: A Critical Survey of Bolshevism* (London, 1939)
Stalin, I. V., *Works*, vols 10–13 (Moscow, 1952–5)
———, *Works*, vols 14–16 (London, 1978)
Stites, R., *Revolutionary Dreams: Utopian Vision and Experimental Life in the Russian Revolution* (New York and Oxford, 1989)
Sudoplatov, Pavel, and Anatoli Sudoplatov, *Special Tasks: The Memoirs of an Unwanted Witness – A Soviet Spymaster* (London, 1994)
Suny, Ronald Grigor, 'Beyond Psychohistory: The Young Stalin in Georgia', *Slavic Review* 50, no. 1 (Spring 1991): 48–58
Taniuchi, Y., 'A Note on the Ural-Siberian Method', *Soviet Studies* 33, no. 4 (1981): 518–47

Thorniley, D., *The Rise and Fall of the Soviet Rural Communist Party, 1927–39* (Basingstoke and London, 1988)
Thurston, Robert W., *Life and Terror in Stalin's Russia 1934–1941* (New Haven, CT and London, 1996)
Tiersky, Ronald, *Ordinary Stalinism: Democratic Centralism and the Question of Communist Political Development* (London and Sydney, 1985)
Trotsky, L., *Stalin: An Appraisal of the Man and his Influence* (London, 1968)
———, *Writings of Leon Trotsky, 1929–1940* (ed. Geirge Breitman, Sarah Lovell and Naomi Allen), 13 vols (New York, 1969–73)
———, *The Challenge of the Left Opposition, 1926–27* (ed. Naomi Allen and George Saunders) (New York, 1980)
Tucker, Robert C., *Stalin in Power: The Revolution from Above, 1928–1941* (New York and London, 1990)
———, *Stalin As Revolutionary, 1879–1929* (New York, 1973)
———, *Stalinism: Essays in Historical Interpretation* (New York, 1977)
Tumarkin, Nina, *Lenin Lives! The Lenin Cult in Soviet Russia* (Cambridge, MA, 1997)
Velikanova, Olga, *Making of an Idol: On Uses of Lenin* (Gottingen, 1996)
Viola, Lynne, *The Best Sons of the Fatherland* (Oxford, 1987)
———, *Peasant Rebels under Stalin: Collectivization and the Culture of Peasant Resistance* (New York and Oxford, 1996)
——— (ed.), *Contending with Stalinism* (Ithaca, NY and London, 2002)
———, *The Unknown Gulag: The Lost World of Stalin's Special Settlements* (Oxford, 2007)
Volkogonov, D., *Stalin: Triumph and Tragedy* (London, 1991)
Waller, Michael, *Democratic Centralism: An Historical Commentary* (Manchester, 1981)
Ward, Chris (ed.), *The Stalinist Dictatorship* (London, 1998)
Watson, Derek, *Molotov and Soviet Government: Sovnarkom 1930–41* (Basingstoke, 1996)
———, *Molotov: A Biography* (Basingstoke, 2005)
Westwood, J. N., *Soviet Locomotive Technology during Industrialization 1928–1953* (London, 1982)
Yekelchyk, Serhy, *Stalin's Empire of Memory: Russian-Ukrainian Relations in the Soviet Historical Imagination* (Toronto, 2004)

Works in Other Languages

Cohen, Yves, 'Des lettres comme action. Stalin au début des années 1930 vu depuis le fonds Kaganovich', *Cahiers du monde russe* 38, no. 3 (1997): 307–46
Danilov, V. and A. Berelowitch, 'Les documents de la VCK-OGPU-NKVD sur le campagne sovietique, 1918–1937', *Cahiers du Monde russe* 35, no. 3 (1994): 633–82
Marcucci, Loris, *Il Commissario Di Ferro Stalin: Biografia Politica di Lazar' M. Kaganovic* (Turin, 1997)
Werth, N., 'Une source inedite: les svodki de la Tcheka-OGPU', *Revue des Études Slaves* 66, no. 1 (1994): 17–27
Werth, N. and Gael Moullenc, *Rapports Secrets Soviétiques: La Société Russe dans les Documents Confidentiels 1921–1991* (Paris, 1994)

NAME INDEX

Akimov, S. A. 286n27
Akulov, I. A. 89
Aleksandrov, G. E. 245
Alliluyeva, N. 133, 218, 306n9
Alliluyeva, S. 249
Andreev, A. A. 57, 83, 85, 97, 103, 107, 166–71, 193–5, 207, 302n10, 307n34, 307n44, 310n3, 317 n114, 319n20, 324n67
Andreeva, N. 268
Antipov, N. K. 136, 139
Antonov-Ovseenko, V. 10, 134, 264, 290n21
Aristov, A. P. 257
Arosev, I. Ya. 284n52
Artyunyants 161
Artyunov, B. N. 236
Averbakh, I. L. 158

Bagirov, M. D. 198, 254, 327n6
Baibakov, N. K. 237
Bakaev, I. P. 184
Bakulin, A. V. 197, 199
Balashov, I. D. 186
Balitsky, V. A. 70, 86, 108
Bauman, K. Ya. 85, 106, 145, 147–8
Bazhanov, B. 207–8, 319n21
Bekhterev, V. M. 219
Bel'sky, I. N. 188
Belyakov, N. K. 10, 284n52
Benes, E. 195
Berdyaev, N. A. 6
Berezin, A. 69
Bergavinov, S. A. 104

Beria, L. P. 190, 198, 200, 218, 232, 234–40, 242–3, 245–7, 249–51, 254, 257, 262, 265, 277–8, 327n6
Berman, M. D. 161, 309n124
Beshchev, B. P. 239, 251–2, 257, 259
Bessedovsky, B. 208
Bezymensky, A. I. 157
Birt, R. 219
Blagonravov, G. I. 166, 169, 200
Blat, I. 86
Boky, G. I. 288n110
Bondarenko, I. M. 200
Bosh, E. B. 6–7, 58
Brezanovsky, Ya. E. 136
Brezhnev, L. I. 237, 241, 257, 267
Brzezinski, Z. K. xi
Bubnov, A. 62, 97, 139, 291n46
Budennyi, S. M. 32, 58, 252
Bukharin, N. I. 11, 29, 48–9, 53–5, 57–9, 78, 79, 81, 83–7, 89, 93–6, 98, 102, 103, 112, 118, 120, 185, 187–9, 193, 198–9, 201, 204, 208, 215, 264, 273, 298n70, 304n68
Bulatov, D. A. 136
Bulganin, N. A. 21, 26, 34–5, 146, 155, 157–61, 225, 243, 246, 249–53, 256, 258, 260, 265, 308n61, 309n124, 327n6
Bulushev, A. I. 146

Carr, E. H. xi
Chaplin, C. 139
Chase, W. xi

Chayanov, A. V. 102, 112, 131, 264
Chernenko, K. 267
Chernov, M. A. 109, 150
Chernyak, M. F. 258
Chernyavsky, V. I. 76
Chernyshevsky, N. 211
Chesnokov, D. I. 285n6
Chicherin, G. V. 49
Chubar', V. Ya. 30, 62, 53, 66, 67, 69, 74, 76, 78, 79, 107–9, 133, 170, 194, 223, 229, 233, 257, 264
Chuev, F. xiv, 209, 235, 261–3, 268
Cohen, S. xi, 79
Colton, T. J. 147
Conquest, R. xi, 225

Daniels, R. V. xi
Danishevsky, K. Kh. 22
Dashkovsky, I. 66
Davies, R. W. xi, 112–13
Degtyarev 284n35
Demchenko. M. 68
Dement'ev 319n29
Denikin, A. I. 19, 31–2, 175
Deutscher, I. xi, 98, 287n45, 287n56, 296n13, 298n90
Dickens, C. 4
Dimitrov, G. 195, 206
Dogadov, A. I. 88, 291n46
Donenko, N. Ye. 147
Doroshkevich 68
Dostoevsky, F. 18
Drobnis, Ya. N. 187
Duranty, W. 301n97, 310n6
Durnovo, P. N. 8
Dzerzhinsky, F. E. 23, 25, 38, 48–9, 53, 73, 168, 198
Dzevaltovsky, I. I. 284n52

Eideman, R. P. 161
Eikhe, R. I. 105, 126

Eisenstein, S. 139
Eismont, V. V. 131
Eletskaya 213–14
Eliava, Sh. Z. 288n110
Emshanov, A. I. 191
Engels, F. 163, 210, 251, 253
Enver Pasha 35, 38
Erdman, N. 138
Essad-Bey 208
Evdokimov, E. G. 86
Evdokimov, G. E. 184
Evseev, E. 268

Fedorov, G. F. 22, 286n27
Fedorov, V. S. 319n29
Fefer, I. 245, 326n136
Firin, S. G. 158–9
Fitzpatrick, S. xi
Frank, S. 6
Friedrich, C. J. xi
Frunze, M. 15–16, 33, 48–9, 62, 288n110
Furtseva, E. A. 259

Gaister, S. 166
Gamarnik, Ya. B. 7, 109, 194, 257
Gartman 87
Genghis Khan 84
Getty, J. Arch xi, 141, 185
Ginsburg. M. Ya. 152
Girsh, B. 326n136
Gnedin, E. A. 142
Golosheikin, F. I. 288n110
Gopner, S. I. 8
Gorbachev, M. S. 267–9
Gorky, M. 4, 138, 139, 158
Grabar', I. 155
Grabovsky 5
Gramsci, A. 17
Graziosi, A. xiii
Gregor, A. J. 204
Grin'ko, G. G. 63, 68–70, 73, 78, 108, 169
Grizodubova, V. 232

Gromyko, A. A. 267
Gulyi, K. 65, 69

Hegel, G. W. F. 215
Himmler, H. 314n23
Hitler, A. 142, 165, 205, 245
Hughes, J. 8
Hugo, V. 4
Hunter, H. 175

Ioffe, A. A. 37, 58
Isaev, B. 170
Itkin, D. 284n35
Ivanov, A. A. 69

Jasny, Naum 165, 186

Kabakov. I. D. 93
Kadar, J. 255
Kaganovich, Aron M. (brother) 2, 3, 6, 218
Kaganovich, Israil M. (brother) 2, 3, 6, 218
Kaganovich, Mosei B. (father) 2
Kaganovich, Mikhail M. (brother) 2–6, 125, 218, 232–5, 250, 251, 253, 258, 264, 324n53
Kaganovich, P. K. 32, 47, 288n104, 290n23, 320n38
Kaganovich, Yuli L. (son) 217
Kaganovich, Yuli M. (brother) 2–6, 218, 321n70 and 71
Kaganovicha (née Dudinskaya), G. (mother) 2
Kaganovicha, Maia L. (daughter) 35, 217, 218, 268
Kaganovicha, Maria M. (wife) 12, 15, 35, 217, 258, 261
Kaganovicha, Rachel M. (sister) 2–3
Kahan, S. xiv
Kalinin, M. I. 29, 32, 49, 52, 67, 88, 97, 104, 124, 145, 155, 194, 198, 207, 218, 221, 234, 291n46, 302n10, 304n67, 317n114, 319n20

Kamenev, L. B. 29, 46–7, 49, 53–9, 62–4, 67, 72, 84, 152, 160, 172, 181, 184–5, 264, 289n9, 292n73
Kapitonov, L. V. 253
Kaplan 319n29
Karponsov, A. G. 324n67
Kautsky, K. 32
Kerzhentsev, P. 138
Khachaturov, T. S. 232
Khataevich, M. M. 12, 43, 85, 119
Khaustov, F. P. 284n52
Khlevniuk, O. V. xii–xiii, 201
Khrabovitsky, A. V. 158
Khrennikov, S. A. 87
Khrulev, A. V. 237, 324n67
Khrushchev, N. S. 9, 76, 78, 140, 146, 150, 155–9, 161–2, 167, 195, 198, 201, 223–5, 232, 235–6, 241–7, 249–53, 255–60, 262, 265–7, 269, 275, 277–8, 284n39, 319n20, 327n6
Khvylovy, M. 68–70, 71
Kipnis, I. 241
Kirkizh, K. O. 63, 76
Kirov, S. M. 38, 57–8, 124–5, 134–5, 140–1, 143, 162, 172, 183, 192, 206–7, 212, 214, 223, 226, 304n67, 319n20
Kiselev, A. S. 92
Kishkin, V. A. 169
Klement'ev, Yu. V. 258, 319n29
Klimenko, I. 63–4, 76
Knyazev, I. A. 188–9
Kogan, L. I. 159, 161, 306n15, 309n124
Kolchak, A. V. 19, 30
Kollontai, A. M. 36–8
Kolman, A. E. 223
Kondratiev, N. D. 112, 131, 264
Kornilov, L. G. 12
Kornyushin, F. 69, 76
Korotkov, I. I. 48
Kosarev, A. V. 90, 109, 193–4
Kosior, I. V. 126

Kosior, S. V. 8, 79, 103, 107–9, 114, 125, 126, 133, 212, 223, 257, 264
Kosygin, A. N. 267
Kovalev, G. B. 324n67
Kovalev, Lt. Gen. I. V. 234, 238, 324n67
Kraevsky 286n27
Krasin, G. B. 152
Krasin, L. B. 45–6
Kravchenko, V. 223, 322n84
Krestinsky, N. N. 29, 199
Kritsman, L. 102
Krivonos, P. F. 173, 200
Krupskaya, N. K. 31, 53–5, 67, 116, 147–8, 212, 232
Krylenko, N. V. 10, 13, 284n52, 285n71
Krzhizhanovsky, G. M. 81, 319n20
Kudrevatov, S. K. 167, 175
Kuibyshev, V. V. 11, 35, 42, 46, 49, 54, 58–9, 73, 75, 80–1, 86, 88, 97, 102–3, 118, 124–5, 127, 134–5, 137, 141–2, 159, 166–7, 206–7, 212, 237, 271–2, 288n110, 291n46, 294n83, 302n10, 304n67, 319n20
Kumanev, G. A. xiv, 169
Kun, B. 37
Kursky, D. I. 44, 48–9
Kuznetsov, A. A. 243
Kuznetsov, N. G. 234
Kviring, E. I. 62, 73, 78

Ladovsky, N. A. 152
Larin, Yu. 27, 71–2, 152
Larina, A. 98, 185
Larri, Ya. 209
Lazarevsky, A. A. 171
Le Corbusier (Jeanneret, C-E.) 152
Lebed', D. Z. 67
Lenin, V. I. ix, 5–6, 10, 13–6, 18, 22–3, 25, 27–9, 31–3, 35–9, 42, 43–6, 48–51, 54–5, 57–9, 61, 73, 82, 83, 91, 93, 96, 102, 111, 115–16, 124, 128, 148, 163, 203, 206, 207, 212, 214, 225, 252–3, 261, 263, 265, 269, 272, 289n9
Lepa, A. K. 42
Levin, L. G. 219
Lewin, M. xi
Liber, M. 12
Liebknecht, K. 25
Liebknecht, W. 4
Lifshits, Ya. A. 169, 185–6, 188, 191, 223
Likhachev, I. A. 161
Linden, C. A. xii
Litvinov, M. M. 142, 180, 233
Litvin-Sedoi, Z. 47
Lobanov 66
Lobov, S. S. 174
Lominadze, V. V. 131
Lukashin 317n120
Luxemburg, R. 25
Lyons, E. 323n84
Lysenko, T. D. 255
Lyubchenko, P. P. 114
Lyubimov. I. E. 174, 197

Machiavelli, N. x
Maior (Maiorov) 284n35
Maksimov, V. 28
Maksimovich, K. 72, 78
Maksimovsky, V. N. 123
Malashkin, S. I. 25
Malenkov, G. M. 146, 150, 178, 195–6, 225, 235–6, 238–43, 247, 249–53, 256–9, 262, 265, 267, 324n85, 327n6
Malin, V. N. 323n52
Malinovsky, Marshall R. Ya. 258
Manning, R. xi
Mao Tse-tung 256
Marachkovsky, S. V. 184
Mar'in, A. I. 319n29
Marcucci, L. xiv
Martov, Yu. O. 14

Marx, K. 54, 154, 163, 251
Matskevich, V. V. 255
Matusov 161
May, E. 152
Medvedev, A. 64, 67
Medvedev, R. xiv, 39, 150, 155, 225, 235, 258, 321n67
Medvedev, S. P. 38, 57, 160
Mekhlis, L. Z. 265
Mekhonoshin, K. A. 10, 15, 284n52, 285n71
Mekk, K. N. von 87
Mel'nikov, K. S. 152
Mel'nikov, L. G. 327n6
Menzhinsky, V. R. 86
Mezhlauk, V. I. 23, 169, 175, 194, 197, 31n50
Mikhailov, N. M. 246
Mikheenko, A. 64, 69
Mikhoels, S. M. 245, 326n136
Mikoyan, A. I. 57–8, 83, 95, 97, 103, 109, 124–5, 127, 134, 170, 174, 185, 189–90, 193–5, 198, 201, 206–7, 212, 217, 234–6, 238, 240, 242–3, 246–7, 249, 250–3, 255–6, 258, 265–7, 275, 277, 317n14, 324n67, 327n6
Mil'shtein, S. R. 200, 234
Milyutin, V. P. 9
Mirbach, Count W. 21
Miroshnikov, P. I. 317n120
Mitskevich, S. I. 42
Moiseenko, V. 64, 39
Molotov, V. M. 10, 32, 42, 48–9, 52, 54, 58–60, 62, 78, 80, 85–6, 88, 95, 97–8, 101, 103, 105, 107–10, 113–15, 119, 123–8, 130, 134–5, 138–9, 141–2, 145, 154–5, 158, 166, 169–70, 175–6, 184–7, 190, 193–4, 198, 200, 207–10, 212, 214–15, 217–18, 232–6, 239–40, 242–4, 246–7, 249–65, 267–8, 271, 274, 276–8, 291n46, 292n73, 299n28, 301n97, 302n10, 304n67, 310n3, 315n61, 316n89, 317n14, 319n20, 319n21, 323n24, 327n6
Mordovtsev 31
Moskalenko, Marshall K. S. 251
Mrachkovsky, S. V. 184
Muralov, N. I. 24, 187
Mussolini, B. 142, 205
Myasnikov, A. F. 12–3
Nabatchikov, A. M. 258
Nakhaev, A. S. 140
Naumov, O. V. 186
Nefedov, I. A. 196
Nekrasov, V. 245
Nevsky, V. I. 10, 191, 284n52, 284n53
Nicholas II 1, 9
Nicolaevskii, B. 125, 133
Nikolaenko 192, 257
Nove, A. xi

Obraztsov, V. N. 169, 171
Odintsov, A. 79
Okhlopkov 42
Ordzhonikidze, G. K. 35, 38, 57–8, 86, 88, 97, 101, 104–5, 117–19, 124–7, 130–1, 134, 135, 140–2, 162, 166, 169–70, 172–4, 176, 179, 180–4, 186, 187–90, 192–3, 201, 204, 206–7, 210, 212, 217–18, 223, 226, 235, 250, 264, 273, 304n67, 310n9, 319n20
Ordzhonikidze, P. K. (Papulia) 190
Osinsky, V. V. 28, 83, 290n21
Osipenko, P. 232

Pashukanis, E. B. 137
Patolichev, N. S. 241
Pen'kov, N. 85
Pervukhin, M. G. 234, 246, 253, 255–6, 258, 327n6
Peters, Ya. Kh. 22, 35, 136, 146–7, 160, 307n41
Petlyura, S. 13, 108
Petrov, Gen. I. E. 237

Petrovsky, G. I. 23, 57, 62–7, 69–70, 74, 76–8, 84
Pilsudski, J. 70
Pipes, R. xi
Platonov, A. 139
Pletnev, D. D. 219
Podgorny, N. V. 257, 259
Podvoisky, N. I. 10–11, 15–6, 42, 284n52, 285n71
Pokrovsky, M. 137
Polyansky, D. S. 257, 259
Ponomarenko, P. K. 327n6
Popov, G. M. 243
Popov, M. M. 114
Poskrebyshev, A. N. 136, 189
Pospelov, P. N. 253, 259
Postnikov, A. M. 169, 311n50
Postyshev, P. P. 67–8, 76, 79, 114, 126, 191, 198, 211, 223, 257, 264, 300n64, 303n57
Pravdin 36
Preobrazhensky, E. A. 36, 44, 56, 290n13, 290n21
Privorotskaya, L. M. 7
Privorotskatya, M. M.: *see* Kaganovich, Maria M. 7
Privorotsky, T. M. 12–3, 35
Pyatakov, Yu. L 6–7, 56, 73, 185, 187–8, 190, 204, 208, 290n21

Rabinovich, A. A. 326n136
Radchenko, A. 63, 65, 76
Radek, K. V. 188
Rakosi, M. 254
Rakovsky, Kh. 75–6
Rakitina 213–14
Rancour-Lafferiere, D. 219
Raskol'nikov, F. F. 22, 24, 221
Raskova, M. 323
Redens, S. F. 108, 146
Ree, E. van x
Ribbentrop J. von 233
Rigby, T. H. xiii
Robespierre, M. de 77, 264
Rodionov, N. 259

Rolland, R. 139
Romanov, I. P. 19
Rosenfeld, N. A. 172
Rotert, P. P. 156–7
Rozengolts, A. P. 24, 290n21
Rozmirovich, E. F. 284n52
Rudzutak, Ya. E. 38, 57, 103, 124, 130, 136–7, 166, 200, 288n110, 302n10, 303n57, 304n67, 319n20
Rukhimovich, M. I. 63, 73, 125, 166, 194, 200, 232
Rumyantsev, I. P. 115, 195
Russell, Lord Bertrand xii
Rykov, A. I. 46, 49, 53, 57–8, 72, 76, 81, 83–4, 86, 89, 94, 98, 112, 123, 127, 155, 185, 188–9, 193, 198–9, 208, 298n70
Ryndin, K. V. 146, 306n15, 307n38, 307n41, 307n48, 309n109, 309n119, 309n121
Ryutin, M. N. 131

Sabsovich, L. M. 152
Saburov, M. Z. 243, 246, 250, 253, 256, 258, 327n6
Safarov, G. I. 35–7
Sakharov, V. V. 284n52
Sapronov, T. V. 28, 290n21
Sarkis (Sarkisov), S. A. 119, 173
Schapiro, L. xi
Sedin, I. K. 234
Segal', G. M. 178
Seleznev, P. I. 237
Semashko, A. Ya. 10, 284n52
Semashko, N. A. 19, 30
Semin, S. I. 215
Serdyuk, Z. T. 259
Serebryakov, L. P. 47, 188, 290n21
Serge, V. 206
Sergushev, M. S. 21, 25–6, 28–31, 34–5, 43
Serov, I. A. 256–7
Shakhurin, A. I. 234
Shanin, A. M. 169, 187

Shaposhnikov, B. M. 234
Shapoval, Yu. xiv
Shashko, Z. A. 324n67
Shcherbakov, A. S. 197, 265, 307n37
Sheboldaev, B. P. 85, 110
Sheinin, L. A. 7
Shelekhes, I. S. 286n27
Shelepin, A. 258
Shemaev 10
Shepilov, D. T. 255
Shevchenko, T. G. 7
Shilkin, P. M. 327n23
Shirshov, P. P. 324n67
Shkiryatov, M. F. 47, 109–10, 195–6, 303n57, 304n67
Shlyapnikov, A. G. 36, 38, 57, 160
Shtange, G. V. 215
Shumsky, A. Ya. 63, 65–72, 74, 78, 80, 115, 242
Shumyatsky, B. 139
Shvernik, N. M. 83, 85, 89, 118, 119, 193, 194, 201, 236, 251, 252, 259, 327n6
Shvetsov, D. N. 87
Skrypnik, N. A. 63, 66–7, 69, 71–2, 78–9, 107, 114
Skvortsov-Stepanov, I. I. 47
Slovatinskaya, T. K. 319n29
Smirnov, A. P. 93, 131
Smirnov, I. N. 24, 184
Smirnov, V. 101
Souvarine, B. 205
Sokolnikov, G. Ya. 23, 33, 34, 36, 37, 48, 53–6, 83–4, 160, 185, 188, 292n73
Solodub, P. 66, 68–9
Solov'ev 319n29
Solts, A. A. 47, 161, 316n72
Souvarine, B. 205, 290n23, 311n45, 319n10, 319n23
Spiridonova, M. 10
Stakhanov, A. 173
Stalin, I. V. ix–xv, 7, 10, 15, 16, 25, 27, 29, 32, 34–9, 42, 44–68, 70, 73–4, 76–88, 90, 92, 94–9, 101–3, 105–21, 123–42, 145–50, 152–3, 154–57, 159–60, 162–4, 165–78, 180–2, 183–87, 189–90, 192–202, 203–14, 217–28, 229–47, 249–50, 252–4, 256–9, 261–9, 271–9, 281n6, 291n6, 302n8, 302n10, 304n67, 310n3, 310n6, 311n46, 312n75, 312n87, 314n5, 316n89, 317n114, 319n20
Stasova, E. 31–2, 35, 309n132, 319n29
Sten, I. 215
Stetsky, A. I. 83, 136, 211
Stites, R. 204, 209
Stolypin, P. A. 1, 5–8, 17, 102
Strakhov, N. I. 237
Stroganov, V. 76
Sudoplatov, P. 242
Sukhomlin, K. 68
Sulimov, D. E. 85, 200
Suslov, M. A. 237, 245
Svanidze, M. 217
Sverdlov, Ya. M. 11, 14–5, 19, 23, 28
Sverdlova, K. T. 28
Syrtsov, S. I. 42, 49, 95, 131, 291n46, 302n10

Taube 87
Taubman, W. 162
Terekhov, P. 76
Thorez, M. 254
Thurston, R. xi
Timasheff, N. S. 204
Timoshenko, S. K. 234
Tolmachev, G. G. 131
Tomsky, M. P. 37, 49, 53, 55–8, 76, 81, 83–5, 88–90, 94, 98, 112, 118, 296n33
Trifonov, V. 285n71
Trotsky, L. D. ix, 7, 15–16, 20, 22, 24, 26–7, 29–32, 36, 39, 42, 44–9, 52, 54–9, 61–2, 73, 82–3, 99, 168, 184–5, 188, 191, 194, 204–6, 208, 212, 225, 264, 289n126, 314n21

Tselyuk, M. 293n39
Tucker, R. C. 219
Tukhachevsky. Marshall M. N. 142, 165, 176, 180, 194, 264
Tyulenev, I. V. 237

Uborevich, I. P. 194–5
Ugarov, F. 65
Uglanov, N. A. 49, 53–4, 57–8, 84–5, 145, 147, 150, 152, 187, 291n46
Ul'rikh, V. V. 140, 184
Ulam, A. xi
Ustrialov, N. V. 54
Utesov, L. O. 139

Vaganyan, V. 71–2
Vailiev, A. A. 196
Vakhrushev, V. V. 233
Vannikov, B. L. 235
Vardin, I. 54
Varekis, I. M. 85
Vasiliev A. 10
Vatsetis, I. I. 24
Veinberg, G. D. 8, 284n35
Vitvitsky 326n136
Vladimirsky, B. E. 214
Vladimirsky, M. F. 42, 47
Volkogonov, D. 124, 220, 224–5, 240, 251
Volkov, M. A. 199
Vorob'ev, Ya. Z. (Kats) 22, 26, 29, 31, 35, 286n27
Vorob'evaya, R. (Grinshpon) 7
Voroshilov, K. E. 27, 58, 97, 124–5, 128, 134, 138, 141, 161, 166, 170, 172, 184, 189–90, 192–4, 198, 201, 206–7, 212, 217, 234, 236, 243, 246, 249–53, 256–7, 259, 265, 277–8, 304n67, 317n114, 319n20
Voznesensky, N. A. 229, 232, 234, 236, 238, 240, 242, 243, 247
Vyshinsky, V. V. 119, 184

Weber, M. 282
Wheatcroft, S. G. xiii, 113
Wrangel, P. N. 19

Yagoda, G. G. 109, 141, 163, 165, 184–6, 199, 250, 264
Yakir, I. E. 68, 194, 223, 257, 300n64
Yakovlev, Ya. A. 102, 104, 111
Yaroslavsky, E. M. 38, 53, 136, 303n57, 304n67, 319n20
Yartsev, V. V. 199
Yenukidze, A. S. 58, 92, 136, 160, 171
Yezhov, N. I. 104, 126, 136–7, 167–8, 170–2, 174, 179, 181, 183–6, 188–90, 193–4, 198, 200, 208, 211, 217–18, 250, 261, 264, 273, 314n23, 317n114
Yudenich, N. N. 19, 32
Yurenev, K. K. 24, 285n71
Yurkin, T. A. 109, 111–12

Zaitsev, F. 9, 284n38, 285n84
Zaks, V. G. 21
Zatonsky, V. P. 8, 15, 63, 67, 69, 70, 76, 135
Zelensky, I. A. 47
Zemlyachka, R. S. 37, 42, 47
Zhdanov, A. A. 83, 116, 135–36, 138, 168, 185, 189, 194, 200, 207, 214, 229, 232, 240, 242–3, 245, 277–8
Zhdanov, V. I. 87
Zhemchuzhina, P. 243
Zholtovsky, V. I. 155
Zhuk, S. Ya. 159
Zhukov, Marshall G. K. 239, 256, 258
Zhuravlev, P. V. 199
Zimin, N. N. 166, 169, 188, 223, 311n50
Zinoviev, G. E. 23, 27–9, 36, 45–7, 49–50, 53–9, 62–3, 67, 71–2, 83, 160, 181, 184–5, 188, 264, 291n45, 292n73

SUBJECT INDEX

Abyssinia (Ethiopia) 142
Academy of Sciences 155, 160
agriculture 1, 53, 56, 64–5, 66–7,
    73, 77, 81–4, 87, 91, 93, 95, 97,
    101–3, 107, 110–14, 117, 120–1,
    123, 129, 131, 133–5, 137, 140,
    143, 147–50, 163, 241, 253, 255,
    260, 271–2
  collectivization 77, 85, 90, 85,
    98, 101–6, 108, 111. 113–17,
    120–1, 126, 129, 131, 143, 145,
    147–8, 164, 183, 202, 209,
    218, 223, 253, 264, 272 (see also
    'dekulakization')
  collective farms (*kolkhozy*) 73, 95,
    101–3, 105, 107–8, 110–13,
    115–16, 129, 137, 146, 148–50,
    160, 203, 214, 255
  grain procurement 77–8, 82–4,
    93–5, 103, 108–9, 110–11,
    115–16, 150, 272
  grain requisitioning 20, 30, 34, 37,
    80, 93, 120
  peasant agriculture 65, 73, 77, 102
  state farms (*sovkhozy*) 73, 106,
    111–13, 116, 137, 240
All-Russian Central Executive
    Committee (VTsIK) 14, 15, 20,
    23, 32
All-Russian Congress of Soviets
  V Congress 21
  VII Congress 32
All Stalin's Men (Medvedev) xiv, 225

All-Union Dispatchers Conference
    167
All-Union Meeting on Soviet
    Construction 95
All-Union Railway Workers' Day 180,
    232
Amsterdam 55–6
Anarchists 5, 20, 196
Anti-Party Group 256–8, 274
anti-Semitism 3, 62, 64, 78, 155, 233,
    240–1, 245, 257, 268, 277, 278
  pogroms 3, 6
Architectural Planning Commission
    (Arkhplan) 154
Argumenty i fakty 268
Armenia 195
Austro-Hungary 8
Azerbaidzhan 198, 254

Baikal–Amur line 231, 234
Baku 198, 231
Baltic states 233
Baltic–White Sea canal (Belomor) 159
Barnaul 94
Bashkirya 93, 195
Bashmachi 33, 38
Beilis case 5
Belarus 11; *see also* Byelorussia
Berlin 150, 157, 207
Bessarabia 233
Birobidzhan 139, 215, 245
Black Hundreds 5, 6
Bol'shevik, 71, 72, 93, 215

Bolshevik Party 5–7, 10–14, 16, 21, 30, 33, 36, 41, 43, 45, 50–1, 197, 204, 206, 227
  Military Organization 9–12, 14, 17, 27, 271
  All-Russian Bureau of Military Party Organization 10, 15
  All-Russian Collegium for Organising the Red Army 15–6
Bolshevik ethics x, xii, xiv, 17, 33, 44, 51, 190, 205, 209, 277
  moral nihilism 204
Bolshevik leaders x, 22, 32–3, 45, 148, 176, 217
  social background 210
  teoretiki/praktiki 206
Bolshevism x, 2, 4, 6, 17m39, 44, 48, 91, 172, 203, 206, 208, 221, 227, 271–2, 275–6; *see also* Leninism; Stalinism
  cultic aspects xiv, 48, 99, 203
Borot'bists 63, 68–9, 71
Brest-Litovsk, Treaty of 15, 20, 21
Britain 19, 142, 154, 255
British General Strike 55, 81
budget 53, 65, 74, 128, 218
Bukovina 233
Bulletin' Oppositsii 168
Bund 5, 6, 12
Byelorussia 2–3, 11, 13, 161, 176, 195, 214, 232, 245

cadres 45–6, 49, 65, 79, 85, 87, 89, 91–2, 101, 104, 106, 112, 119, 121, 123, 126–8, 130–1, 134, 137, 139, 143, 147–8, 171–2, 175–6, 178, 180–1, 183, 189–92, 197, 199–201, 229, 231, 233, 257, 259, 266, 273–4, 277; *see also* education and training
censorship 128, 138
Central Asia 33, 37–8, 49; *see also* Turkestan
Central Asia Bureau 38

Central Black Earth region 85, 104–5
Central Executive Committee (TsIK) of the Congress of Deputies 95, 163, 167, 175, 176, 180
Chayanovshchina 131
Cheka 13, 20–7, 29, 30–1, 38, 41, 166
  Nizhnyi Cheka 20–7, 29–31, 286n15
  Voronezh Cheka 31
Chelyabinsk 116, 195
Chernobyl' 2, 3
Chervonyi shliakh 65, 70
Chinese Communist Party 81
Chinese Eastern Railway 191, 196
Christian Science Monitor 168
cinema 128, 138–9, 163, 215
Civil War xiv, 9–10, 14, 19–21, 30, 32, 38, 41, 43, 48, 59, 64, 73, 88, 102, 109, 120, 139, 146, 206–7, 214, 217, 223, 271, 275
  Eastern Front 22, 26, 30–1, 206
  Revolutionary Military Council of the Eastern Front 22
  Southern front 27, 31–2
Cold War 240
Colonial Revolution in Turkestan (Safarov) 35
Commission of Party Control (CPC) 136–7, 166, 167, 169, 273
Commission of Soviet Control (CSC) 136–7, 169
communism x–xii, 41, 65, 89, 118, 208, 261, 267–8; *see also* Leninism
Communist Academy 91, 96, 137
Communist Party of USSR 64, 75, 102, 104
  Central Committee 10, 12, 15, 19, 23, 26, 27, 28, 29, 30–1, 33, 34, 36, 37, 38, 43, 46–9, 55, 56, 59, 62, 63, 73, 75, 79, 84–91, 103, 106, 108, 111, 117, 118, 126, 127, 128, 134–7, 143, 147–9, 160, 161, 168, 171, 175, 176,

SUBJECT INDEX

180, 182, 185–6, 192–3, 197, 202, 207, 209, 224, 222, 233, 235–6, 238, 241, 246, 250–1, 253, 256–8, 265

Central Committee plenums 49–50, 52, 56–7, 62, 65, 69, 73–6, 78–9, 83, 88, 93, 96, 100–103, 114, 116–17, 153, 158, 174, 176, 178, 188–90, 198, 214, 230, 241, 250, 255–6, 258

Central Committee resolution 85, 86, 95, 102, 112, 124, 152, 153, 154, 176, 179, 254

Central Committee–Central Control Commission joint plenums 47, 49, 56, 57, 62, 71, 83, 94, 110–12, 114, 116, 131, 134

Central Committee–Sovnarkom resolutions 119, 156, 160, 163, 166, 170, 172, 230

Central Committee–Sovnarkom Transport Commission 166–7, 169–70, 310n9

Central Control Commission 54, 90, 97, 109, 130
  Presidium 71, 89, 93

Central Control Commission-Rabkrin 45, 46, 58, 88, 97, 101, 102, 124, 125, 127, 134, 136
  abolition of 136–7, 143

Conferences
  XIII 48, 50
  XIV 50, 52
  XV 57, 74
  XVIII 234–5

Congresses
  VIII 26, 28–9
  X 36, 48,
  XI 38, 42, 53, 57
  XII 45, 63
  XIII 48, 50
  XIV 53–4, 55, 67, 72
  XV 49, 75–6, 78, 82–3, 97

XVI 90, 101, 104, 105, 106, 117, 124, 127–30, 145
XVII 115–16, 118–19, 130, 131, 134–5, 141, 151, 159, 166, 178, 212
XVIII 230–1
XIX 246–47
XX 252–54, 257, 263
XXII 201, 259–61
XXVIII 268

Organizational Bureau (Orgburo) 28, 29, 43, 47, 50, 54, 85, 97, 126, 127, 133, 135, 136, 143, 165, 168, 207, 209, 232
  commission on cinema 139
  commission on soviets 12
  party instructors 43, 43, 85, 137, 143

Politburo 28–9, 37, 42, 47–9, 53–7, 60, 62, 67, 69–70, 73, 74, 77–81, 84–5, 89, 93–5, 97–8, 103, 105, 107, 109–11, 113–14, 116, 118–19, 120–1, 123–8, 130–1, 133–40, 141–3, 145–6, 148, 152, 154–6, 157–9, 162–3, 166–70, 174, 177, 184–6, 188–90, 194–5, 197, 199, 200, 202, 210, 212, 217, 222, 224, 232–6, 240–1, 244–6, 246, 257, 265–7, 269, 274, 278
  decisions 111, 125, 195
  decline of 126, 133, 194
  meetings 85, 126, 133, 143, 194, 240
  membership 29, 48, 49, 124
  polling of members (opros) 126

Politburo commissions 97, 107, 118, 131, 141, 158, 166, 170, 240
  foreign policy 210, 261
  economic policy 194
  defence 96, 231 (*see also* Sovnarkom/Politburo Defence Committee)

on the repression of Stalin
era 254, 253
on the repression of the
Stalin era 200, 269
Politburo–Presidium of CCC joint
plenums 89, 93, 110–11
Presidium (replaces Politburo) 243,
246, 249–50, 253–5, 256–8,
260–1, 266–7, 269
    bureau 246, 250–1
Secretariat xiv, 23, 27–8, 30–1,
42–4, 46–9, 54, 58–9, 79, 85, 97,
101, 104, 112, 119, 121, 126–8,
133, 143, 136, 147, 162, 165,
168, 193, 207, 245, 250–1, 255,
258, 271, 276
    departments 42, 126–7, 136,
290n36
        Administrative Affairs 127,
136, 168
        Agitation and Propaganda
Department 49
        Agricultural Sector
(Selkhozotdel) 111, 112,
120, 136
        Culture-Propaganda Sector
136
        Industrial Sector 136
        Leading Party Organs
(ORPO) 136
        Organization and
Assignment Department
(Orgraspred) 49
        Organization and
Instruction Department
(Orgotdel) 42–3, 46–7, 49
        Planning-Finance-Trade
Sector 136
        Records and Assignment
Department (Uchraspred)
42, 46, 49
        Secret Department/Special
Sector 127, 136
        Transport Sector 136, 166

Women's Department
(Zhenotdel) 104, 272
Poor Peasants 104
Communist Party activists (*aktiv*)
8, 11, 17, 23, 30, 32, 41, 47,
55–6, 72, 76–7, 84–5, 89, 91,
98–9, 103–4, 106, 108–10, 115,
120, 146–7, 160, 185, 192–3,
199–200, 206, 215, 245–6, 252,
271, 275
Communist Party membership 6,
23, 27, 42, 50, 83, 128–9, 130
    education of party members
50, 129, 189
    proletarianization of party
128–9, 143, 272
    purge of party ranks 35, 50,
110, 116, 119, 128, 130, 143,
148, 160, 168, 273
    recruitment drive 50, 128–9
    (*see also* Lenin enrolment)
Communist Party of Western
Ukraine (KPZU) 71–2, 76
Communist International
(Comintern) 72, 142
    V Congress 72
    VI Congress 94
    VII Congress 142
Conference of Marxist Agronomists
137
Constituent Assembly 12–4,
19, 30
constitutions 1, 9, 35
    Stalin Constitution (1936)
231
Council of Ministers (successor of
Sovnarkom) 240, 242–3, 250–2,
258, 260–1
    Bureau 242
    Bureau of Transportation
and Communications 251
    Committee on Labour and
Wages 252
    Ministry of Defence 250, 258

SUBJECT INDEX

Ministry for Construction Materials Industry 240, 242–3, 255
Ministry for Heavy Industrial Construction 242
Ministry of Transport 251
State Economic Commission 255
State Committee for Material and Technical Supplies of the National Economy (Gossnab) 243
courts 104, 109, 167, 169–70, 178
Cossacks 13, 110
Crimea 37, 245
Criminal Code 44, 84
cultural policy 69, 137–9
'cultural revolution' 87, 99, 128
Czechoslovak Legion 22, 23
Czechoslovakia 195

'Declaration of the 83' 71
defence, of USSR 56, 72, 129, 140, 141, 161, 165, 180, 191, 202, 231, 234, 242, 252
'dekulakization' 53, 55, 101–5, 107, 115, 120, 164, 183, 209, 218
Democratic Centralists 28, 39
de-Stalinization 249, 254, 259, 260, 267, 274, 278
Dmitrov camp 159
Dnepropetrovsk 64, 67, 70, 76, 78, 119, 185
Dneprostroi 73–4
Dnieper dam 64, 73–4
Doctors' Plot 245–6, 266
Don River 32
Donetsk 119, 173, 185, 197
Donbass 8–9, 17, 64, 67, 69, 76, 78, 79, 86, 118–19, 151, 156, 187, 197, 199, 201, 230, 241
Duma 7

economic councils (*sovnarkhozy*) 255, 269
edinonachalie (one-man management) 135
education and training 86–7, 91, 112, 123, 128, 130, 134, 137, 138; *see also* intelligentsia: creation of new Soviet intelligentsia
proletarianization of education 28
role of *vuzy, vtyzy, tekhnikums* 131
Efremov district 150
Egypt 255
Ekaterinoslav 6, 8, 64; *see also* Dnepropetrovsk
Eksploitatsiya zheleznykh dorog 171
'enemies of the people' 171, 196, 198
'enemy syndrome' x, 44, 88, 90, 115, 120, 130, 137, 140, 141, 149, 160, 175, 177, 179, 180, 183, 184, 186–93, 196, 197, 198, 201, 202, 206, 209, 217, 219, 221, 225, 226, 228, 244, 256, 257, 264, 265, 266, 273, 274, 275, 276, 278
engineers 45, 86–7, 98, 130–1, 156–7, 164, 168, 172, 179–80, 191, 193, 197, 271
espionage 86, 88, 149, 189, 190–1
Europe 55, 72, 152–5, 160, 186, 231, 250
European revolution 14, 19, 41
'extraordinary measures' 94
Ezhenedelnik 'Pravdy' 29

famine 33, 37, 107, 109, 111–15, 120, 121, 123, 133–6, 143, 149, 156, 161, 165, 171, 183, 212, 240, 264, 272, 300n64
Far East 1, 115, 232
Far East territory 113
fascism 76, 134, 142, 195, 205
Finland 233, 235
First World War 8, 17

Five-Year Plans 97, 103
  First Five-Year Plan 111, 130–1, 152, 173, 202, 253, 272
  Second Five-Year Plan 129, 135, 150–1, 156, 158, 160, 167, 188, 231
  Third Five-Year Plan 232, 234
  Fourth Five-Year Plan 240
food supplies 16, 19, 21, 23, 29, 30–2, 34, 43, 89, 114, 148
  rationing 93, 116, 117, 141, 150
forced labour 159, 247; *see also* Gulag
foreign intelligence (subversion, espionage and wrecking) 86, 140
foreign policy/affairs 55–6, 81, 98, 141–2, 194, 210, 251–2, 254–5, 260, 266; *see also* Nazi–Soviet Pact
foreign trade 45, 218, 243
France 19, 142, 255
French Revolution 77

Georgian peasant revolt 51
Germany 8, 21, 130, 170, 180, 205, 238, 240, 250, 259
  Nazi Germany 142, 233–5
  Gestapo 195
  Wehrmacht 195, 237
gigantism/gigantomania 230, 232
Glavlit: *see* censorship
Gomel' 11–3, 17, 43, 161, 214
Gosplan 73, 81, 87, 101, 121, 125, 130, 151, 154, 156, 158–9, 167, 169, 171, 173, 212, 229–30, 234, 243
Great Patriotic War 235–9
Great Terror ix, xii, 165, 172, 183–202, 203, 205, 218, 231, 264, 272–4
  'fifth column' argument 201
  Order No. 00447 195
  Polish operation 195
  scale of repression 202, 231
Green movement 30

Gudok 178
Gulag 120, 159, 218, 247, 249, 250, 251, 264, 272–3; *see also* forced labour

Harbin 191
Holocaust 245
Hungary
  Hungarian Communist Party 255
  Hungarian Uprising 254–5

Industrial Academy 146
industrialization 1, 49, 56, 72–6, 80, 82, 85, 88–91, 93, 95, 97–8, 101–2, 113–15, 117, 123, 125, 131, 152–3, 232, 272; *see also* Five-Year Plans
industry 6, 30, 36–7, 52–3, 64–5, 72–5, 81–4, 86–7, 88, 80, 97, 102–3, 106, 117–21, 129–31, 135, 139–40, 143, 148–51, 158, 165, 168, 173, 176, 180–1, 183, 187, 189, 191, 194, 197–8, 200, 223, 230–7, 240, 243, 255, 258, 273–4
  factories, works and mines
    24-i zavod 150
    Aivazov 10
    AMO 150
    Azovstal 241
    Bobrikovsky (Stalinogorsk) chemical works 151
    Briansk 8
    Briansk Arsenal 30
    Dynamo 150
    Elektrozavod 150
    Frunze 151
    Goznak 150
    Kaganovich Ball Bearing Works 151
    Kauchyk 150
    Kharkov Tractor Works 200
    Krasnyi Bogatyr' 150
    Krasnyi Postavshchik 37, 48

SUBJECT INDEX 361

Kolomensky locomotive works 151
Kommunar 119
Kulebansky 21
Mercury 16
New Putilov 9
New Tula (Novotula) 151
Nikolaev 75
Novaya Etna 30
Proletarsky locomotive repair works 201
Ruchenkov mines 9
Serp i Molot 150
Sharikopodshipnik 215
Tormoznoi 150
Sormovo 20–1, 23, 26, 30, 75
Stalin Motor Works (ZIS) 150
Trekhgorka 215
Ugreshansky chemical works 151
Urals Potash Works 258, 261
Vladimir Ilich 35, 150
Voronezh locomotive repair works 201
Voskresensky chemical works 151
Vyksynsky 21, 23
Zaporozhstal 241

sectors
    aircraft 151, 234, 236
    aluminium 198
    chemicals 150, 151, 161, 198
    coal 73, 86, 118–19, 151, 173, 197, 230–1, 233, 238, 240–1
    construction materials 240, 255, 258
    copper 197
    defence 150, 232–4
    fuel 230–1
    gas 231
    gold 198

    machine building 73, 75, 150, 151, 152
    metallurgy 74, 75, 121, 151, 197, 241
    oil 198, 231, 233–4, 237
    peat 230
    rubber 196, 198
    textiles 150–2
    timber 200
trusts and combines
    Donugol' 86
    Gipromez 87
    Glavmetall 87
    Gomzy 87
    Kramatorsk 74
    Yugostal 73, 74
    Yuzhmashtrest 73, 75
Institute of Agrarian Marxists 102
Institute of History 137
Institute of Red Professors 96, 137
Institute of Soviet Construction 52, 91–2, 137
Institute of Soviet State and Law 96
intelligentsia 68, 70, 86–7, 114, 131, 230, 231
    creation of Soviet intelligentsia 86, 131, 230–1
International Federation of Trade Unions (IFTU) 55–6
Israel 245, 255
Italy 205
Ivanovo 148–50, 195–6, 215
Izhev 22
Izvestiya 63, 168, 215
Izvestiya TsK RKP(b) 215
Izvestiya Turk TsIK 36

Japan 1, 19, 115, 142, 165, 177, 180, 233, 239
jazz 139
Jews 2–6, 17, 197, 215, 217, 233, 241, 245–6, 255, 268; *see also* anti-Semitism
Jewish homeland 245

Jewish Anti-Fascist Committee (JAFC) 245
Joint Opposition 54–8, 70–1, 74–6, 80, 81–2, 92, 98, 99
justice (revolutionary) 3, 5, 23, 88, 52, 265, 269; *see also* Military Tribunal (Civil War); Military Revolutionary Committee (MRC); Red Terror

Kabany 2–3, 8, 320n47
Kadets 20
Kaganovich, L. M.
  aides 208, 237, 258, 319n29
  conception of socialism 17–8, 48, 51, 99, 209, 275
  cult of 134, 159–61, 164, 169, 237, 259
  early employment 4–5, 8–9
  education and upbringing 1–4, 17
  family life 217–18
  health 4, 217, 268
  Jewish ix, 2–5, 7, 8, 11, 12, 17, 62, 139, 197, 209, 210, 215, 217, 233, 241, 245, 246, 255, 258, 268, 275, 277
  pseudonyms 8, 9, 13, 32, 284n39
  psychology 17, 223, 226–7, 244, 274, 277–9
  trade unionist 7, 8, 17, 271
  on architecture 138, 154, 162
  on the arts and cinema 128, 137–9
  on the Bolshevik left 38–9, 51, 271, 276
  on the Cheka 20–7, 30, 38, 166
  on democracy 50, 90, 209
  on industrialization 73–5, 80, 90–1, 96–9, 115
  on law and socialist legality 24, 32, 52, 78, 96, 113, 251
  on NEP 38, 49, 54, 68, 72, 80, 81, 92
  on party instructors 85, 137, 143, 272
  on party organization 17, 26–8
  on *politotdely* 112, 116, 166, 272
  on Right Opposition 98, 101
  on soviets 32, 51–3, 91–3
  on Stakhanovite/Krivonosovite movement 173–4, 177–9, 181–2, 193, 197, 273
  on trade unions 36, 39, 55–6, 88–90, 98, 117–19, 128–29, 193
  on USM 93–5, 103, 120, 272
  relations with Lenin 5, 10, 16, 22, 25, 31, 33, 35, 36, 38, 39, 50, 51, 54, 55, 57–8, 59, 73, 82–3, 91, 93, 96, 115, 116, 124, 163, 214, 225, 253, 261, 263, 269
  relations with Stalin 42, 50–1, 59, 207–9, 212–15, 222–3, 226–7, 243–4, 261–5
    as acolyte of 226–7
    as deputy to 123–43, 145, 167
    promoter of Stalin's cult 99, 115, 226, 227, 254, 273
  relations with other leaders
    Andreev 103, 168, 193
    Beria 235, 242, 245, 250–1
    Budennyi 32, 252
    Bulganin 21, 26, 34–5, 146, 159, 161, 250, 252, 258, 265
    Bukharin 53–5, 59, 78–9, 87, 95–6, 185, 188, 208, 264
    Khrushchev ix, 9, 76, 146, 155–8, 161, 162, 223, 224, 235, 241–2, 243–4, 249, 250, 252–3, 255–60, 262, 266–7, 275, 278
    Kosior 8, 79, 108, 125, 212, 223, 264
    Kuibyshev 11, 35, 42, 46, 73, 97, 212
    Malenkov 146, 225, 235, 242, 258, 265
    Mikoyan 125, 185, 198, 212, 235–6, 265

Molotov 42, 58, 59, 101, 135, 142, 208, 209–10, 212, 244, 253–4, 261–2
Ordzhonikidze 97–8, 117, 118, 119, 125, 173, 174, 179, 180–1, 186, 190, 212, 223, 273
Sokolnikov 53, 55, 84, 185
Tomsky 55–6, 76, 85, 88–9, 90, 94, 118
Trotsky 7, 27, 39, 47, 55–6, 85, 91, 96, 185–6, 208
Voroshilov 125, 201, 212, 250, 252, 253, 259
Vosnesensky 229–30, 233–4, 243, 247
Yagoda 141, 250, 264
Yakir 68, 194, 223, 257
Yezhov 126, 167–8, 174, 179, 181, 183, 185–6, 200, 250, 264
Zhdanov 138, 162, 214, 232, 242–3
role in collectivization 101–17, 145
role in the Great Terror 183–202, 272, 274
    as critic of mass repression 177–8, 180, 183, 187, 202
role in the Second World War 224, 236, 239–40, 274
    in the RSDLP 9–10
    work in Council of Ministers 240–3, 250–2, 258, 260–1
    work in Fuel Commissariat 233
    work in Military Organization 9–11, 14, 17, 271
    work in Ministry of Construction Building Materials 240, 242–3, 255
    work in Moscow party organization 47, 84–5, 99, 129, 145–64, 165, 214, 272–3
    work in Nizhnyi Novgorod 19–31, 38, 75, 146–7, 209, 271
    work in NKPS 162, 165–82, 191–7, 198–202, 229–30, 231, 234–7, 238–9
    work in NKTyazhProm 189–90, 196–8, 201, 210
    work in the Oil Commissariat 233–4
    work in the Orgburo 48–50, 52, 85, 126–7, 135–6, 139, 143, 165, 167, 209, 232
    work in the Secretariat 42, 44, 46–9, 54, 58, 85, 101, 104, 126–7, 136, 143, 147, 162, 165, 167, 207, 232
    work in Polese 12–13
    work in Turkestan 33–39, 49
    work in Voronezh 31–3, 35, 43, 52, 214, 271
    as theorist and writer 95–7, 262
        Kak postroena RKP (Bol'shevikov) 50
        Kak postroena VKP (Bol'shevikov) 51
        Kak stroitsa sovetskaya vlast' 32
        Pamyatnaya knizhka sovetskogo stroitelya 35
        Pamyatne zapiski rabochego, kommunista-bol'shevika, profsoyuznogo, partiinogo i sovetskogo rabotnika xiv, 261
Kalinin (town) 145, 151
Kaluga 145
Katyn massacre 37, 264
Kazakhstan 92–4, 107, 115
Kazan 22, 24, 30
Kemerovo trial 187
KGB (Committee of State Security) 253, 257
Khalkhin Gol 233
Kharkov 54, 56, 63, 64, 72, 76, 78, 86, 110, 111, 114, 200
Khochava 4

Kiev 2–9, 13, 15, 16, 17, 64–5, 67, 70, 75, 76, 191, 218
Kiev Bolshevik Party organization 3–8, 284n35
Kievskaya Mysl' 7
Kishinev 3
Kislovodsk 46
Kokand 33
Kolkhoztsentr 102
Kolomna 145
Komsomol, All-Union 32, 44, 49, 87, 88, 90–1, 98, 104, 109, 129, 131, 136, 163, 178, 194, 215
  Central Committee 53, 129, 194
  X Congress 178
Komsomol, Ukrainian 65, 86
Komsomolskaya Pravda 88
Kommunist 65
Komuch 22
Kozlov 105
Krasnaya armiya 65
Krasnaya zvezda 240
Krasnoarmeisk 110
Krasnodar 195, 237
Krasnoyarsk locomotive depot 177, 191
Kremlin 59, 62, 133, 155, 156, 163, 172–3, 177, 197, 215–17, 219, 236, 239, 245–6, 251–2, 258
Krivoi Rog 185, 187, 198
Krivonosite movement 173–4, 176; *see also* Stakhanovism/ Stakhanovites
Kronstadt revolt 36, 57
Kuban 110, 113, 153, 259, 272
Kuibyshev (town) 195, 237
Kuntsevo 240
Kursk 35, 195
Kuzbass coalfield 187, 199, 230

labour unrest and strikes 5, 7–9, 12, 20, 30, 31, 37, 41, 46, 148; *see also* workers
Lake Khasan 233

leader cult 240; *see also* Stalin, cult of personality; Kaganovich, L. M. cult of
League of Nations 142
Left Communists 15, 42, 96
Left SRs 14, 19, 20–2, 26, 29, 54
legitimacy, legitimation crisis xiv, 1, 14, 41, 240, 259, 267, 269
Lenin ix, 6, 18, 57, 111, 115, 163, 214, 217, 238, 251, 253
  'What is to Be Done?' 6, 42, 50–1, 59, 272
  'On Cooperation' 44, 55
  'Testament' 44, 48, 59
Lenin enrolment 50–1, 58, 128, 272; *see also* Communist Party membership, recruitment drive
Lenin Institute 127
Leningrad 52–4, 58, 87, 140, 160, 162, 168, 195, 201, 233, 243
Leningrad 240
'Leningrad Affair' 243
Leningrad Opposition 52–4, 58, 99
Leningradskaya Pravda 54
Leninism xii, 25, 47, 49–50, 59, 64, 91, 148, 204, 211, 227, 241, 244, 261, 263, 271–2
Let History Judge (Medvedev) 225
light industry 135, 150–1, 197
London 153
Lubyanka 3
Lubyanka building 154

Machiavellianism x, 25, 218, 220, 227, 275; *see also* Bolshevik ethics
Machine Tractor Stations (MTS) 112, 116, 150, 255
Magnitogorsk 129
Manchuria 115, 140, 165, 233
Mariupol 77
Martynovich 3
Marx-Engels-Lenin Institute 253
Marxism-Leninism: *see* Leninism
Melitopol' 8

Mensheviks 5–7, 9–10, 13–14, 16, 20, 22, 30, 54, 83, 85, 93, 130, 168, 191, 211, 264
Mexico 142
Military Revolutionary Committee (MRC) 22
  in Nizhnyi Novgorod 22–4, 38, 286n27
  in Polese 13
  in Tashkent 34, 38
  in Voronezh 31–2, 38
Military Revolutionary Council (Revvoensovet) 22, 34, 62
military tribunal 25, 140, 237
militarization of administration 46, 224
  of economic administration 46, 137, 143, 272
  of labour 36
  of party 31, 38, 48, 98
  of railways 166, 180, 237
militia 104
Minsk 12, 13, 16, 17, 245
Mogiliev 12–3, 17
Morals or Class Norms (Preobrazhensky) 44
Moscow 11–3, 15, 21–3, 30–3, 35, 37–8, 43–4, 47, 53–5, 58, 64–5, 68–71, 74, 78–9, 84–6, 89–92, 99, 103, 106, 109, 115–18, 128–9, 134–6, 140–1, 145–64, 165, 167–8, 170, 173, 180, 187–8, 196, 207, 214, 217, 223–4, 253, 256, 261, 272–3
  agriculture 145–6, 147–50
  buildings and locations
    Bolshoi Theatre 32, 198
    Byelorussian station 214
    Church of Christ the Saviour 155
    Donskoi Monastery 269
    Frunze Embankment 268
    Gorky Park 162, 173, 180, 196, 232
    Iversky Gates 156
    Kitaigorod 156
    Kropotkinskaya embankment 155
    Lenin Hills 155, 258
    Okhotnyi ryad 162
    Prospekt Marx 154
    Red Square 156, 189
    Rechnoi Vokzal 163
    St. Basil's 156
    Spassky Tower 217
    Sokol'niki Park 162, 232
    Sukharev Tower 155
    Yaroslavl station 83
  districts 146, 148, 149, 156,
    Bauman 147
    Krasnaya Presnaya 147, 261
    Orekhovo-zuevsky 147
    Rogozhsko-Simonovsky 85
    Sokol'niki 147
    Zamoskvorech'e 37, 47
  industry 150–2
  transport 147, 151, 152, 156, 158, 163
  urban redevelopment and housing 152–6
Moscow city party committee (*gorkom*) 8, 35, 118, 146, 196, 223, 253
  bureau 11, 252
  district party committees (*raikoms*) 47, 105, 108, 116, 147
  first secretary 28
  oppositionist influence in 47, 147, 184, 160, 226
  party cells 36, 47, 49, 52, 129
Moscow City Trade Union Council 89
Moscow Duma 156
Moscow Metro 153, 156–8, 161–4, 214, 253, 273
  Metrostroi 156, 161, 168, 310n140
Moscow Military District 251
Moscow–Volga canal 153, 158–9, 161, 163–4, 273

Moskanalstroi 159
Moscow OGPU 146
Moscow party conferences 28, 146
  IV province and third city party conference 159
Moscow party Control Commission 146, 160
  purge of oppositionists 184
Moscow Province Party Committee (*obkom*) 147–8, 162
  first secretary 28
Murom 21

nationalities policy 36, 37, 43, 45, 61, 63, 71, 82, 114
Nazi–Soviet Pact 233, 263
Nazism 161, 205, 215, 233
NEP xii, 37–8, 41, 43–5, 49, 53–4, 59, 61, 72, 79–80, 81–3, 92, 94–5, 98, 101–2, 106–7
NeoNEP 107, 149
New York 153
New York Times 117
nihilism 6, 11, 21, 44, 204, 211
Nizhegorodskaya kommuna 24–7
Nizhnyi Novgorod 19–31, 38, 53, 75, 91, 146, 147, 207, 209, 214–15, 218, 271
Nizhnyi Novgorod party organization 19–31, 91
  Province Party Conference
    IV 21
    V 24
    VI 26, 27, 28
    VII 31
  Nizhnyi Novgorod Soviet 26
  province soviet executive committee 20–2, 26, 29, 30–2
    II Province Congress of Soviets 21
Northern Territory 104
North Caucasus 85–6, 103, 109–10, 113, 115, 121, 195, 237
Novodevichy cemetery 133, 251, 269

NKPS 125, 126, 139, 162–82, 186–91, 193, 197–200, 202, 207, 210, 214, 223–4, 229–30, 234, 236–9, 247, 257, 259, 273, 311n46, 314n27, 324n67, 324n79
  Collegium 191, 199, 200
  Locomotive Administration 173
  Operational Administration 170–1
  Political Administration 43, 63, 86, 112, 136, 166, 169, 188, 237 (*see also politotdely*, on the railways)
  Sector of Control 169
  Scientific Technical Council 170
  Soviet 178–9
NKVD 140, 141, 154, 159, 165, 168–9, 175, 177, 181, 184–6, 190, 193, 195–201, 202, 234, 236, 254, 261, 264
  Transport Department 169, 187, 199–200

October Manifesto 1
October Revolution 12, 14, 17, 35, 72, 75, 83, 115, 157, 206, 252, 264
Odessa 3, 75, 76, 239
OGPU/GPU 43, 87, 110, 104, 109–10, 112–13, 140–1, 146, 148, 159, 161
Old Bolsheviks 10, 16, 42, 47, 57
Omsk 177
O natsional'noi kulture (Vaganya) 71
oppositionists 181, 184, 188, 190–1, 205, 226; *see also* Right Opposition
Orekhovo-Zuevo 145
Order of Lenin 150, 163, 217, 238, 251
Orenburg 187, 195, 257

Palace of Soviets 155, 164
Palestine 245
Panama Canal 158
Paris 153

Paris Commune 51, 83
Partinnoe stroitel'stvo 215
peasants 1–3, 8, 12, 14–5, 20–2, 25, 29–30, 33–6, 38, 41, 43, 45, 49, 49, 51–7, 63–5, 71–4, 77, 80–3, 91, 93, 95, 97–8, 101–3, 106–7, 111, 113, 115–17, 121, 131, 148–50, 174, 203, 206–7, 259, 264, 272
  committees of poor peasants (*kombedy*) 20, 21, 29, 53, 64, 74, 77
  'kulaks' 2, 20–2, 25, 35, 52–6, 66–8, 70, 73–4, 77, 80, 83–4, 86, 91–5, 98, 101–16, 120, 137, 148, 160, 177–8, 190–1, 195, 264, 272
  middle peasants 2–3, 20–1, 29–30, 52–5, 64, 70, 77–8, 83–4, 92–5, 102–5
  poor peasants 2–3, 20–1, 54, 55, 64, 77, 92, 93, 94, 95, 103, 146
  well-to-do peasants 2, 55, 65, 84, 110
peasant resistance 20–2, 25, 30, 37, 41, 51, 102, 104–5, 114
Perm 25, 176, 258
Petrograd 10–15, 21, 23, 30, 32, 37
Pioneers 129, 218
planning 87, 96, 136, 151–4, 164, 170, 180, 199, 215, 230, 232, 255, 268
'Platform of the 46' 46
Plekhanov Institute 47
Poland 70, 233, 234, 255
Polish United Workers Party 255
Podol'sk 145
Polese 2, 11–3, 15
politotdely 31, 112, 160
  in agriculture 112, 116–17, 121, 137, 150, 272
  on the railways 166, 170, 178, 187–9, 190–1, 200, 238, 273
Prague 252
Pravda 23, 26, 27, 28, 29–30, 45, 47, 70, 105, 124, 168, 171, 174, 177, 199, 253

press 4, 15, 21, 23, 24, 25, 42, 88, 113, 138, 158–9, 168, 185–6, 253, 261
Procuracy 105–6, 119, 140, 141, 181, 185, 188,
  Chief Procuracy of the Railways 188
Proletarskaya revolyutsiya 137
Provisional Government 9, 13–4, 16
'public sphere' xiv, 90, 97, 99, 120, 143, 204, 209
public opinion (popular opinion) xii, xiv, 20, 97, 99, 204, 259
purges 50, 197, 198, 218, 230, 263

Rabotnitsa 217
railways 140, 151, 160–1, 162, 165–82, 186–8, 191–2, 194, 197, 199, 210, 230–4, 236–9, 252, 257, 273–4; see also NKPS
  accident rate 166–9, 170–2, 175, 178–9, 187, 191, 199, 230, 31n46
  efficiency drive 88, 161, 163, 172–3, 180–1, 210–11, 230, 237–8, 271–3
  Krivonosovite movement 173–6, 179, 200, 231, 233, 238
  'limiters' 173–8, 191
  line administrations 187, 237
    Donetsk 166, 173, 187, 191, 199
  purge of railways 87, 160, 168, 175–6, 178, 185, 191, 193–8, 200, 233, 238
  research institutes 171, 180, 231
    Scientific Technical Research Institute of Operations 167, 170–1, 175
    Scientific Research Institute of Railway Transport 171
    Scientific Research Institute of Track and Construction 171
    Institute for the Reconstruction of Traction 178

Central Scientific Research Institute of Railway Construction 178
Red Army 14–6, 20, 24, 26–7, 29, 30–2, 38, 41, 63, 76, 82, 95, 97, 106, 109, 112, 166, 171, 190, 194, 198, 231, 233
Red Banner of Labour 176, 233
Red Guards 12, 14, 16, 20, 33, 285n71
Red International of Trade Unions (Profintern) 55–6
Red Terror 22–6, 38, 207, 271
Repubblica 268
religion 208
repression 1, 5, 21, 24–5, 29, 44, 86, 104, 109, 111, 113, 119, 131, 140, 143, 146, 171, 174, 177–8, 180–1, 183, 185–8, 193, 196, 200–2, 223, 226–27, 234, 245, 254, 256–7, 259, 261, 267, 269, 272–3; *see also* Red Terror; Great Terror
  during the Great Terror 165, 172, 183, 188, 196, 201–3, 205, 218, 231, 264, 272–4
  of bourgeois specialist 27, 78, 86–7, 98, 130–1, 207
  of Central Committee members 222
  of military high command 194
  of Politburo members 222, 229, 243, 251
  of railway personnel 166–7, 171–2, 200–201, 254, 257, 259
  of non-Russian nationals 195 (*see also* Katyn massacre)
'revolutionary legality' 52, 265; *see also* repression
Right Opposition 98, 101
'Rightists' 53, 72, 80, 81, 84, 85, 88–9, 91, 94–8, 102, 106, 112, 123–4, 131, 141, 147, 156, 185, 187, 188, 193–5, 262, 272
Rostov 110, 195, 241
RSFSR 34, 35, 64, 72

Rubtsovsk 94
Russia 1, 8, 14, 37, 44–5, 54, 56, 168, 207, 263–4
Russian Association of Proletarian Writers (RAPP) 138
Russian Orthodox Church 43, 44, 148, 155
Russification 68–9
Russo–Japanese War
  1904–5 3
  1945 176
Rybinsk 21
Ryutin platform 131

Samara 22, 42, 58
Saratov 9–11, 195
Saratov RSDLP 10
  military organization 10
secret police 43, 86, 133, 140, 251, 273; *see also* Cheka; OGPU/GPU; NKVD; NKGB 238
  MVD 241, 250
  MGB 250, 253
  KGB 253, 256–7
Semipalatinsk 92
Serpukhov 145
Shakhty affair 78, 86–8, 91, 130–1, 140, 191–2
Shuia 44
Siberia 83, 93–5, 105, 116, 146
Siberian Territorial Party Committee 79, 94
Simbirsk 22, 32
Smirnov-Eismont-Tolmachev group 131–2
Smolensk 13, 92, 92, 195
Smolensk scandal 92
'Socialism in One Country' 49, 55, 57, 74
socialist property 111–12
socialist realism 138
Socialist Revolutionary Party 1, 5, 6, 9, 10, 11, 13–4, 22, 27, 44, 199; *see also* Left SRs

Solikamsk 258
Sotsialisticheskii transport 178
Sotsialisticheskii vestnik 168, 211–12
Sovetskaya kultura 268
Sovnarkom 15, 19–21, 23, 27,
    44, 46, 69, 84, 119, 123,
    125–7, 135–7, 142, 154, 156,
    159, 163, 166–7, 169–70, 172–3,
    194, 197, 199, 212, 229–30,
    232, 235, 238, 240; *see also*
    Communist Party of the USSR,
    Central Committee–Sovnarkom
    resolutions
  Bureau 235, 238, 242–3, 246,
    250–2
  State Committee for Grain
    Procurement (KomZag) 109, 150
  Commission of Implementation 136
  Council of Labour and Defence
    (STO) 64, 84, 135, 158–9, 167,
    194
  Council for the Defence Industries
    234
  Council for Fuel and Electricity
    Industry 234
  Economic Council 235
  People's Commissariats
    NKFin 53, 169
    NKInDel 49, 142
    NKPros RSFSR 87
    NKPS (*see* NKPS)
    NKRKI (Rabkrin) 45, 117
    (*see also* Central Control
    Commission-Rabkrin)
    NKSovkhoz 109, 111–12
    NKTyazhProm 118, 125,
      135, 140, 159, 165, 169, 173,
      180–2, 188–91, 196–9, 202,
      210, 229–31, 259
    NKVMDel 15
    NKZem 102, 104–5,
      111–12, 119, 126
    Gosplan 73, 81, 87, 101,
      121, 125, 130, 151, 154, 156,
      158–9, 167, 169, 171, 173,
      212, 229–30, 234, 243
    Vesenkha 49, 62, 63, 73, 75,
      80, 81, 88, 101, 119, 121,
      125, 165
    PC for Armaments 235
    PC for Aviation Industry
      233–4
    PC for Coal Industry 233
    PCfor Defence 176
    PC for Defence Industries 233
    PC for Foreign Trade 45,
      218, 243
    PC for Fuel Industries 230
    PC of Justice 44, 63
    PC for Light Industry 197
    PC for Nationalities 33
    PC for Oil Industry 233
    PC for Procurement 31, 34
  Sovnarkom/Politburo Defence
    Committee 142, 194, 232–3,
    234–5
sovnarkhoz reforms 255, 260
Soyuzkino: *see* cinema
Spanish Civil War 142, 201
Stakhanovism/Stakhanovites 173–81,
    182–3, 197, 199, 200, 231,
    233, 238, 273; *see also* railways,
    Krivonosovite movement
  First All-Union Congress 173
Stalin, I. V. (see also entry in name
    index)
  cult of personality 123, 134, 240, 244,
    259, 275, 253–4, 257, 265, 269
  despot/tyrant x–xiii, 202–3, 205,
    218, 222, 227, 229, 239, 249,
    253, 265–6, 268, 274, 276–8
  dictator x–xiii, 120, 123, 131, 133,
    143, 165, 190, 203, 205, 206,
    209, 211, 212, 222, 227, 229,
    263, 267, 273, 276
  faction xiii, 80, 97–9, 120,
    124, 207
  'general line' 90, 105, 111, 134

inner circle or 'leading group' xiii,
  49, 58, 123–6, 194, 222, 229,
  238, 242, 271, 302n10
'left turn' 81, 97
meetings in his Kremlin office 133,
  245, 304nn74–5
psychology of x, xii, 105, 202,
  218–21, 227, 242, 267
relations with his deputies xii–xiii, 69,
  123–4, 138, 140, 143, 145, 162,
  164, 183–4, 186, 190, 194, 202–5,
  207–9, 212, 218, 220, 222–9,
  242–3, 262, 254, 266, 271–9
Tsaritsyn group 58, 206
works 137, 240–1, 258, 261
  'Dizzy with Success' 105,
    134, 145, 148, 150, 192
  Questions of Leninism 263
  Foundations of Leninism 50,
    263
  *The Economic Problems of
    Socialism in the USSR* 246
Stalinism xii, 117, 203–5, 209, 222,
  239, 244, 263, 269
  developmental dictatorship xii, 41,
    123, 131, 138, 142, 204
  dictatorship of the proletariat 22,
    24, 27, 32, 41, 45, 51, 54, 78, 92,
    96, 103, 104, 177, 273
  political religion xiv, 6, 48, 130, 203,
    208
  'revolution from above' 87, 99, 101,
    113, 115, 120, 121, 133, 130,
    142, 202, 203, 272, 279
  Stalinist culture 203–6
  Stalinist ethics 204
  High Stalinism 222, 239
Stalingrad 238
Stavka 13, 236–7
State Defence Committee (GKO)
  236–8
  Evacuation Council 236
  Operative Bureau 238
  Transport Commission 237

Stavropol 237
STO: *see* Sovnarkom, Council of
  Labour and Defence (STO)
Sto sorok besed s Molotovym (Chuev) 261
Supreme Court 140, 188
  Military Collegium 140, 177, 184,
    188–9, 199
  Transport Collegium 187–8
Supreme Soviet 189–90, 197–8, 214,
  218, 234, 238, 251–2
  Presidium 218, 251
  Budget Commission 218
Sverdlov University 50
Sverdlovsk 195, 197
Syrtsov-Lominadze group 131

Tashkent 33–8, 42, 58, 197, 214, 271
  Tashkent Soviet 33
TASS 185
Tatary 195
taxation 29, 37, 45, 51, 54, 55, 61, 65,
  74, 93, 101, 107, 141, 149
technical intelligentsia 231; *see also*
  engineers
Terror x–xi, 86, 207, 251, 271; *see also*
  Red Terror; Great Terror
  Lenin's view 32, 43–4
  Stalin's view 49
  Trotsky's view 32–33
  anti-state acts 86, 88, 94, 112, 113,
    140, 1248, 171, 241, 250
  as a facet of despotic/tyrannical rule
    202, 203, 205, 222, 274
  impact on the ruling group 223,
    226–7, 229
Terrorism and Communism (Trotsky) 32
Tiblisi 237
Tomsk 177
totalitarianism x–xiii, 143, 205
trade 45–6, 73, 81–2, 84, 87, 103, 107,
  114, 130, 149, 151, 218, 243
  collective farm trade 107, 110, 149
trade unions 7–8, 24, 31, 36–9, 42,
  49, 50, 54–6, 58, 65, 71, 80,

SUBJECT INDEX 371

82, 88, 89, 90, 98, 117–19,
128–29, 169, 193, 215, 217, 224,
261, 271–3; *see also* VTsSPS;
Ukrainian trade unions
Traktortsentr 102
Trans-Caucasus 35, 190, 198
trials, political or show trials 192, 218,
251, 254, 259, 269
  'Anti Soviet Bloc of Rights and
Trotskyites' 199
  'Anti-Soviet Trotskyite Centre' 188
  'Anti-Soviet Unified Trotskyite-
Zinovievite Centre' 184
  Industrial Party 87, 130
  Labouring Peasants Party 130
  Menshevik Buro 130
  Metro-Vickers 140
  Shakhty 78, 86, 91, 130–1, 140,
191–2
  Socialist Revolutionaries 44
Trotskyism 49, 106, 272
Trotskyist opposition 75, 77,
181, 271
support for 47–8
'Trotskyists' 47, 56, 58, 75, 83, 85,
91, 96, 97, 101, 106, 117, 123,
137–8, 141, 160, 162, 168,
171–2, 177, 178, 181, 184–8,
189–91, 193, 194, 195–6, 198–9,
205, 256
Trud 197
Tula 30, 145, 151
Turkestan 19, 33–8, 42–3, 53, 73,
146, 147, 214
Turkestan bureau (Turkburo) 33–5,
37, 38
Turkestan Commission of the
Russian Communist Party
(Turkkomission) 33–5, 37,
288n10
Turkestan Communist Party 33, 34,
35, 36, 37–8
  V Congress 34
  VI Congress 38

Turkestan Sovnarkom 34
IX Congress of Soviets of Turkestan
35
NKRKI 34, 288n115
PC of Social Welfare 35
'Twenty-five thousanders' 90, 104, 106

Uglanovshchina 147
Ukraina 65
Ukraine 1–17, 54, 57, 58, 61–76,
78–81, 86, 98, 101, 104, 107–10,
114–16, 121, 125, 133, 143, 146,
147, 185, 191, 195, 240, 241–2,
245, 247, 257, 272
Ukrainian Academy of Science 241
Ukrainian Central Executive
Committee 63, 65, 74
  IX All-Ukrainian Congress of
Soviets 63, 64
Ukrainian Communist Party 53, 61,
62–3, 66–7, 69, 71–2, 74–6,
83–4, 257, 259
  Central Committee 62, 64, 65, 67,
71–2, 86, 107
  Central Committe plenums 57, 62,
63, 65, 69, 73, 75, 76, 78, 79,
114, 241
    Information-Statistical
Department 64
  Central Control Commission 71, 76
  Central Committee–Central Control
Commission joint resolutions 71,
76, 77, 114
  membership 65, 293n37
  Party Conferences 74
    III Party Conference 114
  Party Congresses
    IX Congress 54, 63, 67
    X Congress 72, 75
  Politburo 62, 63, 65, 66, 67, 68. 69,
70, 73, 74, 78, 79, 114, 126, 241,
294n83
    commission on Ukrainization
65, 70

commission for investigating
the frontier 70–71
Politburo–Presidium CCC
joint resolution 75
Ukrainian Institute of Marxism-
Leninism 64, 241
Ukrainian anti-communist
intelligentsia 68, 70, 114
Ukrainian congress of trade unions 76
Ukrainian language 66, 294n83
Ukrainian Military District 68, 194
Ukrainian nationalism 5, 66, 114–15,
241
Ukrainian Sovnarkom/Council of
Ministers 63, 79, 108, 114, 241
Gosplan 68
OGPU/GPU 64, 70, 77, 86–7,
108–10
Ministry of Agriculture 241
MVD 241, 250
NKPros 65, 70
Procuracy 241
Vesenkha 62–3, 73, 75, 80–1
Ukrainian trade unions 63, 65–6, 71,
76, 80, 88
Ukrainian Writers Union 242
Ukrainian Institute of Marxism-
Leninism 64, 241
Ukrainization 61, 64–72, 76, 78–80,
114
Ukrainskii Bol'shevik 71
Union of Soviet Architects 154
Urals 75, 81, 85, 93–4, 101, 121, 151,
231, 239
Urals Province Party 93
IX Urals Province Party Conference
94
Urals-Siberian method (USM) 93–5,
103, 120, 272
USA xi, xiv, 2, 19, 113, 129, 142, 170,
179, 231, 238, 254, 260
USSR xii, 56, 61–4, 71–2, 74, 75, 92,
97, 106, 117, 130, 139–41, 145,
150, 154, 160, 161, 164, 165,
179–80, 205, 206, 209, 210, 230,
231, 232, 233, 234, 236, 239, 240,
245, 246, 250, 255, 263, 269

Vechernaya Moskva 158
Vichuga 148
Vienna 153, 207
Virgin Lands 251
Vitebsk 13
Volga 20, 23, 29–30, 85, 93
Lower Volga region 85, 104, 107,
115
Central Volga region 85, 104, 107
Volga flotilla 30
Voronezh 19, 31–3, 38, 42, 43, 52,
147, 195, 201, 214, 271
VTsSPS 36–7, 49, 55–6, 76, 84, 88–9,
117–18, 193–4, 230; *see also* trade
unions
Presidium 88–9, 193
IV Congress of Trade Unions 37
VII Congress of Trade Unions 88
IX Congress of Trade Unions 118

War Communism 21, 37, 41, 55, 84
war scare of 1927 70, 75, 86, 97, 98
Warsaw 255
Western province 115, 195
'White Guardists' 20, 22, 72, 178,
187, 191
Winter (Finnish) War 233, 235
workers 173, 179–81, 183, 197, 199,
273; *see also* Stakhanovism/
Stakhanovites
railway workers 5, 12–13, 33, 35,
36, 139, 166–8, 172, 173, 176,
177, 179, 180, 190, 196, 215,
231, 232, 256, 324n78
textile workers 148
metal workers 9, 36, 56, 197
miners 9, 56, 230, 231
shock workers 89, 112, 113,
117–19, 129, 158, 173, 197
training of workers 178, 187

worker resistance 37, 77, 102,
    104, 106, 107, 110–11, 167,
    170, 179–80, 193, 197, 226
Workers' Opposition 36–9, 57–8,
    289n126
World War I: *see* First World War
wrecking and sabotage 86–7, 112,
    179, 180–1, 183–4, 187–93, 198

Yaroslavl 21, 26, 195–6
Yezhovshchina 201
Yuzovka 8–9, 78

Zaporozhe 76, 77, 236, 241
Zionism 16, 215, 241–2, 243, 245,
    255, 268
Zvezda 240

www.ingramcontent.com/pod-product-compliance
Lightning Source LLC
Chambersburg PA
CBHW021815300426
44114CB00009BA/193